2005 Song Writer's Market

Ian Bessler, Editor

Michael Schweer, Assistant Editor

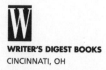

WRITER'S DIGEST BOOKS
CINCINNATI, OH

If you would like to be considered for a listing in the next edition of *Songwriter's Market*, send a SASE (or SAE and IRC) with your request for a questionnaire to *Songwriter's Market—* QR, 4700 East Galbraith Road, Cincinnati OH 45236. Please indicate in which section you would like to be included.

Editorial Director, Writer's Digest Books: Barbara Kuroff
Managing Editor, Writer's Digest Annual Books: Alice Pope

Writer's Digest Books website: www.writersdigest.com.
Writer's Market website: www.writersmarket.com.

2005 Songwriter's Market. Copyright © 2004 by Writer's Digest Books. Published by F+W Publications, 4700 East Galbraith Road, Cincinnati, Ohio 45236. Printed and bound in the United States of America. All rights reserved. No part of this book may be reproduced in any form or by any electronic or mechanical means including information storage and retrieval systems without written permission from the publisher, except by reviewers who may quote brief passages to be printed in a magazine or newspaper.

International Standard Serial Number 0161-5971
International Standard Book Number 1-58297-276-1

Cover design by Nick and Diane Gliebe, Design Matters

Interior design by Clare Finney

Attention Booksellers: This is an annual directory of F+W Publications. Return deadline for this edition is December 31, 2005.

Contents

ADVANCED ARTICLES

THE MARKETS

From the Editor

I recently saw an aphorism that said, "If we don't know where we're going, we'll probably get there." On its face, it's a bit nonsensical, but it also makes an important point about the need for songwriters to have a clear idea of what they want, to build a clear picture in their minds, and to see it happening within a certain time frame. After all, in a few years you're going to wind up *somewhere*, so why not choose your destination?

For those of you new to this book, a good first step is to flip this page over and look at the **Quick-Start Guide** on page 2. After that read the Getting Started articles starting on page 5, especially **How Do I Avoid the Rip-Offs?**, page 19.

Nashville enthusiasts should check out these three articles: **PRO's: The Way to Go?**, by Jim Melko, on page 40; **Moving to a Music Hub**, by C.J. Watson, on page 50; and the Insider Report with **ASCAP Featured Artist/Writer of December 2003, Shannon Lawson**, on page 96. Aspiring Nashville songwriters should also consider joining **Nashville Songwriters Association International** (see their listing in the Organizations section on page 326).

There are several articles and interviews performing pop songwriters should find useful and inspirational: **Use Publicity to Help Your Songwriting**, by music publicist Anne Leighton, on page 45; **Building a Support Team for Today's Market**, by producer Scott Mathews, on page 69. Insider Reports with pop songwriter **Lindy Robbins (Clay Aiken, Faith Hill)** on page 32, and **independent singer/songwriter Bibi Farber** on page 160 offer useful perspectives on pop songwriting and online music licensing.

This year's article by music publisher Rusty Gordon, **Commercial Songwriting: Creative Secrets for Success**, on page 57, should be useful to songwriters hoping to build a creatively satisfying, yet commercial, songwriting style. Also, look at **Mid-Atlantic Song Contest: Editor's Report from the 2003 Awards Show** on page 75 and the Insider Report with **singer/songwriter Rachael Sage** on page 180 to see how songwriters of all types are using song contests to help build their careers.

So, there is a lot of information and advice to draw upon in this edition, and if you have carefully considered your goals and where you want to go with your songwriting, you can use this information to build a path to your chosen destination.

Ian C. Bessler
songmarket@fwpubs.com
www.writersdigest.com

Quick-Start

New to Songwriter's Market?

his "Quick-Start" guide is designed to lay it out for you step by step. Each step shows you where to find the information you need in *Songwriter's Market*, from basic to more advanced.

Use this as guide to launch your songwriting career. Look over the whole list once, then go back and read each article completely. They will show you new facets of the music industry and reinforce what you already know. Good luck!

1. Join a songwriting organization. Connecting with other songwriters and learning from their experience will save you a lot of trouble starting out. Organizations help you learn about the music business, polish your songwriting and help you make contacts who can take you to the next level.

- Organizations, page 326

2. Learn about the music business. Protect yourself with knowledge. Learn how money is really made in the music business and avoid scams. Go to songwriting workshops and music conferences.

- How Do I Avoid the Rip-Offs?, page 19
- Royalties: Where Does the Money Come From?, page 28
- What About Copyright?, page 32
- What About Contracts?, page 36
- Career Songwriting: What Should I Know?, page 34
- PRO's: The Way to Go?, page 40
- Moving to a Music Hub, page 50
- Building the Business Team for Today's Market, page 69
- Use Publicity to Help Your Songwriting Career, page 45
- Workshops & Conferences, page 351
- Publications of Interest, page 369

3. Develop your songwriting skill. Get letterhead, have your songs critiqued, make contacts and subscribe to songwriting/music magazines. Start building your catalog of songs. If you also perform, start developing your performance skills and build a following.

- Commercial Songwriting: Creative Secrets for Success, page 57
- Music Resources on the Internet, page 64
- Organizations, page 326
- Workshops & Conferences, page 351
- Publications of Interest, page 369
- Websites of Interest, page 376

4. Choose your best three songs and make a demo recording.
- Demo Recordings: What Should I Know?, page 13
- What About Copyright?, page 32

5. Learn how to spot rip-offs.
- How Do I Avoid the Rip-Offs?, page 19
- What About Copyright?, page 32
- What About Contracts?, page 36

6. Decide which arm(s) of the music business you will submit your songs to.
- Where Should I Send My Songs?, page 9
- Submission Strategies, page 23
- Music Publishers Section Introduction, page 80
- Record Companies Section Introduction, page 141
- Record Producers Section Introduction, page 197
- Managers & Booking Agents Section Introduction, page 225
- Advertising, Audiovisual & Commercial Music Firms Section Introduction, page 260
- Contests & Awards Section Introduction, page 312

7. Find companies open to your style of music and level of experience or use your contacts at Organizations and Performing Rights Organizations (ASCAP, BMI, SESAC) to get a referral and permission to submit. Be picky about where you send your material. Do not waste your time and effort submitting to every company listed in this book without regard to whether they want your style of music.
- Where Should I Send My Songs, page 9
- Openness to Submissions Index, page 415
- Category Indexes, page 388

8. Locate companies in your area.
- Geographic Index, page 425

9. Read the listings and decide which companies to submit to and whether they are appropriate for you (pay special attention to the **Music** subhead and also the royalty percentage they pay). Do additional research through trade publications, the Internet and other songwriters.
- The Markets, page 80
- Publications of Interest, page 369
- Websites of Interest, page 376

10. Find out how to submit. Read information under the How to Contact subhead of each listing. Learn the etiquette involved in contacting companies. Learn how to package your demo in a professional way. Learn how to avoid getting ripped off.
- *Songwriter's Market*: How Do I Use It?, page 7
- How Do I Submit My Demo?, page 15
- Quiz: Are You Professional?, page 26
- How Do I Avoid the Rip-Offs?, page 19

11. Call the companies and verify their submission policy has not changed. Also check to make sure the contact person is still there.

12. Send your submission package according to each company's directions. Read the information under the How to Contact subhead in each listing again.
- Quiz: Are You Professional?, page 26
- How Do I Submit My Demo?, page 15
- What About Copyright?, page 32

13. Decide whether to sign with a company.
- Royalties: Where Does the Money Come From?, page 28
- How Do I Avoid the Rip-Offs?, page 19

14. Have an entertainment attorney look over any contract before you sign.

15. After signing, how do you get paid?

Songwriter's Market

How Is It Put Together?

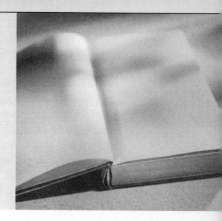

The following articles are for songwriters who have never used this book before and are new to the music industry. This is all important information—especially for first-time readers of *Songwriter's Market*—so don't skip straight to the listings. There's a lot to learn, but it's been rewritten for clarity and simplicity. Taking a little time now to educate yourself can save you a lot of trouble later and save you from having to learn a lot of things the hard way.

How do I use *Songwriter's Market?*

First, take a minute to get to know the book and how it's put together. Here's a rundown of *what* is in the book, followed by:

What you'll find inside this book

Songwriter's Market is a big book and can seem overwhelming at first. But don't worry, it's not that tough to find your way around the book. Here's a quick look at how it's put together.

The book has six basic parts:

1. Articles about the music business and songwriting craft
2. Introductions to each section of listings
3. Listings of music companies and organizations
4. Insider Reports
5. Indexes
6. Lists of websites, magazines, books, and other useful extras

Music biz and songwriting articles

These range from articles on the basics of how the music business works—the essentials, laid out in plain English, of how songwriters and artists make money and advance their careers—to articles with more detail and depth on business and creativity, written by music industry insiders with many years of experience in the trenches.

Section intros and listings—the "meat" of the book

There are 11 sections in the book, from Music Publishers and Record Companies to Contests & Awards. Each section begins with an introduction detailing how the different types of companies function—what part of the music industry they work in, how they make money, and what you need to think about when approaching them with your music.

The listings are the heart of *Songwriter's Market*. They are the names, addresses and contact information of music biz companies looking for songs and artists, as well as descriptions of the types of music they are looking for.

What are Insider Reports?

Insider Reports are interviews with songwriters, performers and music industry honchos working at all levels in the music business. By showing how others have achieved success, you learn by example. By peeking behind the curtain of record labels, music publishers and others, you understand more about how the industry works. You learn how the businessmen think, and how to work that to your advantage. Reading them gives you an important edge over songwriters and performers who don't. Insider Reports are scattered throughout the listings and are listed in the Table of Contents.

Songwriter's Market

How Do I Use It?

The quick answer is that you should use the indexes to find companies who are interested in your type of music, then read the listings for details on how they want the music submitted. For support and help of all sorts, join a songwriting or other music industry association. Become a student of the music industry. (Also see the Quick-Start guide on page 2.)

How does *Songwriter's Market* "work"?

The listings in *Songwriter's Market* are packed with a lot of information. It can be intimidating at first, but they are put together in a structured way to make them easy to work with. Take a few minutes to get used to how the listings are organized, and you'll have it down in no time. For more detailed information about how the listings are put together, skip ahead to Where Should I Send My Songs? on page 9.

What are the general rules for working with listings?

Look at A Sample Listing Decoded on page 11 for an example of how a typical listing is put together. The following are general rules about how to use the listings.

1. **Read the entire listing** to decide whether to submit your music! Do not use this book as a mass mailing list! If you blindly mail out demos by the hundreds, you'll waste a lot of money on postage, annoy a lot of people, and your demos will wind up in the trash.
2. **Jump to the "Music" section in each listing.** This will tell you what kind of music the company is looking for. If they want rockabilly only and you write heavy metal, don't submit.
3. **Pay close attention to submission instructions** shown under "How to Contact" and follow them to the letter. A lot of listings are very particular about how they want submissions packaged. Pay close attention. If you do not follow their instructions, they will probably throw your submission in the garbage. You have been warned! If you are confused about their directions, call, e-mail or write to the company for clarification.
4. **If in doubt, contact the company for permission to submit.** This is a good general rule. Many companies don't mind if you send an unsolicited submission, but some will want you to get special permission from them. Contacting a company first is also a good way to find out their latest music needs. This is also a chance to briefly make contact on a personal level (but don't wear out your welcome!)
5. **Be courteous, be efficient** and always have a purpose to your personal contact—

DO NOT WASTE THEIR TIME! If you call, always have a reason for making contact—permission to submit, checking on guidelines, following up on a demo, etc. These are solid reasons to make personal contact, but once you have their attention do not wear out your welcome! Always be polite! Always have an upbeat, pleasant attitude when you call (even if you are feeling frustrated or uptight at that particular moment)!

6. **Check for a preferred contact.** A lot of listings have a designated contact person shown after a bolded "**Contact**" in the heading. This is the person you should contact with questions or address you're submission to.

7. **Read the "Tips" section.** This part of the listing provides extra information on how to submit or what it might be like to work with the company.

This is just the beginning. For more detailed information about the listings, see Where Should I Send My Songs? on page 9 and the sidebar with the sample listing called A Sample Listing Decoded on page 11. Also see Quiz: Are You Professional? on page 26.

Frequently asked questions

1. **How do these companies get listed in the book anyway?** No company pays to be included—all listings are free. The listings come from a combination of research the editor does on the music industry and questionnaires requested by companies who want to be listed (many of them contact us to be included). All questionnaires are screened for known sharks and to make sure they meet our requirements (see How Do I Avoid the Rip-Offs? on page 19 for details of what makes us reject or remove a listing).

2. **Why aren't other companies I know about listed in the book?** We may have sent them a questionnaire, but they did not return it, were removed for complaints, went out of business, specifically asked not to be listed, could not be contacted for an update, etc.

3. **What's the deal with companies that don't take unsolicited submissions?** In the interest of completeness, the editor will sometimes include listings of crucial music companies he thinks you should be aware of. Major labels such as Capitol Records and Warner Bros. fall under this category. You want to at least have some idea of what their policies are, don't you? If a company is closed to unsolicited submissions, you can do either of two things: 1) don't submit to them; or 2) find a way around the roadblock by establishing a relationship or finding a backdoor of some kind (charming them on the phone, through managers, producers, artists, entertainment attorneys, or the fabled Seven Degrees of Separation—i.e. networking like crazy).

4. **A company said in their listing they take unsolicited submissions. My demo came back unopened. What happened?** Some companies needs change rapidly and may have changed since we contacted them for this edition of the book. This is another reason why it's often a good idea to contact a company before submitting.

Where Should I Send My Songs?

t depends a lot on whether you write mainly for yourself as a performer, or if you just write and want someone else to pick up your song for their recording (usually the case in country music, for example). Are you mainly a performing songwriter or a non-performing songwriter? This is important is figuring out what kind of companies to contact, as well as how you contact them. (For more detail, skip to Submission Strategies on page 23.)

What if I'm a non-performing songwriter?

Many well-known songwriters are not performers in their own right. Some are not skilled instrumentalists or singers, but they understand melody, lyrics and harmony and how they go together. They can write great songs, but they need someone else to bring it to life through skilled musicianship. A non-performing songwriter will usually approach music publishers first for access to artists looking for songs, as well as artists' managers, their producers and their record companies. On the flip side, many incredibly talented musicians can't write to save their lives and need someone else to provide them with good songs to perform. (For more details on the different types of companies and the roles they play for performing songwriters, see the section introductions for Music Publishers on page 80, Record companies on page 141, Record Producers on page 197, and Managers & Booking Agents on page 225. Also see Submission Strategies on page 23.)

What if I am a performing songwriter?

Many famous songwriters are also famous as performers. They are skilled interpreters of their own material, and they also know how to write to their own particular talents as musicians (which can often be quirky and unique to them). In this case, their intention is also usually to sell themselves as a performer in hopes of recording and releasing an album, or they have an album and want to find gigs and people who can help guide their careers. They will usually approach record companies or record producers first, on the basis of recording an album. For gigs and career guidance, they talk to booking agents and managers.

A smaller number also approach publishers in hopes of getting others to perform their songs, much like non-performing songwriters. Some music publishers in recent years have also taken on the role of developing artists as both songwriters and performers, or are connected to a major record label, so performing songwriters might go to them for these reasons. (For more details on the different types of companies and the roles they play for performing songwriters, see the section introductions for Music Publishers on page 80, Record companies on page 141, Record Producers on page 197, and Managers & Booking Agents on page 225. Also see Submission Strategies on page 23.)

Types of music companies

- **Music Publishers**—evaluate songs for commercial potential, find artists to record them, finds other uses for the songs such as film or TV, collects income from songs, protects copyrights from infringement

- **Record Companies**—sign artists to their labels, finance recordings, promotion and touring, releases songs/albums to radio and TV

- **Record Producers**—works in the studio and records songs (independently or for a record company), may be affiliated with a particular artist, sometimes develop artists for record labels, locates or co-writes songs if an artist does not write their own

- **Managers & Booking Agents**—works with artists to manage their careers, finds gigs, locates songs to record if the artist does not write their own

How do I use *Songwriter's Market* to narrow my search?

Once you've identified whether you are primarily interested in getting others to perform your songs (non-performing songwriter) or you perform your own songs and want a record deal, etc., there are several steps you can then take:

1. **Identify what kind of music company you wish to approach.** Based on whether you're a performing or non-performing songwriter, do you want to approach a music publisher for a publishing deal? Do you want to approach a record producer because you need somone to help you record an album in the studio? Maybe you want to approach a producer in hopes that an act he's producing needs songs to complete their album. Also see Submission Strategies on page 23 and the Section Introductions for Music Publishers on page 80, Record companies on page 141, Record Producers on page 197, and Managers & Booking Agents on page 225.

2. **Check for companies based on location.** Maybe you need a manager located close by. Maybe you need to find as many Nashville-based companies as you can because you write country and most country publishers are in Nashville. In this case start with the Geographic Index on page 425. You can also tell Canadian and Foreign listings by the icons in the listing (see A Sample Listing Decoded below and on page 11).

3. **Look for companies based on the type of music they want.** Some companies want country. Some record labels want only punk rock. Check the Category Indexes on page 388 for a list of music companies broken down by the type of music they are interested in.

4. **Look for companies based on how open they are to beginners.** Some companies are more open than others to beginning artists and songwriters. Maybe you are a beginner and it would help to approach these companies first. Some music publishers are hoping to find that wild card hit song and don't care if it comes from an unknown writer. Maybe you are just starting out looking for gigs or record deals, and you need a manager willing to help build your band's career from the ground up. Check the Openness to Submissions Index on page 415.

For more information on how to read the listings, see A Sample Listing Decoded on page 11.

A SAMPLE LISTING DECODED
What do the little symbols at the beginning of the listing mean?
Those are called "icons," and they give you quick information about a listing with one glance. Here is a list of the icons and what they mean:

Openness to submissions

- ◯ means the company is open to beginners' submissions, regardless of past success
- ◑ means the company is mostly interested in previously published songwriters/well-established acts*, but will consider beginners
- ◉ these companies do not want submissions from beginners, only from previously published songwriters/well-established* acts
- ∅ companies with this icon only accept material referred by a reputable industry source**
- * Well-established acts are those with a following, permanent gigs or previous record deal
- ** Reputable industry sources include managers, entertainment attorneys, performing rights organizations, etc.

Other icons

- ✿ means the listing is Canadian
- ⊕ means the listing is based overseas (Europe, Britain, Australia, etc.)
- Ⓝ indicates a listing is new to this edition
- ✓ means there has been a change in the contact information: contact name, phone number, fax, e-mail or website
- ♈ is for companies who have won an industry award of some type
- ▦ shows a company places songs in films or television shows (excluding commercials)

SPECIFIC
CONTACT
NAMES

EASY-TO-USE
REFERENCE
ICONS

TERMS OF
AGREEMENT

DETAILED
SUBMISSION
GUIDELINES

WHAT THEY'RE
LOOKING FOR

INSIDER
ADVICE

Ⓝ◯◑▦ BANANA RECORDS
3115 Hiss Ave., Baltimore MD 21234. Phone/fax: (410)663-5915. E-mail: theunholythree@yahoo.com. Website: www.theunholythree.com. **Contact:** Ron Brown, President. Record company, music publisher (Infinite Publishing) and record producer (Ronald Brown). Estab. 1990. Releases 30 singles, 20 LPs and 20 CDs/year. Pays standard royalty to artists on contract; statutory rate to publisher per song on record.
How to Contact: Submit demo tape by mail. Unsolicited submissions are OK. Prefers cassette with 3 songs and lyric sheet. Include SASE. Responds in 3 weeks.
Music: Mostly top 40/commercial, pop/ballads and alternative. Released "Crack of the Universe," written and recorded by Jesse Brown (pop) on Global; The Unholy Three (album), written and recorded by Ronnie B. (commercial), released 2002 on Banana Records.
Tips: "A good singer works hard at his craft. A hit song has good punch and a lot of talent."

Additional resources

For More Info

Songwriter's Market lists music publishers, record companies, producers and managers (as well as advertising firms, play producers and classical performing arts organizations) along with specifications on how to submit your material to each. If you can't find a certain person or company you're interested in, there are other sources of information you can try.

The Recording Industry Sourcebook, an annual directory published by Norris-Whitney Communications, lists record companies, music publishers, producers and managers, as well as attorneys, publicity firms, media, manufacturers, distributors and recording studios around the U.S. Trade publications such as *Billboard* or *Variety*, available at most local libraries and bookstores, are great sources for up-to-date information. These periodicals list new companies as well as the artists, labels, producers and publishers for each song on the charts.

CD booklets and cassette j-cards can also be valuable sources of information, providing the name of the record company, publisher, producer and usually the manager of an artist or group. Use your imagination in your research and be creative—any contacts you make in the industry can only help your career as a songwriter. See Publications of Interest on page 369.

Demo Recordings

What Should I Know?

What is a "demo"?

The demo, shorthand for *demonstration recording*, is the most important part of your submission package. They are meant to give music industry professionals a way to hear all the elements of your song as clearly as possible so they can decide if it has commercial potential.

Should I send a cassette or a CD?

More and more music industry people want CDs, although the cassette is still commonly accepted. A few companies want demos sent on CD only. It's getting cheaper and easier all the time to burn recordings onto CDR ("CD-Recordable"), so it is worth the investment to buy a burner or borrow one. Other formats such as DAT ("Digital Audio Tape") are rarely requested.

What should I send if I'm seeking management?

Some companies want a video of an act performing their songs. Most want VHS format videocassettes. A few ask for video on DVD. Check with the companies for specific requirements.

How many songs should I send, and in what order and length?

Most music industry people agree that three songs is enough. Most music professionals are short on time, and if you can't catch their attention in three songs, your songs probably don't have hit potential. Also, put three *complete songs* on your demo, not just snippets. Make sure to put your best, most commercial song first. An up-tempo number is usually best. If you send a cassette, *put all the songs on one side of the cassette and cue the tape to the beginning of the first song so no time is wasted fast-forwarding or rewinding.*

Should I sing my own songs on my demo?

If you can't sing well, you may want to find someone who can. There are many places to check for singers and musicians, including songwriters organizations, music stores and songwriting magazines. Some aspiring professional singers will sing on demos in exchange for a copy they can use as a demo to showcase their singing.

Should I use a professional demo service?

Many songwriters find professional demo services to be a convenient if they don't have time or the resources to put together musicians on their own. For a fee, a demo service will produce your songs in their studio using in-house singers and musicians (this is pretty common in

Nashville). Many of these advertise in music magazines, songwriting newsletters and bulletin boards at music stores. Make sure to hear samples of work they've done in the past. Some are mail-order businesses—you send a rough tape of your song or the sheet music, and they produce and record a demo within a month or two. Be sure you find a service that will let you have some control over how the demo is produced, and tell them exactly how you want your song to sound. As with studios, shop around for a service that fits your needs and budget. (Some will charge as low as $300 for three songs, while others may go as high as $3,000 and boast a high-quality sound—shop around and use your best judgment!)

Should I buy equipment and record demos myself?

If you have the drive and focus to learn good recording technique, yes. If not, it might be easier to have someone else do it. Digital multi-track recorders are now easily available and within reasonable financial reach of many people. For performing songwriters in search of record deals, the actual sound of their recordings can often be an important part of their artistic concept. Having the "means of production" within their grasp can be crucial to artists pursuing the independent route. But, if you don't know how to use the equipment, it may be better to go into a professional studio.

How elaborate and full should the demo production be if I'm a non-performing songwriter?

Many companies in *Songwriter's Market* tell you what they prefer. If in doubt, contact them and ask. In general, country songs and pop ballads can often be demoed with just a vocal plus guitar or piano, although many songwriters in those genres still prefer to get a more complete recording with drums, guitars and other backing instruments. Up-tempo pop, rock and dance demos usually need a more full production.

What kind of production do I need if I'm a performing songwriter?

If you are a band or artist looking for a record deal, you will need a demo that is as fully produced as possible. Many singer/songwriters record their demos as if they were going to be released as an album. That way, if they don't get a deal, they can still release it on their own. Professionally pressed CDs are also now easily within reach of performing songwriters, and many companies offer graphic design services for a professional-looking product.

How Do I Submit My Demo?

Y ou have three basic options for submitting your songs: submitting by mail, submitting in person and submitting over the Internet (the newest and least widely accepted option at this time).

SUBMITTING BY MAIL

Should I call, write or e-mail first to ask for permission or submission requirements?

This is always a good idea, and many companies ask you to contact them first. If you call, be polite, brief and specific. If you send a letter, make sure it is typed and to the point. Include a typed SASE they can use to reply. If you send an e-mail, again be professional and to the point. Proofread your message before you send it, and then be patient. Give them some time to reply. Do not send out mass e-mails or otherwise spam their e-mail account.

What do I send with my demo?

Most companies have specific requirements, but here are some general pointers:

- Read the listing carefully and submit *exactly* what they ask for, in the exact way they ask. It's also a good idea to call first, just in case they've changed their submission policies.
- Listen to each demo to make sure they sound right and are in the right order (see Demo Recordings: What Should I Know? on page 13).
- If you use cassettes, make sure they are cued up to the beginning of the first song.
- Enclose a *brief*, typed cover letter to introduce yourself. Tell them what songs you are sending and why you are sending them. If you are pitching your songs to a particular artist, say so in the letter. I you are an artist/songwriter looking for a record deal, you should say so. Be specific.
- Include *typed* lyric sheets or lead sheets, if requested. Make sure your name, address and phone number are on each sheet.
- Neatly label each tape with your name, address and phone number, along with the names of the songs in the order they appear on the tape.
- Include a SASE with sufficient postage and large enough to return all your materials. **Warning: Many companies do not return materials, so read each listing carefully!**
- If you submit to companies in other countries, include a self-addressed envelope (SAE) and International Reply Coupon (IRC), available at most post offices. Make sure the envelope is large enough to return all of your materials.
- Pack everything neatly. Neatly type or write the company's address and your return address so they are clearly visible. Your package is the first impression a company has of you and your songs, so neatness counts!

Submission Mailing Pointers

Send your package with bubble wrap or in a **padded envelope** to protect pieces.

Laser Print all text on computer for a professional look.

Include **lyric sheets** with your demo and label each song section (verse, chorus, etc.).

Keep **cover letter brief** and let the song speak for itself.

Be sure to enclose sufficient **return postage** for all your materials.

If you send a **cassette,** make sure you've cued the tape to the beginning of the first song.

Include **contact information** on every piece.

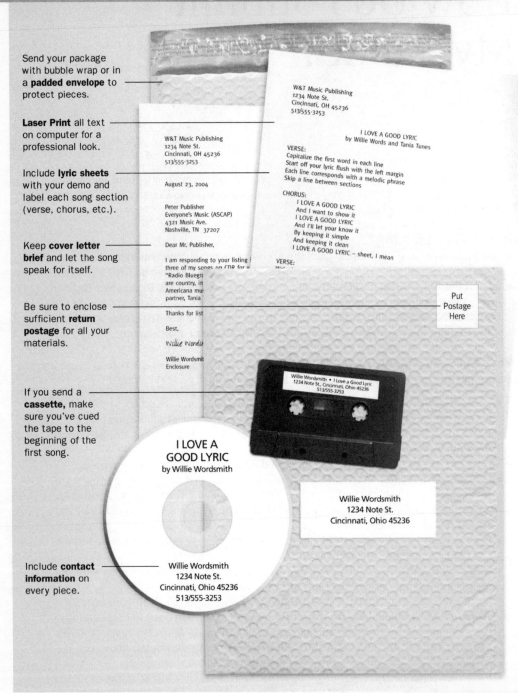

W&T Music Publishing
1234 Note St.
Cincinnati, OH 45236
513/555-3253

I LOVE A GOOD LYRIC
by Willie Words and Tania Tunes

VERSE:
Capitalize the first word in each line
Start off your lyric flush with the left margin
Each line corresponds with a melodic phrase
Skip a line between sections

CHORUS:
I LOVE A GOOD LYRIC
And I want to show it
I LOVE A GOOD LYRIC
And I'll let your know it
By keeping it simple
And keeping it clean
I LOVE A GOOD LYRIC – sheet, I mean

VERSE:

W&T Music Publishing
1234 Note St.
Cincinnati, OH 45236
513/555-3253

August 23, 2004

Peter Publisher
Everyone's Music (ASCAP)
4321 Music Ave.
Nashville, TN 37207

Dear Mr. Publisher,

I am responding to your listing
three of my songs on CDR for
"Radio Bluegr
are country, in
Americana mu
partner, Tania

Thanks for list

Best,

Willie Wordsm

Willie Wordsmit
Enclosure

Put Postage Here

Willie Wordsmith • I Love a Good Lyric
1234 Note St., Cincinnati, Ohio 45236
513/555-3253

I LOVE A
GOOD LYRIC
by Willie Wordsmith

Willie Wordsmith
1234 Note St.
Cincinnati, Ohio 45236

Willie Wordsmith
1234 Note St.
Cincinnati, Ohio 45236
513/555-3253

- Mail first class. Stamp or write "First Class Mail" on the package and the SASE you enclose.
- **Do not use registered or certified mail unless requested!** Most companies will not accept or open demos sent by registered or certified mail for fear of lawsuits.
- Keep records of the dates, songs and companies you submit to.

Is it OK to send demos to more than one person or company at a time?
It is usually acceptable to make simultaneous submissions. One exception is when a publisher, artist or other industry professional asks to put your song "on hold."

What does it mean when a song is "on hold"?
This means they intend to record the song and don't want you to give the song to anyone else. This is not a guarantee, though. Your song may eventually be returned to you, even if it's been on hold for months. Or it may be recorded and included on the album. If either of these happens, you are free to pitch your song to other people again.

How can I protect myself from my song being put "on hold" indefinitely?
You can, and should, protect yourself. Establish a deadline for the person who asks for the hold (for example, "You can put my song on hold for [number of] months."), or modify the hold to specify you will still pitch the song to others but won't sign another deal without allowing the person with the song on hold to make you an offer. Once you sign a contract with a publisher, they have exclusive rights to your song and you may not pitch it to other would-be publishers.

SUBMITTING IN PERSON
Is a visit to New York, Nashville or Los Angeles to submit in person a good idea?
A trip to one of the major music hubs can be valuable if you are organized to make the most of it. You should have specific goals and set up appointments before you go. Some industry professionals are difficult to see and may not feel meeting out-of-town writers is a high priority. Others are more open and even encourage face-to-face meetings. By taking the time to travel, organize and schedule meetings, you can appear more professional than songwriters who submit blindly through the mail.

What should I take?
Take several copies of your demo and typed lyric sheets of each of your songs. More than one company you visit may ask you to leave a copy for them to review. You can expect occasionally to find a person has cancelled an appointment, but want you to leave a copy of your songs so they may listen and contact you later. (Never give someone the only or last copy of your demo if you absolutely want it returned, though.)

Where should I network while visiting?
Coordinate your trip with a music conference or make plans to visit ASCAP, BMI or SESAC offices while you are there. For example, the South by Southwest Music Conference in Austin and the NSAI Spring Symposium often feature demo listening sessions, where industry professionals listen to demos submitted by songwriters attending the seminar. ASCAP, BMI and SESAC also sometimes sponsor seminars or allow aspiring songwriters to make appointments with counselors who can give them solid advice.

How do I deal with rejection?
Many good songs have been rejected simply because they were not what the publisher or record company was looking for at that particular point. Do not take it personally. If few

people like your songs, it does not mean they are not good. On the other hand, if you have a clear vision for what your particular songs are trying to get across, specific comments can also teach you a lot about whether your concept is coming across as you intended. If you hear the same criticisms of your songs over and over—for instance, the feel of the melody isn't right or the lyrics need work—give the advice serious thought. Listen carefully and use what the reviewers say constructively to improve your songs.

SUBMITTING OVER THE INTERNET
Is it OK to submit over the Internet?
It can be done, but it's not yet widely accepted. There can still be problems with audio file formats. Although e-mail is more common now if you look through the listings in *Songwriter's Market*, not all music companies are necessarily equipped with computers or Internet access sufficient to make the process easy. But it shows a lot of promise for the future. Web-based companies like Tonos.com or TAXI, among many others are making an effort to connect songwriters and industry professionals over the Internet. The Internet is proving important for networking. Tunesmith.net has extensive bulletin boards and allow members to post audio files of songs for critique. Stay tuned for future developments.

If I want to try submitting over the Internet, what should I do?
First, send an e-mail to confirm whether a music company is equipped to stream or download audio files properly (whether mp3 or real audio, etc.). If they do accept demos online, one strategy becoming common is build a website with audio files that can be streamed or down-loaded. Then, when you have permission, send an e-mail with links to that website or to particular songs. All they have to do is click on the link and it launches their web browser to the appropriate page. Do not try to send mp3s or other files as attachments. They are often too large for the free online e-mail accounts people commonly use, and they may be mistakenly erased as potential viruses.

How Do I Avoid the Rip-Offs?

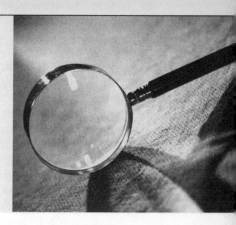

The music industry has its share of dishonest, greedy people who will try to rip you off by appealing to your ambition, by stroking your ego or by claiming special powers to make you successful—for a price, of course. Most of them use similar methods, and you can prevent a lot of heartbreak by learning to spot them and stay away.

What is a "song shark"?

"Song sharks," as they're called, prey on beginners—songwriters unfamiliar with how the music industry works and what the ethical standards are. Two general signs of a song shark are:

- Song sharks will take *any* songs—quality doesn't count.
- They're not concerned with future royalties, since they get their money up front from songwriters who think they're getting a great deal.

What are some of the more blatant rip-offs?

A request for money up front is the most common element. Song sharks may ask for money in the form of submission fees, an outright offer to publish your song for a fee or an offer to re-record your demo for a sometimes hefty price (with the implication that they will make your song wildly successful if you only pay to have it re-demoed in *their studio*). There are many variations on this theme.

If you write lyrics, but not music

- **You must find a collaborator.** The music business is looking for the complete package: music plus lyrics. If you don't write music, find a collaborator who does. The best way to find a collaborator is through songwriting organizations. Check the Organizations section (page 326) for songwriting groups near you.

- **Don't get ripped-off.** "Music mills" advertise in the back of magazines or solicit you through the mail. For a fee they will set your lyrics or poems to music. The rip-off is that they may use the same melody for hundreds of lyrics and poems, whether it sounds good or not. Publishers recognize one of these melodies as soon as they hear it.

Here is a list of rules that can help you avoid a lot of scams:

- **DO NOT SELL YOUR SONGS OUTRIGHT!** It's unethical for anyone to offer such a proposition. If your song becomes successful after you've sold it outright, you will never get royalties for it.
- **Never pay any sort of "submission fees," "review fees," "service fees," "filing fees," etc.** Reputable companies review material free of charge. If you encounter a company in this book who charges to submit, report them to the editor. If a company charges "only" $15 to submit your song, consider this: *if "only" 100 songwriters pay the $15, this company has made an extra $1,500 just for opening the mail!*
- **Never pay to have your songs published.** A reputable company interested in your songs assumes the responsibility and cost of promoting them, in hopes of realizing a profit once the songs are recorded and released. If they truly believe in your song, they will accept the costs involved.
- **Do not pay a company to pair you with a collaborator.** It's much better to contact a songwriting organization that offers collaboration services to their members.
- **Never pay to have your lyrics or poems set to music.** This is a classic rip-off. "Music mills"—for a price—may use the same melody for hundreds of lyrics and poems, whether it sounds good or not. Publishers recognize one of these melodies as soon as they hear it.
- **Avoid "pay-to-play" CD compilation deals.** It's totally unrealistic to expect this will open doors for you. These are mainly a money-maker for the music company. CDs are cheap to manufacture, so a company that charges $100 to include your recording on a CD is making a killing. They claim they send these CDs to radio stations, producers, etc., but they usually wind up in the trash or as drink coasters. Music industry professionals have no incentive to listen to them. Everybody on the CD paid to be included, so it's not like they were carefully screened for quality.
- **Avoid "songpluggers" who offer to "shop" your song for an upfront fee or retainer.** This practice is not appropriate for *Songwriter's Market* readers, many of whom are beginners and live away from major music centers like Nashville. Professional, established songwriters in Nashville are sometimes known to work on a fee basis with songpluggers they have gotten to know over many years, *but the practice is controversial even for professionals.* Also, the songpluggers used by established professionals are very selective about their clients and have their own reputation to uphold. Companies who offer you these services but barely know you or your work are to be avoided. Also, contracting a songplugger by long distance offers little or no accountability—they take your money and then you have no real way of knowing what they're doing on your behalf, if anything.
- **Avoid paying a fee up front to have a publisher make a demo of your song.** Some publishers may take demo expenses out of your future royalties (a negotiable contract point usually meant to avoid endless demo sessions), but avoid paying up front for demo costs for a song signed to a publisher.
- **No record company should ask you to pay them or an associated company to make a demo.** The job of a record company is to make records and decide which artists to sign *after* listening to demo submissions.
- **Read all contracts carefully before signing.** And don't sign any contract you're unsure about or that you don't fully understand. It is well worth paying an attorney for the time it takes him to review a contract if you can avoid a bad situation that may cost you thousands.
- **Before entering a songwriting contest, read the rules carefully.** Be sure what you're giving up in the way of entry fees, etc., is not more than what you stand to gain by

winning the contest. See the Contests & Awards section on page 312.

- **Verify any situation about an individual or company if you have any doubts at all.** Contact the company's Performing Rights Society—ASCAP, BMI, SESAC or SOCAN (in Canada). Check with the Better Business Bureau in the company's town, or contact the state attorney general's office. Contact professional organizations you're a member of and inquire about the reputation of the company.
- **If a record company or other company asks you to pay expenses up front, be careful.** Record producers commonly charge up front to produce an artist's album. Small indie labels sometimes ask a band to help with recording costs (but seek less control than a major label might). It's up to you to decide to whether or not it is a good idea. Talk to other artists who have signed similar contracts before you sign one yourself. Research companies to find out if they can deliver on their claims, and what kind of distribution they have. Visit their website, if they have one. Beware of any company that won't let you know what it has done in the past. If a company has had successes and good working relationships with artists, it should be happy to brag about them.

I noticed record producers charge to produce albums. Is this bad?

No. Just remember what your goals are. If you write songs, but do not sing or perform, you are looking for publishing opportunities with the producer instead of someone who can help you record an album or CD. If you are a performing artist or band, then you might be in the market to hire a producer, in which case you will most likely pay them up front (and possibly give them a share in royalties or publishing, depending on the specific deal you negotiate). For more information see the Record Producers section introduction on page 197 and Royalties: Where Does the Money Come From? on page 28.

How do I file a complaint?

Write to the *Songwriter's Market* editor at: 4700 E. Galbraith Rd., Cincinnati OH 45236. Include:

- A complete description of the situation, as best you can describe it.
- Copies of any materials a company may have sent you that we may keep on file.

If you encounter situations similar to any of the "song shark" scenarios described above, let us know about it.

Will it help me avoid rip-offs if I join a songwriting organization?

Yes. You will have access to a lot of good advice from a lot of experienced people. You will be able to research and compare notes, which will help you avoid a lot of pitfalls.

What should I know about contracts?

Negotiating a fair contract is important. You must protect yourself, and there are specific things you should look for in a contract (see What About Contracts? on page 32).

Are companies that offer demo services automatically bad?

No, but you are not obligated to make use of their services. Many music companies have their own or related recording studios, and with good recording equipment becoming so cheap and easy to use in recent years, a lot of them are struggling to stay afloat. This doesn't mean a company is necessarily trying to rip you off, but use your best judgment. In some cases, a company will submit a listing to *Songwriter's Market* for the wrong reasons—to pitch their demo services instead of finding songs to sign—in which case you should report them to the *Songwriter's Market* editor.

Submission Strategies

NON-PERFORMING SONGWRITERS

Here's a short list of avenues non-performing songwriters can pursue when submitting songs:

1. Submit to a music publisher. This is the obvious one. Look at the information under "**Music**" in the listing to see examples of a publisher's songs and the artists they've found cuts with. Do you recognize the songs? Have you heard of the artists? Who are the writers? Do they have cuts with artists you would like to get a song to?

2. Submit to a record company. Are the bands and artists on the record company's roster familiar? Do they tend to use outside songs on their albums? When pursuing this angle, it often helps to contact the record company first. Ask if they have a group or artist in development who needs material.

3. Submit to a record producer. Do the producer's credits in the listings show songs written by songwriters other than the artist? Does he produce name artists known for using outside material? Be aware that producers themselves often write with the artists, so your song might also be competing against the producer's songwriting.

4. Submit to an artist's manager. If an artist needs songs, their manager is a prime gateway for your song. Contact the manager and ask if he has an act in need of material.

5. Join a songwriting organization. Songwriting organizations are a good way to make contacts. You'll discover opportunities through the contacts you make that others might not hear about. Some organizations can put you in direct contact with publishers for song critique sessions. You can increase your chances of a hit by co-writing with other songwriters. Your songs will get better because of the feedback from other members.

6. Approach Performing Rights Organizations (PROs). PROs like ASCAP and BMI have songwriter counselors who can sometimes (if they think you're ready) give you a reference to a music company. This is one of the favored routes to success in the Nashville music scene.

PERFORMING SONGWRITERS

This is a bit more complicated, because there are a lot of different avenues available.

Finding a record deal.

This is often a performing songwriter's primary goal. Get a record deal and release an album. Here are some possible ways to approach it:

1. Approach a record company for a record deal. This is another obvious one. Independent labels will be a lot more approachable than major labels, who are usually deluged with demos. Independent labels give you more artistic freedom, while major labels will demand more compromise, especially if you do not have a previous track record. A compromise between the two is to approach one of the "fake indie" labels owned a major. You'll get more of the benefits of an indie, but with more of the resources and connections of a major label.

2. Approach a record producer for a development deal. Some producers sign artists, produce their album and develop them like a record company and then approach major labels for distribution deals. This has advantages and drawbacks. For example, the producer gives you guidance and connections, but it can also be harder to get paid because you are signed to the producer and not the label.

3. Get a manager with connections. The right manager with the right connections can make all the difference in getting a record deal.

4. Ask a music publisher. Publishers are taking on more and more of a role of developing performing songwriters as artists. Many major publishers are sister companies to record labels and can shop you for a deal when they think you're ready.

5. Approach an entertainment attorney. Entertainment attorneys are a must when it comes to negotiating record contracts, and some moonlight by helping artists make connections for record deals (they will get their cut, of course).

6. Approach PROs. ASCAP and BMI can counsel you on your career and possibly make a referral. They also commonly put on performance showcases where A&R ("artist and repertoire") people from record labels attend to check out new artists.

Finding a producer to help with your album

Independently minded performing songwriters often find they need help navigating the studio when it comes time to produce their own album. In this case, the producer often works for an upfront fee from the artist, for a percentage of the royalty when the album is released and sold, or a combination of both.

Things to keep in mind when submitting a demo to a producer on this basis:

1. Is the producer known for a particular genre or "sound"? Many producers have a signature sound to their studio productions and are often connected to specific genres. Phil Spector had the "Wall of Sound." Bob Rock pioneered a glossy metal sound for Metallica and The Cult. Daniel Lanois and Brian Eno are famous for the atmospheres they created on albums by U2. Look at your favorite CDs to see who produced. Use these as touchstones when approaching producers to see if they are on the same wavelength as you.

2. What role does a particular producer like to take in the studio. The "**Tips**" section of *Songwriter's Market* Record Producers listings often have notes from the producer about how they like to work with performing songwriters in the studio. Some work closely as a partner with the artist on developing arrangements and coaching performances. Some prefer final authority on creative decisions. Think carefully about what kind of working relationship you want.

Finding a manager

Many performing songwriters eventually find it necessary to find a manager to help with developing their careers and finding gigs. Some things to keep in mind when looking:

1. Does the manager work with artists in my genre of music? A manager who typically works with punk rock bands may not have as many connections useful to an aspiring country singer-songwriter. A manager who mainly works with gospel artists might not know what to do with a hedonistic rock band.

2. How big is the manager's agency? If a manager is working with multiple acts, but has a small (or no) staff, you might not get the attention you want. Some of the listings have information in the heading about the agency's staff size.

3. Does the manager work with acts from my region? You can check the Geographic

Index on page 425 to check for management agencies located near your area. Many of the listings also have information in their headings provided by the companies describing whether they work with regional acts only or artists from any region.

4. Does the manager work with name acts? A manager with famous clients could work wonders for your career. Or you could get lost in the shuffle. Use your best judgment when sizing up a potential manager and be clear with yourself about the kind of relationship you would like to have and the level of attention you want for your career.

5. If I'm a beginner, will the manager work with me? Look in the Openness to Submissions Index on page 415 to find companies open to beginners. Some may suggest extensive changes to your music or image. On the other hand, you may have a strong vision of what you want to do and need a manager who will work with you to achieve that vision instead of changing you around. Decide for yourself how much you are willing to compromise in good faith.

Remember that a relationship between you and a manager is a two-way street. You will have to earn each other's trust and be clear about your goals for mutual success.

Quiz: Are You Professional?

Okay, everybody! Take out your submission package and let's take a look. Hmm . . . very interesting. I think you're well on your way, but you should probably change a few things.

We asked record companies, music publishers and record producers, "What do songwriters do in correspondence with your company (by phone, mail or demo) that screams 'amateur'?" Take this quiz and find out how professional you appear to those on the receiving end of your submission. The following are common mistakes songwriters make all the time. They may seem petty, but, really, do you want to give someone an excuse not to listen to your demo? Check off the transgressions you have committed.

BY MAIL YOU SENT:

- ☑ anything handwritten (lyrics, cover letters, labels for cassettes). Today there is no excuse for handwritten materials. Take advantage of your local library's typewriters or businesses that charge by the hour to use a computer. And don't even think about using notebook paper.
- ☑ materials without a contact name *and* phone number. Put this information on *everything*.
- ☑ lyrics only. Music companies want music and words. See the If You Write Lyrics, But Not Music sidebar on page 19.
- ☑ insufficient return postage, an envelope too small to return materials, no SASE at all, or a "certified mail" package. If you want materials returned, don't expect the company to send it back on their dime with their envelope—give them what they need. Certified mail is unnecessary and annoying; first class will suffice.
- ☑ long-winded, over-hyped cover letters, or no cover letter at all. Companies don't need (or want) to hear your life story, how many instruments you play, how many songs you've written, how talented you are or how all your songs are sure-fire hits. Briefly explain why you are sending the songs (e.g., your desire to have them published) and let the songs speak for themselves. Double check your spelling too.
- ☑ over-packaged materials. Do not use paper towels, napkins, foil or a mountain of tape to package your submission. Make the investment in bubble wrap or padded envelopes.
- ☑ photos of your parents or children. As much as you love them, your family's pictures or letters of recommendation won't increase your chances of success (unless your family is employed by a major music company).
- ☑ songs in the style the company doesn't want. Do not "shotgun" your submissions. Read the listings carefully to see if they want your style of music.

YOU CALLED THE CONTACT PERSON:

☑ to check on the submission only a couple days after it was received. Read the listings to see how soon (or if) they report back on submissions. Call them only after that time has elapsed. If they are interested, they will find a way to contact you.

☑ excessively. It's important to be proactive, but check yourself. Make sure you have given them enough time to respond before you call again. Calling every week is inappropriate.

☑ armed with an angry or aggressive tone of voice. A bad attitude will get you nowhere.

WITH THE DEMO YOU PROVIDED:

☑ no lyric sheet. A typed sheet of lyrics for each song is required.

☑ poor vocals and instrumentation. Spending a little extra for professionals can make all the difference.

☑ a poor-quality cassette. The tape should be new and have a brand name.

☑ long intros. Don't waste time—get to the heart of the song.

☑ buried vocals. Those vocals should be out front and clear as a bell.

☑ recordings of sneezes or coughs. Yuck.

SCORING

If you checked 1-3: Congratulations! You're well within the professional parameters. Remedy the unprofessional deeds you're guilty of and send out more packages.

If you checked 4 or more: Whoa! Overhaul your package, let someone check it over, and then fire away with those impeccably professional submissions!

Royalties

Where Does the Money Come From?

NON-PERFORMING SONGWRITERS
How do songwriters make money?
The quick answer is that songwriters make money through rights available to them through the copyright laws. For more detail, keep reading and see the article What About Copyright? on page 32.

What specific rights make money for songwriters?
There are two primary ways songwriters earn money on their songs: Performance Royalties and Mechanical Royalties.

What is a performance royalty?
When you hear a song on the radio, on television, in the elevator, in a restaurant, etc. the songwriter receives royalties, called "Performance Royalties." Performing Rights Organizations (ASCAP, BMI and SESAC in the U.S.A.) collect payment from radio stations, television, etc. and distribute those payments to songwriters (see below).

What is a mechanical royalty?
When a record company puts a song onto a CD, cassette, etc. and distributes copies for sale, they owe a royalty payment to the songwriter for each copy they press of the album. It is called a "mechanical royalty" because of the mechanical process used to mass produce a copy of a CD, cassette or sheet music. The payment is small per song (see the "Royalty Provisions" subhead of the Basic Song Contract Pointers sidebar on page 38), but the earnings can add up and reach massive proportions for songs appearing on successful major label albums. ****Note: This royalty is totally different from the artist royalty on the retail price of the album.****

Who collects the money for performance and mechanical royalties?
Performing Rights Organizations collect performance royalties. There are three organizations that collect performance royalties: ASCAP, BMI and SESAC. These organizations arose many years ago when songwriters and music publishers gathered together to press for their rights and improve their ability to collect fees for the use of their songs. ASCAP, BMI and SESAC collect fees for the use of songs and then pass along the money to their member songwriters and music publishers.

Mechanical rights organizations collect mechanical royalties. There are three organizations that collect mechanical royalties: The Harry Fox Agency (HFA), The American Mechanical Rights Agency (AMRA) and The Songwriters Guild of America (SGA). These three organizations collect mechanical royalties from record companies of all sizes—major labels, mid-size and independents—and pass the royalties along to member music publishers and songwriters.

MUSIC PUBLISHING ROYALTIES

How do songwriters hook up with this system to earn royalties?

For **Performance Royalties**, individual songwriters **affiliate** with a Performing Rights Organization of their choice, and register their songs in the PRO database. Each PRO has a slightly different method of calculating payment, different ownership, and different membership structure, so choosing a PRO is an individual choice. Once a songwriter is affiliated and has registered their songs, the PROs then collect fees as described above and issue a check to the songwriter.

For **Mechanical Royalties**, three different things can happen:

1. The songwriter is signed to a publisher that is affiliated with The Harry Fox Agency. The Harry Fox Agency collects the mechanical royalties and passes them along to the publisher. The publisher then passes these along to the songwriter within 30 days. This case usually happens when a songwriter is signed to a major publisher and has a song on a major label album release.

2. The songwriter is not signed to a publisher and owns exclusive rights to his songs, and so works with AMRA or The Songwriters Guild of America, who cut a check directly to the songwriter instead of passing them to the publisher first.
3. They are signed to a publisher, but the songs are being released on albums by independent labels. In this case, the songwriter often works with AMRA since they have a focus on the independent music publishing market.

PERFORMING SONGWRITERS/ARTISTS
How do performing songwriters make money?
Performing songwriters and artists (if they write their own songs) make money just like non-performing songwriters, as described above, but they also make money through royalties made on the retail price of an album when it is sold online, in a store, etc.

What about all the stories of performing songwriters getting into bad deals?
The stories are generally true, but if they're smart, performing songwriters usually can hold on to the money they would be owed as songwriters (performing and mechanical royalties). But when it comes to retail sale royalties, all they will usually see is an "advance"—essentially a loan—which must then be paid off from record sales. You will not see a royalty check on retail sales until you're advance is paid off. If you are given a $600,000 advance, you will have to pay back the record company $600,000 out of your sales royalties before you see any more money.

Do performing songwriters and artists get to keep the advance?
Not really. If you have a manager who has gotten you a record deal, he will take his cut. You will probably be required in the contract to pay for the producer and studio time to make the album. Often the producer will take a percentage of subsequent royalties from album sales, which comes out of your pocket. Then there are also music video costs, promotion to radio stations, tour support, paying sidemen, etc. Just about anything you can think of is eventually paid for out of your advance or out of sales royalties. There are also deductions to royalties usually built in to record company contracts that make it harder to earn out an advance.

What should a performing songwriter wanting to sign with a major label do?
Their best option is to negotiate a fair contract, get as big of an advance as possible, and then manage that advance money the best they can. A good contract will keep the songwriting royalties described above completely separate from the flow of sales royalties, and will also cut down on the number of deductions the record company builds into the contract. And because of the difficulty in earning out any size advance or auditing the record company, it makes sense to get as much cash up front as you can, then to manage that as best you can. You will need a good lawyer.

RECORD COMPANIES, PRODUCERS AND MANAGERS & BOOKING AGENTS
How do music publishers make money?
A publisher works as a songwriter's agent, looks for profitable commercial uses for the songs he represents, and then takes a percentage of the profits. This is typically 50% of all earning from a particular song—often referred to as the *publisher's share*. A successful publisher stays in contact with several A&R reps, finding out what upcoming projects are in need of new material, and whether any songs he represents will be appropriate.

How do record companies make money?

Record companies primarily make their money from profits made selling CDs, cassettes, DVDs, etc. Record companies keep most of the profit after subtracting manufacturing costs, royalties to recording artists, distribution fees and the costs of promoting songs to radio (which for major labels can reach up to $300,000 per song). Record companies also usually have music publishing divisions that make money performing all the functions of publishers.

How do record producers make money?

Producers mostly make their money by charging a flat fee up front to helm a recording project, by sharing in the royalties from album sales, or both. A small independent producer might charge $10,000 (or sometimes less) up front to produce a small indie band, while a "name" producer such as Bob Rock, who regularly works with major label bands, might charge $300,000. Either of these might also take a share in sales royalties, referred to as "points"— as in "percentage points." A producer might say, "I'll produce you for $10,000 and 2 points." If an artist is getting a 15% royalty an album sales, then two of those percentage points will go to the producer instead. Producers also make money by co-writing with the artists to get publishing royalties, or they may ask for part of the publishing from songs written by outside songwriters.

How do managers make money?

Most managers make money by taking a percentage commission of their clients' income, usually 10-25%. If a touring band finishes a show and makes a $2,000 profit, a manager on 15% commission would get $300. If an artist gets a $40,000 advance from a mid-size label, the manager would get $6,000. Whether an artist's songwriting income is included in the manager's commission comes down to negotiation. *The commission should give the manager incentive to make things happen for your career, so avoid paying flat fees up front.*

Music Biz Basics

What About Copyright?

How am I protected by the copyright laws?

Copyright protection applies to your song the instant you it them down in fixed form—a recording, sheet music, lead sheet, etc. This protection lasts for your lifetime plus 70 years (or the lifetime of the last surviving writer, if you co-wrote the song with somebody else). When you prepare demos, place notification of copyright on all copies of your song—the lyric sheets, lead sheets and labels for cassettes, CDs, etc. The notice is simply the word ''copyright'' or the symbol © followed by the year the song was created (or published) and your name: © 2005 by John Q. Songwriter.

What parts of a song are protected by copyright?

Traditionally, the melody line and the lyrics are eligible for copyright. Period. Chords and rhythm are virtually never protected. An incredibly original arrangement can sometimes qualify, but the original copyright owner of the song must agree to it and they usually don't). Sound recordings can also be copyrighted, but this applies strictly to the actual sounds on the recording, not the song itself (this copyright is usually owned by record companies).

What songs are not protected?

Song titles or mere ideas for music and lyrics cannot be copyrighted. Very old songs in the ''public domain'' are not protected. You could quote a melody from a Bach piece, but you could not then stop someone else from quoting the same melody in their song.

When would I lose or have to share the copyright?

If you *collaborate* with other writers, they are assumed to have equal interests unless you state some other arrangement, in writing. If you write under a *work-for-hire* arrangement, the company or person who hired you to write the song then owns the copyright. Sometimes your spouse may automatically be granted an interest in your copyright as part of their *spousal rights*, which might then become important if you got divorced.

Should I register my copyright?

Registering you copyright with the Library of Congress gives the best possible protection. Registration establishes a public record of your copyright—even though a song is copyrighted whether or not it is registered—and could prove useful in any future court cases involving the song. Registration also entitles you to a potentially greater settlement in a copyright infringement lawsuit.

How do I register my song?

To register your song, request government form PA from the Copyright Office. Call the 24-hour hotline at (202)707-9100 and leave your name and address on the messaging system. Once you receive the PA form, you must return it, along with a registration fee and a CD (or tape) and lead sheet of your song. Send these to the Register of Copyrights, Copyright Office, Library of Congress, Washington DC 20559. It may take several months to receive your certificate of registration from the Copyright Office, but your songs are protected from the date of creation, the date of registration will reflect the date you applied. For more information, call the Copyright Office's Public Information Office at (202)707-3000 or visit their website at http://lcweb.loc.gov/copyright.

echo – www.copyright .gov

Government resources

For More Info

The Library of Congress's copyright website is your best source for current, complete information on the subject of copyright. Not only can you learn all you could possibly wish to know about intellectual property rights and U.S. copyright law (the section of the U.S. Code dealing with copyright is reprinted there in its entirety), but you can also download copyright forms directly from the site. The site also includes links to other copyright-related web pages, many of which will be of interest to songwriters, including ASCAP, BMI, SESAC, and the Harry Fox Agency. Check it out at **http://lcweb.loc.gov/copyright**.

Music Biz Basics

How likely is it that someone will try to steal my song?

Copyright infringement is very rare. But, if you ever feel that one of your songs has been stolen—that someone has unlawfully infringed on your copyright—you must prove that you created the work and that the person you are suing had access to your song. Copyright registration is the best proof of a date of creation. You *must* have your copyright registered in order to file a lawsuit. Also, it's helpful if you keep your rough drafts and revisions of songs, either on paper or on tape.

Why did song sharks start soliciting me after I registered my song?

This is one potential, unintended consequence of registering your song with the Library of Congress. The copyright indexes are a public record of your songwriting, and song sharks often search the copyright indexes and mail solicitations to songwriters who live out away from major music centers such as Nashville. They figure these songwriters don't know any better and are easy prey. *Do not allow this possibility to stop you from registering your songs!* Just be aware, educate yourself, and then throw the song sharks' mailings in the trash.

What if I mail a tape to myself to get a postmark date on a sealed envelope?

The "poor man's copyright" has not stood up in court, and is not an acceptable substitute for registering your song. If you feel it's important to shore up your copyright, register it with the Library of Congress.

Career Songwriting

What Should I Know?

What career options are open to songwriters who do not perform?

The possibilities range from a beginning songwriter living away from a music center like Nashville who lands an occasional single-song publishing deal, to a staff songwriter signed to a major publishing company. And then there are songwriters like Desmond Child who operate independently, have developed a lot of connections, work with numerous artists and set up their own independent publishing operations.

What is "single-song" songwriting about?

In this case, a songwriter submits songs to many different companies. One or two songs gain interest from different publishers, and the songwriter signs separate contracts for each song with each publisher. The songwriter can then pitch other songs to other publishers. In Nashville, for instance, a single-song contract is usually the first taste of success for an aspiring songwriter on his way up the ladder. Success of this sort can induce a songwriter to move to a music center like Nashville (if they haven't already), and is a big boost for a struggling songwriter already living there. A series of single-song contracts often signals a songwriters' maturing skill and marketability.

What is a "staff songwriter"?

A staff songwriter usually works for a major publisher and receives a monthly stipend as an advance against the royalties he is likely to earn for the publisher. The music publisher has exclusive rights to everything the songwriter writes while signed to the company. The publisher also works actively on the writer's behalf to hook him or her up with co-writers and other opportunities. A staff songwriting position is highly treasured by many because it offers a steady income, and in Nashville is a sign the songwriter has "arrived."

What comes after the staff songwriting position?

Songwriters who go to the next level have a significant reputation for their ability to write hit songs. Famous artists seek them out, and they often write actively in several markets at once. They often write on assignment for film and television, and commonly keep their own publishing companies to maximize their income.

As my career grows what should I do about keeping track of expenses, etc.?

You should keep a ledger or notebook with records on all financial transactions related to your songwriting—royalty checks, demo costs, office supplies, postage, travel expenses, dues to organizations, class and workshop fees, plus any publications you purchase pertaining to songwriting. You may also want a separate checking account devoted to your songwriting activities. This will make record keeping easier and help to establish your identity as a business for tax purposes.

What should I know about taxes related to songwriting income?

Any royalties you receive will not reflect taxes or any other mandatory deductions. It is your responsibility to keep track of income and file the correct tax forms. For specific information, contact the IRS or talk to an accountant who serves music industry clients.

Music Biz Basics

What About Contracts?

CO-WRITING
What kind of agreements do I need with co-writers?

You may need to sign a legal agreement between you and a co-writer to establish percentages you will each receive of the writer's royalties. You will also have to iron out what you will do if another person, such as an artist, wants to change your song and receive credit as a co-writer. For example, in the event, a major artist wants to cut your song for her album—but also wants to rewrite some lyrics and take a share of the publishing—you and your co-writer need to agree whether it is better to get a song on an album that might sell millions (and make a lot of money) or pass on it because you don't want to give up credit. The situation could be uncomfortable if you are not in sync on the issue.

When do I need a lawyer to look over agreements?

When it comes to doing business with a publisher, producer or record company, you should always have the contract reviewed by a knowledgeable entertainment attorney. As long as the issues at stake are simple, the co-writers respect each other, and they discuss their business philosophies before writing a song together, they can probably write up an agreement without the aid of a lawyer.

SINGLE-SONG CONTRACTS
What is a single-song contract?

A music publisher offers a single-song contract when he wants to sign one or more of your songs, but doesn't want to hire you as a staff songwriter. You assign your rights to a particular song to the publisher for an agreed-upon number of years, so that he may represent the song and find uses profitable for both of you. This is a common contract and will probably be the first you encounter in your songwriting career.

What basic elements should every single-song contract contain?

Every contract should have the publisher's name, the writer's name, the song's title, the date and the purpose of the agreement. The songwriter also declares the song is a original work and he is creator of the work. The contract *must* specify the royalties the songwriter will earn from various uses of the song, including performance, mechanical, print and synchronization royalties.

How should the royalties usually be divided in the contract?

The songwriter should receive no less than 50% of the income his song generates. That means the songwriter and publisher split the total royalties 50/50. The songwriter's half is

When does 50% equal 100%?

NOTE: the publisher's and songwriter's share of the income are sometimes referred to as each being 100%—for 200% total! You might hear someone say, "I'll take 100% of the publisher's share." **Do not be needlessly confused!** If the numbers confuse you, ask for the terms to be clarified.

Tip

called the "writer's share" and the publisher's half is called the "publisher's share." If there is more than one songwriter, the songwriters split the writer's share. Sometimes, successful songwriters will bargain for a percentage of the publisher's share, negotiating what is basically a co-publishing agreement. For a visual explanation of how royalties are collected and flow to the songwriter, see the chart called Music Publishing Royalties on page 29.

What should the contract say about a "reversion clause"?

Songwriters should always negotiate for a "reversion clause," which returns all rights back to the songwriter if some provision of the contract is not met. Most reversion clauses give a publisher a set amount of time (usually one or two years) to work the song and make money with it. If the publisher can't get the song recorded and released during the agreed-upon time period, the songwriter can then take his song to another publisher. The danger of *not* getting some sort of reversion clause is that you could wind up with a publisher sitting on your song for the entire life-plus-70-years term of the copyright—which may as well be forever.

Is a reversion clause difficult to get?

Some publishers agree to it, and figure if they can't get any action with the song in the first year or two, they're not likely to ever have much luck with it. Other publishers may be reluctant to agree to a reversion clause. They may invest a lot of time and money in demoing and pitching a song to artists and want to keep working at it for a longer period of time. Or, for example, a producer might put a song on hold for a while and then go into a lengthy recording project. A year can easily go by before the artist or producer decides which songs to release as singles. This means you may have to agree to a longer time period, be flexible and trust the publisher has your best mutual interests in mind. Use your best judgment.

What other basic issues should be covered by a single-song contract?

The contract should also address these issues:

- will an advance be paid, and if so, how much will the advance be?
- when will royalties be paid (annually or semiannually)?
- who will pay for demos—the publisher, songwriter or both?
- how will lawsuits against copyright infringement be handled, including the cost of lawsuits?
- will the publisher have the right to sell its interest in the song to another publisher without the songwriter's consent?
- does the publisher have the right to make changes in a song, or approve changes by someone else, without the songwriter's consent?
- the songwriter should have the right to audit the publisher's books if he feels it is necessary and gives the publisher reasonable notice.

Basic song contract pointers

Tips

The following list, taken from a Songwriters Guild of America publication, enumerates the basic features of an acceptable songwriting contract:

1 **Work for Hire.** When you receive a contract covering just one composition, you should make sure the phrases "employment for hire" and "exclusive writer agreement" are *not* included. Also, there should be no options for future songs.

2 **Performing Rights Affiliation.** If you previously signed publishing contracts, you should be affiliated with either ASCAP, BMI or SESAC. All performance royalties must be received directly by you from your performing rights organization and this should be written into your contract.

3 **Reversion Clause.** The contract should include a provision that if the publisher does not secure a release of a commercial sound recording within a specified time (one year, two years, etc.), the contract can be terminated by you.

4 **Changes in the Composition.** If the contract includes a provision that the publisher can change the title, lyrics or music, this should be amended so that only with your consent can such changes be made.

5 **Royalty Provisions.** You should receive fifty percent (50%) of all publisher's income on all licenses issued. If the publisher prints and sells his own sheet music, your royalty should be ten percent (10%) of the wholesale selling price. The royalty should not be stated in the contract as a flat rate ($.05, $.07, etc.).

6 **Negotiable Deductions.** Ideally, demos and all other expenses of publication should be paid 100% by the publisher. The only allowable fee is for the Harry Fox Agency collection fee, whereby the writer pays one half of the amount charged to the publisher for mechanical rights. The current mechanical royalty collected by the Harry Fox Agency is 8.5 cents per cut for songs under 5 minutes; and 1.65 cents per minute for songs over 5 minutes.

7 **Royalty Statements and Audit Provision.** Once the song is recorded, you are entitled to receive royalty statements at least once every six months. In addition, an audit provision with no time restriction should be included in every contract.

8 **Writer's Credit.** The publisher should make sure that you receive proper credit on all uses of the composition.

9 **Arbitration.** In order to avoid large legal fees in case of a dispute with your publisher, the contract should include an arbitration clause.

10 **Future Uses.** Any use not specifically covered by the contract should be retained by the writer to be negotiated as it comes up.

Where else can I go for advice on contracts?

The Songwriters Guild of America has drawn up a Popular Songwriter's Contract which it believes to be the best minimum songwriter contract available (see the Ten Basic Points Your Contract Should Include sidebar above). The Guild will send a copy of the contract at no charge to any interested songwriter upon request (see the Songwriters Guild of America listing in the Organizations section on page 326). SGA will also review—free of charge—any contract offered to its members, and will check it for fairness and completeness. Also see these two books published by Writer's Digest Books: *The Craft and Business of Songwriting*, by John Braheny and *Music Publishing: A Songwriter's Guide*, by Randy Poe.

Music Biz Basics

PRO's

The Way to Go?

by Jim Melko

You're ready to take the plunge: you're going to visit Nashville and present your songs to the industry. But where do you start? Who should you call? How does all this work, anyway? Is there anyone you can talk to when you don't have any contacts?

As a workshop coordinator for the Nashville Songwriters Association International, I have often encouraged members of our Dayton/Cincinnati chapter to schedule their first appointments with representatives from the three major performing rights organizations (PRO's): ASCAP, BMI, and SESAC. The primary purpose of the PRO is to collect royalties from any public performance of your song to a listening audience—radio, television, the Internet, concerts, etc. (They do not collect royalties for tangible recordings—CD's, cassettes, videotapes, etc.)

"Why would I want to visit a PRO if none of my songs are making any money right now?" you may ask. Well, most successful publishers will not meet with you unless you are referred to them by a PRO.

"Why would the PRO want to meet with me if my songs aren't making any money?" As a songwriter you represent potential - the potential of writing songs that may someday earn royalties. If a PRO focused only on the writers who are already earning income and never cultivated new writers, it would not last long.

A MARRIAGE MADE IN BUSINESS

So it seems simple enough: you're a songwriter who believes you have already written potential hits—and the PRO wants to find potential hit songwriters. Obviously, this is a perfect marriage—right?

Right! But (you knew there had to be a "but") let's take a closer look at the elements of that marriage.

When you look at it that way, it isn't quite so perfect a match. On your side is belief; on the PRO's side is business.

As a workshop coordinator for more than ten years, I have seen plenty of songwriters who believe that what has to change in the above marriage is on the PRO's side; somehow, those in the music industry must set aside their low and arbitrary standards and recognize the incredible talent in the songwriter—the PRO just needs to believe.

The songwriters I've seen who make headway in the business, however, realize that

---

JIM MELKO has been a staff writer for a Nashville music publisher and has also been a co-coordinator since 1993 for the Songwriter's Workshop at Southbrook, the Dayton/Cincinnati chapter of NSAI (Nashville Songwriters Association International). See the NSAI listing in the Organizations section of this book.

- You're a songwriter.
- You believe you can write hits.

- The PRO wants to find potential hit songwriters.
- The PRO's business is to collect royalties from public performances.

songwriting is a business and understand that a PRO is a prospective business partner. Ralph Murphy, ASCAP's Vice President for International and Domestic Membership in Nashville, puts it this way: "Two percent of our 161,000 members generate income in royalties through ASCAP. 14.8% of royalties collected by ASCAP go to our cost of doing business—which includes all the services ASCAP provides both to earning writers and to aspiring songwriters—including the salaries and benefits of the writer relations staff." He then notes, "The time I spend with an aspiring songwriter represents a financial cost to ASCAP. If I have to prioritize a requested meeting with one of the songwriters who pays our bills versus a songwriter who is not yet published, I will of course have to give the professional songwriter priority."

That may sound like there is, once again, no hope for the aspiring songwriter—but remember the other part of the PRO side: finding potential hit songwriters. Somehow, the PRO must balance its need to survive and grow by finding new hit songwriters with its fundamental purpose—to collect performance royalties. How can you, then, get "found"?

ONE PART OF THE TOTAL PLAN

The three PRO representatives I interviewed were unanimous in their first recommendation: "Get involved with a local songwriting organization," says Caroline Davis, Director of Media Relations for BMI in Nashville. All three PRO's prefer songwriters to provide references when asking for an appointment; a referral from the leader of a reputable local organization is considered acceptable. Tim Fink, Associate Vice President for Writer/Publisher Relations at SESAC, advises, "Get involved in a local group to find out what's going on and who to contact. We take references from other writers, publishers, song camp personnel, NSAI chapter leaders, attorneys, managers, etc."

"Network, network, network, network, network!" says ASCAP's Ralph Murphy. "You must be self-motivated, because the successful songwriters are not always the most talented. I have seen tremendously talented people who won't make it because they don't understand the business of music. It is a lifestyle—you 'bank' your relationships for the day when success is possible."

SESAC's Tim Fink agrees, "If your local organization brings in industry professionals, go—not to get your songs critiqued, but to find out what that person is all about so you can submit to that person later! 'Pitch-a-Thons' are not so much about pitching songs—very few ever lead to cuts—they're more about meeting the people who are in the industry."

Just as important as local involvement and networking is a knowledge of the music business. Both Murphy and Fink stress that it is critical to do your homework. By sponsoring weekly workshops orienting the songwriter to the music industry, both BMI and ASCAP have taken proactive approaches to avoid having their writers relations repeatedly waste time going over the basics.

ASCAP provides weekly "straight talk" sessions as an orientation not only to ASCAP but to the music business itself. BMI provides similar sessions called the BMI Roundtable and workshops in the craft of songwriting, led by Jason "Change My Mind" Blume, author of 6 Steps to Songwriting Success. BMI's Caroline Davis notes that Blume's sessions usually include either a song critique or a pitching session to a local publisher. In these sessions, writers hear reactions not only to their own songs but those of their peers—"more detailed feedback than a fifteen-minute session with a writer's representative would provide," says Davis.

The ASCAP and BMI sessions are free, and you do not have to be an affiliated member with either PRO to attend—but BMI does request that you register in advance because of limited space. ASCAP also offers a series called "ASCAP's Music Business 101 for Songwriters" which hosts a variety of guest speakers from the music industry on a wide range of topics (see the ASCAP event calendar on the Web).

HOW ACCESSIBLE ARE THE PRO'S?

BMI prides itself on an "open door policy," says Caroline Davis. Any songwriter can call in advance and request an appointment; however, BMI will understandably give preference to affiliated members. ASCAP focuses its time on affiliated members, but will consider meeting with unaffiliated members who come with industry referrals.

SESAC is the lesser-known of the three PRO's, with a very different approach to accessibility (it should be noted that the author is a member of SESAC). The organization is much smaller, offering 3 to 4 writer relations representatives for a membership of about 8,000 members. By contrast, ASCAP has 7 representatives for a membership of about 161,000 members, while BMI has 11 representatives for about 300,000 members.

SESAC is selective in its membership; by the time a songwriter becomes a member, he or she will already have established a relationship with several staff members. Fink explains, "We're trying to spread it around, so that if I get hit by a truck tomorrow, there are several reps who know who the writer is and what's going on with him or her. If you call here for me and you don't get me, you know these other people and can go to them instead." Fink believes this kind of accessibility also breeds accountability, so that SESAC staff feel driven to keep their individual members happy and successful.

A songwriter seeking membership with SESAC must first be able to demonstrate that he or she has "something going on," says Fink. "Our receptionist will get that call and ask, 'How do you know us? What have you been doing so far?' If the writer has significant activity requiring representation or is associated with someone we know, we'll set up a meeting. We will then listen to a tape or CD to determine if there is a potential advantage to a relationship: does this writer have the potential to write songs that will need representation?"

That potential is what drives the relationship between songwriter and any of the three PRO's. ASCAP's Murphy explains, "It costs about one million dollars to promote a single. That song is a script for a lyrical conversation between an artist and his or her audience, which can be someone listening to the radio while driving to work at 7 a.m." He points out, "A song is a product; like a hamburger stand sells hamburgers, the publisher, artist, and record company sell songs. As a staff songwriter, you are an employee to the publisher who is putting on the line his or her salary, 401k, health insurance, car, and family's future!" That is a risky venture, says Murphy: "If they said 'no' to songwriters 100% of the time, they'd be right 95% of the time. When someone signs you, that person is literally putting his or her job on the line."

BUSINESS IS THE BOTTOM LINE

BMI's Davis says, "We're here to help you with the business part, which is just as important as the music part. You can't make the music you want to make if everything else is not in line. In any kind of profitable venture, you've got to take of business. We want to educate songwriters about the licensing and make them realize that they themselves are each small businesses."

SESAC's Fink agrees: "Songwriting is a business. A lot of people don't see it that way because of the creativity involved. They don't realize that a lot of songwriters have to get up every day and go to work to produce a commercial product."

So if the PRO likes what you're doing, what will they do for you? In general, they will refer you to publishers. That, however, is not likely to happen in the first visit. Murphy says he has "never seen someone come in the first time and hand over a hit. It requires an investment of yourself—you must physically be here a minimum of three to five years." He points out, "My referrals are one of my products. To refer you to a publisher, I would have to be willing to consider signing you myself."

Murphy's referral standard reflects the standards of the other PRO's as well. Fink responds, "It's a good criteria. Publishers will set up meetings with writers I refer because I only send the really good ones." He adds, "Sometimes I work with a writer for years before I make a referral. I worked with one writer for two years and kept telling him, 'You're really good, but you need to get better.' He became frustrated, and I warned him, 'Don't create a bad buzz about yourself by meeting with people before you're ready. Better to have no reputation than a bad reputation in this town.' But he was hungry for a publishing deal, so he switched to another PRO and ended up in a bad publishing deal. When that deal ended, he came back to SESAC."

SHOULD I MOVE TO NASHVILLE?

Murphy also stresses the importance of the writer's reputation, not only for quality but also for personality. "Personality is a huge factor! I have seen great songwriters go nowhere because they couldn't relate well to others." He adds, "Being published is a partnership—you can't have a long-distance partnership. There is an interaction required." BMI's Davis adds, "Nashville's music industry is a very small community, and people keep running into each other. That's why it's so important to live here."

Fink, however, differs from his colleagues on the necessity of living in Nashville. He states, "You do not have to be present to win; you just have to be available to pick up the prize. I am one of the few people in Nashville who will say that - but you must be involved in a songwriting community, visit Nashville regularly, and make maximum use of your time while present."

SHOULD I AFFILIATE AS A FIRST STEP?

Finally, is it in your best interests to affiliate? Both BMI's Davis and SESAC's Fink concur that it is best to keep your options open. Says Davis, "You owe it to yourself to look around and investigate all three PRO's. You're going to learn a lot by talking to as many people as possible. I believe BMI will stand up in comparison." Fink notes, "I've tended to preach that a 'life rule' is to keep your options open. It is easy to get affiliated with the other PRO's and then end up with no one who is into what you're doing, but a lot of writers feel like they can't have a relationship with someone at the other PRO's until they do the paperwork. At SESAC, we do the opposite: we develop the relationship before we affiliate you."

In general, you have to belong to ASCAP to meet with a writer's representative. ASCAP's Murphy, however, points out that if you haven't found someone who believes in your music, it's "not a matter of getting to the right person, it's a matter of writing the right song."

Planning a visit to Nashville

Tips

So how can the writer plan to make maximum use of that time? Here are suggestions assembled from all three PRO representatives:

1. Call at least two weeks ahead for an appointment if you want to meet with a PRO representative.

2. Check out the PRO web sites. Read articles about all the awards banquets and other songwriting functions to learn who the "hot" songwriters are.

3. Plan your first trip for a week and a half.

4. Come the week before Tin Pan South (a week-long event featuring hit songwriters every night in clubs across town—sponsored by NSAI in the spring).

5. Meet with NSAI, the Songwriters Guild, cowriters, and anyone else you know.

6. Find out what meetings and events are being sponsored by the PRO's and sign up in advance.

7. Find someone doing a demo session and sit in on it to see how it's done.

8. Spend the next week going to all of the Tin Pan South shows.

9. Take a day to evaluate what you saw over that week.

10. If you feel you can compete, go home and start writing.

11. If you can't, keep songwriting as a hobby.

Tim Fink adds, "Don't go to the Bluebird Café just on Sunday night. I will often see visiting writers on Monday who say, 'I went to the Bluebird Sunday night, and I'm a lot better than they are.' That's not what's going on in this town. That show is for out-of-towners trying to get to perform there. Instead, go to the 9:30 shows on Tuesday, Wednesday, and Thursday and see the pros. If you can stack up against what they're doing, then let's talk. Compare yourself to the industry, not so much to your peers."

Use Publicity

To Help Your Songwriting Career

by Anne Leighton

One way to get people to talk about your song is to do a little publicity, and this article shows you the basics. The premise in hyping your songwriting talent in the media is quite similar to approaching publishers, except the media companies that hype songwriters and performers are usually newspapers, magazines, websites, television, and radio stations. The main differences are that up-and-coming songwriters need not have exclusives with any media outlets, and a contract is usually not required unless a publication wants to reprint your lyrics.

WHAT IS PUBLICITY?

Publicity is the act of finding as much media space as possible to cover you and your art. From its most simple and complicated actions, publicity is goal setting. Once a publicist has a project, he creates a media kit, then develops a media outreach plan and a list of media outlets that might be interested in the music or performer. The publicist sets a schedule to service the media through mailing, faxing, emailing, and calling them.

As a songwriter, you're creative enough to adapt the tools I describe later in this article toward spreading the word about your songs. Just as it takes time and thought to create your music, some detail must be given to an outreach plan. Research is important for building a media list (see below) and takes time. It also takes time to rewrite bios and press releases, plus schedule photo shoots.

Please note, there is a pecking order the media uses to cover musicians. Most important are the artists who always seem to be on TV, in the daily paper and on the radio—they're why people buy newspapers and listen to the radio. Next are shock stories when a musician, who has charted at one time in his career, is involved with controversy. After that the media focuses on artists coming to town (with emphasis on the most famous ones). In between outlets wanting the fame, shock, and show stories are those in need of relevant pieces on good deeds, current events and the bizarre ("man bites dog"). Your job is to think of ways to be relevant to a variety of media.

WHAT ARE THE BASIC TOOLS?

A basic media kit should include your bio, a press release, photograph or photo composite, plus your music. Media kits must be adaptable for different purposes. Booking agents use

ANNE LEIGHTON is a working music publicist, who believes artists can create their own career opportunities. She is an adjunct professor at Baruch College, and has authored *Using Your Art & the Media to Comfort People* (Free To Run Books). She also writes publicity articles for *Inside Connection*, a musician's magazine.

them for shows. Managers help artists find record and publishing deals, and publicists find media attention from radio, print, TV, and Internet outlets. In the beginning, you're the manager, agent, and publicist. It's possible to convince the media to cover music with just a recording and press release.

A one page bio

Read profiles about actors and musicians in the local newspaper. Notice these articles offer information about the artist's career history and how it relates to a current project. A lot of the papers just reprint bios pre-written by publicists. Here is how to create one:

- Create a one page story that explains who you are in relation to your current music. (If you're creating a bio for a band, list the group members and their instruments.)
- The bio should written in the third person; use "he," "she" or "they" instead of "I."
- The first paragraph should focus on who you are and what you're interested in publicizing. If you can, show how your current songs relate to your personality as a performer.
- The second paragraph explains how you started all this music-making.
- The third paragraph shows how you developed your current songs.
- The final paragraph explains your goals (shows, projects, plans) in regard to the enclosed songs.
- The act's name should be at the top of the page.
- Reread the bio and include one or two quotes from you explaining important points of your life as a musician.
- After you've edited and reread the bio out loud, let a literate friend proofread the final version so it has excellent grammar and perfect spelling.

Press release

An event-related press release always has a format:

- It has a headline that says something is happening on a specific date and location. This includes the release of a CD. The headline gives the act's name and what they're going to do on what date. "JON SMITH TO PLAY SUMMIT, NJ ON JULY 10."
- The first paragraph has the name of the artist and what he's doing when and where. Give contact info. "MARY SMITH is having a record release party at the Dew Drop Inn, 123 Main Street Briarcliff Manor, NY on July 10 at 8 pm. Admission is $5. The venue phone is 123-456-7890."
- Paragraph two offers information about the event or artist, depending on which is most relevant to your campaign. If your song, "Be Strong" is to help raise funds for local charity, then write about the event, that people will be singing it once an hour for a week until $20,000 is raised to fund a women's abuse center.
- The third paragraph should offer information on the songwriter.
- Include the lyrics.
- Develop templates you can use again and again. I like using templates for touring press releases and have stock lines on my artists. I just insert the locations and venue information on their dates.
- After writing your press release, have someone proofread it.

Photographs

Here are pointers for effective publicity photographs:

- Have photos shot that are reflective of your onstage personality. Are you an aggressive rock and roller or a stylish crooner? Look at posed photos with articles in newspapers.

When John Taylor left Duran Duran, he wanted to be perceived as a gentleman but with a casual flare. Always a student of "cool," he needed his photo to be attractive to journalists and fans. He wore a suit without a tie, and unbuttoned his shirt down to his sternum.

- Even if you're a sweaty rock and roller, make sure we can see your eyes. In addition to appearing relaxed on camera, the photographer made sure we could see John Taylor's eyes. (Lou Peretta, who publishes *Swank*, insists the eyes are the most important feature of all the ladies in his magazines.)
- Whether you use an expensive photographer in a fancy studio or a friend takes snapshots on the street, it's important to plan photo sessions in order to be happy with the results.
- I recommend the affordable three-picture composite of ABC Pictures' Layout "D." (www.abcpictures.com, 888-526-5336). A composite with two vertical photos and one horizontal (or vice versa) photo gives art directors more of an opportunity to use your picture when they're pasting up the calendar at deadline.
- Always include contact information on your photos, including phone, e-mail, website. Also, make sure to note who's who (from left to right) if the act is a band.

Song description sheets

Frank Zappa once said, "Talking about music is like dancing about architecture." But, when it comes to publicity, you'll just have to grit your teeth and frame your music in the best way possible using words. The song description sheet is an important tool for doing this, and here are pointers for putting one together:

- Make two song sheets, one for song lyric descriptions and a sheet for film and television music supervisors. Assuming you have a 12-song CD, these would be one page each.
- The page of song lyric descriptions explains what the songs are about and how you wrote them. Each song has a one-to-three-sentence description that shows its style, theme, and tempo. For instance Queen's "We Will Rock You/We Are the Champions," would be described this way: "First half of the song is gang vocals and claps with repeated male chorus, 'We will rock you.' Segue into metal-style guitar solo, and then a slow and mellow male vocal singing about 'paying his dues.' Builds up into dramatic vocal chorus of 'We Are the Champions of the World.' "
- The music supervision sheet should be sent along with your recording to film and television music supervisors. Note ownership for the synch, recording and publishing rights of all songs. Include contact information for whomever administers the song, you or your music publisher.
- All your tools should always include contact information, especially phone and e-mail. List your website. Media people may want to get in touch with you before you follow up.
- Obviously the music is important. Include a CD and with contact information. (In fact, if you release a CD, that is news and worth some write ups locally and hopefully on a national level.)

HOW TO USE YOUR PUBLICITY TOOLS

Be in touch with your goals as a songwriter and think up a dozen avenues to hype yourself. The goal is to receive attention for your music. (While it would be an ultimate goal to be featured on MTV, examine where your career really is and what you think you can do for yourself the next year.) Choose one or two relevant ideas you can pursue with a publicity campaign. Did you record a demo or release a full-blown CD. Is your song about trying to establish a national holiday? Does it give attention to a group of people? Is a poet reading your lyrics in public? Did you have a successful collaboration with a famous producer? Can a lyric make it on to a greeting card that you design and sell at a local shop? Are you teaching?

Carefully analyze the particular media market you live in. The challenge in major markets like Los Angeles, New York City, Nashville, Philadelphia, San Francisco and Chicago is finding neighborhood papers and college radio shows. It's worth your time to send releases and photos to every appropriate outlet. In the beginning send your full kits to the folks with whom you have a realistic chance of placement, especially college radio and neighborhood papers near the venue you're playing. If you're not doing anything in a particular town, don't waste the money and time sending them anything, unless you have a friend working at a local station. Always let your friends with ties to media outlets know about your work. Focus on your current activities and gigs.

If you're a performing songwriter, call local media outlets when you get a gigs at clubs, bookstores, schools, and so on. Get the names (with correct spelling) of who covers music and send them press releases. Make follow-up calls after you send your kit and ask for an interview or, at least, a listing of your show.

Seek out media coverage when a recording artist cuts your song. In the 1980s I helped my songwriting coach Dianne Baumgartner find regional attention for her song "Who's the Lucky Girl" when a Louisiana-based singer named Becky Birdwell released a recording of it. We simply used the single and a photocopied one page press release typed on Baumgartner's manual typewriter. We sent it to the monthly countywide glossy magazine, an arts paper, a local women's newspaper, and the daily newspaper. All of them gave her coverage.

I also wrote a women's news piece, which included Baumgartner's story and analysis of a hit song, "Sister Christian" by Night Ranger. The reporter for the local arts newspaper devoted three paragraphs to the topic, and included some songwriting advice from Baumgartner. The daily paper put her achievement in the local good news network. She was most proud of the glossy magazine, because a reporter visited her for an interview and then a photographer came by to snap a photo of Baumgartner and her cat Henry.

Through the years, she continued to have her songs placed with a variety of singers and media projects, and has been invited to be on public radio. She has always done her publicity work herself. These days, the local media call *her* and ask "What's new?"

Depending on your contacts, create an event or charity record with area performers. Does your song slam or endorse a politician? The New York Post has covered obscure artists who picked on New York City's mayor. They may also preview a great cause. Tell the media. It's possible to receive attention for your art. Convince friends to donate services like studio time and pressing, then produce a CD for a favorite cause.

As an example, I worked on publicity for a single about homelessness called "Crying in the Night" by NightFlyte. I wrote a press release explaining how the single became reality, typed up the lyrics, and contacted a variety of media outlets including radio and television. The attention generated for the record empowered the songwriter, Mindy Meyers, to get out and perform. She had a few other friends who also wrote, and they put together a group to sing original and traditional folk songs at homeless shelters, churches, songwriter alliances, and clubs. Soon local papers gave blurbs about their gigs. Public radio played the record, as did a national TV news report on homelessness. One day Meyers received a check from her licensing organization for 600 dollars. She promptly sent the check to the Coalition for the Homeless.

HOW TO DEVELOP YOUR MEDIA LIST

Just as your career, songs, and press kit evolves, so does your media contact list as you discover new outlets for your publicity campaigns. Pick up newspapers and magazines at stores, banks, supermarkets. Look in the TV and radio section of your city's paper to find out the radio stations in the area; pay attention to stations that are at 91.1 and under—those are college stations. The Yellow Pages lists media outlets.

Listen to radio stations and watch the local cable TV channel. Discover shows that can give you attention. People at regional TV and radio stations seem to wear a couple of hats in show biz. An overnight DJ might have a cable variety show. Someone working traffic at the local TV station may also be managing musicians on the side.

These websites have leads of music media: www.indie-music.com, www.starpolish.com, www.indiemusic.com. The best print directories for the media are: The Musicians Atlas, (local bookstore, website: www.musiciansatlas.com) and Writer's Market (local bookstore, website: www.writersdigest.com). In addition to their music publications, also look up general, small, or literary publications and topics relevant to your songs.

Finally, if you're doing shows in other towns, the local promoter should be able to give you leads. In addition, use www.newsdirectory.com and do a Google search for media or newspapers, radio, with the name of the town.

There are many outlets that will offer attention for your music. Make acquaintances with writers at neighborhood newspapers, call them to find out who covers music. If someone doesn't respond to your call, e-mail them. Send them your kit. After a week, make a polite follow up to see if they'd like an interview. It's important to listen to what the writer says. He may say, "I haven't listened, can you call me next week on Thursday afternoon?" He may prefer an e-mail interview. Honor the request. He may ask for a color photo; see if a print or slide will do or if you should e-mail a high resolution JPEG or on a disc.

The more people you tell about your music, the better the chance that word will spread about your career. You never know who may open the door that gets your songs talked about all day and night.

Advanced Articles

Moving to a Music Hub

by C.J. Watson

I f you want to be a surfer, Landlock, Nebraska isn't the place to do it; you have to be where the waves are. To be a professional songwriter, you have to be where you can make some waves. One of the most important things you can do for your career is to move to a city with a music industry presence.

Planning ahead

Don't just sell your house, rent a U-Haul, and go. There are things you need to do, know, and think about before you pack up and head out for Music Row, Tin Pan Alley, or Hollywood. Making a permanent move is a big deal. A little planning can make the transition a much smoother one.

Surveillance and reconnaissance

The first thing you need to decide is which hub is right for you. While the top three hubs (Nashville, L.A., and New York) have a little of everything, many of the smaller hubs specialize in one or two genres and don't offer much to songwriters outside those styles.

Scenes sometimes change overnight, but you can generally find the following genres (and maybe more) in the following places:

Songwriting organizations

For More Info

A songwriting organization's branch office in a given hub can be a great source of information. If you're a member of NSAI or SGA, have your local coordinator hook you up with members in various hubs and ask them about the town, the scene, and other information you should know before making a visit.

C.J. WATSON is the author of *The Everything Songwriting Book* (Adams Media). He has recorded a #10 Indie Country single, and worked as an Artist Development Representative. His songs have been recorded by James Otto (Mercury), Mustang Sally (Curb), Patt Webb (Flatrock), and Jason Whitehorn (Arista). He's currently a full-time staff songwriter for Blue Desert Entertainment in his hometown of Nashville, TN.

- New York City: pop, hip-hop, R&B, jazz, rock, alt, punk, house, show tunes, new age, classical, experimental, blues
- Nashville: country, pop, gospel, alt-country, Americana, Christian contemporary music singer/songwriter, alt, bluegrass, new folk, roots rock
- Los Angeles: pop, hip-hop, salsa, rock, country, alt, punk, new age, Christian contemporary music, classical
- Seattle: alt, grunge, nu-metal, hardcore
- Austin: country, alt-country, singer/songwriter, Western swing, blues, rock
- Atlanta: nu-soul, hip-hop, R&B
- Detroit: hip-hop
- Dallas: country, Western swing, jazz, blues
- Miami: dance, salsa
- Bakersfield, CA: country
- New Orleans: Dixieland, zydeco
- Chicago: blues
- Memphis: blues, R&B
- Cleveland/Toledo: polka (not a good way to get rich)

Make some trips to your prospective new home to get a feel for the place and the people. Make friends who can clue you in and help you find your way around. Most importantly, see if it's the right hub for the kind of writing you want to do.

Finding a place

Before you move to a music hub, decide what living arrangement will suit your needs best. Do you need a house or an apartment? Will you buy, rent, or lease? How close do you want to be to the publishing district or your place of work? Ask your friends (the ones you made during your scouting trips) about things like the bad parts of town, traffic patterns, and where to get a good pizza after midnight.

Find some friends

Tip

It's good to fit in, but don't be afraid to let people know where you're from. In most hubs, there are people from all over. Odds are you can hook up with some homies, which gives you some instant friends with whom you already have a lot in common and helps when you get homesick.

Finding a job

Just because you're making the transition to professional songwriting doesn't mean that the bills will magically pay themselves. You're going to need a job in your new hometown, probably for several years. If you have a marketable trade or a college degree, a headhunter service might help you find the right job. If not, the classifieds are a good place to look. If you can live cheaply, find something with flexible hours, so that you have time to schedule co-writing sessions and publisher meetings.

No more money gigs?

The job you won't find in a music hub is a decent-paying music gig. If you're used to making a living as a musician or singer, you're out of luck. The competition for gigs in these places is tough and some people will play for free or even pay to play just to be seen. It's not so bad in New York, but in Nashville, L.A., or Austin it's tough to get a paying gig. Most of the musicians who play the strip in Nashville play for tips only. It's common to see players from the touring bands of big stars playing for tips on their time off just so that they can stay visible in the scene and maybe reunite with friends for a couple of days or weeks before hitting the road. While finding a paying gig in some hubs can be tough, hubs can be great places to learn by watching big stars and famous songwriters up close.

Digging in

When you make your move, don't waste time. Set up a routine as soon as possible. Don't kill yourself: The object is to set up a sustainable situation that moves you steadily toward your goals. Set up a writing routine. Renew contacts with people you've met and schedule co-writes. Get to know the writer's hangouts. Don't think you're going to take over the town in two weeks. This is going to take a while. You're here for the long haul; treat it that way.You may have to make some adjustments. If you've never lived in a big city, be prepared for culture shock in places like New York and L.A., where Kamikaze cabdrivers, gridlock, and crime might be new experiences for you. If you're heading down to Nashville or Atlanta, get ready for sweet tea, hot summers, and bugs you've only seen in movies. In any hub over a hundred miles from your home, people may talk, drive, and eat differently. The sooner you embrace the culture of your hub, the sooner you'll stop looking like a tourist.

Spend some time networking

No matter which hub you land in, you need to meet people—and as many as possible. The music business is about relationships, and you can't have relationships with people you don't know. You need to make the acquaintance of writers, publishers, producers, musicians, artists, and potential artists—the people you need to know in order to do what you're here to do.

Hi, my name is . . .

Rule number one: You don't meet many people hanging around your apartment watching TV. As a matter of fact, put your TV in the closet, so that it's still in good shape when you have to pawn it for demo money. Don't worry, there will still be *Seinfeld* reruns when you have a mantel full of Grammies and all the time in the world to watch them. Get out there and meet some people! Where? Well, if you did your homework, you should have a list of hangouts and a couple of friends who can introduce you to their friends and friends of friends. Get to it!

Be who you are

Don't be someone you're not. It's easy to put on airs because you want to impress people and fit in. If you're a performer, you can probably patter with anyone for half an hour (or

Hobbies and networking

Tip

Sports and other hobbies can be a great networking tool and a sanity saver. Find some friends who like what you like—fishing, opera, roller blading, whatever—and make a regular thing of it. If you don't golf, learn. Golf is the greatest networking sport in the biz and the sport of choice for many publishers.

however long the breaks are in the clubs you played on the road). The difference here is that you really need to get to know these people and they need to know you. Publishers have B.S. detectors so sensitive that they can spot a politician twenty miles away. They'll see you coming. Your goal is to end up working with these people and you'll have to be yourself when you do that.

Find your tribe

Find people you like who like you. You're going to be here awhile, maybe the rest of your life. Do you want to do business with people you don't like? Someone who sees your potential and likes you as a person may take you under his or her wing. Someone who sees your potential but doesn't like you probably won't. Spend your time with people you relate to and trust; they'll be more likely to want you to succeed. Add to that the fact that you'll be much happier this way, and that's a win/win situation.

Writer's nights

In certain clubs and cafés, the writers rule. Most of these are "originals only" venues where a cover tune can get you laughed off the stage. When you move to a hub, writer's nights may be the center of your world for the first few years. A writer's night is the best place to make friends, network, test-market songs, and learn how things work. You don't get paid for this gig, unless opportunities are worth something to you.

The host, usually a well-respected songwriter, decides who plays and when, and you'll probably have to audition. If you pass, the host will book you for a round in which you take turns playing songs with two to four other songwriters. Eventually, you may get to pick the other people for your round or even get to do a solo feature of several songs by yourself.

Being seen

You might see anybody at a writer's night, from the other newbies to hit writers, publishers, A&R reps, and even the occasional celebrity. This means these people will see you as well. No matter what night of the week or what time it is, there could be someone important in the room or about to walk in at any moment, so be at your best, both onstage and off. Before you get tipsy and dance on the tables, tell a tasteless joke, or insult someone in public, think carefully; if you're lucky, these are the people you'll be dealing with for the rest of your life.

But, I can't sing!

Tip

If you absolutely can't carry a two-ounce tune in a five-gallon bucket, you have two options for the writer's nights: Either hire a singer or rely on your co-writers to do the singing. You might even book a round of your co-writers somewhere.

Being heard

Each host may have slightly different rules; learn them. There is a code of etiquette for writer's nights. The faster you learn it, the more quickly you'll be accepted into the songwriting community. The following writer's night rules are adapted from the July 22, 2001 edition of the *Nashville Rant* e-zine. Nashville writer's night hosts Camille Schmidt, Barbara Cloyd,

Respect the law

Important

Laws in hub cities and among clubs vary. Ask before bringing minors to a gig. Sneaking a drink into a writer's club, even bottled water, could get it shut down. In Tennessee, a club can get busted for unlicensed dancing, and you really don't want to be known as the person who got the writer's club closed down.

C.J. Watson, Debbie Champion, Jack Scott, and Lee Rascone provided source material for the article.

How to play writer's nights without getting shot or, worse, ignored

1. When you arrive (early!), check in with the host. Ask where to tune and store your instrument. Tune with an electronic tuner *before* your round. Be ready and set up quickly: If you waste three minutes getting ready, someone loses a song.

2. Spend money, bring friends, come early, and stay late. Hosts usually work on a percentage. Promoting the gig means you are market minded and motivated, which are as important as talent in this business. If you stay to hear other people, they are more likely to come hear you. (Remember the part about bringing friends?)

3. Talk as much as you like . . . as much as you like *others* to talk during *your* songs.

4. You were a star back home? Winning the Ox Booger, South Dakota Talent Show, and Potato Auction three years in a row doesn't count for much now. Get over it and start making a name *here*. Nobody will ever compliment you on the vastness of your ego.

5. A seven-minute song is not going to win you many friends. You just burned up three-and-a-half minutes of someone else's time on an uncuttable song. Ax that intro where you soulfully strum 32 bars of "E." Most of us know "E" too. It doesn't impress us; get to the hook. Don't talk about the song for half an hour. If they can't tell what it's about by *listening to the song*, there's a problem.

6. Be nice to the host/sound person. This is like the rule that says not to annoy anyone who's going to touch your food. Be polite and quick during soundcheck. Don't ask for reverb in the monitor; it causes problems. If you don't like your voice, practice. Get a guitar with a pickup. If you can play, play. If you don't play, bring someone to play for you; backup tracks are for karaoke singers.

7. Be nice to the waitstaff. Most of the people working at a writer's club are songwriters and/or friends with some big writers. If they like you, they'll say nice things about you. If they don't, you will not only die of thirst, but you may die in obscurity as well. Also, you may soon be a waitress or bartender, so be nice, tip what you can, and remember that it takes as long to bring you a glass of water as it does to bring a quadruple shot of Wild Turkey with a flaming pink umbrella.

8. Skill with harmony or a lead instrument can be valuable assets, but ask before jumping in. Practice with friends and learn parts for each other's songs. Four drunks doing the same exact thing on acoustic guitars is not "ensemble" playing.

Being proactive

Fame is not going to come find you; you have to hunt it down and grab it by the throat. Many brilliant songwriters remain undiscovered because they think that writing great songs is enough. It's not; you have to get them recorded and heard and keep at it until somebody gets it. You are not a planet or a scientific theory; no one is going to discover you unless you get someone's attention. Don't "gherm" people, but you can ask questions and advice of anyone you know. [*An example of gherming—a Nashville expression—is to accost established hit songwriters and shove your tapes and CDs at them, and is considered bad etiquette—Editor*] You can also watch the incoming newbies and be the first person to befriend those with talent and potential.

Publisher appointments

Tip

Getting appointments with publishers is much like telemarketing. If you know someone with telemarketing experience, ask for pointers. Develop a "script" so you know what to say and practice until it's second nature. Compare notes with friends about what works and what doesn't.

Most importantly, keep trying. If someone is too busy for a meeting, ask if you can send a CD or call back at a better time. When you have a meeting, get as much feedback as possible. Get specifics; if someone says, "Your lyrics need work," ask if there are particular areas that need improvement. Find out which writers a publisher likes and study their songs. If a publisher says you can come back in a month or even a year, follow up on it and make sure you have some great new songs for the next meeting. If a host doesn't book you for a round after playing the open mike, ask for feedback and work harder to get in. Proving that you are focused and relentless will impress people as much as having talent.

Setting goals

Time has a way of flying by when you get settled in somewhere. Set goals to make sure that you are making progress. Sometimes your ultimate goal (a #1 hit, a Grammy, or a house in the Bahamas) can seem unreachable. Setting short-term and intermediate goals can help you stay positive and focused and keep you on track as you journey toward the big ones.

Keep lists of your goals; as you accomplish a goal and cross it off your list, you can replace it with a new goal. Examine the ways in which some goals support others. Here's a simplified example of a probability goal chain, where every step builds on the goal results from the last level to reach toward the next:

- If you put in the time and the effort, you'll learn more and write more.
- If you learn and write enough, you'll probably come up with a great song.
- If you write enough great songs and have enough publisher meetings, you'll probably get a single-song contract or a staff deal.
- If you get enough single-song contracts or work hard enough at your staff-writing job, you'll probably get some holds.
- If you get enough holds, you'll probably get a single.
- If you get enough singles, you'll probably get a hit.
- If you get enough hits, you'll probably get a #1 hit, a Grammy, or a house in the Bahamas.

See? It's easy. All you have to do is accomplish one set of goals to make the next set easier to reach. Of course, it still requires hard work and commitment, but focusing on your work allows you to go further and faster.

What kind of goals?

Tip

Goals aren't "one size fits all." Some goals may be bigger or smaller to you than they are to others. If you just started lessons, getting onstage with your guitar is a bigger deal than if you grew up playing it.

Keeping the faith

The hardest thing to do is to keep on believing, but it's also the most important. Getting cuts is a sales job and belief is the foundation of sales. If you don't believe in the product (your songs), you're in the wrong business—find something else to do.

Sooner or later, and probably more than once, you will feel like giving up. Being prepared for this will help you get through it. Build a support group of people you believe in who also believe in you. Keep track of your progress and acknowledge even the little victories. Once a year, listen through your catalog to see how much you've learned. It can be hard to see how far you've come without looking back.

Commercial Songwriting

Creative Secrets for Success

by H. Rusty Gordon

I teach a college level course in the Business of Music and the Crafting of Commercially Viable Songs. My first seminar was in the Fall of 1970. Since that time, my primary commitment has always been to provide songwriters with the songwriting techniques and skills necessary to compete successfully in the commercial marketplace.

One thing I've found again and again is that aspiring pro songwriters consistently create songs publishers and record producers turn down time after time. They become lost in the competitive shuffle without knowing why their songs are non-commercial. Also, many would-be professionals do not know how to write on demand like the established track record songwriters. To compete, aspiring professionals must better utilize both the conscious and subliminal aspects of creativity, inspiration and craft to boost their songwriting skills.

For example, writer's block is the nemesis of the songwriting industry, and there are a number of things that cause or lead to this enemy of creativity. The pressure and stress of performing can eat into the time a songwriter might otherwise use for writing new songs. The songwriter's personal life can become stressful, make them feel pressured, frustrated, and anxious, and lead to a loss of concentration. Since most songwriters believe that song ideas should come to them naturally and spontaneously, when the ideas stop coming easily, they are at a loss over what to do.

Many successful songwriter/performers also find themselves in this trap. If artists are on deadline to write songs for their next album, panic can set in. They get in this bind due to a conflict between their creative selves and their business commitment to market their current record and exploit themselves with a grueling performing schedule. The time, mood, and necessary inspiration for writing songs doesn't arrive when these obstacles are present.

Inconsistent creativity results in an uneven playing field, and demands techniques for triggering ideas with reliability and shaping those song ideas along competitive lines. Let's level that playing field!

TRIGGERING INSPIRATION

A songwriter's mind should be a fertile field of ideas and language flexibility, and a songwriter should be able to generate a wide range of variations on common themes. This is often easier

H. RUSTY GORDON has been an artist's consultant and manager, record producer, song publisher, lyricist, even producer/promoter, and the creator of a college course entitled "The Business of Music." She has been presenting music business seminars and songwriter's workshops since 1970. Her company, Rustron-Whimsong Music Productions specializes in the production of benefits, music festivals, and special events.

said than done. But, there is room for conscious choice. Writing lyrics is part inspiration with a lot of method thrown in. If we can't control inspiration, then let us concentrate on method and approach inspiration by the back door.

Learn to activate your "creative space"

Pay attention and see if you can identify circumstances or activities that tend to trigger songs for you. Every writer has patterns of behavior and external experiences that lead to the songwriting mode. Consider what you are doing and how you are doing it when a song seems to write itself and the ideas are flowing naturally. Have you suddenly come up with ideas while driving your car? Are you just sitting calmly and strumming your guitar in a rhythm pattern when a song idea, a title, or an interesting riff pops into your head? Have ideas come to you when you were relaxing in the great outdoors, watching the flow of water in a river, a lake or the ocean? Does Mother Nature act as a catalyst when you enjoy a forest, hike trails or admire a beautiful vista?

You may notice many activities conducive to your creativity are rhythmic, feed an ever-changing flow of visual stimuli, or engage your linear, task-oriented left brain so that your right brain is free to create associations and slip into something resembling a dream state. When in need of inspiration, seek out these activities and trigger that state of consciousness.

So when song ideas dry up, take the time to put yourself in a conducive stimulating or calming environment, whatever your preference. Get away from the "same old" routines. Take something to write on, your instrument and a tape recorder. Taking other people or your pets with you will be a distraction. Create your own space, your own rhythm and free your imagination. The key to unlock a writer's block is always there and within reach.

Expand your focus

When looking for ideas, songwriters tend to focus in one of two ways—internal or external. Most songwriters naturally create from the internal and focus on their own personal emotional experiences. This exclusive focus can limit the possible viewpoints and themes for the listener to identify with, and therefore limit the songwriter's potential audience. A limited audience equals limited commercial possibilities. (This doesn't mean every individual song you write must cover all possible bases of theme and viewpoint and be all things to all people. As I discuss below, it's very important for songwriters to write many varied songs and cover as much ground as possible in the selection of topics, themes or concepts.)

Externally sourced, or "method" songwriting, takes its concepts from the real life experiences of people the songwriter knows or from the imagination of the songwriter who creates a lyrical work of fiction and tells a story in song. Writing for musical theater, motion pictures, children's music, television theme songs, topical, socio-political, historical, or patriotic themes are examples of songs created externally by choice, or as a result of a contracted request for songs on a specific theme. Music industry contract songwriters can become very successful at creating theme-identified songs upon request by their employer. For many songwriters, this requires the conscious cultivation of observation skills and a willingness to consciously shift their focus from internal concerns to the world around them.

Fill the well using lists

A songwriter's mind must be fertile and nourished by words, phrases, titles and raw ideas that can blossom into songs, and the "song concept list" is a useful tool for bringing song concept ideas to the surface. Create one for yourself in a handy notebook and use it to collect concepts you think will be great for future songs. Carry it around with you. Wherever you are and whatever you're doing, when you get an idea that could make a great song, waste no time in writing it down. Refer to this list to trigger your creative process when nothing seems to be coming into focus naturally.

When you have an experience that is remarkable, or find you can identify with someone else's experience, consider it a possible song concept and write it down. When you see something on television or in a film and it inspires you, create a song concept from it. If something said on a radio talk show or a news program grabs your attention and makes you angry, sad, happy or determined to take action, write it down. Concepts for songs are everywhere around you, all the time, and if you take the time to notice and look a little past the obvious, you will find a potpourri of choices and ideas you might otherwise miss.

Review the songs you have already written

When you look back over your catalog isolate the concepts and themes you were exploring at the time you wrote each song. Do any of these concepts still apply to newer songs you are writing today? You may discover all the songs written over a specific period of time mainly addressed personal issues from that time frame of your life as a songwriter, but ignored other topics, concepts, or viewpoints. You may find you write mainly from your own innermost emotions and that these familiar patterns are hard to break.

Even if the most-repeated theme is "love won and/or lost" the songwriter must consciously try to approach the issue from different directions. Otherwise, the songwriter in search of a good concept for a new song may easily become caught up in personal experience and issues and inadvertently stifle their commercial potential. A songwriter's catalog needs variety to be commercially competitive. Their body of work should cover many different themes and include a variety of viewpoints on common themes the listener may identify with.

Why is listener identification so important? When a song absorbs the listener through the magic of good storytelling and clever manipulation of theme, the listener feels disappointed when the song is over. They want to hear the song and have that experience again and again and again. This reaction translates to money in the bank. Once a new song on the radio hooks a customer, a consumer has been born. The next step is the purchase of the record product and an appreciation for the artist as a performer. Like any other business winning loyal customers (a "fan base" for performing artists) and new consumers builds success.

You may find this simple act of analyzing your song catalog and brainstorming new angles and viewpoints on old themes triggers the excitement and inspiration you have been looking for.

SHAPING INSPIRATION WITH CRAFT

Once you've found your inspiration, it's time to shape that inspiration with effective craft techniques. Since your aim is to be competitive in the marketplace, these tried and true techniques for shaping inspired raw ideas into commercial songs will put you ahead of the game while inspiration is fresh, and you will waste less time.

Build "definitive melody"

A "definitive melody" repeats the same notes exactly from section to section while the lyrics change each time. Verses need definitive melody and once the songwriter has picked the melody (note pattern) for the first verse, the lyrics for the remaining verses should be edited to that note pattern. Good definitive melody means a song is flexible and can be easily covered by other artists and produced with many different arrangements. (A commercially viable chorus keeps the same set of lyrics each time the chorus is repeated. A chorus and a bridge also require one definitive note pattern *different* from the verse melody.)

Songwriters who write verse lyrics to meter and rhythm instead of to a specific note pattern, create verses that each have a slightly different melody. The phrases in the first verse will be different in the subsequent verses because of this. Doing this creates the problem of run-away lyric, wandering phrasing, and rambling melody. These are very common problems found in the songs of songwriters who do not pay much attention to note patterns. Loosely structured verses make a song less commercially viable for single-song marketing. They could be adequate album cuts for the singer-songwriter's own album product, but they would be too eclectic and loosely crafted for the serious marketing of an individual song.

Spot weak melody and recompose/rewrite

Weak melody is easy to detect. If a songwriter knows they tend to be lyric dominant, they should pay special attention to their melodies. One way to review a melody without the words is to sing it into a tape recorder using sounds, not words. Sing *la la la* or *dum dum dum*, or whatever sound you are partial to and record the entire song that way. Listen to it many times and try to evaluate if this melody can stand on its own without words. If it falls on its face without the words, the melody will require a revamping or a complete replacement. With this in mind, songwriters should check through their song catalog for songs they think are worth the time to workshop and rebuild with definitive melody. Sometimes a song you've almost forgotten can be given a second life (and renewed commercial viability) with a dose of careful crafting.

Focus on titles, primary phrases, hooks, and tags

Titles should be selected from a phrase in the song that stands out lyrically and melodically, and these will usually be spotlighted in strategic areas at the beginning or end of a song section. Careful planning of a chorus should render at least one phrase that stands out well enough to be the title of the song. An average song title usually has no more than eight syllables. In selecting your title, try to avoid titles that have already been successfully exploited in the commercial music industry. Titles are important, especially for selling songs to the public. Make them memorable!

Hooks can be a catchy part of the melody or they can be a section of words and music (usually a phrase) often found in the chorus. Publishers and record producers are always on the lookout for strong hooks. If you have created a phrase that is catchy, hard to forget, and really puts something special into a song, you have created a hook!

Tags are short phrases of words and melody that are repeated to emphasize a thought. They are used most often at the end of a song. Tags wind the song down, repeating over and over until the sound gets lower and fades away. Commercial producers often use this technique in the studio as part of the arrangement. Songs that have a tag phrase in their chorus or at the end of the last verse are prepared for tag arrangements.

Watch out for verse redundancy

Give special attention and take your time with your verse lyrics. Your chorus is the attention getter, but the verses explain your reasons for writing. Don't shortchange your verses. Apply your wordsmith skills to present them in a logical and sensible sequence, as in a story. If the verses tell a story, the chorus can elaborate on the primary point the song is trying to make.

Redundancy occurs when verse after verse is saying the same thing over and over, just using different words. When this happens, the songwriter stifles the song's ability to hold the listener's interest and to evolve to reach conclusion. If any verse in a song can fall in any sequence, the song's concept will not progress.

Develop your rhyming skills

How the songwriter works with rhyming is a crucial song element publishers look at when they review a song. Rhyming helps to unify the end of lyrical lines with one another. Rhyming makes a song easier to sing and easier to remember. When careful attention is not paid to rhyming, it is easy to fall into a very predictable pattern. If a listener who has never heard a song before is asked to guess what the rhyme word will be at the end of a line and they guess

Consider collaboration

Tip

The great majority of songwriters are "lyric dominant." This means they find lyric writing easier than composing the melody or note pattern for a song. Maybe 10% of songwriters are "melody dominant" and find lyrics don't come easily or at all. In both cases, a songwriter who is very strong in either lyrics or music, may seek a collaborating partner to write songs with. Finding a collaboration that works well between two or more people isn't easy, but when it works, the results can be exceptional. About 30% of songwriters can balance the relationship between words and music, where lyric dominance or melody dominance is hardly noticeable. Song-writers who can identify their strengths and weaknesses can work to improve the balance.

Wherever the story or circumstances of a song take the listener, it's imperative the listener be willing to go. Both the melody and the lyrics working together provide the elements that entice the listener to make the song their own, so be realistic about your strengths and weaknesses and find collaborators who can complement your abilities.

correctly, that's a problem. All songwriters should have a rhyming dictionary'. Don't settle for the easy rhyming patterns. Craft your lyrical lines so they can end in rhymes that are not easily second-guessed. The old "moon/ june/ spoon" rhyming patterns have become over-used and predictable. Don't take the easy way out!

Focus on who, what, where, when, why and how
A good lyric should reveal bits and pieces of what is realistically happening within the song's storyline by carefully intermingling details of who, what, where, when, and why.

- **WHO** Who are the people in a lyric's storyline? What about them is significant, interesting, poignant, special, troublesome, or difficult? Bring out the individual characteristics, behavior, personality, style, or attitude that makes them come alive in the song.
- **WHAT** What is the song trying to reveal, explain, express or amplify? Like a short story, a song is focusing on a storyline revealing a small segment of life experience. But the song has only three or four minutes of communication time between the songwriter and the listening potential consumer. Clearly develop and identify the reasons for writing the song and don't wander off into confusion.
- **WHERE** Where, if the song is not just emotional expression, does the song describe things happening—places, atmosphere, weather, colors, inside or outside, venues and seasons? Using descriptive phrases and words usually enhances song lyrics and makes them more interesting.
- **WHEN** When is functional to time—past, present or future. When does the song's theme or concept take place? Is the song reminiscing, or reviewing the past? Is what's happening in the song occurring in the here and now or is the song's focus on the future? This includes combinations of all three, moving backward and forward in time.
- **WHY** Why is personal to the songwriter and contains the reasons and motivations for the creation of the song. It is good creative expression and direction for the songwriter to explore his reasons for writing a song, but only after he allows all his creative ideas

to flow as naturally as possible. Don't second-guess your inspirations while they are in progress. When the song reaches completion in the songwriter's mind, then the review of why the song was written may be revealing and empowering.

- **HOW** How is about the specifics of using the techniques of songwriting craft to the best advantage of each song a songwriter creates. Songcraft guides the songwriter through the many variables that are tried and kept or discarded during the song's creative evolution. It comprises the songwriter's skills and personal confidence in himself. It guides the song from the first to the last syllable and note.

TAKING IT TO THE MARKET

Creativity and craft obviously have to happen before you can even think about marketing your songs. But, if you've incorporated the suggestions I've outlined above, then you are already on track to build the sort of songs that achieve success in the marketplace, and you have saved yourself time, effort and frustration.

Building "standards"

If a songwriter creates one song that becomes a "standard," they will be fixed for life, and a focus on melody and lyrics early in the writing process, rather than arrangement and production style, widens the "standard potential" for any song. For example, in certain styles of commercial music, the words of a song are secondary to the arrangement and production techniques used to record the song. Studio production techniques can sometimes cover for significant lyric and melodic weaknesses, and become a trendy "hit" sound for its time, but this type of song often doesn't translate into other styles or arrangements and has a short shelf life. Once this trend in recording style runs its course, the song almost never becomes a standard. The song has its run, slips from consumer interest, and does not generate further royalties from other recording artists who could have cut the song on their own records with new arrangements and production. It doesn't generate royalties from translation into foreign languages and release in foreign countries.

On the other hand, if a song is strong on the basic level—lyrics and melody—and is of the caliber to be a standard, and the songwriters are lucky, the song may in time be picked up by the "golden-oldie" radio stations, be cut by other artists over many years, be translated into foreign languages, etc. This is how standards are born, and if you've developed accessible song concepts and crafted these with strong definitive melody and strong lyrics from the beginning, you already have the focus and elements in place that could lead to a standard.

Effective demos and copyright

If you are not a performing songwriter looking for both a publishing and a record label combination deal, the demos you present do not require the depth of arrangement a performing artist's original song does. As a freelance songwriter, your demo can be arranged simply with just a vocal and piano or guitar. The vocal will make or break the demo so get someone who can sing well. Have the song clearly reflect the style of music you believe it fits best. Don't get suckered by sound studios who want to charge you lots of money for more complicated arrangements. If a song is selected by a publisher, it's the publisher's responsibility to produce a demo. Remember, if you have written a song with definitive melody that can be arranged in different styles, keeping the demo simple makes it easier for industry professionals to take notice of that fact. They will not become lost in an overpowering arrangement or lose interest from one that does not do the song justice.

I also sincerely encourage songwriters to invest in their own home recording studio. Pick the price range you can afford. A 2-track or 4-track set-up will suffice to record a clear, clean demo that allows a reviewer to hear a dominant vocal and simple instrumentation in the background.

Remember, *a song with strong lyrics and definitive melody can be sung a cappella.* The addition of instruments and arrangements should only help the song sound better. Note: the actual basic song you copyright with the Library of Congress is comprised strictly of melody (note pattern) and the words that are sung with those notes. Chord progressions and arrangement ideas are not copyrightable. Even when you send the library of Congress a completely arranged version of a song, the words and melody are the focus of the song, and are carried by the singer's voice (which should then be the focus of the demo arrangement). The instrumental arrangement is superfluous when it comes to copyright. It is also advisable that songwriters copyright all songs they plan to market to the music industry before they begin distributing them. If you plan to record, manufacture, and sell your original songs to the public, **copyright them first!**

Copyright notes

For More Info

Songwriters should Copyright their songs individually or in collections. Using the Library of Congress form PA to register for copyright gives the songwriter ownership of the exclusive rights to their songs, covering any future arrangement created for the songs by others. Form PA gives the songwriter world-wide protection for any and all uses of each song registered.

The Library of Congress form SR is used to register sound recordings for copyright. The owner of the exclusive rights to a sound recording captures the rights to only the specific arrangements of the songs on that specific sound recording. Record labels, independent record producers and songwriters with demos to distribute or sell, use form SR.

Expand your catalog or "body of work"
A word of caution! In today's music market, the singer-songwriter with less than 100 songs in their catalog may be steering themselves into a corner, allowing little latitude for rescue. The songs chosen by a record label for a debut CD will be the 10 most commercially viable songs as selected by A&R, producers, and arrangers. The songs that remain are the second stage selections for a subsequent album that will also require newer songs not available for selection the first time around. The more songs a songwriter has when they contract with a label, the less stressful their career will be. Publishers also appreciate a songwriter who has a sizable song catalog/body of work.

FINDING THE BALANCE
The serious songwriter is pursuing the kind of creative lifestyle and success only the music industry can provide. That success can be incalculable in today's world. By presenting these techniques and insights, it's my hope songwriters can take their creativity to the limit and open their minds to new options, new creative directions and a self confidence that will carry them past the inevitable failures and rejections to the breakthrough.

I especially want songwriters to keep writing and turning out wonderful songs. I want them to write songs people will treasure and remember and songs that will make a difference in people's lives. Hopefully, the elements of inspiration and songcraft I've discussed will help you take control of your creativity and build a career that is both artistically and commercially satisfying.

Advanced Articles

Internet Music Resources

by Brian Austin Whitney

When asked to write an article on songwriter resources on the Internet, I initially thought I should simply list all the most helpful sites I have found over the years. But there are already quite a few articles and online resources that do a great job of supplying an all-inclusive laundry list.

Instead, what you will find below is a smaller number of sites (in a wide variety of areas) with more in-depth explanations on why those sites (and others like them) are of use to you as a songwriter. It isn't meant to be all-inclusive, but to provide a benchmark so you can succeed and thrive on your own as you expand your own searches to additional sites and resources. Because companies come and go each year and sometimes change their business structure, please be sure to check with each for their current status and policies.

SIZE UP THE COMPETITION

In my opinion there's nothing better you can do to help your songwriting talent than listen to as much great music as you can. Even though the radio and mass media today play less and less diverse music, the Internet is crawling with musical talent, and if you have a fast connection listening to it is just a click away. Here's the best site for songwriters who want to size up the competition:

CD Baby (www.cdbaby.com)

Why is this site important to songwriters? Two main reasons:

You can browse and find out what's really going on in your genre(s) of music. Remember, you can't compete in the music business until you clearly understand what the competition is doing. Until you've listened to the best of your peers, you won't fully understand how good you need to be just to be in the game. This site offers commercially viable artists who haven't been hyper-filtered by mass media, meaning you'll find far more creative diversity and cutting edge material. Write country songs? Listen to what up-and-coming country artists are doing. Compose experimental electronic noise? No problem. You'll find oodles of it. If you have a fast connection, you can listen in real time by streaming.

Networking opportunities abound! CD Baby's site includes bios and backgrounds on

BRIAN AUSTIN WHITNEY is the founder of Just Plain Folks, the largest grassroots music organization with members worldwide. The organization educates, inspires, promotes, and networks members through both online and face-to-face events and activities. Members include everything from #1 songwriters, artists, and music industry professionals to those just getting started. Visit their website at www.justplainfolks.org or send e-mail to info@jpfolks.com.

the artists and recordings. Even better, they allow you to e-mail the artists directly (something you can rarely do with mass market artists). The artists on CD Baby may be among your best candidates to record your music if what you do is compatible with what they do. Even if they don't record other writers' music they probably work in circles with artists who do. Songwriters need to network with people actively making the types of music they write. An endless number of good things can happen via networking, including things you'd never predict.

There are no better allies for you as a songwriter than artists with great talent who are also rising up the ranks in their careers. So, if you find an artist who blows you away, buy their CD, and send them a note saying "I was so moved by your music I had to own a copy of it myself. I totally get what you are doing musically. And by the way, I write songs and have one you might want to consider for your next project." Little things that like will jump you to the head of your networking class. Nothing gains an artist's interest faster than sincere praise. In addition, if you are a songwriter and an artist, CD Baby has become the pathway to getting your music on the large Internet digital music services alongside the major label artists. See the CD Baby site for details.

GET INVOLVED IN ON-LINE COMMUNITIES

Building a network of friends and peers is crucial to long term success. Though it would be great to start at the top with the most successful people in the business, it's more realistic to make friends with the people who are on the rise at the same time you are. Here are three community websites that offer a lot of opportunities to mix it up with your peers:

The Muse's Muse (www.musesmuse.com)

This is probably the single finest songwriting-focused resource site on the Net. An outstanding monthly e-mail newsletter, "Muse's News," comes packed with educational articles, opportunities, and even music reviews. There is an extensive library of articles, CD Reviews, tips and links to resources of all types on the site. If you want to find something related to songwriting, this should be your first stop. There's also a very active message board community, with places to get feedback on your lyrics and give some back to others.

Indie-Music (www.indie-music.com)

This is probably the most diverse resource/information site of the three. It covers a broad amount of information relevant to both artists and songwriters. They recently added a premium membership service for a fee, but there is still a great deal of free information to be found, as well as a message board and other helpful information.

Just Plain Folks (www.jpfolks.com)

This is the largest grassroots music organization in the world and accordingly has the most active song and lyric feedback message boards of the three sites. Their focus is on networking, both on line and face to face. There are local chapters, member showcases and roadtrips, a large mentor staff to answer questions and share their experiences as well as the world's largest music awards program and a large Internet radio station to help promote their members music. They also have an e-mail newsletter, "Just Plain Notes," with educational and inspirational articles and updates.

STUDY SONGWRITING ONLINE

After taking advantage of the free resources offered by the above sites, you may also want some formal structured education on the craft of songwriting. There are two great options for songwriters who may not be able to attend a university program on songwriting, but who still want the structure offered in that type of program:

Berklee Online: (www.berkleemusic.com)

This one is presented by the Berklee College of Music and offers college credits.

Song U: (www.songu.com)

This program is presented by successful Nashville staff writers Danny Arena and Sara Light along with a team of additional songwriting educators from around the world.

Though these programs have different benefits and approaches, the people running them are highly respected in the music community. They both offer free resources such as chat rooms, message boards and information, as well as an actual curriculum, which is fee-based, similar to a college course. I highly recommend you visit their sites if you'd like a formal, structured, online classroom type of learning opportunity.

POST YOUR MUSIC ONLINE

One of the best things about the Net is that you can quickly and easily put your music up for people to check out, co-writers to fiddle with, publishers to listen to, and fans and peers to learn about and sample your work. There are three primary ways to post your songs on the net:

Your own website

Your own site website (such as www.yourname.com) is a great way to "hang your shingle" out in the cyber world, and is becoming the best and easiest way for people to find each other, communicate, and do business of all types. But to be found, you have to have a presence, and it's less and less expensive and complicated to do these days.

Use a hosting site

If you want your own site, but you aren't a web designer, I suggest going to a hosting company. Find one that is simple to use and straightforward, with templates for people with music files, video content and graphics to post. The best option I have come across is **Hostbaby.com (www.hostbaby.com)**. They are well-suited to get you up and running and even have a free trial period so you can test out their services without spending a dime. The people at CDBaby.com run Hostbaby.com and they understand the needs and desires of songwriters and musicians better than anyone else I have found.

A page on one of the many mp3 and file-streaming sites

If you'd rather not set up your own customized site, there are still other options. Many people are aware of popular sites like mp3.com, but there are some additional ones that aren't as mammoth. Two sites you might want to check out which are popular with songwriters who like to post their works in progress are **Songramp.com (www.songramp.com)** and **Soundclick.com (www.songclick.com)**. These types of sites can usually include some bio info, different types of streaming and often have both free and pay options depending on what you need. In many cases you can be up and running in a short time. Be sure to carefully read what extra benefits you get for any monthly fees.

JOIN PERFORMING RIGHTS ORGANIZATIONS
ASCAP (www.ascap.com), BMI (www.bmi.com), and SESAC (www.sesac.com)

Of course, if you want to earn money from airplay or publish your work, you should affiliate yourself with one of the U.S. Performing rights organizations—ASCAP, BMI, and SESAC. (You can quickly finds lists for all non-USA PROs by doing a web search).

Each site allows you to search for song titles, writers, and artists who have cut various songs for the songs they represent. (This is important if you want to see how many other versions there are of your "unique" song title—you may find dozens or even hundreds of previous uses of any given title!) I strongly suggest you contact all three to learn more about what they have to offer. Each organization also offers various programs to develop the writing skills of their members. (For more information, see their listings in the Organizations section of this book).

Sound Exchange (www.soundexchange.com)

In addition, if you are a songwriter who performs your own material, you should also check out this new Digital Performance Rights Organization which is responsible for collecting performance royalties (as opposed to mechanical royalties) when your music is played on the Internet.

MAKE YOUR VOICE HEARD IN WASHINGTON, DC

With the rapid changes in technology, it is hard to keep up with the changes in laws that affect songwriters. The voices of media and public interests are important to be heard in this discussion, but so are the voices of the songwriters and artists who are the most affected by many of these new laws and technologies. There is one organization in particular that is at the forefront of protecting current and future rights of songwriters and recording artists as well as the public at large.

The Future of Music Coalition: (www.futureofmusic.org)

The Future of Music Coalition is a not-for-profit collaboration between members of the music, technology, public policy and intellectual property law communities. The FMC seeks to educate the media, policymakers, and the public about music/technology issues, while also bringing together diverse voices in an effort to come up with creative solutions to some of the challenges in this space. The FMC also aims to identify and promote innovative business models that will help musicians and citizens to benefit from new technologies. If you want your voice to be heard, I highly recommend that you get involved with this great organization.

FIND COMMERCIAL OUTLETS FOR YOUR MUSIC

There's another type of website that can actually help you make contacts and find commercial opportunities for your music. Each charges a fee, but they provide legitimate services and tools to help you)

TAXI (www.taxi.com)

Founded in 1992, TAXI is the oldest and most respected company in its field, but is also the most often misunderstood. In a nutshell, TAXI acts as an independent A&R company for many major and independent record labels, publishers, producers, movie and television music supervisors and so on. They post and e-mail opportunity listings to members for songs needed by these industry companies and in turn accept submissions from their members hoping to fill those needs. They use a staff of in house A&R experts (often the same people major labels themselves use) to screen the music that comes in and narrow it down to those songs that best fit the listing. If a song isn't suitable for a listing, TAXI (unless otherwise noted) will provide a written critique of the song, including reasons why it wasn't appropriate (or good enough) for that listing. If a song does meet the criteria for that listing, TAXI forwards the song directly to the decision maker who needs the song. TAXI also accepts submissions online and offers a lot of extras to members, including a free music conference called the TAXI Road Rally (considered by many to be the best in the industry).

Advanced Articles

Songcatalog.com (www.songcatalog.com) and Songscope.com (www.songs cope.com)

Some online companies will host your songs on file for potential industry buyers to browse and in some cases provide pitch sheets and other services. Songcatalog.com and Songscope.com are two companies worth checking out in this field.

Reminder: Be sure to carefully read exactly what all these and similar companies do and how they do it. They can each be a valuable tool; but if you purchase the wrong tool or don't really understand how to use it properly, even the best mechanic can't make it do the job. Also remember, no company can make a poorly written song a success. *You have to be writing songs that are both excellent AND in demand by those who are looking.* And having the perfect song is meaningless if you don't have access.

BE CAUTIOUS

The music industry lives and breathes on relationships, sometimes taking years to form. But, the Internet has become a haven for scam artists who claim a shortcut to success as long as you pay their price. If someone contacts you about your music and you've never met them, be very cautious. There is no shortage of great music for legitimate business people to use, so there is no real need for someone to randomly spam songwriters to drum up business— unless the only business they are in is making money off the hopes and dreams of unsuspecting songwriters!

It's easy to get caught up in the excitement when someone shows interest in our songs. But the moment money enters into the picture, you need to check with your resources (including all the folks mentioned earlier in this article) and peers to make sure you aren't being scammed. It's not always easy to tell, but you owe it to yourself and your family to do your homework and fully investigate the credibility of anyone asking you for money. Post questions on message boards (most mass scam artists have hit up thousands of others and they'll be happy to fill you in). You wouldn't buy a car from someone randomly finding you on the street, so don't try to buy your dream of success from someone randomly finding you on the web!

USE YOUR MOST POWERFUL CAREER BUILDING TOOL

The Internet is probably the most cost effective and efficient tool songwriters have ever been given. But for all its potential, sometimes people forget to do the little things that can lead to most positive return for the time and effort. What am I referring to? What's the magical and nearly free tool that you have at your disposal? The simple thank-you note of course.

We all understand that artists and writers appreciate positive feedback from fans. But we often forget that people who do the work to help artists and writers succeed appreciate some positive recognition for their work as well. A smart songwriter doesn't forget that writing a simple thank-you note can be the most important words they ever write for their career. If you read an article that helps you, write the author a thank-you note. If you attend a music conference or seminar, send the organizers a thank-you note. If you find a song that moves you on line, e-mail the artist and the writer a note and tell them. In fact, the more you thank people, the more those same people will work to earn your thanks again. Keep in mind, a positive email thanking someone has a magical way of getting to people you could normally never reach with a phone call.

So don't forget to thank the people who have helped you along the way and they won't forget you the next time you cross their path. These little acts of appreciation are so simple to do and thanks to e-mail so instantaneous in their effect it's amazing. Yet so few songwriters actually do it that when one does, people will take notice. And being noticed at the right time by the right person can make the difference between a successful career in music and a lifetime in artistic oblivion.

Building the Business Team

for Today's Market

by Scott Mathews

Let's say you are a budding performer who writes good songs, and you are expressing yourself through music and having a ton of fun. That, my friend, is success! Don't ever lose what you have found.

Now, let's say as your songs get better, people acknowledge you are in fact gifted, and you gain momentum to the point where you realize music is not just another crazy dream, but something you wish to pursue as a career. I hereby pronounce you a professional artist! You may now kiss yourself.

Wow, a real bona fide artist—wait, that means you have a real job! Yes, you are among the blessed in that you have wisely chosen a field of endeavor you are passionate about—but a job is a job nonetheless. It doesn't take long to find that a career doing what you love may involve more tasks and details than you can handle alone. It may be time to build a support team—usually some combination of producers, lawyers and managers—to handle business tasks on your behalf and help grow that facet of your career, while you focus on letting the artistic juices flow.

The first step in building your team is assessing your current strengths and weaknesses in areas outside of performing and writing. Do you want to record an album but are clueless about how to work in a studio? Are you overwhelmed with phone calls organizing gigs and rehearsals? Are you long on talent but short on industry connections? Is a record company or publisher waving contracts in your face, but you're scared of the legalese and want to make sure it's a fair deal? Are you just plain clueless about what your next step should be?

Set goals for where you want your career to go and make a checklist of everything you need to get done to move toward those goals. We live in a "do it yourself" time with little or no development or direction coming from record companies. Artists must now develop their own act well before deals are done, so it's up to them to get ready for the big time. Figure out what kind of helping hand you need most to help guide the masses to your music. Who should you turn to first?

Multi-platinum contributor **SCOTT MATHEWS** of Hit or Myth Productions has produced, recorded or performed with a range of artists including John Hiatt, Van Morrison, Keith Richards and John Lee Hooker. His songs have been cut by artists such as Barbra Streisand and Dave Edmunds. See his listing in the Record Producers section. "Not affiliated with scottmathewsmusic.com or scottmathewsproductions.com. Beware of these and other impostors using the name 'Scott Mathews.' " E-mail him at hitormyth@aol.com.

PRODUCERS, PROGRESS & PROCEEDS

One major hurdle to get over in the music business is the need to present your work in a fully-realized form so that everyone who hears "gets it." This means documenting your music the best you can, usually in a recording studio. Recorded music can travel places you can't go, be heard by many different people, and present your music to interested ears when you can't be there in person to perform it live. It can also make money for you through your own sales efforts or from licensing it to an interested label. So, it needs to be as good as you can make it—great songs, great sound, and great performances.

In my experience, when you prove you can deliver a killer, marketable record, that's the time good managers, attorneys and record execs will come out of the woodwork seeking you—and you then end up with a much better deal because hold the goods and you don't need a record company's expensive money to complete the project. Plus, the all-important "creative control" is built into a situation where you have proven your own commercial potential on the front end.

Sound advice for the new music industry

With today's digital recording technology, you can make a great record for a fraction of the hundreds of thousands of dollars big labels like to throw at recording projects. And at the end, you own the masters and keep the profits. But, it's not always as easy as it might seem. For the amount of money you spend buying your own recording equipment and learning to use it, you could hire a producer and save a lot of time by making use of his or her expertise and musical knowledge to get what you want.

Making a truly great record requires technical expertise in recording, arranging skills, and a lot of knowledge about how people tick, especially temperamental artists. An inexperienced artist who tries to self-produce may well find herself staring into a microphone, frustrated and stuck, while precious studio time burns away her budget. An artist in this situation needs a producer to guide her through the process of recording and help her get the best bang for her buck in terms of performance and time spent in the studio.

Beware of big promises

Important

You must understand there are absolutely no guarantees for success after the record is made. The moment a producer (or anyone else) makes such guarantees, you know you are working with an excitable amateur or a scam artist. There are simply too many variables to consider, and every creative/ business endeavor is unique. Good fortune comes from many sources— contacts, determination, quality, timing, and yes, plain old good luck. You can only lay plans, make your best efforts, and hope for the best.

When hiring a producer, you should first seek a person with complementary creative drives who can help you make the best possible record. He or she should then also have reasonable contacts in the industry and a plan to help the record get the recognition it deserves. Not all producers can actually offer all of this, but that doesn't stop many from representing themselves as people who can practically guarantee quick-and-easy record deals and instant rock stardom (for a price). As a producer, I strive to make successful records and careers, but I also demand that reality and honest expectations are weighed out and realized by all parties.

The right producer can also be a great long-term creative partner, and help you make great strides in developing your sound, either as an individual singer/songwriter or a band, even before you go into the studio. Good producers understand how instruments blend, support one another, and in turn support the vocal and lyrics, which is the real focus of any effective arrangement.

If you are a band, a good producer can be an objective sounding board, hear the overall picture of your sound, and point out aspects of how you play together as a group that can be tightened up. This will save you time, both as a performing group and in the studio. The version of yourself a good producer can conjure in the studio will also help you see the big picture for yourself and help you move forward on your sound with new direction and focus.

For singer/songwriters, the right producer can frame their songs in new and startling ways they may not have considered and open up whole new vistas of sound for them to explore. Since the artist and producer are not trying to capture a particular band sound, there is actually more freedom to explore styles or radical sounds.

A good producer can also help artists hone their songs to absolute perfection before they go in the studio, and open artists up to whole new areas of songwriting they may not have considered. A good producer can suggest ways for bands to rethink the basic outlines of verse and chorus, or take a singer/songwriter's basic vocal and melody and suggest small changes in phrasing that take it to the next level (or even take the basic vocal and build completely new chords and rhythms around it).

Beware of the Spec Deal

Tip

A word of caution regarding finding the right producer and development deal: beware the "spec" offer that provides free studio time but commits you to giving away publishing rights or other valuable assets. As a recording artist, the publishing generated by your songs will likely represent the first royalties you see and will continue to be a main source of income as long as you control the copyrights. Most record company accounting techniques can be frustrating to say the least but your songs are earning money (your writer's and publishing share) in a fair and equitable way. That's why I chose "Hang On To Your Publishing" as the name for my own music publishing company—that says it all.

A proven new approach

I've encouraged artists I work with to build from an independent stance, and it's paying off for them. In just the past couple of months, I have had a band in America signed to a major label (Atlantic). Another band in Canada is now being seriously courted by senior vice-presidents at several major labels, while a singer/songwriter from England has just finished her CD and found distribution through Universal on an independent label. A few months ago, I had an artist from Belgium go to #1 in Europe for six weeks with a single from a CD we did for his small home spun label. I'm beginning to feel like Nero, making music and careers while Rome (the old industry model) burns! Development rocks!

These results have all come because I believe in the artists and the artists believe in themselves and in my abilities as their producer. We set out to make the rest of the world believe by building their careers based on the fact that great, timeless records speak volumes more than a great gig to a small room of people only interested in the bar. Recorded music can be sent around the world in seconds and be preserved forever. Once the recordings are finished, we stay busy spreading the word high and low. We find fans one by one and some of those fans are in important places such as record companies, management companies, law firms, agencies, etc. The idea is this: if we will build it—they will come. Because, in today's music industry if we don't empower ourselves to build it, we are only fooling ourselves if we think a large corporation will come along and build it for us.

MANAGERS, MOMENTUM & MONEY

I began in the music *business*, now it's called the music *industry*. Anyone can start a business but it takes several large corporations to start an industry. Frankly, I prefer to treat music like a business and fit into the industry while remaining independent. I encourage any self-respecting artist to follow that logic. It's healthy to know how one fits into the overall industry (and how they get paid!), but staying true to your artistic vision is key. Who will be able to share that vision and help you in your day-to-day duties as a business? A great manager can.

An effective artist manager can help lead you where you need to be and keep you on track once you get there. A manager often handles all of the "office-related" work your business conducts such as bookkeeping, booking appearances, publishing and recording deals, press, etc., not to mention being a good friend and confidante (much like your producer should be).

The right manager will understand your artistic vision and help you achieve your goals. A good manager can provide useful advice, draw upon industry connections you do not possess, represent you in business negotiations (in some cases playing the bad cop, so you can be the good guy), and take the load of day-to-day business chores off your back so you have more time to write, practice, and rehearse.

Yes, there is a lengthy laundry list of activities a good manager handles, but be warned— a bad manger can hang you out to dry, *so make sure you choose carefully based on your goals and make sure this business relationship is fulfilling a bona fide need for your career*. The entertainment field is rife with managers who have amassed huge sums of money by being world-class ambulance chasers. This type tends to watch for when an artist or band has generated enough heat on their own, and then pounces on them with their charm and smarm. This school of manager is usually cheesy enough to promise the moon. If they time it right, it can be a quick way for them to step in and collect a full commission on all the years of hard labor an artist has put in. When there are hundreds of thousands of dollars at stake, that 15 or 20% is one fat payday for the heat-seeking missile type of management.

There are countless heartbreaking stories to be told of artists being overly eager to sign any deal. They sign away a large percentage to the wrong party and then find themselves dirt poor. Ouch! So, when inking a management deal, I suggest every artist negotiate a fair percentage accurately reflecting what has been earned, by whom and when. You might even ask a manager to work with you on a trial basis before signing formally. Let them earn their keep and prove they can enhance your career.

LAWYERS, GUNS AND MONEY

You will need an established entertainment attorney if people are throwing contracts at you. Shop around and find someone with the knowledge to know what's up and the honesty to keep your costs down.

Sometimes I feel I have single-handedly paid for at least one of the two towers in Century City where so many of the L.A.-based entertainment law firms operate. Okay, that is an absurd stretch of the truth, but early in my career, I spent much of the money I earned on attorney's fees. I don't mean to bash lawyers—heaven knows, there have been a ton of overpaid producers in the record business!—but, I've concluded the only thing worse than learning from expensive lessons is not learning from expensive lessons.

I still see my fair share of lawyer bills—can't live without them—but there are strategies I've found for making every dollar you spend on legal fees more effective:

- **Be cautious about paying attorneys on a retainer basis when starting out.** It's better not to set lawyers up on extra long retainers and let them run amuck. Pay for their services only when you need them for specific, limited issues. You will save money, and the lawyer will not be tempted to exceed his authority and meddle with your career.
- **Hire specialists for specific needs.** I commonly hire a person who is an expert in whatever area of concern for which I am in need of advice. A certain lawyer whose expertise is publishing is who I will talk to regarding a situation involving my songs. An attorney who deals in accounting might be who I'd call when there is a dispute over royalties. (That would never happen in this industry—right?)
- **Watch and learn.** After many years in the business, I began to see a pattern of entertainment lawyers negotiating record production deals in pretty much the same fashion from one deal to the next. I paid attention, asked a lot of questions and therefore learned a whole lot from my attorneys (and I still do). When I discovered I could apply much of that information to new agreements myself, I took a more active role in the process and set up my own system. Now my company can deal directly in certain areas in which we're well-versed.

Most of the lawyers I have used proved to be smart—some brilliant. I learned from the best and the cost of that education was worth every penny. Still, in the overall scheme of things, I believe the people who make the music should share in the monetary proceeds more than the people who don't make the music.

In the end, it comes down to the old saying that "knowledge is power." If you know the game, you will be able not only to talk to your attorney about what your needs are (and understand your attorney, which can be no small feat) but also be empowered to deal directly with many concerns that involve your day-to-day dealings.

Don't knock before you rock

Tip

Even if you are currently capable of running the entire show yourself, without the aid (or expense) of your own team of "people," be aware that most high-powered industry mucky-mucks do not have an open door policy towards new talent. Due to the sheer volume of solicitations, a "gatekeeper" system is in place, and only known managers, producers or attorneys are allowed to present the case for a new artist. However, it is my experience that there is simply no reason to bring a lawyer into play until your act is developed enough that you are ready to be shopped. You only knock when you are ready to rock!

QUICK RESULTS? YOU MUST CONSULT

It isn't always the right move to hand over all the reins of your business concerns. But, there may be specific help available in the form of consultants you access on an "as needed" basis as opposed to hiring them full-time.

Due to huge industry layoffs, many qualified people are deciding they don't want to work for giant corporations. Some of the most talented that have done great work for various labels now offer their services as consultants. They can be hired to help emerging artists answer big and small questions along the way. The guidance and advice from someone who has been in the industry long enough to know what to look out for and at the same time is current enough to keep an eye on new developments can be a fantastic guiding light to an up-and-comer.

So, do you smell team spirit? Go out and assemble the best you can find, based on your needs. This is no time to be shy . . . wrong business for that. Search out who can help you and present yourself in a professional and ambitious way.

The Mid-Atlantic Song Contest

Editor's Report from the 2003 Awards Show

by Ian Bessler

The Songwriters Association of Washington (SAW) held the awards ceremony for the Mid-Atlantic Song Contest on November 24, 2003 at the Hard Rock Café in downtown Washington, D.C. Once again, the ceremony encompassed and recognized a wide array of talented performers and writers, in all styles from all across the country, many of them at early stages in promising careers.

Lori Kelley, Grand Prize Winner

This year's Grand Prize Winner, and Gold Award winner in the Country category, was Lori Kelley of Centreville, VA., for "It Was A Great Day, " about the frustration of not being able to do what you *want* to do, because of all the things in your life you think you *have* to do. This year, the Grand Prize again consisted of $1,000, a three-year Songwriters Association of Washington membership, and a free one-year membership in TAXI, the online A&R service. It was my honor as editor of *Songwriter's Market* to present the Grand Prize Award to Lori Kelley, and interview her afterward.

Lori Kelley

Photo by Ian Bessler

Kelley had been a member of SAW for several years after moving to the Washington D.C. area in the early '90s, and had been entering songs into the contest since 1994, and had earned several honorable mentions over the years, but had not had a breakthrough until this year. When asked how she knew her writing was ready to compete in a contest format, she mentioned that even though she had long been submitting songs to the contest, she now believes she only recently turned a corner. "I think it took until last year. By that time I felt like I was so much better as a songwriter. I started writing when I was sixteen, but I didn't seriously start writing until I was thirty, when I had two small babies and had nothing to do but get my guitar out and start writing songs again."

Although she performs regularly every week with her performing partner, Cletus Kennelly, Kelley hopes that her song contest win can open doors to music publishers and help her fulfill her ambition to have other artists cut her songs. "That's my hope as a songwriter, to get other people to sing my songs. I enjoy writing songs and performing them near home in my Washington, D.C. area, but I don't want to go on tour and leave my family. So, I'm hoping some other great singer can go off and do that for me!"

IAN BESSLER has been editor of *Songwriter's Market* since the 2001 edition.

Kyler England, Second Place Overall

The Second Place Overall Winner, and winner of the Gold Award in Rock/Alternative, was singer/songwriter Kyler England (also the winner of the 2002 North Carolina Songwriters Competition) for "Something So Beautiful," a song from her new album, *A Flower Grows in Stone*, about a friend who grew out of a difficult upbringing. For this song, she won $500, a free two-year SAW membership, and a free one-year membership to TAXI. England networks extensively and knows many songwriters who enter contests. "I heard about it from some other songwriters in New York who had actually won or placed in different categories before," she says. "I'm also on a lot of mailing lists with other songwriters, and so I hear a lot about competitions other writers are winning."

Kyler England

Photo by Ian Bessler

When asked how many songs she submits, England says, "I usually just submit one to every contest because I don't have enough money to submit multiple songs to multiple contests. And it's a hard choice. On my new record, "Something So Beautiful" is closest to my heart, so I submitted it to a couple of contests, but I usually try to 'spread the love around' and send three or four songs to different contests."

Although she writes mainly for her own performance, England is open to any opportunities to write for other artists. "I write primarily for myself," she says, "because I love performing, and singing has always been my number one love. But, I've been doing some co-writing in Nashville, and I think the idea is that some of those songs will be plugged to artists there. It's not something I'm aiming directly for, but I would definitely be interested in that."

Matt Singer, Gold Award in Hip-Hop/Dance/Urban

Singer/songwriter Matt Singer, winner of the Gold Award in Hip-Hop/Dance/Urban and the Contest Director's Award for "Man With A Can," an acoustic-guitar backed urban rap telling of an encounter with a sage homeless man, heard about the Mid-Atlantic Song Contest through the Contests & Awards section of this book. "I found out about the contest through the *Songwriter's Market*," he says. "It mentioned Mid-Atlantic as one of the reliable song contests."

Matt Singer

Photo by Ian Bessler

He also said he enjoyed the opportunity to bring some recognition to himself and to hip-hop as a genre of writing. "I am motivated by unusual forms of hip-hop. I like when people stretch the boundaries, and the hip-hop you hear on the radio is often not the most ground-breaking, creative stuff you can hear. I think for the most part, even people that love hip-hop a lot of times really concentrate on the background of it and the beat, the thing that makes the mood. I'm really attentive to the lyrics that MC's sing, and I always judge the quality of an MC by their ability to say things intelligently and with rhythm."

When asked what doors he hoped his contest win could open for him, Singer emphasized that the enjoyment he got from the act of writing and performing was his prime motivation and he wants to take things one step at a time. "I haven't gotten that far," he says. "I'm really into winning a contest for the first time with my songs, and I feel like it's a big step for me. I'm just excited to watch everyone else play."

Dwayne Henry (a.k.a. Storm the Unpredictable)
Gold Award in Children's

Dwayne Henry (a.k.a. hip-hop performer "Storm the Un-predictable") won the Grand Prize in the 2002 Mid-Atlantic Song Contest for "Get Your Weight Up," and was back in 2003 to receive a Gold Award in the Children's category for "It's My Culture." Like Singer, Henry also enjoys the recognition and legitimacy the contest has brought to hip-hop as a form of songwriting, and is eager to push the boundaries of hip-hop in terms of the subject matter it can address, including hip-hop addressed directly to children as listeners. "This song was written specifically for chil-dren, even though after I finished with it, and with the cli-mate and atmosphere of the world and the way things are,

Dwayne Henry

Photo by Ian Bessler

it also ended up being something adults can get into. I guess it's the reverse of most of music, which is written for adults but children can listen to it and still get something from it. But it's speaking directly to children about a lot of the different things they may be going through. You can make music listenable for children, but that doesn't mean they can understand everything that is going on. At the same, you can write a song that has no cursing in it, but the subject matter of it is so heavy the children can't really get it. So that was why I wanted to do—something that could be geared more toward them, so they can really get into it and have fun with it.

It turns out his previous win in the contest has opened some doors for him as a hip-hop performer and as a writer. "It was a big boost as far as my press kit, because I was able to put the certificate right there in the front, so it was one of the first things people saw. It showed that I was doing more than just performing at some club. I guess you could say it pumped me up a notch as far as some of the other hip-hop artists in the area - and not just locally in this region, but beyond. It has also opened doors for me as far as performing in high schools and elementary schools and places like that. And, having a songwriting award made people a lot more open to inviting me to come in and talk with their students, not just talk with them about what it's like to be a hip-hop artist, but speak about the creative aspect of songwriting and the genre of hip-hop music."

His previous contest win and recognition as a writer also brought opportunities to widen his career and write on assignment for clients. "It afforded me a lot of other opportunities as far as doing commercials and things like that," he says. "With the coverage that came from this in the *Washingtonian Magazine*, some people sought me out and said, 'Well, you know we have this product, this thing that we're trying to do, and we saw that you won this contest. Do you think you could write something for us for this commercial?' Without my win in the contest, more than likely they would have just looked at me as another rapper. But when you say *songwriter* that brings such a distinction to what you're doing, and I think it gained me another level of respect from a whole other segment of people."

Because of the wider field he's discovered as a writer, and not just performer, Henry advises all would-be songwriters to write about as many different topics as they can. "Don't restrict yourself or think you have to write about one certain thing," he says. "And that's no matter what genre you're working in. Definitely be versatile."

Wendy Kraizel, Gold and Silver in Pop/R&B

Songwriter Wendy Kraizel swept the Gold and Silver awards in Pop/R&B with two songs, "This Is Your Time" (Gold) and "Don't Ever Stop" (Silver). She credited reading a copy of *Songwriter's Market* with inspiring her to get serious and do something with her songwriting,

Advanced Articles

and also with arming her with the necessary information to present her music with a professional attitude. "I've always loved to write music and play piano, but I had never done anything with it," she says. "Then I went through a bunch of life changes, and started to get more emotional in my singing and writing. I picked up a copy of *Songwriter's Market*, I saw that there were all types of contests, and it inspired me to make a demo CD and hopefully pursue a bit of a career in writing songs. I thought the Mid-Atlantic Song Contest was a great place to get some credibility if I placed in anything, and I've been fortunate enough to place Gold and Silver for Pop and R&B. And it's definitely because of the *Songwriter's Mar-*

Wendy Kraizel

ket. If I had not picked it up, I would never have been inspired to do something with it. I find it a very inspirational book, and I've noticed they have them for all types of different careers, and I think it's inspiring for all ages to get involved in something having to do with their talent."

Kraizel chose early on to write songs in a wide range of genres, and found a reasonably-priced demo studio able to produce her vocals with stylistically convincing backing tracks. "I looked in the yellow pages for someplace that did recording in my area," she says. "And even though I only wrote piano accompaniment—very basic—in a recording studio they can help you write the other ends of the music, and you get to approve all the different sounds they're bringing into it. It's a lot easier than I ever thought it would be."

Then, when it came time to pick songs to submit to the contest, she had many options regarding which contest categories she could submit to. "I thought the best approach for me was to concentrate more on the writing side of it. For the demo CD, I picked five songs, one that was country-ish, one that was rock-and-roll, one that was pop and R&B, one that had a bit of rap, and one that was more of a ballad. And I chose each of those five to show a different range of writing ability."

Kasaan Hammon, Silver for Hip-Hop/Dance/Urban

Multi-talented singer/songwriter/manager Kasaan Hammon of New York won the Silver Award in Hip-Hop/Dance/Urban for her song, "Magnet (In My Pants)," a crowd-pleasing party song. She originally wrote the song just for laughs, but it soon took on a life of its own. "I wrote it kind of as a joke, responding to the Spice Girls and all those type of acts," she says, "because I was a 'serious' songwriter and I was upset. So, I wrote 'Magnet' really as a personal joke between me and my friends. But finally I just decided to go record it, and ended up getting a bit of radio play. And it keeps coming back. One of those ones you write half-kidding, but then it never goes away!"

Kasaan Hammon

At the same time, she advises songwriters to go ahead and pursue those crazy, insistent song ideas to their conclusion, even if the song idea seems silly or clashes with the songwriter's self-image. "Just put it out there," she says. "I had 'Magnet' for five years, and it took five years to grow on me. But, when practicing it for tonight, it was the first time I thought, 'Wow, I actually kind of like this song!' If it's there, then there's a reason, and just get it out. If you feel it or not, put it down on paper or put it down on tape, and it may come out a completely different way than you expected."

Hammon is enthusiastic about song contests and the sort of exposure it can bring to a songwriter. It's just a matter of knowing your craft and then having the confidence to submit your work. "Just put it out there," she says. "Definitely. You never ever know what something is going to lead to. The more you put yourself out there, and the more people you meet, the greater your opportunities for exposure."

The power of a great song

Contest organizer Jean Bayou is also enthusiastic about the level of talent she's seen through the contest, and enjoys the opportunity to help these songwriters be heard by the public. "The best part of my job is getting to hear all sorts of incredibly talented people express themselves in so many different, creative ways. I am always amazed at the number of amateur songwriters out there, across all genres, who produce such excellent work. The quality of writing in many instances is way above what is out there on the commercial market, and the Mid-Atlantic Song Contest is proud to provide a conduit for these songwriters." She cautions that there is "no magic pill," though, and says that the "most important thing to remember is to keep on writing and keep on trying . . . it's all an inevitable part of the process of becoming a successful songwriter."

Music Publishers

Music publishers find songs and then get them recorded. In return for a share of the money made from your songs, they work as an agent for you by plugging your songs to recording artists, taking care of paperwork and accounting, setting you up with co-writers (recording artists or other songwriters), and so on.

HOW DO MUSIC PUBLISHERS MAKE MONEY FROM SONGS?

Music publishers make money by getting songs recorded onto albums, Film and TV soundtracks, commericals, etc.and other areas. While this is their primary function, music publishers also handle administrative tasks such as copyrighting songs, collecting royalties for the songwriter, negotiating and issuing synchronization licenses for use of music in films, television programs and commercials, arranging and administering foreign rights, auditing record companies and other music users, suing infringers, and producing new demos of the music submitted to them. In a small, independent publishing company, one or two people may handle all these jobs. Larger publishing companies are more likely to be divided into the following departments: creative (or professional), copyright, licensing, legal affairs, business affairs, royalty, accounting and foreign.

HOW DO MUSIC PUBLISHERS FIND SONGS?

The *creative department* is responsible for finding talented writers and signing them to the company. Once a writer is signed, it is up to the creative department to develop and nurture the writer so he will write songs that create income for the company. Staff members often put writers together to form collaborative teams. And, perhaps most important, the creative department is responsible for securing commercial recordings of songs and pitching them for use in film and other media. The head of the creative department, usually called the "professional manager," is charged with locating talented writers for the company.

HOW DO MUSIC PUBLISHERS GET SONGS RECORDED?

Once a writer is signed, the professional manager arranges for a demo to be made of the writer's songs. Even though a writer may already have recorded his own demo, the publisher will often re-demo the songs using established studio musicians in an effort to produce the highest-quality demo possible.

Once a demo is produced, the professional manager begins shopping the song to various outlets. He may try to get the song recorded by a top artist on his or her next album or get the song used in an upcoming film. The professional manager uses all the contacts and leads he has to get the writer's songs recorded by as many artists as possible. Therefore, he must be able to deal efficiently and effectively with people in other segments of the music industry, including A&R personnel, recording artists, producers, distributors, managers and lawyers. Through these contacts, he can find out what artists are looking for new material, and who may be interested in recording one of the writer's songs.

WHERE THE MONEY COMES FROM

After a writer's songs are recorded, the other departments at the publishing company come into play.

- The *licensing and copyright departments* are responsible for issuing any licenses for use of the writer's songs in film or TV and for filing various forms with the copyright office.
- The *legal affairs department and business affairs department* works with the professional department in negotiating contracts with its writers.
- The *royalty and accounting departments* are responsible for making sure that users of music are paying correct royalties to the publisher and ensuring the writer is receiving the proper royalty rate as specified in the contract and that statements are mailed to the writer promptly.
- Finally, the *foreign department*'s role is to oversee any publishing activities outside of the United States, to notify subpublishers of the proper writer and ownership information of songs in the catalogue and update all activity and new releases, and to make sure a writer is being paid for any uses of his material in foreign countries.

LOCATING A MUSIC PUBLISHER

How do you go about finding a music publisher that will work well for you? First, you must find a publisher suited to the type of music you write. If a particular publisher works mostly with alternative music and you're a country songwriter, the contacts he has within the industry will hardly be beneficial to you. Each listing in this section details, in order of importance, the type of music that publisher is most interested in; the music types appear in **boldface** to make them easier to locate. It's also very important to submit only to companies interested in your level of experience (see A Sample Listing Decoded on page 11). You will also want to refer to the Category Index at the end of this section, which lists companies by the type of music they work with. Publishers placing music in film or TV will be proceded by a ◾ (see the Film & TV Index for a complete list of these companies).

Do your research!

It's important to study the market and do research to identify which companies to submit to.

- Many record producers have publishing companies or have joint ventures with major publishers who fund the signing of songwriters and who provide administration services. Since producers many times have an influence over what is recorded, targeting the producer/publisher can be a useful avenue.
- Since most publishers don't open unsolicited material, try to meet the publishing representative in person (at conferences, speaking engagements, etc.) or try to have an intermediary intercede on your behalf (for example, an entertainment attorney; a manager, an agent, etc.).
- As to demos, submit no more than 3 songs.
- As to publishing deals, co-publishing deals (where a writer owns part of the publishing share through his or her own company) are relatively common if there is interest in a writer.
- Are you targeting a specific artist to sing your songs? If so, find out if that artist even

considers outside material. Get a copy of the artist's latest album, and see who wrote most of the songs. If they were all written by the artist, he's probably not interested in hearing material from outside writers. If the songs were written by a variety of different writers, however, he may be open to hearing new songs.

- Check the album liner notes, which will list the names of the publishers of each writer. These publishers obviously have had luck pitching songs to the artist, and they may be able to get your songs to that artist as well.

- If the artist you're interested in has a recent hit on the *Billboard* charts, the publisher of that song will be listed in the "Hot 100 A-Z" index. Carefully choosing which publishers will work best for the material you write may take time, but it will only increase your chances of getting your songs heard. "Shotgunning" your demo packages (sending out many packages without regard for music preference or submission policy) is a waste of time and money and will hurt, rather than help, your songwriting career.

Once you've found some companies that may be interested in your work, learn what songs have been successfully handled by those publishers. Most publishers are happy to provide you with this information in order to attract high-quality material. Ask the publisher for the names of some of their staff writers, and give them a call. Ask their opinion of how the publisher works. Keep in mind as you're researching music publishers how you get along with them personally. If you can't work with a publisher on a personal level, chances are your material won't be represented as you would like it to be. A publisher can become your most valuable connection to all other segments of the music industry, so it's important to find someone you can trust and feel comfortable with.

Independent or major company?

Also consider the size of the publishing company. The publishing affiliates of the major music conglomerates are huge, handling catalogs of thousands of songs by hundreds of songwriters. Unless you are an established songwriter, your songs probably won't receive enough attention from such large companies. Smaller, independent publishers offer several advantages. First, independent music publishers are located all over the country, making it easier for you to work face-to-face rather than by mail or phone. Smaller companies usually aren't affiliated with a particular record company and are therefore able to pitch your songs to many different labels and acts. Independent music publishers are usually interested in a smaller range of music, allowing you to target your submissions more accurately. The most obvious advantage to working with a smaller publisher is the personal attention they can bring to you and your songs. With a smaller roster of artists to work with, the independent music publisher is able to concentrate more time and effort on each particular project.

SUBMITTING MATERIAL TO PUBLISHERS

When submitting material to a publisher, always keep in mind that a professional, courteous manner goes a long way in making a good impression. When you submit a demo through the mail, make sure your package is neat and meets the particular needs of the publisher. Review each publisher's submission policy carefully, and follow it to the letter. Disregarding this information will only make you look like an amateur in the eyes of the company you're submitting to.

Listings of companies in Canada are preceded by a ❧ , and international markets are designated with a 🌐 . You will find an alphabetical list of these companies at the back of the book, along with an index of publishers by state.

Icons

For more instructional information on the listings in this book, including explanations of symbols ( ), read the article *Songwriter's Market: How Do I Use It?* on page 7.

For More Info

PUBLISHING CONTRACTS

Once you've located a publisher you like and he's interested in shopping your work, it's time to consider the publishing contract—an agreement in which a songwriter grants certain rights to a publisher for one or more songs. The contract specifies any advances offered to the writer, the rights that will be transferred to the publisher, the royalties a songwriter is to receive and the length of time the contract is valid.

- When a contract is signed, a publisher will ask for a 50-50 split with the writer. *This is standard industry practice*; the publisher is taking that 50% to cover the overhead costs of running his business and for the work he's doing to get your songs recorded.
- It is always a good idea to have a publishing contract (or any music business contract) reviewed by a competent entertainment lawyer.
- There is no "standard" publishing contract, and each company offers different provisions for their writers.

Make sure you ask questions about anything you don't understand, especially if you're new in the business. Songwriter organizations such as the Songwriters Guild of America (SGA) provide contract review services, and can help you learn about music business language and what constitutes a fair music publishing contract. Be sure to read What About Contracts? on page 36 for more information on contracts. See the Organizations section, beginning on page 326 of this book, for more information on the SGA and other songwriting groups.

When signing a contract, it's important to be aware of the music industry's unethical practitioners. The "song shark," as he's called, makes his living by asking a songwriter to pay to have a song published. The shark will ask for money to demo a song and promote it to radio stations; he may also ask for more than the standard 50% publisher's share or ask you to give up all rights to a song in order to have it published. Although none of these practices is illegal, it's certainly not ethical, and no successful publisher uses these methods. *Songwriter's Market* works to list only honest companies interested in hearing new material. (For more on "song sharks," see How Do I Avoid the Rip-Offs? on page 19.)

ADDITIONAL PUBLISHERS

There are **more publishers** located in other sections of the book! On page 139 use the list of Additional Publishers to find listings within other sections who are also music publishers.

☑ A TA Z MUSIC

P.O. Box 1014, St. George UT 84771-1014. Phone/fax: (435)688-1818. E-mail: info@acecrazy.com. Website: www.acecrazy.com. **Contact:** Kyle Garrett, professional manager (pop/r&b/hip-hop). Music publisher. Estab. 1999. Publishes 8 songs/year; publishes 2 new songwriters/year. Staff size: 4. Pays standard royalty.

How to Contact *We only accept material referred to us by a reputable industry source (manager, entertainment attorney, etc.)* Prefers DVD/CD/CDR or VHS videocassette with lyric sheet. "Be sure to include lyric sheets!" Include SASE.

Music Mostly **pop**, **r&b** and **hip-hop**; also **rock**, **dance** and **alternative country**. Published "Five Thousand New Angels" (single by Ace); and "Power of USA" (single by Ace) from *9-11* (album), recorded by Ace (pop), released 2001 on "Diferent" Album.

Tips "Put a lot of effort into your submission . . . it'll show. Never take a submission lightly . . . it'll show! Go to as many songwriter workshops as possible and refine your craft. Send only great songs . . . *not* good songs."

☑ ABALORN MUSIC (ASCAP)

P.O. Box 5537, Kreole Station, Moss Point MS 39563-1537. (228)475-0059. "No collect calls." Estab. 1974. **Contact:** Joe F. Mitchell, executive vice president/general manager. First Vice President: Justin F. Mitchell. Second Vice President: Jonita F. Mitchell. Music publisher and record company (Missile Records).

   • Also see the listing for Bay Ridge Publishing in this section and the listing for Missile Records in the Record Companies section.

Affiliate(s) Bay Ridge Publishing Co. (BMI).

How to Contact *"Please don't send us anything until you contact us by phone or in writing and receive submission instructions. You must present your songs the correct way to get a reply.* Always whenever you write to us, be sure you include a #10 business-size envelope addressed back to you with a first class USA postage stamp on the envelope. We reply back to you from the SASE you send to us. All songs sent for review must include sufficient return postage. No reply made back to you without SASE or return of material without sufficient return postage. **Absolutely no reply postcards—only SASE**. If you only write lyrics, do not submit. We only accept completed songs, so you must find a collaborator. We are not interested in reviewing homemade recordings." Prefers CD (first choice) or cassette with 3-8 songs and lyrics to songs submitted. Responds in 2 months. "A good quality demo recording will always get preference over a poor recording."

Music All types and styles of songs. "Mississippi, Mississippi" (single by Kadish Millett) and "Innocent Little One" (single by Bob Levy) from *If It Takes All Night* (album), recorded by Christian Ramsey (modern pop country), released on Missile Records.

Tips "Our doors are always open to young recording artists who are exceptional talented and want to make a name for themselves in the music business. Your success is our success. We will work with you to reach your goal. We also are in the business of getting your professionally-recorded album of 10-12 well-produced and well-written, radio-ready songs placed with record companies in the USA and foreign countries for the possibility of record deals. Here is what we have gotten for some artists: $850,000 record deal for Charity (religious singing group) on Big Easy (USA) in 2001; $500,000 record deal for Vance Greek on Dime-A-Dozen (Germany) in 2002; and a $150,000 record deal for Randell Ruthledge (country) on Dime-A-Dozen (Germany) in 2003. Two more artists are under consideration as of 2004, and others may be considered. Missile Records, Abalorn Music (ASCAP) and Bay Ridge Publishing Co. (BMI) are listed in some well-known publications such as the *Billboard International Buyer's Guide*, *Mix Master Directory*, *Industrial Source Book*, *Pollstar*, *Yellow Pages of Rock* and other publications. Some well-known recording artists born and raised in Mississippi include Elvis Presley, Conway Twitty, B.B. King and Faith Hill. The Moss Point, MS area music scene is also home to nationally-known rock group Three Doors Down, who sold more than 10 million of their CD albums and singles. Singers and songwriters thinking about doing professional recording, give us a call before you make that move. We can save you money, time, headaches, heartaches and troubles you may run into. We know what to do and how to do it to benefit you and get the best results."

☑ ABEAR PUBLISHING (BMI)/SONGTOWN PUBLISHING (ASCAP)

323 N. Walnut St., Murfreesboro TN 37130. (615)890-1878. Fax: (615)890-3771. E-mail: ron@icofm.com. **Contact:** Ron Hebert.

☒ ◯ ALEXANDER SR. MUSIC (BMI)

PMB 364, 7100 Lockwood Blvd., Boardman OH 44512. (330)782-5031. Fax: (330)782-6954. E-mail: dap@netdot com.com. Website: www.dapentertainment.com. **Contact:** LaVerne Chambers, promotions. Owner: Darryl Alexander. Music publisher, record company (DAP Entertainment), music consulting, distribution and promotional services and record producer. Estab. 1992. Publishes 12-22 songs/year; publishes 2-4 new songwriters/year. Staff size: 3. Pays standard royalty.

• Also see the listing for DAP Entertainment in the Record Producers section of this book.

How to Contact *Write first and obtain permission to submit.* Prefers cassette with 4 songs and lyric sheet. "We will accept finished masters (CD) for review." Include SASE. Responds in 2 months. "No phone calls or faxes please."

Film & TV Places 2 songs in TV/year. Music Supervisor: Darryl Alexander. Recently published "Love Never Fails in Saturday Night Live" (through DSM); "Feel Your Love" and "You Are So Beautiful" for the film *The Doctor Is Upstairs*, both written and recorded by Darryl Alexander.

Music Mostly **contemporary jazz** and **urban gospel**; also **R&B**. Does not want rock, gangsta rap, heavy metal or country. Published "Plumb Line" (single by Herb McMullan/Darryl Alexander) from *Diamond In The Sky* (album), recorded by Darryl Alexander (contemporary jazz); "3rd Eye" and "Too Late For Love" (singles) from *Diamond In The Sky* (album), written and recorded by Darryl Alexander (contemporary jazz), all released 2004 on DAP Entertainment.

Tips "Send only music in styles that we review. Submit your best songs and follow submission guidelines. Finished masters open up additional possibilities. Lead sheets may be requested for material we are interested in. Must have SASE if you wish to have CD returned. No phone calls, please."

☑ ☐ ALIAS JOHN HENRY TUNES (BMI)

11 Music Square E., Suite 607, Nashville TN 37203. (615)255-4437. E-mail: bobbyjohnhenry@bellsouth.net. **Contact:** Bobby John Henry, owner. Music publisher and record producer. Publishes 3 songs/year; publishes 1 new songwriter/year. Staff size: 3. Pays standard royalty.

How to Contact Send by mail. Prefers cassette or CD with 3 songs and lyric sheet. Does not return material. Responds in 6 months only if interested.

Music Mostly **country**, **rock** and **alternative**. Does not want rap. Published *Mr. Right Now* (album by Kari Jorgensen), recorded by "Hieke" on Warner Bros. (rock); and *Nothing to Me* (album by B.J. Henry), recorded by Millie Jackson on Spring.

Tips "Focus and rewrite, rewrite, rewrite."

⊕ ☑ ☐ ALL ROCK MUSIC

Phone: (31) 186-604266. Fax: (32) 0186-604366. Website: www.collectorrecords.nl. **Contact:** Cees Klop, president. Music publisher, record company (Collector Records) and record producer. Estab. 1967. Publishes 40 songs/year; publishes several new songwriters/year. Staff size: 3. Pays standard royalty.

Affiliate(s) All Rock Music (England).

• Also see the listings for Collector Records in the Record Companies and Record Producers sections of this book.

How to Contact Submit demo tape by mail. Unsolicited submissions are OK. Prefers cassette. SAE and IRC. Responds in 2 months.

Music Mostly **'50s rock**, **rockabilly** and **country rock**; also **piano boogie woogie**. Published *Rock Crazy Baby* (album), written and recorded by Art Adams (1950s rockabilly), released 2001; *Bobby Crain-Rock-A-Sock-A-Hop* (album), written and recorded by Bobby Crain (1950s rocker), released 2003; and *Marvin Jackson* (album), written and recorded by Marvin Jackson (1950s rockers), released 2004, all on Collector Records.

Tips "Send only the kind of material we issue/produce as listed."

☐ ALLEGHENY MUSIC WORKS

1611 Menoher Blvd., Johnstown PA 15905. (814)255-4007. E-mail: TunedOnMusic@aol.com. Website: www.all eghenymusicworks.com. **Contact:** Al Rita, managing director. Music publisher and record company (Allegheny Records). Estab. 1991. Staff size: 2. Pays standard royalty.

Affiliate(s) Allegheny Music Works Publishing (ASCAP) and Tuned on Music (BMI).

• Also see the listings for Allegheny Music Works in the Record Companies section and The Leads Sheet in Publications of Interest section of this book.

How to Contact *Write first and obtain permission to submit.* "Include SASE for reply. E-mail queries are acceptable. NO Phone Calls! We will not reply to voice mail requests. Responds usually in 1-3 weeks to regular mail requests and usually within 48 hours to e-mail queries. If we are not interested in your material, we will sometimes offer suggestions on other markets to try."

Music Mostly **country**; also **pop**, **A/C**, **R&B**, **novelty**, **Halloween** and **inspirational**. Does not want rap, metal or x-rated lyrics. Published "Flying In the Sky" (single by Penny Towers Wilber) from *Halloween Bash* (album), recorded by Victor R. Vampire (pop/novelty/Halloween), released 2000 on Allegheny.

Tips "Bookmark our website and check it regularly, clicking on *Songwriter Opportunities.* Each month, as a free service to songwriters, we list a new artist or company looking for songs. Complete contact information is included. For a deeper insight into the type of material our company publishes, we invite you to read the customer reviews on amazon.com to our 2000 best seller Halloween album release, *Halloween Bash.*"

☑ ⏸ ALLISONGS INC. (ASCAP, BMI)

2132 Elm Hill Pike, Nashville TN 37214. (615)313-8764. E-mail: info@allisongs.com. Website: www.allisongs.c om. President: Jim Allison. Professional Manager: Stacy Hogan. Music publisher, record company (ARIA Records) and record producer (Jim Allison). Estab. 1985. Publishes 50 songs/year. Staff size: 4. Pays standard royalty.

Affiliate(s) Jim's Allisongs (BMI), Songs of Jim Allison (BMI) and Annie Green Eyes Music (BMI).

- Reba McEntire's "What Am I Gonna Do About You," published by AlliSongs, Inc., was included on her triple-platinum album, *Greatest Hits*.

How to Contact Submit demo tape by mail. Unsolicited submissions are OK. Send CD and lyric sheet. Does not return material. Responds in 6 weeks only if interested.

Music Mostly **country** and **pop**. Published "Beautiful World" (single by Anne Delana Reeves/Billy Montana/ Jim Allison) from *Beautiful World* (album), recorded by Sheri Porter (alternative country), released 2001 on ARIA Records; and "Montgomery to Memphis" (single by Anne Delana Reeves/Billy Montana) from *Lee Ann Womack* (album), recorded by Lee Ann Womack (country), released 1997 on Decca Records.

Tips "Send your best—we will contact you if interested. No need to call us. It will be listened to."

⏸ ⏸ ALPHA MUSIC INC. (BMI)

747 Chestnut Ridge Rd., Chestnut Ridge NY 10977. (845)356-0800. Fax: (845)356-0895. E-mail: alpha@trfmusic. com. **Contact:** Michael Nurko. Music publisher. Estab. 1931. Pays standard royalty.

Affiliate(s) Dorian Music Publishers, Inc. (ASCAP) and TRF Music Inc.

- Also see listing for TRF Production Music Libraries in the Advertising, Audiovisual & Commercial Music Firms section of this book.

How to Contact "We accept submissions of new compositions. Submissions are not returnable."

Music All categories, mainly **instrumental** and **acoustic suitable for use as production music**, including **theme and background music** for television and film. "Have published over 50,000 titles since 1931."

⏸ AMERICATONE INTERNATIONAL

1817 Loch Lomond Way, Las Vegas NV 89102-4437. (702)384-0030. Fax: (702)382-1926. E-mail: jjj@americaton e.com. Website: www.americatone.com. President: Joe Jan Jaros. Estab. 1975. Publishes 25 songs/year. Pays variable royalty.

Affiliate(s) Americatone Records International, Christy Records International USA, Rambolt Music International (ASCAP).

- Also see the listing for Americatone Records International in the Record Companies section of this book.

How to Contact Submit demo tape by mail. Unsolicited submissions OK. Prefers cassettes, "studio production with top sound recordings." Include SASE. Responds in 1 month.

Music Mostly **country**, **R&B**, **Spanish** and **classic ballads**. Published "Romantic Music," written and recorded by Chuck Mymit; "Explosion" (by Ray Sykora), recorded by Sam Trippe; and "From Las Vegas" (by Ladd Staide), recorded by Robert Martin, all on Americatone International Records.

⏸ ANTELOPE PUBLISHING INC.

P.O. Box 55, Rowayton CT 06853. **Contact:** Tony LaVorgna, owner/president. Music publisher. Estab. 1982. Publishes 5-10 new songs/year; publishes 3-5 new songwriters/year. Pays standard royalty.

How to Contact Submit demo tape by mail. Unsolicited submissions are OK. Prefers cassette with lead sheet. Does not return material. Responds in 1 month "only if interested."

Music Only **bebop** and **1940s swing**. Does not want anything electronic. Published *Inspiration* (album), written and recorded by T. LaVorgna (jazz); *Please Stay* (album by Nicole Pasternak), recorded by Cathy Gale (1940s swing), both on Antelope; *Nightcrawler* (album by Tommy Dean), recorded by Swing Fever on Alto Sound (jazz); and "Latin Blues," recorded by David Budway.

Tips "Put your best song first with a short intro."

☑ ⏸ ARAS MUSIC (ASCAP)

P.O. Box 100215, Palm Bay FL 32910-0215. Phone/fax: (328)988-0250. E-mail: savpublishing@aol.com. Website: www.outbackrecords.com. President: Bill Young. **Contact:** Amy Young (country, contemporary Christian, pop, alternative, jazz and latin) or Bruce Marion (piano and instrumental). Music publisher and record company (Outback Records). Member Academy of Country Music, Country Music Association. Estab. 1996. Pays standard royalty.

Affiliate(s) SAV Music (BMI), Outback Records and PARDO Music (SESAC).

How to Contact Submit tape/CD by mail. Please no phone calls. E-mail OK. No MP3s. "We do not return any material. We will contact only when we can use."

Music Mostly **country** and **contemporary Christian**. Also music suitable for motion pictures. Does not want rap or classical. Published "That Fifty Seven Chevy" (single by A. Webb) from *That Fifty Seven Chevy*, recorded by Aaron Russell (country); "Little House in the Country" (single by A. Dycus) from *Paris Moon* (album), recorded by Amanda Dycus (country); and "One More Day" (single by T. Stice) from *Just Send Me Roses* (album), recorded by Kelly Weaver (country), all released 2003 on Outback Records.

Tips "When recording a demo, have an artist in mind. We pitch to major labels and major artists, so please submit studio-quality demos with typed lyric sheets. If you submit a marketable product, we will put forth 100% effort for you."

☐ AUDIO MUSIC PUBLISHERS (ASCAP)

449 N. Vista St., Los Angeles CA 90036. (818)362-9853. Fax: (323)653-7670. E-mail: parlirec@aol.com. Website: www.parlirec.com. **Contact:** Len Weisman, professional manager. Owner: Ben Weisman. Music publisher, record company and record producer (The Weisman Production Group). Estab. 1962. Publishes 25 songs/year; publishes 10-15 new songwriters/year. Staff size: 10. Pays standard royalty.

• Also see the listings for Queen Esther Music Publishers in the Music Publishers section of this book; the Weisman Production Group in the Record Producers section of this book and Parliament Records in the Record Companies section of this book.

How to Contact Submit demo tape by mail. Unsolicited submissions are OK. "No permission needed." Prefers cassette with 3-10 songs and lyric sheet. "We do not return unsolicited material without SASE. Don't query first; just send tape." Responds in 6 weeks. "We listen; we don't write back. If we like your material we will telephone you."

Music Mostly **pop**, **R&B** and **rap**; also **dance**, **funk**, **soul** and **gospel**. Does not want heavy metal. "Crazy About You" (single) and *Where Is Love* (album), both written by Curtis Womack; and *Don't Make Me Walk Away* (album by Debe Gunn), all recorded by Valerie (R&B) on Kon Kord.

☑ BAGATELLE MUSIC PUBLISHING CO. (BMI)

P.O. Box 925929, Houston TX 77292. (713)680-2160 or (800)845-6865. **Contact:** Byron Benton, President. Music publisher, record company and record producer. Publishes 40 songs/year; publishes 2 new songwriters/year. Pays standard royalty.

Affiliate(s) Floyd Tillman Publishing Co.

• Also see the listing for Bagatelle Record Company in the Record Companies section of this book.

How to Contact Submit demo tape by mail. Unsolicited submissions are OK. Prefers cassette (or videocassette) with any number of songs and lyric sheet. Include SASE.

Music Mostly **country**; also **gospel** and **blues**. Published "Everything You Touch" (single), written and recorded by Johnny Nelms; "This Is Real" and "Mona from Daytona" (singles), written and recorded by Floyd Tillman, all on Bagatelle Records.

☑ BAIRD MUSIC GROUP (BMI)

P.O. Box 42, 1 Main St., Ellsworth PA 15331. E-mail: ronssong@charterpa.net. **Contact:** Ron Baird, president. Music publisher, record company (La Ron Ltd. Records), record producer (Ron Baird Enterprises). Estab. 1999. Publishes 5-12 songs/year. Pays standard royalty.

Affiliate(s) Baird Family Music (ASCAP).

• Also see the listing for Ron Baird Enterprises in the Record Producers section of this book.

How to Contact Submit demo tape by mail. Unsolicited submissions are OK. "No certified mail." Prefers cassette only with 2-4 songs and lyric sheet. Does not return submissions. Responds only if interested.

Music Mostly **country** and **country rock**. Does not want hip-hop, gospel/religious or R&B.

Tips "Don't give up!"

☑ BAITSTRING MUSIC (ASCAP)

2622 Kirtland Rd., Brewton AL 36426. (334)867-2228. **Contact:** Roy Edwards, president. Music publisher and record company (Bolivia Records). Estab. 1972. Publishes 20 songs/year; publishes 10 new songwriters/year. Hires staff songwriters. Pays standard royalty.

Affiliate(s) Cheavoria Music Co. (BMI)

• Also see the listings for Cheavoria Music in this section, Bolivia Records in the Record Companies section, and Known Artist Productions in the Record Producers section of this book.

How to Contact Submit demo tape by mail. Unsolicited submissions are OK. Prefers cassette with 3 songs and lyric sheet. Does not return material. Responds in 1 month.

Music Mostly **R&B**, **pop** and **easy listening**; also **country**. Published "Forever and Always," written and recorded by Jim Portwood (pop); and "Make Me Forget" (by Horace Linsley) and "Never Let Me Go" (by Cheavoria Edwards), both recorded by Bobbie Roberson (country), all on Bolivia Records.

☑ ◻ BARKIN' FOE THE MASTER'S BONE (ASCAP)

405 Broadway St. Suite 900, Cincinnati OH 45202-3329. (513)241-6489. Fax: (513)241-9226. E-mail: autoredcurtis@aol.com. Website: www.1stbook.com. Company Owner (rock, R&B): Kevin Curtis. Professional Managers: Shonda Barr (country, jazz, pop, rap); Betty Barr (gospel, soul, soft rock). Music publisher. Estab. 1989. Publishes 4 songs/year; publishes 1 new songwriter/year. Staff size: 4. Pays standard royalty.

Affiliate(s) Beat Box Music (ASCAP) and Feltstar (BMI).

How to Contact Submit demo tape by mail. Unsolicited submissions are OK. Prefers CD (or VHS videocassette) with 3 songs. Include SASE. Responds in 2 weeks.

Music Mostly **top 40** and **pop**; also **soul**, **gospel**, **rap** and **jazz**. Does not want classical. Published "Lover, Lover" (single by J Tea/Jay B./Skylar) from *The Time Has Come* (album), recorded by J-Trey (rap), released 2003 on East Side Records; "Been A Long Time" (single by J Tea/Jay B./Skylar), from *The Time Has Come* (album), recorded by J-Trey (rap), released 2003 on East Side Records; "No Worries" (single by Mejestic/7-Starr/D-Smooy/Hardhead), from *Home Grown* (album), recorded by Low Down Boyz (rap), released 2002 on Untamed Records.

☑ BAY RIDGE PUBLISHING CO. (BMI)

P.O. Box 5537, Kreole Station, Moss Point MS 39563-1537. (228)475-0059. "No collect calls." Estab. 1974. **Contact:** Joe F. Mitchell, executive vice president/general manager. First Vice President: Justin F. Mitchell. Second Vice President: Jonita F. Mitchell. Music publisher and record company (Missile Records).

- Also see the listing for Abalorn Music in this section and the listing for Missile Records in the Record Companies section of this book.

Affiliate(s) Abalorn Music (ASCAP).

How to Contact *"Please don't send us anything until you contact us by phone or in writing and receive submission instructions. You must present your songs the correct way to get a reply.* Always whenever you write to us, be sure you include a #10 business-size envelope addressed back to you with a first class USA postage stamp on the envelope. We reply back to you from the SASE you send to us. All songs sent for review must include sufficient return postage. No reply made back to you without SASE or return of material without sufficient return postage. **Absolutely no reply postcards—only SASE.** If you only write lyrics, do not submit. We only accept completed songs, so you must find a collaborator. We are not interested in reviewing homemade recordings." Prefers CD (first choice) or cassette with 3-8 songs and lyrics to songs submitted. Responds in 2 months. "A good quality demo recording will always get preference over a poor recording."

Music All types and styles of songs. "Mississippi, Mississippi" (single by Kadish Millett) and "Innocent Little One" (single by Bob Levy) from *If It Takes All Night* (album), recorded by Christian Ramsey (modern pop country), released on Missile Records.

Tips "Our doors are always open to young recording artists who are exceptional talented and want to make a name for themselves in the music business. Your success is our success. We will work with you to reach your goal. We also are in the business of getting your professionally-recorded album of 10-12 well-produced and well-written, radio-ready songs placed with record companies in the USA and foreign countries for the possibility of record deals. Here is what we have gotten for some artists: $850,000 record deal for Charity (religious singing group) on Big Easy (USA) in 2001; $500,000 record deal for Vance Greek on Dime-A-Dozen (Germany) in 2002; and a $150,000 record deal for Randell Ruthledge (country) on Dime-A-Dozen (Germany) in 2003. Two more artists are under consideration as of 2004, and others may be considered. Missile Records, Abalorn Music (ASCAP) and Bay Ridge Publishing Co. (BMI) are listed in some well-known publications such as the *Billboard International Buyer's Guide*, *Mix Master Directory*, *Industrial Source Book*, *Pollstar*, *Yellow Pages of Rock* and other publications. Some well-known recording artists born and raised in Mississippi include Elvis Presley, Conway Twitty, B.B. King and Faith Hill. The Moss Point, MS area music scene is also home to nationally-known rock group Three Doors Down, who sold more than 10 million of their CD albums and singles. Singers and songwriters thinking about doing professional recording, give us a call before you make that move. We can save you money, time, headaches, heartaches and troubles you may run into. We know what to do and how to do it to benefit you and get the best results."

⊕ ☑ BEARSONGS

Box 944, Birmingham, B16 8UT England. Phone: 44-021-454-7020. Managing Director: Jim Simpson. Professional Manager: Junet Kenny. Music publisher and record company (Big Bear Records). Member PRS, MCPS. Publishes 25 songs/year; publishes 15-20 new songwriters/year. Pays standard royalty.

- Also see the listings for Big Bear Records in the Record Companies section and Big Bear in the Record Producers section of this book.

How to Contact Submit demo tape by mail. Unsolicited submissions are OK. Prefers CD. Does not return material. Responds in 3 months.

Music Mostly **blues** and **jazz**. Published *Blowing With Bruce* and *Cool Heights* (by Alan Barnes), recorded by

Bruce Adams/Alan Barnes Quintet; and *Blues For My Baby* (by Charles Brown), recorded by King Pleasure & The Biscuit Boys, all on Big Bear Records.

Tips "Have a real interest in jazz, blues, swing."

BIG FISH MUSIC PUBLISHING GROUP

11927 Magnolia Blvd., Suite 3, N. Hollywood CA 91607. (818)984-0377. President, CEO and Music Publisher: Chuck Tennin. Producer: Gary Black (country, pop, adult contemporary, rock, crossover songs, other styles). Professional Music Manager: Lora Sprague (jazz, New Age, instrumental, pop rock, r&b). Professional Music Manager: B.J. (pop, TV, film and special projects). Professional Music & Vocal Consultant: Zell Black (country, pop, gospel, rock, blues). Producer Independent Artists: Darryl Harrelson—Major Label Entertainment (country, pop and other genres). Music publisher, record company (California Sun Records) and production company. Estab. 1971. Publishes 10-20 songs/year; publishes 5-10 new songwriters/year. Staff size: 7. Pays standard royalty. "We also license songs and music copyrights to users of music, especially TV and film."

Affiliate(s) Big Fish Music (BMI) and California Sun Music (ASCAP).

How to Contact *Write first and obtain permission to submit.* Include SASE for reply. "*Please do not call.* After permission to submit is confirmed, we will assign and forward to you a submission code number allowing you to submit up to 4 songs maximum, preferably on CD or cassette. Include a properly addressed cover letter, signed and dated, with your source of referral (*Songwriter's Market*) with your assigned submission code number and SASE for reply and/or return of material. Include lyrics. *Unsolicited material will not be accepted.* That is our Submission Policy to review outside and new material." Responds in 2 weeks.

Film & TV Places 6 songs in TV/year. Recently published "Even the Angels Knew" (by Cathy Carlson/Craig Lackey/Marty Axelrod); "Stop Before We Start" (by J.D. Grieco); "Oh Santa" (by Christine Bridges/John Deaver), all recorded by The Black River Girls in *Passions* (NBC); licensed "A Christmas Wish" (by Ed Fry/Eddie Max), used in *Passions* (NBC); "Girls Will Be Girls" (by Cathy Carlson/John LeGrande), recorded by The Black River Girls, used in *All My Children* (ABC); "The Way You're Drivin' Me" and "Ain't No Love 'Round Here' " (by Jerry Zanandrea), both recorded by The Black River Girls, used in *Passions* (NBC).

Music Country, including **country pop**, **country A/C** and **country crossover** with a cutting edge; also **pop**, **pop ballads**, **adult contemporary**, **uplifting**, **praise**, **worship**, **spiritual**, and **inspirational adult contemporary gospel** with a powerful message, **instrumental background and theme music** for TV & films, New Age/instrumental jazz and **novelty type songs** for all kinds of commercial use. Published "If Wishes Were Horses" (single by Billy O'Hara); "Purple Bunny Honey" (single by Robert Lloyd/Jim Love); "Leavin' You For Me" (single by J.D. Grieco); "Move That Train" (single by Robert Porter); "Happy Landing" (by T. Brawley/B. Woodrich); "Girls Will Be Girls" (single by Cathy Carlson/John LeGrande); "You Should Be Here With Me" (single by Ken McMeans); "Stop Before We Start" (single by J.D. Grieco); "The Way You're Drivin' Me" and "Ain't No Love 'Round Here' " (singles by Jerry Zanandrea), all recorded by Black River Girls on California Sun Records; "Let Go and Let God" and "There's A Power in Prayer" (singles by Corinne Porter/Molly Finkle), recorded by Molly Pasutti, released on California Sun Records.

Tips "Demo should be professional, high quality, clean, simple, dynamic, and must get the song across on the first listen. Good clear vocals, a nice melody, a good musical feel, good musical arrangement, strong lyrics and chorus—a unique, catchy, clever song that sticks with you. Looking for unique country and pop songs with a different edge that can crossover to the mainstream market for ongoing Nashville music projects and songs for a hot female country trio that crosses over to adult contemporary and pop with great lush, warm harmonies that reach out to middle America and baby boomers and their grown up children (25 to 65). Also, catchy uptempo songs with an attitude, meaningful lyrics (Shania Twain style), and unique pop songs (Celine Dion style) for upcoming album projects and song pitches. Also, soundtrack music of all types (melodic, uplifting, moody, mystique, orchestral, mind soothing, pretty, action packed, etc.) for new film production company and upcoming film and TV projects. Demo should be broadcast quality."

BIXIO MUSIC GROUP & ASSOCIATES/IDM MUSIC (ASCAP)

111 E. 14th St., Suite 140, New York NY 10003. (212)695-3911. Fax: (212)967-6284. E-mail: sales@bixio.com and mail@idmmusic.com. Website: www.bixio.com and www.idmmusic.com. General Manager: Johannes in der Muhlen. Administrator: Miriam Westercappel (all styles). A&R Director: Tomo (all styles). Office Manager: Courtney Stack-Slutsky. Administrative Assistant: Karlene Evans (soundtracks). Creative Director: Robert Draghi (all styles). Senior Creative Director/Producer: Tomo. A&R: Claudene Neysmith (world/New Age). Music publisher, record company and rights clearances. Estab. 1985. Publishes a few hundred songs/year; publishes 2 new songwriters/year. Staff size: 6. Pays standard royalty.

How to Contact *Does not accept unsolicited material.*

Music Mostly **soundtracks**. Published "La Strada Nel Bosco," included in the TV show *Ed* (NBC); "La Beguine Du Mac," included in the TV show *The Chris Isaac Show* (Showtime); and "Alfonsina Delle Camelie," included in the TV show *UC: Undercover* (NBC).

☑ ☒ ○ BLACK MARKET ENTERTAINMENT RECORDINGS (ASCAP, BMI)

936 Harwell St. NW, Atlanta GA 30314. (404)367-8130. Fax: (404)357-8630. E-mail: smolt@bmerecordings.com. **Contact:** Sloane L. Molot, A&R assistant. Music publisher and record company (B.M.E. Records). Estab. 1992. Staff size: 7.

Affiliate(s) SWOLE Music (ASCAP).

How to Contact Submit demo tape by mail. Unsolicited submissions are OK. Prefers CD/CDR with cover letter. "Please do not call; enclose mailing and email address." Does not return material. Responds in 1 month.

Film & TV Places 3 songs in film and 1 song in TV/year. Music Supervisor: Vincent Phillips. Recently published "I Like Dem" (by J. Smith/S. Norris), recorded by Li'l Jon and the Eastside Boyz; "Kissable Spot" (by Jonathan Smith), recorded by Devon, both placed in *Big Momma's House*; and "Trick Busta" (by Hardnett/Anderson/Bryon), recorded by Lyrical Giants, placed in *Sex and the City*.

Music Mostly **rap** and **r&b**; also **rock** and **alternative**. Published "Bia, Bia" (single by J. Smith/S. Norris/T. Shaw/S. Martin) from *Put Yo Hood Up* (album), recorded by Lil Jon and the Eastside Boyz (rap), released 2001 on BME/TVT; "Shut Up" (single by R. McDowell/J. Jones/D. Green/R. Lewis) from *Right Quick* (album), recorded by Jim Crow (rap), released 2001 on Noontime/Interscope; and "I Like Dem" (single by J. Smith/S. Norris) from *We Still Crunk* (album), recorded by Lil Jon and the Eastside Boyz (rap), released 2000 on BME Recordings.

Tips "Put your best foot forward. Submit only the best stuff you have. First impressions are important."

☒ ○ BLACK STALLION COUNTRY PUBLISHING (BMI)

P.O. Box 368, Tujunga CA 91043. Fax: (818)364-1250. E-mail: kenn.king@verizon.net. **Contact:** Kenn Kingsbury, president. Music publisher, management firm and book publisher (*Who's Who in Country & Western Music*). Member CMA, CMF. Publishes 2 songs/year; publishes 1 new songwriter/year. Pays standard royalty.

How to Contact Submit demo tape by mail. Unsolicited submissions are OK. Prefers cassette with 3 songs and lyric sheet. Include SASE. Responds in 1 month.

Music Mostly **jazz** and **country**.

○ BLUE DOG PUBLISHING AND RECORDS

P.O. Box 3438, St. Louis MO 63143. (314)646-0191. Fax: (314)646-8005. E-mail: chillawack@worldnet.att.net. Website: www.bluedogpublishing.com. **Contact:** Matt Davis, A&R. Music publisher and record company. Estab. 1999. Pays standard royalty or payment negotiable.

How to Contact *Contact first and obtain permission to submit.*

Music Mostly **Christian**, **pop**, **rock** and **country**. Published "All Fall Down" (single by Bob Bender/Matt Davis/Steve Gendron) from *Phone Home* (album), recorded by 5th Degree (heavy/hard); "Still in Love With You" (single by Tiffany Kappler) from *Ariel* (album), recorded by Ariel (pop); and *All That and More* (album), written and recorded by Jeff Reulback (country/ballad), all released 2000 on Blue Dog Publishing and Records.

Tips "Call first. Be professional. If we are interested, we will call back."

☑ ⊕ ○ BME PUBLISHING

P.O. Box 450224, Cologne Germany 50877. Phone: (049)221-9472000. Fax: (049)221-9502278. E-mail: BME-Records@Z-online.de. **Contact:** Dr. Dietmar Barzen. Music publisher, record company and record producer. Estab. 1993. Pays standard royalty to artists on contract.

How to Contact Submit demo tape by mail. Unsolicited submissions are OK. Prefers cassette, DAT or CDR with 3-5 songs and lyric sheet. SAE and IRC. Responds in 1 month.

Music Mostly **pop/AC**, **rock** and **commercial dance/hip-hop**; also **MOR**.

☑ ○ BMG MUSIC PUBLISHING

1540 Broadway, 28th Floor, New York NY 10036-4098. (212)930-4000. Fax: (212)930-4263. Website: www.bmg musicsearch.com. Beverly Hills office: 8750 Wilshire Blvd., Beverly Hills CA 90211. (310)358-4700. Fax: (310)358-4727. **Contact:** Scott Francis, president BMG songs. Nashville office: 1400 18th Ave. S., Nashville TN 37212. (615)858-1300. Fax: (615)858-1330. Music publisher.

How to Contact *BMG Music Publishing does not accept unsolicited submissions.*

Music Published "All Night Long" (single by F. Evans/R. Lawrence/S. Combs/S. Crawford), recorded by Faith Evans featuring Puff Daddy on Bad Boy; and "Ain't Enough Roses" (single by L. Brokop/S. Hogin/B. Reagan), recorded by Lisa Brokop on Columbia (country).

○ BOURNE CO. MUSIC PUBLISHERS (ASCAP)

5 W. 37th St., New York NY 10018. (212)391-4300. Fax: (212)391-4306. E-mail: bourne@bournemusic.com. Website: www.bournemusic.com. **Contact:** Professional Manager. Music publisher. Estab. 1917. Publishes educational material and popular music.

Affiliate(s) ABC Music, Ben Bloom, Better Half, Bogat, Burke & Van Heusen, Goldmine, Harborn, Lady Mac and Murbo Music.

How to Contact *Does not accept unsolicited submissions.*

Music Piano/vocal, **band pieces** and **choral pieces**. Published "Amen" and "Mary's Little Boy Child" (singles by Hairston); "When You Wish Upon a Star" (single by Washington/Harline); and "Unforgettable" (single by Irving Gordon).

☑ ◖ ALLAN BRADLEY MUSIC (BMI)

835 E. Buckeyewood Ave., Orange CA 91030. (626)441-4453. E-mail: melodi4ever@earthlink.com. Website: http://allanlicht.ontheweb.com. **Contact:** Allan Licht, Owner. Music publisher, record company (ABL Records) and record producer. Estab. 1993. Publishes 10 songs/year; publishes 5 new songwriters/year. Staff size: 2. Pays standard royalty.

Affiliate(s) Holly Ellen Music (ASCAP).

• Also see the listing for ABL Records in the Record Companies section of this book.

How to Contact Submit demo tape by mail. Unsolicited submissions are OK. Prefers cassette with 3 songs and lyric sheet. "Send only unpublished works." Does not return material. Responds in 2 weeks only if interested.

Music Mostly **A/C, pop** and **R&B**; also **country** and **Christian contemporary**. Does not want hard rock. Published *Time to Go* (album), written and recorded by Alan Douglass; *The Sun that Follows the Rain* (album by R.K. Holler/Rob Driggers), recorded by Michael Cavanaugh (pop), released 1999; and *Only In My Mind* (album by Jonathon Hansen), recorded by Allan Licht, all on ABL Records.

Tips "Be open to suggestions from well-established publishers. Please send only songs that have Top 10 potential. Only serious writers are encouraged to submit."

◖ BRANSON COUNTRY MUSIC PUBLISHING (BMI)

P.O. Box 2527, Broken Arrow OK 74013. (918)455-9442. Fax: (918)451-1965. E-mail: bransoncm@aol.com. **Contact:** Betty Branson, A&R. Music publisher. Estab. 1997. Publishes 5 songs/year; publishes 4-5 new songwriters/year. Pays standard royalty.

How to Contact Submit demo tape by mail with lyric sheet. Unsolicited submissions are OK. Prefers CD or cassette with 3-5 songs and lyric sheet. Does not return material. Responds in 3 weeks only if interested.

Music Mostly **traditional country** and **upbeat country**. Published "Sharin Sharon" (CD single), written and recorded by Roger Wayne Manard (country), released 2001; "Odds Are" (video single by Dale Ray/Allison Rae), recorded by Chris Lowther and the Sidewinder Band (country), released 2004; "Fools Night Out" (CD single by Keith/DaCosta/Bristol), recorded by Chris Lowther (country), released 2004; and "Toy Soldier" (CD single by Teena Eaton), recorded by Carol Shull (country), released 2004.

Tips "Send good quality demo capable of competing with airplay top 40. Put your 'attention getter' up front and build from that point as the listener will give you about 10-15 seconds to continue listening or turn you off. Use a good hook and keep coming back to it."

☑ ▥ ▨ ◖ BSW RECORDS (BMI)

P.O. Box 2297, Universal City TX 78148. Fax: (210)653-3989. E-mail: bswr18@wmconnect.com. **Contact:** Frank Willson, President. Music publisher, record company and record producer (Frank Willson). Estab. 1987. Publishes 26 songs/year; publishes 14 new songwriters/year. Staff size: 5. Pays standard royalty.

Affiliate(s) WillTex Music and Universal Music Marketing (BMI).

• This company has been named Record Label of the Year ('94-'01) by the Country Music Association of America. Also see the listings for BSW Records in the Record Companies section, Frank Wilson in the Record Producers section, and Universal Music Marketing in the Managers & Booking Agents section of this book.

How to Contact Submit demo tape or CD by mail. Unsolicited submissions are OK. Prefers cassette or CD with 3 songs, lyric sheet and cover letter. Include SASE. Responds in 2 months.

Film & TV Places 2 songs in film/year.

Music Mostly **country**, **blues** and **soft rock**. Does not want rap. Published *These Four Walls* (album), written and recorded by Dan Kimmel (country); and *I Cried My Last Tear* (album by T. Toliver), recorded by Candeeland (country), both released 1999 on BSW Records.

◖ BUG MUSIC, INC. (ASCAP, BMI)

1645 N. Vine St., Penthouse, Hollywood CA 90028. (323)466-4352. Fax: (323)466-2366. E-mail: buginfo@bugmusic.com. Website: www.bugmusic.com. Vice President of Creative: Eddie Gomez. Creative Manager: Sasha Ross. Creative Assistant: Nissa Pedraza. **Nashville:** 1026 16th Ave. S., Nashville TN 37212. (615)726-0782. Fax: (615)726-0784. Creative Director: John Allen; Creative Manager: Drew Hale. **New York:** 347 W. 36th St., Suite 1203, New York NY 10018. (212)643-0925. Fax: (212)643-0897. Senior Vice President: Garry Valletri. Music publisher. Estab. 1975. "We handle administration."

Affiliate(s) Bughouse (ASCAP).

How to Contact *Does not accept unsolicited submissions.*

Music All genres. Published "You Were Mine" (by E. Erwin/M. Seidel), recorded by Dixie Chicks on Monument.

☒ ⊘ BUGLE PUBLISHING GROUP (ASCAP, BMI)

14724 Ventura Blvd., Penthouse Suite, Sherman Oaks CA 91403. (818)461-1706. Fax: (818)461-1739. Senior Vice President: Stevo Glendining. Music publisher. Estab. 1992. Publishes 5 songs/year. Staff size: 1. Hires staff songwriters. Pays standard royalty.

Affiliate(s) I.R.S. Songs/Firstars Music (ASCAP) and I.R.S. Music, Inc./Illegal Songs, Inc. (BMI).

How to Contact *Does not accept unsolicited submissions.*

Music Mostly **country** and **pop/rock**. Published *Love Or the Lack Of* (by Rich Wayland), recorded by Daryle Singeltary; and *Then There's You* (by Pat MacDonald), recorded by The Wilkinsons (country), both on Giant; and *The Reason* (by Greg Wells), recorded by Celine Dion on Sony (pop).

Tips "Research the market and make sure your songs have a credible lyric; songs impact the listener and must be moving enough to cause excitement!"

☐ BURIED TREASURE MUSIC (ASCAP)

524 Doral Country Dr., Nashville TN 37221. **Contact:** Scott Turner, owner/manager. Music publisher and record producer (Aberdeen Productions). Estab. 1972. Publishes 30-50 songs/year; publishes 3-10 new songwriters/year. Pays standard royalty.

Affiliate(s) Captain Kidd Music (BMI).

● Also see the listing for Aberdeen Productions in the Record Producers section of this book.

How to Contact Submit demo tape by mail. Unsolicited submissions are OK. Prefers cassette or VHS videocassette with 1-4 songs and lyric sheet. Responds in 2 weeks. "Always enclose SASE if answer is expected."

Music Mostly **country**, **country/pop** and **MOR**. Does not want rap, hard rock, metal, hip-hop or alternative. Published "It Just Ain't Right" (single by Scott Turner/John Marascalco), recorded by Tina Turner (R&B/pop), released 2004 on E.M.I.; and "I Still Can't Say Goodbye" (single by Bob Blinn/Jimmy Moore) from a *C.B.S./Sony Compilation*, recorded by Chet Atkins, released 2004 on C.B.S.

Tips *"Don't send songs in envelopes that are 15"x 20", or by registered mail. The post office will not accept tapes in regular business-size envelopes. Also . . . always enclose a SASE. Submission without same aren't answered because of the wealth of tapes that come in."*

☑ ☐ BURNSONGS (ASCAP)

1110 17th Ave. S. #3, Nashville TN 37212-2221. E-mail: e@burnsongs.com. Website: www.burnsongs.com. **Contact:** Ernie Petrangelo. Music publisher, record company (Da'ville Records, and record producer (Ernie Petrangelo). Estab. 1986. Publishes 13 songs/year; publishes 3 new songwriters/year. Staff size: 1. Pays standard royalty.

Affiliate(s) Raproductions.com (BMI).

How to Contact Submit demo tape by mail. Unsolicited submissions are OK. Prefers cassette or CD/CDR with 3 songs, lyric sheet and cover letter. Include SASE. Responds in 2-3 weeks only if interested.

Film and TV Places 2 songs in film/year. Music supervisor: Ernie Petrangelo. Recently published "Instruments Of Destruction" and "Aw S#!t What Are We Gonna Do Now!" (by Burns/Serpa/Ward), recorded by NRG2 in *Transformers—The Movie* (released to DVD).

Music Mostly **hip-hop**, **rap** and **r&b**; also **urban pop**, **rock/rap** and **pop/rock/alternative**. Does not want country, "unless it's very different, edgy and hip." Recently published "Instruments Of Destruction," "Aw S#!t What Are We Gonna Do Now!" (singles by Burns/Serpa/Ward) and "Come And Get It" (single by Burns/Ward) from *Transformed* (album), recorded by NRG2 (heavy metal), released 2001 on Da'Ville Records.

Tips "Please submit the best quality demo you can afford. We are interested in hit quality material with great hooks. Raps must be interesting & have meaning. No thugged-out material please. No excessive profanity. If you are an artist, please send a photo and bio with your package."

☐ ⊘ CENTERGY MUSIC GROUP

130 Seaboard Lane, Franklin TN 37607. (615)370-9869.

Affiliate(s) ASCAP, BMI, SESAC

How to Contact No unsoliicited submissions. Responds only if interested.

Music Southern Gospel, church inspirational, Christian country.

☑ CHEAVORIA MUSIC CO. (BMI)

2622 Kirtland Rd., Brewton AL 36426. (334)867-2228. **Contact:** Roy Edwards, president. Music publisher, record company (Bolivia Records) and record producer (Known Artist Production). Estab. 1972. Publishes 20 new songwriters/year. Pays standard royalty.

Affiliate(s) Baitstring Music (ASCAP).

- Also see the listings for Baitstring Music in this section, Bolivia Records in the Record Companies section, and Known Artists Productions in the record Producers sections of this book.

How to Contact *Write first and obtain permission to submit.* Prefers cassette with 3 songs and lyric sheet. Does not return material. Responds in 1 month.

Music Mostly **R&B**, **pop** and **country**; also **ballads**. Published "Forever and Always" (single), written and recorded by Jim Portwood on Bolivia Records (country).

☑ CHELSEA MUSIC GROUP

7118 Peach Court, Brentwood TN 37207. (615)373-5223.

☆ ☑ CHRISTMAS & HOLIDAY MUSIC (BMI)

24351 Grass St., Lake Forest CA 92630. (949)859-1615. E-mail: justinwilde@christmassongs.com. Website: www.christmassongs.com. **Contact:** Justin Wilde, president. Music publisher. Estab. 1980. Publishes 8-12 songs/year; publishes 8-12 new songwriters/year. Staff size: 1. "All submissions must be complete songs (i.e., music and lyrics)." Pays standard royalty.

- See their website for most current address before mailing.

Affiliate(s) Songcastle Music (ASCAP).

How to Contact Submit demo CD or cassette by mail. Unsolicited submissions are OK. *Do not call.* "First class mail only. Registered or certified mail not accepted." Prefers CD or cassette with no more than 3 songs with lyric sheets. Do not send lead sheets or promotional material, bios, etc." Include SASE but does not return material out of the US. Responds only if interested.

Film & TV Places 4-5 songs in TV/year. Published "Mr. Santa Claus" in *Casper's Haunted Christmas*.

Music Strictly **Christmas**, **Halloween**, **Hanukkah**, **Mother's Day**, **Thanksgiving**, **Father's Day** and **New Year's Eve music** in every style imaginable: easy listening, rock, R&B, pop, blues, jazz, country, reggae, rap, children's secular or religious. *Please do not send anything that isn't a holiday song.* Published "It Must Have Been the Mistletoe" (single by Justin Wilde/Doug Konecky) from *Christmas Memories* (album), recorded by Barbra Streisand (pop Christmas), released 2001 by Columbia; "What Made the Baby Cry?" (single by Toby Keith) and "You've Just Missed Christmas" (single by Penny Lea/Buzz Smith/Bonnie Miller) from *The Vikki Carr Christmas Album* (album), recorded by Vikki Carr (holiday/Christmas), released 2000 on Delta; and "Mr. Santa Claus" (single by James Golseth) from *Casper's Haunted Christmas* soundtrack (album), recorded by Scotty Blevins (Christmas), released 2000 on Koch International.

Tips "We only sign one out of every 100 submissions. Please be selective. If a stranger can hum your melody back to you after hearing it twice, it has 'standard' potential. Couple that with a lyric filled with unique, inventive imagery, that stands on its own, even without music. Combine the two elements, and workshop the finished result thoroughly to identify weak points. Submit to us only when the song is polished to perfection. Submit positive lyrics only. Avoid negative themes like 'Blue Christmas.'"

☑ ☑ SONNY CHRISTOPHER PUBLISHING (BMI)

P.O. Box 9144, Ft. Worth TX 76147-2144. (817)367-0860. E-mail: ebbycondra@aol.com. **Contact:** Sonny Christopher, CEO. Music publisher, record company and record producer. Estab. 1974. Publishes 20-25 new songs/year; publishes 3-5 new songwriters/year. Staff size: 1. Pays standard royalty.

How to Contact *Write first, then call and obtain permission to submit.* Prefers cassette with lyric sheet. Include SASE (#10 or larger). Responds in 3 months.

Music Mostly **country**, **rock** and **blues**. Published *Did They Judge Too Hard* (album by Sonny Christopher), recorded by Ronny Collins (collins@abilene.com.) on Sonshine Records.

Tips "Be patient. I will respond as soon as I can. A songwriter should have a studio-cut demo with a super vocal. I am one who can hear a song with just acoustic guitar. Don't be hesitant to do a rewrite. To the young songwriter: *never, never* quit."

☑ CHRYSALIS MUSIC GROUP

(formerly Chrysalis Music), 8500 Melrose Ave., Suite 207, Los Angeles CA 90069. (310)652-0066. Fax: (310)652-2024. Website: www.chrysalismusic.com. **Contact:** Mark Friedman, vice president of creative services. **Nashville:** 1204 16th Ave. S., Nashville TN 37212. (615)327-4797. Fax: (615)327-1903. **Contact:** Trisha Brantley, Todd Chapman, Stephanie Greene, Shawn Heflin. Music publisher. Estab. 1968.

How to Contact *Chrysalis Music does not accept any submissions.*

Music Published "Sum 41" (single by Outcast); "Light Ladder" (single by David Gray). Administer David Lee Roth; Andrea Boccelli.

☑ ⊘ CLEARWIND PUBLISHING (SESAC)/LADY MARION PUBLISHING (ASCAP)/SUNSCAPE PUBLISHING (BMI)

256 S. Robertson Blvd., Suite 6100, Beverly Hills CA 90211. (310)629-6420. E-mail: clearwindpub@earthlink.net. **Contact:** A&R Director. Music publisher, sub-publisher, music licensing and personal management company (Sapphire Management). Estab. 1983. Publishes 12-15 songs/year; sub-publishes over 25. Staff size: 1. Pays standard royalty and collects standard fees for administration of sub-publishing and licensing deals.
 • "Our main focus is international, specifically the Asia/Pan-Pacific Region and Europe."
How to Contact *Write to obtain permission to submit.* "Do NOT call! Unsolicited submissions will be returned unopened." Prefers CD, DVD with no more than 3 songs and typed lyric sheet (with promo pack and photo if applicable). Does not return material. Will respond before 3 months after receipt.
Music Mostly **pop**, **rock**, **metal**, **R&B**, **jazz**, **smooth jazz**, **rap** and **hip-hop**. Recently sub-published "Somewhere Tonight" and "Too Late" (singles by Peter Roberts/Scott Cross); and "OOH Yea" (single by Peter Roberts/Dorothy Sea Gazely) all from *Heart of Gold*(album), recorded by Lisa Frazier (R&B/dance), released 2000 on Universal Discopui (Italy), Imperial Teichiku (Japan) and AVEX.

🌐 ◯ R.D. CLEVÈRE MUSIKVERLAG

Postfach 2145, D-63243 Neu-Isenburg, Germany. Phone/fax: 01212-510612 440. E-mail: rdc.in@web.de. **Contact:** Tony Hermonez, professional manager. Music publisher. Estab. 1967. Publishes 700-900 songs/year; publishes 40 new songwriters/year. Pays standard royalty.
Affiliate(s) Big Sound Music, Hot Night Music, Lizzy's Blues Music, Max Banana Music, R.D. Clevère-Cocabana-Music, R.D. Clevère-Far East & Orient-Music, and R.D. Clevère-America-Today-Music.
How to Contact Submit demo tape by mail. "No oversized envelope, dimensions up to 10×15 inches only." Unsolicited submissions are OK. Prefers CD, mini-disk or cassette with "no limit" on songs and lyric sheet. SAE and 2 IRCs. Responds in 2 months.
Music Mostly **pop**, **disco**, **rap**, **rock**, **R&B**, **country**, **ethno** and **folk**; also **musicals** and **classic/opera**. "No jazz, free style or instrumental music."

☑ ⊘ COAL HARBOR MUSIC (BMI)

P.O. Box 148027, Nashville TN 37868-0579. (615)883-2020. E-mail: coalharborbmi@aol.com. Website: www.coalharbormusic.com. **Contact:** Jerry Ray Wells, president. Music publisher, Record company (Coal Harbor Music), Record producer (Jerry Ray Wells), also recording studio, demo services, sheet music, number charts, management and booking services, artist development. Estab. 1990. Publishes 21 songs/year; publishes 4 new songwriters/year. Staff size: 2. Pays standard royalty.
 • Also see the listing for Coal Harbor Music in the Record Companies Record section of this book.
How to Contact Send CD with 3-5 songs, lyric sheet and cover letter. Does not return submissions. Responds in 3 months if interested.
Music Mostly **country**, **gospel** and **bluegrass**; also **contemporary Christian**, **Christmas** and **pop/rock**. Does not want heavy metal, rap, hard rock/grunge. Released "Storms of Life" (single/comp disc) written and recorded by Angela Baker Wells (2004); "So Good to Know" (single) from All I Need (album), written and recorded by Damon Westfaul (country Gospel), released 2004 on Coal Harbor/Shoreline Music; "You" (single) from Unraveled (album), written and recorded by Anne Borgen (contemporary Christian), released 2004 on Coal Harbor.
Tips "Write from the heart-the listener knows. Join songwriter organizations, go to seminars, co-write, etc. When submitting material send everything on one cassette or CD. Don't send two CDs and one cassette and tell us what song or track numbers to listen to. We don't have time. Put your best song first, even if it is a ballad. Keep writing; we ARE looking for GREAT songs!"

🆕 ⊘ COME ALIVE COMMUNICATIONS, INC. (ASCAP)

348 Valley Rd., Suite 1, West Grove PA 19390-0436. (610)869-3660. Fax: (610)869-3660. E-mail: info@comealivemusic.com. Website: www.comealivemusic.com. Professional Managers: Joseph L. Hooker (pop, rock, jazz); (Bridget G. Hylak (spiritual, country, classical). Music publisher, record producer and record company. Estab. 1985. Publishes 4 singles/year. Staff: 7. Pays standard royalty of 50%.
 • Come Alive Communications received a HIS Ministries Award in 1996.
How to Contact *Call first to obtain permission to submit a demo.* For song publishing submissions, prefers CD/CDR with 3 songs, lyric sheet, and cover letter. Does not return submissions. Responds only if interested.
Music Mostly **pop**, **easy listening**, **contemporary Christian**, and **patriotic**; also **country** and **spiritual**. Does not want obscene, suggestive, violent, or morally offensive lyrics. Produced "In Search of America" (single)

from *Long Road to Freedom* (album), written and recorded by J. Hooker (patriotic), released 2003 on ComeAliveMusic.com.

☐ ⊘ COPPERFIELD MUSIC GROUP/PENNY ANNIE MUSIC (BMI)/TOP BRASS MUSIC (ASCAP)/ BIDDY BABY MUSIC (SESAC)

1400 South St., Nashville TN 37212. (615)726-3172. **Contact:** Ken Biddy, president/CEO.

How to Contact Contact first and obtain permission to submit a demo. Does not return submissions. Responds only if interested.

Music Mostly **country**; also **pop**, **contemporary gospel**, and **modern bluegrass**. Does not want rap or heavy/metal/rock. Recently published "Daddy Won't Sell the Farm" from *Tatoos and Scars* (album), recorded by Montgomery Gentry (country).

☑ ◯ CORELLI MUSIC GROUP (BMI/ASCAP)

P.O. Box 2314, Tacoma WA 98401-2314. (253)798-5281. E-mail: corellismusicgroup@yahoo.com. Website: www.JerryCorelli.com. **Contact:** Jerry Corelli, owner. Music publisher, record company (Ωmega III Records), record producer (Jerry Corelli/Angels Dance Studio) and booking agency (Tone Deaf Booking). Estab. 1996. Publishes 12 songs/year; publishes 6 new songwriters/year. Staff size: 3. Pays standard royalty.

Affiliate(s) My Angel's Songs (ASCAP); Corelli's Music Box (BMI).

How to Contact Submit demo by mail. Unsolicited submissions are OK. "No phone calls asking to submit." Prefers cassette or CD with 3 songs, lyric sheet and cover letter. "We want songs with a message and overtly Christian. Make sure all material is copyrighted." Include SASE. Responds in 2 months.

Music Mostly **contemporary Christian**, **soft rock Christian** and **Christmas**; also **love songs**, **ballads** and **new country**. Does not want rap, hip-hop, southern gospel or songs without lyrics. Published "I Believe in Jesus Christ" (single by Jared Holt), "Great I Am" (single by Joe May/Kristin Black) and "Righteous Man" (single by Jerry Corelli) from *Righteous Man* (album), recorded by Jerry Corelli (contemporary Christian), released 2003 on Omega III Records.

Tips "Success is obtained when opportunity meets preparation! If a SASE is not sent with demo, we don't even listen to the demo. Be willing to do a re-write. Don't send matrial expecting us to place it with a Top Ten artist. Be practical. Do your songs say what's always been said, except differently? Don't take rejection personally."

☑ THE CORNELIUS COMPANIES (BMI, ASCAP, SESAC)

Dept. SM, 1719 West End Ave., Suite 805-E, Nashville TN 37203. (615)321-5333. E-mail: corneliuscomps@aol.com. Website: www.corneliuscompanies.com. **Contact:** Ron Cornelius, owner/manager. Music publisher and record producer (Ron Cornelius). Estab. 1986. Publishes 60-80 songs/year; publishes 2-3 new songwriters/year. Occasionally hires staff writers. Pays standard royalty.

Affiliate(s) RobinSparrow Music (BMI), Strummin' Bird Music (ASCAP) and Bridgeway Music (SESAC).

How to Contact *Write or call first and obtain permission to submit.* Submit demo tape by mail. Unsolicited submissions are OK. Prefers CD, DAT or cassette with 2-3 songs. Include SASE. Responds in 2 months.

Music Mostly **country** and **pop**; also **positive country**, **gospel** and **alternative**. Published songs by Confederate Railroad, Faith Hill, David Allen Coe, Alabama and over 50 radio singles in the positive Christian/country format.

Tips "Looking for material suitable for film."

☑ ⊕ ▦ ⊘ CTV MUSIC (GREAT BRITAIN)

Television Centre, St. Helier, Jersey JE1 3ZD Channel Islands Great Britain. Phone: (1534)816816. Fax: (1534)816817. E-mail: gordon.destecroix@channeltv.co.uk. Website: www.channeltv.co.uk. **Contact:** Gordon De Ste. Croix, director of special projects. Music publisher of music for TV commercials, TV programs and corporate video productions. Estab. 1986. Staff size: 1. Pays standard royalty.

How to Contact *Does not accept unsolicited submissions.*

Music Mostly **instrumental**, for TV commercials and programs.

☑ ◯ CUPIT MUSIC GROUP (ASCAP, BMI)

P.O. Box 121904, Nashville TN 37212. (615)731-0100. Fax: (615)731-3005. E-mail: info@cupitmusic.com. Website: www.cupitmusic.com. **Contact:** Publishing Division. Music publisher, record producer, record company, entertainment division and recording studio. Estab. 1986. Staff size: 8. Pays standard royalty.

Affiliate(s) Cupit Memaries (ASCAP) and Cupit Music (BMI).

● Also see the listing for Jerry Cupit Productions in the Record Producers section. Cupit Music's "What If He's Right" was number 1 on the CCRB Chart for ten consecutive weeks, and was named Song of the Year.

How to Contact *Please visit cupitmusic.com for our submission policy.* Prefers CD with lyric sheet. "We will return a response card." Include SASE. Usually responds in 2 months.

Shannon Lawson

Smokin' (Blue)grass in Music City

Before sitting down to talk about life in Music City, singer-songwriter Shannon Lawson wants to get one thing straight: "I'm a Kentucky boy, not a Nashville guy," he laughs, raising his pint glass. He pauses for a moment and his smile widens before he adds, "Well, I guess I'm a Nashville guy now since I've been there six years."

Both statements are true. Lawson is a down-home Kentucky man at heart. He spent his early years in Taylorsville, a rural town about 45 minutes outside of Louisville, hanging tobacco with his father and uncles by day and gathering again at night for their favorite family pastime: bluegrass.

At 18, the extraordinarily proficient guitarist committed himself to his music, leaving college to tour full-time with Top Hat, a seasoned local blues musician. Lawson continued to play and sing the blues through the early '90s, though he longed to return to his musical roots. He decided to form a new group, The Galoots, a wildly popular regional act that infused his beloved bluegrass with rock and country sounds. Though fans throughout the Midwest embraced the few albums The Galoots released independently, Lawson needed a new challenge. "I felt like I really hit the ceiling. I needed to do something other than just play clubs all the time," he says. "I'd never explored the publishing industry; it was a mystery to me."

It was time to make the move to Nashville. Just two days after returning from his honeymoon, Lawson and his new wife packed up and headed down Interstate I-65 to Music City. "It was a challenge to go down there and see if I could make something happen," remembers Lawson. "I moved because I wanted to be a performer and get a record deal, but also because I wanted to understand how the songwriting business worked. There's no better place in the country to learn the craft of songwriting while also learning the publishing business."

But the decision to move to Nashville was not something Lawson made on a whim. "I'd actually tried to move down there a year before, but something about it just wasn't right. I'm the kind of person that trusts my gut," he says. "Timing is everything in your life, so I just waited another year and ended up moving."

Lawson acknowledges that songwriters must be sure that they are secure enough, especially financially, before moving to Nashville. He was close enough to Louisville to travel home and play live shows when he was short on cash during his first year, but if you don't have that luxury, make sure you can survive even when the market is slow.

"The songwriting industry can be a hard thing to break into, especially over the last few years," he says. "Part of the reason is because songs are staying on the market longer. It used to be that a musician would record an album every year; now it's more like every two years." This naturally reduces the amount of songs that songwriters can hope to sign with recording artists. "The publishers sell less cuts a year. That's less revenue, and they can't sign as many writers, so it's harder for writers to find a job," he explains.

In addition to the financial aspect, songwriters must also ensure their catalog is ready for the transition. So what's a good indicator that you're ready for Nashville? Get feedback from open mic nights, other musicians, and from your audiences. "Pay attention to the response you're getting at home," says Lawson. "If you're getting a massive amount of positive feedback from strangers—not just your best friend or family members—then that's a pretty good gauge." Make sure you have an extensive repertoire, too; you won't be able to survive with only one or two polished songs.

It's also a good idea to license your music. Lawson chose ASCAP before he left Louisville. The ASCAP appealed to him because it's set up as a guild, owned by its members, and it offers many support services. His membership proved to be a smart decision; ASCAP chose Lawson as its "featured artist/writer" in December 2003. [For more information, check out www.ascap.com or see the American Society of Composers and Publishers (ASCAP) listing on pg. 328 of this book.]

If you realize that your catalog is not *quite* ready, Lawson suggests you attend a writing workshop to stretch your boundaries. "I believe that for people just breaking into songwriting, workshops are great," he says. "It really cracks the door open and introduces you to co-writing, which for a lot of people is a very strange idea. In Nashville, that's just how it works. You'll sit down with someone you've never met before and try to write a song with them. It's pretty interesting, really."

Not only should songwriters try their hand at co-writing (or at writing solo, if that's their weaker skill), but Lawson notes workshops are also an invaluable tool for "learning how to take criticism and smooth out your craft" and for networking. "When I first moved down to Nashville, I did a workshop with NSAI, and it was cool. You hook up with very established writers who are married to the craft, and they want to help people," he says.

Speaking of networking, Lawson confirms that the old adage "Nashville is built on friendships" is entirely true, so make the move with an open heart, a pocket full of business cards, and a Rolodex. "You'll make friends with other professional players, and favors are traded all the time. You're not going to get along with everybody, but it definitely works like that," Lawson says. "There's a lot of hiring of friends, and people help each other out."

Case in point: Once Lawson arrived in Nashville, he called upon his old pals The Galoots and booked three shows at The Station Inn. He invited several industry representatives—publishers, songpluggers, and other writers—in attempt to announce his arrival and get the music community talking. "Once there's a buzz, things start moving really quickly," he says. "We started creating this buzz with the first show; by the second show we had a bigger audience and invited more industry people; and by the third show, I had six publishing deal offers and two production deal offers."

After the showcase, Lawson accepted a publishing deal with Extreme Writers Group. As his demo circulated around the city, so did praise for his powerful voice and his energetic stage performance. After a legendary show in which Lawson jumped off the stage for an a cappella bluegrass version of Marvin Gaye's "Let's Get it On," MCA Nashville Chairman Bruce Hinton and label President Tony Brown offered him a contract. Lawson released one album with MCA, *Chase the Sun* (2002), before deciding that he favored the natural, dynamic sound of his live shows to the layered, over-produced version of himself heard on the record.

Looking for a better fit for his music, Lawson parted ways with MCA in 2003 and with EWG in 2004, but he wasn't discouraged. He continued to write, record, and tour, and he has since partnered with Equity Music Group, the label that also houses Clint Black. This experience has been an entirely different one for Lawson. "This label is very artist-friendly, which is why I'm there. Basically, they want me to make the record I want to make," says Lawson.

The lesson here is to stay true to your work. If you find yourself with a major-label or large-house publishing contract but it doesn't feel like the right home for you or your music, don't be afraid to keep looking. Songwriting is a hectic—often frustrating—business marked by "extreme highs and lows," admits Lawson, and there can be a lot of pressure to conform to a narrow, mass-market sound. "You want to be an asset to your label, but take from that what you need and leave the rest," he advises. Use the pressure to tighten your sound, but also recognize the endless possibilities in your songwriting. "The wonderful thing about writing is that you have no boundaries. And its fun," he says.

While he's finishing up his first record on the Equity label, Lawson divides his time between touring, writing, and family life. If you find yourself juggling a job, a family, and your music, too, Lawson suggests carving out a "regular workday" for yourself, even if it's just a few hours. "I'll go in at 10 a.m. and write until 2 or 3 in the afternoon. Sometimes I'll have two sessions a day— maybe a 10-2 and then a 3-6 or so. Sometimes I'll even go home again and write until midnight with somebody. I just squeeze it in whenever I can," he says. The important thing is to stay productive.

But productivity isn't all you need. If you're packing up your truck for the move to Music City, Lawson says you must take a strong backbone, a solid work ethic, the sensitivity to write what's inside you, and most importantly, an unbending belief in what you're doing. "Oh, and a trust fund wouldn't hurt," he laughs.

Seems like a sense of humor is a good thing to take along, too.

— Lauren Mosko

Lauren Mosko is the assistant editor for *Children's Writer's & Illustrator's Market* and *Artist's & Graphic Designer's Market* (Writer's Digest Books). Before contributing to the Market Books series, she worked as a music journalist, editor, and critic for the alternative press.

Music Mostly **country, bluegrass, blues, pop, gospel** and **instrumental**. Does not want rap, hard rock or metal. Published "What If He's Right" (single by Jerry Cupit) from *Memarie* (album), recorded by Memarie, released 2000 on HotSong Records; and "I'm Not Homeless" (single by Jerry Cupit/Ken Mellons/Randy Roberts) from *Wings of a Dove* (album), recorded by Ken Mellons, released 2000 on Curb Records.

◪ CURB MUSIC

47 Music Square East, Nashville TN 37203. (615)321-5080. Fax: (615)321-9532. Website: www.curb.com. **Contact**: Meredith Stewart DeVoursney.

◪ JOF DAVE MUSIC (ASCAP)

1055 Kimball Ave., Kansas City KS 66104. (913)593-3180. **Contact:** David Johnson, CEO. Music publisher, record company (Cymbal Records). Estab. 1984. Publishes 30 songs/year; publishes 12 new songwriters/year. Pays standard royalty.

How to Contact *Contact first and obtain permission to submit.* Prefers cassette or CD. Include SASE. Responds in 1 month.

Music Mostly **gospel** and **R&B**. Published "The Woman I Love" (single) from *Sugar Bowl* (album), written and recorded by King Alex, released 2001 on Cymbal Records.

✓ 🖼 ⊘ THE EDWARD DE MILES MUSIC COMPANY (BMI)

28 E. Jackson Bldg., 10th Floor, #S627, Chicago IL 60604-2263. (773)509-6381. Fax: (312)922-6964. Website: www.edmsahara.com. **Contact:** Professional Manager. Music publisher, record company (Sahara Records), record producer, management, bookings and promotions. Estab. 1984. Publishes 50-75 songs/year; publishes 5 new songwriters/year. Hires staff songwriters. Pays standard royalty.

- Also see the listings for Edward De Miles in the Record Producers and Managers & Booking Agents sections, and Sahara Records And Filmworks Entertainment in the Record Companies section of this book.

How to Contact *Write first and obtain permission to submit.* Prefers cassette with 1-3 songs and lyric sheet. Does not return material. Reponds in 1 month.

Music Mostly **top 40 pop/rock**, **R&B/dance** and **country**; also **musical scores for TV, radio, films and jingles**. Published "Dance Wit Me" and "Moments" (singles), written and recorded by Steve Lynn on Sahara Records (R&B).

Tips "Copyright all songs before submitting to us."

🅽 ⊘ DEL CAMINO MUSIC PUBLISHING (BMI)

5010 S. Twelfth Ave., Tucson AZ 85706. (520)573-7274. Fax: (520)573-3325. **Contact:** Luis Lopez, president. Music publisher and record producer. Estab. 1985. Pays standard royalty.

How to Contact Submit demo tape by mail. Unsolicited submissions are OK. Prefers cassette with 3 songs and lyric and lead sheet. "Include copy of properly copyrighted form." Does not return material.

Music Mostly **Latin/Spanish**, **Tex-Mex/pop** and **country rock**. Published "Te Quiero Tanto, Tanto" (single by Epifanio Gonzalez) from *La Leyenda Viva* (album), recorded by Lorenzo De Montecloro, released 2001 on Fonovisa Records; "Mi Mejor Regalo" (single by Armando Antonio Negrete) from *De Chichuahua Para Ti* (album), recorded by Polo Urias Y Su Maquina Norteña, released 2001 on Fonovisa Records; and "Tu Llegada" (single by Martin Miranda) from *Juego Peligroso* (album), recorded by Amenaza Norteña, released 2001 on Sony Records.

Tips "Make sure your songs have good commercial potential. Have a clean sounding demo and clearly typed lyric sheet."

✓ ⊘ DELEV MUSIC COMPANY

7231 Mansfield Ave., Philadelphia PA 19138-1620. (215)276-8861. Fax: (215)276-4509. E-mail: delevmusic@msn.com. President/CEO: W. Lloyd Lucas. A&R: Darryl Lucas. Music publisher. Publishes 6-10 songs/year; publishes 6-10 new songwriters/year. Pays standard royalty.

Affiliate(s) Sign of the Ram Music (ASCAP) and Delev Music (BMI).

How to Contact *Does not accept unsolicited material. Write or call first to obtain permission to submit.* Prefers CD or cassette with 1-3 songs and lyric sheet. "We will not accept certified mail." Does not return material. Responds in 3 months.

Music Mostly **R&B ballads** and **dance-oriented**; also **pop ballads**, **crossover** and **country/western**. No gangsta rap. Published "Angel Love" (single by Barbara Heston/Geraldine Fernandez) from *The Silky Sounds of Debbie G* (album), recorded by Debbie G (light R&B/easy listening), released 2000 on Blizzard Records; *Variety* (album), produced by Barbara Heston and Carment Lindsay, released on Luvya Records; and "Ever Again" by Bernie Williams, released 2003 on SunDazed Records.

Tips "Persevere regardless if it is sent to our company or any other company. Believe in yourself."

🅽 🌐 ⊘ DEMI MONDE RECORDS & PUBLISHING LTD.

Foel Studio, Llanfair Caereinion, POWYS, Wales. Phone/fax: (01938)810758. E-mail: demi-monde@dial.pipex.com. Website: www.demi.monde.co.uk/demimonde. **Contact:** Dave Anderson, managing director. Music publisher, record company (Demi Monde Records & Publishing Ltd.), record producer (Dave Anderson). Member MCPS. Estab. 1983. Publishes 50-70 songs/year; publishes 10-15 new songwriters/year. Pays standard royalty.

How to Contact Submit demo tape by mail. Unsolicited submissions are OK. Prefers cassette or VHS videocassette with 3-4 songs. Does not return material. Responds in 6 weeks.

Music Mostly **rock**, **R&B** and **pop**. Published "I Feel So Lazy" (by D. Allen), recorded by Gong (rock); "Phalarn Dawn" (by E. Wynne), recorded by Ozric Tentacles (rock); and "Pioneer" (by D. Anderson), recorded by Amon Dual (rock), all on Demi Monde Records.

⊘ DISNEY MUSIC PUBLISHING (ASCAP, BMI)

500 S. Buena Vista St., Burbank CA 91521-6182. (818)569-3228. **Contact:** Brian Rawlings, vice president of music publishing.

Affiliate(s) Seven Peaks Music and Seven Summits Music.

How to Contact *Call first and obtain permission to submit.* Does not return material.

☐ DREAM SEEKERS PUBLISHING (BMI)

21 Coachlight Dr., Danville IL 61832-8240. (615)822-1160. **Contact:** Jerry Webb, professional manager. President: Sally Sidman. Music publisher. Estab. 1993. Publishes 25-50 songs/year; publishes 15-20 new songwriters/year. Pays standard royalty.

Affiliate(s) Dream Builders Publishing (ASCAP).

How to Contact Submit demo tape by mail. Unsolicited submissions are OK. "Please do not call to request permission—just submit your material. There are no code words. We listen to everything." Prefers cassette or CD with 2 songs and lyric sheet. "If one of your songs is selected for publishing, we prefer to have it available on CD for dubbing off copies to pitch to artist." Include SASE. Responds in 6 weeks.

Music Mostly **country**. "All types of **country** material, but mostly in need of uptempo songs, preferably with positive lyrics." Does not want rap, jazz, classical, children's, hard rock, instrumental or blues. Published "Not Done Yet" (single by Coley McCabe/Mark Collie) from *Alabama Love Story* (album), recorded by Mark Collie (country), released 2004; "A Dad Like That" (single by Jamie Champa) from *Ken Mahon* (album), recorded by Ken Mahon (country), released 2003; and "City Lights" (single by Kim Caudill) from *So Far So Good* (album), recorded by Avery Lovey (country), released 2004.

Tips "Be willing to work hard to learn the craft of songwriting. Be persistent. Nobody is born a hit songwriter. It often takes years to achieve that status."

☑ ⊘ DREAMWORKS SKG MUSIC PUBLISHING

331 N. Maple Dr., Suite 300, Beverly Hills CA 90210. (310)288-7700. Website: www.dreamworkspublishing.com. Music publisher and record company (DreamWorks Records).

How to Contact *DreamWorks SKG Music Publishing does not accept unsolicited submissions.*

◐ DUANE MUSIC, INC. (BMI)

382 Clarence Ave., Sunnyvale CA 94086. (408)739-6133. **Contact:** Garrie Thompson, President. Music publisher and record producer. Publishes 10-20 songs/year; publishes 1 new songwriter/year. Pays standard royalty.

Affiliate(s) Morhits Publishing (BMI).

How to Contact Submit demo tape by mail. Unsolicited submissions are OK. Prefers 1-2 songs. Include SASE. Responds in 2 months.

Music Mostly **blues**, **country**, **disco** and **easy listening**; also **rock**, **soul** and **top 40/pop**. Published "Little Girl" (single), recorded by The Syndicate of Sound & Ban (rock); "Warm Tender Love" (single), recorded by Percy Sledge (soul); and "My Adorable One" (single), recorded by Joe Simon (blues).

◐ EARITATING MUSIC PUBLISHING (BMI)

P.O. Box 1101, Gresham OR 97030. Website: www.earitating.com. Music publisher. Estab. 1979. Pays individual per song contract, usually greater than 50% to writer.

How to Contact Submit demo by mail. Unsolicited submissions are OK. Prefers CD or CD-R with lyric sheet. "Submissions should be copyrighted by the author. We will deal for rights if interested." Does not return material. Responds only if interested.

Music Mostly **rock, country** and **folk**. Does not want rap.

Tips "Melody is most important, lyrics second. Style and performance take a back seat to these. A good song will stand with just one voice and one instrument. Also, don't use staples on your mailers."

◐ EARTHSCREAM MUSIC PUBLISHING CO. (BMI)

8377 Westview Dr., Houston TX 77055. (713)464-GOLD. E-mail: sarsjef@aol.com. Website: www.soundartsrecording.com. Contact: Jeff Wells; Peter Verheck. Music publisher, record company and record producer. Estab. 1975. Publishes 12 songs/year; publishes 4 new songwriters/year. Pays standard royalty.

• Also see the listings for Surface Records in the Record Companies section and Sound Arts Recording Studio in the Record Producers section of this book.

Affiliate(s) Reach For The Sky Music Publishing (ASCAP).

How to Contact Submit demo tape by mail. Unsolicited submissions are OK. Prefers cassette or videocassette with 2-5 songs and lyric sheet. Does not return material. Responds in 6 weeks.

Music Mostly **new rock, country, blues** and **top 40/pop**. Published "Baby Never Cries" (single by Carlos DeLeon), recorded by Jinkies on Surface Records (pop); "Telephone Road" (single), written and recorded by Mark May on Icehouse Records (blues); and "Do You Remember" (single by Barbara Pennington), recorded by Perfect Strangers on Earth Records (rock).

☑ ⊕ ☐ EDITION ROSSORI

Hietzinger Hptstr 94, Vienna A-1130 Austria. Phone: +43(1)876 24 00. Fax: +43(1)879 54 64. Website: www.poppate.com. **Contact:** Mario Rossori, manager. Music publisher and management agency. Estab. 1990. Publishes 150 songs/year; publishes 10 new songwriters/year. Staff size: 2. Pays negotiable royalty.

How to Contact Submit demo tape by mail. Unsolicited submissions are OK. Does not return material. Responds in 2 months.

Music Mostly **pop, dance** and **rock**. Does not want jazz. Published *Welsfischer au Wolpedelta* (album), written and recorded by Heinz on Universal (rock).

☑ ⬭ EGYPTIANMAN PRODUCTIONS (ASCAP)

(formerly May Peace Be Upon You Music), 4855 E. Warner Rd., Suite 24-169, Phoenix AZ 85044. (602)212-6735. Fax: (775)942-0589. E-mail: info@egyptianmanproductions.com. Website: www.egyptianmanproduction s.com. CEO/Writer/Publisher/President: Carlos C. Muhammad. Music publisher. Estab. 1996.

Affiliate(s) May Peace Be Upon You Music (ASCAP).

How to Contact Submit demo CD by mail. Unsolicited submissions are OK. Prefers CD with 3-4 songs, lyric sheet, 8×10 b&w glossy and bio on a floppy disk. "Do not call. In cover letter say whether you are seeking a publishing or record deal." Include SASE. Responds in 3 weeks.

Music Mostly **r&b, pop/r&b, hip-hop, rap, heavy metal, rock, punk rock, pop, alternative**; also **soft rock, Latin, contemporary country, inspirational** and **jazz**. "Deep into the Night" and "Seasons of Your Love" (singles by Carlos Muhammad/Brendan Woodward/Alex Hamilton); and "Risk Taker" (single by Brendan Woodward/Alex Hamilton) from *Aren B* (album), recorded by Aren B (R&B), released April 2003 on Egyptian-man Productions.

☑ ⬭ ELECTRIC MULE PUBLISHING COMPANY (BMI)/NEON MULE MUSIC (ASCAP)

1500 Clifton Ln., Nashville TN 37215. E-mail: emuleme@aol.com. **Contact**: Jeff Moseley, President.

⬭ EMANDELL TUNES

10220 Glade Ave., Chatsworth CA 91311. (818)341-2264. Fax: (818)341-1008. **Contact:** Leroy C. Lovett, Jr., president/administrator. Music Publisher. Estab. 1979. Publishes 6-12 songs/year; publishes 3-4 new songwriters/year. Pays standard royalty.

Affiliate(s) Ben-Lee Music (BMI), Birthright Music (ASCAP), Em-Jay Music (ASCAP), Northworth Songs, Chinwah Songs, Gertrude Music (all SESAC), Andrask Music, Australia (BMI), Nadine Music, Switzerland.

How to Contact *Write first and obtain permission to submit.* Prefers cassette, videocassette or CD with 4-5 songs and lead or lyric sheet. Include bio of writer, singer or group. Include SASE. Responds in 6 weeks.

Music Mostly **inspirational, contemporary gospel** and **choral**; also **strong country** and **light top 40**. Published "Under My Skin" and "Colorada River" (singles by Diana/Kim Fowley), recorded by Diana, released 2001 on WFL Records; and "Runaway Love" (single by Gil Askey), recorded by Linda Clifford (new gospel), released 2001 on Sony Records.

Tips "We suggest you listen to current songs. Imagine how that song would sound if done by some other artist. Keep your ear tuned to new groups, bands, singers. Try to analyze what made them different, was it the sound? Was it the song? Was it the production? Ask yourself these questions: Do they have that 'hit' feeling? Do you like what they are doing?"

Ⓝ ⬭ EMF PRODUCTIONS

1000 E. Prien Lake Rd., Suite D, Lake Charles LA 70601. Phone/fax: (337)474-0435. E-mail: emfprod@aol.com. Website: www.emfproductions.com. President: Ed Fruge. Music publisher and record producer. Estab. 1984. Pays standard royalty.

• Also see the listing for EMF Productions in the Record Companies section of this book.

How to Contact Submit demo tape by mail. Unsolicited submissions are OK. Prefers cassette or VHS videocassette with 4 songs and lyric sheet. Does not return material. Responds in 6 weeks.

Music Mostly **R&B, pop** and **rock**; also **country** and **gospel**.

☑ ⬭ EMI CHRISTIAN MUSIC PUBLISHING

P.O. Box 5085, Brentwood TN 37024. (615)371-6800. Website: www.emicmg.com. Music publisher. Publishes 100 songs/year; publishes 2 new songwriters/year. Hires staff songwriters. Pays standard royalty.

Affiliate(s) Birdwing Music (ASCAP), Sparrow Song (BMI), His Eye Music (SESAC), Ariose Music (ASCAP), Straightway Music (ASCAP), Shepherd's Fold Music (BMI), Songs of Promise (SESAC), Dawn Treader Music (SESAC), Meadowgreen Music Company (ASCAP), River Oaks Music Company (BMI), Stonebrook Music Company (SESAC), Bud John Songs, Inc. (ASCAP), Bud John Music, Inc. (BMI), Bud John Tunes, Inc. (SESAC).

How to Contact *"We do not accept unsolicited submissions."*

Music Published "Concert of the Age" (by Jeffrey Benward), recorded by Phillips, Craig & Dean; "God Is In Control," written and recorded by Twila Paris, both on StarSong Records; and "Faith, Hope and Love" (by Ty Lacy), recorded by Point of Grace on Word Records.

Tips "Come to Nashville and be a part of the fastest growing industry. It's nearly impossible to get a publisher's attention unless you know someone in the industry that is willing to help you."

☑ ⊘ EMI MUSIC PUBLISHING

1290 Avenue of the Americas, 42nd Floor, New York NY 10104. (212)492-1200. **Santa Monica:** 2700 Colorado Ave., Suite 100, Santa Monica CA 90404. (310)586-2700. Fax: (310)586-2758. Website: www.emimusic.com. Contact: Jodi Gerson; Big Jon. Music publisher.

How to Contact *EMI does not accept unsolicited material.*

Music Published "All Night Long" (by F. Evans/R. Lawrence/S. Combs), recorded by Faith Evans featuring Puff Daddy on Bad Boy; "You" (by C. Roland/J. Powell), recorded by Jesse Powell on Silas; and "I Was" (by C. Black/P. Vassar), recorded by Neal McCoy on Atlantic.

Tips "Don't bury your songs. Less is more—we will ask for more if we need it. Put your strongest song first."

☑ ⊘ EMSTONE MUSIC PUBLISHING (BMI)

Box 398, Hallandale FL 33008. (305)936-0412. E-mail: webmaster@emstonemusicpublishing.com. **Contact:** Michael Gary, Creative Director. President: Mitchell Stone. Vice President: Madeline Stone. Music publisher. Estab. 1997. Pays standard royalty.

How to Contact Submit demo CD by mail with any number of songs and lyric sheets. Unsolicited submissions are OK. Does not return material. Responds only if interested.

Music Everything except classical and opera. Published "www.history" (single by Tim Eatman) and "Gonna Recall My Heart" (single by Dan Jury) from *No Tears* (album), recorded by Cole Seaver and Tammie Darlene, released on CountryStock Records; and "I Love What I've Got" (single by Heather and Paul Turner) from *The Best of Talented Kids* (compilation album) recorded by Gypsy.

Tips "We only send publishing contracts to writers whose songs exhibit a spark of genius. Anything less can't compete in the music industry."

⊕ ⊘ EVER-OPEN-EYE MUSIC (PRS)

Wern Fawr Farm, Pencoed, MID, Glam CF356NB United Kingdom. Phone: (01656)860041. **Contact:** M.R. Blanche, managing director. Music publisher and record company (Red-Eye Records). Member PPL and MCPS. Estab. 1980. Publishes 6 songs/year. Staff size: 3. Pays negotiable royalty.

How to Contact Submit demo tape by mail. Unsolicited submissions are OK. Prefers CD. Does not return material. Responds in 2 months.

Music Mostly **R&B, gospel** and **pop**; also **swing**. Published "Snake Hips" and "Eclection" (singles by Burton/Jones); and "Life Insurance" (single by Steve Finn), all recorded by Tiger Bay on Red-Eye Records.

▨ ⊘ FAMOUS MUSIC PUBLISHING COMPANIES

10635 Santa Monica Blvd., Suite 300, Los Angeles CA 90025. (310)441-1300. Fax: (310)441-4722. Website: www.syncsite.com. President: Ira Jaffe. Vice President, Film and TV: Stacey Palm. Vice President/Urban: Brian Postelle. Senior Creative Director: Carol Spencer (rock/pop/alternative). Senior Creative Director/Latin: Claribell Cuevas. New York office: 1633 Broadway, 11th Floor, New York NY 10019. (212)654-7433. Fax: (212)654-4748. Chairman and CEO: Irwin Z. Robinson. Executive Vice President, Finance and Administration: Margaret Johnson. Vice President Catalogue Development: Mary Beth Roberts. Creative Director: Tanya Brown. Nashville office: 65 Music Square East, Nashville TN 37212. (615)329-0500. Fax: (615)321-4121. Vice President: Pat Finch (country). Senior Creative Director: Curtis Green. Music Publisher. Estab. 1929. Publishes 500 songs/year. Hires staff songwriters. Staff size: 100. Pays standard royalty.

Affiliate(s) Famous Music (ASCAP) and Ensign Music (BMI).

How to Contact *Famous Music does not accept unsolicited submissions.*

Film & TV Famous Music is a Paramount Pictures' company. Music Supervisors: Stacey Palm and Delly Ramin. Published "My Heart Will Go On" (by James Homer/Wil Jennings), recorded by Celine Dion in *Titanic*.

Music Mostly **rock, urban, R&B, country** and **Latin**. Published "I Hope You Dance" (single by Tia Sellers/Michael Dulaney), recorded by Lee Ann Womack; and "He Wasn't Man Enough" (single by Fred Jerkins III), recorded by Toni Braxton.

◯ FIFTH AVENUE MEDIA, LTD.

19 W. 21st St., #603A, New York NY 10010. (516)295-3922. Fax: (516)295-6872. E-mail: fifthavmed@aol.com. Website: www.thefirm.com/fifthavenue. Professional Managers: Bruce E. Colfin (rootsy bluesy rock/reggae, Jam Bands/alternative rock/heavy metal); Jeffrey E. Jacobson (hip-hop/R&B/dance). Music publisher and record company (Fifth Avenue Media, Ltd.). Estab. 1995. Publishes 2 songs/year. Staff size: 4. Pays standard royalty.

Music Published "Analog" (single by Paul Byrne) from *Paul Byrne & the Bleeders* (album), recorded by Paul Byrne (pop rock), released 2001 on Independent.

⊕ 🔊 💿 FIRST TIME MUSIC (PUBLISHING) U.K. (PRS, MCPS)

Sovereign House, 12 Trewartha Road, Praa Sands, Penzance, Cornwall TR20 9ST United Kingdom. Phone: (01736)762826. Fax: (01736)763328. E-mail: panamus@aol.com. Website: www.songwriters-guild.com. **Contact:** Roderick G. Jones, managing director. Music publisher, record company (First Time Records), record producer (Panama Music Library) and management firm (First Time Management and Production Co.). Member MCPS. Estab. 1986. Publishes 500-750 songs/year; 20-50 new songwriters/year. Staff size: 6. Hires staff writers. Pays standard royalty; "50-60% to established and up-and-coming writers with the right attitude."

Affiliate(s) Scamp Music Publishing, Panama Music Library, Musik Image Library, Caribbean Music Library, Psi Music Library, ADN Creation Music Library, Heraldic Production Music Library, Promo Sonor International, Eventide Music, Melody First Music Library, Panama Music Ltd.

How to Contact Submit demo tape by mail. Unsolicited submissions are OK. Prefers cassette, CD/CDR or VHS videocassette "of professional quality" with unlimited number of songs and lyric or lead sheets. Responds in 1 month. SAE and IRC required for reply.

Film & TV Places 200 songs in film and TV/year. "Copyrights and phonographic rights of Panama Music Limited and its associated catalogue idents have been used and subsist in various productions broadcasts and adverts produced by major and independent production companies, television, film/video companies, radio broadcasters (not just in the UK, but in various countries world-wide) and by commercial record companies for general release and sale. In the UK & Republic of Ireland they include the BBC networks of national/regional television and radio, ITV network programs and promotions (Channel 4, Border TV, Granada TV, Tyne Tees TV, Scottish TV, Yorkshire TV, HTV, Central TV, Channel TV, LWT, Meridian TV, Grampian TV, GMTV, Ulster TV, Westcountry TV, Channel TV, Carlton TV, Anglia TV, TV3, RTE (Ireland), Planet TV, Rapido TV, VT4 TV, BBC Worldwide, etc.), independent radio stations, satellite Sky Television (BskyB), Discovery Channel, Learning Channel, National Geographic, Living Channel, Sony, Trouble TV, UK Style Channel, Hon Cyf, CSI, etc., and cable companies, GWR Creative, Premier, Spectrum FM, Local Radio Partnership, Fox, Manx, Swansea Sound, Mercury, 2CRFM, Broadland, BBC Radio Collection, etc. Some credits include copyrights in programs, films/videos, broadcasts, trailers and promotions such as Desmond's, One Foot in the Grave, EastEnders, Hale and Pace, Holidays from Hell, A Touch of Frost, 999 International, and Get Away."

Music All styles. Published "Limerick Vales" (single) from *Rambling Boy* (album), recorded by T.R. Dallas (country), released 2003 on Temple Records; "Toulit Pequit" (single) from *Gypsy Soul* (album), recorded by Negrita (flamenco/gypsy music), released 2004 on Promo Sonor International Records; and "Horsehead Nebula" (single) from *Light From Orlon* (album), recorded by Kevin Kendle (New Age instrumental), released 2004 on Eventide Records.

Tips "Have a professional approach—present well produced demos. First impressions are important and may be the only chance you get. Writers are advised to join the Guild of International Songwriters and Composers in the United Kingdom."

🔊 ◯ FRESH ENTERTAINMENT (ASCAP)

1315 Simpson Rd., Atlanta GA 30314. Phone/fax: (770)642-2645. E-mail: whunter1122@yahoo.com. **Contact:** Willie W. Hunter, managing director. Music publisher and record company. Publishes 5 songs/year. Staff size: 4. Hires staff songwriters. Pays standard royalty.

Affiliate(s) !Hserf Music (ASCAP), Blair Vizzion Music (BMI) and Santron Music (BMI).

How to Contact Submit demo tape by mail. Unsolicited submissions are OK. Prefers cassette or videocassette with 3 songs and lyric sheet. "Send photo if available." Include SASE. Responds in 6 weeks.

Film & TV Places 1 song in TV/year. Published the theme song for BET's *Comic Vue* (by Charles E. Jones), recorded by Cirocco.

Music Mostly **rap**, **R&B** and **pop/dance**. Published *Ancestral Spirits* (album), written and recorded by Robert Miles (jazz), released 2004 on Sheets of Sound/Fresh Entertainment; and *My Life My Hustle* (album), written and recorded by Jamal Smith (rap/hip-hop), released 2004 on Vision Vibe/Fresh Entertainment.

◯ BOB SCOTT FRICK ENTERPRISES

404 Bluegrass Ave., Madison TN 37115-5307. Phone/fax: (615)865-6380. E-mail: bob_scott_frick@juno.com. **Contact:** Bob Frick, owner. Music publisher, record company (R.E.F.) and record producer. Estab. 1961. Publishes 25 songs/year; publishes 2 new songwriters/year. Staff size: 2. Pays standard royalty.

Affiliate(s) Sugarbakers Music (ASCAP) and Frick Music Publishing Co. (BMI).

How to Contact Submit demo tape by mail. Unsolicited submissions are OK. Prefers cassette with 2 songs and lyric sheet. Include SASE. Responds in 3 weeks.

Music Mostly **Christian** and **country**. Does not want rock. Published *Come Home Daddy* (album by Bill Herold) (country); *It's All Right* (album by Gerald Cunningham) (country); *If You Need A Miracle* (album by Don Blunkall) (gospel), all recorded by Bob Scott Frick on R.E.F.; and *Songs You Requested*, *The Stylist* and *Big Band Requests*, all recorded by Bob Scott Frick.

☑ ◔ FRICON MUSIC COMPANY (BMI)

1048 S. Ogden Dr., Los Angeles CA 90019. (323)931-7323. Fax: (323)938-2030. E-mail: fricon@comcast.net. President: Terri Fricon. **Contact:** Madge Benson, professional manager. Music publisher. Estab. 1981. Publishes 25 songs/year; publishes 1-2 new songwriters/year. Staff size: 6. Pays standard royalty.

Affiliate(s) Fricout Music Company (ASCAP) and Now and Forever Songs (SESAC).

How to Contact *Contact first and obtain permission to submit.* Prefers cassette with 1-2 songs and lyric or lead sheet. "Prior permission must be obtained or packages will be returned." Include SASE. Responds in 2 months.

Music Mostly **country**.

☑ ◯ FURROW MUSIC (BMI)

P.O. Box 4121, Edmond OK 73083-4121. E-mail: furrowmusic@sbcglobal.net. **Contact:** G.H. Derrick, owner/ publisher. Music publisher, record company (Gusher Records) and record producer. Estab. 1984. Publishes 10-15 songs/year. Staff size: 1. Pays standard royalty.

How to Contact Submit demo tape by mail. Unsolicited submissions are OK. Prefers CD or cassette with 1 song and lyric sheet. (If submission is on CD, will accept up to 10 songs). "One instrument and vocal is OK for demo." Include SASE. Responds in 2 weeks.

Music Mostly **country** and **cowboy**.

Tips "Have your song critiqued by other writers (or songwriter organizations) prior to making the demo. Only make and send demos of songs that have a universal appeal. Make sure the vocal is out front of the music. Never be so attached to a lyric or tune that you can't rewrite it. Don't forget to include your SASE with all submissions."

◔ G MAJOR MUSIC (BMI)

P.O. Box 3331, Fort Smith AR 72913-3331. Fax: (501)782-0842. E-mail: JerryGlidewell@juno.com. Professional Managers: Alex Hoover (country/southern rock/gospel); Jerry Glidewell (contemporary country/pop). Music publisher. Estab. 1992. Publishes 10 songs/year; publishes 3 new songwriters/year. Staff size: 2. Pays standard royalty.

How to Contact Submit demo tape by mail. Unsolicited submissions are OK. Prefers cassette or CD. Submit up to 3 songs. Include SASE. Responds in 3 weeks.

Music Mostly **country**, **traditional country** and **pop**; also **contemporary Christian**. Published *In Competition With a Truck* (album by Elaine Woolsey), recorded by Libby Benson (country); "Question of Heart" (single by Jerry Glidewell), recorded by Brian Bateman (country); and "Step Out Into the Sun" (single by Chad Little/ Jerry Glidewell), recorded by Libby Benson (Christian contemporary), all on MBS.

Tips "We are looking for radio-friendly hits for the country market. We use a top songplugger in Nashville. Remember, your song has to be so good that people will spend their hard earned money to hear it over and over again."

◯ ALAN GARY MUSIC (ASCAP, BMI)

P.O. Box 179, Palisades Park NJ 07650. President: Alan Gary. Creative Director: Fran Levine. Creative Assistant: Harold Green. Music publisher. Estab. 1987. Publishes a varying number of songs/year. Staff size: 3. Pays standard royalty.

How to Contact Submit demo tape by mail. Unsolicited submissions are OK. Prefers cassette or VHS videocassette with lyric sheet. Include SASE.

Music Mostly **pop**, **R&B** and **dance**; also **rock**, **A/C** and **country**. Published "Liberation" (single by Gary/ Julian), recorded by Les Julian on Music Tree Records (A/C); "Love Your Way Out of This One" (single by Gary/Rosen), recorded by Deborah Steel on Bad Cat Records (contemporary country); and "Dueling Rappers" (single by Gary/Free), recorded by Prophets of Boom on You Dirty Rap! Records (rap/R&B).

◓ GEO MUSIC

23 Music Square E., Nashville TN 37203. (615)242-9999. Fax: (615)242-9994. **Contact:** George Johnson.

Affiliate(s) ASCAP, BMI.

How to Contact Submit CD with lyric sheet, lead sheet, and cover letter. See website for submission policy. Does not return submissions.

Music **country**, **country pop**. Published "Good Morning Beautiful," written by Tom Cerney and Zach Lyle, recorded by Steve Holy in *Blue Moon* (album), released in 2001.

☑ ▢ GLAD MUSIC CO. (ASCAP, BMI, SESAC)

14340 Torrey Chase, Suite 380, Houston TX 77014. (281)397-7300. Fax: (281)397-6206. E-mail: hwesdaily@glad musicco.com. Website: www.gladmusicco.com. **Contact:** Wes Daily, A&R Director (country). Music publisher, record company and record producer. Estab. 1958. Publishes 10 songs/year; publishes 10 new songwriters/year. Staff size: 4. Pays standard royalty.

Affiliate(s) Bud-Don (ASCAP) and Rayde (SESAC).

How to Contact *Write first and obtain permission to submit or to arrange personal interview.* Prefers CD with 3 songs, lyric sheet and cover letter. Does not return material. Responds in 2 weeks. SASE or e-mail address for reply.

Music Mostly **country**. Does not want weak songs. Published *Love Bug* (album by C. Wayne/W. Kemp), recorded by George Strait, released 1995 on MCA; *Walk Through This World With Me* (album), written and recorded by George Jones and *Race Is On* (album by D. Rollins), recorded by George Jones, both released 1999 on Asylum.

☑ ▢ THE GOODLAND MUSIC GROUP INC.

P.O. Box 24454, Nashville TN 37202. (615)269-7071. Fax: (615)269-0131. E-mail: bheffron@aristomedia.com. Website: www.thegoodlandgroup.com. **Contact:** Brian Heffron, publishing coordinator. Estab. 1988. Publishes 50 songs/year; 5-10 new songwriters/year. Pays standard royalty.

Affiliate(s) Goodland Publishing Company (ASCAP), Marc Isle Music (BMI) and Gulf Bay Publishing (SESAC).

How to Contact Submit demo tape by mail. Unsolicited submissions are OK. Include SASE with first class postage.

Music Mostly **country/Christian**, but open to **all styles**. "We are now listening to **pop, hip-hop, rock, dance** for publishing consideration." Published "Just Lookin" (single by Vaughan Daniel/Pete Strawn), recorded by Scott Hisey (country), released 2003 on Dead Man Walking.

☑ ▣ ▢ GOODNIGHT KISS MUSIC (BMI)

10153½ Riverside Dr. #239, Toluca Lake CA 91601. (831)479-9993. Website: www.goodnightkiss.com. **Contact:** Janet Fisher, managing director. Music publisher, record company and record producer. Estab. 1986. Publishes 6-8 songs/year; publishes 4-5 new songwriters/year. Pays standard royalty.

• Goodnight Kiss Music specializes in placing music in movies and TV, but also pitches major label acts.

Affiliate(s) Scene Stealer Music (ASCAP).

How to Contact "Check our website or subscribe to free newsletter (www.goodnightkiss.com) to see what we are looking for and to obtain codes. Packages must have proper submission codes, or they are discarded." Prefers CD or cassette with 1-3 songs and lyric sheet. Send SASE for reply. Does not return material. Responds in 6 months.

Film & TV Places 3-5 songs in film/year. Published "I Do, I Do, Love You" (by Joe David Curtis), recorded by Ricky Kershaw in *Road Ends*; "Bee Charmer's Charmer" (by Marc Tilson) for the MTV movie *Love Song*; "Right When I Left" (by B. Turner/J. Fisher) in the movie *Knight Club*.

Music All modern styles. Published and produced *Addiction: Highs & Lows* (CD), written and recorded by various artists (all styles), released 2004; *Tall Tales of Osama Bin Laden* (CD), written and recorded by various artists (all styles parody), released 2004; and *Troops & Allies* (CD), written and recorded by various artists (all styles), slated release 2005, all on Goodnight Kiss Records.

Tips "The absolute best way to keep apprised of the company's needs is to subscribe to the online newsletter. Only specifically requested material is accepted, as listed in the newsletter (what the industry calls us for is what we request from writers). We basically use an SGA contract, and there are never fees to be considered for specific projects or albums. However, we are a real music company, and the competition is just as fierce as with the majors."

▢ R.L. HAMMEL ASSOCIATES, INC.

P.O. Box 531, Alexandria IN 46001-0531. E-mail: rlh@rlhammel.com. Website: www.rlhammel.com. **Contact:** A&R Department. President: Randal Hammel. Music publisher, record producer and consultant. Estab. 1974. Staff size: 3-5. Pays standard royalty.

Affiliate(s) Ladnar Music (ASCAP) and Lemmah Music (BMI).

How to Contact Submit demo tape by mail. Unsolicited submissions are OK. Prefers cassette, CD, DAT or VHS/8mm videocassette with 3 songs and typed lyric sheet. "Please notate three (3) songs—no time to listen to a full project." Does not return material. Responds ASAP.

Music Mostly **pop, Christian** and **R&B**; also **MOR**, **rock** and **country**. Published *Lessons For Life* (album by Kelly Hubbell/Jim Boedicker) and *I Just Want Jesus* (album by Mark Condon), both recorded by Kelly Connor on Impact Records.

Music Publishers

⊞ ☐ HAPPY MELODY

VZW, Paul Gilsonstraat 31, 8200 St-Andries, Belgium. Phone: 00 32 50-316380. Fax: 00 32 50-315235. **Contact:** Eddy Van Mouffaert, general manager. Music publisher, record company (Jump Records) and record producer (Jump Productions). Member SABAM S.V., Brussels. Publishes 100 songs/year; publishes 8 new songwriters/year. Staff size: 2. Pays standard royalty via SABAM S.V.

How to Contact Submit demo CD or tape by mail. Unsolicited submissions are OK. Prefers CD. Does not return material. Responds in 2 weeks.

Music Mostly **easy listening**, **disco** and **light pop**; also **instrumentals**. Published *Dikke Berta* and *Da Da Da* (albums by Ricky Mondes), both recorded by Guy Dumon on BM Studio (Flemish); and *Onze Vader* (album by David Linton), recorded by De Korenaar on Korenaar (profane).

Tips "Music wanted with easy, catchy melodies (very commercial songs)."

⊘ HESFREE PRODUCTIONS & PUBLISHING COMPANY

(formerly Hes Free Productions & Publishing Company), 3711 E. 29th, P.O. Box 1214, Bryan TX 77806-1214. (979)268-3263. Fax: (979)775-5261. E-mail: hesfreeprodandpubco@yahoo.com. Website: www.hesfreeproduct ions.com. President/CEO/Owner: Brenda M. Freeman-Heslip (gospel); Producer of Songwriting: Marcus Franklin. Vice President/Owner: Rochelle Heslip (R&B). Vice President/Executive Producer: Donell Travis. Senior Director of R&B, Gospel & Rappers: Cyril Roberson (rap). Music publisher and record producer. Estab. 2001.

  • Also see the listings for HesFree Productions & Publishing in the Record Producers and Managers & Booking Agents sections of this book.

How to Submit *We only accept material referred to us by a reputable industry source (manager, entertainment attorney, etc.).* Include CD/CDR. Does not return submissions. Responds in 4-6 weeks only if interested. "Make sure you copyright all of your material through the Library of Congress in Washington, D.C."

Music Mostly **R&B**, **gospel**, **rap** and **rock**. Published "Texas Boys" (single by Chris Idlebird), recorded by Chris Idlebird and Vicki Diggs (rap), released 2002; "Walk through the Rays" (single by Donell Travis), recorded by Donell Travis and Ralatraneka Mercer (rap), released 2002.

Tips "We will ensure that each project is complete with professionalism, with the highest technology methods possible. Additionally, our goal is to publish and record over 200 songs annually."

⊞ ▨ ⊘ HEUPFERD MUSIKVERLAG GmbH

Ringwaldstr. 18, Dreieich 63303 Germany. Phone/fax: (06103)86970. E-mail: heupferd@t-online.de. **Contact:** Christian Winkelmann, general manager. Music publisher and record company (Viva La Difference). GEMA. Publishes 30 songs/year. Staff size: 3. Pays "royalties after GEMA distribution plan."

Affiliate(s) Song Bücherei (book series). "Vive La Difference!" (label).

How to Contact *Does not accept unsolicited submissions.*

Film & TV Places 1 song in film/year. Published "El Grito Y El Silencio" (by Thomas Hickstein), recorded by Tierra in *Frauen sind was Wunderbares*.

Music Mostly **folk**, **jazz** and **fusion**; also **New Age**, **rock** and **ethnic music**. Published "Mi Mundo" (single by Denise M'Baye/Matthias Fürstenberg) from *Havana—Vamos A Ver* (album), recorded by Havana (Latin), released 2003 on Vive La Difference.

▨ ⊘ HICKORY LANE PUBLISHING AND RECORDING (ASCAP, SOCAN)

19854 Butternut Lane, Pitt Meadows BC V3Y 2S7 Canada. (604)465-1258. **Contact:** Chris Urbanski, president. Music publisher, record company and record producer. Estab. 1988. Hires staff writers. Publishes 30 songs/year; publishes 5 new songwriters/year. Pays standard royalty.

How to Contact *Does not accept unsolicited submissions.*

Music Mostly **country** and **country rock**. Published "There She Goes" (single by Matthias Urbanski/Chris Urbanski/Marina Lum), recorded by Chris Michaels (country/rock), released 2002 on Hickory Lane Records; "Mama Liked the Roses" recorded by Chris Michaels (ballad), released 2004 on Hickory Lane Records; "Something Old Is New Again" (single by Chris Urbanski/Alex Bradshaw/John Middleton), recorded by Chris Michaels (country), released 2002 on Hickory Lane Records.

Tips "Send us a professional quality demo with the vocals upfront. We are looking for hits, and so are the major record labels we deal with. Be original in your approach, don't send us a cover tune."

▨ ☐ HIS POWER PRODUCTIONS AND PUBLISHING (ASCAP, BMI)

1304 Canyon, Plainview TX 79072-4740. (806)296-7073. Fax: (806)296-7111. E-mail: dcarter@texasonline.net. Professional Managers: Darryl Carter (R&B, gospel, country rock); T. Lee Carter (pop, new rock, classic rock). Music publisher, record company (Lion and Lamb), record producer and management and booking agency (End-Time Management & Booking Agency). Estab. 1995. Publishes 4-10 songs/year; publishes 3 new songwriters/year. Staff size: 4. Hires staff songwriters. Pays negotiable royalty.

Affiliate(s) Love Story Publishing (BMI).
- The song "Heal Me," published by His Power, was awarded a 1998, 1999, 2000, 2001 and 2002 ASCAP Popular Award.

How to Contact *Write or call first and obtain permission to submit.* Prefers cassette, CD or DAT with 1-5 songs and lyric sheet. Include SASE. "No material returned without SASE." Responds ASAP.

Music Mostly **power gospel, pop, new rock, classic rock, country rock gospel** and **adult contemporary gospel**; also **R&B, jazz, Christ-oriented Christmas music, pro-life and family**. Looking for unconventional styles and structure. Does not want negative-based lyrics of any kind. Published "She Used to Be Me" (single), written and recorded by Crystal Cartier on Love Story (blues); "It's His Life" (single), written and recorded by Mike Burchfield (country gospel), released on Lion and Lamb Records.

Tips "Be serious. We are only interested in those who have meaning and substance behind what is created. Music is an avenue to change the world. Submit what comes from the heart. Don't be in a hurry. Good music has no time limits. And yet, time will reward the desire you put into it. Be willing to embark on newly designed challenges that will meet a new century of opportunity and needs never before obtainable through conventional music companies."

☐ HITSBURGH MUSIC CO. (BMI)

P.O. Box 1431, 233 N. Electra, Gallatin TN 37066. (615)452-0324. Promotional Director: Kimolin Crutcher. A&R Director: K'leetha Gilbert. Executive Vice President: Kenneth Gilbert. **Contact:** Harold Gilbert, President/General Manager. Music publisher. Estab. 1964. Publishes 12 songs/year. Staff size: 4. Pays standard royalty.

Affiliate(s) 7th Day Music (BMI).

How to Contact Submit demo tape by mail. Unsolicited submissions are OK. Prefers cassette or quality videocassette with 2-4 songs and lead sheet. Prefers studio produced demos. Include SASE. Responds in 6 weeks.

Music Mostly **country gospel** and **MOR**. Published "Georgia Boy" (single by Donald Layne), recorded by The Swingsters (MOR), released 2000 on Southern City; and "Disorder at the Border" (single), written and recorded by Donald Layne, released 2001 on Southern City.

⚅ ☐ HITSOURCE PUBLISHING (BMI)

1324 Oakton, Evanston IL 60202. (847)328-4203. Fax: (847)328-4236. E-mail: hitsource@earthlink.net. **Contact:** Al Goldberg, president. Music publisher. Estab. 1986. Publishes 3-12 songs/year; publishes 1-2 new songwriters/year. Pays standard royalty.

Affiliate(s) Grooveland Music (ASCAP) and KidSource Publishing (BMI).

How to Contact *Write or e-mail first and obtain permission to submit.* "Sometimes we are not actively plugging songs." Prefers CD or cassette with 3 songs and lyric sheet. Does not return material. Responds in 2 months.

Music Mostly **pop, country** and **rock**.

Tips "Ask yourself the following questions: Does this song come from the heart? Will an artist be willing to risk his career by recording this song? Have you critiqued the song yourself and rewritten it yet?"

☒ ☐ HOLY SPIRIT MUSIC (BMI)

P.O. Box 31, Edmonton KY 42129. (270)432-3183. **Contact:** W. Junior Lawson, president. Music publisher. Member GMA, International Association of Gospel Music Publishers and Southern Gospel Music Association. Estab. 1973. Publishes 4 songs/year; publishes 2 new songwriters/year. Staff size: 1. Pays standard royalty.

How to Contact Submit demo tape by mail. Unsolicited submissions are OK. Prefers cassette with 2 songs and lyric sheet. Include SASE. Responds in 3 weeks.

Film & TV Places 1 song in film and 1 song in TV/year. Published "I'm Making Plans To See Jesus" (by Gregory A. Pollard), recorded by The Florida Boys in *Saved By Grace*.

Music Mostly **Southern gospel** and **country gospel**. Does not want rock gospel or contemporary gospel. Published "United We Stand, America" (single by Catherine E. Ray) from *Artists With A Message* (album), recorded by Reconcile, released 2002 on First Love Records; "If You Know" (single by Steven W. Perry) from *Artists With A Message* (album), recorded by Lori Long, released 2002 on First Love Records; and "Excuses" (single by Harold S. Lecke) from *More Than Ever* (album), recorded by Pensacola Christian College Singers, released 2002 on Independent.

Tips Send "good clear cut tape with typed copy of lyrics."

☑ ⊕ ☒ ⊘ INTOXYGENE SARL

(formerly Pas Mal Publishing SARL), 283 Fbg St. Antoine, Paris 75011 France. Phone: 011(33)1 43485151. Fax: 011(33)1 43485753. E-mail: infos@intoxygene.com. Website: www.intoxygene.com or www.theyounggods.com. **Contact:** Jammes Patrick, managing director. Music publisher. Estab. 1990. Staff size: 1. Publishes 5-10 songs/year. Pays 50% royalty.

How to Contact *Does not accept unsolicited submissions.*

Film & TV Places 3 songs in film and 2 songs in TV/year.

Music Mostly **new industrial** and **metal** as well as lounge, electronic, and ambient. Does not want country, pop or jazz. Published *Second Nature Lucidogen Astromic* (album), written and recorded by The Young Gods (alternative), released October 2000 on Intoxygene.

☑ ○ IRON SKILLET MUSIC (ASCAP, BMI, SESAC)

6337 Murray Lane, Brentwood TN 37027. (615)371-0646. Fax: (615)370-0353. E-mail: info@countryalbums.c om. Website: www.countryalbums.com. **Contact:** Jack Schneider, president. Vice President: Claude Southall. Office Manager: Nell Tolson. Music publisher, record company (Rustic Records Inc.) and record producer. Estab. 1984. Publishes 20 songs/year. Pays standard royalty.

Affiliate(s) Covered Bridge Music (BMI), Town Square Music (SESAC), Iron Skillet Music (ASCAP).

How to Contact Submit demo tape or CD by mail. Unsolicited submissions are OK. Prefers CD with 3-4 songs and lyric sheet. Include SASE. Responds in 3 months.

Music Mostly **country**. Published "In Their Eyes" (single by Jamie Champa); "Take Me As I Am" (single by Bambi Barrett/Paul Huffman); and "Yesterday's Memories" (single by Jack Schneider), recorded by Colte Bradley (country), to be released 2003.

Tips "Send three or four traditional country songs, novelty songs 'foot-tapping, hand-clapping' gospel songs with strong hook for male or fale artist of duet. Enclose SASE (manilla envelope)."

🌐 ○ ISLAND CULTURE MUSIC PUBLISHERS (BMI)

Chateau Bordeaux, St. John U.S. Virgin Islands 00830. Phone/fax: (340)693-5353. E-mail: L_monsanto@hotmail .com. **Contact:** Liston Monsanto, Jr., president. Music publisher and record company (Island King Records). Estab. 1996. Publishes 10 songs/year; publishes 3 new songwriters/year. Hires staff songwriters. Staff size: 3. Pays standard royalty.

How to Contact Submit demo tape by mail. Unsolicited submissions are OK. Prefers cassette with 8 songs and lyric sheet. Send bio and 8×10 glossy. Does not return material. Responds in 1 month.

Music Mostly **reggae**, **calypso** and **zouk**; also **house**. Published "Jah Give Me Life" (single by Chubby) from *Best of Island King* (album), recorded by Chubby (reggae), released 2003 on Island King Records; "When People Mix Up" (single by Lady Lex/ L. Monsanto/Chubby) from *Best of Island King* (album, recorded by Lady Lex (reggae), released 2003 on Island King Records; "I Am Real" (single by L. Monsanto) from *Best of Island King* (album), recorded by Lady Lex (reggae), released 2003 on Island King Records.

Ⓝ ○ IVORY PEN ENTERTAINMENT (ASCAP)

P.O. Box 1097, Laurel MD 20725. (301)490-4418. Fax: (301) 490-4635. E-mail: ivorypen@comcast.net. Website: www.uwritethehit.com. Professional Managers: Steven Lewis (hip-hop/rap, R&B, inspirational); Sonya Lewis (pop, jazz, A/C). Music publisher. Estab. 2003. Publishes 10 songs/year. Staff size: 4. Pays standard royalty.

How to Contact Submit demo by mail. Unsolicited submissions are OK. Prefers CD/CDR with 3-5 songs and cover letter. Include SASE. Does not return material without SASE. Responds in 1 month. "Don't forget contact info! Always be professional when you submit your work to any company."

Music Mostly **R&B**, **hip-hop**, and **inspirational/gospel**; also **jazz**, **adult contemporary**, and **pop/rock**. Published One Dose (album), written and recorded by Jeremy Wills Project (hip-hop), released on Ivory Pen Entertainment.

Tips: "Learn your craft and don't steal from other musicians. Be original. Ivory Pen Entertainment is a music publishing company with distribution that caters to the producer and aspiring artist. We release CDs of music tracks (no vocals) for aspiring singers and songwriters to use for their demos. This enables you, the aspiring recording artist or songwriter to cut your recording costs in half, if not more. Ivory Pen also allows you to send your completed demo to record companies if you are an artist or to publishing companies if you are a songwriter, meanwhile, the producer gets paid every time his/her tracks are used. All CDs are licensed under Ivory Pen Entertainment (ASCAP) and sell for $15.99."

⊿ JANA JAE MUSIC (BMI)

P.O. Box 35726, Tulsa OK 74153. (918)786-8896. Fax: (918)786-8897. E-mail: janajae@janajae.com. Website: www.janajae.com. **Contact:** Kathleen Pixley, secretary. Music publisher, record company (Lark Record Productions, Inc.) and record producer (Lark Talent and Advertising). Estab. 1980. Publishes 5-10 songs/year; publishes 1-2 new songwriters/year. Staff size: 8. Pays standard royalty.

How to Contact Submit demo tape by mail. Unsolicited submissions are OK. Prefers CD or VHS videocassette with 3-4 songs and typed lyric and lead sheet if possible. Does not return material. Responds only if accepted for use.

Music Mostly **country**, **bluegrass**, **jazz** and **instrumentals** (**classical** or **country**). Published *Mayonnaise* (album by Steve Upfold), recorded by Jana Jae; and *Let the Bible Be Your Roadmap* (album by Irene Elliot) recorded by Jana Jae, both on Lark Records.

☒ ◌ JAELIUS ENTERPRISES (ASCAP, BMI)

P.O. Box 459, Royse City TX 75189. (972)636-9230. Fax: (972)636-0036. E-mail: jaelius@flash.net. Website: www.jaelius.com. **Contact:** James Cornelius, managing director. Music publisher. Staff size: 2. Pays standard royalty.

Affiliate(s) Jaelius Music (ASCAP), Hitzgalore Music (BMI), Air Rifle Music (ASCAP) and Bee Bee Gun Music (BMI).

How to Contact *Write or call first and obtain permission to submit.* Prefers cassette. Include SASE. Responds in 6 weeks.

Film & TV Places 2 songs in film/year. Recently published "Night Has a Thousand Eyes" (by Wayne/Weisman/Garrett), recorded by Anita Kelsey in *Dark City*; and "Feeling in Love," written and recorded by J.J. Cale in *Lawn Dogs*.

Music Mostly **gospel.** Published "Make a Joyful Noise" and "I Know" (singles), recorded by Olivia Mojica (gospel); "Where Would I Be Without Your Love" (single), recorded by Lee Mays (gospel); "God Gives His Love International" (single), recorded by Michelle Deck (gospel).

Tips "Today's market requires good demos. Strong lyrics are a must."

⊕ ◻ JA/NEIN MUSIKVERLAG GMBH

Oberstr. 14 A, D-20144, Hamburg Germany. Fax: (+49)40 448850. E-mail: janeinmv@aol.com. General Manager: Mary Dostal. Music publisher, record company and record producer. GEMA. Publishes 50 songs/year; publishes 5 new songwriters/year. Staff size: 3. Pays 60% royalty.

Affiliate(s) Pinorrekk Mv., Star-Club Mv. and Wunderbar Mv. (GEMA).

How to Contact Submit audio (visual) carrier by mail. Unsolicited submissions are OK. Prefers cassette, CDR or VHS videocassette. Enclose e-mail address. Responds in 2 months.

Music Mostly **jazz, klezmer, pop, rap** and **rock.** Published *Groovology* (album) written and recorded by Axel Zwingenberger and Gottfried Boettger (boogie woogie & blues), released 2004 on Vagabond; *Horizons* (album) written and recorded by Gottfried Boettger (ragtime/jazz), released 2004 on Vagabond.

Tips "We do not return submitted material. Send A-Side songs or extraordinary works/ideas only, please. Write what you expect from collaboration. If artist, enclose photo. If CS, leave three seconds between tracks. Enclose lyrics. Be fantastic!"

◻ JERJOY MUSIC (BMI)

P.O. Box 1264, 6020 W. Pottstown Rd., Peoria IL 61654-1264. (309)673-5755. Fax: (309)673-7636. E-mail: uarltd@AS.com or banbr1@hotmail.com. Website: www.unitedcyber.com. **Contact:** Jerry Hanlon, professional manager. Music publisher and record company (Universal-Athena Records). Estab. 1978. Publishes 6 songs/year; publishes 6 new songwriters/year. Staff size: 3. Pays standard royalty.

Affiliate(s) Kaysarah Music (ASCAP); Abilite Music (BMI).

  • Also see the listing for Kaysarah Music in this section and UAR Records in the Record Companies section of this book.

How to Contact "We accept unsolicited submissions. We **DO NOT** return phone calls." Prefers cassette or CD with 4-8 songs and lyric sheet. Include SASE "for reply only and/or mailing materials and postage if you wish everything returned to you. **We do not critique work unless asked.**" Simple demos—vocal plus guitar or keyboard are acceptable. We DO NOT require a major demo production to interpret the value of a song. Responds in 2 weeks.

Music Mostly **country.** Published "For Old Loves Sake," "Never Mind" and "You Don't Have to Tell Me" (singles by Norma Owen) and "Just An Ordinary Woman" (single by J.J. Jan Cole), recorded by Melanie Hiatt (country); "All Your Little Secrets" and "The Girl From Central High" (singles by Ron Czikall), recorded by Tracy Wells (country); "Inching My Way Toward Heaven" and "Rainbows in Heaven" (singles by J.W. Rhea/Marilyn Westerhoff/Danny Blakey), recorded by Danny Blakey (country), all released on UAR Records.

Tips "Don't submit any song that you don't honestly feel is well constructed and strong in commercial value. Be critical of your writing efforts. Be sure you use each and every one of your lyrics to its best advantage. 'Think Big!' Make your songs tell a story and don't be repetitious in using the same or similar ideas or words in each of your verses. Would your musical creation stand up against the major hits that are making the charts today? Think of great hooks you can work into your song ideas."

Ⓝ JODA MUSIC (BMI)

P.O. Box 100, Spirit Lake IA 51360. (712)336-2859. President: John Senn. A&R Director: Wes Weller. Music publisher and record company. Estab. 1970. Publishes 10 songs/year. Pays standard royalty.

Affiliate(s) Okoboji Music (BMI).

How to Contact Prefers cassette with no more than 4 songs and lyric sheet. "Keep demos short." Include SASE. Responds in 3 weeks.

Music Mostly **light rock**, **country** and **gospel**. Published "Beer & Popcorn" (by Dave Peterson), recorded by Ralph Lundquist (country); "Change is Going to Come" (by Roger Hughes), recorded by Silver $ Band (pop); and *Ain't Like it Used to Be*, (by Dave Petersen and John Senn), recorded by Brent (pop), all on IGL Records.

✓ ◯ QUINCY JONES MUSIC

6671 Sunset Blvd., #1574A, Los Angeles CA 90028. (323)957-6601. E-mail: info@quincyjonesmusic.com. Music publisher.

How to Contact *Quincy Jones Music does not accept unsolicited submissions.*

◯ JPMC MUSIC INC. (BMI)

P.O. Box 526, Burlington VT 05402. (802)860-7110. Fax: (802)860-7112. E-mail: music@jpmc.com. Website: www.jpmc.com. **Contact:** Jane Peterer, president. Music publisher, record company (JPMC Records) and book publisher. Estab. 1989. Publishes 20 songs/year; publishes 10 new songwriters/year. Pays standard royalty.

Affiliate(s) GlobeSound Publishing (ASCAP) and GlobeArt Publishing Inc. (BMI).

How to Contact Submit a demo tape by mail. Unsolicited submissions are OK. Prefers "professional" DAT, CD or cassette with 3 songs and lyric sheet. "If submitting a CD, indicate which three tracks to consider, otherwise only the first three will be considered." Include SASE. Responds in 2 months. See website for complete guidelines.

Music Mostly **pop/R&B**, **jazz** and **gospel**; also **country** and **instrumental**. Published "Ode to Ireland" (single by Breschi), recorded by Breschi/Cassidy on Pick Records (instrumental); and "Ici Paris" (single), written and recorded by Michael Ganian.

Tips "We are in constant communication with record and film producers and will administer your work on a worldwide basis. We also publish songbooks for musicians and fans, as well as educational and method books for students and teachers."

JUST A NOTE (ASCAP, BMI)

P.O. Box 39261, Louisville KY 40233. (502)777-4539. E-mail: TalkToHeath@insight.bb.com. Website: www.TalkToHeath.com. **Contact:** John V. Heath, general partner. Music publisher, record companies (Hillview, Estate) and record producer (MVT Productions). Estab. 1979. Publishes 35 songs/year; publishes 10-15 new songwriters/year. Pays standard royalty.

Affiliate(s) Two John's Music (ASCAP).

How to Contact Submit demo tape by mail. Unsolicited submissions are OK. "Or e-mail me." Prefers cassette or VHS videocassette with 3 songs and lead sheet. Include SASE. Responds in 1 month.

Music Mostly **pop**, **country**, **R&B** and **MOR**; also **gospel**. Published *Old Age* and *Rose* (albums), written and recorded by Mark Gibbs on Hillview Records; and *Area Code 502* (album), written and recorded by Adonis on Estate Records.

Tips "As we are an international company, please have access to lead sheet. Since this takes time to do, we do charge for this service. Our sub-publishers require lead sheets."

◯ KAUPPS & ROBERT PUBLISHING CO. (BMI)

P.O. Box 5474, Stockton CA 95205. (209)948-8186. Fax: (209)942-2163. Website: www.makingmusic4u.com. **Contact:** Kristy Ledford, A&R coordinator (all styles). Production Manager (country, pop, rock): Rick Webb. Professional Manager (country, pop, rock): Bruce Boun. President: Nancy L. Merrihew. Music publisher, record company (Kaupp Records), manager and booking agent (Merri-Webb Productions and Most Wanted Bookings). Estab. 1990. Publishes 15-20 songs/year; publishes 5 new songwriters/year. Pays standard royalty.

How to Contact *Write first and obtain permission to submit.* Prefers cassette or VHS videocassette (if available) with 3 songs maximum and lyric sheet. "If artist, send PR package." Include SASE. Responds in 6 months.

Music Mostly **country**, **R&B** and **A/C rock**; also **pop**, **rock** and **gospel**. Published "Prisoner of Love" (single by N. Merrihew/Rick Webb), recorded by Nanci Lynn (country/rock/pop); "Excuse Me, But That Ain't Country"; "I Thank You Father" and "On the Other Side" (singles by N. Merrihew/B. Bolin), recorded by Bruce Bolin (country/rock/pop); and "Did You Think That I Thought That You Liked Me" (single by N. Merrihew/B. Bolin), recorded by Nanci Lynn (country/rock/pop) and Cheryl (country/rock/pop), all released on Kaupp Records.

Tips "Know what you want, set a goal, focus in on your goals, be open to constructive criticism, polish tunes and keep polishing."

☐ KAYSARAH MUSIC (ASCAP)

P.O. Box 1264, 6020 W. Pottstown Rd., Peoria IL 61654-1264. (309)673-5755. Fax: (309)673-7636. E-mail: uarltd@A5.com. Website: www.unitedcyber.com. **Contact:** Jerry Hanlon, owner/producer. Music Publisher, record company, and record producer. Estab. 2000. Publishes 2 new songwriters/year. Staff size: 3. Pays standard royalty.

Affiliate(s) Jerjoy Music (BMI); Abilite Music (BMI).

● Also see the listing for Jerjoy Music in this section and UAR Records in the Record Companies section of this book.

How to Contact Submit demo tape by mail. Unsolicited submissions are OK. Prefers cassette or CD with 4 songs and lyric sheet and cover letter. Include SASE. Responds in 2 weeks.

Music Mostly **traditional country**, **modern country** and **country gospel**; also **Irish country**, **Irish ballads** and **Irish folk/traditional**. Recently published "It's Too Late For Goodbye" (single by Dorothy Wallace) and "A World Without You" (single by Sue Rapp) from *Candlelight and Wine* (album), recorded by Jackie Nelson (modern country), released 2001 on Irish Records.

Tips "Be honest in comparing your material to commercially recorded works."

⬛ ☐ KEYSHAVON MUSIC PUBLISHING (BMI)

530 Broadway St., Platteville WI 53818. (608)348-3555. E-mail: Topcat@mhct.net. **Contact:** Christopher Isabell, owner. Music Publisher. Estab. 2001. Pays standard royalty.

How to Contact Submit demo tape by mail. Unsolicited submissions are OK. Prefers cassette or CD with 5 songs and lyric and lead sheet. "Please copyright your songs." Include SASE. Responds in 1 month.

Music All types.

Tips "Make sure your song is well written with a professional demo. We need hits. Also, please read all you can about the music industry."

☐ LAKE TRANSFER PRODUCTIONS & MUSIC (ASCAP, BMI)

11300 Hartland St., North Hollywood CA 91605. (818)508-7158. **Contact:** Jim Holvay, professional manager (pop, R&B, soul); Tina Antoine (hip-hop, rap); Steve Barri Cohen (alternative rock, R&B). Music publisher and record producer (Steve Barri Cohen). Estab. 1989. Publishes 11 songs/year; publishes 3 new songwriters/year. Staff size: 6. Pay "depends on agreement, usually 50% split."

Affiliate(s) Lake Transfer Music (ASCAP) and Transfer Lake Music (BMI).

How to Contact *Does not accept unsolicited submissions.*

Music Mostly **alternative pop**, **R&B/hip-hop** and **dance**. Does not want country & western, classical, New Age, jazz or swing. Published "Tu Sabes Que Te Amo (Will You Still Be There)" (single by Steve Barri Cohen/Rico) from *Rico: The Movement II* (album), recorded by Rico (rap/hip-hop), released 2004 on Lost Empire/Epic-Sony; "When Water Flows" (single by Steve Barri Cohen/Sheree Brown/Terry Dennis) from *Sheree Brown "83"* (album), recorded by Sheree Brown (urban pop), released 2004 on BBEG Records (a division of Saravels, LLC); and "Fair Game" (single by LaTocha Scott/Steve Barri Cohen) soundtrack from the movie *Fair Game* (album), recorded by LaTocha Scott (R&B/hip-hop), released 2004 on Raw Deal Records, College Park, Georgia. "All our staff are songwriters/producers. Jim Holvay has written hits like 'Kind of a Drag' and 'Hey Baby They're Playin our Song' for the Buckinghams. Steve Barri Cohen has worked with every one from Evelyn 'Champagne' King (RCA), Phantom Planets (Epic), Meridith Brooks (Capitol) and Dre (Aftermath/Interscope)."

Tips "Trends change, but it's still about the song. Make sure your music and lyrics have a strong (POV) point of view."

☐ LARI-JON PUBLISHING (BMI)

P.O. Box 216, Rising City NE 68658. (402)542-2336. **Contact:** Larry Good, owner. Music publisher, record company (Lari-Jon Records), management firm (Lari-Jon Promotions) and record producer (Lari-Jon Productions). Estab. 1967. Publishes 20 songs/year; publishes 2-3 new songwriters/year. Staff size: 1. Pays standard royalty.

How to Contact Submit demo CD by mail. Unsolicited submissions are OK. Prefers CD with 5 songs and lyric sheet. "Be professional." Include SASE. Responds in 2 months.

Music Mostly **country**, **Southern gospel** and **'50s rock**. Does not want rock, hip-hop, pop or heavy metal. Published "Bluegrass Blues" and "Carolina Morning" (singles by Larry Good) from *Carolina Morning* (album), recorded by Blue Persuasion (country), released 2002 by Bullseye; "Those Rolling Hills of Glenwood" (single by Tom Campbell) from *Single* (album), recorded by Tom Campbell (country), released 2001 by Jeffs-Room-Productions.

☑ ☐ LCS MUSIC GROUP

P.O. Box 7809, Dallas TX 75209. E-mail: chris@dallastexas.cc. Website: www.homesweethomerecords.com. Professional Managers: Chris Christian (pop/Christian); Dawn Lally. Music publisher, record company and record producer. Estab. 1981. Publishes 2,000 songs/year. Staff size: 3. Hires staff songwriters. Pays standard royalty.

Affiliate(s) Home Sweet Home Music/Bug and Bear Music (ASCAP), Chris Christian Music (BMI) and Monk and Tid (SESAC).

How to Contact Submit demo tape by mail. Unsolicited submissions are OK. Prefers CD, DAT or videocassette. Include name, phone number and e-mail on CD or tape. Does not return material. Responds if interested.

Music Does not want quartet music.

Tips "Keep writing until you get good at your craft. Co-write with the best you can—always put phone number on tape or CD's."

☑ ◯ TRIXIE LEIGH MUSIC

1728 Crimson Tree Way #D, Edgewood MD 21040. (410)538-8262. **Contact:** Rick Solimini, Music Publisher. E-mail: trixieleighmusic@webtv.net. Music publisher and record company (Cherasny Records). Estab. 1997. Publishes 4 songs/year; publishes 4 new songwriters/year. Hires staff writers. Staff size: 4. Pays standard royalty.

How to Contact *Write first and obtain permission to submit.* Prefers cassette with 3 songs and lyric and lead sheets. Include SASE. Responds in 1 month.

Music Contemporary **Christian**. Does not want secular, rap, opera or hard rock. Published "Be" (single by Rick Solimin) from *Restore My Soul* (album), recorded by Donna Bente (contemporary Christian), released 2004; "You've Given me Life" (single by Rick Solimini) from *Restore My Soul* (album), recorded by Sherri Freeman (contemporary Christian), released 2004; and "Clothed" (single by Rick Solomini) from *Restore My Soul* (album), recorded by Redemption (contemporary Christian), released 2004, all on Cherasny Records.

Tips "Be consistent in learning the craft of songwriting."

◯ LEXINGTON ALABAMA MUSIC PUBLISHING (BMI)

3596 County Rd. 136, Lexington AL 35648. Phone/fax: (256)229-8814. Email: LampMusic@cs.com. **Contact:** Darrell Glover, owner. Professional Managers: Roy Crabb (R&B); Ann Glover (country); Grady Glover (rock). Music publisher and record company (Lamp Records). Estab. 1981. Publishes 35 songs/year; publishes 5 new songwriters/year. Staff size: 4. Pays standard royalty.

Affiliate(s) Northwest Alabama Music Publishing (BMI).

How to Contact Submit demo tape by mail. Unsolicited submissions are OK. Prefers CD or CD-R with 3 songs, lyric sheet and cover letter. "Find a new way of expressing old ideas." Does not return material. Responds only if interested.

Music Mostly **country**, **southern rock** and **R&B**; also **comedy**, **gospel** and **Christmas**. Does not want rap, hard rock and classical. Published "Candlelight Opera" (single), written and recorded by Mark Narmore (country); *Let's Make the World Noisy* (album by Curtis Hall), recorded by Apul (rock), both released 2000 on Lamp Records; and "He Pours Out His Spirit" (single), written and recorded by Gary Springer (gospel), released 2001 on Lamp Records.

⬇ ▣ ◯ LILLY MUSIC PUBLISHING (SOCAN)

61 Euphrasia Dr., Toronto ON M6B 3V8 Canada. (416)782-5768. Fax: (416)782-7170. **Contact:** Panfilo DiMatteo, president. Music publisher and record company (P. & N. Records). Estab. 1992. Publishes 20 songs/year; publishes 8 new songwriters/year. Staff size: 3. Pays standard royalty.

Affiliate(s) San Martino Music Publishing and Paglieta Music Publishing (CMRRA).

How to Contact Submit demo tape by mail. Unsolicited submissions are OK. Prefers cassette (or videocassette if available) with 3 songs and lyric and lead sheets. "We will contact you only if we are interested in the material." Responds in 1 month.

Film & TV Places 12 songs in film/year.

Music Mostly **dance**, **ballads** and **rock**; also **country**. Published "Give It To Me (Annick) Artist" (single by Jaz Singh) from *Wonder* (album), recorded by Annick (dance), released 2004 on P&N Records.

◯ LINEAGE PUBLISHING CO. (BMI)

P.O. Box 211, East Prairie MO 63845. (573)649-2211. **Contact:** Tommy Loomas, professional manager. Staff: Alan Carter and Joe Silver. Music publisher, record producer, management firm (Staircase Promotions) and record company (Capstan Record Production). Pays standard royalty.

How to Contact Submit demo tape by mail. Unsolicited submissions are OK. Prefers cassette with 2-4 songs and lyric sheet; include bio and photo if possible. Include SASE. Responds in 2 months.

Music Mostly **country, easy listening, MOR, country rock** and **top 40/pop**. Published "Let It Rain" (single by Roberta Boyle), recorded by Vicarie Arcoleo on Treasure Coast Records; "Country Boy" (single), written and recorded by Roger Lambert; and "Boot Jack Shuffle" (single by Zachary Taylor), recorded by Skid Row Joe, both on Capstan Records.

LITA MUSIC (ASCAP)

2831 Dogwood Place, Nashville TN 37204. (615)269-8682. Fax: (615)269-8929. Website: http://songsfortheplan et.com. **Contact:** Justin Peters, president. Music publisher. Estab. 1980.
Affiliate(s) Justin Peters Music, Platinum Planet Music and Tourmaline (BMI).
How to Contact Submit demo by mail. Unsolicited submissions are OK. Prefers CD with 5 songs and lyric sheet. Does not return material. "Place code '2005' on each envelope submission."
Music Mostly **Southern gospel/Christian**, **country** and **classic rock**. Published "No Less Than Faithful" (single by Don Pardoe/Joel Lyndsey), recorded by Ann Downing on Daywind Records, Jim Bullard on Genesis Records and Melody Beizer (#1 song) on Covenant Records; "No Other Like You" (single by Mark Comden/Paula Carpenter), recorded by Twila Paris and Tony Melendez (#5 song) on Starsong Records; "Making A New Start" and "Invincible Faith" (singles by Gayle Cox), recorded by Kingdom Heirs on Sonlite Records; and "I Don't Want To Go Back" (single by Gayle Cox), recorded by Greater Vision on Benson Records; "Lost In The Shadow of the Cross" (single by James Elliott and Steven Curtis Chapman) recorded by Steven Curtis Chapman on Spawn Records.

✅ 🖉 LOVE & LAUGHTER MUSIC (ASCAP)

14628 Cortina Dr., La Mirada CA 90638. (562)946-2022. Fax: (562)946-6413. E-mail: contact@loveandlaughterm usic.com. Website: www.loveandlaughtermusic.com. **Contact:** Joey Arreguin or Lisa Manor, owners. Music publisher and record producer. Estab. 1987. Publishes 12 songs/year; publishes 4 new songwriters/year. Staff size: 8. Pays standard royalty.
Affiliate(s) Jamin Max Music (BMI).
● Love & Laughter Music was the winner of the ASCAP Plus Award from 1998-2002. Also see the Love & Laughter Music listing in the Record Producers section of this book.
How to Contact Submit demo by mail. Unsolicited submissions are OK. Prefers CD with 3-4 songs, lyric/lead sheet and cover letter. Does not return submissions. Responds only if interested.
Film & TV Places 2 songs in film and 4 songs in TV/year. Music supervisor: Barbara Jordan. Recently published "It Won't Be Long" (by Lisa Manor/Joey Arreguin), recorded by Lisa Manor in *Details* on Cinemax, and "Starlite & You" (by Lisa Manor/Joey Arreguin), in *All My Children* and *One Life to Live* on ABC.
Music Mostly **Latin**, **contemporary jazz** and **R&B**; also **rock**, **hip-hop**, **country** and **contemporary Christian**. Published *Someone's Gotta Say It* (album written by Rick Dodd/Joey Arreguin/Lisa Manor), recorded by Kecia Lewis (gospel), released 2002 on Kebar Entertainment.
Tips "Strong melody, hooks and lyrics a must! We would rather receive one hit song with all the commercial appeal than 4 or 5 songs that still need work and development. Only send the 'cream of the crop' material."

Ⓝ 🖉 SCOTT LYNCH & COMPANY

40 Music Square E., Nashville TN 37203. (615)259-9506.

🖸 M & T WALDOCH PUBLISHING, INC. (BMI)

4803 S. Seventh St., Milwaukee WI 53221. (414)482-2194. VP, Creative Management (rockabilly, pop, country): Timothy J. Waldoch. Professional Manager (country, top 40): Mark T. Waldoch. Music publisher. Estab. 1990. Publishes 2-3 songs/year; publishes 2-3 new songwriters/year. Staff size: 2. Pays standard royalty.
How to Contact Submit demo tape by mail. Unsolicited submissions are OK. Prefers cassette with 3-6 songs and lyric or lead sheet. "We prefer a studio produced demo tape." Include SASE. Responds in 3 months.
Music Mostly **country/pop**, **rock**, **top 40 pop**; also **melodic metal**, **dance**, **R&B**. Does not want rap. Published "It's Only Me" and "Let Peace Rule the World" (by Kenny LePrix), recorded by Brigade on SBD Records (rock).
Tips "Study the classic pop songs from the 1950s through the present time. There is a reason why good songs stand the test of time. Today's hits will be tomorrow's classics. Send your *best* well-crafted, polished song material."

🖉 MAGIC MESSAGE MUSIC (ASCAP)

P.O. Box 9117, Truckee CA 96162. E-mail: alanred@telis.org. Website: www.alanredstone.com. Owner: Alan Redstone. Music publisher and record company (Sureshot Records). Estab. 1979. Publishes 6 songs/year; publishes 1 new songwriter/year. Staff size: 1. Pays standard royalty.
How to Contact *Write or call first and obtain permission to submit or submit demo tape by mail.* Unsolicited submissions are OK. Include SASE. Responds in 1 week.
Music Mostly **comedy**, **novelty** and **parody**; also **blues**. Does not want rap, soul, top 40, New Age or instrumental.

⊘ MAJOR ENTERTAINMENT (BMI)

(formerly Majestic Control), 331 W. 57th St. #173, New York NY 10019. (212)489-1500. Fax: (212)489-5660. E-mail: info@majorentertainment.com. CEO: Matt "Half Pint" Davis. President: Tatiana Sampson. Music publisher, promotions and public relations. Estab. 1983.

How to Contact Submit demo tape by mail. Unsolicited submissions are OK. Prefers CD with 3 songs. Include SASE. Responds in 2 months.

Music Mostly **rap** and **R&B**. Artists include Soul IV Real, Father MC and Tre-8.

☑ 📺 ⊘ MANUITI L.A. (ASCAP)

% Rosen Music Corp., 4007 W. Magnolia Blvd., Burbank CA 91505. (310)230-6040. Fax: (310)230-4074. E-mail: assistant@rosenmusiccorp.com. **Contact:** Steven Rosen, president. Music publisher and record producer. "The exclusive music publishing company for writer/producer Guy Roche."

How to Contact *Does not accept unsolicited material.*

Film & TV Recently published "As If," recorded by Blaque in *Bring It On*; "Turn the Page," recorded by Aaliyah in *Music of the Heart*; and "While You Were Gone," recorded by Kelly Price in *Blue Streak*.

Music Mostly **pop** and **R&B**. Published "What A Girl Wants" (single), recorded by Christina Aguilera (pop); "Almost Doesn't Count" (single), recorded by Brandy (R&B) on Atlantic; "Beauty" (single), recorded by Dru Hill (R&B) on Island; and "Under My Tree" (single), recorded by *NSync on RCA.

Tips "Do your homework on who you are contacting and what they do. Don't waste yours or their time by not having that information."

⊘ MANY LIVES MUSIC PUBLISHERS (SOCAN)

80 Corley Ave., Toronto ON M4E 1V2 Canada. (416)690-9552. U.K. 0776 154 4302 E-mail: pmilner@sympatico. ca. **Contact:** Paul C. Milner, publisher. Music publisher. Estab. 1997. Pays standard royalty.

How to Contact Submit song demo by mail. Unsolicited submissions are OK. Prefers CD and lyric sheet (lead sheet if available). Does not return material. Responds in 3 months if interested.

Music All styles. Released *Your Friend Phil* (album), written and recorded by Phil Morris(Christian), released 2002 on Healing Heart; *Temptation* (album), various writers, arrangement by Paul Milner, Patrizia, Dan Cutrona (rock/opera),will be released in 2003 on United One Records.

☑ ⊘ JOHN WELLER MARVIN PUBLISHING (ASCAP)

P.O. Box 99232, Cleveland OH 44199. (330)733-8585. Fax: (330)733-8595. E-mail: stephanie.arble@jwmpublish ing.net. Website: www.jwmpublishing.net. **Contact:** Stephanie Arble, President. Music Publisher. Estab. 1996. Pays standard royalty.

How to Contact Submit demo tape by mail. Unsolicited submissions are OK. Prefers cassette, CD or VHS and lyric or lead sheet. Responds in 6 weeks.

Music All genres, mostly **pop**, **R&B**, **rap**; also **rock**, and **country**. Published "Downloading Files" (single by S. Arble/R. Scott), recorded by Ameritech Celebration Choir (corporate promotional). "We work with a promoter, booking major label artists, and we're also involved in television and corporate promotional recordings."

☑ 📺 ⊘ MASTER SOURCE (ASCAP, BMI)

28030 Dorothy Dr., Suite 201, Agoura Hills CA 91302. (818)706-9000. Fax: (818)706-1900. E-mail: info@masters ource.com. Website: www.mastersource.com. Owner: Marc Ferrari. Creative Director: Josh Kessler. Music publisher. Estab. 1993. Publishes 100 songs/year; publishes 20 new songwriters/year. Pays standard royalty.

Affiliate(s) Red Engine Music (ASCAP) and Revision West (BMI).

How to Contact *Call first and obtain permission to submit.* Prefers CD with up to 5 songs and lyric sheet. No guaranteed response.

Film & TV Published music for *As Good As It Gets* (film); *Wag The Dog* (film); and *Touched By An Angel* (TV).

Music All contemporary styles. Mostly **reggae/salsa**, **rap/urban** and **ethnic**; also **country**, **jazz** and **world beat**.

Tips "We specialize in film and TV placements. Master quality recordings a must!"

⊘ MAVERICK MUSIC

9348 Civic Center Dr., Beverly Hills CA 90210. (310)385-7800. Website: www.maverick.com. Music publisher and record company (Maverick).

How to Contact *Maverick Music does not accept unsolicited submissions.*

Ⓝ 🍁 ▢ MAYFAIR MUSIC (BMI)

2600 John St., Unit 219, Markham ON L3R 3W3 Canada. (905)475-1848. Fax: (905)474-9870. **Contact:** John Loweth, A&R director. Music publisher, record company (MBD Records), music print publisher (Music Box

Dancer Publications), record producer and distributor. Member CMPA, CIRPA, CRIA. Estab. 1979. Publishes 20-30 songs/year; publishes 3-5 new songwriters/year. Pays standard royalty.

How to Contact Submit demo CD/CDR by mail. Unsolicited submissions are OK. Prefers CD/CDR with 2-5 songs. Does not return material. Responds in 3 weeks.

Music Mostly **instrumental**.

Tips "Strong melodic choruses and original-sounding music receive top consideration."

☑ ⊠ ⊘ McCONKEY ARTISTS AGENCY MUSIC PUBLISHING (BMI)

8701 Lookout Mountain Ave., Los Angeles CA 90046-1817. (323)690-3389. Fax: (323)463-2558. E-mail: mcconke yagency@sbcglobal.net. Website: www.mcconkeyartistagency.com. **Contact:** Mack K. McConkey, managing director. Music publisher. Estab. 1998. Publishes 12 songs/year; publishes 5 new songwriters/year. Staff size: 5. Pays standard royalty.

Affiliate(s) Vinegower Music (ASCAP).

How to Contact Submit CD by mail. Unsolicited submissions are OK. Prefers CD with 1-5 songs and lyric sheet and cover letter. "Please send us a professional CD, as well as a typed or computer-printed lyric sheet and cover letter." Does not return material. Responds in 6 months.

Film & TV Places 2 songs in TV/year. Published "Chinese Cowboy" (single by Sosa/Keesee/McConkey), recorded by The Mess (alternative rock) in an indie film production *What's This?* to be released 2003. Also published "California" (single by Kevin Kos), recorded by Strychnine (modern rock) in a MTV series *The Osbournes* to be released 2003 season.

Music All types. Published "California" (single by Kevin Kos) from *Strychnine II* (album), recorded by Strychnine (modern rock), released 2003 on Vinegower Records; "Chinese Cowboy" (single by Nestor Sosa/John Keesee/Mack McConkey) from *The Mess*, recorded by The Mess (alternative), released 2003 on Vinegower Records; and "Protection" (single by Al Villanueva) from *Protection* (album), recorded by Red Fish Blue Fish (alternative rock), released 2003 on Vinegower Records.

Tips "Provide the best quality package on your songs. Also send the songs you feel are hits. Do not bother sending album filler material."

☐ JIM McCOY MUSIC (BMI)

25 Troubadour Lane, Berkeley Springs WV 25411. (304)258-9381. E-mail: mccoytroubadour@aol.com. Website: www.troubadourlounge.com. **Contact:** Bertha and Jim McCoy, Owners. Music publisher, record company (Winchester Records) and record producer (Jim McCoy Productions). Estab. 1973. Publishes 20 songs/year; publishes 3-5 new songwriters/year. Pays standard royalty.

Affiliate(s) New Edition Music (BMI).

How to Contact Submit demo tape by mail with lyric sheet. Unsolicited submissions are OK. Prefers cassette or CD with 6 songs. Include SASE. Responds in 1 month.

Music Mostly **country**, **country/rock** and **rock**; also **bluegrass** and **gospel**. Published "Stand By Lover" (single by Earl Howard/Jim McCoy) from *Earl Howard Sings His Heart Out* (album), recorded by Earl Howard (country), released 2002 on Winchester; "Let Her" and "Same ole Town" (singles by Tommy Hill), recorded by R. Lee Gray (country), released 2002 on Winchester.

⊠ ⊘ McJAMES MUSIC INC. (BMI)

1724 Stanford St., Suite B, Santa Monica CA 90404. Also: 701 Hollow Rd., Nashville TN 37205. (310)259-8889. Fax: (419)781-6644. E-mail: info@mcjamesmusic.com. Website: www.mcjamesmusic.com. Professional Managers: Tim James (country/pop); Steven McClintock (pop/country). Music publisher, record company (37 Records) and record producer (Steven McClintock). Estab. 1977. Publishes 10 songs/year. Staff size: 3. Pays standard royalty. Does administration and collection for all foreign markets for smaller publishers and writers.

Affiliate(s) 37 Records (ASCAP) and McJames Music, Inc. (BMI).

How to Contact *Only accepts material referred by a reputable industry source.* Prefers cassette with 2 songs and cover letter. Does not return material. Responds in 6 months.

Film & TV Places 2 songs in film and 3 songs in TV/year. Music Supervisor: Tim James. Recently published "Look At Me Now" recorded by SIXWIRE for Warner Brothers Records, "Three Songs in a Little Inside" written and recorded by Matt and Gunnar Nelson and Cathy Anne.

Music Mostly **country**, **pop** and **dance**; also **bluegrass** and **alternative**. Does not want rap or classical. Published *That's What Love Is* (by S. McClintock/T. Douglas), recorded by Mark Vance (country) on Sony; *Keeps Bringing Me Back* (by S. McClintock/V. Shaw), recorded by Victoria Shaw (easy listening) on Taffita; and *Don't Let This Plan* (by S. McClintock/R. Irving), recorded by Steven McClintock (country) on 37 Records. Recent cover by ATC on BMG/Universal with "If Love is Blind," selling over 300,000 CDs in less than 6 months; single by new Warner Bros. act Six Wire called "Look At Me Now," recent duet by Victoria Shaw and Richard

Schneider on Universal Holland with the song "Loved By You." Place three songs in the new Sony Play Station with the writer/artist Chad Petry.

Tips "Write a song we don't have in our catalog or write an undeniable hit. We will know it when we hear it."

🌐 ⊘ MENTO MUSIC GROUP

Symphony House, Winterhuder Weg 142, D-22085, Hamburg Germany. Phone: (040)22716552 + -53. Fax: (040)22716554. E-mail: mento_music@t-online.de. **Contact:** Arno H. Van Vught, general manager. Professional Manager: Michael Frommhold. Music publisher and record company (Playbones Records). Estab. 1970. Pays standard royalty.

Affiliate(s) Auteursunie, Edition Lamplight, Edition Melodisc, Massimo Jauch Music Productions and Marathon Music.

How to Contact Submit demo tape by mail. Unsolicited submissions are OK. Prefers cassette with 3-4 songs. "Put your strongest/best song first. Put your name and address on the inside sleeve of the tape. If you have a fax number, inform us. Tell us in a typed cover letter what you want/what you are looking for." Does not return material. Responds in 3 weeks.

Music Mostly **instrumental**, **pop**, **MOR**, **country**, **background music** and **film music**. Does not want classical. Published "Vergessen wir die Mark" (single by DP/Volker Frank), recorded by Volker Frank (pop), released 2001; *Paradise* (album), written and recorded by Anna C. Nova (pop), released 2001 on Playbones Records; *Lord of the Dance* (album), written and recorded by Wolfgang Bauer (world music), released 2001 on Playbones Records.

🖼 ⊘ MIDI TRACK PUBLISHING (BMI)/ALLRS MUSIC PUBLISHING CO. (ASCAP)

P.O. Box 1545, Smithtown NY 11787. (718)767-8995. E-mail: allrsmusic@aol.com. Website: www.geocities.com/allrsmusic. **Contact:** Renee Silvestri, president. Music publisher, record company (MIDI Track Records), music consultant, artist management. Voting member of NARAS (The Grammy Awards), CMA, SGMA, SGA. Estab. 1994. Staff size: 5. Publishes 3 songs/year; publishes 2 new songwriters/year. Pays standard royalty.

Affiliate(s) Midi-Track Publishing Co. (BMI).

How to Contact *Write or e-mail first to obtain permission to submit. "We do not accept unsolicited submissions."* Prefers CD or cassette with 3 songs, lyric sheet and cover letter. "Make sure your CD or cassette tape is labeled with your name, mailing address, telephone number, and e-mail address. We do not return material." Responds via e-mail in 3 months.

Film & TV Places 1 song in film/year. Published "Why Can't You Hear My Prayer" (single by F. John Silvestri/Leslie Silvestri), recorded by Iliana Medina in a documentary by Silvermine Films.

Music Mostly **country**, **gospel**, **top 40**, **r&b**, **MOR** and **pop**. Does not want showtunes, jazz, classical or rap. Published "Why Can't You Hear My Prayer" (single by F. John Silvestri/Leslie Silvestri), recorded by five-time Grammy nominee Huey Dunbar of the group DLG (Dark Latin Groove), released on Trend Records (other multiple releases, also recorded by Iliana Medina and released 2002 on MIDI Track Records); "Chasing Rainbows" (single by F. John Silvestri/Leslie Silvestri), recorded by Tommy Cash (country), released on MMT Records (including other multiple releases); "Because of You" (single by F. John Silvestri/Leslie Silvestri), recorded by Iliana Medina, released 2002 on MIDI Track Records, also recorded by three-time Grammy nominee Terri Williams, released on KMA Records; also recorded by Vicki Leigh (country) from Grand Ole Opry member Ernie Ashworth's *Ernie Ashworth and Friends* (album), released 2001 on KMA Records; also recorded as a duet by Ernie Ashworth and Terri Williams, released 2003 on KMA Records; and "Why Do You Lie Next to Me" (single by F. John Silvestri/Leslie Silvestri), recorded by Terri Williams, released 2002 on International Productions.

Tips "Attend workshops, seminars, join songwriters organizations and keep writing, you will achieve your goal."

✓ ○ THE MIGHTY BLUE MUSIC MACHINE

13497 99th Ave., Seminole FL 33776. E-mail: mightyblue@joinmail.com. **Contact:** Tony Blue, GM. Music publisher. Estab. 1995. Staff size: 3-5. Pays standard royalty.

Affiliate(s) Earth Groovz (ASCAP) and Songs From Out of the Blue (BMI).

How to Contact *Write first and obtain permission to submit.* Include SASE. "No phone calls, please." Prefers cassette or CD with 1-3 songs and lyric sheets. "Send 'studio' quality demo with typed lyric sheets." Include SASE. Responds in 3 months. "We do not return tapes or CDs."

Music Mostly **rock (acoustic)**, **country** and **pop**; also **blues**, **Christian/gospel**, **R&B**, **jazz** and **dance**. Does not want violent lyrics. "Be positive—be original."

Tips "Submit only professional 'studio' quality demos (invest in your craft) and be very patient."

⚑ ◙ MONTINA MUSIC (SOCAN)

Box 702, Snowdon Station, Montreal, QC H3X 3X8 Canada. **Contact:** David P. Leonard, professional manager. Music publisher and record company (Monticana Records). Estab. 1963. Pays negotiable royalty.
Affiliate(s) Saber-T Music (SOCAN).
How to Contact Unsolicited submissions are OK. Prefers CD. SAE and IRC. Responds in 3 months.
Music Mostly **top 40**; also **bluegrass, blues, country, dance-oriented, easy listening, folk, gospel, jazz, MOR, progressive, R&B, rock** and **soul**. Does not want heavy metal, hard rock, jazz, classical or New Age.
Tips "Maintain awareness of styles and trends of your peers who have succeeded professionally. Understand the markets to which you are pitching your material. Persevere at marketing your talents. Develop a network of industry contacts, first locally, then regionally, nationally and internationally."

◙ MOON JUNE MUSIC (BMI)

4233 SW Marigold, Portland OR 97219. (507)777-4621. Fax: (503)277-4622. **Contact:** Bob Stoutenburg, President. Music publisher. Estab. 1971. Staff size: 1. Pays standard royalty.
How to Contact Submit demo tape by mail. Unsolicited submissions are OK. Prefers cassette or CD with 2-10 songs.
Music Mostly **country**.

◙ THE MUSIC BRIDGE (ASCAP, BMI)

P.O. Box 661918, Los Angeles CA 90066-1918. (310)398-9650. Fax: (310)398-4850. E-mail: thebridge@aol.com. Website: http://themusicbridge.com. **Contact:** David G. Powell, president. Music publisher and music supervision. Estab. 1992.
How to Contact *Only accepts material referred by a reputable industry source.* Does not return material. Responds in 2 months.

◙ THE MUSIC ROOM PUBLISHING GROUP

P.O. Box 219, Redondo Beach CA 90277. (310)316-4551. **Contact:** John Reed, president/owner. Music publisher and record producer. Estab. 1982. Pays standard royalty.
Affiliate(s) MRP (BMI).
How to Contact *Not accepting unsolicited material.*
Music Mostly **pop/rock/R&B** and **crossover**. Published "That Little Tattoo," "Mona Lisa" and "Sleepin' with an Angel" (singles by John E. Reed) from *Rock With An Attitude* (album), recorded by Rawk Dawg (rock), released 2002 on Music Room Productions®.

◙ MUST HAVE MUSIC (ASCAP/BMI)

P.O. Box 801181, Santa Clarita CA 91380-1181. (661)645-7618. Fax: (661)799-3732. E-mail: info@musthavemusic.com. Website: www.musthavemusic.com. **Contact:** Kenneth R. Klar, managing director. Music publisher and music library. Estab. 1990. Pays standard royalty.
Affiliate(s) Must Have More Music (ASCAP); Must Have Music (BMI).
How to contact Submit demo by mail. Unsolicited submissions are OK. Prefers CD with lyric sheet and cover letter. Does not return submissions. Responds in 2 months.
Film & TV Music supervisor: Ken Klar, managing director.
Music Mostly **pop/r&b, pop/country** and **rock**; also **AAA, adult contemporary,** and **contemporary Christian/ gospel**. Does not want instrumental music. "We only work with completed songs with lyric and vocal." Published "Come to the Table" (single by Ken Klar/Steve Massey) from *Worship Leader Magazine's Song Discovery, Vol. 26* (album), recorded by various artists, released 2002 on Worship Leader; "Fool" (single by Ken Klar) from *If You Want My Love* (album), recorded by Jennifer Young (pop/R&B), released 2002 on Independent; and "Blame It On My Heart" (single by Ken Klar/Steve Kirman) fom *Blame It On My Heart* (album), recorded by Steve Kirwan (adult contemporary), released 2001 on Independent.
Tips "Write what you know and what you believe. Then re-write it!"

⚑ ◙ NAKED JAIN RECORDS (ASCAP)

P.O. Box 4132, Palm Springs CA 92263-4132. (760)325-8663. Fax: (760)320-4305. E-mail: info@nakedjainrecords.com. Website: www.nakedjainrecords.com. **Contact:** Dena Banes, vice president/A&R. Music publisher, record company and record producer (Dey Martin). Estab. 1991. Publishes 40 songs/year; publishes 2 new songwriters/year. Staff size: 5. Pays standard royalty.
Affiliate(s) Aven Deja Music (ASCAP).
How to Contact *Write or call first and obtain permission to submit or to arrange personal interview.* Prefers cassette or CD with 3 songs, lyric sheet and cover letter. Does not return material. Responds in 2 weeks.
Film & TV Places 10 songs in TV/year. Music Supervisors: Dey Martin (alternative). Recently published "Yea

Right'' (single), written and recorded by Lung Cookie in Fox Sports TV; ''Just Ain't Me'' (single), written and recorded by Lung Cookie in ESPN-TV; and ''Speak Easy'' (single), written and recorded by Lung Cookie in ESPN-TV.

Music Mostly **alternative rock**. Does not want country.

Tips ''Write a good song.''

🌐 🔾 NERVOUS PUBLISHING

5 Sussex Crescent, Northolt, Middlesex UB5 4DL England. Phone: +44(020) 8423 7373. Fax: +44(020) 8423 7773. E-mail: nervous@compuserve.com. Website: www.nervous.co.uk. **Contact:** Roy Williams, owner. Music publisher, record company (Nervous Records) and record producer. MCPS, PRS and Phonographic Performance Ltd. Estab. 1979. Publishes 100 songs/year; publishes 25 new songwriters/year. Pays standard royalty; royalties paid directly to US songwriters.

• Nervous Publishing's record label, Nervous Records, is listed in the Record Companies section.

How to Contact Submit demo tape by mail. Unsolicited submissions are OK. Prefers cassette with 3-10 songs and lyric sheet. ''Include letter giving your age and mentioning any previously published material.'' SAE and IRC. Responds in 3 weeks.

Music Mostly **psychobilly**, **rockabilly** and **rock** (impossibly fast music—e.g.: Stray Cats but twice as fast); also **blues**, **country**, **R&B** and **rock** ('50s style). Published *Trouble* (album), recorded by Dido Bonneville (rockabilly); *Rockabilly Comp* (album), recorded by various artists; and *Nervous Singles Collection* (album), recorded by various artists, all on Nervous Records.

Tips ''Submit *no* rap, soul, funk—we want *rockabilly*.''

🔾 A NEW RAP JAM PUBLISHING

P.O. Box 683, Lima OH 45802. E-mail: just_chilling_2002@yahoo.com. Professional Managers: William Roach (rap, clean); James Milligan (country, 70s music, pop). **Contact:** A&R Dept. Music publisher and record company (New Experience/Grand Slam Records, Pump It Up Records, and Rough Edge Records). Estab. 1989. Publishes 30 songs/year; publishes 2-3 new songwriters/year. Hires staff songwriters. Staff size: 6. Pays standard royalty.

Affiliate(s) Party House Publishing (BMI), Creative Star Management, and Rough Edge Records.

How to Contact *Write first to arrange personal interview or submit demo tape by mail.* Unsolicited submissions are OK. Prefers cassette with 3-5 songs and lyric or lead sheet. Include SASE. Responds in up to weeks.

Music Mostly **R&B**, **pop**, **blues** and **rock/rap**; also **contemporary**, **gospel**, **country** and **soul**. Published ''Can't Play a Playa'' and ''Get Your Own'' (singles by David Fawcett) from *Enter the Mind* (album), recorded by Devious 01 (rap), released 2002 on Pump It Up Records; ''The Broken Hearted'' (single by Carl Milligan/James Milligan) from *The Final Chapter* (album), recorded by T.M.C. the milligan conection (R&B gospel), released 2003/2004 on New Experience/Pump It Up Records.

Tips ''We are seeking hit artists of the 1970s and 1980s who would like to be re-signed, as well as new talent and female solo artists. Send any available information supporting the group or act. We are a label that does not promote violence, drugs or anything that we feel is a bad example for our youth. Establish music industry contacts, write and keep writing and most of all believe in yourself. Use a good recording studio but be very professional. Just take your time and produce the best music possible. Sometimes you only get one listen. Make sure you place your best song on your demo first. This will increase your chances greatly. If you're the owner of your own small label and have a finished product, please send it. And if there is interest we will contact you. Also be on the lookout for our new blues label Rough Edge Records and Rough Edge Entertainment now reviewing material. Please be aware of the new sampling laws and laws for digital downloading. It is against the law. People are being jailed and fined for this act. Do your homework. Read the new digital downloading contracts carefully or seek legal help if need be. Good luck and thanks for considering our company.''

☑ 🔾 NEWBRAUGH BROTHERS MUSIC (ASCAP, BMI)

228 Morgan Lane, Berkeley Springs WV 25411-3475. (304)258-3656. E-mail: Nbtoys@verizon.net. **Contact:** John S. Newbraugh, owner. Music publisher, record company (NBT Records BMI/ASCAP). Estab. 1967. Publishes 124 songs/year. Publishes 14 new songwriters/year. Staff size: 1. Pays standard royalty.

Affiliates NBT Music (ASCAP) and Newbraugh Brothers Music (BMI).

How to Contact Submit demo tape by mail. Unsolicited submissions are OK. Prefers cassette or CD with any amount of songs, a lyric sheet and a cover letter. Include SASE. Responds in 6 weeks.

Music Mostly **rockabilly**, **hillbilly**, **folk** and **bluegrass**; also **rock**, **country**, and **gospel**. ''We will accept all genres of music except songs with vulgar language.'' Published ''Moonshine Stomp'' (single by Del Clark) from *Hot Rod Daddy* (album), recorded by The Rhythmatics (rockabilly), released 2003; ''Messin Around'' (single by Nic Nilsson) from *Don't Wear Me Out* (album), recorded by Uncle Nic and the Alternators (rock), released 2003; and ''Trainman'' (single by John Modaff) from *Ride The Train—Volume Three* (album), recorded by Good Enough (folk), released in 2004, all on NBT Records.

Tips "Find out if a publisher/record company has any special interest. NBT, for instance, is always hunting 'original' train songs. Our 'registered' trademark is a train and from time to time we release a compilation album of all train songs. We welcome all genres of music for this project."

�"N" ◯ NEWCREATURE MUSIC (BMI)

P.O. Box 1444, Hendersonville TN 37077-1444. (615)452-3234. E-mail: lmarkcom@bellsouth.net. **Contact:** Bill Anderson, Jr., president. Professional Manager: G.L. Score. Music publisher, record company, record producer (Landmark Communications Group) and radio and TV syndicator. Publishes 25 songs/year; publishes 2 new songwriters/year. Pays standard royalty.

Affiliate(s) Mary Megan Music (ASCAP).

How to Contact *Contact first and obtain permission to submit.* Prefers cassette or videocassette with 4-10 songs and lyric sheet. Include SASE. Responds in 6 weeks.

Music Mostly **country**, **gospel**, **jazz**, **R&B**, **rock** and **top 40/pop**. Published *Glory* and *Popcorn, Peanuts and Jesus* (albums by Harry Yates), both recorded by Joanne Cash Yates on Angel Too Records (gospel); and *Were You Thinkin' Of Me* (album), written and recorded by Jack Mosley on Landmark Records (country).

◐ NORTHWEST ALABAMA MUSIC PUBLISHING CO. (BMI)

3596 County Rd. 136, Lexington AL 35648. Phone/fax: (256)229-8814. E-mail: LampMusic@cs.com. Professional Managers: Erica Hand (country, soft rock); Kimberley Glover (gospel, R&B); D. Glover (rock, pop). Music Publisher and record company (Harmony House Records). Estab. 2000. Publishes 10 songs/year; publishes 2 new songwriters/year. Staff size: 3. Hires staff writers. Pays standard royalty.

Affiliate(s) Lexington Alabama Music Publishing (BMI).

How to Contact Submit demo tape by mail. Unsolicited submissions are OK. Prefers cassette or CD with 3 songs, a lyric sheet and cover letter. "If you send unsolicited materials please label it as such in correspondence. List the name of your manager or contact person and the phone number as well as address with SASE for response." Does not return material. Responds only if interested.

Music Mostly **country**, **pop** and **rock**; also **R&B**, **gospel** and **southern rock**. Does not want classical. Published "Let It Go" (single by Mark Terry), recorded by Mark Anthony (country); "Heirlooms" (single), written and recorded by Kellie Flippo (pop); and "Southern Girls" (single by Teena Hartsfield), recorded by Rex & the Rockets (R&B), all released 2000 on Harmony House Records.

Tips "Don't try to critique your own songs."

⟨img⟩ ◐ OLD SLOWPOKE MUSIC (BMI)

P.O. Box 52681, Tulsa OK 74152. (918)742-8087. E-mail: ryoung@cherrystreetrecords.com. Website: www.cher rystreetrecords.com. **Contact:** Steve Hickerson, Professional Manager. President: Rodney Young. Music publisher and record producer. Estab. 1977. Publishes 24-36 songs/year; publishes 2-3 new songwriters/year. Staff size: 2. Pays standard royalty.

How to Contact *Does not accept unsolicited submissions.*

Film & TV Places 1 song in film/year. Recently published "Samantha," written and recorded by George W. Carroll in *Samantha*.

Music Mostly **rock**, **country** and **R&B**; also **jazz**. Published *Promise Land* (album), written and recorded by Richard Neville on Cherry Street Records (rock).

Tips "Write great songs. We sign only artists who play an instrument, sing and write songs."

◯ ONTRAX COMPANIES (ASCAP)

P.O. Box 769, Crown Point IN 46308. (219)736-5815. **Contact:** Professional Manager. Music publisher and record producer. Estab. 1991. Publishes 30 songs/year; 7 new songwriters/year. Staff size: 5. Pays standard royalty.

How to Contact Submit demo tape by mail. Unsolicited submissions are OK. Prefers CD (but will accept cassette) with 1-6 songs. "Tapes and CDs should be mailed in as small a package as possible, preferrably in a small bubble mailer. All items must be labeled and bear the proper copyright notice. We listen to all submissions in the order they arrive. No phone calls please." Does not return submissions. Responds only if interested.

Music Mostly **pop/rock**, **country** and **crossover country**. Does not want heavy metal or rap. Published "(For The) Workin' Man" (single by Drasich/Leigh) from *County Line Road* (album), recorded by D&L Station (country rock), released 2004 on Canyonsongs; "On My Mind's Shelf" (single by E. Steaton/A. Lovington) from *Carousel* (album), recorded by Sounding Bored (pop/rock), released 2004 on Come Away Records; and "Open The Door" (single by L. Buggs/A. Forham/G. Cathramy) from *Five To Seven* (album), recorded by Twice Bitten (country), released 2004 on Onward Up Records.

Tips "Please do not include SASEs or response cards. We will not respond unless interested in publishing the song. You need just request permission to submit. Again, small packages please, 6×9 maximum."

Music Publishers

✪ ORCHID PUBLISHING (BMI)

Bouquet-Orchid Enterprises, P.O. Box 1335, Norcross GA 30091. Phone/fax: (770)339-9088. **Contact:** Bill Bohannon, president. Music publisher, record company, record producer (Bouquet-Orchid Enterprises) and artist management. Member: CMA, AFM. Publishes 10-12 songs/year; publishes 3 new songwriters/year. Pays standard royalty.

How to Contact Submit demo tape by mail. Unsolicited submissions are OK. Prefers cassette or CD with 3-5 songs and lyric sheet. "Send biographical information if possible—even a photo helps." Include SASE. Responds in 1 month.

Music Mostly **religious** ("Amy Grant, etc., contemporary gospel"); **country** ("Garth Brooks, Trisha Yearwood-type material"); and **top 100/pop** ("Bryan Adams, Whitney Houston-type material"). Published "Blue As Your Eyes" (single), written and recorded by Adam Day; "Spare My Feelings" (single by Clayton Russ), recorded by Terri Palmer; and "Trying to Get By" (single by Tom Sparks), recorded by Bandoleers, all on Bouquet Records.

✪ PEERMUSIC (ASCAP, BMI)

5358 Melrose Ave., Suite 400, Los Angeles CA 90038. (323)960-3400. Fax: (323)960-3410. Website: www.peermusic.com. Music publisher and artist development promotional label. Estab. 1928. Publishes 600 songs/year (worldwide); publishes 1-2 new songwriters/year. Hires staff songwriters. Royalty standard, but negotiable.

Affiliate(s) Peer Southern Organization (ASCAP) and Peer International Corporation (BMI).

How to Contact *"We do NOT accept unsolicited submissions. We only accept material through agents, attorneys and managers."* Prefers CD and lyric sheet. Does not return material. Responds in 6 weeks.

Music Mostly **pop**, **rock** and **R&B**. Published music by David Foster (writer/producer, pop); London Jones (writer/producer, R&B, pop) and bands Jimmies Chicken Shack, Joe 90, Shelly Peiken (writer, pop) and Tricky Stewart (R&B, writer/producer).

◻ JUSTIN PETERS MUSIC (BMI)

P.O. Box 271056, Nashville TN 37227. (615)269-8682. Fax: (615)269-8929. Website: http://songsfortheplanet.com. **Contact:** Justin Peters, president. Music publisher. Estab. 1981.

Affiliate(s) Platinum Planet Music, Tourmaline (BMI) and LITA Music (ASCAP).

How to Contact Submit demo by mail. Unsolicited submissions are OK. Prefers CD with 5 songs and lyric sheet. Does not return material. "Place code '2005' on each envelope submission."

Music Mostly **pop**, **reggae**, **country** and **comedy**. Published "Saved By Love" (single), recorded by Amy Grant on A&M Records; "Love's Not a Game" (single), recorded by Kashief Lindo on VP Records; "A Gift That She Don't Want" (single), recorded by Bill Engvall on Warner Brother Records; and "I Wanna Be That Man" (single), recorded by McKameys on Pamplin Records, all written by Justin Peters.

✪ PHOEBOB MUSIC

5181 Regent Dr., Nashville TN 37212. (615)832-4199. **Contact:** Phoebe Binkley.

Affiliate(s) BMI.

How to Contact We do not wand unsolicited submissions.

Music Country, Christian, and theatre.

✪ PIANO PRESS (ASCAP)

P.O. Box 85, Del Mar CA 92014-0085. (619)884-1401. Fax: (858)459-3376. E-mail: pianopress@aol.com. Website: www.pianopress.com. **Contact:** Elizabeth C. Axford, M.A., owner. Music publisher. Publishes songbooks & CD's for music students and teachers. Estab. 1998. Licenses 32-100 songs/year; publishes 1-24 new songwriters/year. Staff size: 5. Pays standard print music and/or mechanical royalty; composer retains rights to songs.

How to Contact *Write or call first and obtain permission to submit.* Prefers cassette or CD with 1-3 songs, lyric and lead sheet, cover letter and sheet music/piano arrangements. "Looking for children's songs for young piano students and arrangements of public domain folk songs of any nationality." Currently accepting submissions for *Kidtunes II.* Include SASE. Responds in 2-3 months.

Music Mostly **children's**, **folk songs** and **funny songs**; also **teaching pieces, piano arrangements, lead sheets with melody, chords and lyrics** and **songbooks**. Does not want commercial pop, R&B, etc. Published "I Can" (single by Tom Gardner) from *Kidtunes* (album), recorded by The Uncle Brothers (children's), released 2002 by Piano Press; "Rock & Roll Teachers" (single by Bob King) from *Kidtunes* (album), recorded by Bob King & Friends (children's), released 2002 by Piano Press; and "It Really Isn't Garbage" (single by Danny Einbender) from *Kidtunes* (album), recorded by Danny Eibende/Pete Seeger/et al. (children's), released 2002 by Piano Press.

Tips "Songs should be simple, melodic and memorable. Lyrics should be for a juvenile audience and well-crafted."

PLATINUM PLANET MUSIC, INC. (BMI)

2831 Dogwood Place, Nashville TN 37204. (615)269-8682. Fax: (615)269-8929. Website: http://songsfortheplan et.com. **Contact:** Justin Peters, president. Music publisher. Estab. 1997.

Affiliate(s) Justin Peters Music, Tourmaline (BMI) and LITA Music (ASCAP).

How to Contact Submit demo by mail. Unsolicited submissions are OK. Prefers CD with 5 songs and lyric sheet. Does not return material. "Place code '2005' on each envelope submission."

Music Mostly **r&b, dance** and **country**; also represents many Christian artists/writers. Published "Happy Face" (single by Dez Dickerson/Jordan Dickerson), recorded by Squirt on Absolute Records; "Welcome To My Love" (single by Mike Hunter), recorded by Kyndl on PPMI; "Love's Not A Game" (single), written and recorded by Kashief Lindo on Heavybeat Rewards; "Dancing Singing" (single by A. Craig/Justin Peters) recorded by Dan Burda on Independent; and "Loud" (single), written and recorded by These Five Down on Absolute Records.

☑ ☑ POLLYBYRD PUBLICATIONS LIMITED (ASCAP, BMI, SESAC)

P.O. Box 261488, Encino CA 91426. (818)506-8533. Fax: (818)506-8534. E-mail: pplzmi@aol.com. Website: www.pplzmi.com. Branch office: 333 Proctor St., Carson City NV 89703. (818)884-1946. Fax: (818)882-6755. **Contact:** Dakota Hawk, vice president. Professional Managers: Cisco Blue (country, pop, rock); Tedford Steele (hip-hop, R&B). Music publisher, record company (PPL Entertainment) and Management firm (Sa'mall Management). Estab. 1979. Publishes 100 songs/year; publishes 25-40 new songwriters/year. Hires staff writers. Pays standard royalty.

Affiliate(s) Kellijai Music (ASCAP), Pollyann Music (ASCAP), Ja'Nikki Songs (BMI), Velma Songs International (BMI), Lonnvanness Songs (SESAC), PPL Music (ASCAP), Zettitalia Music, Butternut Music (BMI), Zett Two Music (ASCAP), Plus Publishing and Zett One Songs (BMI).

How to Contact *Write first and obtain permission to submit*. No phone calls. Prefers cassette or CD videocassette with 4 songs and lyric and lead sheet. Include SASE. Responds in 2 months.

Music Published "Believe" (single by J. Jarrett/S. Cuseo) from *Time* (album), recorded by Lejenz (pop), released 2001 on PRL/Credence; *Rainbow Gypsy Child* (album), written and recorded by Riki Hendrix (rock), released 2001 on PRL/Sony; and "What's Up With That" (single by Brandon James/Patrick Bouvier) from *Outcast* (album), recorded by Condottieré (hip-hop), released 2001 on Bouvier.

Tips "Make those decisions—are you really a songwriter? Are you prepared to starve for your craft? Do you believe in delayed gratification? Are you commercial or do you write only for yourself? Can you take rejection? Do you want to be the best? If so, contact us—if not, keep your day job."

☑ PORPOISEFUL PUBLISHING/KADALANA MUSIC

56 Music Square W., Nashville TN 37203. (615)320-7555. Fax: (615)320-0007.

☑ PORTAGE MUSIC (BMI)

16634 Gannon W., Rosemount MN 55068. (952)432-5737. E-mail: lmlp34@juno.com. President: Larry LaPole. Music publisher. Publishes 5-20 songs/year. Pays standard royalty.

How to Contact *Does not accept unsolicited submissions.*

Music Mostly **country** and **country rock**. Published "Lost Angel," "Think It Over" and "Congratulations to Me" (by L. Lapole), all recorded by Trashmen on Sundazed.

Tips "Keep songs short, simple and upbeat with positive theme."

☑ ☐ PREJIPPIE MUSIC GROUP (BMI)

P.O. Box 816, Van Buren Twp. MI 48152. E-mail: prejippie@comcast.com. Website: www.prejippie.com. Professional Manager: Victoria Henderson. **Contact:** Bruce Henderson, president. Music publisher, record company (PMG Records) and record producer (PMG Productions). Estab. 1990. Publishes 50-75 songs/year; publishes 2-3 new songwriters/year. Hires staff writers. Staff size: 3. Pays standard royalty.

How to Contact Submit demo tape by mail. Unsolicited submissions are OK. Prefers cassette or CD with 3-4 songs and lyric sheet. "No phone calls please." Include SASE. Responds in 6 weeks.

Music Mostly **alternative R&B, alternative rock, techno/house** and **experimental**. Does not want country, gospel, show tunes or lyrics only. Published "Do What I Can Do Right" (single), written and recorded by Bourgeoisie Paper Jam (funk/rock); and "2001 Bass Blizzard" (single), written and recorded by Tony Webb (jazz) all on PMG Records.

Tips "We're always looking for new approaches to traditional genres. We want to hear vocals, lyrics and music that is passionate and takes a chance, but still keeps hooks that are solid."

☐ PRESCRIPTION COMPANY (BMI)

Box 222249, Great Neck NY 11021. (415)553-8540. Fax: (415)553-8541. E-mail: medmike525@aol.com. President: David F. Gasman. Vice President of Sales: Bruce Brennan. Vice President of Finance: Robert Murphy. Music publisher and record producer. Staff size: 7. Pays standard royalty.

• Also see the listing for The Prescription Co. in the Record Producers section of this book.

How to Contact *Write or call first and obtain permission to submit.* Prefers cassette with any number of songs and lyric sheet. ''Send all submissions with SASE (or no returns).'' Responds in 1 month.

Music Mostly **bluegrass**, **blues**, **children's** and **country**, **dance-oriented**; also **easy listening**, **folk**, **jazz**, **MOR**, **progressive**, **R&B**, **rock**, **soul** and **top 40/pop**. Published ''The World's Most Dangerous Man,'' ''Here Comes Trouble'' and ''Automated People'' (singles by D.F. Gasman) from *Special EP No. 1* (album), all recorded by Medicine Mike (rock), released 2003 on Prescription.

Tips ''Songs should be good and written to last. Forget fads—we want songs that'll sound as good in ten years as they do today. Organization, communication and exploration of form are as essential as message (and sincerity matters, too).''

✓ ☒ ◑ THEODORE PRESSER CO. (ASCAP, BMI, SESAC)

588 N. Gulph Rd., King of Prussia PA 19406. (610)592-1222. Fax: (610)592-1229. E-mail: presser@presser.com. Website: www.presser.com. **Contact:** Laurie Albert, Editorial Assistant. Music publisher. Estab. 1783. Publishes 200 songs/year; publishes 3 new songwriters/year. Staff size: 51. Pays standard royalty; 10% on print.

Affiliate(s) Theodore Presser, Beekman, Oliver Ditson, John Church, Elkan-Vogel (ASCAP), Merion Music (BMI) and Mercury Music (SESAC).

How to Contact Submit music ms by mail. Tape or CD can supplement score. Unsolicited submissions are OK. Prefers cassette and score. Include SASE. Responds in 2 months.

Film & TV Places 12 songs in film and 14 songs in TV/year.

Music Mostly **serious concert music**, **sacred and secular choral** and **educational music**. Does not want popular music.

Tips ''Write honest, high quality music and send it to us, following our submission guidelines which you can receive via e-mail or on our website.''

◑ PRITCHETT PUBLICATIONS (BMI)

P.O. Box 725, Daytona Beach FL 32114-0725. (904)252-4848. Fax: (904)252-7402. E-mail: CharlesVickers@USA Link.com. Website: www.ZYWorld.com/CharlesVickers. **Contact:** Charles Vickers, Vice President. Music publisher and record company (King of Kings Record Co., Pickwick/Mecca/International Records). Estab. 1975. Publishes 21 songs/year; publishes 12 new songwriters/year.

Affiliate(s) Alison Music (ASCAP), Charles H. Vickers Music Associates (BMI) and QuickSilver Encrease Records Inc.

How to Contact *Write first and obtain permission to submit.* Prefers cassette with 6 songs and lyric or lead sheet. Does not return material.

Music Mostly **gospel**, **rock-disco** and **country**.

✓ ☒ ○ QUARK, INC.

P.O. Box 7320, FDR Station, New York NY 10150. (212)741-2888. Fax: (845)708-0113. E-mail: pactimeco@aol.c om. **Contact:** Curtis Urbina, manager. Professional Manager: Michelle Harris (alternative/pop). Music publisher, record company (Quark Records) and record producer (Curtis Urbina). Estab. 1984. Publishes 12 songs/year; 2 new songwriters/year. Staff size: 4. Pays standard royalty.

Affiliate(s) Quarkette Music (BMI), Freedurb Music (ASCAP), Pacific Time Entertainment and Quark Records.

How to Contact Prefers CD only with 2 songs. No cassettes. Include SASE. Responds in 2 months.

Film & TV Places 10 songs in film/year. Music Supervisor: Curtis Urbina (pop/dance).

Music Mostly **pop** and **dance music** (all genres). Does not want anything short of a hit. Published ''Keep on Keeping On'' (single by M. Serio) from *Entertainers* (album), recorded by Belmondo (pop), released 2002 on Pacific Time Entertainment; ''Your Lucky Day'' (single by K. Katahgiotis) from *Your Lucky Day* (album), recorded by Kimon (pop/rock), released 2002 on Ultrascene Entertainment; and ''Throwback'' (single by E. Cohen) from *Party Time* (album), recorded by DJ Strobe (dance), released 2002 on Quark Records.

◑ QUEEN ESTHER MUSIC PUBLISHERS (ASCAP)

449 N. Vista St., Los Angeles CA 90036. (323)653-0693. E-mail: unclelenny@aol.com. **Contact:** Len Weisman, owner. Record producer, personal manager, music publisher. Estab. 1980. Publishes 30-50 songs/year.

• Also see the listings for Audio Music Publishers in the Music Publishers section of this book; Parliament Records in the Record Companies section and The Weisman Production Group in this section of this book.

How to Contact Send demo CD or cassette with 3-10 songs. Include SASE. We only return in prepaid large envelopes.

Music Mostly **r&b**, **soul**, **rap** and **2nd gospel**. No rock or metal. Now working on ''E'morey'' CD; ''Jusuan'' CD; and ''Jewel With Love'' CD.

🌐 ◌ R.T.L. MUSIC

White House Farm, Shropshire TF9 4HA England. Phone: (01630)647374. Fax: (01630)647612. **Contact:** Tanya Woof, international A&R manager. Professional Managers: Ron Dickson (rock/rock 'n roll); Katrine LeMatt (MOR/dance); Xavier Lee (heavy metal); Tanya Lee (classical/other types). Music publisher, record company (Le Matt Music) and record producer. Estab. 1971. Publishes approximately 30 songs/year. Pays standard royalty.

Affiliate(s) Lee Music (publishing), Swoop Records, Grenouille Records, Check Records, Zarg Records, Pogo Records, R.T.F.M. (all independent companies).

How to Contact Submit demo tape or CD by mail. Unsolicited submissions are OK. Prefers CD, cassette, MDisc or DVD (also VHS 625/PAL system videocassette) with 1-3 songs and lyric and lead sheets; include still photos and bios. "Make sure name and address are on CD or cassette." Send IRC. Responds in 6 weeks.

Music All types. Published "Time Bombs" (single by Phill Dunn), recorded by Orphan (rock), released 2000 on Pogo; *Phobias* (album), recorded by Orphan (rock), released 2000 on Pogo; and *The Best Of* (album), recorded by Emmitt Till (rock/blues), released 2000 on Swoop.

🖼 ⊘ RAINBOW MUSIC CORP. (ASCAP)

45 E. 66 St., New York NY 10021. (212)988-4619. Fax: (212)861-9079. **Contact:** Fred Stuart, vice president. Music publisher. Estab. 1990. Publishes 25 songs/year. Staff size: 2. Pays standard royalty.

Affiliate(s) Tri-Circle (ASCAP).

How to Contact *Only accepts material referred by a reputable industry source.* Prefers CD with 2 songs and lyric sheet. Include SASE. Responds in 1 week.

Film & TV Published "You Wouldn't Lie To An Angel, Would Ya?" (single by Diane Lampert/Paul Overstreet) from *Lady of the Evening* (album), recorded by Benté Boe (country), released 2003 on Mega International Records; "Gonna Give Lovin' A Try" (single by Cannonball Adderley/Diane Lampert/Nat Adderley) from *The Axelrod Chronicles* (album), recorded by Randy Crawford (jazz), released 2003 on Fantasy Records; and "Gonna Give Lovin' A Try" (single by Cannonball Adderley/Diane Lampert/Nat Adderley) from *Day Dreamin'* (album), recorded by Laverne Butler (jazz), released 2002 on Chesky Records.

Music Mostly **pop**, **R&B** and **country**; also **jazz**.

◌ RED SUNDOWN MUSIC

P.O. Box 609, Pleasant View TN 37212. (615)746-0844. Fax: (615)746-2771. **Contact:** Ruby Perry, Victory Miller.

Affiliates BMI.

How to Contact Does not accept unsolicited submissions. Submit CD and cover letter. Does not return submissions.

Music **country**, **rock**, and **pop**. Does not want rap or hip-hop. Published "Cowboy Cadillac" (single by Denise Benson and Paul Stanich) from *She Can Run* (album), recorded by Pamela Sue Wright (country), released in 1998 on Red Sundown Records.

📺 ⊘ REN ZONE MUSIC (ASCAP)

P.O. Box 3153, Huntington Beach CA 92605. (714)596-6582. Fax: (714)596-6577. E-mail: renzone@socal.rr.com. **Contact:** Keith Wolzinger, president. Music publisher. Estab. 1998. Publishes 14 songs/year; publishes 2 new songwriters/year. Staff size: 2. Pays standard royalty.

● This company won a Parents Choice 1998 Silver Honor Shield.

How to Contact *Does not accept unsolicited submissions.*

Music Mostly **klezmer** and **children's**. Does not want rap, punk or holiday music. Published "Walk Like the Animals" (single by Dayle Lusk) from *Tumble 'n' Tunes* (album), recorded by Dayle Lusk/Danielle Ganya (children's); "Surf Town" (single by Dayle Lusk) from *City Song at Huntington Beach* (album), recorded by Lisa Worshaw (pop); and "Snowboardin' (single by Stephanie Donatoni) from *Sea Cliff Tunes* (album), recorded by Lisa Worshaw (children's), all released 2000 on Ren Zone. Recent klezmer releases include *Glazele Wine* and *Classic American Klezmer.*

Tips "Submit well-written lyrics that convey important concepts to kids on good quality demos with easy to understand vocals."

✓ ⊘ RHINESTONE COWBOY MUSIC (ASCAP)

P.O. Box 22971, Nashville TN 37202. (615)554-1293.

Affiliate(s) ASCAP.

How to Contact Contact first and obtain permission to submit a demo. Submit demo CD with 5 songs. Responds only if interested.

⊠ ◯ RHYTHMS PRODUCTIONS (ASCAP)

P.O. Box 34485, Los Angeles CA 90034. **Contact:** Ruth White, president. Music and multimedia publisher. Member NARAS. Publishes 4 titles/year. Pays negotiable royalty.

Affiliate(s) Tom Thumb Music.

How to Contact Submit tape with letter outlining background in educational children's music. Include SASE. Responds in 2 months.

Music "We're only interested in **children's songs** and interactive programs that have educational value. Our materials are sold in schools and homes, so artists/writers with an 'edutainment' background would be most likely to understand our requirements." Published "Professor Whatzit®" series including "Adventures of Professor Whatzit & Carmine Cat" (cassette series for children); "Musical Math," "Musical Reading" and "Theme Songs."

◯ RONDOR MUSIC INTERNATIONAL/ALMO/IRVING MUSIC, A UNIVERSAL MUSIC GROUP COMPANY

2440 Sepulveda Blvd., Suite 119, Los Angeles CA 90064. (310)235-4800. Fax: (310)235-4801. Website: www.um pg.com/spotlight/dsp_catalog.asp?ID=483. Creative Staff Assistant: Alana Downey. Nashville office: 1904 Adelicia Ave., Nashville TN 37212. (615)321-0820. Fax: (615)327-1018. Music publisher. Estab. 1965.

Affiliates Almo Music Corp. (ASCAP) and Irving Music, Inc. (BMI).

How to Contact *Does not accept unsolicited submissions.*

◯ RUSTRON MUSIC PUBLISHERS (BMI)

1156 Park Lane, West Palm Beach FL 33417-5957. (561)686-1354. E-mail: rmp_wmp@bellsouth.net. **Contact:** Sheelah Adams, office administrator. Professional Managers: Rusty Gordon (adult contemporary, acoustic, electric, New Age fusions, children's, cabaret); Ron Caruso (all styles); Davilyn Whims (folk fusions, country, blues). Music publisher, record company, management firm and record producer (Rustron Music Productions). Estab. 1972. Publishes 100-150 songs/year; publishes 10-20 new songwriters/year. Staff size: 9. Pays standard royalty.

Affiliate(s) Whimsong Publishing (ASCAP).

How to Contact Submit demo tape or CD by mail. Cover letter should explain reason for submitting and what songwriter needs from Rustron-Whimsong. Unsolicited submissions are OK. For freelance songwriters we prefer CD or cassette with 1-3 songs and typed lyric sheets. For performing songwriters we prefer CD with up to 15 songs. "Clearly label your tape container or jewel box. We don't review songs on websites." SASE required for all correspondence. No exceptions. Responds in 4 months.

Music Mostly **pop** (ballads, blues, theatrical, cabaret), **progressive country** and **folk/rock**; also **R&B** and **New Age** instrumental fusions with classical, jazz or pop themes and women's music. Does not publish rap, hip-hop, new wave, youth music, hard rock, heavy metal or punk. Published "Jah Jah Jamaica" (single) from *Jah Jah Jamaica* (album), written and recorded by Jeremy White & Kalliope (Yankee reggae), released 2003 on Whimsong; "Everglades Everlasting" (single) from *Everglades Everlasting* (album), written and recorded by Song On A Whim (children's music), released 2003 on Rustron Records; and "Banyon Tree Blues" (single) from *Everglades Everlasting* (album), written and recorded by The Dinner Key Boys (folk-rock blues), released 2004 on Whimsong Records.

Tips "Accepting performing songwriter's CD for full product review of all songs on CD. Write strong hooks. Keep song length 3½ minutes or less. Avoid predictability—create original lyric themes. Tell a story. Compose definitive melody. Tune in to the trends and fusions indicative of commercially viable new music for the new millennium. Songs reviewed for single-song marketing must be very carefully crafted."

◯ SALT WORKS MUSIC (ASCAP, BMI)

80 Highland Dr., Jackson OH 45640-2074. (740)286-1514 or (740)286-6561. Professional Managers: Jeff Elliott (country/gospel); Mike Morgan (country). Music publisher and record producer (Mike Morgan). Staff size: 2. Pays standard royalty.

Affiliate(s) Salt Creek Music (ASCAP) and Sojourner Music (BMI).

How to Contact Submit demo by mail. Unsolicited submissions are OK. Prefers cassette or CD. Include SASE. Responds in 2 weeks.

Music Mostly **country**, **gospel** and **pop**. Does not want rock, jazz or classical. Published "The Tracks You Left On Me" (single by Ed Bruce/Jeff Elliott/MikeMorgan) and "Truth Is I'm A Liar" (single by Jeff Elliott/Mike Morgan) from *This Old Hat* (album), recorded by Ed Bruce (country), released 2002 on Sony/Music Row Talent.

◯ TIM SCOTT MUSIC GROUP (BMI)

The Associate Group, L.L.C., P.O. Box 91079, Springfield MA 01139. (866)214-1286, ext. 100 (toll free). Fax: (509)351-4379. E-mail: simpleandsafe@aol.com. **Contact:** Timothy Scott, president. Music publisher and record company (Keeping It Simple and Safe). Estab. 1993. Publishes 20-50 songs/year. Staff size: 20. Hires staff writers. Pays standard royalty.

Affiliates Tim Scott Music (ASCAP).

• Also see the listing for Night Owl Records (formerly Keeping It Simple & Safe) in the Record Companies section of this book.

How to Contact Submit demo tape by mail. Unsolicited submissions are OK. Prefers cassette with 3-5 songs and lyric sheet. Include SASE. Responds in 3 months.

Music Mostly **R&B** and **pop**; also **country**, **rock** and **gospel**. Published ''By the Way'' (single), written and recorded by Larry ''TCP'' Smith (top 40), released 2002 on Hurricane Records; ''Without You'' (single by Sammy Jones/Robert Johnson), from *Distant* (album), recorded by Soft Touch (R&B), released 2002 on Night Owl Records; and ''My Heart Beats (For You)'' (single by Ann Jackson/William Jackson) from *Heart to Heart* (album), recorded by Ann Jackson (country), released 2002 on Night Owl Records.

Tips Always send your best material first.

◒ SEGAL'S PUBLICATIONS (BMI)

P.O. Box 507, Newton MA 02159. (617)969-6196. **Contact:** Charles Segal. Music publisher and record producer (Segal's Productions). Estab. 1963. Publishes 80 songs/year; publishes 6 new songwriters/year. Pays standard royalty.

Affilate(s) Charles Segal's Publications (BMI) and Charles Segal's Music (SESAC).

How to Contact Submit demo tape by mail. Unsolicited submissions are OK. Prefers CD or VHS videocassette with 3 songs and lyric or lead sheet. Does not return material. Responds only if interested.

Music Mostly **rock**, **pop** and **country**; also **R&B**, **MOR** and **children's songs**. Published ''A Time to Care'' (by Brilliant/Segal), recorded by Rosemary Wills (MOR); ''Go to Bed'' (by Colleen Segal), recorded Susan Stark (MOR); and ''Only In Dreams'' (by Chas. Segal), recorded by Rosemary Wills (MOR), all on Spin Records.

Tips ''Besides making a good demo cassette, include a lead sheet of music—words, melody line and chords. Put your name and phone number on CD.''

◒ SELLWOOD PUBLISHING (BMI)

170 N. Maple, Fresno CA 93702. Phone/fax: (559)255-1717. E-mail: tracsell@aol.com. **Contact:** Stan Anderson, owner. Music publisher, record company (TRAC Record Co.) and record producer. Estab. 1972. Publishes 10 songs/year; publishes 3 new songwriters/year. Pays standard royalty.

• Also see the listings for Trac Record Co. in the Record Companies and Record Producers sections of this book.

How to Contact Submit demo tape—unsolicited submissions are OK. Prefers cassette, CD or VHS videocassette with 2 songs and lyric sheet. Include SASE. Responds in 3 weeks. ''Submit professional studio demos only.''

Music Mostly **traditional country**, **southern gospel** and **country**. Does not want rock 'n' roll, rap or heavy metal. Published ''City Days & Country Nights'' (single by Jon Jensen) from *Back to Country* (album); ''Sweet Deliverance'' (single by H.C. ''Chuck'' House/Mary Miller) from *Back to Country* (album); and ''Headed Right Out The Wrong Door'' (single by Johnny Spears) from *Back to Country* (album), all recorded by H.C. ''Chuck'' House (country), released 2004 on TRAC Records.

Tips ''We're looking for all styles of country, especially uptempo dance types. A good storyline is important.''

◒ SEVENS INTERNATIONAL (ASCAP)/SEVENTH NOTE MUSIC (BMI)

23 Music Square E., Suite 400, Nashville TN 37203. **Contact:** Mike Stanglin.

✓ ◒ SHAWNEE PRESS, INC.

P.O. Box 1250, Marshalls Creek PA 18335. (570)476-0550. Fax: (570)476-1250. (570)476-0550. Fax: (570)476-5247. E-mail: shawnee-info@shawneepress.com. Website: www.ShawneePress.com. **Contact:** Cherie Troester, Editorial Assistant. Director of Church Music Publications (sacred choral music): Joseph M. Martin. Director of School Music Publications (secular choral music): Greg Gilpin. Professional Managers: Patricia Thor Straten-Mohr (Mark Foster Music Division); Ed Esposito (instrumental, no strings); David Angerman (handbell music); Joseph Martin (piano-sacred only). Music publisher. Estab. 1917. Publishes 150 songs/year. Staff size: 35. Pays negotiable royalty.

Affiliate(s) GlorySound, Harold Flammer Music, Mark Foster Music, Wide World Music, Concert Works.

How to Contact Submit manuscript. Unsolicited submissions are OK. See website for guidelines. Prefers manuscript; recording required for instrumental submissions; recordings optional for choral submissions. Include SASE. Responds in 4 months. ''No unsolicited musicals or cantatas.''

Music Mostly **church/liturgical**, **educational choral** and **instrumental**. No musicals or contatas.

Tips ''Submission guidelines appear on our website.''

☑ ⛶ ◷ SHU'BABY MONTEZ MUSIC

P.O. Box 28816, Philadelphia PA 19151. (215)473-5527. E-mail: shubabyschuler@yahoo.com. Website: http://smm.indiegroup.com. **Contact:** Leroy Schuler, president. Music publisher. Estab. 1986. Publishes 25 songs/year; publishes 10 new songwriters/year. Pays standard royalty.

• Also see the listing for Shu'Baby Montez Music in the Record Producers section of this book.

How to Contact *Contact first and obtain permission to submit.* Prefers CD with 3 songs and lyric sheet. Include SASE. Responds in 5 weeks.

Film & TV Places 3 songs in film/year.

Music Mostly **R&B**, **dance**, **hip-hop** and **pop**. Does not want country. Published "Special Lady" (single by Shubaby Schuler/Saleem Jefferson), recorded by Saleem (R&B); "Who Knowz" (single), written and recorded by Gary Lloyd (R&B); and "Money" (single by Tony Bennett/Shubaby Schuler), recorded by Tony Bennett (R&B), all released 2004 on Urban Logic Records.

Tips "Keep the music simple, but with nice changes. Don't be afraid to use altered chords."

⛶ ⊕ SIEGEL MUSIC COMPANIES

Rindermarkt 16, 80331, Munich Germany. Phone: +49-89-29069-0. Fax: +49-89-29060-277. E-mail: jupiter-records@writeme.com. Website: www.jupiter-records.de. President (pop/MOR): Ralph Siegel. Managing Director (pop/MOR): Joachim Neubauer. Professional Manager (rock/heavy metal): Walter Wicha. Professional Manager (pop/dance): Maria Glauben. Professional Manager (pop/MOR): Helfard V. Schenckendorff. Professional Manager (pop/dance): Sonja Jeschke. Music publisher, record company, (Jupiter Records and 69-Records) and record producer. Estab. 1948. GEMA. Publishes 1,500 songs/year; publishes 50 new songwriters/year. Hires staff songwriters. Pays 60% according to the rules of GEMA.

Affiliate(s) Sounds of Jupiter, Inc. (USA), Gobian Music (ASCAP) and Symphonie House Music (ASCAP).

How to Contact Submit demo tape or CD by mail. Unsolicited submissions are OK. SAE and IRC. Responds in 2 months.

Music Mostly **pop**, **rock** and **dance**; also **soul** and **black music**. Published "Privacy" (by Ralph Siegel/John O'Flynn), recorded by Bianca Shomburg (pop); and "Abrakadabra" (by Ralph Siegel/Nicole Seibert), recorded by Nicole, both on Jupiter; and "Dormi" (by Giacomo Puccini), recorded by Albano Carrisi on WEA Records (classical).

Tips "If you believe that your song could be a #1 in the charts, please submit it!"

◐ SILICON MUSIC PUBLISHING CO. (BMI)

222 Tulane St., Garland TX 75043-2239. President: Gene Summers. Vice President: Deanna L. Summers. Public Relations: Steve Summers. Music publisher and record company (Front Row Records). Estab. 1965. Publishes 10-20 songs/year; publishes 2-3 new songwriters/year. Pays standard royalty.

• Also see the listing for Front Row Records in the Record Companies section of this book.

How to Contact Submit demo tape by mail. Unsolicited submissions are OK. Prefers cassette with 1-2 songs. Does not return material. Responds ASAP.

Music Mostly **rockabilly** and **'50s material**; also **old-time blues/country** and **MOR**. Published "Almost Persuaded," "Someone Somewhere," and "Who Stole The Marker" (singles) all recorded by Gene Summers on Crystal Clear Records (rockabilly). Also publishing "I'm Gonna Find Me Some Neon" (b/w); and "Mr. Radio Face" (singles), written and recorded by Joe Hardin Brown, released 2002 on Mister Rock Records. New CD to be released in 2002 with 10 newly published Silicon songs.

Tips "Hear our latest published songs by clicking on to: mp3.com/shawnsummers. We are very interested in '50s rock and rockabilly *original masters* for release through overseas affiliates. If you are the owner of any '50s masters, contact us first! We have releases in Holland, Switzerland, England, Belgium, France, Sweden, Norway and Australia. We have the market if you have the tapes! Our staff writers include James McClung, Gary Mears (original Casuals), Robert Clark, Dea Summers, Shawn Summers, Joe Hardin Brown, Bill Becker and Dan Edwards."

⛶ ◷ SILVER BLUE MUSIC/OCEANS BLUE MUSIC

3940 Laurel Canyon Blvd., Suite 441, Studio City CA 91604. (818)980-9588. E-mail: jdiamond20@aol.com. **Contact:** Joel Diamond, president. Music publisher and record producer (Joel Diamond Entertainment). Estab. 1971. Publishes 50 songs/year. Pays standard royalty.

How to Contact *Does not accept unsolicited material.* "No tapes returned."

Film & TV Places 4 songs in film and 6 songs in TV/year.

Music Mostly **pop** and **R&B**; also **rap**, **classical**. Does not want country or jazz. Published "After the Lovin" (by Bernstein/Adams), recorded by Engelbert Humperdinck; "This Moment in Time" (by Alan Bernstein/Ritchie Adams), recorded by Engelbert Humperdinck. Other artists include David Hasselhoff, Kaci (Curb Records), Ike Turner, Andrew Dice Clay, Gloria Gaynor, Tony Orlando, Katie Cassidy and Vaneza.

⊕ ☑ SINUS MUSIK PRODUKTION, ULLI WEIGEL

Geitnerweg 30a, D-12209, Berlin Germany. +49-30-7159050. Fax: +49-30-71590522. E-mail: ulli.weigel@arcor
.de. Website: www.ulli-weigel.de. **Contact:** Ulli Weigel, owner. Music publisher, record producer and screen-
writer. Member: GEMA, GVL. Estab. 1976. Publishes 20 songs/year; publishes 6 new songwriters/year. Staff
size: 3. Pays standard royalty.
Affiliate(s) Sinus Musikverlag H.U. Weigel GmbH.
How to Contact Submit demo tape or CD by mail. Unsolicited submissions are OK. Prefers cassette or CD-R
with up to 10 songs and lyric sheets. Responds in 2 months. "If material should be returned, please send 2
International Reply Coupons (IRC) for cassettes and 3 for a CD. No stamps."
Music Mostly **rock**, **pop** and **New Age**; also **background music for movies**. Published "Simple Story" (single),
recorded by MAANAM on RCA (Polish rock); *Die Musik Maschine* (album by Klaus Lage), recorded by CWN
Productions on Hansa Records (pop/German).
Tips "Take more time working on the melody than on the instrumentation. I am also looking for master-quality
recordings for non-exclusive release on my label (and to use them as soundtracks for TV and movie scripts I
am working on)."

☑ SIZEMORE MUSIC (BMI)

P.O. Box 210314, Nashville TN 37221. (615)356-3453. E-mail: gary@sizemoremusic.com. Website: www.sizem
oremusic.com. Contact: Gary Sizemore. Music publisher, record company (The Gas Co.) and record producer
(G.L. Rhine). Estab. 1960. Publishes 5 songs/year; 1 new songwriter/year. Pays standard royalty.
How to Contact Submit demo tape by mail. Unsolicited submissions are OK. Prefers CD, cassette or VHS
videocassette with lyric sheets. Does not return material. Responds in 2 weeks.
Music Mostly **soul** and **R&B**; also **blues**, **pop** and **country**. Published "Liquor and Wine" and "The Wind,"
written and recorded by K. Shackleford on Heart Records (country); and "She's Tuff" (by Jerry McCain),
recorded by The Fabulous Thunderbirds on Chrysalis Records (blues).

☑ ☑ SME PUBLISHING GROUP (ASCAP/BMI)

2375 County Rd. 1211, Blanchard OK 73010. (405)392-3421. Fax: (405)392-3421. E-mail: smemusic@juno.com.
Professional Managers: Cliff Shelder (southern gospel); Sharon Kinard (country gospel). Music publisher. Estab.
1994. Publishes 6 songs/year; publishes 2 new songwriters/year. Staff size: 2. Pays standard royalty.
Affiliates Touch of Heaven Music (ASCAP) and SME Music (BMI).
How to Contact Submit demo tape by mail. Unsolicited submissions are OK. Prefers cassette or CD/CDR with
3 songs and lyric sheet. Make sure tapes and CDs are labeled and include song title, writer's name and phone
number. Does not return material. Responds only if interested.
Music Mostly **Southern gospel**, **country gospel** and **Christian country**. Does not want Christian rap, rock and
roll, and hard-core country. Released "Miracle For You" (single by Mike Spanhanks) from *In God We Trust*
(album), recorded by Living Sacrifice (southern gospel), released 2003 on Zion; and "Come See A Man" (single
by Mike Spanhanks) from *Keep Your Eyes on The Master* (album), recorded by The Duvalls (southern gospel),
released 2004 on Cross & Crown.
Tips "Always submit good quality demos. Never give up."

☑ ☑ SONY/ATV MUSIC PUBLISHING

(formerly Sony Tree International), 8 Music Square W., Nashville TN 37203. (615)726-8300. Fax: (615)242-
3441. **Santa Monica:** 2100 Colorado Ave., Santa Monica CA 90404. (310)449-2100. **New York:** 550 Madison
Ave., 18th Floor, New York NY 10022. (212)833-8000. Website: www.sonyatv.com.
How to Contact *Sony/ATV Music does not accept unsolicited submissions.*

☑ ☑ SOUND CELLAR MUSIC

703 N. Brinton Ave., Dixon IL 61021. (815)288-2900. E-mail: president@cellarrecords.com. Website: www.cella
rrecords.com. **Contact:** Todd Joos (country, pop, Christian), president. Professional Managers: James Miller
(folk, adult contemporary); Mike Thompson (metal, hard rock, alternative). Music publisher, record company
(Sound Cellar Records), record producer and recording studio. Estab. 1987. Publishes 15-25 songs/year. Publishes 5 or 6 new songwriters/year. Staff size: 7. Pays standard royalty.
How to Contact Submit demo CD by mail. Unsolicited submissions are OK. Prefers CD with 3 or 4 songs and
lyric sheet. Does not return material. "We contact by phone in 3-4 weeks only if we want to work with the
artist."
Music Mostly **metal**, **country** and **rock**; also **pop** and **blues**. Published "Problem of Pain" (single by Shane
Sowers) from *Before the Machine* (album), recorded by Junker Jorg (alternative metal/rock), released 2000;
"Vaya Baby" (single by Joel Ramirez) from *It's About Time* (album), recorded by Joel Ramirez and the All-

Stars (latin/R&B), released 2000; and "X" (single by Jon Pomplin) from *Project 814* (album), recorded by Project 814 (progressive rock), released 2001, all on Cellar Records.

N ● SPRADLIN/GLEICH PUBLISHING (BMI)

4234 N. 45th St., Phoenix AZ 85018-4307. **Contact:** Lee Gleich (rock, pop, movie, country); Paul Spradlin (country), managers. Music publisher. Estab. 1988. Publishes 4-10 songs/year; 2-4 new songwriters. Staff size: 2. Pays standard royalty.

Affiliate(s) Paul Lee Publishing (ASCAP).

How to Contact *Write first and obtain permission to submit.* Prefers cassette with 3 songs and lyric or lead sheet. "It must be very good material, as I only have time for promoting songwriters who really care." Include SASE. Responds in 6 weeks.

Music Mostly **country** geared to the US and European country markets; also **pop**, **rock** and **movie**. Published "Going Slow" (single by Paul Spradlin) from *Goosecreek* (album), recorded by Goosecreek Symphony, released 2000 on Capital; and "Blue Ain't As Blue" and "Frosty Morning" (singles by Kurt McFarland) from *Big Sky* (album), recorded by Kurt McFarland, released 2000 on Big Sky Records.

Tips "I need radio type songs. Please send me only your best. I have pitches to major stars but need great songs. I cannot train writers!"

N ● ● ○ STANDARD MUSIC PUBLISHING (BMI)

Lennox House, 229 Lennox St., Richmond, Vic 3121, Australia. Phone: (61-3)9428-4862. Fax: (61-3)9429 9137. E-mail: music@std.com.an. Managers: Janine Kerr; Adrian Marchesoni. Music publisher and management company (RCM International). Estab. 1994. Publishes a variable number of songs/year; publishes a variable number of new songwriters/year. Staff size: 5. Pays negotiable royalty.

How to Contact *Write first and obtain permission to submit.* Prefers cassette with 6 songs and lyric sheet. Does not return material. Responds in 1 month.

Film & TV Places 1 song in TV/year. Recently published "Burn" (by Reswick/Werfel/Arena), recorded by Tina Arena in *Baywatch*.

Music Mostly **rock** and **pop**; also **country**. Published "Chains" (pop); *Wasn't It Good* (pop); and "Burn" (pop) (by Reswick/Werfel/Arena), all recorded by Tina Arena on Epic (pop).

● STARBOUND PUBLISHING CO. (BMI)

Dept. SM, 207 Winding Rd., Friendswood TX 77546. Phone/fax: (281)482-2346. E-mail: bb207@msn.com. **Contact:** Buz Hart, partner; Lonnie Wright, partner; Jack Duncan, partner. Music publisher, record company (Juke Box Records, Quasar Records and Eden Records) and record producers (Lonnie Wright, Buz Hart, Jack Duncan). Estab. 1970. Publishes 15-30 songs/year; publishes 5-10 new songwriters/year. Pays standard royalty.

How to Contact *Write or call first and obtain permission to submit.* Prefers CD with 3 songs and lyric sheet. Include SASE. Responds in 2 months.

Music Mostly **country**, **R&B** and **gospel**. Does not want rap. Published "If I Had Another Heart" (single by Larry Wheeler/Buz Hart) from *Day One* (album), recorded by Waylon Adams (country), released 1999 on Jukebox Records; "My Biggest Thrill" and "Old Fashioned Girl" (singles by Phil Hamm/Buz Hart) from *This and That* (album), recorded by Raiders of the Lost Heart (country), released 2000 on MP3.com.

N ● ● STILL WORKING MUSIC GROUP (ASCAP, BMI, SESAC)

1625 Broadway, Nashville TN 37203. (615)242-4201. Fax: (615)242-4202. Owner: Barbara Orbison. Music publisher and record company (Orby Records, Inc.). Estab. 1994.

Affiliate(s) Still Working for the Woman Music (ASCAP), Still Working for the Man Music (BMI) and Still Working for All Music (SESAC).

How to Contact *Does not accept unsolicited submissions.*

Film & TV Published "First Noel," recorded by The Kelions in *Felicity*.

Music Mostly **rock**, **country** and **pop**; also **dance** and **R&B**. Published "If You See Him/If You See Her" (by Tommy Lee James), recorded by Reba McIntire/Brooks & Dunn; "Round About Way" (by Wil Nance), recorded by George Strait on MCA; and "Wrong Again" (by Tommy Lee James), recorded by Martina McBride on RCA (country).

Tips "If you want to be a country songwriter you need to be in Nashville where the business is. Write what is in your heart."

● JEB STUART MUSIC CO. (BMI)

P.O. Box 6032, Station B, Miami FL 33101-6032. (305)547-1424. **Contact:** Jeb Stuart, president. Music publisher, record producer (Esquire International) and management firm. Estab. 1975. Publishes 4-6 songs/year. Pays standard royalty.

• Also see the listing for Esquire International in the Record Producers section of this book.

How to Contact Submit demo tape by mail. Unsolicited submissions are OK. Prefers cassette or CD with 2-4 songs and lead sheet. Include SASE. Responds in 1 month.

Music Mostly **gospel**, **jazz/rock**, **pop**, **R&B** and **rap**; also **blues**, **church/religious**, **country**, **disco** and **soul**. Published "Peer Pressure" and "So All Alone," both written and recorded by Jeb Stuart and Cafidia Stuart (R&B), released 2004 on Esquire International.

🖥 ✅ 🖾 ◯ SUCCES

Pijnderslaan 84, 9200 Dendermonde Belgium. Phone: (052)21 89 87. Fax: (052)22 52 60. E-mail: deschuyteneer @hotmail.com. **Contact:** Deschuyteneer Hendrik, director. Music publisher, record company and record producer. Estab. 1978. Publishes 400 songs/year. Hires staff songwriters. Staff size: 4. Pays standard royalty.

How to Contact Submit demo tape by mail. Unsolicited submissions are OK. Prefers cassette or VHS videocassette with 3 songs. SAE and IRC. Responds in 2 months.

Film & TV Places songs in TV. Recently released "Werkloos" (by Deschuyteneer), recorded by Jacques Vermeire in *Jacques Vermeire Show*.

Music Mostly **pop**, **dance** and **variety**; also **instrumental** and **rock**. Published "Hoe Moet Dat Nou" (single by Henry Spider), recorded by Monja (ballad), released 2001 on MN; "Liefde" (single by H. Spider), recorded by Rudy Silvester (rock), released 2001 on Scorpion; and "Bel Me Gauw" (single by H. Spider), recorded by Guy Dumon (ballad), released 2001 on BM Records.

🖾 SUPREME ENTERPRISES INT'L CORP.

12304 Santa Monica Blvd., 3rd Floor, Los Angeles CA 90025. (818)707-3481. Fax: (818)707-3482. E-mail: suprem e2@earthlink.net. **Contact:** Lisa Lew, general manager copyrights. Music publisher, record company and record producer. Estab. 1979. Publishes 20-30 songs/year; publishes 2-6 new songwriters/year. Pays standard royalty.

Affiliate(s) Fuerte Suerte Music (BMI).

How to Contact Submit demo tape by mail. Unsolicited submissions are OK. Prefers cassette. Does not return material. "Please copyright material before submitting." Responds in 3 weeks if interested.

Music Mostly **reggae**, **rap** and **dance**. Published "Paso La Vida Pensando," recorded by Jose Feliciano on Motown Records; "Cucu Bam Bam" (by David Choy), recorded by Kathy on Polydor Records (reggae/pop); and "Mineaita," recorded by Gaby on SEI Records.

Tips "A good melody is a hit in any language."

🖾 SURVIVOR RECORDS/TEN OF DIAMONDS MUSIC (BMI)

120 Hana Hwy. #9, PMB 208, Paia HI 96779. (808)874-5900 or (808)573-3100. E-mail: songwriters@dreammaui. com. Website: www.dreammaui.com. Professional Managers: Greta Warren (pop); Jack Warren (country/ blues). Music publisher and record producer. Estab. 1974. Publishes 2 songs/year plus compilations; publishes 2 new songwriters/year. Staff size: 4. Pays standard royalty.

How to Contact Submit demo by mail. Unsolicited submissions are OK. "Submit no more than 3 songs on CD or cassette. Seeking pop ballad for male artist." Include SASE. Responds in 2 weeks.

Music Mostly **pop**, **country**, **R&B** and **New Age**. Does not want rock. Published "In the Morning Light" (by Jack Warren), recorded by Jason (pop ballad); and "Before the Rain" (by Giles Feldscher), recorded by Jason (pop ballad), both on Survivor.

Tips "Looking for a great single only!"

🖾 T.C. PRODUCTIONS/ETUDE PUBLISHING CO. (BMI)

121 Meadowbrook Dr., Somerville NJ 08876. (908)359-5110. Fax: (908)359-1962. E-mail: tcproductions@rcn.c om. Website: www.vmgmusic.com. President: Tony Camillo. Music publisher and record producer. Estab. 1992. Publishes 25-50 songs/year; publishes 3-6 new songwriters/year. Pays negotiable royalty.

Affiliate(s) We Iz It Music Publishing (ASCAP) and Etude/Barcam (BMI).

How to Contact *Write or call first and obtain permission to submit*. Prefers CD or cassette with 3-4 songs and lyric sheet. Include SASE. Responds in 1 month.

Music Mostly **R&B** and **dance**; also **country** and **outstanding pop ballads**. Published "What the World Needs Now" (single) from *I Take A Stand For Women* (album), recorded by Michelle Parto (pop); *God Loves You* (album), recorded by Faith (spiritual), released 2001 on Faith Records.

🖾 TALBOT MUSIC GROUP (ASCAP, BMI)

2 Music Circle S., Nashville TN 37203. (615)244-6200. Fax: (615)254-8860. E-mail: talbotmusi@aol.com. Music publisher. Estab. 1984. Publishes 40 songs/year. Hires staff songwriters. Pays standard royalty.

Affiliate(s) Talbot Music Publishing, Inc. (BMI), Plainspoken Music Publishing, Inc. (ASCAP) and Harbot (SESAC).

How to Contact *Talbot Music Group does not accept unsolicited submissions.*

Music Published "Austin" (single by David Kent/Kirsti Manna) from *Blake Shelton* (album), recorded by Blake Shelton (country), released 2001 on Giant/Warner Bros.

DALE TEDESCO MUSIC CO. (BMI)

16020 Lahey St., Granada Hills CA 91344. (818)360-7329. Fax: (818)832-4292. **Contact:** Dale T. Tedesco, president. General Manager: Betty Lou Tedesco. Music publisher. Estab. 1981. Publishes 20-40 songs/year; publishes 20-30 new songwriters/year. Staff size: 2-3. Pays standard royalty.

Affiliate(s) Tedesco Tunes (ASCAP).

How to Contact Submit demo tape by mail. Unsolicited submissions are OK. Prefers cassette or CD with 1 song and lyric sheet. Include SASE or postcard for critique. "Dale Tedesco Music hand-critiques all material submitted. Only reviews 1 song. Free evaluation." Include SASE. Responds in 1 month.

Film & TV Places 15 songs in film and 8 songs in TV/year. Published "Trouble on Your Mind," "Redneck Man" and "Logger Time," all written and recorded by Doug Ellis in *Sunset Beach*.

Music Mostly **pop**, **R&B** and **A/C**; also **dance-oriented**, **instrumentals** (for TV and film), **jazz**, **MOR**, **rock**, **soul** and **ethnic instrumentals**. Does not want rap. Published *One Child* (album by David Brisbin), recorded by Ernestine Anderson on Quest Records (jazz).

THISTLE HILL (BMI)

P.O. Box 707, Hermitage TN 37076. (615)320-6071. E-mail: wendy@greyhousestudio.com. **Contact:** Wendy Mazur.

How to Contact Submit demo tape by mail. Unsolicited submissions OK. Submit CD with 3-10 songs. Responds only if interested.

Music Country, pop, rock. Published "I Wanna be Free" (single by Jordon My Coskie) from *I Wanna be Free* (album), recorded by Jordon My Coskie (Americana), released 2003 on Atl! Records.

TIKI ENTERPRISES, INC. (ASCAP, BMI)

195 S. 26th St., San Jose CA 95116. (408)286-9840. Fax: (408)286-9845. **Contact:** Gradie O'Neal, president. Professional Manager: Jeannine O'Neil. Music publisher, record company (Rowena Records) and record producer (Jeannine O'Neal and Gradie O'Neal). Estab. 1967. Publishes 40 songs/year; publishes 12 new songwriters/year. Staff size: 3. Pays standard royalty.

Affiliate(s) Tooter Scooter Music (BMI), Janell Music (BMI) and O'Neal & Friend (ASCAP).

How to Contact Submit demo tape by mail. Unsolicited submissions are OK. Prefers cassette with 3 songs and lyric or lead sheets. Include SASE. Responds in 2 weeks.

Music Mostly **country**, **Mexican**, **rock/pop gospel**, **R&B** and **New Age**. Does not want atonal music. Published "You're Looking Good To Me" (single) from *A Rock 'N' Roll Love Story* (album), written and recorded by Warren R. Spalding (rock 'n' roll), released 2003-2004; "I Am Healed" (single) from *Faith On The Front Lines* (album), written and recorded by Jeannine O'Neal (praise music), released 2003-2004; and "It Amazes Me" (single by David Davis/Jeannine O'Neal) from *The Forgiven Project* (album), recorded by David Davis and Amber Littlefield, released 2003, all on Rowena Records.

Tips "Keep writing and sending songs in. Never give up—the next hit may be just around the bend."

TOURMALINE MUSIC, INC. (BMI)

2831 Dogwood Place, Nashville TN 37204. (615)269-8682. Fax: (615)269-8929. Website: http://songsfortheplan et.com. **Contact:** Justin Peters, president. Music publisher. Estab. 1980.

Affiliate(s) Justin Peters Music (BMI), LITA Music (ASCAP) and Platinum Planet Music.

How to Contact Submit demo by mail. Unsolicited submissions are OK. Prefers CD with 5 songs and lyric sheet. Does not return material. "Place code '2005' on each envelope submissions."

Music Mostly **worship**, **country** and some **classic rock**. Published "Santa Can You Bring My Daddy Home" (single by D. Mattarosa); "The Hurt Is Worth The Chance" (single by Justin Peters/Billy Simon), recorded by Gary Chapman on RCA/BMG Records; and "For So Long" (single by Monroe Jones/Chris McCollum), recorded by GLAD on Benson Records (also recorded by DMB Band, Connie Scot).

TOWER MUSIC GROUP

50 Music Square W., Suite 201, Nashville TN 37203. (615)320-7003. Fax: (615)320-7006. E-mail: castlerecords@ castlerecords.com. Website: www.castlerecords.com. **Contact:** Dave Sullivan, A&R Director. Professional Managers: Ed Russell; Eddie Bishop. Music publisher, record company (Castle Records) and record producer. Estab. 1969. Publishes 50 songs/year; publishes 10 new songwriters/year. Staff size: 15. Pays standard royalty.

Affiliate(s) Cat's Alley Music (ASCAP) and Alley Roads Music (BMI).

How to Contact *See submission policy on website.* Prefers cassette with 3 songs and lyric sheet. Does not return material. "You may follow up via e-mail." Responds in 3 months only if interested.

Film & TV Places 2 songs in film and 26 songs in TV/year. Published "Run Little Girl" (by J.R. Jones/Eddie Ray), recorded by J.R. Jones in *Roadside Prey*.

Music Mostly **country** and **R&B**; also **blues**, **pop** and **gospel**. Published "If You Broke My Heart" (single by Condrone) from *If You Broke My Heart* (album), recorded by Kimberly Simon (country); "I Wonder Who's Holding My Angel Tonight" (single) from *Up Above* (album), recorded by Carl Butler (country); and "Psychedelic Fantasy" (single by Paul Sullivan/Priege) from *The Hip Hoods* (album), recorded by The Hip Hoods (power/metal/y2k), all released 2001 on Castle Records.

Tips "Please contact us via e-mail with any other demo submission questions."

🌐 🎬 📀 TRANSAMERIKA MUSIKVERLAG KG

Wilhelmstrasse 10, 23611 Bad Schwartau, Germany. Phone: 0049-451-21530. E-mail: transamerika@online.de. Website: www.TRANSAMERIKAmusik.de. General Manager: Pia Kaminsky. **Hamburg:** Isestrasse 77, 20149 Hamburg, Germany. Phone: 0049-40-46961527. E-mail: transamerika@t-online.de. Professional Manager: Kirsten Jung. Member: GEMA, PRS, KODA, NCB, APRA. Music publisher and administrator. Estab. 1978. Staff size: 3. Pays 50% royalty if releasing a record; 85% if only administrating.

Affiliate(s) German Fried Music, Screen Music Services Ltd. (London), Cors Ltd. (London), MCI Ltd. (London), Leosong Music Australia Rty. Ltd. (Sydney), MCS Music Ltd. (USA, London), Pacific Electric Music Publishing.

How to Contact "We accept only released materials—no demos!" Submit CD or VHS videocassette. Does not return material. Responds only if interested.

Film & TV Places several songs in film and 2 songs in TV/year.

Music Mostly **pop**; also **rock**, **country**, **film music** and **reggae**.

Tips "We are specializing in administering (filing, registering, licensing and finding unclaimed royalties, and dealing with counter-claims) publishers worldwide."

☑ 🎬 📀 TRANSITION MUSIC CORPORATION (ASCAP, BMI, SESAC)

P.O. Box 8820, Universal City CA 91618-8820. (323)860-7074. Fax: (323)860-7986. E-mail: info@transitionmusic.com. Website: www.transitionmusic.com. Director of Film and Television Music: Jennifer Brown. President: Donna Ross-Jones. Vice President: David Jones. Administration: Mike Dobson. Music publisher. Estab. 1988. Publishes 250 songs/year; publishes 20 new songwriters/year. Variable royalty based on song placement and writer.

Affiliate(s) Pushy Publishing (ASCAP), Creative Entertainment Music (BMI) and One Stop Shop Music (SESAC).

How to Contact Address submissions to: New Submissions Dept. Submit demo tape by mail. Unsolicited submissions are OK. Prefers cassette, DAT or CD with 3 songs. Include SASE. Responds in 5 weeks.

Film & TV "TMC provides music for film, TV and commercials."

Music All styles.

Tips "Supply master quality material with great songs."

☑ 📀 TRIO PRODUCTIONS (BMI, ASCAP)

1026 15th Ave. S., Nashville TN 37212. (615)248-2284. Fax: (615)254-0519. **Contact:** Robyn Taylor-Drake.

Affiliate(s) ASCAP, BMI.

How to Contact Contact first and obtain permission to submit demo. Submit CD with 3-4 songs and lyric sheet. We do not return submissions.

Music **Country** and **bluegrass**.

☑ 📀 TWIN TOWERS PUBLISHING CO.

Dept. SM, 8455 Beverly Blvd., Suite 400, Los Angeles CA 90048. (323)655-5007. President: Michael Dixon. Music publisher and booking agency (Harmony Artists, Inc.). Publishes 24 songs/year. Pays standard royalty.

How to Contact *Call first and get permission to submit.* Prefers cassette with 3 songs and lyric sheet. Include SASE. Responds only if interested.

Music Mostly **pop**, **rock** and **R&B**. Published "Magic," from *Ghostbusters* soundtrack on Arista Records; and "Kiss Me Deadly" (by Lita Ford) on RCA Records.

📀 ULTIMATE PEAK MUSIC (BMI)

P.O. Box 707, Nashville TN 37076. E-mail: something@whatrecords.com. Website: www.whatrecords.com. **Contact:** Danny Crader, creative manager. Music publisher. Estab. 1992. Publishes 35 songs/year; publishes 4 new songwriters/year. Hires staff writers. Staff size: 4. Pays standard royalty.

How to Contact Submit demo tape by mail. Unsolicited submissions are OK. Prefers cassette with 1-6 songs and lyric sheet. Include SASE. Responds in 6 weeks.

Music Publishers

Lindy Robbins

Pop Perspective

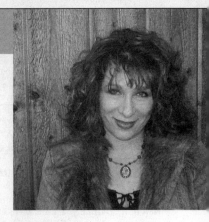

These are productive times for Los Angeles songwriter Lindy Robbins. She's penned two songs, "Shine" and "I Will Carry You," for Clay Aiken's platinum debut, *Measure of a Man*; she has a cut with Jesse McCartney on the Disney soundtrack and in the film *Cinderella Story*; she's renegotiated a new publishing pact with media powerhouse Universal Music Publishing Group; and she's preparing to move into a home she's purchased in the San Fernando Valley's trendy NoHo Arts district.

Make no mistake, Lindy Robbins is no overnight success. A native Angeleno who relocated to New York City in the '80s, Robbins' tale is one of fate, faith, trust, and timing. "It was only two years ago that I had any money at all," she confesses. "I was a late bloomer. I had a publishing deal in 1994 with Rodgers and Hammerstein Music in New York, but I was writing theatrical, cabaret, and art songs and making a living performing. It wasn't until 1997 that I quit performing and decided I wanted to write pop songs. I moved back to L.A. to do that, without a deal, without any money, without anything."

On a fluke, she entered a song in the UniSong International Song Contest and won the grand prize. She was subsequently invited to Ireland for Celtic Harmony, a week-long songwriter retreat organized by Music Bridges (USA) in conjunction with Irish rights society IMRO, where she was cast in intensive writing sessions with hitmakers from around the world. "I had moved back to L.A. with not a fork," says Robbins, "and there I was, on-stage, singing with Lamont Dozier and Brenda Russell. It all happened so fast."

In Ireland, Robbins met Rowana Gillespie of Polygram Music Publishing, who signed her to a deal. (The company has since merged with Universal Music Publishing Group.) In addition to a music publisher, Robbins retains the services of a manger. Still, she never stops hustling up her own opportunities. "No matter what cuts you have, you can never stop working your songs," she emphasizes. She makes regular trips to New York to meet personally with A&R executives at various labels. "I've found that if I make a connection they'll listen to a song later," she says. "We talk about life for a second. It's a human thing."

Robbins earned serious Music City credentials with a Faith Hill cut, "Back To You," and international recognition for "I Dreamed of You," a four and a half million-seller co-written and recorded by dance diva Anastacia. But, unless she is co-writing with an artist, she does not generally write songs with a specific performer in mind, and she cautions writers about becoming what she terms "genre whores." She explains, "Sometimes there are certain types of songs on the radio. You try to copy that trend, and by the time you're shopping those songs the trend has changed. By the time you're pitching yours, A&R execs have heard a hundred of those songs and they want to hear something different. Sometimes you have to start the trend yourself." She shares that on many occasions, it's necessary to turn off the business mind in order to create. "It's like, 'Can we just write a great song today?' Sometimes you have to flow and not think about business—just write. And those are the songs that get cut, because they're fun."

A global perspective is vital for pop songwriters, says Robbins. "I've had great things in the U.S. like Clay Aiken and Faith Hill, but I've gotten by on stuff in England, France and Australia. It's important to investigate other avenues rather than just the U.S. I can go to London and write dance or pop, then go to Nashville and write country, then to New York to write urban. That's what keeps it fresh." Robbins' ability to work quickly makes for a burgeoning catalog. "I can do a song a day easily," she says. "When I'm on a writing trip I'll do 10-15 songs. If 20 percent of them get placed, that makes a huge difference." She writes both melodies and lyrics, and she generally prefers to write with a producer. "I don't work with other writers, except when I'm doing standards or country," she says.

Robbins notes that production is key to getting cuts. "That's the biggest lesson I had to learn. As good as some of my songs were, the tracks weren't good enough and the songs wouldn't get placed. The demos have to sound as good as records." Robbins says that it is common practice now for songwriters to create the words and music, and then share a 20 percent writing credit with a producer to craft the definitive track. "It's worth it. Without a great demo a song can't get placed."

In the mercantile world of high-stakes songwriting, Robbins says that regular trips to Music City keep her centered. "When I get burnt on writing to tracks, I go to Nashville and get in a room with a great collaborator who plays piano or guitar. All my training in theater and cabaret comes into play more there than anywhere else. With country songs you can be funny and clever. In pop you can't be as poetic. I love Nashville. They've opened their arms at the Universal office—and that Faith Hill cut didn't hurt."

One recent trend Robbins observes is that country is reverting back to a rootsier style. "I'm a Valley Girl," she laughs. "I can't relate as much to the whole Southern experience. I try to write about what I know. But that's what I love about collaboration. If I write with somebody who really understands that, they can help me express it. If I'm writing something urban, I'll only write with someone who understands that world. That expands me. Where I excel is pop rock, so people will bring me in because of my expertise. By finding collaborators who do something different than what I do, I get a lot more versatility in my catalog."

One of her newest collaborators is pop-meister David Frank, a writer/producer probably best known for "Genie in a Bottle," the song that launched the career of Christina Aguilera. "David and I have just clicked; we're on the same page creatively. The first thing we wrote together got cut by a new artist, Bree Larson. I've found that helps. If you write with someone and get an immediate response to your collaboration, that's encouraging. There might be someone you've written seven songs with and none of them have gotten cut. You have to think maybe it's not the best situation."

Ease and comfort in the creative process is another collaborative plus. "Sometimes you have to give it more than one shot, but I'm the type of person who likes to go with something and not think about it. If someone keeps saying, 'No, that's not it,' and interrupts the flow, then I just want to go home. It should always be fun."

Robbins' writing tools are simple: a spiral notebook, a pen, a rhyming dictionary, a thesaurus, and a small digital recorder. "I have pages of ideas in a notebook. Every time something comes to me I add to it." Her digital recorder holds 200 songs, but after a song is demoed, Robbins erases the work track to make more room. She has notebooks dating back to 1986. "The good thing about using a notebook is you can go back and look at the work pages," she says. She is also adept at writing to tracks, especially in pop and dance music. "I can close my eyes and just completely sing whatever comes out of my mouth and record ten ideas, then go back and find a verse, pre-chorus and chorus that I like. It's not a thinking process."

Robbins is an increasingly rare breed—a successful songwriter who is not a producer, whose strength is her uncanny ability to write songs under virtually any circumstances in a wide scope of styles. Still, like any artist, the art of songwriting is as much about focus and discipline as it is about inspiration . "There are plenty of days I'm driving to a writing session and I'm thinking, 'I want to go to the mall, I want to go to the movies, I want to go to the beach, I want my mommy,' but you have to force yourself to work hard."

—Dan Kimpel

Dan Kimpel is the author of the best-selling book *Networking in the Music Business* (Writer's Digest Books). Since 1998, he has taught a course based on his book at Sir Paul McCartney's Liverpool Institute for Performing Arts (LIPA) in the U.K. He contributes to a variety of print mediums, and passengers on United Airlines hear Kimpel's interviews with songwriters and recording artists on the United Entertainment Network. He lives in Los Angeles, California.

Music Mostly **country** and **MTV pop/rock**. Published "That Reminds Me" (single by Stephany Delray/Billy Herzig) from *Go* (album), recorded by Rene (pop), released 2003 on What Records; "Concrete Shoes" (single by Stephany Delray) from *Jordan Mycoskie* (album), recorded by Jordan Mycoskie (Americana), released 2002 on Ah! Records; "I Love Animals" (single by Carla Rhodes) from *Carla's Golden Hits Volume 6* (album), recorded by Carla Rhodes (comedy/rock), released 2003 on What Records.
Tips "Listen to the radio and compare your songs to the hits—not for recording quality, but for substance and content and structure—and be objective and realistic and honest with yourself."

⊘ UNIVERSAL MUSIC PUBLISHING
12 Music Circle S., Nashville TN 37203. (615)248-4800. **New York:** 1755 Broadway, 8th Floor, New York NY 10019. **Los Angeles:** 2440 Sepulveda Blvd., Suite 100, Los Angeles CA 90064. (310)235-4700. Website: www.umusicpub.com.
   • In 1999, MCA Music Publishing and PolyGram Music Publishing merged into Universal Music Publishing.
How to Contact *Does not accept unsolicited submissions.*

☑ ⊘ VAAM MUSIC GROUP (BMI)
P.O. Box 29550, Hollywood CA 90029-0550. Phone/fax: (323)664-7765. E-mail: pmarti3636@aol.com. Website: www.vaammusic.com. **Contact:** Pete Martin, president. Music publisher and record producer (Pete Martin/ Vaam Productions). Estab. 1967. Publishes 9-24 new songs/year. Pays standard royalty.
Affiliate(s) Pete Martin Music (ASCAP).
   • Also see the listings for Blue Gem Records in the Record Companies section of this book and Pete Martin/ Vaam Music Productions in the record Producers section of this book.
How to Contact Send CDs or cassette with 2 songs and lyric sheet. Include SASE. Responds in 1 month. "Small packages only."
Music Mostly **top 40/pop**, **country** and **R&B**. "Submitted material must have potential of reaching top 5 on charts."
Tips "Study the top 10 charts in the style you write. Stay current and up-to-date with today's market."

Ⓝ ◯ VALIANT RECORDS & MANAGEMENT
P.O. Box 1, Waveland MS 39576. (228)467-5323. Fax: (228)467-5347. Website: www.vincevance.com and www.vincevance.net. **President:** Andy Stone. Music Publisher. Estab. 1971. Publishes 20 songs/year; publishes 1 new songwriter/year. Staff size: 5. Pays standard royalty of 50%.
Affiliate(s) Brightstone Publishing (ASCAP) and Brightstone Music Publishing (SESAC).
How to Contact Submit demo tape by mail. Unsolicited submissions are OK. Prefers cassette, CD, videocassette with a maximum of 4 songs and lyric sheet, lead sheet, and cover letter. SASE. "No guarantees!" Does not return submissions. Responds only if interested.
Music Mostly **novelty**, *parodies*, **Top 40 country**; also **adult contemporary**, *top 40* and **children's**. No rap or

X-rated material. Published "Cruising the Coast" (single by Terry Houle/Troy Powers/Andy Stone) and "Contents Under Pressure" (single by Troy Powers) from *Cruising the Coast* (album), recorded by Vince Vance (rock), released 2001 on Valiant Records; and "My Valentine" (single by Troy Powers/Ed Loftus/Andy Stone), from a single release, recorded by Vince Vance (AC), released 2002 on Valiant Records.

Tips "Submit clear recordings where we can hear the lyrics, melody, chord structure. Your expertise as an arranger is appreciated, but we find that producers have their own ideas. We have had the best luck with novelty, parodies, holiday songs and mainstream country, but we are looking for hits!"

☑ ☑ VINE CREEK MUSIC

P.O. Box 171143, Nashville TN 37217. (615)366-1326. Fax: (615)367-1073. E-mail: jingle1113@aol.com. **Contact:** Darlene Austin, Brenda Madden. Administration: Jayne Negri. Creative Director: Brenda Madden. Song Plugger: Markham Brown.

How to Contact "Only send material of good competitive quality. We do not return tapes/CDs unless SASE is enclosed."

☑ WALKER PUBLISHING CO. L.L.C. (ASCAP/BMI)

P.O. Box 11084, Birmingham AL 35202-1084. (205)601-4420. Fax: (775)514-8462. E-mail: superior_marketing@ msn.com. Website: www.walkerpublishingco.com. **Contact:** Gary Walker, owner. Professional Managers: Gary Walker (pop/R&B/ country), Charlie Craig (country/new country). Music Publisher, record producer (Charlie Craig Productions). Estab. 2000. Publishes 10 new songs/year; publishes 3 new songwriters/year. Staff size: 3. Hires staff songwriters. Pays standard royalty.

    ● Also see the listing for Charlie Craig Productions in the Record Producers section of this book.

Affiliates Cryptogram Music (ASCAP) and Star Alliance Music (BMI).

How to Contact Submit demo tape by mail. Unsolicited submissions are OK. Prefers CD with 3 songs, lyric sheet and writer's e-mail address. Does not return material. Responds in 6 weeks, via e-mail only. "Submit only professional studio quality demos."

Music Mostly **country**, **new country** and **pop**; also **soft rock**. Does not want rap, hard rock or metal. Published "Dallas Didn't Do It" (single by Craig/Wilkinson/Crosby) from a yet-unnamed album recorded by The Wilkinsons (country); "Tin Can" (single by Charlie Craig/Jerry Cupid) from debut album recorded by Brad & Shelly (country), released on Cupid Records.

Tips "Walker Publishing Co. L.L.C. has partnered with Charlie Craig Productions, owned by legendary writer/producer Charlie Craig—his writing credits include Alan Jackson's 'Wanted'; Travis Tritt's 'Between an Old Memory and Me'; Dolly Parton's 'Chicken Every Sunday'; and Johnny Cash's 'I Would Like to See You Again.' See www.charliecraig.com."

☑ ☑ WARNER/CHAPPELL MUSIC, INC.

10585 Santa Monica Blvd., Third Floor, Los Angeles CA 90025. (310)441-8600. Fax: (310)470-8780. **New York:** 1775 Broadway, 23rd Floor, New York NY 10019. (212)419-2600. Fax: (212)419-2633. **Nashville:** 20 Music Square E., Nashville TN 37203. (615)254-8777. Music publisher.

How to Contact *Warner/Chappell does not accept unsolicited material.*

☑ WEAVER OF WORDS MUSIC (BMI)

P.O. Box 803, Tazewell VA 24651. (276)988-6267. E-mail: cooksong@netscape.net. **Contact:** H.R. Cook, president. Music publisher and record company (Fireball Records). Estab. 1978. Publishes 12 songs/year. Pays standard royalty.

Affiliate(s) Weaver of Melodies Music (ASCAP).

How to Contact Submit demo by mail. Unsolicited submissions are OK. Prefers CD with 3 songs and lyric or lead sheets. "We prefer CD submissions but will accept submissions on cassette." Include SASE. Responds in 3 weeks.

Music Mostly **country**, **pop**, **bluegrass**, **film and television** and **rock**. Published "Zero To Love" (single by H. Cook/Brian James Deskins/Rick Tiger) from *It's Just The Night* (album), recorded by Del McCoury Band (bluegrass), released 2003 on McCoury Music; "Muddy Water" (single by Alan Johnston) from *The Midnight Call* (album), recorded by Don Rigsby (bluegrass), released 2003 on Sugar Hill; and "Ol Brown Suitcase" (single by H.R. Cook) from *Lonesome Highway* (album), recorded by Josh Williams (bluegrass), released 2004 on Pinecastle.

☑ WEMAR MUSIC CORP. (BMI)

836 N. La Cienega Blvd., #276, W. Hollywood CA 90069. Phone/fax: (323)692-1037. **Contact:** Stuart Wiener, President. Music publisher. Estab. 1940. Publishes 30 songs/year; publishes 30 new songwriters/year. Pays standard royalty.

Affiliate(s) Grand Music Corp. (ASCAP).

How to Contact Submit demo tape by mail. Unsolicited submissions are OK. "No phone calls." Include SASE. Responds in 2 months.

Music Mostly **pop**, **country**, **R&B** and **dance**. Published "Dick's Boogie" (single by Johnny Brandon), recorded by Dick Vance (jazz), released 2002 on Direct Source; "Your Old Lady" (single by The Isley Bros.), recorded by The Isley Bros. (R&B), released 2002 on Rhino; "Castle Rock" (single by E. Drake/J. Shirl/A. Seans) from *Frank Sinatra Super Hits Smart Piano* (album), recorded by Bill Cunliffe (pop), released 2002 on Yamaha.

🌐 ◯ BERTHOLD WENGERT (MUSIKVERLAG)

Hauptstrasse 36, D-76327, Pfinztal-Sollingen, Germany. **Contact:** Berthold Wengert. Music publisher. Pays standard GEMA royalty.

How to Contact Prefers cassette and complete score for piano. SAE and IRC. Responds in 1 month. "No cassette returns!"

Music Mostly **light music** and **pop**.

⛏ ◢ WESTWOOD MUSIC GROUP (ASCAP, BMI)

One Main St., Suite 205, Eatontown NJ 07724-3906. (732)380-9400. Fax: (732)380-9433. E-mail: music@westwoodmusicgroup.com. Website: www.westwoodmusicgroup.com. President: Victor Kaply. Vice President/Creative Services: Steve Willoughby. **Film & TV Dept.:** 521 Fifth Ave., 17th Floor, New York NY 10175. (212)619-3500. Fax: (212)619-3588. E-mail: filmmusic@westwoodmusicgroup.com. **Contact:** Steve Willoughby, director of film/TV music. Music publisher. Publishes 30 songs/year; publishes 2 new songwriters/year. Staff size: 4. Pays standard royalty.

How to Contact *Write first and obtain permission to submit.* Prefers CD with 3 songs and lyric sheet. Include SASE. Responds in 6 weeks.

Music Mostly **rock**; also **pop**. Published *13th Child—Legend of the Jersey Devil (Original Motion Picture Soundtrack)*, written and recorded by Peter Calandra; *Home-The Horror Story (Original Motion Picture Soundtrack)*, written and recorded by Brad Hodge (pop/jazz), both released 2002 on Westwood.

Tips "Submit a neat promotional package with bio and lyrics."

◯ WHITE CAT MUSIC

P.O. Box 19720, Fountain Hills AZ 85269. (480)951-3115. Fax: (480)951-3074. Professional Manager: Frank Fara. Producer: Patty Parker. Music publisher, record company and record producer. Member CMA, CCMA, BCCMA and BBB. Estab. 1978. Staff size: 2. "50% of our published songs are from non-charted and developing writers." Pays standard royalty.

Affiliate(s) Rocky Bell Music (BMI), How The West Was Sung Music (BMI) and Crystal Canyon Music (ASCAP).

  • Fara and Parker are authors of the book *How to Open Doors in the Music Industry—the Independent Way*. Also see the listing for Comstock Records in the Music Publishers section and Patty Parker in the Record Producers section of this book.

How to Contact "Submit demo by postal mail only. We do not accept audiofiles online." Unsolicited submissions are OK. "Song submission by CD only (no cassettes) with 2-4 songs and lyric sheet. Include SASE if demo is to be returned." Responds in 2 weeks.

Music All styles of **country**—traditional to crossover. Published "Great American Country" (single by Paula Mengarelli/Tom Mengarelli/Jaff Hansel), recorded by Paula Mengarelli (country), released on Comstock; "She's Bad News" (single by Roy G. Ownbey/Alexandria Sheraton), recorded by Jentille (country), released 2001 on Comstock; and "Give Your Love to Me" (single by Michael Ray) from *Reason to Believe* (album), recorded by Derek Carle (country), released on Comstock.

Tips "Have an out front vocal presentation so lyric can be heard. Go easy on long instrumental intros and breaks which distract. Send only two to four songs—medium to up tempo are always in demand. This helps stack the odds in your favor for getting heard."

✅ ◢ WILCOM PUBLISHING (ASCAP)

Box 4456, West Hills CA 91308. (661)285-8032. Fax: (661)285-8032. E-mail: william@wilcompublishing.com. **Contact:** William Clark, Owner. Music publisher. Estab. 1989. Publishes 10-15 songs/year; publishes 1-2 new songwriters/year. Staff size: 2. Pays standard royalty.

How to Contact *Write or call first and obtain permission to submit.* Prefers cassette with 1-2 songs and lyric sheet. Include SASE. Responds in 3 weeks.

Music Mostly **R&B**, **pop** and **rock**; also **country**. Does not want rap. Published "Girl Can't Help It" (single by W. Clark/D. Walsh/P. Oland), recorded by Stage 1 on Rockit Records (top 40).

☑ ◑ SHANE WILDER MUSIC (BMI)

P.O. Box 335687, North Las Vegas NV 89033. (701)395-5624. **Contact:** Shane Wilder, president. Music publisher, record producer (Shane Wilder Productions) and Management firm (Shane Wilder Artists' Management). Publishes 20-40 songs/year.

Affiliate(s) Shane Wilder Artist's Management.

How to Contact Send demo by mail. Unsolicited submissions are OK. "Submit with no more than 5 songs per submission and include lyric sheet." Responds within 30 days.

Music Country songs only.

☒ ◑ WINSTON & HOFFMAN HOUSE MUSIC PUBLISHERS (ASCAP, BMI)

P.O. Box 1415, Burbank CA 91507-1415. Fax: (323)462-8342. E-mail: sixties1@aol.com. **Contact:** Lynne Robin Green, president. Music publisher. Estab. 1958. Publishes 25 songs/year. Staff size: 2. Pays standard royalty.

Affiliate(s) Lansdowne Music Publishers (ASCAP), Bloor Music (BMI) and Ben Ross Music (ASCAP), "also administers 26 other firms."

How to Contact Submit demo tape by mail. Unsolicited submissions are OK. "*Do not query first. Do not call. Do not send lyrics without completed music.*" Prefers cassette with 3 songs maximum and lyric sheet. "*Must include SASE, or no reply!*" Responds in 1 month.

Film & TV Places 45 songs in film and 25 songs in TV/year. Recently published "Dooley" (by Dillard/Jayne) in *Baby Blues*; "Closer Walk With Thee" (by Craver/Henderson) in *Smiling Fish and Goat on Fire*; and "Born to Jump" (by Larry Dunn) in *Olympics 2000*.

Music Mostly **R&B dance**, **ballads**, **hip hop**, **vocal jazz**, **alternative rock** and **R&B**; also **bluegrass**, **Spanish pop** and **pop ballads**. Published "There Is A Time" (single by Mitch Jayne/Rodney Dillard) from *Will the Circle Be Unbroken III* (album), recorded by The Nitty Gritty Dirt Band (bluegrass), released 2003 on Capitol; "Hard Work" (single) from *All About the Benjamins* (soundtrack CD and movie), written and recorded by John Handy (jazz/funk), released 2003 on New Line Records; and "Dooley" (single by Rodney Dillard/Mitch Jayne) from *Shinebox* (album), recorded by The Gourds (bluegrass), released 2003 on Sugarhill Records.

Tips "Be very selective in what you send. 'A' side hit quality single songs only. For film or T.V. submissions you must specify you own all the master rights! Be interesting lyrically and strikingly original melodically. No hard rock, violent or sexist lyrics, novelty or holiday songs. We don't with lyricists only. No instrumental score type music, please. Independent artist's album material most welcome.

◑ WORLD FAMOUS MUSIC CO. (ASCAP)

1364 Sherwood Rd., Highland Park IL 60035. (847)831-3123. E-mail: getchip@interacess.com. **Contact:** Chip Altholz, president. Music publisher and record producer. Estab. 1986. Publishes 25 songs/year; 3-4 new songwriters/year. Pays standard royalty.

How to Contact *E-mail first to obtain permission to submit.* Submit demo tape by mail. Unsolicited submissions are OK. Prefers cassette with 3 songs and lyric sheet. Include SASE. Responds in 1 month.

Music Mostly **pop**, **R&B** and **rock**. Published "Harmony" (single by Altholz/Faldner), recorded by Barry Faldner on Amertel Records (ballad); and "Running" and "Serious" (singles), both written and recorded by Nick Bak on Pink Street Records.

Tips "Have a great melody, a lyric that is visual and tells a story and a commercial arrangement."

☑ ◑ YOUR BEST SONGS PUBLISHING (ASCAP)

1402 Auburn Way N, Auburn WA 98002. (877)672-2520. General Manager: Craig Markovich. Music publisher. Estab. 1988. Publishes 1-5 songs/year; publishes 1-3 new songwriters/year. Query for royalty terms.

How to Contact *Write first and obtain permission to submit.* Prefers CD or cassette with 1-3 songs and lyric sheet. "Submit your 1-3 best songs per type of music. Use separate CDs or cassettes per music type and indicate music type on each CD or cassette." Include SASE. Responds in 3 months.

Music Mostly **country**, **rock/blues** and **pop/rock**; also **progressive**, **A/C**, some **heavy metal** and **New Age**. Published "Sea of Dreams," written and recorded by J.C. Mark on Cybervoc Productions, Inc. (New Age).

Tips "We just require good lyrics, good melodies and good rhythm in a song. We absolutely do not want music without a decent melodic structure. We do not want lyrics with foul language or lyrics that do not inspire some form of imaginative thought."

☑ ☒ ◑ ZETTITALIA MUSIC INTERNATIONAL (ASCAP, BMI)

P.O. Box 261488, Encino CA 91426. (818)506-8533. Fax: (818)506-8534. E-mail: zettworks@aol.com. Website: www.pplzmi.com. **Contact:** Cheyenne Phoenix, A&R. Assistant, A&R: Kaitland Diamond. Music publisher. Estab. 1995. Publishes 40 songs/year; publishes 2 new songwriters/year. Staff size: 2. Hires staff songwriters. Pays standard royalty.

Affiliate(s) Zett One Songs (ASCAP) and Zett Two Music (BMI).

How to Contact *E-mail or write to obtain permission to submit. No phone calls.* "Include SASE or e-mail." Prefers cassette or CD with 3 songs. Include SASE. Responds in 6 weeks.

Film & TV Places 2 songs in film and 4 songs in TV/year.

Music Mostly **pop**, **film music**, **country**, **instrumental** and **R&B**.

Tips "In art, be a good student and stay true to your instincts. In business, be thorough, realistic, flexible and straightforward. Finally, The Golden Rule rules."

✍ ZOMBA MUSIC PUBLISHING (ASCAP, BMI)

138 W. 25th St., 8th Floor, New York NY 10001. (212)727-0016. **Beverly Hills:** 8750 Wilshire Blvd., Beverly Hills CA 90211. (310)358-4200. Website: www.zomba.com. Music publisher. Publishes 5,000 songs/year.

Affiliate(s) Zomba Enterprises, Inc. (ASCAP); Zomba Songs, Inc. (BMI).

How to Contact *Zomba Music Publishing does not accept unsolicited material.* "Contact us through management or an attorney."

Music Mostly **R&B**, **pop** and **rap**; also **rock** and **alternative**. Published ". . . Baby One More Time" (single by M. Martin), recorded by Britney Spears on Jive; "Home Alone" (single by R. Kelly/K. Price/K. Murray), recorded by R. Kelly featuring Keith Murray on Jive; and "Taking Everything" (single by G. Levert/D. Allamby/L. Browder/A. Roberson), recorded by Gerald Levert on EastWest.

ADDITIONAL MUSIC PUBLISHERS

The following companies are also music publishers, but their listings are found in other sections of the book. See the General Index for page numbers, then read the listings for submission information.

A

''A'' Major Sound Corporation
ACR Productions
American Artists Entertainment
Ariana Records
Arkadia Entertainment Corp.
Atlan-Dec/Grooveline Records
Avita Records

B

Banana Records
Barrett Rock 'n' Roll Enterprises, Paul
Blue Wave Productions
Blues Alley Records
Boulevard Music & Publishing
Butler Music, Bill

C

Cacophony Productions
Cambria Records & Publishing
Chattahoochee Records
Circuit Rider Talent & Management Co.
Coppin, Johnny/Red Sky Records
Cosmotone Records
CPA Records
Crawfish Productions

D

DaVinci's Notebook Records
Discmedia

E

Eiffert, Jr., Leo J.
Ellis International Talent Agency, The
Eternal Song Agency, The

F

Final Mix Music
Fireant

G

Garrett Entertainment, Marty
Generic Records, Inc.
Gig Records

Groove Makers' Recordings
Gueststar Records/Entertainment Agency

H

Hailing Frequency Music Productions
Hardison International Entertainment Corporation
Heads Up Int., Ltd.
Heart Music, Inc.
Hi-Bias Records Inc.
Hot Wings Entertainment
Hottrax Records
Huge Production, Inc., A

J

J & V Management
Jay Jay Publishing & Record Co.

K

Kingston Records
Knight Agency, Bob
Kuper Personal Management/Recovery Recordings

L

L.A. Entertainment, Inc.
Lazy Bones Productions/Recordings, Inc.
Levy Management, Rick
Living Eye Productions Ltd.
Lock
Lucifer Records, Inc.

M

Mac-Attack Productions
Marvel Records, Andy

N

Noteworthy Enterprises

O

OCP Publications
On the Level Music!
Only New Age Music, Inc.

Music Publishers

P

Philly Breakdown Recording Co.
Pierce, Jim
Precision Management

R

RAVE Records, Inc.
Riohcat Music
Rival Records
Robbins Entertainment LLC
Ruf Records

S

Satellite Music
Serge Entertainment Group
Sound Works Entertainment Productions Inc.
SRS Productions/Hit Records Network
Stormin' Norman Productions
Studio Seven

T

Tangent® Records
Tari, Roger Vincent

Tas Music Co./Dave Tasse Entertainment
Thump Records, Inc.
TMC Productions
TVT Records

V

Van Pol Management, Hans

W

Warehouse Creek Recording Corp.
Warner Productions, Cheryl K.
Westpark Music—Records, Production & Publishing
Winterland Entertainment Management & Publishing
World Wide Management

X

X.R.L. Records/Music

Y

Young Country Records/Plain Country Records

Record Companies

Record companies release and distribute records, cassettes and CDs—the tangible products of the music industry. They sign artists to recording contracts, decide what songs those artists will record, and determine which songs to release. They are also responsible for providing recording facilities, securing producers and musicians, and overseeing the manufacture, distribution and promotion of new releases.

MAJOR LABELS & INDEPENDENT LABELS

Major labels and independent labels—what's the difference between the two? Major labels are defined as those record companies distributed by one of the "Big 5" distribution companies: BMG Distribution, EMI Music Distribution (EMD), Sony Music Distribution, Warner/Elektra/Atlantic Distribution (WEA) and Universal Music and Video Distribution (UMVD). Distribution companies are wholesalers that sell records to retail outlets. If a label is distributed by one of these major companies, you can be assured any release coming out on that label has a large distribution network behind it. It will most likely be sent to most major retail stores in the United States. Independent labels go through smaller distribution companies to distribute their product. They usually don't have the ability to deliver records in massive quantities as the major distributors do. However, that doesn't mean independent labels aren't able to have hit records just like their major counterparts. A record label's distributors are found in the listings after the **Distributed by** heading.

Many of the companies listed in this section are independent labels. They are usually the most receptive to receiving material from new artists. Major labels spend more money than most other segments of the music industry; the music publisher, for instance, pays only for items such as salaries and the costs of making demos. Record companies, at great financial risk, pay for many more services, including production, manufacturing and promotion. Therefore, they must be very selective when signing new talent. Also, the continuing fear of copyright infringement suits has closed avenues to getting new material heard by the majors. Most don't listen to unsolicited submissions, period. Only songs recommended by attorneys, managers and producers who record company employees trust and respect are being heard by A&R people at major labels (companies with a referral policy have a ⊘ preceding their listing). But that doesn't mean all major labels are closed to new artists. With a combination of a strong local following, success on an independent label (or strong sales of an independently produced and released album) and the right connections, you could conceivably get an attentive audience at a major label.

But the competition is fierce at the majors, so you shouldn't overlook independent labels. Since they're located all over the country, indie labels are easier to contact and can be impor-

The case for independents

Tip

If you're interested in getting a major label deal, it makes sense to look to independent record labels to get your start. Independent labels are seen by many as a stepping stone to a major recording contract. Very few artists are signed to a major label at the start of their careers; usually, they've had a few independent releases that helped build their reputation in the industry. Major labels watch independent labels closely to locate up-and-coming bands and new trends. In the current economic atmosphere at major labels—with extremely high overhead costs for developing new bands and the fact that only 10% of acts on major labels actually make any profit—they're not willing to risk everything on an unknown act. Most major labels won't even consider signing a new act that hasn't had some indie success.

But independents aren't just farming grounds for future major label acts; many bands have long term relationships with indies, and prefer it that way. While they may not be able to provide the extensive distribution and promotion that a major label can (though there are exceptions), indie labels can help an artist become a regional success, and may even help the performer to see a profit as well. With the lower overhead and smaller production costs an independent label operates on, it's much easier to "succeed" on an indie label than on a major.

tant in building a local base of support for your music (consult the Geographic Index at the back of the book to find out which companies are located near you). Independent labels usually concentrate on a specific type of music, which will help you target those companies your submissions should be sent to. And since the staff at an indie label is smaller, there are fewer channels to go through to get your music heard by the decision makers in the company.

HOW RECORD COMPANIES WORK

Independent record labels can run on a small staff, with only a handful of people running the day-to-day business. Major record labels are more likely to be divided into the following departments: A&R, sales, marketing, promotion, product management, artist development, production, finance, business/legal and international.

- The *A&R department* is staffed with A&R representatives (reps) who search out new talent. They go out and see new bands, listen to demo tapes, and decide which artists to sign. They also look for new material for already signed acts, match producers with artists and oversee recording projects. Once an artist is signed by an A&R rep and a record is recorded, the rest of the departments at the company come into play.
- The *sales department* is responsible for getting a record into stores. They make sure record stores and other outlets receive enough copies of a record to meet consumer demand.
- The *marketing department* is in charge of publicity, advertising in magazines and other media, promotional videos, album cover artwork, in-store displays, and any other means of getting the name and image of an artist to the public.

- The *promotion department*'s main objective is to get songs from a new album played on the radio. They work with radio programmers to make sure a product gets airplay.
- The *product management department* is the ringmaster of the sales, marketing and promotion departments, assuring that they're all going in the same direction when promoting a new release.
- The *artist development department* is responsible for taking care of things while an artist is on tour, such as setting up promotional opportunities in cities where an act is performing.
- The *production department* handles the actual manufacturing and pressing of the record and makes sure it gets shipped to distributors in a timely manner.
- People in the *finance department* compute and distribute royalties, as well as keep track of expenses and income at the company.
- The *business/legal department* takes care of contracts, not only between the record company and artists but with foreign distributors, record clubs, etc.
- And finally, the *international department* is responsible for working with international companies for the release of records in other countries.

LOCATING A RECORD LABEL

With the abundance of record labels out there, how do you go about finding one that's right for the music you create? First, it helps to know exactly what kind of music a record label releases. Become familiar with the records a company has released, and see if they fit in with what you're doing. Each listing in this section details the type of music a particular record company is interested in releasing. You will want to refer to the Category Index, located at the end of this section, to help you find those companies most receptive to the type of music you write. You should only approach companies open to your level of experience (see A Sample Listing Decoded on page 11). Visiting a company's website can also provide valuable information about a company's philosophy, the artists on the label and the music they work with.

Networking

Recommendations by key music industry people are an important part of making contacts with record companies. Songwriters must remember that talent alone does not guarantee success in the music business. You must be recognized through contacts, and the only way to make contacts is through networking. Networking is the process of building an interconnecting web of acquaintances within the music business. The more industry people you meet, the larger your contact base becomes, and the better are your chances of meeting someone with the clout to get your demo into the hands of the right people. If you want to get your music heard by key A&R representatives, networking is imperative.

Networking opportunities can be found anywhere industry people gather. A good place to meet key industry people is at regional and national music conferences and workshops. There

Icons

For More Info

For more instructional information on the listings in this book, including explanations of symbols (🅽 ✅ 🆈 🍁 🌐 ◐ ◑ ◒ ⊘), read the article *Songwriter's Market: How Do I Use It?* on page 7.

are many held all over the country for all types of music (see the Workshops and Conferences section for more information). You should try to attend at least one or two of these events each year; it's a great way to increase the number and quality of your music industry contacts.

Creating a buzz

Another good way to attract A&R people is to make a name for yourself as an artist. By starting your career on a local level and building it from there, you can start to cultivate a following and prove to labels that you can be a success. A&R people figure if an act can be successful locally, there's a good chance they could be successful nationally. Start getting booked at local clubs, and start a mailing list of fans and local media. Once you gain some success on a local level, branch out. All this attention you're slowly gathering, this "buzz" you're generating, will not only get to your fans but to influential people in the music industry as well.

SUBMITTING TO RECORD COMPANIES

When submitting to a record company, major or independent, a professional attitude is imperative. Be specific about what you are submitting and what your goals are. If you are strictly a songwriter and the label carries a band you believe would properly present your song, state that in your cover letter. If you are an artist looking for a contract, showcase your strong points as a performer. Whatever your goals are, follow submission guidelines closely, be as neat as possible and include a top-notch demo. If you need more information concerning a company's requirements, write or call for more details. (For more information on submitting your material, see the article Where Should I Send My Songs? on page 9, Demo Recordings: What Should I Know? on page 13 and Quiz: Are You Professional? on page 26.)

RECORD COMPANY CONTRACTS

Once you've found a record company that is interested in your work, the next step is signing a contract. Independent label contracts are usually not as long and complicated as major label ones, but they are still binding, legal contracts. Make sure the terms are in the best interest of both you and the label. Avoid anything in your contract that you feel is too restrictive. It's important to have your contract reviewed by a competent entertainment lawyer. A basic recording contract can run from 40-100 pages, and you need a lawyer to help you understand it. A lawyer will also be essential in helping you negotiate a deal that is in your best interest.

Recording contracts cover many areas, and just a few of the things you will be asked to consider will be: What royalty rate is the record label willing to pay you? What kind of advance are they offering? How many records will the company commit to? Will they offer tour support? Will they provide a budget for video? What sort of a recording budget are they offering? Are they asking you to give up any publishing rights? Are they offering you a publishing advance? These are only a few of the complex issues raised by a recording contract, so it's vital to have an entertainment lawyer at your side as you negotiate.

ADDITIONAL RECORD COMPANIES

There are **more record companies** located in other sections of the book! On page 195 use the list of Additional Record Companies to find listings within other sections who are also record companies.

☐ ABL RECORDS

835 E. Buckeywood Ave., Orange CA 92865. (714)685-9958. E-mail: melodi4ever@earthlink.net. Website: www .ABLmusic.com. **Contact:** Allan Licht, owner. Record company and music publisher (Allan Bradley Music/BMI and Holly Ellen Music/ASCAP). Estab. 1993. Staff size: 2. Releases 10 singles/year. Pays 50% royalty to artists on contract; statutory rate to publisher per song on record.

• Also see the listing for Allan Bradley Music in the Music Publishers section of this book.

How to Contact Submit demo tape by mail. Unsolicited submissions are OK. Prefers cassette with 3 songs and lyric sheet. Does not return material. Responds in 1 month.

Music Mostly **A/C**, **pop** and **R&B**; also **country** and **Christian contemporary**. Released *I'll Keep the Change* (by Betty Kay Miller/Marcia McCaslin), recorded by Dakota Brad (country), released 1999 on ABL Records. Other artists include Tracy Todd, Sam Morrison, Donna West, Jill J. Switzer and Michael Cavanaugh.

Tips "Submit top-notch material with great demos."

☐ ALLEGHENY MUSIC WORKS

1611 Menoher Blvd., Johnstown PA 15905. (814)255-4007. E-mail: TunedOnMusic@aol.com. Website: www.all eghenymusicworks.com. **Contact:** Al Rita, managing director. Labels include Allegheny Records. Record company and music publisher (Allegheny Music Works Publishing/ASCAP and Tuned on Music/BMI). Estab. 1991. Pays 10-12% royalty to artists on contract; statutory rate to publisher per song on record.

How to Contact *Write first and obtain permission to submit.* "Include SASE for reply. E-mail queries are acceptable. Responds ASAP to regular mail requests and usually within 72 hours to e-mail queries. NO PHONE CALLS! If we are not interested in your material, we sometimes offer suggestions on other markets to try."

Music Mostly **country (all styles)**; also **pop**, **A/C**, **R&B**, **inspirational**, **novelty** and **Halloween**. Doe not want rap, metal, or x-rated lyrics. Released "That's My Jack O'Lantern" (single), written and recorded by Neil Hartenburg) from *Halloween Bash* (album) (country), released 2000 on Allegheny.

Tips "Bookmark our website and check it regularly, clicking on *Songwriter Opportunities.* Each month, as a free service to songwriters, we list a new artist or company looking for songs. Complete contact information is included. For a deeper insight into the type of material our company publishes, we invite you to read the customer reviews on amazon.com to our 2000 best seller Halloween album release *Halloween Bash.*"

🌐 ☐ ALPHABEAT

Box 12 01, D-97862 Wertheim/Main, Germany. Phone/fax: (49)9342-84155. E-mail: alphabeat@t-online.de. Website: www.alphabeat-shop.de. **Contact:** Stephan Dehn, owner. A&R Managers (all styles): Marga Zimmermann, Patrick Darr and Stephan Dehn. Record company and record producer. Payment to artists on contract "depends on product."

How to Contact Submit demo tape by mail. Unsolicited submissions are OK. Prefers cassette or PAL videocassette with maximum of 3 songs and lyric sheet. "When sending us your demo tapes, please advise us of your ideas and conditions." SAE and IRC. Responds in 1 month.

Music Mostly **dance/disco/pop**, **synth/pop** and **electronic**; also **R&B**, **hip-hop/rap** and **ballads**.

Tips "We are a distributor of foreign labels. If foreign labels have interest in distribution of their productions in Germany (also Switzerland and Austria) they can contact us. We distribute all styles of music of foreign labels. Please contact our 'Distribution Service' department."

✅ ☐ AMERICAN RECORDINGS

8920 Sunset Blvd., 2nd Floor, W. Hollywood CA 90069. (310)288-5300. Website: www.americanrecordings.c om. A&R: Dino Paredes, George Drakoulias, Antony Bland, Brendon Mendoza. Labels include Too Pure, Infinite Zero, UBL, Venture and Onion. Record company.

Distributed by Sony.

How to Contact Submit demo tape by mail. Unsolicited submissions are OK. Prefers CD, cassette or videocassette with lyric and lead sheet.

Music Released *Unchained*, recorded by Johnny Cash on American Recordings. Other artists include Slayer, System of a Down, The Jayhawks, Rahat Feteh Ali Khan, Paloalto, Noise Ratchet, and The (International) Noise Conspiracy.

✅ ☐ AMERICATONE RECORDS INTERNATIONAL USA

1817 Loch Lomond Way, Las Vegas NV 89102-4437. (702)384-0030. Fax: (702)382-1926. E-mail: jjjamericatone @aol.com. Website: www.americatone.com. Estab. 1985. **Contact:** A&R Director. Labels include The Rambolt Music International (ASCAP), Americatone Publishers (BMI) and Christy Records International. Record company, producer and music publisher. Releases 4-5 CDs and cassettes/year. Pays 10% royalty.

Distributed by Big Band Dist., Otter Music, North County, General, Harbor Export, International Dist., Twinbrook Dist., Gibson Dist.

How to Contact Submit demo CD by mail. Unsolicited submissions are OK. Prefers cassette or CD. Include SASE. Responds in 1 month.

Music Jazz and **Spanish jazz** only. Artists include Raoul Romero and His Jazz Stars Orchestra, Mark Masters and His Jazz Orchestra, Dick Shearer and His Stan Kenton Spirits, Sam Trippe and His Jazz Orchestra, Ladd McIntosh and His Orchestra, Caribbean Jazz, Jazz in the Rain Quintet, Brad Saunders and His Quintet, Bill Perkins and His Jazz Quintet, and the Eugene Shapiro Jazz Quintet. Americatone International USA is also a publisher of piano music and orchestrations.

N ⊕ ☑ AMP RECORDS & MUSIC

Box BM F.A.M.E., London WC1N 3XX United Kingdom. E-mail: markjenkins@beeb.net. Website: www.ampmu sic.demon.co.uk. **Contact:** Mark Jenkins, A&R (New Age, instrumental, ambient, progressive rock). Record company. Estab. 1985. Staff size: 10. Releases 12 CDs/year. Pays negotiable royalty to artists on contract; negotiable rate to publisher per song on record.

Distributed by Shellshock (UK), Eurock/ZNR/NSA (USA), MP (Italy) and Crystal Lake (France).

How to Contact Submit demo tape by mail. Unsolicited submissions are OK. Prefers cassette, CD or DAT with cover letter and press clippings. Does not return material. Responds in 2 months.

Music Mostly **New Age**, **instrumental** and **ambient**; also **progressive rock**, **synthesizer** and **ambient dance**. Does not want ballads, country or AOR. Released *Changing States*, recorded by Keith Emerson (progressive rock); *Tyranny of Beauty*, written and recorded by Tangerine Dream (synthesizer); and *Spirit of Christmas*, written and recorded by various artists (instrumental compilation), all on AMP Records.

Tips "Send a relevant style of music."

☑ ☑ ANGEL RECORDS

(formerly Angel/EMI Records), 150 Fifth Ave., 6th Floor, New York NY 10011. (212)786-8600. Website: www.an gelrecords.com. Record company. Labels include EMI Classics, Manhattan Records, and Virgin Classics.

Distributed by EMI Music Distribution.

How to Contact *Angel/EMI Records does not accept unsolicited submissions.*

Music Artists include Sarah Brightman, Paul McCartney and Bernadette Peters.

☑ ARIANA RECORDS

1312 S. Avenida Polar #A-8, Tucson AZ 85710. (520)790-7324. E-mail: jgasper1596@earthlink.net. Website: www.arianarecords.com. **Contact:** James M. Gasper, president. Vice President (pop, rock): Tom Dukes. Partners: Tom Privett (funk, experimental, rock); Scott Smith (pop, rock, AOR). Labels include Egg White Records. Record company, music publisher (Myko Music/BMI) and record producer. Estab. 1980. Staff size: 4. Releases 2 singles, 4 LPs and 1 compilation/year. Pays negotiable royalty to artists on contract; negotiable rate to publisher per song on record.

Distributed by Impact Music Distributors and Care Free Music.

How to Contact "We are only interested in finished CD projects. *No tapes. No demos.* Unsolicited submissions are OK. Include SASE. Responds in 6 months.

Music Mostly **rock**, **funk**, **jazz**, **anything weird**, **strange** or **lo-fi** (must be mastered to CD). Released "Bloated Floater" (single by Mr. Jimi/Trece Broline/Larry's Fault) from *Bloated Floater* (album), recorded by Bloated Floater (space funk), released 2004 on Ariana Records; "Feel My Face" (single by James Gasper) from *Soledad* (album), recorded by Scuba Tails (electro rock), released 2004 on Ariana Records; and "Smak You Up" (single by Trece Broline/Mr. Jimi/Larry's Fault) from *Headphones Plez*, recorded by Beatnik Grip (trash euro funk), released 2004 on Ariana Records. Other artists include Tom P., Big White Teeth, JTiom, Slim Taco Explosion, and The Miller Boys.

Tips "We're a small company, but working your material is our job. If we like it, we'll sell it! It's a tough business. Keep trying."

☑ ☑ ARISTA RECORDS

888 7th Ave., New York NY 10019. (212)489-7400. Fax: (212)977-9843. Website: www.arista.com. Beverly Hills office: 8750 Wilshire Blvd., 3rd Floor, Beverly Hills CA 90211. (310)358-4600. Nashville office: 7 Music Circle North, Nashville TN 37203. (615)846-9100. Fax: (615)846-9192. Labels include Bad Boy Records, Arista Nashville and Time Bomb Recordings. Record company.

Distributed by BMG.

How to Contact *Does not accept unsolicited material.*

Music Artists include Outkast, Dido, Pink, Usher, Avril Lavigne, Babyface, and Sarah McLachlan.

☑ ☺ ARKADIA ENTERTAINMENT CORP.

34 E. 23rd St., New York NY 10010. (212)533-0007. Fax: (212)979-0266. E-mail: arkadiany@aol.com. Website: www.arkadiarecords.com. **Contact:** A&R Song Submissions. Labels include Arkadia Jazz, Arkadia Classical, Arkadia Now and Arkadia Allworld. Record company, music publisher (Arkadia Music), record producer (Arkadia Productions) and Arkadia Video. Estab. 1995.

How to Contact *Write or call first and obtain permission to submit.*

Music Mostly **jazz**, **classical** and **pop/R&B**; also **world**.

☑ ☺ ASTRALWERKS

104 W. 29th St., 4th Floor, New York NY 10001. Website: www.astralwerks.com. **Contact:** A&R. Record company. Estab. 1979. Releases 10-12 12″ singles and 100 CDs/year. Pays varying royalty to artists on contract; statutory rate to publisher per song.

How to Contact Send submissions to: "Alt: A&R" to address above. No unsolicited phone calls please.

Music Mostly **alternative/indie/electronic**. Artists include Air, Badly Drawn boy, The Beta Band, Chemical Brothers, and Fatboy Slim.

Tips "We are open to artists of unique quality and enjoy developing artists from the ground up. We listen to all types of 'alternative' music regardless of genre. It's about the aesthetic and artistic quality first. We send out rejection letters so do not call to find out what's happening with your demo."

☐ ATLAN-DEC/GROOVELINE RECORDS

2529 Green Forest Court, Snellville GA 30078-4183. (770)985-1686. Fax: (877)751-5169. E-mail: atlandec@prodigy.net. Website: www.ATLAN-DEC.com. President/Senior A&R Rep: James Hatcher. A&R Rep: Wiletta J. Hatcher. Record company, music publisher and record producer. Estab. 1994. Staff size: 2. Releases 3-4 singles, 3-4 LPs and 3-4 CDs/year. Pays 10-25% royalty to artists on contract; statutory rate to publisher per song on record.

Distributed by ATLAN-DEC Records.

How to Contact Submit demo tape by mail. Unsolicited submissions are OK. Prefers CDR and lyric sheet. Does not return material. Responds in 3 months.

Music Mostly **R&B/urban**, **hip-hop/rap** and **contemporary jazz**; also **soft rock**, **gospel**, **dance** and **new country**. Released "Inspiration" (single), recorded by Ebony Moore (R&B/pop), released 2004 on Atlan-Dec/Grooveline Records. Other artists include Furious D (rap/hip-hop) and Mark Cocker (new country).

☑ ☺ ATLANTIC RECORDS

New York: 1290 Avenue of the Americas, New York NY 10104. (212)707-2000. Fax: (212)581-6414. **Los Angeles:** 3400 W. Olive Ave., 3rd Floor, Burbank CA 91505. (818)238-6800. Fax: (310)205-7411. **Nashville:** 20 Music Square East, Nashville TN 37203. (615)272-7990. Website: www.atlanticrecords.com. Labels include Big Beat Records, LAVA, Nonesuch Records, Atlantic Classics and Rhino Records. Record company. Pays negotiable royalty to artists on contract; negotiable rate to publisher per song on record.

Distributed by WEA.

How to Contact *Does not accept unsolicited material.* "No phone calls please."

Music Artists include Matchbox Twenty, Jewel, Sugar Ray, Kid Rock, Luna, P.O.D., The Darkness, and The Corrs.

☺ AVITA RECORDS

P.O. Box 764, Hendersonville TN 37077-0764. (615)824-9313. Fax: (615)824-0797. E-mail: Tachoir@bellsouth.net. Website: www.tachoir.com. **Contact:** Robert Kayre, manager. Record company, music publisher (Riohcat Music, BMI) and record producer (Jerry Tachoir). Estab. 1976. Staff size: 8. Releases 2 LPs and 2 CDs/year. Pays negotiable royalty to artists on contract; statutory rate to publisher per song on record.

• Also see the listing for Riohcat Music in the Managers & Booking Agents section of this book.

How to Contact *Contact first and obtain permission to submit.* We only accept material referred to us by a reputable industry source. Prefers cassette, CD or DAT. Does not return materials. Responds only if interested.

Music Mostly **jazz**. Released *Improvised Thoughts* (album by Marlene Tachoir/Jerry Tachoir/Van Manakas), recorded by Jerry Tachoir and Van Manakas (jazz), released 2001 on Avita Records. Other artists include Van Manakas.

☑ ☺ AVITOR MUSIC

(formerly Seague International Records), P.O. Box 5537 Kreole Station, Moss Point MS 39563-1537. (228)475-0059 "No collect calls, please." **Contact:** Jemiah F. Mitchell, president/owner. Estab. 2003. Releases 10 singles and 5 LPs/year. Pays negotiable royalty to artists on contract; statutory rate to publisher per song on record. "Avitor Music has National and International distribution."

Distributed by Select-O-Hits, CD Baby, and Amazon.Com.

How to Contact *Write or call first for submission instructions.* "Always whenever you write, be sure you include a #10 business-size envelope addressed back to yourself with a first-class USA postage stamp on the envelope. A reply will come back to you using the SASE you include in your mailing when you write. *Absolutely no reply postcards—only SASE.* If you only write lyrics, do not submit; only complete songs reviewed, so you must find a collaborator. Not interested in reviewing homemade recordings." Prefers CD (first choice) or cassette with 3-10 songs along with lyrics to songs submitted. Responds in 2 months.

Music All types and styles of songs. "Recording artists with 10-12 professionally recorded and finished songs ready for release can contact Seague International Records for release and National Distribution. Songs and artist must be outstanding in all respect."

Tips "We are reaching out to find undiscovered, talented writers and singers who deserve a chance to be heard, accepted, and appreciated. We are looking for serious-minded people who are hungry for success and filled with ambition. Singers and songwriters wanting to record professionally, contact Avitor Music before you make a move. Save time and money and problems you could run into. For the best results to benefit you call Avitor Music to get the job done right from the start."

N □ AWAL.COM

P.O. Box 879, Ojai CA 93024. (805)640-7399. Fax: (805)646-6077. E-mail: info@awal.com. Website: www.awal.com. **Contact:** A&R Department. President: Denzyl Feigelson. Record company. Estab. 1996. Staff size: 7. Releases 6 singles, 12 LPs and 12 CDs/year. Pays 50% or negotiable royalty to artists on contract.

Distributed by Valley and on the Internet.

How to Contact Submit demo tape by mail. Unsolicited submissions are OK. Prefers CD with 5 songs, lyric sheet, cover letter and press clippings. Does not return materials. Responds in 1 month if interested.

Music Mostly **pop**, **world** and **jazz**; also **techno**, **teen** and **children's**. Released *Go Cat Go* (album by various), recorded by Carl Perkins on ArtistOne.com; *Bliss* (album), written and recorded by Donna Delory (pop); and *Shake A Little* (album), written and recorded by Michael Ruff, both on Awal Records.

☑ ☺ AWARE RECORDS

2336 W. Belmont Ave., Chicago IL 60618. (773)248-4210. E-mail: info@awarerecords.com. Website: www.awarerecords.com. A&R: Steve Smith. President: Gregg Latterman. Record company. Distributed by Sony and Redeye. Estab. 1993. Staff size: 8. Releases 5 LPs, 1 EP and 3 CD/year. Pays negotiable royalty to artists on contract; statutory rate to publisher per song on record.

Distributed by Sony and RED.

How to Contact *Does not accept unsolicited submissions.*

Music Mostly **rock/pop**. Released *Aware 9* (album), written and recorded by various artists (pop/rock); and *More Sounds from Spaghetti Westerns* (album), recorded by Red Elephant, both on Aware Records. Other artists include John Mayer, Five for Fighting, Riddlin Kid, Alice Peacock and Bleu.

□ BANANA RECORDS

3115 Hiss Ave., Baltimore MD 21234. Phone/fax: (410)663-5915. E-mail: theunholythree@yahoo.com. Website: www.theunholythree.com. **Contact:** Ron Brown, President. Record company, music publisher (Infinite Publishing) and record producer (Ronald Brown). Estab. 1990. Releases 30 singles, 20 LPs and 20 CDs/year. Pays standard royalty to artists on contract; statutory rate to publisher per song on record.

How to Contact Submit demo tape by mail. Unsolicited submissions are OK. Prefers cassette with 3 songs and lyric sheet. Include SASE. Responds in 3 weeks.

Music Mostly **top 40/commercial**, **pop/ballads** and **alternative**. Released "Crack of the Universe," written and recorded by Jesse Brown (pop) on Global; *The Unholy Three* (album), written and recorded by Ronnie B. (commercial), released 2002 on Banana Records.

Tips "A good singer works hard at his craft. A hit song has good punch and a lot of talent."

☑ ☺ BELMONT RECORDS

484 Lexington St., Waltham MA 02452. (781)891-7800. Fax: (781)893-1771. E-mail: jpennycw@rcn.com. **Contact:** John Penny, president. Labels include Waverly Records. Record company and record producer. Pays standard royalty to artists on contract; statutory rate to publisher per song on record.

How to Contact *Write first and obtain permission to submit.* Prefers cassette with 3 songs and lyric sheet. Include SASE. Responds in 3 weeks.

Music Mostly **country**. Released *Barbara Lawrence* (album), recorded by Barbara Lawrence (c&w), released 1999; and *Listen To Me* (album), recorded by Barbara Lawrence (c&w), released 2000; both on Belmont Records. Other artists include Stan Jr., Tim Barrett, Jackie Lee Williams, Robin Right, Mike Walker and Dwain Hathaway.

⊕ BIG BEAR RECORDS

Box 944, Birmingham, B16 8UT, United Kingdom. Phone: 44-021-454-7020. Fax: 44-021-454-9996. A&R Director: Jim Simpson. Labels include Truckers Delight and Grandstand Records. Record company, record producer and music publisher (Bearsongs). Releases 6 LPs/year. Pays 8-10% royalty to artists on contract; 8$\frac{1}{4}$% to publishers for each record sold. Royalties paid directly to songwriters and artists or through US publishing or recording affiliate.

- Big Bear's publishing affiliate, Bearsongs, is listed in the Music Publishers section, and Big Bear is listed in the Record Producers section of this book.

How to Contact Submit demo tape by mail. Unsolicited submissions are OK. Prefers CD. Does not return material. Responds in 3 weeks.

Music **Blues** and **jazz**. Released *I've Finished with the Blues* and *Blues for Pleasure* (by Skirving/Nicholls), both recorded by King Pleasure and the Biscuit Boys (jazz); and *Side-Steppin'* (by Barnes), recorded by Alan Barnes/Bruce Adams Quintet (jazz), all on Big Bear Records. Other artists include Lady Sings the Blues, Drummin' Man and Kenny Baker's Dozen.

☑ 🗹 ⊘ BIG HEAVY WORLD

P.O. Box 428, Burlington VT 05402-0428. (802)865-1140. E-mail: redshift@bigheavyworld.com. Website: www. bigheavyworld.com. **Contact:** James Lockridge, founder/A&R director. Record company. Estab. 1996. Staff size: 12. Releases 3 CDs/year. Pays negotiable royalty to artists on contract; pay varies by project to publisher per song on record.

- This company was given the 1998 Visionary Award by the Women's Rape Crisis Center. Big Heavy World promotes the music of Burlington, Vermont, and its region. Their compilation CDs vary in genre and theme and often benefit humanitarian services.

How to Contact *Big Heavy World does not accept unsolicited submissions.*

Music Compilation projects vary in genre. Released *Pop Pie* (pop); *Pulsecuts Vol II* (alternative); *No Secrets* and *Tonic Two: Core Breach Burlington* (rock/alternative), *242.01 The Bands of Burlington Vermont* (hardcore/ punk/alternative); *Hop 3 An Independent Collection of Rhythms and Melodies from the North Upper Most* (downtempo urban); *Hop 4 A Bumpnthump Electronic Loopngroove Compilation from the Green Mountains* (uptempo hip-hop); *Sullivan Square The Contemporary Folk Collection*; *The 10th Annual Los Angeles Music Awards Sonic Sampler* (eclectic).

Tips "Vermont-based artists are welcome to contact us, both as a record label and online music retail venue."

◻ BLUE GEM RECORDS

P.O. Box 29550, Hollywood CA 90029. (323)664-7765. E-mail: pmarti3636@aol.com. **Contact:** Pete Martin. Record company, music publisher (Vaam Music Group) and record producer (Pete Martin/Vaam Productions). Estab. 1981. Pays 6-15% royalty to artists on contract; statutory rate to publisher per song on record.

- Also see the listings for Vaam Music Group in the Music Publishers section of this book and Pete Martin/ Vaam Music Productions in the Record Producers section of this book.

How to Contact Submit demo tape by mail. Unsolicited submissions are OK. Prefers CD or cassette with 2 songs. Include SASE. Responds in 3 weeks.

Music Mostly **country** and **R&B**; also **pop/top 40** and **rock**.

◻ BLUE WAVE

3221 Perryville Rd., Baldwinsville NY 13027. (315)638-4286. Fax: (315)635-4757. E-mail: bluewave@localnet.c om. Website: www.bluewaverecords.com. **Contact:** Greg Spencer, president/producer. Labels include Blue Wave/Horizon. Record company, music publisher (G.W. Spencer Music/ASCAP) and record producer (Blue Wave Productions). Estab. 1985. Staff size: 1. Releases 3 LPs and 3 CDs/year. Pays variable royalty to artists on contract; statutory rate to publisher per song on record.

Distributed by Select-O-Hits, Action Music, Burnside Dist.

- Also see the listing for Blue Ware Productions in the Managers & Booking Agents section of this book.

How to Contact Submit demo tape by mail. Unsolicited submissions are OK. Prefers cassette or videocassette (live performance only) and as many songs as you like. Include SASE. Responds in 1 month only if interested. "Do not call."

Music Mostly **blues/blues rock**, **roots rock** and **roots R&B/soul**; also **roots country/rockabilly** or **anything with "soul."** Released "Leave Married Women Alone" (single by Jimmy Cavallo) from *The House Rocker* (album), recorded by Jimmy Cavallo (jump blues), released 2002 on Blue Wave; "Sometimes You Gamble" (single by Kim Simmonds) from *Blues Like Midnight* (album), recorded by Kim Simmonds (blues), released 2001 on Blue Wave; and "Motherless World" (single by Pete McMahon) from *Trouble on the Run* (album), recorded by The Kingsnakes (blues), released 2001 on Blue Wave.

Tips "Be able to put the song across vocally."

N ⊘ BMX ENTERTAINMENT

P.O. Box 10857, Stamford CT 06904. Fax: (203)329-1639. Website: www.bmxentertainment.com. **Contact:** Mauris Gryphon, CEO. Labels include Red Tape Records. Record company. Estab. 1984. Releases 7 singles, 7 12″ singles, 7 LPs, 7 EPs and 7 CDs/year. Pays 10-12% royalty to artists on contract.

How to Contact Submit demo tape by mail. Unsolicited submissions are OK. Prefers cassette, CD or VHS videocassette with 4 songs or more. "Send bio, résumé, 8×10 photo, contact information." Include SASE. Responds in 3 weeks.

Music Mostly **top 40**, **country**, **R&B** and **rock**; also **hip-hop**, **pop**, **jazz**, **classical**, **children's**, **New Age**, **gospel** and **salsa**.

🌐 ◯ BOULEVARD MUSIC & PUBLISHING

16 Limetrees, Llangattock, Crickhowell NP8 1IL Wales. Phone: (0044)(0)1873 810142. Fax: (0044)(0)1873 811557. E-mail: boulmusic@aol.com. A&R Director: Kevin Holland-King (MOR/jazz). Labels include Silverword, Associate, Mirabeau. Record company and music publisher (Boulevard Publishing). Estab. 1987. Staff size: 2. Releases 8 singles and 25 CDs/year. Pays negotiable royalty to artists on contract; statutory rate to publisher per song on record.

Distributed by SMG/T.H.E.

How to Contact Submit demo tape by mail. Unsolicited submissions are OK. Prefers cassette, CD or VHS videocassette with 3 songs, lead sheet and cover letter. SAE and IRC. Responds in 1 month.

Music Mostly **MOR**, **rock** and **R&B**; also **country** and **jazz**. Released "I Say Strawberry Fields Forever" (single by P. Eaton/R. Brook), recorded by Ronnie Brock (pop), released 2002 on Wizard; *Every Word* (album), recorded by Mike Doyle (pop ballads), released 2002 on Silverword; and *Neopolitan Love Songs* (album), recorded by Dewi Wyn (classical), released 2002 on Chateau. Other artists include Jeff Hooper, Southlanders, Screemer, Modern Romance, Ashmore, Poe-Alley and Richard Beavis.

Tips "A well-written song is like any masterpiece: hard to find—easy to recognize."

✓ ⊘ BOUQUET RECORDS

Bouquet-Orchid Enterprises, P.O. Box 1335, Norcross GA 30091. (770)814-2420. Fax: (770)339-9088. **Contact:** Bill Bohannon, president. Record company, music publisher (Orchid Publishing/BMI), record producer (Bouquet-Orchid Enterprises) and management firm (Bouquet-Orchid Enterprises). Releases 3-4 singles and 2 LPs/year. Pays 5-8% royalty to artists on contract; pays statutory rate to publishers for each record sold.

How to Contact Submit demo tape by mail. Unsolicited submissions are OK. Prefers cassette or CD with 3-5 songs and lyric sheet. Include SASE. Responds in 1 month.

Music Mostly **religious** (contemporary or country-gospel, Amy Grant, etc.), **country** ("the type suitable for Clint Black, George Strait, Patty Loveless, etc.") and **top 100** ("the type suitable for Billy Joel, Whitney Houston, R.E.M., etc."); also **rock** and **MOR**. Released *Blue As Your Eyes* (by Bill Bohannon), recorded by Adam Day (country); *Take Care of My World* (by Bob Freeman), recorded by Bandoleers (top 40); and *Making Plans* (by John Harris), recorded by Susan Spencer (country), all on Bouquet Records.

Tips "Submit 3-5 songs on a cassette tape with lyric sheets. Include a short biography and perhaps a photo. Enclose SASE."

✓ 🎤 ⊘ BROKEN NOTE RECORDS

P.O. Box 541651, Houston TX 77254. (281)658-6484. **Contact:** Tony Avitia, A&R. Record company. Estab. 1993. Staff size: 3. Releases 4 singles, 6 LPs and 6 CDs/year. Pays negotiable royalty to artists on contract; statutory rate to publisher per song on record.

Distributed by Southwest and Crystal Clear.

● Awarded 1999 Best Local Label by Houston Press

How to Contact Submit demo by mail. Unsolicited submissions are OK. Prefers cassette, CD or VHS videocassette with lyric sheet, cover letter and press clippings. Does not return materials. Responds in 2 months if interested.

Music Mostly **heavy rock**, **rap** and **techno-rock**; also **surf-instrumental**, **hip hop** and **folk**. Released *The Sultry Sounds of Collision* (album), written and recorded by Cult Ceavers (jazzcore); *The Regal Beagle* (album), written and recorded by I-45 (rap); and *Pogo Au-go-go* (album), written and recorded by Bickley (punk), all on Broken Note.

Tips "Be persistent."

✓ ⊘ BSW RECORDS

P.O. Box 2297, Universal City TX 78148. Phone/Fax: (210)653-3989. E-mail: bswr18@wmconnect.com. Website: www.bswrecords.com. President: Frank Willson. Vice Presidents: Frank Weatherly (country, jazz); Regina Willson (blues). Record company, music publisher (BSW Records/BMI), management firm (Universal Music

Marketing) and record producer (Frank Willson). Estab. 1987. Staff size: 5. Releases 18 albums/year. Pays standard royalty to artists on contract; statutory rate to publisher per song on record.

- Also see the listings for BSW Records in the Music Publishers section, Frank Wilson in the Record Producers section and Universal Music Marketing in the Managers & Booking Agents section of this book.

How to Contact Submit demo CD by mail. Unsolicited submissions are OK. Prefers CD (or ³/₄″ videocassette) with 3 songs and lyric sheet. Include SASE. Responds in 6 weeks.

Music Mostly **country**, **rock** and **blues**. Released *Memories of Hank Williams, Sr.* (album), recorded by Larry Butler and Willie Nelson. Other artists include Candee Land, Crea Beal, John Wayne, Sonny Marshall and Bobby Mountain.

◖ C.P.R.

4 West St., Massapequa Park NY 11762. (518)993-3939. E-mail: d.yannacone@aol.com. **Contact:** Denise Yannacone, A&R. Record company. Estab. 1997. Pays negotiable royalty to artists on contract; statutory rate to publisher per song on record.

How to Contact Submit demo tape by mail. Unsolicited submissions are OK. Prefers cassette, CD or DAT with 4 songs and lyric sheet. Does not return material. Responds in 3-4 months.

Music Mostly **uptempos**, **R&B**, **rap**, **rock**, **pop** and **soundtrack**.

Tips "Keep in mind the sky's the limit. Remember when you feel like quitting, there are no short cuts to success. So please submit songs that are well produced."

◖ CAMBRIA RECORDS & PUBLISHING

P.O. Box 374, Lomita CA 90717. (310)831-1322. Fax: (310)833-7442. E-mail: cambriamus@aol.com. **Contact:** Lance Bowling, director of recording operations. Labels include Charade Records. Record company and music publisher. Estab. 1979. Staff size: 3. Pays 5-8% royalty to artists on contract; statutory rate to publisher for each record sold.

Distributed by Albany Distribution.

How to Contact *Write first and obtain permission to submit.* Prefers cassette. Include SASE. Responds in 1 month.

Music Mostly **classical**. Released *Songs of Elinor Remick Warren* (album) on Cambria Records. Other artists include Marie Gibson (soprano), Leonard Pennario (piano), Thomas Hampson (voice), Mischa Leftkowitz (violin), Leigh Kaplan (piano), North Wind Quintet and Sierra Wind Quintet.

◖ CANDYSPITEFUL PRODUCTIONS

2051 E. Cedar St., #8, Tempe AZ 85281. (480)968-7017. E-mail: mandrakerocks@yahoo.com. Website: www.ca ndyspiteful.com. President: William Ferraro. Professional Managers: Maxwell Frye (jazz, rock). Record company, music publisher (Candyspiteful Productions), record producer (Candyspiteful Productions). Estab. 2000. Staff size: 2. Produces 2 singles, 2 albums per year. Pays negotiable royalty to artists; statutory rate to publisher per song on record.

- Also see the listings for Candyspiteful Productions in the Record Producers section and Major Entertainment (formerly Majestic Control) in the Music Publishers section of this book.

How to Contact Submit CD by mail. Unsolicited submissions are OK. Prefers CD/CDR with 3 songs, lyric sheet and cover letter. "Please include a fact sheet, bio, current play dates, etc." Does not return material. Responds only if interested.

Music Mostly **progressive rock**, **rock/pop**. Released *Cloud Nine* (album by Richard Farnsworth), recorded by Thunderhead (hard rock); and "Seven Opus" (single by Sharon Barlow) from *Seven Opus* (album), recorded by Sharon Barlow (pop), both released 2001 on Candyspiteful Productions.

Tips "We are out in the trenches with our artists and fight hard for them. Often in N.Y. and L.A. and we just may be that person standing in the back checking you out."

◖◖◖ CANTILENA RECORDS

6548 Via Sereno, Rancho Murieta CA 95683-9226. (916)354-8651. E-mail: llzz@aol.com. Website: www.cantile narecords.com. A&R: Laurel Zucker, owner. A&R: Dr. J. Baurerly. Record company. Estab. 1993. Releases 5 CDs/year. Pays Harry Fox standard royalty to artists on contract; statutory rate to publishers per song on record.

How to Contact *Write first and obtain permission to submit or to arrange personal interview.* Prefers CD. Does not return material.

Music Classical, jazz, world music. Released "Caliente!" (single by Christopher Caliendo) from *Caliente! World Music for Flute & Guitar* (album), recorded by Laurel Zucker and Christopher Caliendo! (world crossover); *Suites No. 1 & 2 For Flute & Jazz Piano Trio* (album by Claude Bolling), recorded by Laurel Zucker, Joe Gilman, David Rokeach, Jeff Neighbor (jazz); and *HOPE! Music for Flute, Soprano, Guitar* (album by Daniel Akiva, Astor Piazzolla, Haim Permont, Villa-Lobos) (classical/world), recorded by Laurel Zucker, Ronit Widmann-Levy,

Daniel Akiva, all released in 2004 by Cantilena Records. Other artists include Tim Gorman, Prairie Prince, Dave Margen, Israel Philharmonic, Erkel Chamber Orchestra, Samuel Magill, Renee Siebert, Robin Sutherland and Gerald Ranch.

⊘ CAPITOL RECORDS
1750 N. Vine St., Hollywood CA 90028-5274. (323)462-6252. Fax: (323)469-4542. Website: www.hollywoodand vine.com. **Nashville:** 3322 West End Ave., 11th Floor, Nashville TN 37203. (615)269-2000. Labels include Blue Note Records, Grand Royal Records, Pangaea Records, The Right Stuff Records and Capitol Nashville Records. Record company.
Distributed by EMD.
How to Contact *Capitol Records does not accept unsolicited submissions.*
Music Artists include Coldplay, Beastie Boys, Liz Phair, and Auf der Maur.

✔ ▦ ⊘ CAPP RECORDS
P.O. Box 150871, San Rafael CA 94915-0871. (415)457-8617. Fax: (415)453-6990. E-mail: submissions@capcom pany.com. Website: www.capprecords.com. CEO/International Manager: Dominique Toulon (pop, dance, New Age); Creative Manager/A&R: Manus Buchart (dance, techno). President: Rudolf Stember. Vice President/ Publisher: Marc Oshry (pop, rock, dance). Music publisher (Lappster music/ASCAP and CIDC Music/BMI) and record company. Member: NARAS, NCSA, Songwriter's Guild of America. Estab. 1993. Publishes 100 songs/ year; publishes 25 new songwriters/year. Staff size: 8. Pays standard royalty.
Affiliate(s) Cary August Publishing Co./CAPP Company (Germany)/Capp Company (Japan).
How to Contact Submit demo by mail. Unsolicited submissions are OK. Prefers CD, NTSC videocassette or CD-R with 3 songs and cover letter. "E-mail us in advance for submissions, if possible." Include SASE. Only responds if interested.
Film & TV Places 20 songs in film and 7 songs in TV/year. Music Supervisors: Dominique Toulon (pop, dance, New Age); Mark D. D'Elicio (dance, techno). Published "Wish You Were Here" (by Cary August/Marc Oshry/ Brian Wood/Tom Finch), recorded by Cary August for "Café Froth" TV/ad; "Indian Dream" and "Song For the Earth," both written and recorded by Steven Buckner in "Deep Encounters."
Music Mostly **pop, dance** and **techno**; also **New Age**. Does not want country. Released "It's Not a Dream" (single by Cary August/André Pessis), recorded by Cary August on CAPP Records (dance).

⊘ CAPSTAN RECORD PRODUCTION
P.O. Box 211, East Prairie MO 63845. (575)649-2211. **Contact:** Joe Silver or Tommy Loomas. Labels include Octagon and Capstan Records. Record company, music publisher (Lineage Publishing Co.), management firm (Staircase Promotion) and record producer (Silver-Loomas Productions). Pays 3-5% royalty to artists on contract.
How to Contact Unsolicited submissions are OK. Prefers cassette or VHS videocassette with 2-4 songs and lyric sheet. "Send photo and bio." Include SASE. Responds in 1 month.
Music Mostly **country, easy listening, MOR, country rock** and **top 40/pop.** Released "Country Boy" (single by Alden Lambert); and "Yesterday's Teardrops" and "Round & Round" (single), written and recorded by The Burchetts. Other artists include Bobby Lee Morgan, Skidrow Joe, Vicarie Arcole, Fleming and Scarlett Britoni.

⊘ CASE ENTERTAINMENT GROUP/C.E.G. RECORDS, INC.
102 E. Pikes Peak Ave., #200, Colorado Springs CO 80903. (719)632-0227. Fax: (719)634-2274. E-mail: rac@hpi. net. Website: www.newpants.com and www.oldpants.com. **Contact:** Robert A. Case, president. Record company and music publisher (New Pants Publishing/ASCAP, Old Pants Publishing/BMI). Estab. 1989. Releases 3-4 LPs and 3-4 CDs/year. Pays negotiable royalty to artists on contract.
How to Contact Submit demo tape by mail. Unsolicited submissions are OK. Prefers CD with 3-5 songs and lyric sheet. "Include a brief history of songwriter's career. Songs submitted must be copywritten or pending with copyright office." Does not return material. "Our representative will contact you if interested in material."
Music Mostly **pop, rock** and **country**. Released *James Becker* (album), recorded by James Becker (folk), released 2001 on New Pants; *Romancing the Blues* (album), by Kathy Watson (pop), released 2001 on New Pants; and *Stephanie Aramburo* (album), recorded by Stephanie Aramburo (pop), released 2001 on Old Pants.
Tips "Think of the music business as a job interview. You must be able to sell yourself and the music is your baby. You have to be strong and not deal with rejection as a personal thing. It is not a rejection of you, it's a rejection of the music. Most songwriters don't know how to communicate with labels. The best way is to start a friendship with people at the label."

✔ ⊘ CELLAR RECORDS
703 N. Brinton Ave., Dixon IL 61021. (815)288-2900. E-mail: president@cellarrecords.com. Website: www.cella rrecords.com. **Contact:** Todd Joos, president. A&R Department: Bob Brady, Albert Hurst, Jim Miller, Mark

Summers, Jon Pomplin. Record company, music publisher (Sound Cellar Music/BMI) and record producer (Todd Joos). Estab. 1987. Staff size: 6. Releases 6-8 CDs/year. Pays 15-100% royalty to artists on contract; statutory rate to publisher per song on record. Charges in advance "if you use our studio to record."
Distributed by Harvest Media (www.harvest-mg.com).
How to Contact Submit demo CD by mail. Unsolicited submissions are OK. Prefers CD with 3-4 songs and lyric sheet. Does not return material. Responds in 1 month only if interested. "If we like it we will call you."
Music Mostly **metal**, **country**, **rock**, **pop** and **blues**. *"No rap."* Released "With Any Luck at All" (single by Tony Stampley/Randy Boudreaux/Joe Stampley) from *With Any Luck At All* (album), recorded by Cal Stage (pop/country); "Sleeping With a Smile" (single by Tony Stampley/Melissa Lyons/Tommy Barnes) from *With Any Luck At All* (album), recorded by Cal Stage (pop/country); and "Speed of My Life" (single by Jon Pomplin/Todd Joss) from *Declassified* (album), recorded by Project 814 (rock), all released 2001 on Cellar Records. Other artists include Eric Topper, Snap Judgment, Ballistic, Dago Red, Sea of Monsters, Rogue, Kings, James Miller, Vehement, Noopy Wilson, Dual Exhaust, Junker Jorg, The Unknown, Joel Ramirez & the Allstars, Tracylyn, Junk Poet, Cajun Anger, Roman, Flesh Pilgrims, LYZ, and Justice4.
Tips "Make sure that you understand your band is a business and you must be willing to self-invest time, effort and money just like any other new business. We can help you, but you must also be willing to help yourself."

☐ CHATTAHOOCHEE RECORDS
2544 Roscomare Rd., Los Angeles CA 90077. (818)788-6863. Fax: (310)471-2089. E-mail: cyardum@prodigy.net. **Contact:** Robyn Meyers, Music Director/A&R. Music Director: Chris Yardum. Record company and music publisher (Etnoc/Conte). Member NARAS. Releases 4 singles/year. Pays negotiable royalty to artists on contract.
How to Contact Submit demo tape by mail. Unsolicited submissions are OK. Prefers cassette with 2-6 songs and lyric sheet. *Does not return material.* Responds in 2 months only if interested.
Music Mostly **rock**. Released *Don't Touch It Let It Drip* (album), recorded by Cream House (hard rock), released 2000 on Chattahoochee Records. Artists include DNA.

☑ CHERRY STREET RECORDS
P.O. Box 52626, Tulsa OK 74152. (918)742-8087. Fax: (918)742-8003. E-mail: info@cherrystreetmusic.com. Website: www.cherrystreetrecords.com. President: Rodney Young. Vice President: Steve Hickerson. Record company and music publisher. Estab. 1990. Staff size: 2. Releases 2 CD/year. Pays 50% royalty to artists on contract; statutory rate to publisher per song on record.
Distributed by Internet.
How to Contact *Write first and obtain permission to submit.* Prefers cassette or videocassette with 4 songs and lyric sheet. Include SASE. Responds in 4 months.
Music Rock, **country** and **R&B**; also **jazz**. Released *Promise Land* (album), written and recorded by Richard Neville on Cherry Street (rock). Other artists include George W. Carroll and Chris Blevins.
Tips "We sign only artists who play an instrument, sing and write songs. Send only your best four songs."

☑ CHIAROSCURO RECORDS
830 Broadway, New York NY 10003. (212)473-0479. Fax: (845)279-5025. E-mail: jon@chiaroscurojazz.com. Website: www.ChiaroscuroJazz.com. **Contact:** Jon Bates, A&R/operations manager. Labels include Downtown Sound. Record company and record producer (Hank O'Neal, Andrew Sordoni, Jon Bates). Estab. 1973. Releases 12 CDs/year. Pays negotiable royalty to artists on contract; statutory rate to publisher per song on record.
Distributed by Allegro.
How to Contact Submit demo tape by mail. Unsolicited submissions are OK. Prefers cassette, CD, DAT or videocassette with 1-3 songs. Include SASE. Responds in 6 weeks.
Music Mostly **jazz** and **blues**. "A full catalog listing is available on the web at www.chiarascurojazz.com or by calling (800)528-2582. Reissues and new recordings for 2003 by the following artists: Earl Hines, Junior Nance & Joe Temperly, Abdullah Ibrahim and Bobby Hackett."
Tips "We are not a pop label. Our average release sells between 3,000-5,000 copies in the first three years. We do not give cash advances or tour support, and our average budget per release is about $15,000 including all production, printing and manufacturing costs."

☑ CKB RECORDS/HELAPHAT ENTERTAINMENT
527 Larry Court, Irving TX 75060. (214)986-5412. E-mail: spoonfedmusik@juno.com. **Contact:** Tony Briggs, CEO. Record company and production company. Estab. 1999. Staff size: 8. Pays negotiable royalty to artists on contract.
Distributed by Crystal Clear Distribution.
How to Contact Submit demo by mail. Unsolicited submissions are OK. Prefers CD with 4 songs, cover letter and press clippings. Does not return materials. Responds only if interested.

Record Companies

Music Mostly **rap**, **hip-hop** and **R&B**. Released "Body, Body" (single), recorded by T-Spoon (hip-hop), released 2002 on CKB Records; and "We Can't Be Stopped" (single) from *Ouncified* (album), written and recorded by Tha 40 Clique (hip-hop), released 2002 on CKB. Other artists include Baby Tek, Lil' Droop, Shampoo, Deuce Loc, Tré and Laticia Love.

Tips "Be confident, honest and open to ideas."

✅ CLEOPATRA RECORDS
13428 Maxella Ave., PMB 251, Marina del Rey CA 90292. (310)823-0337. Fax: (310)823-5497. **Contact:** Sydney Lanix or Jason Myers. Labels include Hypnotic, Deadline, X-Ray, Cult, Stardust and Purple Pyramid. Record company. Estab. 1991. Releases 5 singles, 10 LPs, 5 EPs and 100 CDs/year. Pays 10-14% royalty to artists on contract; negotiable rate to publisher per song on record.

How to Contact Submit demo tape by mail. Unsolicited submissions are OK. Prefers CD with 3 songs. Does not return material. Responds in 1 month.

Music Mostly **industrial**, **gothic** and **trance**; also **heavy metal**, **space rock** and **electronic**.

✅ ✅ COAL HARBOR MUSIC
P.O. Box 148027, Nashville TN 37214-8027. (615)883-2020. E-mail: info@coalharborbmusic.com. Website: www.coalharbormusic.com. President/Owner: Jerry R. Wells, (country/pop/rock). Vice President: Angela R. Wells (gospel/contemporary Christian). Labels include Coal Harbor. Record company, music publisher (Coal Harbor Music/BMI), record producer (Jerry R. Wells), radio promotion agency, management firm, booking agency, demo services, recording studio, artist development. Estab. 1990. Staff size: 2. Releases 3 singles/year and 4 CDs/year. Pays negotiable royalty to artists on contract; statutory royalty to publisher per song on record.

• Also see the listing for Coal Harbor Music in the Music Publishers section of this book.

Distributed by Self distribution.

How to Contact Send CD with 3-5 songs, lyric sheet, and cover letter. Does not return submissions. Responds only if interested.

Music Mostly **country**, **gospel** and **contemporary Christian**; also **pop**, **rock** and **jazz/bluegrass instrumental**.

✅ 🌐 ⬜ COLLECTOR RECORDS
P.O. Box 1200, 3260 AE oud beyerland Holland. Phone: (31)186 604266. Fax: (31)186 604366. E-mail: cees@collectorrec.com. Website: www.collectorrecords.nl. **Contact:** Cees Klop, president. Manager: John Moore. Labels include All Rock, Downsouth, Unknown, Pro Forma and White Label Records. Record company, music publisher (All Rock Music Publishing) and record producer (Cees Klop). Estab. 1967. Staff size: 4. Release 25 LPs/year. Pays 10% royalty to artist on contract.

How to Contact Submit demo tape by mail. Unsolicited submissions are OK. Prefers cassette. SAE and IRC. Responds in 2 months.

Music Mostly **'50s rock**, **rockabilly**, **hillbilly boogie** and **country/rock**; also **piano boogie woogie**. Released *Rock Crazy Baby* (album), recorded by Art Adams (1950s rockabilly), released 2004; *Rock-A-Sock-A-Hop* (album), recorded by Jimmy Crain (1950's rockers), released 2004, all on Collector Records. Other artists include Henk Pepping.

✅ ✅ COLUMBIA RECORDS
550 Madison Ave., 24th Floor, New York NY 10022. (212)833-4000. Fax: (212)833-4389. **Santa Monica:** 2100 Colorado Ave., Santa Monica CA 90404. (310)449-2100. Fax: (310)449-2743. **Nashville:** 34 Music Square E., Nashville TN 37203. (615)742-4321. Fax: (615)244-2549. E-mail: sonymusiconline@sonymusic.com. Website: www.columbiarecords.com. Labels include So So Def Records and Ruffhouse Records. Record company.

Distributed by Sony.

How to Contact *Columbia Records does not accept unsolicited submissions.*

Music Artists include Aerosmith, Marc Anthony, Beyonce, Bob Dylan, and Patti Smith.

📍 ✅ COMPADRE RECORDS
101 Crawford, Suite 2J, Houston TX 77002. (713)228-3847. Fax: (713)228-3843. E-mail: info@compadrerecords.com. Website: www.compadrerecords.com. **Contact:** Brad Turcotte, president. **Tennessee Office:** 806 Centeroak Dr., Knoxville TN 37920. (615)423-2038. Fax: (615)726-8601. Record company. Estab. 2001.

Distributed by RED/Sony Music.

How to Contact "We can't promise that we will listen to every demo that is sent to us, but we welcome any submission. We enjoy listening to new material and support the creative process. Keep writing, sing loud and keep the spirit alive."

Music Mostly **Americana**. Released *Billy and the Kid* (album), recorded by Billy Joe Shaver; and *James McMur-*

try—Live (album), recorded by James McMurtry, both released 2004 on Compadre. Other artists include Suzy Bogguss, Flaco Jimenez, Kate Campbell, and Kevin Kinney.

☑ ✆ COMPENDIA MUSIC

210 25th Ave. N., Suite 1200, Nashville TN 37203. (615)277-1800. Fax: (615)277-1801. Website: www.compendi amusic.com. Vice President/General Manager, Compendia Label & Intersound: Ric Pepin (country/rock; contemporary jazz); Vice President/General Manager, Light Records: Phillip White (black gospel). Record company. Labels include Compendia, Light Records, Life², Intersound. Pays negotiable royalty to artists on contract; negotiable rate to publisher per song on record.

How to Contact *Write or call first and obtain permission to submit.* Prefers CD with 3 songs. "We will contact the songwriter when we are interested in the material." Does not return material. Responds only if interested.

Music Mostly **country**, **rock**, **gospel** and **classical**. Artists include Joan Osborne, Robert Palmer, Mighty Clouds of Joy.

☑ ◻ COMSTOCK RECORDS LTD.

P.O. Box 19720, Fountain Hills AZ 85269. (480)951-3115. Fax: (480)951-3074. E-mail: fara@comstockrecords.c om. Website: www.comstockrecords.com. Production Manager/Producer: Patty Parker. President: Frank Fara. Record company, music publisher (White Cat Music/ASCAP, Rocky Bell Music/BMI, How the West Was Sung Music/BMI), record producer (Patty Parker) and radio promotion. Member CMA, BBB, CCMA, BCCMA, British CMA and AF of M. "Comstock Records, Ltd. has three primary divisions: Production, Promotion and Publishing. We distribute and promote both our own Nashville productions, as well as already completed country or pop/ rock CDs. We also offer CD design and mastering and manufacturing for products we promote. We can master from a copy of your DAT master or CD." Staff size: 2. Releases 10-12 CD singles, 10-12 albums/year and 5-6 international sampler CDs. Pays 10% royalty to artists on contract; statutory rate to publishers for each record sold. "Artists pay distribution and promotion fee to press and release their masters."

• Comstock Records was named indie Label of the Year at ECMA of Europe's Country Music Awards for 1998 and 1999. Fara & Parker are also authors of the book *How To Open Doors in the Music Industry—The Independent Way* (available through amazon.com).

How to Contact Submit CD by postal mail only. "We do not accept audio files online." Unsolicited submissions are OK. "Submission by CD only (no cassette)." Include SASE. "Enclose stamped return envelope if demo is to be returned." Responds in 2 weeks.

Music Released *Weed and Water* (album by Paul Marshall and various co-writers), recorded by Paul Marshall (country), released on Comstock/Scostepa Music; *Britt Hammond* (album), recorded by Britt Hammond (country). Other artists include Kevin Atwater, Mahoney Brothers, Lorena Prater, Crissy Cummings and Kelli Lidell.

Tips "Go global—good songs and good singers are universal. Country acts from North America will find a great response in the overseas radio market. Likewise U.S. Radio is open to the fresh new sounds that foreign artists bring to the airwaves."

✆ COSMOTONE RECORDS

PMB 412, 3350-A Highway 6 S., Sugar Land TX 77478. E-mail: marianland@earthlink.net. Website: www.maria nland.com/music.html. Record company, music publisher (Cosmotone Music, ASCAP) and record producer (Rafael Brom). Estab. 1984.

Distributed by marianland.com.

How to Contact "We do not accept material at this time." Does not return materials.

Music All types. Released *Angelophany*, *The True Measure of Love*, *All My Love to You Jesus* (albums), and *Rafael Brom Unplugged* (live concert DVD), by Rafael Brom.

✆ CPA RECORDS

15104 Golden Eagle Way, Tampa FL 33625-1545. (813)920-4605. Fax:(813)926-0846. E-mail: al@cparecords.c om. Website: www.cparecords.com. **Contact:** Al McDaniel, president. Labels include Coffee's Productions and Associates. Record company and music publisher (CPA Music Publishing). Estab. 1999. Staff size: 5. Releases 3 singles and 2 albums/year. Pays negotiable royalty to artists on contract; negotiable royalty to publisher per song on record.

How to Contact *Write or call first and obtain permission to submit a demo.* Prefers CD/CDR and VHS videocassette with 3 songs, lyric sheet, lead sheet and cover letter. Include SASE. Responds in 2 weeks.

Music Mostly **gospel/Christian**, **rhythm**, **blues** and **jazz**; also **pop** and **rap**. Does not want country. Released "Somwhere" (single by Al McDaniel) from *"Coffee" Greatest Oldies* (album), recorded by Al "Coffee' McDaniel (jazz), released 2002 on CPA Records; and "The Last Dance" (single by Al McDaniel) from *"Coffee" Greatest Oldies* (album), recorded by Al "Coffee' McDaniel (R&B), released 2002 on CPS Records. Other artists include Sax Kari, Anthony "Big Lou" McDaniel, and Mike and Anita.

Tips "Be marketable, creative, committed to achieving success, and willing to work hard to accomplish your goals."

☑ ○ CRANK! A RECORD COMPANY

Attn: New Rock, 1223 Wilshire Blvd. #823, Santa Monica CA 90403. (310)392-8985. Fax: (310)399-7355. E-mail: fan@crankthis.com. Website: www.crankthis.com. **Contact:** Jeff Matlow. Record company. Estab. 1994. Releases 6 singles, 5 LPs, 2 EPs and 5 CDs/year. Pays negotiable royalty to artists on contract.
Distributed by Southern, Revolver, Lumberjack and Nail.
How to Contact Submit demo by mail. Unsolicited submissions are OK. Prefers CD. "Send whatever best represents your abilities." Does not return material. Responds in 6 weeks.
Music Mostly **indie/alternative rock** and **pop**. Released *Neva Dinova* (album), written and recorded by Neva Dinova; *Mono* (album), written and recorded by The Icarus Line (rock/punk); *Down Marriott Lane!* (album), written and recorded by the Get Set (rock/pop); *The Power of Failing*, written and recorded by Mineral (rock); *Boys Life*, written and recorded by Boys Life (rock); and *Such Blinding Stars for Starving Eyes*, written and recorded by Cursive (rock), all on Crank! Other artists include Fireside, Errortype:11, Onelinedrawing, The Regrets, Sunday's Best and Gloria Record.

○ CREATIVE IMPROVISED MUSIC PROJECTS (CIMP) RECORDS

Cadence Building, Redwood NY 13679. (315)287-2852. Fax: (315)287-2860. Website: www.cadencebuilding.com. **Contact:** Bob Rusch, producer. Labels include Cadence Jazz Records. Record company and record producer (Robert D. Rusch). Estab. 1980. Releases 25-30 CDs/year. Pays negotiable royalty to artists on contract; pays statutory rate to publisher per song on record.
Distributed by North Country Distributors.
● CIMP specializes in jazz and creative improvised music.
How to Contact Submit demo tape or CD by mail. Unsolicited submissions are OK. Prefers cassette or CD. "We are not looking for songwriters but recording artists." Include SASE. Responds in 1 week.
Music Mostly **jazz** and **creative improvised music**. Released *The Redwood Session* (album), recorded by Evan Parker, Barry Guy, Paul Lytton and Joe McPhee; *Sarah's Theme* (album), recorded by the Ernie Krivda Trio, Bob Fraser and Jeff Halsey; and *Human Flowers* (album), recorded by the Bobby Zankel Trio, Marily Crispell and Newman Baker, all released on CIMP (improvised jazz). Other artists include Arthur Blyme, John McPhee, David Prentice, Anthony Braxton, Roswell Rudd, Paul Smoker, Khan Jamal, Odean Pope, etc.
Tips "CIMP Records are produced to provide music to reward repeated and in-depth listenings. They are recorded live to two-track which captures the full dynamic range one would experience in a live concert. There is no compression, homogenization, eq-ing, post-recording splicing, mixing, or electronic fiddling with the performance. Digital recording allows for a vanishingly low noise floor and tremendous dynamic range. This compression of the dynamic range is what limits the 'air' and life of many recordings. Our recordings capture the dynamic intended by the musicians. In this regard these recordings are demanding. Treat the recording as your private concert. Give it your undivided attention and it will reward you. CIMP Records are not intended to be background music. This method is demanding not only on the listener but on the performer as well. Musicians must be able to play together in real time. They must understand the dynamics of their instrument and how it relates to the others around them. There is no fix-it-in-the-mix safety; either it works or it doesn't. What you hear is exactly what was played. Our main concern is music not marketing."

☑ ⊘ CURB RECORDS

47 Music Square E., Nashville TN 37203. (615)321-5080. Fax: (615)327-1964. Website: www.curb.com. **Contact:** John Ozler, A&R coordinator. Record company.
How to Contact Curb Records does not accept unsolicited submissions; accepts previously published material only. *Do not submit without permission.*
Music Released *Everywhere* (album), recorded by Tim McGraw; *Sittin' On Top of the World* (album), recorded by LeAnn Rimes; and *I'm Alright* (album), recorded by Jo Dee Messina, all on Curb Records. Other artists include Mary Black, Merle Haggard, Kal Ketchum, David Kersh, Lyle Lovett, Tim McGraw, Wynonna and Sawyer Brown.

○ ALAN DALE PRODUCTIONS

1630 Judith Lane, Indianapolis IN 46227. (317)786-1630. E-mail: AlanDale2211@aol.com. **Contact:** Alan D. Heshelman, president. Labels include ALTO Records. Record company. Estab. 1990. Pays 10% royalty to artists on contract.
How to Contact *Write or call first and obtain permission to submit or to arrange personal interview.* Prefers cassette with 3 songs. Does not return material. Responds in 10 weeks.
Music Mostly **A/C**, **country**, **jazz**, **gospel** and **New Age**.
Tips "At the present time, we are only looking for vocalists to promote as we promote the songs we write and produce."

☑ ☺ DEARY ME RECORDS

P.O. Box 19315, Cincinnati OH 45219. (859)442-0477. E-mail: jim@dearymerecords.com. Website: www.deary merecords.com. **Contact:** Jim Farmer, director of business & A&R. Record company. Estab. 1995. Staff size: 2. Releases 3 CDs/year. Pays 50% royalty "after we break even."

How to Contact Unsolicited submissions are OK. "Please check our website for submission policy."

Music Mostly **garage rock**, **country punk** and **rockabilly**. Released *This Is Our ~ Music* (album by Matt Hart/Darren Callahan), recorded by Travel (off-beat punk), released 2000 on Deary Me Records; *Tender Trap* (album), recorded by Fairmount Girls (indie rock), released 2001 on Deary Me Records; and *Black Box Broken* (album), recorded by Chalk (indie rock), released 2001 on Deary Me Records. Also released singles by the Greenhornes and Thee Shams (garage rock), and rereleased the Wolverton Brothers first album (country punk).

Tips "We can't do it all. So be absolutely willing to push your release by playing as many shows as possible."

☐ DEEP SOUTH ENTERTAINMENT

P.O. Box 17737, Raleigh NC 27619-7737. (919)844-1515. Fax: (919)847-5922. E-mail: info@deepsouthentertain ment.com. Website: www.deepsouthentertainment.com. Director of Artist Relations: Amy Cox, associate manager. Record company and management company. Estab. 1996. Staff size: 10. Pays negotiable royalty to artists on contract; statutory rate to publisher per song on record.

Distributed by Redeye Distribution, Valley, Select-O-Hits, City Hall, AEC/Bassin, Northeast One Stop, Pollstar and Koch International.

How to Contact Submit demo tape by mail. Unsolicited submissions are OK. Prefers cassette or CD with 3 songs, cover letter and press clippings. Does not return material. Responds only if interested.

Music Mostly **pop**, **modern rock** and **alternative**; also **swing**, **rockabilly** and **heavy rock**. Does not want rap or R&B. Artists include Bruce Hornsby, Little Feat, Mike Daly, SR-71, Stretch Princess, Darden Smith and many more.

☺ DEL-FI RECORDS, INC.

8271 Melrose Ave., Suite 103, Los Angeles CA 90046. (800)993-3534. Fax: (323)966-4805. E-mail: info@del-fi.com. Website: www.del-fi.com. **Contact:** Bob Keane, owner and president. Labels include Del-Fi, Del-Fi Nashville, Donna, Mustang, Bronco and others. Record company. Estab. 1957. Releases 5-10 LPs and 40 CDs/year. Pays negotiable royalty to artists on contract; statutory rate to publisher per song on record.

Distributed by Bayside, Burnside, Action Music, Hep Cat and Get Hip.

- Del-Fi's open door policy is legendary.

How to Contact Submit demo tape by mail. Unsolicited submissions are OK. Prefers cassette or CD. "Please enclose bio information and photo if possible. Send a résumé via fax." Does not return material "unless specified. Allow several weeks." Responds in 1 month.

Music Mostly **rock**, **surf/drag** and **exotica**. Recently released *Out There in the Dark* (album), written and recorded by Outrageous Cherry (rock); and *Cloud Eleven* (album), written and recorded by Cloud Eleven (rock/pop), *Be Pretty, Be Naked, Be Quiet* (album), recorded by the Rumble Bees (comedy). Other artists include The El Caminos.

Tips "Be sure you are making/writing music that specifically meets your own artistic/creative demands, and not someone else's. Write/play music from the heart and soul and you will always succeed on a personal rewarding level first. We are *the* surf label . . . home of the 'Delphonic' sound. We've also released many of the music world's best known artists, including Ritchie Valens and the Bobby Fuller Four."

Ⓝ ⊕ ☺ DEMI MONDE RECORDS AND PUBLISHING, LTD.

Foel Studio, Llanfair Caereinion, Powys, Wales, United Kingdom. Phone/fax: (01938)810758. E-mail: demi.mon de@dial.pipex.com. Website: www.demimonde.co.uk/demimonde. Managing Director: Dave Anderson. Record company, music publisher (Demi Monde Records & Publishing, Ltd.) and record producer (Dave Anderson). Estab. 1983. Releases 5 12" singles, 10 LPs and 6 CDs/year. Pays 10% royalty to artists on contract; statutory rate to publisher per song on record.

Distributed by Pinnacle, Magnum and Shellshock.

How to Contact Submit demo tape by mail. Unsolicited submissions are OK. Prefers cassette with 3-4 songs. Does not return material. Responds in 6 weeks.

Music Mostly **rock**, **R&B** and **pop**. Released *Hawkwind, Amon Duul II & Gong* and *Groundhogs* (by T.S. McPhee), all on Demi Monde Records.

☐ DENTAL RECORDS

P.O. Box 20058 DHCC, New York NY 10017. (212)486-4513. Fax: (212)832-6370. E-mail: rsanford@dentalrecord s.com. Website: www.dentalrecords.com. **Contact:** Rick Sanford, owner. Record company. Estab. 1981. Staff size: 2. Releases 1-2 CDs/year. Pays negotiable royalty to artists on contract; statutory rate to publisher per song on record.

Distributed by Dutch East India Trading.

How to Contact Submit demo tape by mail. Unsolicited submissions are OK. Prefers CD with any number of songs, lyric sheet and cover letter. "Check our website to see if your material is appropriate." Include SASE. Responds only if interested.

Music Pop derived structures, jazz derived harmonies and **neo-classic-wannabee-pretenses**. Does not want urban, heavy metal or hard core. Released *Perspectivism*, written and recorded by Rick Sanford (instrumental), released 2003 on Dental Records. Other artists include Les Izmor.

☐ DISCMEDIA

2134 Newport Blvd., Costa Mesa CA 92627. (949)631-8597. Fax: (949)515-7499. E-mail: irmavideo@hotmail.com. Website: www.discmedia.com. **Contact:** Irma Moller, manager. Producers: Glenn Moller (rock, dance) and Henry Moller (pop). Record company, music publisher (Discmedia) and record producer (Moller Digital Studios). Estab. 1989.

How to Contact Submit demo tape by mail. Unsolicited submissions are OK. Prefers cassette, CD or VHS with 1 or more songs, lyric sheet and cover letter. "Do not call after submitting." Does not return materials. Responds only if interested.

Music Mostly **rock**, **pop** and **dance**; also **bilingual Spanish material** (dance, pop-merengue, rock ballads).

☐ DISCOS FUENTES/MIAMI RECORDS & EDIMUSICA USA

(formerly Miami Records), % Arc Music Group, 254 W. 54th St., 13th Floor, New York NY 10019. (212)246-3333. E-mail: info@arcmusic.com. Website: www.arcmusic.com. **Contact:** Juan Carlos Barguil. Vice President: Jorge Fuentes. President: Alejandro Fuentes. Labels include Discos Fuentes. Record company, music publisher (Edimusica-USA). Estab. 1936. Staff size: 14. Releases 13 singles and 89 CDs/year. Pays negotiable royalty to artists on contract; statutory rate to publisher per song on record.

    ● Edimusica-USA, Discos Fuentes/Miami Publishing Division entered into an administration deal effective August 18, 2000 with Arc Music Group.

Distributed by Miami Records.

How to Contact Submit demo CD/CDR by mail. Unsolicited submissions are OK. Prefers CD/CDR with lyric sheet. Does not return material. Responds only if interested.

Music Mostly **salsa**, **cumbia** and **vallenato**; also **grupera**, **merengue** and **tropical**. Released *Que Lindo Cu* (album) by Rafael Benitez), recorded by Sonora Dinamita (cumbia); *Mi Libertad* (album by Saulo Sanchez), recorded by Fruko y Sostesos (salsa); and *El Majedro (El Viagra)* (album by Elkin Garcia), recorded by Embajadores Vallenatos (vallenato). Other artists include Sonora Carruseles, The Latin Brothers, Los Chiches Vallenatos, Latinos En La Casa, Chambacu, Pastor Lopez, Grupo Mayoral, Los Titanes and Frank La P & Anthony.

Tips "Please keep sending us material. Don't give up if we do not use your first demo."

☑ ⊘ DM RECORDS GROUP

(formerly DM/Bellmark/Critique Records), 301 Yamato Rd., Suite 1250, Boca Raton FL 33431. (561)988-1820. Fax: (561)988-1821. Website: www.dmrecords.com. President: Mark Watson. Record company, music publisher (Bass Tracks & Ashley Watson Publishing) and record producer (Bass 305). Estab. 1992. Releases 16-20 CDs/year. Pays negotiable royalty to artists on contract; 75% statutory rate to publisher per song on record. Labels include Ichiban, Belmark, Wrap Records, Sky Records, Wild Dog Blues, and Altered.

Distributed by Ryko/WEA.

How to Contact Submit CD/CDR by mail. Unsolicited submissions are OK. Prefers CD/CDR. Does not return material. Responds in 2 weeks, if interested.

Music Mostly **southern rap**, **R&B** and **gospel**; also **dance**.

☑ ⊞ ⊘ DREAMWORKS RECORDS

2220 Colorado Ave., Santa Monica CA 90404. (310)365-1000. Fax: (310)865-8059. Website: www.dreamworksrecords.com. **Nashville:** 60 Music Sq. E., Nashville TN 37203. (615)463-4600. Fax: (615)463-4601. Record company and music publisher (DreamWorks SKG Music Publishing). Labels include Interscope, Geffen, and A&M.

How to Contact Material must be submitted through an agent or attorney. *Does not accept unsolicited submissions.*

⊘ DRUMBEAT INDIAN ARTS, INC.

4143 N. 16th St., Suite 1, Phoenix AZ 85016. (602)266-4823. **Contact:** Bob Nuss, president. Labels include Indian House and Sweet Grass. Record company and distributor of American Indian recordings. Estab. 1984. Staff size: 8. Releases 50 cassettes and 50 CDs/year. Royalty varies with project.

• Note that Drumbeat Indian Arts is a very specialized label, and only wants to receive submissions by Native American artists.

How to Contact *Call first and obtain permission to submit.* Prefers cassette or VHS videocassette. Include SASE. Responds in 2 months.

Music Music by American Indians—any style (must be enrolled tribal members). Does not want New Age "Indian style" material. Released *Pearl Moon* (album), written and recorded by Xavier (native Amerindian), released 2000 on Sweet Grass. Other artists include Black Lodge Singers, R. Carlos Nakai, Lite Foot, and Joanne Shenandoah.

Tips "We deal only with American Indian performers. We do not accept material from others. Please include tribal affiliation."

Ⓝ Ⓓ DWELL RECORDS

Attn: A&R, P.O. Box 39439, Los Angeles CA 90039. Website: www.dwellrecords.com. Label Managers: Rex Quick. Record company. Estab. 1991. Staff size: 11. Releases 15 CDs/year.

Distributed by DNA, Navarre, Handleman, BMG and Columbia House.

How to Contact Submit demo tape by mail. Unsolicited submissions are OK. Prefers CD, bio and photo with press clippings. Does not return materials. Responds only if interested.

Music Mostly **extreme heavy music**. Released *Procession to the Infraworld* (album), written and recorded by The Chasm (dark metal); and *Gods of Creation, Death, and Afterlife* (album).

Tips "Submit quality music."

Ⓓ EDMONDS RECORD GROUP

(formerly Yab Yum Records), 1635 N. Cahenga Blvd., 6th Floor, Los Angeles CA 90028. (323)860-1520. Fax: (323)860-1537. Record company.

Distributed by J Records.

How to Contact No accepting unsolicited demos.

Ⓓ ELEKTRA RECORDS

75 Rockefeller Plaza, 17th Floor, New York NY 10019. Website: www.elektra.com. Labels include Elektra Records, Eastwest Records and Asylum Records. Record company.

Distributed by WEA.

How to Contact *Elektra does not accept unsolicited submissions.*

Music Mostly **alternative/modern rock**. Artists include Phish, Jason Mraz, Björk, Busta Rhymes, and Metallica.

Ⓒ EMF RECORDS & AFFILIATES

633 Post, Suite #145, San Francisco CA 94109. (415)273-1421. Fax: (415)752-2442. E-mail: onelinkglobal1@aol.com. **Contact:** Steven Lassiter, director of operations. Vice President, A&R (all styles): Michael Miller. A&R Supervisor (commercial): Robin Taylor. International Producer (world artists): Kimberly Nakamori. Producer/Writer (all or most styles): Joe Tsongo. Labels include Richland Communications, Sky Bent and Urbana Sounds. Record company. Estab. 1994. Staff size: 9. Releases 5 CDs/year. Pays negotiable royalty to artists on contract; statutory rate to publisher per song on record.

Distributed by GTI Marketing and Songo Publishing International.

How to Contact Submit demo CD by mail. Unsolicited submissions are OK. Prefers CD with 3 songs and lyric and lead sheets. Does not return material. Responds in 4 months.

Music Mostly **urban/pop/rock**, **jazz/Latin** and **New Age/classical (crossover)**; also **country**, **world beat** and **ethnic (world)**. Released *Mutual Impact*, written and recorded by Joe Tsongo on EMF Records (New Age); *If I Had Your Love*, written and recorded by Flamé on Richland Communications (soft jazz); and *From The Source* (by B. Flores/A. Jiminez), recorded by Orchestra de Sabor on Urbana Sounds (salsa/Latin jazz). Other artists include Slam Jam.

Tips "Build your fan base and present good images or professional packages as much as possible. Market focus in your genre is a must. Beware of trends in music and film."

☑ Ⓒ ENTOURAGE MUSIC GROUP

11115 Magnolia Blvd., N. Hollywood CA 91601. (818)505-0001. Fax: (818)761-7956. E-mail: guy@E51.biz. Website: www.entouragestudios.com. **Contact:** Guy Paonessa, president. Record company and recording studio. Estab. 1986 (studio); 1995 (label). Releases 4 CDs/year. Pays negotiable royalty to artists on contract; statutory rate to publisher per song on record.

Distributed by Touchwood Distribution.

How to Contact Submit demo tape by mail. Unsolicited submissions are OK. Prefers cassette, CD, DAT or ½″ videocassette with 3-10 songs. "No phone calls please." Include SASE. Responds in 3 months.

Bibi Farber

New Life Through Licensing

Performing songwriter Bibi Farber began her musical career as a teenager in the late-'70s New Wave scene of Sweden. The Swedish New Wavers drew inspiration from punk rock, especially New York punk progenitors Television (featuring virtuosic guitarists/songwriters Richard Lloyd and Tom Verlaine). "I started songwriting when I was a teenager in Sweden and New Wave music was just starting to happen," she says. "I played bass, and everybody was inspired by punk and the whole DIY (Do It Yourself) ethic. It was much more grassroots than America, where unless you were in a major place like New York or L.A., what we now call 'classic rock' still reigned. But in Sweden everyone I was hanging out with was learning an instrument and playing and writing. It was a very vital, vibrant scene."

After six years in Sweden, Farber returned to New York to attend college. She continued writing and performing upbeat pop music throughout the '80s in a band with her sister and another songwriter named Greg Talenfeld. This band stayed together for several years, but didn't find the break they were looking for. "We would have fit on a bill with the Smithereens or Katrina and the Waves," says Farber, "and pop has always been my passion—really strong melodies, upbeat guitars, nice arrangements, harmonies, strings—anything that is "pop" is what I love. We put out an EP, and there were several bands I recorded as much as 10 or 15 songs with, but we never went on to release them or get deals."

In the '90s, Farber finally found a break after making the acquaintance of one of her teenage heroes, Television guitarist Richard Lloyd. Lloyd had maintained a solo career since the '70s and played lead guitar on albums and on tour for "power pop" artist Mathew Sweet. Farber's demo tape found its way into Lloyd's hand, and he subsequently took on the role of producer and musical mentor. This musical relationship led directly to *Firepop*, Farber's first full solo album. "I finally got to make my first record with Richard Lloyd," she says, "which I put out myself, and he's all over the record and plays guitar and produced it. We did a lot of playing, and he ended up having me in his band for four years, which was another fantastic adventure."

Firepop earned positive reviews and Farber sold some copies through her own efforts, but the cost of major promotion and distribution were beyond her resources as an independent artist. (She now estimates the costs of rehearsal and production for *Firepop* amounted to between $15,000 and $18,000 of her own money.) It seemed as if she would have to accept some severe limitations to her financial success as an artist—until she discovered the world of online commercial musical licensing through Pump Audio (www.pumpaudio.com), a small online music licensing company based in upstate New York. Having complete control of her own master tapes and copyrights was beneficial after all. "The icing on the cake," she says, "is that one of the songs from *Firepop*—'Shine,'—ended up in a Kodak commercial! I had some songwriter friends who said 'You should send some stuff to Pump Audio.' They place music to indie filmmakers, sometimes for commercials, and to TV producers when they need incidental music but don't want to build it from the ground up and can't afford real licensing fees—meaning they're not going to buy a Bee-Gees song!"

Farber initially felt skeptical because of a previous negative experience in the world of music licensing. "There was one other licensing possibility that came via a distribution company that later went under owing a lot of people money," she says. "They almost got one of my songs placed in *Daria*, the MTV cartoon show. I still don't know if they did or didn't run it, because I sent them the contract, and from then on it was impossible to reach them! But, let's just say it started fresh with Pump Audio."

In this case, she decided the non-exclusive contract terms were worth a shot, and she quickly scored some small license fees for songs off of *Firepop*. "I said, 'OK. What harm could be done?' It's non-exclusive, there's no fee to sign up," she says, "and they simply catalog your songs according to genre, tempo, etc. When somebody comes calling for something in that genre and tempo, they have your stuff right there online, it comes up, and the client listens to it. I sent them my stuff, got in their system, and got some little license fees of under $200. 'Caroline's Waiting' was actually used in a World Wrestling Federation home video, and I still get these little moneys trickling in from that."

Then she got a call that her song "Shine" was under consideration by Kodak. "They called one day and said, 'We just wanted to call and make sure you have access to the masters of this song, because there is a big company possibly interested, and we just want to make sure you have access to the masters.' And, I thought, 'Wow, OK, well the masters are on 24-track tape. It's not like a little ProTools disk. But, yes, I have access to the masters!' Another week goes by, another few days, and they say, 'OK, now you're one of two people they're considering. It's gone from sixteen songs down to two songs, and one of them is yours.' A few days later, sure enough, they said, 'Your song won!' "

She later received a check for $10,500 (followed by another $1,400 in performance royalties from BMI for the commercial's appearances on television). Although tiny by the standards of a large corporation, it was a windfall for an independent artist like Farber. "That amount was for just thirty seconds of music," she says, "and I didn't even need to go and do anything with the masters. All I did was fax in a contract. It's totally non-exclusive. I'm just not allowed to give it to any other camera manufacturers within the next three years."

The money she received through this deal has gone a long way toward recouping the costs of producing *Firepop* and also facilitated the recording of her new solo record, *Second Kiss*. This time around, she's made sure to build the album's recording process to accommodate the possible requests for alternate mixes and versions. "They call it 'the Splits,' " she says, "and this means they may want the guitar mixed down, or get rid of the guitar, or something. What I am doing is sending them instrumental versions of everything. The new record is recorded mostly on 24-track, although two songs will be recorded in a digital format. But certainly, I want to get geared up and thinking in terms of production music."

Having seen the music industry climate go through drastic changes, she's also grateful that new companies such as Pump Audio have found a place the world, and she hopes other songwriters and artists can pursue this avenue as a realistic alternative to enhance their careers. "Things keep changing," she says. "For every year that goes by, the artists that are selling records, the songs that get to them are more tightly managed. There are fewer doors open. Today, I think songwriters should focus much more on production music—jingles, licensing—and all these other avenues where music is still being purchased."

This is good news for artists such as Bibi Farber who pursue careers as musical artists and songwriters for the love of music. With her new album Second Kiss completed, she remains hopeful about the future, and that good things will manifest at the right time if she pursues her dream with total commitment. "In college I majored in audio engineering, so I guess that was a commitment to be in the music industry by hook or by crook," she says. "I love it more than anything else. And I have tried to go into other things. I took a class in real estate and was just about to get my license last year, and I just said, 'No, no, no! I don't want to be a real estate agent. I'm going to be a songwriter!' And one month later the Kodak thing happened, because I put that record out myself, and I believed in it and loved it and went into debt for it. I just totally lived and died for it. It was such beautiful . . . karma, I guess."

—Ian Bessler

Music Mostly **rock**, **alternative** and **contemporary jazz**; also **alternative country**. Released *The Mustard Seeds*, written and recorded by The Mustard Seeds (alternative rock); *MacAnanys*, written and recorded by MacAnanys (alternative country); and *P.O.L. Sprockett*, recorded by P.O.L. (rock), all on Entourage Records.

☑ ⊘ EPIC RECORDS
550 Madison Ave., 21st Floor, New York NY 10022. (212)833-8000. Fax: (212)833-4054. Senior Vice Presidents A&R: Ben Goldman, Rose Noone. **Santa Monica:** 2100 Colorado Ave., Santa Monica CA 90404. (310)449-2100. Fax: (310)449-2848. Website: www.epicrecords.com. A&R: Pete Giberga, Mike Flynn. Labels include Epic Soundtrax, LV Records, Immortal Records and Word Records. Record company.
Distributed by Sony Music Distribution.
How to Contact *Write or call first and obtain permission to submit* (New York office only). Does not return material. Responds only if interested. *Santa Monica and Nashville offices do not accept unsolicited submissions.*
Music Artists include Celine Dion, Macy Gray, Modest Mouse, Audioslave, Fuel, Jennifer Lopez, B2K, Incubus, Ben Folds.
Tips "Do an internship if you don't have experience or work as someone's assistant. Learn the business and work hard while you figure out what your talents are and where you fit in. Once you figure out which area of the record company you're suited for, focus on that, work hard at it and it shall be yours."

⊘ FIREANT
2009 Ashland Ave., Charlotte NC 28205. Phone/fax: (704)335-1400. E-mail: lewh@fireantmusic.com. Website: www.fireantmusic.com. **Contact:** Lew Herman, owner. Record company, music publisher (Fireant Music) and record producer (Lew Herman). Estab. 1990. Releases several CDs/year. Pays negotiable royalty to artists on contract; statutory royalty to publisher per song on record.
Distributed by CityHall and North Country.
How to Contact Submit demo tape by mail. Unsolicited submissions are OK. Prefers cassette, DAT or videocassette. Does not return material.
Music Mostly **progressive**, **traditional** and **musical hybrids**. "Anything except New Age and MOR." Released *Loving the Alien: Athens Georgia Salutes David Bowie* (album), recorded by various artists (rock/alternative/electronic), released 2000 on Fireant; and *Good Enough* (album), recorded by Zen Frisbee. Other artists include Mr. Peters' Belizean Boom and Chime Band.

🅽 ◯ FIRST POWER ENTERTAINMENT GROUP
5801 Riverdale Rd., Suite 105, Riverdale MD 20737. (301)277-1671. Fax: (301)277-0173. E-mail: powerpla@mail.erols.com. **Contact:** Adrianne Harris, vice president/A&R. Labels include Power Play Records and First Power Records. Record company, recording studio and television show (*StreetJam* and *Phat Trax*). Estab. 1992. Releases 3-5 singles, 2-3 LPs and a variable number of EPs and CDs/year. Pays negotiable royalty to artists on contract; statutory rate to publisher per song on record.
Distributed by Independent Distributor.
How to Contact Submit demo tape by mail. Unsolicited submissions are OK. Prefers cassette, CD, DAT or VHS videocassette. "Send name and contact number and address. Please write clearly. Also, it is imperative to include a photo of the artist or group." Does not return material. Responds in 3 months.
Music Mostly **R&B**, **rap** and **rock**; also **alternative**, **gospel** and **children's**. "We prefer r&b, rap, Gospel, metal, hip hop, rock and alternative. We do not accept 'gansta rap' artists or material. We prefer 'dance, love, reality

and positive' song material and artists." Released *Bunwatcher* (by J. McCoy/M. Butler), recorded by Bad Influence on Power Play (rap/R&B). Other artists include Mothership, Warren Caldwell and Frank Niti.

Tips "Have patience, a professional attitude and devoted commitment to your career. You must also be creative, open to explore new ways to improve your songs from producers and appear at scheduled events in a timely manner. Artists should be focused and ready to work. We also love groups who have a creative and unique gimmick or image."

FIRST TIME RECORDS

Sovereign House, 12 Trewartha Rd., Praa Sands, Penzance, Cornwall TR20 9ST England. Phone: (01736)762826. Fax: (01736)763328. E-mail: panamus@aol.com. Website: www.songwriters-guild.co.uk. **Contact:** Roderick G. Jones, managing director A&R. Labels include Pure Gold Records, Rainy Day Records and Mohock Records, Heraldic Vintage Records, Heraldic Jester Records, Heraldic Creative Disc. Registered members of Phonographic Performance Ltd. (PPL). Record company, music publisher (First Time Music Publishing U.K./MCPS/PRS), management firm and record producer (First Time Management & Production Co.). Estab. 1986. Staff size: 6. Pays variable royalty to artists on contract; statutory rate to publisher per song on record subject to deal.

Distributed by Media U.K. Distributors.

How to Contact Submit demo tape by mail. Unsolicited submissions are OK. Prefers cassette or CD with unlimited number of songs and lyric or lead sheets, but not necessary. SAE and IRC. Responds in 3 months.

Music All styles. Released "Temple Gongs" (single) from *World Music—China & India* (album), recorded by Tim Donovan (instrumental/world music), "Streetwise" (single) from *Electro Urban Funk* (album), recorded by David Jones (electro urban funk), both released 2004 on Panama Productions; and "Ancient Hedgerows" (single) from *Distant Horizons* (album), recorded by Kevin kendle, released 2004 on Eventide/Panama Records.

FLYING HEART RECORDS

Dept. SM, 4015 NE 12th Ave., Portland OR 97212. E-mail: flyheart@teleport.com. Website: http://home.teleport .com/~flyheart. **Contact:** Jan Celt, owner. Record company and record producer (Jan Celt). Estab. 1982. Releases 2 CDs/year. Pays variable royalty to artists on contract; negotiable rate to publisher per song on record.

Distributed by Burnside Distribution Co.

How to Contact Submit demo tape by mail. Unsolicited submissions are OK. Prefers cassette with 1-10 songs and lyric sheets. Does not return material. "SASE required for *any* response." Responds in 3 months.

Music Mostly **R&B**, **blues** and **jazz**; also **rock**. Released *Vexatious Progr.* (album), written and recorded by Eddie Harris (jazz); *Juke Music* (album), written and recorded by Thara Memory (jazz); and *Lookie Tookie* (album), written and recorded by Jan Celt (blues), all on Flying Heart Records. Other artists include Janice Scroggins, Tom McFarland, Obo Addy, Snow Bud and The Flower People.

FRESH ENTERTAINMENT

1315 Simpson Rd. NW, Suite 5, Atlanta GA 30314. Phone/fax: (770)642-2645. E-mail: whunter1122@yahoo.c om. **Contact:** Willie W. Hunter, managing director. Record company and music publisher (Hserf Music/ASCAP, Blair Vizzion Music/BMI). Releases 5 singles and 2 LPs/year. Pays 7-10% royalty to artists on contract; statutory rate to publisher per song on record.

Distributed by Ichiban International and Intersound Records.

How to Contact Submit demo tape by mail. Unsolicited submissions are OK. Prefers cassette or VHS videocassette with at least 3 songs and lyric sheet. Include SASE. Responds in 2 months.

Music Mostly **R&B**, **rock** and **pop**; also **jazz**, **gospel** and **rap**. Released "We Hate Pastor Troy" (single by W. Jackson/Javou/Chosen One) from *Ready For War*, recorded by Swat Team (rap/hip-hop), released 2000 on Armageddon/Milltyme; "Erase The Color Line" (single by M. Warner/J. Smith/J. Lewis) from *EMG-Non Pilation*, recorded by Michael Warner/JS-1/Noray (R&B/hip-hop), released 2000 on EMQ Entertainment; *Ancestral Spirits* (album), written and recorded by Bob Miles (jazz), released 2004 on Sheets of Sound/Fresh Entertainment; *My Life—My Hustle* (album), written by Jamal Smith and recorded by JS-1 (rap/hip-hop), released 2004 on Vision Vibe/Fresh Entertainment. Other artists include Cirocco and Invisible Men.

FRONT ROW RECORDS

Ridgewood Park Estates, 222 Tulane St., Garland TX 75043. **Contact:** Gene or Dea Summers. Public Relations/Artist and Fan Club Coordinator: Steve Summers. A&R: Shawn Summers. Labels include Juan Records. Record company and music publisher (Silicon Music/BMI). Estab. 1968. Releases 5-6 singles and 2-3 LPs/year. Pays negotiable royalty to artists on contract; standard royalty to songwriters on contract.

Distributed by Crystal Clear Records.

• Also see the listing for Silicon Music Publishing Co. in the Music Publishers section of this book.

How to Contact Submit demo tape by mail. Unsolicited submissions are OK. Prefers cassette or VHS videocassette with 1-3 songs. *"We request a photo and bio with material submission."* Does not return material. Responds ASAP.

Music Mostly **'50s rock/rockabilly**; also **country**, **bluegrass**, **old-time blues** and **R&B**. Released "Domino" (single), recorded by Gene Summers on Pollytone Records (rockabilly); "Goodbye Priscilla" and "Cool Baby" (singles), both recorded by Gene Summers on Collectables Records.

Tips "If you own masters of 1950s rock and rockabilly, contact us first! We will work with you on a percentage basis for overseas release. We have active releases in Holland, Switzerland, Belgium, Australia, England, France, Sweden, Norway and the US at the present. We need original masters. You must be able to prove ownership of tapes before we can accept a deal. We're looking for little-known, obscure recordings. We have the market if you have the tapes! We are also interested in country and rockabilly *artists* who have not recorded for awhile but still have the voice and appeal to sell overseas."

☑ ⦿ MARTY GARRETT ENTERTAINMENT

320 West Utica Place, Broken Arrow OK 74011. (918)451-6780. E-mail: musicbusiness@telepath.com. Website: www.storesonline.com/site/musicbusiness. **Contact:** Marty R. Garrett, president. Labels include Lonesome Wind Records. Record company, record producer, music publisher and entertainment consultant. Estab. 1988. Releases 1-2 EPs and 1 CD/year. Pays negotiable royalty to artists on contract; statutory rate to publisher per song on record.

How to Contact *Call or check Internet site first and obtain permission to submit.* Prefers CD or cassette with 4-5 songs and lyric or lead sheet with chord progressions listed. Does not return material. Responds in 2-4 weeks.

Music Mostly **Honky tonk, progressive/traditional country** or **scripturally-based gospel**. Released *I'm Not Over You* (album by Drake/McGuire), recorded by Darla Drake on Comstock Records; *Too Free Too Long* (album by Cliff Voss), recorded by Mark Cypert on Stormy Heart Records; and *Carry Me Over* (album), written and recorded by The Cripple Jimmi Band on Kid Mega Records.

Tips "We help artists secure funding to record and release major label quality CD products to the public for sale through 1-800 television and radio advertising and on the Internet. Although we do submit finished products to major record companies for review, our main focus is to establish and surround the artist with their own long-term production, promotion and distribution organization. Professional studio demos are not required, but make sure vocals are distinct, up-front and up-to-date. I personally listen and respond to each submission received, so check website to see if we are reviewing for an upcoming project."

⦿ GENERIC RECORDS, INC.

433 Limestone Rd., Ridgefield CT 06877. (203)438-9811. Fax: (203)431-3204. E-mail: hifiadd@aol.com. President (pop, alternative, rock): Gary Lefkowith. A&R (pop, dance, adult contemporary): Bill Jerome. Labels include Outback, GLYN. Record company, music publisher (Sotto Music/BMI) and record producer. Estab. 1976. Staff size: 2. Releases 6 singles and 2 CDs/year. Pays 15% royalty to artists on contract; statutory rate to publisher per song on record.

Distributed by Dutch East India.

How to Contact Submit demo tape by mail. Unsolicited submissions are OK. Prefers cassette with 2-3 songs. Include SASE. Responds in 2 weeks.

Music Mostly **alternative rock, rock** and **pop**; also **country** and **rap**. Released "Young Girls" (by Eric Della Penna/Dean Sharenow), recorded by Henry Sugar (alternative/pop); "Rock It," written and recorded by David Ruskay (rock/pop); and *Tyrus*, written and recorded by Tyris (alternative), all on Generic Records, Inc. Other artists include Hifi, Honest, Loose Change and John Fantasia.

Tips "Love what you're doing. The music comes first."

⦿ GIG RECORDS

520 Butler Ave., Point Pleasant NJ 08742. (732)701-9044. Fax: (732)701-9777. E-mail: Indian@gigrecords.com. Website: www.gigrecords.com. **Contact:** Lenny Hip, A&R. Labels include AMPED. Record company and music publisher (Gig Music). Estab. 1998. Staff size: 8. Releases 2 singles, 2 EPs and 15 CDs/year. Pays negotiable royalty to artists on contract; statutory rate to publisher per song on record.

Distributed by Amazon, E-Music, CD Now, Nail and Sumthing.

How to Contact Submit demo tape by mail. Unsolicited submissions are OK. Prefers cassette, CD or VHS videocassette with lyric sheet and cover letter. Does not return materials. Responds ASAP if interested.

Music Mostly **rock** and **electronic**; also **drum & bass, trip-hop** and **hip-hop**. Does not want country. Released *Hungry* (album), recorded by Gum Parker (electronico), released 2003 on Gig Records; *Waiting For You* (album), recorded by Nick Clemons Band (alternative rock/pop), released 2003 on Groove Entertainment; and 3 new releases to come from Michael Ferentino, Amazing Meet Project, Love in Reverse. Other artists include Ned's Atomic Dustbin, Virginia, The Vibrators, Groundswell UK, Nebula Nine, The Youth Ahead, Dryer and Red Engine Nine.

Tips "No egos."

⊠ ⬭ GOTHAM RECORDS

P.O. Box 49425, Los Angeles CA 90049. E-mail: mail@gothamrecords.com. Website: www.gothamrecords.com. **Contact:** John Cross, vice president A&R/retail. Record company. Estab. 1994. Staff size: 3. Releases 8 LPs and 8 CDs/year. Pays negotiable royalty to artists on contract; statutory rate to publisher per song on record.
Distributed by Dutch East India and MS Distributing.
How to Contact Submit demo tape by mail "in a padded mailer or similar package." Unsolicited submissions are OK. Prefers cassette or CD and bios, pictures and touring information. Does not return material. Responds in 6 weeks.
Music Mostly **rock**, **pop**, **alternative** and **AAA**. Released *Nineteenth Soul*, recorded by Liquid Gang (rock); *Supafuzz*, written and recorded by Supafuzz (rock); and *Oh God! Help Our Fans!*, written and recorded by The Loose Nuts (ska), all on Gotham Records. Other artists include Love Huskies.
Tips "Send all submissions in regular packaging. Spend your money on production and basics, not on fancy packaging and gift wrap."

☑ ⬭ GROOVE MAKERS' RECORDINGS

P.O. Box 271170, Houston TX 77227-1170. Phone/fax: (281)403-6279. E-mail: mistamadd@paidnphull.com. Website: www.paidnphull.com. **Contact:** Ben Thompson (R&B, rap), CEO. Labels include Paid In Full Entertainment. Record company, music publisher and record producer (Crazy C). Estab. 1994. Staff size: 4. Releases 3 singles, 2 LPs and 2 CDs/year. Pays negotiable royalty to artists on contract; statutory rate to publisher per song on record.
Distributed by S.O.H..
How to Contact *Write first and obtain permission to submit.* Prefers cassette or CD. Does not return material.
Music Mostly **rap** and **R&B**. Released "They Don't Know" (single by Paul Wall/Mike Jones) from *Chick Magnet* (album), recorded by Paul Wall (rap), released 2004 on Paid In Full; "Down South Pt. II" (single by Ben Thompson III) from *Supa Thugz Pt. II* (album), recorded by Mista MADD (rap), released 2004 on Paid In Full; and "Ballin Is A Habit" (single) from *Grown Man Style* (album), recorded by 50/50 Twin (rap), released 2004 on Paid in Full. Other artists include S.O.U.L., Yung Ro, and Shei Atkins.

☑ ⬭ GUESTSTAR RECORDS, INC.

17321 Ritchie Ave. NE, Sand Lake MI 49343-9475. (616)636-5068. Fax: (775)743-4169. E-mail: gueststarww@wingsisp.com. Website: www.mountainmanww.com **Contact:** Marilyn Dietz, office manager. Record company, management firm (Gueststar Entertainment Agency), record producer and music publisher (Sandlake Music/BMI). Estab. 1967. Staff size: 3. Releases 8 singles, 2 LPs and 2 CDs/year. Pays variable royalty to artist on contract, "depending on number of selections on product; 3½¢/per record sold; statutory rate to publisher per song on record."
Distributed by Guestar Worldwide Music Distributors.
How to Contact Submit demo by mail. "Include contact information." Unsolicited submissions are OK. Prefers CD, cassette or VHS videocassette with lyric and lead sheet. Returns submissions after 1 year if SASE and correct postage are included. Responds in 6 months if contact information is added in kit.
Music Mostly **traditional country**. Released "I'm in Love with a Stranger" (single by Raymond Dietz); and "When Jesus Comes" (single by Raymond Dietz), both from *Best of Mountain Man* (album), recorded by Mountain Man (country), released 2001 on GuestStar. Other artists include Jamie "K" and Sweetgrass Band.
Tips "Songwriters: send songs like you hear on the radio. Keep updating your music to keep up with the latest trends. Artists: send VHS video and press kit with shoulder shot only. E-mail and return address is very important."

⬭ HACIENDA RECORDS & RECORDING STUDIO

1236 S. Staples St., Corpus Christi TX 78404. (361)882-7066. Fax: (361)882-3943. E-mail: info@haciendarecords. com. Website: www.haciendarecords.com. **Contact:** Rick Garcia, executive vice president. Founder/CEO: Roland Garcia. Record company, music publisher, record producer. Estab. 1979. Staff size: 10. Releases 12 singles and 15 CDs/year. Pays negotiable royalty to artists on contract; negotiable rate to publisher per song on record.
How to Contact Submit demo by mail. Unsolicited submissions are OK. Prefers CD or cassette with cover letter. Does not return material. Responds in 6 weeks.
Music Mostly **tejano**, **regional Mexican**, **country** (Spanish or English) and **pop**. Released "Chica Bonita" (single), recorded by Albert Zamora and D.J. Cubanito, released 2001 on Hacienda Records; "Si Quieres Verme Llorar" (single) from *Lisa Lopez con Mariachi* (album), recorded by Lisa Lopez (mariachi), released 2002 on Hacienda; "Tartamudo" (single) from *Una Vez Mas* (album), recorded by Peligro (norteno); and "Miento" (single) from *Si Tu Te Vas* (album), recorded by Traizion (tejano), both released 2001 on Hacienda. Other artists include Ricky Naramzo, Gary Hobbs, Steve Jordan, Grammy Award nominees Mingo Saldivar and David Lee Garza, Michelle, Victoria Y Sus Chikos, La Traizion.

◖ HEADS UP INT., LTD.

23309 Commerce Park Dr., Cleveland OH 44122. (216)765-7381. Fax: (216)464-6037. E-mail: dave@headsup.com. Website: www.headsup.com. **Contact:** Dave Love, president. Record company, music publisher (Heads Up Int., Buntz Music, Musica de Amor) and record producer (Dave Love). Estab. 1980. Staff size: 57. Releases 10 LPs/year. Pays negotiable royalty to artists on contract.

Distributed by Telarc Int. Corp.

How to Contact Submit demo tape by mail. Unsolicited submissions are OK. Prefers CD. Does not return material. Responds in one month.

Music Mostly **jazz**, **R&B** and **pop**. Does not want anything else. Released *Keeping Cool* (album), written and recorded by Joyce Cooling (jazz); *Another Side of Midnight* (album), written and recorded by Marion Meadows (jazz); and *Love Letters* (album), written and recorded by Gerald Veasley (jazz). Other artists include Philip Bailey, Joe McBride, Richard Smith, Robert Perera, Spyro Gyra and Pieces of a Dream.

☑ ◖ HEART MUSIC, INC.

P.O. Box 160326, Austin TX 78716-0326. (512)795-2375. E-mail: info@heartmusic.com. Website: www.heartmusic.com. **Contact:** Tab Bartling, president. Record company and music publisher (Coolhot Music). Estab. 1989. Staff size: 2. Releases 1-2 CDs/year. Pays statutory rate to publisher per song on record.

How to Contact *Not interested in new material at this time.* Does not return material. Responds only if interested.

Music Mostly **rock**, **pop** and **jazz**; also **blues** and **contemporary folk**. Released *Mirror* (album), recorded by Monte Montgomery (pop/rock), released June 1999; *Goodnight Venus* (album), recorded by Libby Kirkpatrick, released in 2003, and *Be Cool Be Kind* (album), recorded by Carla Helmbrecht (jazz), released January 2001.

☑ ▨ ◐ HI-BIAS RECORDS INC.

Attn: A&R Dept., 20 Hudson Dr. (side entrance), Maple ON L6A 1X3 Canada. (905)303-9611. Fax: (905)303-6611. E-mail: info@hibias.ca. Website: www.hibias.ca. **Contact:** Nick Fiorucci, director. Labels include Tilt, Riff, Toronto Underground, Remedy and Club Culture. Record company, music publisher (Bend 60 Music/SOCAN) and record producer (Nick Fiorucci). Estab. 1990. Staff size: 5. Releases 20-30 singles and 2-5 CDs/year. Pays negotiable royalty to artists on contract; statutory rate to publisher per song on record.

Distributed by EMI.

How to Contact Submit demo tape by mail. Unsolicited submissions are OK. Prefers cassette or DAT with 3 songs and lyric sheet. Does not return material. Responds in 6 weeks.

Music Mostly **dance**, **house**, **club**, **pop** and **R&B**. Released "Hands of Time" (single by N. Fiorucci/B. Cosgrove), recorded by Temperance; "Now That I Found You" (single by B. Farrinco/Cleopatra), recorded by YBZ; and "Lift Me Up" (single), written and recorded by Red 5, all on Hi-Bias (dance/pop). Other artists include DJ's Rule.

◐ HOLLYWOOD RECORDS

500 S. Buena Vista St., Old Team Bldg., Burbank CA 91521-1840. (818)560-5670. Fax: (818)845-4313. Website: www.hollywoodrecords.com. Senior Vice President of A&R: Geoffrey Weiss. Senior Vice President of A&R (soundtracks): Mitchell Leib. Vice Presidents: Jon Lind, Eric Clinger. **New York:** 320 7th Ave., Brooklyn NY 11215. (718)832-0860. Fax: (718)832-0869. Website: www.hollywoodrec.com. Executive Director: Jason Jordan. Labels include Acid Jazz Records, Mountain Division Records and Bar/None Records. Record company.

How to Contact *Hollywood Records does not accept unsolicited submissions.* Queries accepted only from a manager or lawyer.

Music Artists include Hilary Duff, Jess McCartney, Breaking Benjamin, and Los Lobos.

◐ HOT WINGS ENTERTAINMENT

429 Richmond Ave., Buffalo NY 14222. (716)884-0248. E-mail: dahotwings@aol.com. **Contact:** Dale Anderson, president. Record company and music publisher (Buffalo Wings Music/BMI). Estab. 1994. Staff size: 1. Releases 2 CDs/year. Pays 10-15% to artists on contract; statutory rate to publisher per song on record.

How to Contact *Call first and obtain permission to submit.* Prefers cassette or CD with 3 or more songs. Does not return material. Responds in 2 months.

Music Mostly **folk/acoustic**, **alternative rock** and **jazz**. (Preference to artists from Upstate New York.) Released *Like Being Born* (album), written and recorded by Alison Pipitone (folk/rock); *Flavor* (album by Geoffrey Fitzhugh Perry), recorded by Fitzhugh and the Fanatics (blues/rock); and *Everything Counts* (album), written and recorded by Gretchen Schulz (pop/R&B), all on Hot Wings Records.

◐ HOTTRAX RECORDS

1957 Kilburn Dr., Atlanta GA 30324. (770)662-6661. E-mail: hotwax@hottrax.com. Website: www.hottrax.com. **Contact:** Oliver Cooper, vice president, A&R. Labels include Dance-A-Thon and Hardkor. Record company and music publisher (Starfox Publishing). Staff size: 6. Releases 8 singles and 3-4 CDs/year. Pays 5-15% royalty to artists on contract.

Distributed by Get Hip Inc.

• Also see the listing for Alexander Janoulis Productions/Big Al Jano Productions in the Record Producers section of this book.

How to Contact *Write first and obtain permission to submit.* Prefers CDR with 3 songs and lyric sheet. Does not return material. Responds in 6 months. "When submissions get extremely heavy, we do not have the time to respond/return material we pass on. We do notify those sending the most promising work we review, however."

Music Mostly **blues/blues rock**, some **top 40/pop**, **rock** and **country**; also **hardcore punk** and **jazz-fusion**. Released *Starfoxx* (album), written and recorded by Starfoxx (rock); *Lady That Digs The Blues* (album), recorded by Big Al Jano's Blues Mafia Show (blues rock); and *Vol. III, Psychedelic Era. 1967-1969* (album), released 2002 on Hottrax. Other artists include Big Al Jano, Sammy Blue and Sheffield & Webb.

☒ ◒ IDOL RECORDS PUBLISHING

P.O. Box 720043, Dallas TX 75372. (214)826-4365. Fax: (214)370-5417. E-mail: info@idolrecords.com. Website: www.Idol-Records.com. **Contact:** Erv Karwelis, president. Record company. Estab. 1992. Releases 2-3 singles, 30 LPs, 2-3 EPs and 15-20 CDs/year. Pays negotiable royalty to artists on contract; negotiable rate to publisher per song on record.

Distributed by Cargo and Hepcat Dist..

How to Contact See website at www.idolrecords.com for submission policy. No phone calls or e-mail follow-ups.

Music Mostly **rock**, **pop** and **alternative**. Released *Onward Quirky Soldiers* (album), recorded by Chomsky (alternative); *Distance and Clime* (album), recorded by Centro-Matic (alternative); and *Falling Hard in the Key of E* (album), recorded by Macavity (alternative), all released 2001 on Idol Records. Other artists include Pervis, Billyclub, Old 97's, Hoarse, Feisty Cadavers, The American Fuse and Watershed.

◒ IMAGINARY RECORDS

P.O. Box 66, Whites Creek TN 37189-0066. Phone/fax: (615)299-9237. E-mail: jazz@imaginaryrecords.com. Website: www.imaginaryrecords.com. **Contact:** Lloyd Townsend, proprietor. Labels include Imaginary Records, Imaginary Jazz Records. Record company. Estab. 1981. Staff size: 1. Releases 1-3 CDs/year. Pays negotiable royalty to artists on contract; statutory rate to publisher per song on record.

Distributed by North Country, Harbor Record Export and Imaginary Distribution.

How to Contact *Write first to obtain permission to submit.* "We do not act as a publisher placing songs with artists." Prefers CD with 3-5 songs, cover letter and press clippings. Include SASE. Responds in 4 months if interested.

Music Mostly **mainstream jazz**, **swing jazz** and **classical**. Does not want country, rap, hip-hop or metal. Released *Fifth House* (album), recorded by New York Trio Project (mainstream jazz), released 2001; *Triologue* (album), recorded by Stevens, Siegel, and Ferguson (mainstream jazz), released 2001; and *Perspectives* (album), written and recorded by the Tom Dempsey/Tim Ferguson Quartet (jazz), released 2003.

Tips "Be patient, I'm slow. I'm primarily considering mainstream jazz or classical—other genre submissions are much less likely to get a response."

☒ ◒ INNER SOUL RECORDS, INC.

1750 N. Collins St., Suite 208, Richardson TX 75080. (972)231-8993. Website: www.innersoulrecords.com. **Contact:** Dorie Dorsey, head of A&R dept. Record company. Estab. 1995. Releases 2 singles, 2 LPs/year. Pays negotiable royalty to artists on contract.

How to Contact Submit demo tape by mail. Unsolicited submissions are OK. Prefers cassette. Mail submissions to 1240 W. 9th St., Port Arthur TX 77640. Does not return material. Responds in 2 months.

Music Mostly **rap** and **R&B**. Released "Mr. 25/8" (single by DJ DMD) from *Thirty-Three: Live from Airoshima* (album), recorded by DJ DMD (hip-hop), released 2001 on Inner Soul Records; "25 Lighters" (single by DJ DMD/Lil Ke Ke/Fat Pat) from *Twenty-Two: P.A. Worldwide* (album), recorded by DJ DMD (hip-hop), released 1998 on Inner Soul/Electra Records; and "So Real" (single by DJ DMD/DJ Screw and Screwed Up Click) from *Eleven* (album), recorded by DJ DMD (hip-hop), released 1996 on Inner Soul.

Tips "Please be as professional as possible with your submissions. A complete package (bio, cassette, photo) is preferred."

☒ ☒ ◒ INTERSCOPE/GEFFEN/A&M RECORDS

2220 Colorado Ave., Santa Monica CA 90404. (310)865-1000. Fax: (310)865-7908. **New York:** 1755 Broadway, 8th Floor, New York NY 10019. (212)841-8000. Website: www.interscoperecords.com. Labels include Death

Row Records, Nothing Records, Rock Land, Almo Sounds, Aftermath Records and Trauma Records. Record company.

- As a result of the PolyGram and Universal merger, Geffen and A&M Records have been folded into Interscope Records.

How to Contact *Does not accept unsolicited submissions.*

Music Released *Fush Yu Mang*, recorded by Smash Mouth; and *The Dirty Boogie*, recorded by The Brian Setzer Orchestra. Other artists include U2 and Marilyn Manson.

☑ ⦿ ISLAND/DEF JAM MUSIC GROUP

825 Eighth Ave., 29th Floor, New York NY 10019. (212)333-8000. Fax: (212)603-7654. Website: www.islanddefjam.com. **Los Angeles:** 8920 Sunset Blvd, 2nd Floor, Los Angeles CA 90069. (310)276-4500. Fax: (310)242-7023. Executive A&R: Paul Pontius. Labels include Mouth Almighty Records, Worldly/Triloka Records, Blackheart Records, Private Records, Slipdisc Records, Thirsty Ear, Blue Gorilla, Dubbly, Little Dog Records, Rounder and Capricorn Records. Record company.

How to Contact *Island/Def Jam Music Group does not accept unsolicited submissions. Do not send material unless requested.*

Music Artists include Bon Jovi, Ja Rule, Jay-Z and Ludacris.

⦿ J RECORDS

745 Fifth Ave., 6th Floor, New York NY 10151. (646)840-5600. Website: www.jrecords.com.

How to Contact *J Records does not accept unsolicited submissions.*

Music Artists include Faithless, Alicia Keys, and Annie Lennox.

☑ ⦿ JIVE RECORDS

8750 Wilshire Blvd., Beverly Hills CA 90211. (310)358-4200. Website: www.jiverecords.com. Labels include LaFace, So So Def and Verity Records.

Distributed by BMG.

How to Contact *Does not accept unsolicited material.* "Contact us through management or an attorney."

Music Mostly **R&B**, **pop** and **rap**. Artists include Justin Timberlake, R. Kelly, Britney Spears, Too Short, Petey Pablo and Nivea.

Tips "Make the best material possible."

⦿ ⦿ JUPITER RECORDS

Rinkermarkt 16, 80331 Munchen Germany. E-mail: contact@jupiter-records.de. Website: www.jupiter-records.de. Owner: Ralph Siegel. Record company and record producer.

How to Contact Submit demo tape or CD by mail. Unsolicited submissions are OK. SAE and IRC. Responds in 2 months.

Music Mostly **pop**, **rock** and **dance**; also **soul** and **Black music**.

Tips "If you believe that your song could be No. 1 on the charts, please submit it!"

☑ ⦿ KAUPP RECORDS

Box 5474, Stockton CA 95205. (209)948-8186. **Contact:** Melissa Glenn. Record company, music publisher (Kaupps and Robert Publishing Co./BMI), management firm (Merri-Webb Productions) and record producer (Merri-Webb Productions). Estab. 1990. Releases 1 single and 4 LPs/year. Pays standard royalty to artists on contract; statutory rate to publisher per song on record.

Distributed by Merri-Webb Productions and Cal-Centron Distributing Co.

How to Contact *Write first and obtain permission to submit or to arrange personal interview.* Prefers cassette or VHS videocassette with 3 songs. Include SASE. Responds in 3 months.

Music Mostly **country**, **R&B** and **A/C rock**; also **pop**, **rock** and **gospel**. Released "I Thank You Father" and "On the Other Side(singles by N. Merrihew/B. Bolin), recorded by Bruce Bolen; and "Did You Think That I Though That You Liked Me" (single by N. Merrihew/B. Bolin), recorded by Cheryl, all on Kaupp Records.

⦿ ⦿ KILL ROCK STARS

120 N.E. State #418, Olympia WA 98501. E-mail: krs@killrockstars.com. Website: www.killrockstars.com. **Contact:** Slim Moon, CEO. Record company. Estab. 1991. Releases 6-8 singles, 6 LPs, 4-6 EPs and 18 CDs/year. Pays 50% of net profit to artists on contract; negotiated rate to publisher per song on record.

Distributed by Mordam, Caroline, Dutch East India, Revolver, Bayside, Valley, Rotz, Pacific Coast One Stop and AEC.

How to Contact *Write first and obtain permission to submit.* Prefers CD. Does not return material.

Music Mostly **punk rock, neo-folk or anti-folk** and **spoken word**. Artists include Sleater-Kinney, Phranc, and Bikini Kill.

(pop guitar punk); *Julie Ruin*, written and recorded by Kathleen Hanna (punk); and *Frumpies One Piece*, written and recorded by Frumpies (punk), all on Kill Rock Stars. Other artists include Thrones, Emily's Sassy Lime, Long Hind Legs, Mocket and Free Kitten.

Tips "Send a self-released CD. Prefer working with touring acts, so let us know if you are playing Olympia, Seattle or Portland. Particularly interested in young artists with indie-rock background."

⬤ KINGSTON RECORDS

15 Exeter Rd., Kingston NH 03848. (603)642-8493. E-mail: kingstonrecords@ttlc.net. Website: www.kingstonrecords.com. **Contact:** Harry Mann, coordinator. Record company, record producer and music publisher (Strawberry Soda Publishing/ASCAP). Estab. 1988. Releases 3-4 singles, 2-3 12″ singles, 3 LPs and 2 CDs/year. Pays 3-5% royalty to artists on contract; statutory rate to publisher per song.

How to Contact *Write first and obtain permission to submit.* Prefers cassette, DAT, 15 ips reel-to-reel or videocassette with 3 songs and lyric sheet. Does not return material. Responds in 2 months.

Music Mostly **rock, country** and **pop**; "no heavy metal." Released *Two Lane Highway* and *Armand's Way* (albums), written and recorded by Armand Learay (rock); and *Count the Stars* (album), written and recorded by Doug Mitchell, released 1999, all on Kingston Records.

Tips "Working only with N.E. and local talent."

ⓝ ⬜ LANDMARK COMMUNICATIONS GROUP

P.O. Box 1444, Hendersonville TN 37077. E-mail: lmarkcom@bellsouth.net. **Contact:** Bill Anderson, Jr., president (all styles). Professional Manager (western): Dylan Horse. Labels include Jana and Landmark Records. Record company, record producer, music publisher (Newcreature Music/BMI and Mary Megan Music/ASCAP) and management firm (Landmark Entertainment). Releases 10 singles, 8 LPs and 8 CDs/year. Pays 5-7% royalty to artists on contract; statutory rate to publisher for each record sold.

How to Contact Submit demo tape by mail. Unsolicited submissions are OK. Prefers 7½ ips reel-to-reel or cassette with 4-10 songs and lyric sheet. Include SASE. Responds in 1 month.

Music Mostly **country/crossover, gospel, jazz, R&B, rock** and **top 40/pop**. Released *The Gospel Truth* (album by various artists), recorded by Vernon Oxford on Rocade (country); *The Yates Family 25 Year Anniversary* (album by various artists), recorded by Joanne Cash Yates on Jana (gospel); and *Nothin' Else Feels Quite Like It* (album), written and recorded by various artists on Landmark (positive country).

Tips "Be professional in presenting yourself."

⬤ LARI-JON RECORDS

P.O. Box 216, Rising City NE 68658. (402)542-2336. **Contact:** Larry Good, owner. Record company, management firm (Lari-Jon Promotions), music publisher (Lari-Jon Publishing/BMI) and record producer (Lari-Jon Productions). Estab. 1967. Staff size: 1. Releases 15 singles and 5 LPs/year. Pays varying royalty to artists on contract.

How to Contact Submit demo tape by mail. Unsolicited submissions are OK. Prefers CD's with 5 songs and lyric sheet. Include SASE. Responds in 2 months.

Music Mostly **country, gospel-Southern** and **'50s rock**. Released "Glory Bound Train" (single), written and recorded by Tom Campbell; *The Best of Larry Good* (album), written and recorded by Larry Good (country); and *Her Favorite Songs* (album), written and recorded by Johnny Nace (country), all on Lari-Jon Records. Other artists include Kent Thompson and Brenda Allen.

⬤ LARK RECORD PRODUCTIONS, INC.

P.O. Box 35726, Tulsa OK 74153. (918)786-8896. Fax: (918)786-8897. E-mail: janajae@janajae.com. Website: www.janajae.com. **Contact:** Kathleen Pixley, vice president. Record company, music publisher (Jana Jae Music/BMI), management firm (Jana Jae Enterprises) and record producer (Lark Talent and Advertising). Estab. 1980. Staff size: 8. Pays negotiable royalty to artists on contract; statutory rate to publisher per song on record.

How to Contact Submit demo tape by mail. Unsolicited submissions are OK. Prefers CD or VHS videocassette with 3 songs and lead sheets. Does not return material. Responds only if interested.

Music Mostly **country, bluegrass** and **classical**; also **instrumentals**. Released "Fiddlestix" (single by Jana Jae); "Mayonnaise" (single by Steve Upfold); and "Flyin' South" (single by Cindy Walker), all recorded by Jana Jae on Lark Records (country). Other artists include Syndi, Hotwire and Matt Greif.

🌐 ⬜ LOCK

Coachhouse, Mansion Farm, Liverton Hill, Sandway, Maidstone, Kent ME172NJ England. Phone/fax: (01622)858300. E-mail: info@eddielock.com. Website: www.eddielock.co.uk. **Contact:** Eddie Lock, A&R. Record company, music publisher (Lock 'n' S) and record producer (Carpe Diem). Estab. 1988. Staff size: 2.

Releases 10 singles/year. Pays negotiable royalty to artists on contract; statutory rate to publisher per song on record.

Distributed by Unique and Essential.

How to Contact Submit demo CD by mail. Unsolicited submissions are OK. Prefers CD. Does not return material.

Music Mostly **dance** and **house**. Released "Quiero Bailar La Salsa" (single by Eddie Lock/Dylan Burns), recorded by Lock & Burns (house); "Work So Hard" (single by Dylan Burns/James Lock), recorded by Yardmen (house), both released 2004 on Lock; and "Situation" (single by Robbie Rivera/Marc Sacheli), recorded by Kings of Tribal (Robbie Rivera) (tribal), released 2003 on Lock.

◖ LUCIFER RECORDS, INC.

P.O. Box 263, Brigantine NJ 08203-0263. (609)266-2623. Fax: (609)266-4870. **Contact:** Ron Luciano, president. Labels include TVA Records. Record company, music publisher (Ciano Publishing and Legz Music), record producer (Pete Fragale and Tony Vallo), management firm and booking agency (Ron Luciano Music Co. and TVA Productions). "Lucifer Records has offices in South Jersey; Palm Beach, Florida; and Las Vegas, Nevada."

How to Contact *Call or write to arrange personal interview.* Prefers cassette with 4-8 songs. Include SASE. Responds in 3 weeks.

Music Mostly **dance**, **easy listening**, **MOR**, **rock**, **soul** and **top 40/pop**. Released "I Who Have Nothing," (single), by Spit-N-Image (rock); "Lucky" (single), by Legz (rock); and "Love's a Crazy Game" (single), by Voyage (disco/ballad). Other artists include Bobby Fisher, Jerry Denton, FM, Zeke's Choice, Al Caz, Joe Vee and Dana Nicole.

☑ ☒ ◖ MAKOCHÉ RECORDING COMPANY

208 N. Fourth St., Bismarck ND 58501. (701)223-7316. Fax: (701)255-8287. E-mail: info@makoche.com. Website: www.makoche.com. **Contact:** Lisa Dowhaniuk, A&R assistant. Labels include Makoché and Chairmaker's Rush. Record company and recording studio. Estab. 1995. Staff size: 5. Releases 4 CDs/year. Pays negotiable royalty to artists on contract; statutory rate to publisher per song on record.

Distributed by DNA, Music Design, Four Winds Trading, Zango Music and New Leaf Distribution.

- Makoché is noted for releasing quality music based in the Native American tradition. Recognized by the Grammys, Nammys, New Age Voice Music Awards and C.O.V.R. Music Awards.

How to Contact *Call first and obtain permission to submit.* "Please submit only fiddle and American Indian-influenced music." Include SASE. Responds in 2 months.

Music Mostly **Native American**, **flute** and **fiddle**. Released *Edge of America* (album), written and recorded by Annie Humphrey (folk), released 2004 on Makoché; and *Togo* (album), written and recorded by Andrew Vasquez (Native American flute), released on Makoché 2004; *Way of Life* (album), recorded by Lakota Thunder (drum group), released on Makoché 2004. Other artists include Gary Stroutsos, Bryan Akipa, Keith Bear, Andrew Vasquez, Lakota Thunder, Sissy Goodhouse and Kevin Locke.

Tips "We are a small label with a dedication to quality."

☒ ◖ MALACO RECORDS

P.O. Box 9287, Jackson MS 39286-9287. (601)982-4522. E-mail: malaco@malaco.com. Website: www.malaco.com. Executive Director: Jerry Mannery. Record company. Estab. 1986. Releases 20 projects/year. Pays variable royalty to artists on contract; statutory rate to publisher per song.

How to Contact Submit demo tape by mail. Unsolicited submissions are OK. Prefers cassette or CD. Does not return material.

Music Mostly **traditional** and **contemporary gospel**. Artists include Mississippi Mass Choir, The Bonner Brothers, Lou Rawls, Men of Standard, Mississippi Children's Choir, Bryan Wilson, The Pilgrim Jubilees, Lillian Lilly, Dorothy Norwood, The Sensational Nightengales, The Angelic Gospel Singers, Carolyn Traylor, Christopher Brinson and Rudolph Stanfield & New Revelation.

☒ ◖ ANDY MARVEL RECORDS

(formerly Alyssa Records), 302 Bluepoint Rd. W., Holtsville NY 11742. President: Andy Marvel. Labels include Ricochet Records. Record company, music publisher (Andy Marvel Music/ASCAP, Bing Bing Bing Music/ASCAP and Andysongs/BMI) and record producer (Marvel Productions). Estab. 1981. Staff size: 3. Releases 12-15 singles, 1 12" single and 4 LPs/year. Pays standard royalty to artists on contract; statutory rate to publisher per song on record.

How to Contact Submit demo by mail. Unsolicited submissions are OK. Prefers CD with 3 songs and lyric sheet. Does not return material. "Do not call." Responds in 1 month.

Music Mostly **pop**, **R&B** and **top 40**; also **country**.

⚑ ⊘ MAVERICK RECORDS

9348 Civic Center Dr., Beverly Hills CA 90210. (310)385-7800. Fax: (310)385-7711. Website: www.maverick.c om. CEO/Head of A&R: Guy Oseary. A&R: Russ Rieger, Jason Bentley, Danny Strick, Berko Weber, Michael Goldberg. Record company.

Distributed by WEA.

Music Released *Under Rug Swept* (album); *Supposed Former Infatuation Junkie* (album) and *Jagged Little Pill* (album), both recorded by Alanis Morissette; *The Spirit Room* (album), recorded by Michelle Branch; *Tantric* (album), recorded by Tantric; and *Ray of Light* (album), recorded by Madonna. Other artists include Deftones, Home Town Hero, Mest, Michael Lee, Me'shell Ndegeocello, Muse, Onesidezero, Prodigy and Paul Oakenfold.

Ⓝ ⊠ ⊘ MAYFAIR MUSIC

2600 John St., Unit 219, Markham ON L3R 3W3 Canada. (905)475-1848. **Contact:** John Loweth, A&R. Record company, music publisher (MBD Records). Estab. 1979. Pays 10% royalty to artists on contract; statutory rate to publisher per song on record.

- Mayfair Music is also listed in the Music Publishers section.

How to Contact Submit demo CD/CDR by mail. Unsolicited submissions are OK. Prefers CD/CDR only with 4 songs. Does not return material. Responds in 3 weeks.

Music Mostly **instrumental**. Current acts include Frank Mills and Paul Saulnier.

⚑ ⊘ MCA NASHVILLE

(formerly MCA Records), 60 Music Square E., Nashville TN 37203. (615)244-8944. Fax: (615)880-7447. Website: www.mca-nashville.com. Record company and music publisher (MCA Music).

How to Contact MCA Records cannot accept unsolicited submissions.

Music Artists include Tracy Byrd, George Strait, Vince Gill, The Mavericks and Trisha Yearwood.

☑ ◻ MEGAFORCE RECORDS

(formerly Megaforce Worldwide Entertainment), P.O. Box 63584, Philadelphia PA 19147. (215)922-4612. Fax: (509)757-8602. E-mail: gregaforce@aol.com. Website: www.megaforcerecords.com. **Contact: Robert John, President. General Manager: Missi Callazzo. Record company. Estab. 1983. Staff size: 5. Releases 6 CDs/ year. Pays various royalties to artists on contract; ³/₄ statutory rate to publisher per song on record.**

Distributed by Ryko Distributions.

How to Contact *Contact first and obtain permission to submit.*

Music Mostly **rock**. Artists include Clutch, God Lives Underwater, S.O.D., and Fozzy.

Ⓝ ⊘ METAL BLADE RECORDS

2828 Cochran St., Suite 302, Simi Valley CA 93065. (805)522-9111. Fax: (805)522-9380. E-mail: metalblade@met alblade.com. Website: www.metalblade.com. **Contact:** Kim Macleery, vice president creative services. Record company. Estab. 1982. Releases 20 LPs, 2 EPs and 20 CDs/year. Pays negotiable royalty to artists on contract.

How to Contact Submit demo CD by mail. Unsolicited submissions are OK. CD with 3 songs. Does not return material. Responds in 3 months.

Music Mostly **heavy metal** and **industrial**; also **hardcore**, **gothic** and **noise**. Released "Gallery of Suicide," recorded by Cannibal Corpse; "Voo Doo," recorded by King Diamond; and "A Pleasant Shade of Gray," recorded by Fates Warning, all on Metal Blade Records. Other artists include Grip Inc., Galactic Cowboys, Sacred Reich, Bolt Thrower, Kings X, Mercyful Fate, Flotsam and Jetsam and Six Feet Under.

Tips "Metal Blade is known throughout the underground for quality metal-oriented acts."

Ⓝ ⊘ MIGHTY RECORDS

150 West End, Suite 6-D, New York NY 10023. Manager: Danny Darrow. Labels include Mighty Sounds & Filmworks. Record company, music publisher (Rockford Music Co./BMI, Stateside Music Co./BMI and Corporate Music Publishing Co./ASCAP) and record producer (Danny Darrow). Estab. 1958. Releases 1-2 singles, 1-2 12″ singles and 1-2 LPs/year. Pays standard royalty to artists on contract; statutory rate to publisher per song on record.

How to Contact Submit demo tape by mail. Unsolicited submissions are OK. "No phone calls." Prefers cassette or CD with 2 songs and lyric sheet. Does not return material. Responds in 1 month only if interested.

Music Mostly **pop**, **country** and **dance**; also **jazz**. Released "Let There Be Peace" (single by Danny Darrow) from *Let There Be Peace* (album), recorded by Danny Darrow (spiritual); "Doomsday" (single by Robert Lee Lowery and Danny Darrow) from *Doomsday* (album), recorded by Danny Darrow (Euro jazz); and "Impulse" (single by Danny Darrow) from *Impulse* (album), recorded by Danny Darrow (Euro jazz), all released 2004 on Mighty Records.

☑ MISSILE RECORDS

P.O. Box 5537, Kreole Station, Moss Point MS 39563-1537. (228)475-0059. "No collect calls!" Estab. 1974. **Contact:** Joe F. Mitchell, executive vice president/general manager. First Vice President: Justin F. Mitchell. Second Vice President: Jonita F. Mitchell. Record company and music publisher (Abalorn Music/ASCAP, Bay Ridge Publishing/BMI) and record producer. Releases 28 singles and 10 LPs/year. Pays "10-16% royalty to new artists on contract, higher rate to established artists"; statutory rate to publisher for each record sold. "Missile Records has National and International Distribution."

• Also see the listing for Bay Ridge Publishing and Abalorn Music in the Music Publishers section.

Distributed by Star Sound Music Distributors, Hits Unlimited, Action Music Sales, Inc., Allegro Corp., Big Easy Distributing, Select-O-Hits, Total Music Distributors, Music Network, Impact Music, Universal Record Distributing Corporation, Dixie Rak Records & Tapes, Navaree Corporation, Curtis Wood Distributors, Big Daddy Music Distribution Co., ATM Distributors, HL Distribution, Bayside Distribution, Blue Sky Distribution, Alamo Record Distributors and MDI Distribution.

How to Contact *"Please don't send us anything until you contact us by phone or in writing and receive submission instructions. You must present your songs the correct way to get a reply."* Always whenever you write to us, be sure you include a #10 business-size envelope addressed back to you with a first class USA postage stamp on the envelope. We reply back to you from the SASE. All songs sent for review must include sufficient return postage. No reply made back to you without SASE or return of material without sufficient return postage. **Absolutely no reply postcards—only SASE.** If you only write lyrics, do not submit. We only accept completed songs, so you must find a collaborator. We are not interested in reviewing homemade recordings." Prefers CD (first choice) or cassette with 3-8 songs and lyrics to songs submitted. Responds in 2 months. A good quality demo recording will always get preference over a poor recording.

Music All types and styles of songs. Released "Excuse Me Lady" and "When She Left Me" (singles by Rich Wilson); "Everyone Gets A Chance (To Lose In Romance)" and "I'm So Glad We Found Each Other" (singles by Joe F. Mitchell), from *Excuse Me Lady* (album), recorded by Rich Wilson (country/western); "Rose Up On A Stem" (single by Joe F. Mitchell), from *My Kind of Kountry* (album), recorded by Jerry Piper (country); "Southern Born" and "Old Folks Know" (singles by Christian Ramsey); "Innocent Little One" (single by Bob Levy), "Pretty Lady Come Closer" (single by David L. Resler) and "She Was Sittin' Pretty" (single by Jim Hendricks) all from *If It Takes All Night* (album), recorded by Christian Ramsey (modern pop country), all released on Missile Records. Other artists include Moto (reggae), Jackie Lambarella (country pop), Sarah Cooper (pop/R&B), Della Reed (contemporary Christian), Metellica (heavy metal), Coco Hodge (alternative) and Lady Love (rap).

Tips "Our doors are always open to young recording artists who are exceptionally talented and want to make a name for themselves in the music business. Your success is our success. We will work with you to reach your goal. We also are in the business of getting your professionally-recorded album of 10-12 well-produced and well-written, radio-ready songs placed with record companies in the USA and foreign countries for the possibility of record deals. Here is what we have gotten for some artists: $850,000 record deal for Charity (religious singing group) on Big Easy (USA) in 2001; $500,000 record deal for Vance Greek on Dime-A-Dozen (Germany) in 2002; and a $150,000 record deal for Randell Ruthledge (country) on Dime-A-Dozen (Germany) in 2003. Two more artists are under consideration as of 2004, and others may be considered. Missile Records, Abalorn Music (ASCAP) and Bay Ridge Publishing Co. (BMI) are listed in some well-known publications such as the *Billboard International Buyer's Guide*, *Mix Master Directory*, *Industrial Source Book*, *Pollstar*, *Yellow Pages of Rock* and other publications. Some well-known recording artists born and raised in Mississippi include Elvis Presley, Conway Twitty, B.B. King and Faith Hill. The Moss Point, MS area music scene is also home to nationally-known rock group Three Doors Down, who sold more than 10 million of their CD albums and singles. Singers and songwriters thinking about doing professional recording, give us a call before you make that move. We can save you money, time, headaches, heartaches and troubles you may run into. We know what to do and how to do it to benefit you and get the best results"

☐ MODAL MUSIC, INC. ™

P.O. Box 6473, Evanston IL 60204-6473. (847)864-1022. E-mail: info@modalmusic.com. Website: www.modal music.com. President: Terran Doehrer. Assistant: J. Distler. Record company and agent. Estab. 1988. Staff size: 2. Releases 1-2 LPs/year. Pays negotiable royalty to artists on contract; negotiable rate to publisher per song on record.

How to Contact Submit demo tape by mail. Unsolicited submissions are OK. Prefers CD or cassette with bio, PR, brochures, any info about artist and music. Does not return material. Responds in 4 months.

Music Mostly **ethnic** and **world**. Released *Dance The Night Away* (album by T. Doehrer), recorded by Balkan Rhythm Band℗; *Sid Beckerman's Rumanian (D. Jacobs)* (album), recorded by Jutta & The Hi-Dukes℗; and *Hold Whatcha Got* (album), recorded by Razzemetazz℗, all on Modal Music Records. Other artists include Ensemble M'chaiya℗, Nordland Band℗ and Terran's Greek Band℗.

Tips "Please note our focus is ethnic. You waste your time and money by sending us any other type of music. If you are unsure of your music fitting our focus, please call us before sending anything. Put your name and contact info on every item you send!"

MONTICANA RECORDS

P.O. Box 702, Snowdon Station, Montreal QC H3X 3X8 Canada. **Contact:** David P. Leonard, general manager. Record company, record producer (Monticana Productions) and music publisher (Montina Music/SOCAN). Estab. 1963. Staff size: 1. Pays negotiable royalty to artists on contract.
How to Contact Submit demo tape by mail. Unsolicited submissions are OK. Prefers CD. Include SASE.
Music Mostly **top 40**, **blues**, **country**, **dance-oriented**, **easy listening**, **folk** and **gospel**; also **jazz**, **MOR**, **progressive**, **R&B**, **rock** and **soul**.
Tips "Be excited and passionate about what you do. Be professional."

DOUG MOODY PRODX

(formerly Doug Moody Productions), P.O. Box 6271, Oceanside CA 92052-6271. E-mail: dmprodx@aol.com. Website: www.MysticRecordsHQ.com. Labels include Clock. Music publisher (Mystic Records USA & UK, Doug Moody Music USA & UK). Estab. 1968. Releases 73 LPs and 20 CDs/year. Pays 10% royalty to artists on contract.
How to Contact Only open to groups who perform. Include SASE.
Music Mystic thrash, **punk** and **blues**, **50s** and **60s** music for Clock Records. Does not want pop, classical, religious. Released *Maximum Rock 'n' Roll* (album), written and recorded by NOFX (mystic); and *Happy Organ* (album), written and recorded by Dave Baby Cortez (clock).
Tips "Make a master ready for release."

NATION RECORDS INC.

6351 W. Montrose 333, Chicago IL 60634. E-mail: info@nationrecords.com. Website: www.nationrecords.com. **Contact:** Phil Vaughan, A&R. Record company. Estab. 1996. Releases 5 CDs/year. Pays negotiable royalty to artists on contract; statutory rate to publisher per song on record.
Distributed by Midwest Artist Distribution.
How to Contact *Contact first and obtain permission to submit.* Prefers CD with lyric sheet. Does not return material. Responds in 6 months.
Music All types. Released *American Stories* (album by Bob Young); and *Steve & Johnnie Present Life After Dark* (album), both on Nation Records Inc. Other artists include The Buckinghams, Pete Special and World Class Noise.

NBT RECORDS

228 Morgan Lane, Berkeley Springs WV 25411-3475. (304)258-3656. E-mail: nbtoys@verizon.net. **Contact:** John S. Newbraugh, owner. Record company, music publisher (Newbraugh Brothers Music/BMI, NBT Music/ASCAP). Estab. 1967. Staff size: 1. Releases 4 singles and 52 CDs/year. Pays negotiable royalty to artists on contract; statutory royalty to publishers per song on record.
Distributed by "Distribution depends on the genre of the release. Our biggest distributor is perhaps the artists themselves, for the most part, depending on the genre of the release. We do have product in some stores and on the Internet as well.
How to Contact Submit demo by mail. Unsolicited submissions are OK. Prefers CD or cassette with any amount of songs, lyric sheet and cover letter. Include SASE. Responds in 4-6 weeks.
Music Mostly **rockabilly**, **hillbilly**, **folk** and **bluegrass**; also **rock**, **country** and **gospel**. Does not want any music with vulgar lyrics. "We will accept all genres of music except songs that contain vulgar language." Released "Momma Likes To Boogie" (single by Dale Brooks) from *Hot Rod Daddy* (album), recorded by The Rhythmatics (rockabilly); "Nonstop Holiday" (single by Kurt Christensen) from *Don't Wear Me Out* (album), recorded by The Gyros (rock); and "Clackty Clack" (single by A.V. "Sonny" May/Steven Cooper) from *Ride the Train—Volume Three* (album), recorded by William Ray (country), all released 2004 on NBT Records.
Tips "We are best known for our rockabilly releases. Reviews of our records can be found on both the American and European rockabilly websites. Our 'registered' trademark is a train. From time to time, we put out a CD with various artists featuring original songs that use trains as part of their theme. We use all genres of music for our train releases. We have received train songs from various parts of the world. All submissions on this topic are welcomed."

NERVOUS RECORDS

5 Sussex Crescent, Northolt, Middlesex UB5 4DL England. Phone: 44(20)8423 7373. E-mail: nervous@compuserve.com. Website: www.nervous.co.uk. **Contact:** R. Williams, managing director. Record company (Rage Records), record producer and music publisher (Nervous Publishing and Zorch Music). Member: MCPS, PRS,

PPL, ASCAP, NCB. Releases 10 CDs/year. Pays 8-12% royalty to artists on contract; statutory rate to publisher per song on records. Royalties paid directly to US songwriters and artists or through US publishing or recording affiliate.

• Nervous Records' publishing company, Nervous Publishing, is listed in the Music Publishers section.

How to Contact Submit demo tape by mail. Unsolicited submissions are OK. Prefers cassette with 4-15 songs and lyric sheet. SAE and IRC. Responds in 3 weeks.

Music Mostly **psychobilly** and **rockabilly**. ''No heavy rock, AOR, stadium rock, disco, soul, pop—only wild rockabilly and psychobilly.'' Released ''Extra Chrome'', written and recorded by Johnny Black; ''It's Still Rock 'N' Roll to Me'', written and recorded by The Time. Other artists include Restless Wild and Taggy Tones.

◙ NEURODISC RECORDS, INC.

3801 N. University Dr., Suite 403, Ft. Lauderdale FL 33351. (954)572-0289. Fax: (954)572-2874. E-mail: info@neurodisc.com. Website: www.neurodisc.com. President: Tom O'Keefe. Label Manager: John Wai. Record company and music publisher. Estab. 1990. Releases 3 singles, 10 LPs and 10 CDs/year. Pays negotiable royalty to artists on contract; 75% ''to start'' to publisher per song on record.

Distributed by Capital Records/EMI.

How to Contact Submit demo CD by mail. Unsolicited submissions are OK. Prefers CD, DAT or VHS videocassette. Include SASE. Responds only if interested.

Music Mostly **electronic**, **dance**, **New Age**, and **electro-bass**; also **rap**. Released albums from Peplab, Etro Anime, Tastexperience, Ryan Farish & Amethystium, as well as Bass Lo-Ryders and Bass Crunk. Other artists include Eric Hansen, Bella Sonus and NuSound as well as DJ's Suzy Solar, Vicious Vic, Andy Hughes and Scott Stubbs.

▢ NIGHT OWL RECORDS.

(formerly Keeping It Simple and Safe, Inc.), P.O. Box 91079, Springfield MA 01139-1079. (866)214-1286, ext. 107 (toll free) or (413)883-2527. Fax: (509)351-4379. E-mail: nightowlrecord@aol.com. **Contact:** New Talent Department. Labels include Grand Jury Records, Second Time Around Records and Southend-Essex Records. Record company. Estab. 1993. Releases 3 singles 2 CDs/year. Pays 12-25% royalty to artists on contract; statutory rate to publisher per song on record.

Distributed by Tim Scott Music Group (BMI) music publisher.

• Also see the listing for Tim Scott Music Group in the Music Publishers section of this book.

How to Contact Submit demo package by mail. Unsolicited submissions are OK. Prefers cassette or CD with 3-5 songs and lyric sheet. Include SASE. Responds in 1 month.

Music Mostly **pop**, **R&B**, and **rap**; also **country**, **rock** and **gospel**. Released ''By The Way'' (single), written and recorded by Larry ''TCP'' Smith (top 40), released 2002 on Hurricane Records; ''Without You'' (single by Sammy Jones/Robert Johnson) from *Distant* (album), recorded by Soft Touch (r&b), released 2002 on Night Owl Records; and ''My Heart Beats (For You)'' (single by Ann Jackson/William Jackson) from *Heart Two Heart* (album), recorded by Ann Jackson (country), released 2002 on Night Owl Records.

Tips ''Always include in cover letter whether you are asking for a publishing or a recording record deal.''

☒ ◙ NIGHTMARE RECORDS

7751 Greenwood Dr., St. Paul MN 55112. (763)784-9654. Fax: (763)784-7914. E-mail: info@nightmarerecords.com. Website: www.nightmarerecords.com. Contact: Lance King. Record company, distributor and management firm (Jupiter Productions). Estab. 1983. Pays 10-15% royalty to artists on contract.

Distributed by US: Best Buy stores, Sam Goody/Musicland/Media Play/On Cue, Blockbuster Music, Nightmare-Records.com, Dream Disc, Perris Records, Dynasty Music, Two Guys Music, Wildside Imports, Molten Metal, Impulse Music, Alta Mira, Amazon.com, D.S.B. Music, Echo Rider/Music Works, Generations Underground, Lasers Edge, CD Baby, Outer Limites, Moremetal.com, Sentinel Steel, Restless & Wild, CD's and More, Amazing-cds.com, Sounds of Metal, Seven Gates, Must Have Music, Oarfin Records & Distribution, Select-O-Hits, Neh Records, Phoenix Records, Metal Mayhem Music, Century Media, The Sounds of Metal, Rasputin Music, Loud Distribution. Foreign: Bertus Distribution (Netherlands), Bee Bee Records/Distribee (Netherlands), Mega Rock Distribution (Sweden), Nordic Metal (Denmark), Scrape Records (Canada), HMV (Canada), Lament Distribution (Mexico), Steel Gallery (Greece), Sleazy Rider (Greece), Sun Records, Sounds Machine (Italy), Heavencross (Spain), Leyenda (Spain), The Rock Shop (Spain), JPM Music (Chile), Rising Sun (Germany), Lobel Music (GeK), Concrete (Germany), War of Horns Records (Germany), Discos Sun Records (Spain), Rockhouse Records (Holland), Hellion Records (Germany), DSB (Germany), AOR Basement (UK), Diskheaven (Japan), Sheer Records (Czech Republic), Music Hunter (Finland), Heavy Sound Rock Shop (Sweden), Lament Distributions (Mexico). Christian: Holy Rollers, The Crossing (CDHC), Christian Demo Clearing House, M8, Spring Arbor, C.M.P. (Australia), Rugged Cross, Rad Rockers, Bibles Plus, Ultimatum Music, Blast Beats Music, Nordic Mission, Something More Christian Bookstore, ClassicGod.com.

How to Contact Submit demo tape by mail. Unsolicited submissions are OK. Prefers cassette or CD with 3 songs. Include brief bio, photo and press clippings (if available). Does not return material. Responds only if interested.

Music Mostly **hard rock-metal**, with a special interest in **progressive metal**. Released *Untitled* (by King/Barilla), recorded by The Kings Machine (rock); *From Cradle to Grave* (by Petrick/Cassidy), recorded by Malicious (rock); and *Pavlov's Dog's* (by Stevenson/Christensen), recorded by Conditioned Response (rock), all on Nightmare. Current acts include Godhead (Southern fried grunge), Visionary (progressive metal), Balance of Power (progressive metal), Cains Alibi (power metal), Empyria (progressive power metal), Antithesis (progressive thrash metal), USM (Nu-metal) and Sonic Boom (industrial dance).

Tips "Be patient, persistent and positive! We're busy and we know what were looking for, if we like what we hear, we'll call you ASAP."

☐ NORTH STAR MUSIC

22 London St., E. Greenwich RI 02818. (401)886-8888 or (800)346-2706. Fax: (401)886-8880. E-mail: info@northstarmusic.com. Website: www.northstarmusic.com. **Contact:** Richard Waterman, president. Record company. Estab. 1985. Staff size: 15. Releases 12-16 LPs/year. Pays 9% royalty to artists on contract; ³⁄₄ statutory rate to publisher per song on record.

Distributed by Alliance, Goldenrod and Lady Slipper.

How to Contact Submit demo CD by mail. Unsolicited submissions are OK. Prefers finished CD. Does not return material. Responds in 2 months.

Music Mostly **instrumental, traditional** and **contemporary jazz, New Age, traditional world (Cuban, Brasilian, singer/songwriter, Hawaiian and Flamenco)** and **classical**. Released *Sacred* (album), written and recorded by David Tolk (inspirational), released 2003; *An Evening In Tuscany* (album), written and recorded by Bruce Foulke/Howard Kleinfeld (contemporary instrumental), released 2004; *Always & Forever* (album), written and recorded by David Osborne (piano), released 2003, all on North Star Music. Other artists include Judith Lynn Stillman, David Osborne, Emilio Kauderer, Gerry Beaudoin, Cheryl Wheeler and Nathaniel Rosen.

☐ OCP PUBLICATIONS

P.O. Box 18030, 5536 NE Hassalo, Portland OR 97213. **Contact:** Paulette McCoy, director, music publications. Labels include Candleflame and NALR. Record company, music publisher and record producer. Estab. 1977. Releases 20 LPs and 10 CDs/year. Pays 10% royalty to artists on contract; negotiable rate to publisher per song on record.

How to Contact Submit demo tape or CD by mail. Unsolicited submissions are OK. Requires lead sheets (with chords, melody line and text minimum) with *optional* demo tape/CD. Prefers cassette with lead sheet. "Detailed submission information available upon request." Include SASE. Responds in 3 months.

Music Mostly **liturgical, Christian/listening** and **children's Christian**; also **choral Christian anthems** and **youth Christian anthems**. Released *Set Free* (album), written and recorded by Steve Angrisano (youth gospel); *Cry the Gospel* (album), written and recorded by Tom Booth (youth gospel); and *Spirit & Song* (hymnal with 9 CDs), written and recorded by various (youth gospel), all released 1999 on OCP. "There are over 80 artists signed by OCP."

Tips "Know the Catholic liturgy and the music needs therein."

⊠ ☻ OGLIO RECORDS

P.O. Box 404, Redondo Beach CA 90277. Fax: (310)791-8670. Contact: Kevin Knight. Record company. Estab. 1992. Releases 20 LPs and 20 CDs/year. Pays negotiable royalty to artist on contract; statutory rate to publisher per song on record.

How to Contact *Write first and obtain permission to submit.* Accepts demos in all formats. Does not return material. Responds in 6 weeks.

Music Mostly **alternative rock** and **comedy**. Released *Shine* (album), recorded by Cyndi Lauper (pop); *Live At The Roxy* (album), recorded by Brian Wilson (rock); *Team Leader* (album), recorded by George Lopez (comedy).

☐ ONLY NEW AGE MUSIC, INC.

8033 Sunset Blvd. #472, Hollywood CA 90046. (323)851-3355. Fax: (323)851-7981. E-mail: info@newagemusic.com. Website: www.newagemusic.com or www.newageuniverse.com. **Contact:** Suzanne Doucet, president. Record company, music publisher and consulting firm. Estab. 1987.

How to Contact *Call first and obtain permission to submit.* Does not return material.

Music Mostly **New Age**; also **world music**.

Tips "You should have a marketing strategy and at least a small budget for marketing your product."

✷ OUTSTANDING RECORDS

P.O. Box 2111, Huntington Beach CA 92647. (714)377-7447 or (800)749-8469. Fax: (714)377-7468. Website: www.outstandingmusic.com. **Contact:** Earl Beecher, owner. Labels include Morrhythm. Record company, music publisher (Earl Beecher Publishing/BMI and Beecher Music Publishing/ASCAP) and record producer (Earl Beecher). Estab. 1968. Staff size: 1. Releases 40 CDs/year. Pays $2/CD royalty to artists on contract; statutory rate to publisher per song on record.

Distributed by Sites on the Internet and "through distribution companies who contact me directly, especially from overseas."

How to Contact Submit demo by mail. Unsolicited submissions are OK. Prefers CD or videocassette (VHS) with 3 songs, lyric sheet, photo and cover letter. Include SASE. Responds in 3 weeks.

Music Mostly **jazz, rock** and **country**; also **everything else especially Latin**. Does not want music with negative, anti-social or immoral messages.

Tips "Keep selections short (three to three and a half minutes. Short intros and fade outs, if any). No dirty language. Do not encourage listeners to use drugs, alcohol or engage in immoral behavior. I'm especially looking for upbeat, happy, danceable music."

✷ ◻ P. & N. RECORDS

61 Euphrasia Dr., Toronto ON M6B 3V8 Canada. (416)782-5768. Fax: (416)782-7170. **Contact:** Panfilo Di Matteo, president, A&R. Record company, record producer and music publisher (Lilly Music Publishing). Estab. 1993. Staff size: 2. Releases 10 singles, 20 12″ singles, 15 LPs, 20 EPs and 15 CDs/year. Pays 25-35% royalty to artists on contract; statutory rate to publisher per song on record.

How to Contact Submit demo tape by mail. Unsolicited submissions are OK. Prefers cassette or videocassette with 3 songs and lyric or lead sheet. Does not return material. Responds in 1 month only if interested.

Music Mostly **dance, ballads** and **rock**. Released *Only This Way* (album), written and recorded by Angelica Castro; *The End of Us* (album), written and recorded by Putz, both on P. & N. Records (dance); and "Lovers" (single by Marc Singer), recorded by Silvana (dance), released 2001 on P. and N. Records.

✷ ◻ PACIFIC TIME ENTERTAINMENT

P.O. Box 7320, FDR Station, New York, NY 10150. (212)741-2888. Fax: (845)708-0113. E-mail: pactimeco@aol.com. Website: www.pactimeco.com. **Contact:** Curtis Urbina, president. Record company. Estab. 1998. Staff size: 4. Releases 2 singles and 20 CDs/year. Pays negotiable royalty to artists on contract; ¾ rate to publisher per song on record.

Distributed by Navarre Corporation.

How to Contact *Call first and obtain permission to submit.* Prefers CD with 3 songs. Responds in 1 month.

Music Film scores. Released "The Son's Room" (single by N. Piovani) from *The Son's Room* (album), recorded by Nicola Piovani (soundtrack); and "Keep on Keeping On" (single by M. Serio) from *Entertainers* (album), recorded by Bel Mondo (pop), both released 2001 on Pacific Time Entertainment. Other artists include Nana Simpoulos, Jimmy Earl, Psonica, Mark P. Adler and Scotch Egg.

✷ PARLIAMENT RECORDS

449 N. Vista St., Los Angeles CA 90036. (323)653-0693. E-mail: parlirec@aol.com. Website: www.parlirec.com **Contact:** Ben Weisman, owner. Record company, record producer (Weisman Production Group) and music publisher (Audio Music Publishers, Queen Esther Music Publishing). Estab. 1965. Produces 30 singles/year. Fee derived from sales royalty when song or artist is recorded.

  • Also see the listings for Audio Music Publishers and Queen Esther Music Publishing in the Music Publishers section and Weisman Production Group in the Record Producer section.

How to Contact Submit demo by mail. Unsolicited submissions are OK. Prefers CD or cassette with 3-10 songs and lyric sheet. Include SASE. "Mention Songwriter's Market. Please make return envelope the same size as the envelopes you send material in, otherwise we cannot send everything back." Responds in 6 weeks.

Music Mostly **R&B, soul, dance, rap,** and **top 40/pop**; also **gospel** and **blues**. Arists include Rapture 7 (gospel), Wisdom (male gospel singers), and chosen Recovery Ministry (female gospel group).

Tips "Parliament Records will also listen to 'tracks' only. If you send tracks, please include a letter stating what equipment you record on—ADAT, Protools or Roland VS recorders."

✷ PICKWICK/MECCA/INTERNATIONAL RECORDS

P.O. Box 725, Daytona Beach FL 32115. (386)252-4849. Fax: (386)252-7402. E-mail: CharlesVickers@aol.com or KingofKingsCV@aol.com. **Contact:** Clarence Dunklin, president. Record company and music publisher (Pritchett Publications). Estab. 1980. Releases 20 singles, 30 LPs and 30 CDs/year. Pays 5-10% royalty to artists on contract; negotiable rate to publisher per song on record.

How to Contact Submit demo tape by mail. Unsolicited submissions are OK. Prefers cassette with 12 songs and lyric or lead sheet. Does not return material.

Music Mostly **gospel**, **disco** and **rock/pop**; also **country**, **ballads** and **rap**. Released *Give It To Me Baby* (album by Loris Doby), recorded by Gladys Nighte; *Baby I Love You* (album), written and recorded by Joe Simmon; and *I Love Sweetie* (album by Doris Doby), recorded by Bobby Blane.

☑ ◐ PLATEAU MUSIC

P.O. Box 947, White House TN 37188. (615)654-8131. Fax: (615)654-8207. E-mail: nville93@comcast.com. Website: www.plateaumusic.com. **Contact:** Tony Mantor, owner. Record company and record producer. Estab. 1990. Staff size: 1. Pays negotiable royalty to artists on contract; statutory rate to publisher per song on record.

How to Contact Submit demo by mail. Unsolicited submissions are OK. Prefers CD with 4 songs and lyric sheet. Does not return material. Responds only if interested. "Include an e-mail address and we will respond quicker."

Music Mostly **country**, **R&B** and **rock/pop**. Released "On My Way to You" (single) from *On My Way to You* (album), recorded by Nina Sharp (country), released 2003-2004; "Child of the City" (single by Michael Constantino) (rock/pop), released 2004; "Fly" (single) from *Did You Miss Me*, recorded by Rani (R&B), released 2004-2005, all on Plateau Music. Other artists include Carlynne DeVine, Nina Sharp, Charles Walsh and Jason Lee Ward.

Tips "Be prepared to work harder than you ever have in singing if you sing for Plateau Music. We are a development music company that works with a singer to get the most out of them. We develop and manage the client until they are ready to be shopped to potential management and major record labels. We do very few independent releases. Our focus is getting the singer radio ready and radio friendly so they may have an opportunity to succeed in music. We take tride in the Quality of our work and the opportunity it gives the singers that we record. Plateau Music has a good repuration in Nashville and will not drop quality, so again be prepared for a lot of hard work."

☑ 🌐 ◐ PLAYBONES RECORDS

Symphony House, Eppendorfer Weg 7, D-20259 Hamburg Germany. Phone: (040)22716552 + -53. Fax: (040)22716554. E-mail: mento_music@t-online.de. **Contact:** Arno H. van Vught, head of A&R. Producer: Arno van Vught. Labels include Rondo Records. Record company, music publisher (Mento Music Group) and record producer (Arteg Productions). Estab. 1975. Releases 30 CDs/year. Pays 8-16% royalty to artists on contract; statutory rate to publisher per song on record.

How to Contact Submit demo tape by mail. Unsolicited submissions are OK. Prefers CD-R with 3-4 songs. Put your strongest/best song first. "Put your name and address on the inside sleeve of the tape. If you have a fax number, inform us. Tell us in a typed cover letter what you want/what you are looking for." Does not return material. Responds in 3 weeks.

Music Mostly **instrumentals**, **country** and **jazz**; also **background music**, **rock** and **gospel**. Released *Paradise* (album), written and recorded by Anna C. Nova (pop); "Vergessen wir die Mark" (single by DP/Volker Frank), recorded by Volker Frank (pop); and *Lord of the Dance* (album), written and recorded by Wolfgang Bauer (world music), all released 2003/2004 on Playbones Records. Other artists include Ellen Obier, Volker Frank, Dianna Jēan, Bianca 4 Harry.

☑ ◯ PMG RECORDS

P.O. Box 816, Van Buren Township MI 48152. E-mail: prejippie@comcast.net. Website: www.presjippie.com. **Contact:** Bruce Henderson, president. Record company, music publisher (Prejippie Music Group/BMI) and record producer (PMG Productions, Prejippie Music Group). Estab. 1990. Staff size: 3. Releases 6-12 12″ singles, 2 LPs and 2 EPs/year. Pays 40% royalty to artists on contract; statutory rate to publisher per song on record.

- Publishes *Direct Hitz*, a newsletter "where other independents can learn how to work effectively in the music business today."

Distributed by Dancefloor and Win.

How to Contact Submit demo tape by mail. Unsolicited submissions are OK. Prefers CD or VHS videocassette with 3-4 songs and lyric sheet. "Include photo if possible. No calls please." Include SASE. Responds in 6 weeks.

Music Mostly **funk/rock**, **alternative R&B**, **alternative rock**, **experimental** and **techno/dance**. Released *Tony Webb's Bass Christmas* (album), written and recorded by Tony Webb (alternative jazz) on PMG Records. Other artists include Urban Transit and the Prejippies.

Tips "Be very original in your approach to a song: concentrate on creating an interesting arrangement; concentrate on having at least one good hook; and put some thought into creating interesting lyrical themes."

◐ POP RECORD RESEARCH

10 Glen Ave., Norwalk CT 06850. E-mail: horar@earthlink.net. Director: Gary Theroux. Estab. 1962. Pays statutory rate to publisher per song on record.

● Also see their listing in the Organizations section.

How to Contact Submit demo tape by mail. Unsolicited submissions are OK. Prefers CD, cassette or VHS videocassette. Does not return material.

Music Mostly **pop**, **country** and **R&B**. Released "The Declaration" (single by Theroux-Gilbert), recorded by An American; "Thoughts From a Summer Rain" (single), written and recorded by Bob Gilbert, both on Bob Records; and "Tiger Paws" (single), written and recorded by Bob Gilbert on BAL Records. Other artists include Gary and Joan, The Nightflight Singers and Ruth Zimmerman.

Tips "Help us keep our biographical file on you and your career current by sending us updated bios/press kits, etc. They are most helpful to writers/researchers in search of accurate information on your success."

☑ ◯ POWERBLAST WORLDWIDE (formerly Powerblast Recordings)

P.O. Box 402721, Miami Beach FL 33140. (305)335-2529. Website: www.powerblastworldwide.com. CEO: Ernest W. Coleman. Record company. Estab. 1992. Staff size: 4. Releases 4 CDs/year. Pays negotiable royalty to artists on contract; statutory rate to publisher per song on record.

Distributed by Various one-stop distributors and online e-commerce sites on the Internet.

How to Contact Submit demo tape by mail. Unsolicited submissions are OK. Prefers CD, cassette or videotape (VHS) with 3 songs and cover letter. Include SASE. Responds in 1 month if interested.

Music Mostly **hip-hop/rap**, **alternative**, **jazz** and **r&b**. Does not want country. Released *Born Official* (album), recorded by Rising Sun; *Spookopolis* (album), by Cutty B. Spooky; *Destructive Communication* (album), written and recorded by Bombthreat (hardcore hip hop); *Death Becomes All of 'Em* (album), written and recorded by Cutty B. Spooky; *Explosive Material* (album), written and recorded by Bombthreat (hardcore hip-hop); and *Heat* (album), written and produced and recorded by The G. Other artists include Skandal D Ruckus Man, Gino Vega, Terror, Benny Haze and Mayhem Stompabitch.

Tips "Be professional when making contact or approaching our company."

☑ ◑ PPL ENTERTAINMENT GROUP

P.O. Box 261488, Encino, CA 91426. (818)506-8533. Fax: (818)506-8534. E-mail: a&r@pplzmi.com. Website: www.pplentertainmentgroup.com. **Contact:** Cisco Crowe, vice president A&R. Vice President A&R: Dakota Kelly. Vice President, A&R: Kaitland Diamond. General Manager: Jim Sellavain. President, Creative: Suzette Cuseo. Labels include Bouvier, Credence and JBK. Record company, music publisher (Pollybyrd Publications), management firm (Sa'mall Management) and distributor (Malibu Trading Company). Estab. 1979. Staff size: 15. Releases 10-30 singles, 12 12″ singles, 6 LPs and 6 CDs/year. Pays 10-15% royalty to artists on contract; statutory rate to publisher per song on record.

Distributed by Sony and The Malibu Trading Company.

How to Contact *E-mail and obtain permission to submit.* Prefers CD, cassette or videocassette with 3 songs. Include SASE. Responds in 6 weeks.

Music Released "Step Into the Light" (single) and "He's Coming" (single) from *J.R. Perry* (album), written and recorded by J.R. Perry (gospel), released 2003 on PPL/Sony; "Bigg Leggeded Woman" (single by Buddy Wright) from *Destiny* (album), recorded by Buddy Wright (blues), released 2003 on PPL; *Ghost* (album), recorded by The Band AKA, written and produced by J. James Jarrett; "Step Aside" (single by Gary Johnson) from *Step Aside* (album), recorded by Gary J., released 2003 on PPL/Sony. Other artists include Phuntaine, Condottiere and Gary J.

◑ PRAVDA RECORDS

6311 N. Neenah, Chicago IL 60631. (773)763-7509. Fax: (773)763-3252. E-mail: pravdausa@aol.com. Website: pravdamusic.com. **Contact:** Mo Goodman, director of A&R. A&R (pop/rock): Matt Favazza. Labels include Bughouse. Record company. Estab. 1985. Releases 3-6 singles, 1 EP and 5-6 CDs/year. Pays 10-15% royalty to artists on contract; statutory rate to publisher per song on record.

Distributed by Hep Cat, Alliance and Carrot Top.

How to Contact Submit demo tape by mail. Unsolicited submissions are OK. Prefers cassette or CD with 3-4 songs. Does not return material. "Will contact only if interested."

Music Mostly **rock**. Released *Variations On A Goddamn Old Man* (album), recorded by Cheer-Accident (alternative), released 2002 on Pravda; *Vodka & Peroxide* (album), recorded by The Civil Tones (r&b), released 2003 on Pravda; and *album title TBA* (album), recorded by The Goldstars (garage), released 2003 on Pravda. Other artists include Tiny Tim, Frantic Flattops, Gringo, Javelin Boot, The Slugs, The New Duncan Imperials and Legendary Stardust Cowboy.

Tips "Be nice! Tour behind your release, don't take yourself too seriously."

☑ ◙ PRIORITY RECORDS

6430 Sunset Blvd., Hollywood CA 90028. (323)467-0151. Website: www.priorityrecords.com. Labels include No Limit Records, Rawkus Records, Hoo-Bangin' Records and Duck Down Records. Record company.

Distributed by EMD.

How to Contact *Does not accept unsolicited submissions.*

Music Artists include Ice Cube, Snoop Dogg, Big Moe and Dilated People.

🔊 QUARK RECORDS

P.O. Box 7320, FDR Station, New York NY 10150 or 4 E. 12th St., New York NY 10003. (212)741-2888. E-mail: quarkent@aol.com. **Contact:** Curtis Urbina, president (pop, dance). A&R: Michelle Harris (alternative). Labels include Pacific Time Entertainment. Record company and music publisher (Quarkette Music/BMI and Freedurb Music/ASCAP). Estab. 1984. Releases 6 singles and 3 LPs/year. Pays negotiable royalty to artists on contract; ³/₄ statutory rate to publisher per song on record.

How to Contact *Call first and obtain permission to submit.* Prefers CD with 2 songs. Include SASE. Responds in 6 weeks.

Music Mostly **dance/pop**. Released "Throwback" (single by E. Cohen) from *Party Time* (album), recorded by DJ Strebe (dance); "Being With You" (single by M. Adler) from *Flagstaff, AZ* (album), recorded by Mark P. Adler (pop); and "Ant & The Sky" (single by C. Urbina) from *Highbridge Gardens* (album), recorded by Curtis Urbina (spoken word), all released 2002 on Quark Records.

☐ RADICAL RECORDS

77 Bleecker St., Suite C2-21, New York NY 10012. (212)475-1111. Fax: (212)475-3676. E-mail: info@radicalrecords.com. Website: www.radicalrecords.com. **Contact:** Johnny Chiba, A&R. Record company. "We also do independent retail distribution for punk, hardcore music." Estab. 1986. Staff size: 7. Releases 1 single and 6 CDs/year. Pays 14% royalty to artists on contract; statutory rate to publisher per song on record.

Distributed by City Hall, Revelation, Select-O-Hits, Revolver, Choke.

How to Contact *E-mail first for permission to submit demo.* Prefers cassette or CD. Does not return material. Responds in 1 month.

Music Mostly **punk** and **hardcore**. Released *Too Legit for the Pit—Hardcore Takes the Rap* (album), recorded by various; *Punk's Not Dead—A Tribute to the Exploited* (album), recorded by various; *Fresh Out of Give-a-Fucks* (album), recorded by Submachine; and *East Coast of Oi!* (album), recorded by various. Other artists include The Agents, Social Scare, Blanks 77 and Inspector 7.

Tips "Create the best possible demos you can and show a past of excellent self-promotion."

🔊 RAVE RECORDS, INC.

Attn: Production Dept., 13400 W. Seven Mile Rd., Detroit MI 48235. E-mail: info@raverecords.com. Website: www.raverecords.com. **Contact:** Carolyn and Derrick, production managers. Record company and music publisher (Magic Brain Music/ASCAP). Estab. 1992. Staff size: 2. Releases 2-4 singles and 2 CDs/year. Pays various royalty to artists on contract; statutory rate to publisher per song on record.

Distributed by Action Music Sales.

How to Contact Submit demo CD by mail. Prefers CD with 3 songs, lyric sheet. "Include any bios, fact sheets, and press you may have. We will contact you if we need any further information. Does not return materials.

Music Mostly **alternative rock** and **dance**. Artists include Cyber Cryst, Dorothy, Nicole and Bukimi 3.

🔊 RAZOR & TIE ENTERTAINMENT

214 Sullivan St., Suite 4A, New York NY 10012. (212)473-9173. E-mail: info@razorandtie.com. Website: www.razorandtie.com. Record company.

How to Contact *Does not accept unsolicited material.*

Music Released *The Beauty of the Rain* (album) by Dar Williams; *The Sweetheart Collection* by Frankie & The Knockouts; *Everybody's Normal But Me* by Stuttering John; and *Marigold* (album) by Marty Lloyd, all on Razor & Tie Entertainment. Other artists include Graham Parker, Marshall Crenshaw and Toshi Reagon.

✅ 🎙 🔊 RCA RECORDS

1540 Broadway, 36th Floor, New York NY 10036. (212)930-4936. Fax: (212)930-4447. Website: www.rcarecords.com. A&R: Donna Pearce. **Beverly Hills:** 8750 Wilshire Blvd., Beverly Hills CA 90211. (310)358-4105. Fax: (310)358-4127. Senior Vice President of A&R: Jeff Blue. **Nashville:** 1400 18th Ave. S., Nashville TN 37212. A&R Director: Jim Catino. Labels include Loud Records, Deconstruction Records and Judgment/RCA Records. Record company.

Distributed by BMG.

How to Contact *RCA Records does not accept unsolicited submissions.*

Music Artists include The Strokes, Dave Matthews Band, Clay Aiken, Christina Aguilera, and Velvet Revolver.

Rachael Sage

Conquers With Song Contests

New York City-based singer-songwriter Rachael Sage reports that the very first contest she ever won was a coloring contest for a Hello Kitty poster at her local Hallmark card shop. The confidence she gained that day eventually grew into great rewards in her busy career as a creator and performer of thoughtful and complex pop. She has since been honored by a litany of music competitions, including the CSN Producer Project (First Prize, 2004), the 10th International *Billboard* Songwriting Contest (Winner, 2002), the John Lennon Songwriting Contest (Grand Prize, 2001), and the Great American Songwriting Contest (Winner, 2001).

Sage began to teach herself piano at the age of five. Early interest in classical composers gave way to a love of renowned songwriters such as Elvis Costello, Carole King, and Laura Nyro. From her childhood attendance at the School of American Ballet through her graduation with a Drama degree from Stanford University, the muse continually lead her to music. Upon returning from college in California, she began attending the Actors Studio MFA program, but left for work in national commercials and voiceovers. At the age of twenty-four, she began her own label, Mpress Records.

Sage's independent releases to date include *Morbid Romantic, Smashing the Serene, Painting of a Painting, Illusion's Carnival,* and her most recent CD, *Public Record.* Her sixth release, *Balance and Burlesque,* is due out by Fall 2004.

I see that you won the Grand Prize in the John Lennon Songwriting Contest.
That was in 2001, I think.

Which song won it for you?
It was for "Pictures They Took" on *Painting of a Painting.*

Do you have a feeling for why your song was chosen? Do you have a sense of the various contests and what they are looking for?
You know, it's funny. There are certain contests that actually give you written evaluations and I really love those. The Great American Song Contest gave me little grade sheets and there was a point system. There are different categories like "How strong is the hook?" or "How is the production?" But on that one, it was more of a general, overall kind of an evaluation where my CD was given to the different celebrity panelists and was just passed around and posted to the site. They just listened to the different songs and I guess it must have grabbed them in some way.

It was kind of fun for me because it was the Rock category which we entered on kind of a whim. I'm not really that known for being much of a rocker per se, but a dear friend had helped me produce "Pictures They Took" and she kind of put it a little bit in that direction with the rhythm track and all, otherwise I probably would have entered it in Pop. Sometimes putting yourself in a category where you're a little bit different from what everyone else is doing can work in your favor. I guess that was the case.

Who produced the track?

Jo Davidson. She was in an artists' collective called Urban Muse with me. At one point she said, "You know, that song's gotta go on your record." I had just completed, or I thought I had completed *Painting of a Painting* and I said, "no." She said, "That's a good song. Let me produce it for you." We went into the studio and knocked it out. I really owe it to her that track got recorded.

Tell me a little more about some of the other contests you've won or been a part of. I know there was the *Billboard* Songwriting Contest . . .

Well, I'll mention one that was more recent. There's CSN Producer Project. We were really excited because they have a really cool angle. They were evaluating female artists based on their production skills. It was sponsored by Chick Singer Night. I didn't really know about it until I started seeing it listed on some of these women's artist collective sites like GoGirls Music and Indiegrrl.com. Just on a whim I entered my song "Bravedancing." At one point I was a finalist alongside my very good friends Edie Carey and Jenny Bruce and that was fun. A little while later, I got word that I had received First Prize. I won a bunch of cool gear that I've already started to use in my home studio. I had some insecurities going into the studio about whether I could produce myself without that support, that mirror that a co-producer can provide, so this was a particularly fun and gratifying win.

Billboard . . . that's been around for a long time. All of us get our applications in the mail. If you go to any music store, they'll find a way to track you down and send you their material! "My Precious Love" was the song that won in that one, and that won in R&B, which was kind of fun because I don't consider myself an R&B artist. So I think what's cool is that they really do demonstrate that they're not just evaluating production or the sonic quality. They really look into songs.

How are you feeling now about your latest release, *Public Record* (August 2003)? Are your personal favorites on the CD the same songs that are getting notice?

The first song I felt the strongest about on *Public Record* was "Bravedancing" because it was my favorite one to write. It was a little mini account of what I was doing for the whole record. Now I'm leaning toward "What If" because it's a little more relevant to where I'm at right now.

I've been joking lately that "What If" is kind of my version of the four questions on Passover, which of course ask "Why do we celebrate Passover? Why is this night different from all other nights?" "What If" is my version, asking "Why am I single?"

I am very curious about how your independent label, Mpress Records, works. When last we talked, you had a staff of two.

I have one full-time brilliant genius—Margo Parks—helping me and a few other part-time young ladies working on bookings and retail and radio.

I think survival is probably the key. You reach the point where you are receiving more inquiries and requests to perform or to record than you can handle just on your own. So you make a bold move and you reach out and you try to find someone who can help handle that workload. That shift for me came back in 1998 when I received an invitation to tour with Ani DiFranco, and I realized I was in over my head. So I think there were certain opportunities that came up that pushed me to the edge of whether or not I could handle all of the work and all of the logistics. It challenged me, and then I navigated my way through it and consulted a lot of people for advice. There are many aspects of running a label—it's trial and error, really. We're still figuring it out. By no means are we finished learning. We're learning everyday.

So, what are some of the ways that the contests have helped your career?

I think the biggest way that entering contests has helped me is that it is another area where you're developing contacts and making connections that will stay with you. For instance, it's been a couple of years since I won the John Lennon contest, but I recently got a call from the fellow who runs the contest and he'd recommended me as someone who could participate on a panel at South By Southwest. They needed a keyboard player to demonstrate new software. And I just thought that was really, really cool that it's not just "Wham, bam, thank you, Ma'am" and you know, on to the next. They have winners every year, and they are working really hard and have their hands full, but they also kept me in mind for something like that. And so it's just building your family and widening your circle to folks on your team in a really broad sense.

Also, a lot of these contests sponsor showcases and events at conferences. USA Songwriting Contest is really wonderful at presenting different winners from past years together, in-the-round, and in different booths. I jump to participate in those because it is a great way to meet other artists and to introduce your music to their audiences and friends and just widen your fan base.

I guess it helps on your short bio, too, when someone goes to introduce you. They may not know a damn thing about you up until they say "Rachael Sage—John Lennon Songwriting Contest!" It's a chance to bond when you're in Michigan and you are trying to introduce yourself.

—*Robin Renee*

N ⊕ ∅ RED SKY RECORDS

P.O. Box 27, Stroud, Glos. GL6 0YQ United Kingdom. Phone: 01453-836877. Fax: 01453-836877. Website: www.redskyrecords.co.uk. **Contact:** Johnny Coppin, producer. Record company and record producer (Johnny Coppin). Estab. 1985. Staff size: 1. Releases 1 album/year. Pays 8-10% to artists on contract; statutory rate to publisher per song on record.

Distributed by ADA, CM.

How to Contact *Write first and obtain permission to submit.* Does not return material. Responds in 6 months.

Music Mostly **rock/singer-songwriters**, **modern folk** and **roots music**. Released *The Dolan Brothers* (album), written and recorded by Dolan Brothers (blues); *A Journey* (album), written and recorded by Johnny Coppin (singer/songwriter); and *Dead Lively!* (album), written and recorded by Paul Burgess (folk) on Red Sky Records. Other artists include David Goodland.

☑ ○ REDEMPTION RECORDS

P.O. Box 10238, Beverly Hills CA 90213. (323)666-0221. E-mail: info@redemption.net. Website: www.redempti on.net. A&R Czar: Ryan D. Kuper (indie rock, power pop, rock, etc.). Record company. Estab. 1990. Staff size: varies. Releases 2-3 singles, 2-3 EPs and 2-3 CDs/year. Pays standard royalty to artists on contract; statutory rate to publisher per song on record.

Distributed by Navarre and others.

How to Contact *Does not accept unsolicited material. E-mail to obtain permission to submit.* Submit demo CD by mail or send mp3 link by e-mail. "Include band's or artist's goals." Does not return material. Responds only if interested.

Music Mostly **indie rock** and **power pop**. Artists include The Working Title, Race For Titles, Schatzi, Motion

City Soundtrack, The Remedy Session, Musico, and the *Redemption Versus Series* featuring indie rock bands from different geographical locations.
Tips "Be prepared to tour to support the release. Make sure the current line-up is secure."

⊞ ◪ RED-EYE RECORDS
Wern Fawr Farm, Pencoed, Mid-Glam CF35 6NB United Kingdom. Phone: (01656)86 00 41. **Contact:** M.R. Blanche, managing director. Record company and music publisher (Ever-Open-Eye Music/PRS). Estab. 1979. Releases 4 singles and 2-3 LPs/year. Pays negotiable royalty to artists on contract; statutory rate to publisher per song on record.
How to Contact Submit demo tape by mail. Unsolicited submissions are OK. Prefers cassette, VHS videocassette or CD with 4 songs. SAE and IRC. Does not return material.
Music Mostly **R&B**, **rock** and **gospel**; also **swing**. Released "River River" (single by D. John), recorded by The Boys; and "Billy" (single by G. Williams); and "Cadillac Walk" (single by Moon Martin), both recorded by the Cadillacs, all on Red-Eye Records. Other artists include Cartoon and Tiger Bay.

◪ REPRISE RECORDS
3300 Warner Blvd., 4th Floor, Burbank CA 91505. (818)846-9090. Fax: (818)840-2389. Website: www.repriserec ords.com. Labels include Duck and Sire. Record company.
Distributed by WEA.
How to Contact *Reprise Records does not accept unsolicited submissions.*
Music Artists include Eric Clapton, Guster, Josh Groban, The Distillers, and Neil Young.

◪ ◪ RIVAL RECORDS
204 W. Fifth St., Lorain OH 44052. (440)244-5324. Fax: (440)244-5349. E-mail: info@rivalrecords.com. Website: www.RivalRecords.com. **Contact:** Scotti C. Campana, president. Record company, music publisher (Campana Music Publishing/ASCAP) and record producer. Estab. 1998. Staff size: 8.
How to Contact Submit demo (CD only) by mail with 3 songs, lyric sheet, cover letter, photo and press clippings. Unsolicited submissions are OK. Does not return submissions. Responds in 6 weeks.
Music Mostly **R&B**, **hip-hop** and **pop**. Released "You Played Me" (single by David Tolliver), recorded by Men at Large; and "Something About You" (single by Scotti Campana), recorded by Soul, both on Rival Records (R&B). Other artists include Danny and S.O.S.C.

◪ ROAD RECORDS
P.O. Box 2620, Victorville CA 92393. E-mail: staff@askland.net. Website: www.roadrecords.com. **Contact:** Conrad Askland, president. Record company, record producer (Road Records) and music publisher (Askland Publishing). Estab. 1989. Produces 6 singles and 10 albums/year.
How to Contact Prefers at least 3 songs with lyric and lead sheet. Does not return submissions. Responds only if interested."We accept complete songs, soundtracks and ambient recordings."
Music Mostly **alternative**, **modern country** and **dance**; also **orchestral instrumental**. Does not want jazz. Released "You're the Best Lie" (single by Gailyn Addis and Conrad Askland) from *Gailyn Addis* (album), recorded by Gailyn Addis (pop/AC), released 2001 on Road Records.
Tips "Do not submit what you think we are looking for. A lot of our projects are 'on the edge.' We are looking for people that have a different, original sound. We supply music for dozens of companies worldwide."

◪ ◪ ROBBINS ENTERTAINMENT LLC
159 W. 25th St., 4th Floor, New York NY 10001. (212)675-4321. Fax: (212)675-4441. E-mail: info@robbinsent.c om. Website: www.robbinsent.com. **Contact:** John Parker, vice president, A&R/dance promotion. Record company and music publisher (Rocks, No Salt). Estab. 1996. Staff size: 8. Releases 25 singles and 12-14 CDs/year. Pays negotiable royalty to artists on contract; statutory rate to publisher per song on record.
Distributed by BMG.
How to Contact Accepts unsolicited demos as long as it's dance music. Prefers CD with 2 songs or less. "Make sure everything is labeled with the song title information and our contact information. t his is important in case the CD and the jewel case get separated. Do not call us and ask if you can send your package. The answer is yes."
Music Commercial **dance** only. Released top 10 pop smash, "Heaven" (single), recorded by DJ Sammy, as well as Hot 100 records from Rockell, Lasgo, Reina and K5. Other artists include Ian Van Dahl, Andain, Judy Torres, Marly, Dee Dee, Milky, Kreo and many others.
Tips "Do not send your package 'Supreme-Overnight-Before-You-Wake-Up' delivery. Save yourself some money. Do not send material if you are going to state in your letter that, 'If I had more (fill in the blank) it would sound better.' We are interested in hearing your best and only your best. Do not call us and ask if you can send your package. The answer is yes. We are looking for dance music with crossover potential."

▢ ROLL ON RECORDS®

112 Widmar Pl., Clayton CA 94517. (925)833-4680. E-mail: rollonrecords@aol.com. **Contact:** Edgar J. Brincat, owner. Record company and music publisher (California Country Music). Estab. 1985. Releases 2-3 LPs/cassettes/year. Pays 10% royalty to artists on contract; statutory rate to publisher per song on record.

Distributed by Tower.

How to Contact Submit demo tape by mail. Unsolicited submissions are OK. Do not call or write. Prefers CD's or cassette with 3 songs and lyric sheet. Include SASE and phone number. Responds in 6 weeks.

Music Mostly **contemporary/country**, **MOR** and **R&B**; also **pop**, **light rock** and **modern gospel**. Released "Broken Record" (single by Horace Linsley/Dianne Baumgartner), recorded by Edee Gordon on Roll On Records; *Maddy* and *For Realities Sake* (albums both by F.L. Pittman/Madonna Weeks), recorded by Ron Banks/ L.J. Reynolds on Life Records/Bellmark Records.

Tips "Be patient and prepare to be in it for the long haul. A successful songwriter does not happen overnight. It's rare to write a song today and have a hit tomorrow. If you give us your song and want it back, then don't give it to us to begin with."

⃞ ▢ ROTTEN RECORDS

Attn: A&R Dept., P.O. Box 56, Upland CA 91786. E-mail: rotten@rottenrecords.com. Website: www.rottenrecords.com. President: Ron Peterson. Promotions/Radio/Video: Andi Jones. Record company. Estab. 1988. Releases 3 LPs, 3 EPs and 3 CDs/year.

Distributed by Shock (Australia), Sonic Rendezvous (UK), DNA, Smash (US) and St. Clair (Canada).

How to Contact Submit demo tape by mail. Unsolicited submissions are OK. Prefers CD. Does not return material.

Music Mostly **rock**, **alternative** and **commercial**; also **punk** and **heavy metal**. Released *Paegan Terrorism . . .* (album), written and recorded by Acid Bath; *Kiss the Clown* (album by K. Donivon), recorded by Kiss the Clown; and *Full Speed Ahead* (album by Cassidy/Brecht), recorded by D.R.T., all on Rotten Records.

Tips "Be patient."

▢ ROWENA RECORDS

195 S. 26th St., San Jose CA 95116. (408)286-9840. Fax: (408)286-9845. E-mail: onealproduction@juno.com. Owner/A&R (country, Mexican, gospel): Grady O'Neal. A&R (all styles): Jeannine O'Neal. Record company and music publisher (Tiki Enterprises). Estab. 1967. Staff size: 3. Releases 8-12 LPs and 8-12 CDs/year. Pays negotiable royalty to artists on contract; pays statutory rate to publisher per song on record.

• Also see the listing for Tiki Enterprises Inc. in the Music Publishers section of this book.

How to Contact Submit demo tape by mail. Unsolicited submissions are OK. Prefers cassette with 2 songs and lyric sheet. Include SASE. Responds in 2 weeks.

Music Mostly **gospel**, **country** and **pop**; also **Mexican** and **R&B**. Released "It Amazes Me" (single by David Davis/Jeannine O'Neal) from *Forgiven*, recorded by Amber Littlefield/David Davis (Christian), released 2003-2004; "I'm Healed" (single by Jeannine O'Neal) from *Faith On the Front Lines*, recorded by Jeannine O'Neal, released 2004; and "You're Looking Good to Me" (single by Warren R. Spalding) from *A Rock 'N' Roll Love Story*, recorded by Warren R. Spalding, released 2003-2004, all on Rowena Records.

⃞ ▢ RUF RECORDS

162 N. 8th St., Kenilworth NJ 07033. (908)653-9700. E-mail: rufpublicist@aol.com. **Contact:** Mike DeUrso, marketing manager. General Manager: Ira Leslie. Record company, music publisher and record producer (Thomas Ruf). Estab. 1993. Releases 12 CDs/year. Pays negotiable royalty to artists on contract; statutory rate to publisher per song on record.

Distributed by IDN.

• Ruf is known for releasing blues.

How to Contact Write or call Mike to obtain permission to submit. Does not return material. Responds in 1 week.

Music Mostly **blues**, **rock** and **R&B**. Ruf America artist roster includes Luther Allison, Walter Trout, Ana Popovic, Omar and The Howlers, Candye Kane, and Bernard Allison.

▢ RUSTIC RECORDS

6337 Murray Lane, Brentwood TN 37027. (615)371-0646. Fax: (615)370-0353. E-mail: Jschneiderassoc@aol.com. President: Jack Schneider (country). Vice President: Claude Southall (country). Manager: Nell Tolson (gospel). Record company and music publisher (Iron Skillet Music/ASCAP, Covered Bridge/ BMI, Town Square/ SESAC). Estab. 1979. Staff size: 4. Releases 2 albums/ year. Pays negotiable royalty to artists on contract; statutory royalty to publisher per song on record.

● Also see the listings for Iron Skillet Music in the Music Publishers section of this book.
Distributed by Select-O-Hits.
How to Contact Submit demo by mail. Unsolicited submissions are OK. Prefers CD, cassette or videocassette with 3-4 songs, lyric sheet and cover letter. Include SASE. Responds in 4-5 weeks.
Music Mostly **traditional country**, **novelty**, and **old-time gospel**. Released "Ain't It Amazing" (single by C. Southall/ J. Schneider), "In Their Eyes" (single by Jamie Champa) and "You Got It All" (single by Bobby Reed) from *Ain't It Amazing (What One Little Screw Will Do)* (album), all recorded by Colte Bradley (traditional country), released in 2002 on Rustic Records. Other artists include Tanya Stanbridge and Holt Wilson.
Tips "Submit a professional demo."

☑ ○ RUSTRON MUSIC PRODUCTIONS

1156 Park Lane, West Palm Beach FL 33417-5957. (561)686-1354. E-mail: rmp_wmp@bellsouth.net. **Contact:** Sheelah Adams, office administrator. Executive Director: Rusty Gordon (folk fusions, blues, women's music, adult contemporary, electric, acoustic, New Age instrumentals, children's, cabaret). Director A&R: Ron Caruso. Associate Director of A&R: Kevin Reeves (pop, country, blues, R&B, jazz). Labels include Rustron Records and Whimsong Records. "Rustron administers 20 independent labels for publishing and marketing." Record company, record producer, management firm and music publisher (Whimsong/ASCAP and Rustron Music/ BMI). Estab. 1970. Releases 5-10 CDs/year. Pays variable royalty to artists on contract. "Artists with history of product sales get higher percent than those with no sales track record." Pays statutory rate to publisher.
How to Contact *Songwriters may write or call first to discuss your submission* or submit demo tape or CD by mail. Unsolicited submissions are OK. Prefers CD with up to 15 songs and typed lyric sheets. Cassette is limited to 3 songs. "Include cover letter with complete information regarding your submission with your promo pack. If singer/songwriter has independent product (cassette or CD) produced and sold at gigs—send this product." SASE required for all correspondence, no exceptions. Responds in 4 months.
Music Mostly **mainstream** and **women's music**, **adult contemporary electric acoustic**, **pop (cabaret, blues)** and **blues (R&B, country and folk)**; also **New Age fusions** (instrumentals), **modern folk fusions**, **environmental**, **socio-political**, **children's music** and **light jazz**. Released "Banyon Tree Blues" (single) from *Banyon Tree Blues* (album), written and recorded by The Dinner Key Boys (folk-rock blues), released 2004 on Whimsong Records; "Jah Jah Jamaica" (single) from *Jah Jah Jamaica* (album), written and recorded by Jeremy White & Kalliope (yankee reggae), released 2003 on Whimsong Records; and "Everglades Everlasting" (single) from *Everglades Everlasting* (album), written and recorded by Song On A Whim (children's music), released 2003 on Rustron Records.
Tips "Find your own unique style; write well crafted songs with unpredictable concepts, strong hooks and definitive melody. New Age composers: evolve your themes and add multi-cultural diversity with instruments. Don't be predictable. Don't over-produce your demos and don't drown vocals. Send cover letter clearly explaining your reasons for submitting. Carefully craft songs for single-song marketing."

☑ SABTECA RECORD CO.

P.O. Box 10286, Oakland CA 94610. (510)465-2805. Fax: (510)832-0464. E-mail: vitaminsun@aol.com. **Contact:** Duane Herring, president. Production Coordinator (pop, R&B, jazz): Sean Herring. Secretary (pop, R&B, country): Lois Shayne. Labels include André Romare Records. Record company and music publisher (Sabteca Music Co./ASCAP, Toyiabe Music Co./BMI). Estab. 1980. Releases 3 singles and 1 12″ single/year. Pays 10% royalty to artists on contract; statutory rate to publisher per song on record.
Distributed by Sabteca.
How to Contact *Write first and obtain permission to submit.* Prefers cassette with lyric sheet. Include SASE. Responds in 1 month.
Music Mostly **R&B**, **pop** and **country**. Released "Walking My Baby Home," "What Can I Do" and "Jenny Rose" (singles by Reggie Walker) from *Reggie Walker* (album), all recorded by Reggie Walker (pop), released 2002 on Andre Domare Records/Sabteca.
Tips "Determination and persistence are vital."

○ SAFIRE RECORDS

5617 W. Melvina, Milwaukee WI 53216. Phone/fax: (414)444-3385. **Contact:** Darnell Ellis, president. A&R Representatives: Darrien Kingston (country, pop); Reggie Rodriqez (world, Latin, Irish). Record company, music publisher (Ellis Island Music/ASCAP), record producer (Darnell Ellis) and management firm (The Ellis International Talent Agency). Estab. 1997. Staff size: 2. Releases 3 singles, 3 LPs, 1 EP and 3 CDs/year. Pays negotiable royalty to artists on contract; statutory rate to publisher per song on record.
● Also see the listing for The Ellis International Talent Agency in the Managers & Booking Agents section of this book.
How to Contact Submit demo tape by mail. Unsolicited submissions are OK. Prefers cassette or CD with 3-4

songs. Does not return material. Responds in 2 months. "We will respond only if we are interested."

Music Mostly **country**, **pop**, **mainstream pop**, all styles of **rock** and anything else except **rap** or **hip-hop**. Artists include Tracy Beck. Released "Ribbons and Bows" (single by Tracy Beck) from *Let The Wind Carry Me* (album), recorded by Tracy Beck (blues, alt. country/acoustic/roots), released 2002 on Safire Records.

Tips "Songwriters need to get back to the basics of songwriting: great hooklines, strong melodies. We would love to hear from artists and songwriters from all over the world. And remember, just because someone passes on a song it doesn't mean that it's a bad song. Maybe it's a song that the label is not able to market or the timing is just bad."

☑ ☒ ⊘ SAHARA RECORDS AND FILMWORKS ENTERTAINMENT

28 E. Jackson Bldg., 10th Floor #S627, Chicago IL 60604-2263. (773)509-6381. Fax: (312)922-6964. Website: www.edmsahara.com. **Contact:** Edward De Miles, president. Record company, music publisher (EDM Music/BMI, Edward De Miles Music Company) and record producer (Edward De Miles). Estab. 1981. Releases 15-20 CD singles and 5-10 CDs/year. Pays $9^{1}/_{2}$-11% royalty to artists on contract; statutory rate to publishers per song on record.

How to Contact *Does not accept unsolicited submissions.*

Music Mostly **R&B/dance**, **top 40 pop/rock** and **contemporary jazz**; also **TV-film themes**, **musical scores** and **jingles**. Released "Hooked on U," "Dance Wit Me" and "Moments" (singles), written and recorded by Steve Lynn (R&B) on Sahara Records. Other artists include Lost in Wonder, Dvon Edwards and Multiple Choice.

Tips "We're looking for strong mainstream material. Lyrics and melodies with good hooks that grab people's attention."

⊘ SALEXO MUSIC

P.O. Box 18093, Charlotte NC 28218-0093. (704)392-2477. E-mail: salexo@bellsouth.net. **Contact:** Samuel Obie, president. Record company. Estab. 1992. Releases 1 CD/year.

How to Contact *Write first and obtain permission to submit.* Prefers cassette with 3 songs and lyric sheet. Include SASE. Responds in 1 month.

Music Mostly **contemporary gospel** and **jazz**. Released *A Joyful Noise* (album), recorded by Samuel Obie with J.H. Walker Unity Choir (gospel), released 2003, Macedonia Baptist Church; and "Favor" (single) from *Favor*, written and recorded by Samuel Obie (contemporary gospel), released 2004 on Salexo Music.

Tips "Make initial investment in the best production."

⊕ ☑ ◯ SATELLITE MUSIC

34 Salisbury St., London NW8 8QE United Kingdom. Phone: (+44)207-402-9111. Fax: (+44)207-723-3064. E-mail: eliot@amimedia.co.uk. Website: www.amimedia.co.uk. **Contact:** Eliot Cohen, CEO. Director: Ray Dorset. Labels include Saraja and Excalibur. Record company and music publisher. Estab. 1976. Staff size: 10. Releases 5 singles, 3 LPs and 3 CDs/year. Pays negotiable royalty to artists on contract; statutory rate to publisher per song on record.

Distributed by S. Gold & Sons and Total Home Entertainment.

How to Contact Submit demo tape by mail. Unsolicited submissions are OK. Prefers cassette, CD, DAT or VHS videocassette with 4 songs, cover letter and press clippings. SAE and IRC. Responds in 6 weeks.

Music Mostly **dance**, **disco** and **pop**. Does not want blues, jazz or country. Released "In the Snow" (by Ray Dorset), recorded by Mungo Jerry on BME (pop).

⊘ SILTOWN RECORDS

1 Park Plaza, Suite 600, Irvine CA 92614. (949)474-5050. Fax: (949)367-1078. E-mail: asp@siltown.com. Website: www.siltown.com. **Contact:** Alban Silva, CEO. Vice President/A&R: Greg Jensen. A&R, Christian/Gospel: Barbara Anderson. A&R, Rap/Hip Hop. Record company. Estab. 1998. Staff size: 4. Releases 2 singles and 2 CDs/year.

Distributed by On website.

How to Contact Submit demo tape by mail. Unsolicited submissions are OK. Prefers CD, DAT with lyric sheet, cover letter and press clipping. Does not return material. Responds in 6 weeks. See website for submission guidelines.

Music Mostly **pop/rock**, **Christian** and **country**; also **rap**, **hip-hop**, **all genres**.

Tips "Submit songs and music that are preferably in digital mode. Submit lyric sheet and send only your best CD. If your are interested in free exposure of your music, submit CD, a recent color photograph of band, and a short biography of thirty words or less. Please visit our website for format."

◙ SILVER WAVE RECORDS

P.O. Box 7943, Boulder CO 80306. (303)443-5617. Fax: (303)443-0877. E-mail: info@silverwave.com. Website: www.silverwave.com. **Contact:** James Marienthal. Record company. Estab. 1986. Releases 3-4 CDs/year. Pays varying royalty to artists on contract and to publisher per song on record.

How to Contact *Call first and obtain permission to submit.* Prefers CD. Include SASE. Responds only if interested.

Music Mostly **Native American** and **world**.

◙ SIN KLUB ENTERTAINMENT, INC.

P.O. Box 2507, Toledo OH 43606. (419)537-9293. E-mail: esthree@buckeye-express.com. Website: www.sinklu b.com. (419)475-1189. President/A&R: Edward Shimborske III. Labels include Sin-Ka-Bob Records. Record company, music publisher (Morris St. James Publishing) and record producer (ES3). Estab. 1990. Releases 1 single, 1 LP and 5 CDs/year. Pays negotiable royalty to artists on contract; statutory rate to publisher per song on record.

Distributed by Cargo.

How to Contact Submit demo tape by mail. Unsolicited submissions are OK. Prefers cassette or CD with 3 songs and lyric sheet. "Send a good press kit (photos, bio, articles, etc.)." Does not return material. Responds in 1 month.

Music Mostly **harder-edged alternative**, **punk** and **metal/industrial**; also **rap**, **alternative** and **experimental**. Released *Urban Witchcraft* (album), recorded by Thessalonian Dope Gods (industrial), released 1994; *All Balled Up* (album), recorded by Bunjie Jambo (punk), released 1996, both on Sin Klub. Other artists include Kid Rock, Dan Hicks, Lucky Boys Confusion, Crashdog, The Geminus Sect, Evolotto, Lazy American Workers, The PB Army and The Dead Heroes.

☑ ◙ SMALL STONE RECORDS

P.O. Box 02007, Detroit MI 48202. Fax: (248)541-6536. E-mail: sstone@smallstone.com. Website: www.smallst one.com. Owner: Scott Hamilton. Record company. Estab. 1995. Staff size: 1. Releases 2 singles, 2 EPs and 10 CDs/year. Pays negotiable royalty to artists on contract; statutory rate to publisher per song on record.

Distributed by Action, Baker & Taylor.

How to Contact Submit CD/CD Rom by mail. Unsolicited submissions are OK. Does not return material. Responds in 2 months.

Music Mostly **alternative**, **rock** and **blues**; also **funk (not R&B)**. Released *Fat Black Pussy Cat*, written and recorded by Five Horse Johnson (rock/blues); *Wrecked & Remixed*, written and recorded by Morsel (indie rock, electronica); and *Only One Division*, written and recorded by Soul Clique (electronica), all on Small Stone Records. Other artists include Acid King, Perplexa, and Novadriver.

Tips "Looking for esoteric music along the lines of Bill Laswell to Touch & Go/Thrill Jockey records material. Only send along material if it makes sense with what we do. Perhaps owning some of our records would help."

◙ SMITHSONIAN FOLKWAYS RECORDINGS

750 9th St. NW, Suite 4100, Washington DC 20560-0953. (202)275-1144. Fax: (202)275-1164. E-mail: folkways@ aol.com. Website: www.folkways.si.edu. **Contact:** Daniel Sheehy, curator/director. Labels include Smithsonian Folkways Recordings, Dyer-Bennet, Cook, Paredon, Folkway, Monitor and Fast Folk. Record company and music publisher. Estab. 1948. Releases 25 CDs/year. Pays negotiable royalty to artists on contract and to publisher per song on record.

Distributed by Koch Entertainment.

How to Contact *Write first and obtain permission to submit or to arrange personal interview.* Prefers CD or DAT. Does not return material. Responds in 6 months.

Music Mostly **traditional US folk music, world music** and **children's music**. Released *We Shall Overcome* (by Pete Seeger), recorded by various artists (folk/Americana), from *Classic Folk Music from Smithsonian Folkways* (album), released 2004; *Goodnight Irene*, written and recorded by by Lead Belly (folk/Americana), from *Lead Belly—Where Did You Sleep Last Night* (album), released 1996; *This Land is Your Land*, written and recorded by Woody Guthrie, from *This Land is Your Land* (album), released 1997; all released by Smithsonian Folkways Recordings. "We only are interested in music publishing associated with recordings we are releasing. Do not send demos of songwriting only."

Tips "If you are a touring artist and singer/songwriter, consider carefully the advantages of a non-museum label for your work. We specialize in ethnographic and field recordings from people around the world."

Ⓝ ◯ SOLANA RECORDS

2440 Great Highway, #5, San Francisco CA 94116. (415)566-0411. E-mail: info@solanarecords.com. Website: www.solanarecords.com. **Contact:** Eric Friedmann, president. Record company, music publisher (Neato Bandito Music) and record producer (Eric Friedmann). Estab. 1992. Staff size: 1. Releases 1 single and 2 CDs/year. Pays negotiable royalty to artists on contract; statutory rate to publisher per song on record.

How to Contact Submit demo tape by mail but please e-mail permissions first. Prefers CD with 3-5 songs, photo and cover letter. Include SASE. Responds in 1 month.

Music Mostly any kind of guitar/vocal-based **rock/pop** and **country**. Does not want rap, hip-hop. Released *Spacious* (by Valerie Moorhead), recorded by Enda (alternative rock); *Livin' the High Life* (by James Cook), recorded by The Wags (hardcore); and *The Grain* (by Rick Ordin), recorded by The Grain (progressive rock). *To Hell with the Road*; *Live at the Sandbox*, recorded b Delectric (Skiffle).Other artists include The Detonators, Eric Friedman and the Lucky Rubes, The Mudkats and Doormouse.

Tips "Be honest and genuine. Know how to write a good song, and know how to sing. Don't send my your resumé or life story please. Big bonus points for Telecaster players."

☑ ◖ SONAR RECORDS & PRODUCTION

2342 20th St., Suite A, Santa Monica CA 90405. Fax: (310)392-1973. E-mail: info@sonarproductions.com. Website: www.sonarproductions.com. Artist Development: Ken Moody (Moodini). Vice President Urban Music: William Collins. A&R: Geo Clinton and Shana Holyfield. Labels include Sounds of New Artist Recordings. Record producer (Sonar, Moodini). Estab. 1994. Staff size: 4. Releases 3 singles, 1 LP, and 1 CD/year. Pays 12% royalty to artists on contract; statutory rate to publisher per song on record.

Distributed by WEA.

How to Contact Submit demo tape by mail. Unsolicited submissions are OK. Prefers CD. Does not return material. Responds in 1 month if interested.

Music Mostly **r&b**, **positive rap**, **hip-hop** and **gospel**; also **contemporary gospel.** Artists include Locaine, XL, OX, Peaches and Huzzy, Sons of Abraham and Shank.

Tips "Invest in yourself and others will follow."

◖ SONY MUSIC

550 Madison Ave., New York NY 10022. Website: www.sonymusic.com.

How to Contact *For specific contact information see the listings in this section for Sony subsidiaries Columbia Records, Epic Records and Sony Nashville.*

◖ SONY MUSIC NASHVILLE

34 Music Square E., Nashville TN 37203. (615)742-4321. A&R: Mark Brown. Labels include Columbia, Epic, Lucky Dog Records, Monument.

How to Contact *Sony Music Nashville does not accept unsolicited submissions.*

◖ SOUND GEMS

P.O. Box 801, South Eastern PA 19399. Website: www.soundgems.com. CEO: Frank Fioravanti. A&R Director: Trish Wassel. Record company and music publisher (Melomega Music, Meloman Music). Estab. 1972. Staff size: 3. Pays negotiable royalty to artists on contract; statutory rate to publisher per song on record.

Distributed by EMI, Sony, Warner.

How to Contact Submit demo tape by mail. Unsolicited submissions are OK. Prefers cassette, CD with lyric sheet, cover letter and press clipping. "Do not send registered or certified mail." Does not return material. Responds only if interested.

Music R&B only. Released "Be Thankful" (single by William Devaughn) from *Bones* (soundtrack album), recorded by William DeVaughn (r&b), released 2001 on PRI; and "Limo Dream" (single by Hopkins/Rakes/Fioravanti), recorded by Corey (r&b), released 2001 on Sound Gems; and "Girl I Wanna Take You Home" (single by Rueben Cross), recorded by Corey Wims (R&B/neo-soul), released 2002 on Sound Gems.

Tips "Be sure your style fits our catagory. Submit R&B material only."

◖ SOUTHLAND RECORDS, INC.

P.O. Box 1547, Arlington TX 76004-1547. (817)461-3280. E-mail: SteveReed@SouthlandRecords.com. Website: www.SouthlandRecords.com. **Contact:** Steve Reed, president. Record company and record producer (Steve Reed). Estab. 1980. Releases 12 CDs/year. Pays negotiable royalty to artists on contract; statutory rate to publisher per song on record.

How to Contact Submit demo tape or CD by mail. Unsolicited submissions are OK. Prefers cassette or CD with 4 songs, lyric and lead sheet, cover letter and press clippings. Does not return material. Responds in 3 months.

Music Country only. Artists include Leon Rausch, Rob Dixon, Bob Willis & the Texas Playboys, Ron Gaddis, Tommy Allsup, Jake Hooker, Curtis Potter and Darrell McCall.

⟦N⟧ ⟦Ø⟧ SUGAR HILL RECORDS

P.O. Box 55300, Durham NC 27717-5300. E-mail: info@sugarhillrecords.com. Record company. Estab. 1978.
• Welk Music Group acquired Sugar Hill Records in 1998.

How to Contact *No unsolicited submissions.* "If you are interested in having your music heard by Sugar Hill Records or the Welk Music Group, we suggest you establish a relationship with a manager, publisher, or attorney that has an ongoing relationship with our company."

Music Mostly **Americana**, **bluegrass**, and **country**. Artists include Albert Lee, Nickel Creek, Lonesome River Band, Del McCoury Band, New Grass Revival, Gray Larsen, Marty Stuart, and Psychograss.

⟦N⟧ ⟦⟧ ⟦Ø⟧ SUN-SCAPE ENTERPRISES LIMITED

P.O. Box 793, Station F, Toronto ON M4Y 2N7 Canada or 65 High Ridge Rd., Suite 103, Stamford CT 06905. 1-800-437-1454. E-mail: info@sun-scape.com. Website: www.sun-scape.com. Estab. 1973. Releases 2 LPs and 2 CDs/year. Pays negotiable royalty to artists on contract.

Distributed by Christie and Christie, Music Design, Valley Records, New Leaf Distributing and Backroads.
• See the listing for Star-Scape in the Classical & Performing Arts section.

How to Contact *Call first and obtain permission to submit.* Call for submission requirements. Does not return material. Responds in 1 month.

Music Mostly **choral**, **new age** and **contemporary classical**. Released *Promethean Fire, Arrival of the Unexpected* and *Let Robots Melt* (albums), all written and recorded by Kenneth G. Mills (New Age); and *Tonal Persuasions, Vol. II* (album), written by Kenneth G. Mills/various, recorded by New Star-Scape Singers (choral), all on Sun-Scape Records.

⟦⟧ ⟦Ø⟧ SURFACE RECORDS

8377 Westview, Houston TX 77055. (713)464-4653. Fax: (713)464-2622. E-mail: jeffwells@soundartsrecording. com. Website: www.soundartsrecording.com. **Contact:** Jeff Wells, president. A&R: Peter Verkerk. Record company, music publisher (Earthscream Music Publishing Co./BMI) and record producer (Jeff Wells). Estab. 1996. Releases 4 CDs/year. Pays negotiable royalty to artists on contract; statutory rate to publisher per song on record.

Distributed by Earth Records.

How to Contact Submit demo tape by mail. Unsolicited submissions are OK. Prefers cassette or CD with 4 songs and lyric sheet. Does not return material. Responds in 6 weeks.

Music Mostly **country**, **blues** and **pop/rock**. Released *Everest* (album), recorded by The Jinkies; *Joe "King" Carrasco* (album), recorded by Joe "King" Carrasco; and *Perfect Strangers* (album), recorded by Perfect Strangers, all on Surface Records (pop). Other artists include Rosebud.

⟦⟧ ⟦⟧ SYNERGY RECORDS

1609 Harwood St., Suite 7, Vancouver BC V6G 1Y1, Canada. (604)687-5747. Fax: (604)687-8528. E-mail: darren @synergyrecords.com. Website: www.synergyrecords.com. Project Manager: Darren Staten. Record company, music publisher (Nubian Music) and record producer (Darren Staten). Estab. 1998. Staff size: 3. Releases 2 singles and 2 LPs. Pays negotiable royalty to artists on contract; statutory rate to publisher per song on record.

Distributed by Fusions Distribution.

How to Contact Submit demo tape by mail. Unsolicited submissions are OK. Prefers cassette, CD with 3-4 original or cover songs, or singing a cappela, cover letter and a full body shot photo. Does not return material. Responds in 3 weeks.

Music Mostly **dance-pop**, **dance**, and **R&B**. Does not want punk, folk, rock, hard rock, traditional country.

Tips "We are looking to develop artists from scratch for Rhythm oriented music genres. All potential artists must be driven, committed, talented, and have an interesting image."

⟦⟧ TANGENT® RECORDS

P.O. Box 383, Reynoldsburg OH 43068-0383. (614)751-1962. Fax: (614)751-6414. E-mail: info@tangentrecords.c om. Website: www.tangentrecords.com. **Contact:** Andrew Batchelor, president. Director of Marketing: Elisa Batchelor. Record company and music publisher (ArcTangent Music/BMI). Estab. 1986. Staff size: 3. Releases 10-12 CDs/year. Pays negotiable royalty to artists on contract; statutory rate to publisher per song on record.

How to Contact Submit demo tape or CD by mail. Unsolicited submissions are OK. Prefers CD, with minimum of 3 songs and lead sheet if available. "Please include a brief biography/history of artist(s) and/or band, including musical training/education, performance experience, recording studio experience, discography and photos (if available)." Does not return material. Responds in 3 months.

Music Mostly **artrock** and **contemporary instrumental/rock instrumental**; also **contemporary classical**, **world beat**, **jazz/rock**, **ambient**, **electronic**, and **New Age**.

Tips "Take the time to pull together a quality CD or cassette demo with package/portfolio, including such relevant information as experience (on stage and in studio, etc.), education/training, biography, career goals, discography, photos, etc. Should be typed. We are *not* interested in generic sounding or 'straight ahead' music. We are seeking music that is innovative, pioneering and eclectic with a fresh, unique sound.''

◖ TEXAS MUSIC CAFÉ

1823 Crow Dr., Waco TX 76705. (254)867-3372. E-mail: info@texasmusiccafe.com. Website: www.texasmusicc afe.com. **Contact:** Chris Ermoian, president. Labels include E-Cleff Records Inc. Television show. Estab. 1987. Staff size: 3. Releases 10 singles and 10 CDs/year. Pays negotiable royalty to artists on contract.
Distributed by PBS, Hastings, Sony.
How to Contact Submit demo by mail. Unsolicited submissions are OK. Prefers CD, videocassette (VHS) with sample songs. Does not return material. Responds only if interested.
Music Only all original written material. Released *Live At the Texas Music Café, Vol 1 and 2*, written and recorded by various (eclectic).
Tips ''Be willing to travel to Texas to be taped.''

◖ THUMP RECORDS, INC.

3101 Pomona Blvd., Pomona CA 91768. (909)595-2144. Fax: (909)598-7028. E-mail: info@thumprecords.com. Website: www.thumprecords.com. President A&R: Bill Walker. Vice President of A&R and General Manager: Pebo Rodriguez. Labels include Thump Street and Fama Records. Record company and music publisher (Walk-Lo/ASCAP, On the Note/BMI). Estab. 1990. Releases 10 singles, 36 LPs, 6 EPs and 36 CDs/year. Pays 10% (negotiable) royalty to artists on contract; ¾ statutory rate to publisher per song on record.
How to Contact Submit demo tape by mail. Unsolicited submissions are OK. Prefers CD/CDR, lyric sheet, biography and 8×10 photo. Include SASE. Responds in 1 month.
Music Mostly **dance**, **rap** and **ballads**; also **oldies**, **classic rock** and **regional Mexican**. Released ''DJ Girl'' (single by Katalina). Other artists include Art Banks TDWY, Don Cisco and Jonny Z.
Tips ''Provide Thump with positive upbeat music that has universal appeal.''

◖ TOMMY BOY RECORDS

32 W. 18th St., Penthouse, New York NY 10011. (212)388-8300. Fax: (212)388-8400. E-mail: mail@tommyboy.c om. Website: www.tommyboy.com. Record company. Labels include Penalty Recordings, Outcaste Records, Timber and Tommy Boy Gospel.
Distributed by WEA.
How to Contact Call to obtain current demo submission policy.
Music Artists include Everlast, Screwball, Amber and Capone-N-Noreaga.

◖◖ TON RECORDS

4474 Rosewood Ave., Los Angeles CA 90004. (323)644-9733. Fax: (323)467-7737. E-mail: tonmusic@earthlink.n et. Website: www.tonrecords.com. Vice President: Jay Vasquez. Labels include 7″ collectors series and Ton Special Projects. Record company and record producer (RJ Vasquez). Estab. 1992. Releases 6-9 LPs, 1-2 EPs and 10-11 CDs/year. Pays negotiable royalty to artists on contract; statutory rate to publisher per song on record.
Distributed by MS, Com Four, Rotz, Subterranean, Revelation, Get Hip, Impact, Page Canada and Disco Dial.
How to Contact Submit demo tape by mail. Unsolicited submissions are OK. Prefers cassette or CD. Include SASE. Responds in 1 month.
Music Mostly **new music**; also **hard new music**. Released *Intoxicated Birthday Lies*, recorded by shoegazer (punk rock); *The Good Times R Killing Me*, recorded by Top Jimmy (blues); and *Beyond Repair*, recorded by Vasoline Tuner (space rock), all on Ton Records. Other artists include Why? things burn, Hungry 5 and the Ramblers.
Tips ''Work as hard as we do.''

◖ TRAC RECORD CO.

170 N. Maple, Fresno CA 93702. Phone/fax: (209)255-1717. E-mail: tracsell@aol.com. **Contact:** Stan Anderson, owner. Record company, record producer and music publisher (Sellwood Publishing/BMI). Estab. 1972. Releases 5 singles, 5 LPs and 2 CDs/year.
    ● Also see the listings for Trac Record Co. in the Record Producers section of this books and Sellwood Publishing in the Music Publishers section.
How to Contact Submit demo tape by mail. Unsolicited submissions are OK. Prefers cassette, CD or VHS videocassette with 2-3 songs and lyric sheet. ''Demo must be clear and professionally recorded.'' Include SASE. Responds in 3 weeks.
Music Country, **all styles** and **southern gospel**. Released ''City Days & Country Nights'' (single by Jon Jensen)

from *Back to Country* (album); "Sweet Deliverance" (single by H.C. "Chuck" House/Mary Miller) from *Back to Country* (album); and "Headed Right Out The Wrong Door" (single by Johnny Spears) from *Back to Country* (album), all recorded by H.C. "Chuck" House (country), released 2004 on TRAC Records.

✔ ◪ TRANSDREAMER RECORDS

P.O. Box 1955, New York NY 10113. (212)741-8861. Fax: (509)757-8602. E-mail: gregaforce@aol.com. Website: www.transdreamer.com. **Contact:** Greg Caputo. President: Robert John. Marketing Savant: Greg Caputo. Record company. Estab. 2002. Staff size: 5. Released 4 CDs/year. Pays negotiable rate to artists on contract; 3/4 statutory rate to publisher per song on record.

• Also see the listing for Megaforce in this section of the book.

Distributed by Ryko Distributions.

How to Contact *Contact first and obtain permission to submit.*

Music Mostly **alternative/rock**. Artists include Bill Ricchini, Fonzie, and Wellwaer Conspiracy.

◪ TRILOKA

23852 PCH #745, Malibu CA 90265. (310)996-7200. **Contact:** Tom Frouge, senior vice president. Record company. Estab. 1990. Releases 10 LPs and 10 CDs/year. Pays negotiable royalty to artists on contract.

How to Contact *Write first and obtain permission to submit.* Prefers cassette, CD or DAT. Does not return material.

Music Mostly **dance**, **world beat**, **new instrumental** and **jazz**. Released *Trance Planet Vol. 1-3*, written and recorded by various artists (world); *Beggars & Saints*, written and recorded by Jai Uttal (world); and *Garden of Dreams*, written and recorded by Ali Akbar Khan (world), all on Triloka.

N ◪ TVT RECORDS

23 E. Fourth St., New York NY 10003. (212)979-6410. Website: www.tvtrecords.com. **Contact:** A&R. Labels include Tee Vee Toons, TVT Soundtrax, 1001 Sundays. Record company and music publisher (TVT Music). Estab. 1986. Releases 25 singles, 20 12″ singles, 40 LPs, 5 EPs and 40 CDs/year. Pays varying royalty to artists on contract; statutory rate to publisher per song on record.

How to Contact Send e-mail to demo-help@tvtrecords.com to receive information on how to submit your demo.

Music Mostly **alternative rock**, **rap** and **techno**; also **jazz/R&B**. Released *Home*, recorded by Sevendust; *Hoopla*, recorded by Speeches; and *Retarder*, recorded by The Unband.

Tips "We look for seminal, ground breaking, genre-defining artists of all types with compelling live presentation. Our quest is not for hit singles but for enduring important artists."

◻ UAR RECORDS (Universal-Athena Records)

Box 1264, 6020 W. Pottstown Rd., Peoria IL 61654-1264. (309)673-5755. Fax: (309)673-7636. E-mail: uarltd@A5.com or banbr1@hotmail.com. Website: www.unitedcyber.com/uarltd. **Contact:** Jerry Hanlon, A&R director. Record company and music publisher (Jerjoy Music/BMI). Estab. 1978. Staff size: 1. Releases 3 or more CDs/year. Pays standard royalty to artists on contract; statutory rate to publisher for each record sold.

How to Contact Unsolicited submissions are OK. "We *do not* return phone calls." Prefers CD or cassette with 3-5 songs and lyric sheet. Include SASE. "*We do not critique work unless asked.*" Responds in 2 weeks. "Simple demos—vocal plus guitar or keyboard—are acceptable. We *do not* require a major demo production to interpret the value of a song."

Music Mostly **country**. Released "Kingdom I Call Home," "We Could" (counry), recorded by Danny Blakey and "Millionaires in Love" and "Since I've Found You" (country and religious), recorded by Micah Spayer. "For Old Loves Sake" recorded by Melanie Hiatt.

◪ UNIVERSAL RECORDS

1755 Broadway, 7th Floor, New York NY 10019. (212)373-0600. Fax: (212)373-0726. Website: www.universalre cords.com. Universal City office: 70 Universal City Plaza, 3rd Floor, Universal City CA 91608. (818)777-1000. Vice Presidents A&R: Bruce Carbone, Tse Williams. Labels include Uptown Records, Mojo Records, Republic Records, Bystorm Records and Gut Reaction Records. Record company.

• As a result of the 1998 PolyGram and Universal merger, Universal is the world's largest record company.

How to Contact *Universal Records in California does not accept unsolicited submissions.* The New York office *only* allows you to call first and obtain permission to submit.

✔ ◪ VAI DISTRIBUTION

109 Wheeler Ave., Pleasantville NY 10570. 1-800-477-7146 or (914)769-3691. Fax: (914)769-5407. E-mail: inquir ies@vaimusic.com. Website: www.vaimusic.com. President: Ernest Gilbert. Record company, video label and

distributor. Estab. 1983. Pays negotiable royalty to artists on contract; other amount to publisher per song on record.

How to Contact *Does not accept unsolicited material.*

Music Mostly **opera (classical vocal)**, **classical (orchestral)** and **classical instrumental/piano**. Released *Susannah* (album by Carlisle Floyd), recorded by New Orleans Opera Orchestra and Chorus, on VAI Audio. Other artists include Jon Vickers, Rosalyn Tureck, Evelyn Lear and Thomas Stewart.

⬧ VALTEC PRODUCTIONS

721 E. main St., #206, Santa Maria CA 93454. (805)928-8559. E-mail: info@valtec.net. Website: www.valtec.net. **Contact:** J. Anderson and J. Valenta, owner/producers. Record company and record producer (Joe Valenta). Estab. 1986. Releases 20 singles, 15 LPs and 10 CDs/year. Pays negotiable royalty to artists on contract; statutory rate to publisher per song on record.

How to Contact Submit demo tape by mail. Unsolicited submissions are OK. Prefers DAT with 4 songs and lyric sheet. Does not return material. Responds in 2 months.

Music Mostly **country**, **top 40** and **A/C**; also **rock**. Released *Just Me* (album by Joe Valenta) and *Hold On* (album by Joe Valenta/J. Anderson), both recorded by Joe Valenta (top 40); and *Time Out (For Love)* (album by Joe Valenta), recorded by Marty K. (country), all on Valtec Records.

✓ ⬦ ⬧ THE VERVE MUSIC GROUP

1755 Broadway, 3rd Floor, New York NY 10019. (212)331-2000. Fax: (212)331-2064. Website: www.vervemusic group.com. A&R Director: Dahlia Ambach. A&R Coordinator: Heather Buchanan. **Los Angeles:** 100 N. First St., Burbank CA 91502. (818)729-4804. Fax: (818)845-2564. Vice President A&R: Bud Harner. A&R Assistant: Heather Buchanan. Record company. Labels include Verve, GRP, Blue Thumb and Impulse! Records.

● Verve's Diana Krall won a 1999 Grammy Award for Best Jazz Vocal Performance; Wayne Shorter won Best Jazz Instrumental Solo; and the Charlie Haden Quartet West won Best Instrumental Arrangement with Vocals.

How to Contact *The Verve Music Group does not accept unsolicited submissions.*

Music Artists include Roy Hargrove, Diana Krall, George Benson, Al Jarreau, John Scofield, Natalie Cole, David Sanborn.

✓ ⬧ VIRGIN RECORDS

5750 Wilshire Blvd., Los Angeles CA 90036. (323)692-1100. Fax: (310)278-6231. New York office: 150 5th Ave., 3rd Floor, New York NY 10016. (212)786-8200. Fax: (212)786-8343. Website: www.virginrecords.com. Labels include Rap-A-Lot Records, Pointblank Records, SoulPower Records, AWOL Records, Astralwerks Records, Cheeba Sounds and Noo Trybe Records. Record company.

Distributed by EMD.

How to Contact Virgin Records does not accept recorded material or lyrics unless submitted by a reputable industry source. "If your act has received positive press or airplay on prior independent releases, we welcome your written query. Send a letter of introduction accompanied by all pertinent artist information. Do not send a tape until requested. All unsolicited materials will be returned unopened."

Artists include Lenny Kravitz, Janet Jackson, Mick Jagger, Nikka Cosla, Ben Harper, Boz Scaggs and Moth.

⬔ ⬧ WAREHOUSE CREEK RECORDING CORP.

P.O. Box 102, Franktown, VA 23354. (757)442-6883. E-mail: warehouse@esva.net. Website: www.warehousecr eek.com. President: Billy Sturgis. Record company, music publisher (Bayford Dock Music) and record producer (Billy Sturgis). Estab. 1993. Staff size: 1. Releases 11 singles and 1 CD/year. Pays negotiable royalty to artists on contract; statutory rate to publisher per song on record.

Distributed by City Hall Records.

How to Contact Submit demo tape by mail. Unsolicited submissions are OK. Prefers cassette, CD, DAT or VHS videocassette with lyric sheet. Does not return material.

Music Mostly **R&B**, **blues** and **gospel**. Released *Greyhound Bus* (album by Arthur Crudup); *Going Down in Style* (album by Tim Drummond); and *Something On My Mind* (album by George Crudup), all recorded by Crudup Brothers on Warehouse Creek Records (blues).

⬦ ⬧ WARNER BROS. RECORDS

3300 Warner Blvd., 3rd Floor, Burbank CA 91505. (818)846-9090. Fax: (818)953-3423. **New York:** 75 Rockefeller Plaza, New York NY 10019. (212)275-4500. Fax: (212)275-4596. A&R: James Dowdall, Karl Rybacki. **Nashville:** 20 Music Square E., Nashville TN 37203. (615)748-8000. Fax: (615)214-1567. Website: www.wbr.com. Labels include American Recordings, Eternal Records, Imago Records, Mute Records, Giant Records, Malpaso Records and Maverick Records. Record company.

Distributed by WEA.

How to Contact *Warner Bros. Records does not accept unsolicited material.* All unsolicited material will be returned unopened. Those interested in having their tapes heard should establish a relationship with a manager, publisher or attorney that has an ongoing relationship with Warner Bros. Records.

Music Released *Van Halen 3* (album), recorded by Van Halen; *Evita* (soundtrack); and *Dizzy Up the Girl* (album), recorded by Goo Goo Dolls, both on Warner Bros. Records. Other artists include Faith Hill, Tom Petty & the Heartbreakers, Jeff Foxworthy, Porno For Pyros, Travis Tritt, Yellowjackets, Bela Fleck and the Flecktones, Al Jarreau, Joshua Redmond, Little Texas and Curtis Mayfield.

N ▦ ☑ WESTPARK MUSIC—RECORDS, PRODUCTION & PUBLISHING

P.O. Box 260227, Rathenauplatz 4, 50515 Cologne Germany. Phone: (49)221 247644. Fax: (49)221 231819. E-mail: westparkmusic@aol.com. Website: www.westparkmusic.com. **Contact:** Ulli Hetscher. Record company and music publisher. Estab. 1986. Staff size: 3. Releases 10-12 CDs/year. Pays 9-18% royalty to artists on contract.

Distributed by Indigo (Germany), Music & Words (Netherlands), Musik Ver Trieb (Switzerland), Ixthucu (Austria), Resistencia (Spain), Mega Musica (Italy), Digelius (UK, Proper Finland).

How to Contact *Write first and obtain permission to submit* or submit demo tape by mail. Unsolicited submissions are OK. Prefers cassette with 5-6 songs and lyric sheets. Does not return material. Responds in 4 months.

Music "Check website."

Tips "Check website first, if possible. Don't send country, mainstream rock/pop or MOR. Mark cassettes clearly. Save yourself money by sending just the CD and booklet (no box and no tray). Don't include stamps (we cannot use them). Send e-mail with brief description first."

☑ WINCHESTER RECORDS

% McCoy, Route 2, Box 114, Berkeley Springs WV 25411. (304)258-9381. E-mail: mccoytroubadour@aol.com. Website: www.troubadourlounge.com. **Contact:** Jim or Bertha McCoy, owners. Labels include Master Records and Real McCoy Records. Record company, music publisher (Jim McCoy Music, Clear Music, New Edition Music/BMI), record producer (Jim McCoy Productions) and recording studio. Releases 20 singles and 10 LPs/year. Pays standard royalty to artists; statutory rate to publisher for each record sold.

How to Contact *Write first and obtain permission to submit.* Prefers CD with 5-10 songs and lead sheet. Include SASE. Responds in 1 month.

Music Mostly **bluegrass, church/religious, country, folk, gospel, progressive** and **rock**. Released "Runaway Girl" (single by Earl Howard/Jim McCoy) from *Earl Howard Sings His Heart Out* CD, recorded by Earl Howard (country), released 2002 on Winchester; *Jim McCoy and Friends Remember Ernest Tubb* (album), recorded by Jim McCoy (country), released January 2003 on Winchester; *The Best of Winchester Records* (album), recorded by RileeGray/J.B. Miller/Jim McCoy/Carroll County (country), released 2002 on Winchester.

N ☑ WIND-UP ENTERTAINMENT

72 Madison Ave., 8th Floor, New York NY 10016. (212)251-9665. Website: www.winduprecords.com. **Contact:** A&R. Record company. Estab. 1997. Releases 6-7 CDs/year. Pays negotiable royalty to artists on contract; statutory rate to publisher per song on record.

Distributed by BMG.

How to Contact *Write first and obtain permission to submit.* Prefers cassette, CD, DAT or videocassette. Does not return material or respond to submissions.

Music Mostly **rock, folk** and **hard rock**. Released *Weathered* (album) and *Human Clay* (album), written and recorded by Creed (rock); *Sinner* (album) by Drowning Pool; and *Stretch Princess* (album), written and recorded by Stretch Princess (rock), released 1998, all on Wind-Up.

Tips "We rarely look for songwriters as opposed to bands, so writing a big hit single would be the rule of the day."

N ☑ WORD RECORDS & MUSIC

25 Music Square W, Nashville TN 37203. Website: www.wordrecords.com. Record company.

Distributed by Epic/Sony.

How to Contact *Word Records does not accept unsolicited submissions.*

Music Released *Blaze*, recorded by Code of Ethics; *Steady On*, recorded by Point of Grace; and *Past the Edges*, recorded by Chris Rice, all on Word.

☐ WORLD BEATNIK RECORDS

20 Amity Lane, Rockwall TX 75087. Fax: (972)771-0853. E-mail: tropikalproductions@juno.com. Website: www.tropikalproductions.com. **Producers:** J. Towry (world beat, reggae, ethnic, jazz); Jembe (reggae, world beat, ethnic); Arik Towry (ska, pop, ragga, rock). Labels include World Beatnik Records. Record company and record producer (Jimi Towry). Estab. 1983. Staff size: 4. Releases 6 singles, 6 LPs, 6 EPs and 6 CDs/year. Pays negotiable royalty to artists on contract; statutory rate to publisher per song on record.

Distributed by Midwest Records, Southwest Wholesale, Reggae OneLove, Ejaness Records, Ernie B's, CD Waterhouse and Borders.

How to Contact Submit demo tape by mail. Unsolicited submissions are OK. Prefers cassette, DAT, mini disk or VHS videocassette with lyric sheet. Include SASE. Responds in 2 weeks.

Music Mostly **world beat, reggae** and **ethnic**; also **jazz, hip-hop/dance** and **pop**. Released *I and I* (album by Abby I/Jimbe), recorded by Abby I (African pop); *Rastafrika* (album by Jimbe/Richard Ono), recorded by Rastafrika (African roots reggae); and *Vibes* (album by Jimbe/Bongo Cartheni), recorded by Wave (worldbeat/jazz), all released 2001/2002 on World Beatnik. Other artists include Ras Richi (Cameroon), Wisdom Ogbor (Nigeria), Joe Lateh (Ghana), Dee Dee Cooper, Ras Lyrix (St. Croix), Ras Kumba (St. Kitts), Gary Mon, Darbo (Gambia), Ricki Malik (Jamaica), Arik Miles, Narte's (Hawaii), Gavin Audagnotti (South Africa) and Bongo (Trinidad).

🌐 ◻ X.R.L. RECORDS/MUSIC

White House Farm, Shropshire TF9 4HA England. Phone: (01630)647374. Fax: (01630)647612. **Contact:** Xavier Lee, International A&R Manager. A&R: Tanya Woof. UK A&R Manager: Cathrine Lee. Labels include Swoop, Zarg Records, Genouille, Pogo and Check Records. Record company, record producer and music publisher (Le Matt Music, Lee Music, R.T.F.M. and Pogo Records). Member MPA, PPL, PRS, MCPS, V.P.L. Estab. 1972. Staff size: 11. Releases 30 12″ singles, 20 LPs and 20 CDs/year. Pays negotiable royalty to artists on contract; negotiable rate to publisher for each record sold. Royalties paid to US songwriters and artists through US publishing or recording affiliate.

Distributed by Lematt Music.

How to Contact Submit demo tape by mail. Unsolicited submissions are OK. Prefers CD, cassette, MD, DVD, or VHS 625 PAL standard videocassette with 1-3 songs and lyric sheet. Include bio and still photos. IRC only. Responds in 6 weeks.

Music Mostly **pop/top 40**; also **bluegrass, blues, country, dance-oriented, easy listening, MOR, progressive, R&B, '50s rock, disco, new wave, rock** and **soul**. Released *Now and Then* (album), written and recorded by Daniel Boone (pop rock), released 2000 on Swoop; *The Creepies* (album), recorded by Nightmare (horror rock), released 2000 on Zarg; and *It's a Very Nice* (album), recorded by Groucho (pop), released 2000 on Swoop. Other artists include Orphan, The Chromatics, Mike Sheriden and the Nightriders, Johnny Moon, Dead Fish, Sight 'N' Sound and Mush.

Tips "Be original."

☑ XEMU RECORDS

19 W. 21st St., Suite 503, New York NY 10010. (212)807-0290. Fax: (212)807-0583. E-mail: xemu@xemu.com. Website: www.xemu.com. **Contact:** Dr. Claw, vice president A&R. Record company. Estab. 1992. Staff size: 4. Releases 4 CDs/year. Pays negotiable royalty to artists on contract; statutory rate to publisher per song on record.

Distributed by Redeye Distribution.

How to Contact *Write first and obtain permission to submit.* Prefers cassette with 3 songs. Does not return material. Responds in 2 months.

Music Mostly **alternative**. Released *A is for Alpha* (album), recorded by Alpha Bitch (alternative rock); *Hold the Mayo* (album), recorded by Death Sandwich (alternative rock); *Stockholm Syndrom* (album), recorded by Trigger Happy (alternative rock); and *The Evolution of Despair* (album), recorded by The Love Kills Theory (alternative rock), all released on Xemu Records. Other artists include Malvert P. Redd, The Fifth Dementia, and the Neanderthal Spongecake.

☑ YOUNG COUNTRY RECORDS/PLAIN COUNTRY RECORDS

P.O. Box 5412, Buena Park CA 90620. (909)941-8216. E-mail: swampbasque@msn.com. **Contact:** Leo J. Eiffert, Jr., owner. Labels include Eiffert Records and Napoleon Country Records. Record company, music publisher (Young Country Music Publishing Co./BMI, Eb-Tide Music/BMI) and record producer (Leo J. Eiffert, Jr). Releases 10 singles and 5 LPs/year. Pays negotiable royalty to artists on contract; negotiable rate to publishers per song on record.

 • Also see the listings for Leo J. Eiffert, Jr. in the Record Producers section of this books and Crawfish Productions in the Managers & Booking Agents section.

How to Contact Submit demo tape by mail. Unsolicited submissions are OK. "Please make sure your song or songs are copyrighted." Prefers cassette with 2 songs and lyric sheet. Does not return material. Responds in 1 month.

Music Mostly **country, easy rock** and **gospel music**. Released "Time Table" (single by Leo J. Eiffert, Jr./Larry Settle), recorded by Larry Settle, released 2004 on Eiffert Records; "Burn Out" (single by Leo J. Eiffert, Jr./Mary T. Eiffert), recorded by Mary T. Eiffert; "Picture" (single by Leo J. Eiffert, Jr./Tom "Slim" Lattimer/Stephen F. Curry, Jr.), recorded by Pigeons, both released 2004 on Young Country Records. Other artists include Brandi Holland, Homemade, Crawfish Band and Larry Settle.

ADDITIONAL RECORD COMPANIES

The following companies are also record companies, but their listings are found in other sections of the book. See the General Index for page numbers, then read the listings for submission information.

A

ACR Productions
Alexander Sr. Music
AlliSongs Inc.
American Artists Entertainment
ARAS Music
Atch Records and Productions

B

Backstreet Booking
Baird Music Group
Barrett Rock 'n' Roll Enterprises, Paul
Big Fish Music Publishing Group
Bixio Music Group & Associates/IDM Music
Black Market Entertainment Recordings
Blue Dog Publishing and Records
Blues Alley Records
BME Publishing
Burnsongs

C

Christopher Publishing, Sonny
Conscience Music

D

DaVinci's Notebook Records

E

EAO Music Corporation of Canada
Eternal Song Agency, The

F

Fifth Avenue Media, Ltd.
Final Mix Music
Frick Enterprises, Bob Scott
Furrow Music

G

Glad Music Co.

H

Hailing Frequency Music Productions
Happy Melody

Hardison International Entertainment Corporation
Heupferd Musikverlag GmbH
Hickory Lane Publishing and Recording
His Power Productions and Publishing
Huge Production, Inc., A

I

Island Culture Music Publishers

J

Ja/Nein Musikverlag GmbH
Jay Jay Publishing & Record Co.
JPMC Music Inc.

K

Kickstart Music Ltd.
Kuper Personal Management/Recovery Recordings

L

L.A. Entertainment, Inc.
Lazy Bones Productions/Recordings, Inc.
LCS Music Group
Leigh Music, Trixie
Levy Management, Rick
Lexington Alabama Music Publishing

M

Mayo & Company, Phil
McJames Music Inc.
Mega Truth Records

N

Naked Jain Records
Neu Electro Productions
New Experience Records
Northwest Alabama Music Publishing

O

OTA Productions

P

Philly Breakdown Recording Co.
Pierce, Jim

R
R.T.L. Music
Renaissance Entertainment Group

S
Satkowski Recordings, Steve
Segal's Productions
Shute Management Pty. Ltd., Phill
Sound Works Entertainment Productions Inc.
SRS Productions/Hit Records Network
Starbound Publishing Co.
Still Working Music Group
Stormin' Norman Productions
Strictly Forbidden Artists
Studio Seven
Succes

Supreme Enterprises Int'l Corp.
Swift River Productions

T
Tari, Roger Vincent
Tas Music Co./Dave Tasse Entertainment
TMC Productions
Tower Music Group

V
Van Pol Management, Hans

W
Warner Productions, Cheryl K.
WE Records & Management
World Records

Record Producers

The independent producer can best be described as a creative coordinator. He's usually the one with the most creative control over a recording project and is ultimately responsible for the finished product. Some record companies have in-house producers who work with the acts on that label (although, in more recent years, such producer-label relationships are often non-exclusive). Today, most record companies contract out-of-house, independent record producers on a project-by-project basis.

WHAT RECORD PRODUCERS DO

Producers play a large role in deciding what songs will be recorded for a particular project and are always on the lookout for new songs for their clients. They can be valuable contacts for songwriters because they work so closely with the artists whose records they produce. They usually have a lot more freedom than others in executive positions and are known for having a good ear for potential hit songs. Many producers are songwriters and musicians themselves. Since they wield a great deal of influence, a good song in the hands of the right producer at the right time stands a good chance of being cut. And even if a producer is not working on a specific project, he is well-acquainted with record company executives and artists and can often get material through doors not open to you.

SUBMITTING MATERIAL TO PRODUCERS

It can be difficult to get your tapes to the right producer at the right time. Many producers write their own songs and even if they don't write, they may be involved in their own publishing companies so they have instant access to all the songs in their catalogs. Also, some genres are more dependent on finding outside songs than others. A producer working with a rock group or a singer-songwriter will rarely take outside songs. It's important to understand the intricacies of the producer/publisher situation. If you pitch your song directly to a producer first, before another publishing company publishes the song, the producer may ask you for the publishing rights (or a percentage thereof) to your song. You must decide whether the producer is really an active publisher who will try to get the song recorded again and again or whether he merely wants the publishing because it means extra income for him from the current recording project. You may be able to work out a co-publishing deal, where you and the producer split the publishing of the song. That means he will still receive his percentage of the publishing income, even if you secure a cover recording of the song by other artists in the future. Even though you would be giving up a little bit initially, you may benefit in the future.

Some producers will offer to sign artists and songwriters to "development deals." These can range from a situation where a Svengali-like producer auditions singers and musicians with the intention of building a group from the ground up, to development deals where a producer signs a band or singer-songwriter to his production company, with the intention of developing an act and producing an album to shop to labels (sometimes referred to as a "baby record deal"). You must carefully consider whether such a deal is right for you. In some cases, such a deal will open doors and propel an act to the next level. In other worst-case scenarios, such a deal can result in loss of artistic and career control, with some acts held in contractual bondage for years at a time. Before you consider any such deal, be clear about your goals, the producer's reputation, and the sort of compromises you are willing to make to reach those goals. If you have any reservations whatsoever, don't do it.

The listings that follow outline which aspects of the music industry each producer is involved in, what type of music he is looking for, and what records and artists he's recently produced. Study the listings carefully, noting the artists each producer works with, and consider if any of your songs might fit a particular artist's or producer's style. Then determine whether they are open to your level of experience (see the A Sample Listing Decoded on page 11).

Consult the Category Index at the end of this section to find producers who work with the type of music you write, and the Geographic Index at the back of the book to locate producers in your area.

Icons

For More Info

For more instructional information on the listings in this book, including explanations of symbols ( ), read the article *Songwriter's Market: How Do I Use It?* on page 7.

ADDITIONAL RECORD PRODUCERS

There are **more record producers** located in other sections of the book! On page 223 use the list of Additional Record Producers to find listings within other sections who are also record producers.

⬇ ◙ "A" MAJOR SOUND CORPORATION

80 Corley Ave., Toronto ON M4E 1V2 Canada. (416)690-9552. Fax: (416)690-9482. E-mail: pmilner@sympatico. ca. **Contact:** Paul C. Milner, producer. Record producer and music publisher. Estab. 1989. Produces 8 CDs/ year. Fee derived in part from sales royalty when song or artist is recorded, and/or outright fee from recording artist or record company, or investors.

How to Contact Submit demo CD by mail. Unsolicited submissions are OK. Prefers CD with 5 songs and lyric sheet (lead sheet if available). Does not return material. Responds only if interested in 3 months.

Music Mostly **rock**, **A/C**, **alternative** and **pop**; also **Christian** and **R&B**. Produced *Great is the Privilege of Achievment* (album, written by David Angelis and Paul Derosa and Phil X), recorded by Supervox (rock), released 2002; *Rock Classics* (album, by various writers), recorded by Phe Cullen with Randy Waldman Trio (jazz), released 2002 on United One Records; *Jazz Standards* (album, by various writers), recorded by Phe Cullen with the Norm Amadio Trio (jazz), to be released in 2003 on United One Records; and *Fury* (album, adapted from public domain), recorded by Patricia Pomeroy, Paul Milner and Dan Cutrona, released 2003 on B&B/Edel/Nuff Entertainment.

◻ ABERDEEN PRODUCTIONS

524 Doral Country Dr., Nashville TN 37221. (615)646-9750. **Contact:** Scott Turner, executive producer. Record producer and music publisher (Buried Treasure Music/ASCAP, Captain Kidd/BMI). Estab. 1971. Produces 10 singles, 15-20 12″ singles, 8 LPs and 8 CDs/year. Fee derived from outright fee from recording artist.
   • Also see the listing for Buried Treasure Music in the Music Publishers section of this book.

How to Contact Submit demo tape by mail. Unsolicited submissions OK. Prefers cassette with maximum 4 songs and lead sheet. Include SASE. "No SASE, no reply." Responds in 2 weeks. No "lyrics only."

Music Mostly **country**, **MOR** and **rock**; also **top 40/pop**. Produced "All of the Above" (single by Douglas Bush) from *The Entrance* (album), recorded by Lea Brennan (country/MOR), released 2000. Other artists include Jimmy Clanton.

Tips "Start out on an independent basis because of the heavy waiting period to get on a major label."

✓ ◻ ACR PRODUCTIONS

P.O. Box 5636, Midland TX 79704. (432)687-2702. E-mail: dwaine915@juno.com. **Contact:** Dwaine Thomas, owner. Record producer, music publisher (Joranda Music/BMI) and record company (ACR Records). Estab. 1986. Produces 120 singles, 8-15 12″ singles, 25 LPs, 25 EPs and 25 CDs/year. Fee derived from sales royalty when song or artist is recorded. "We charge for in-house recording only. Remainder is derived from royalties."

How to Contact Submit demo tape by mail. Unsolicited submissions are OK. Prefers cassette or VHS videocassette with 5 songs and lyric sheet. Does not return material. Responds in 6 weeks if interested.

Music Mostly **country swing**, **pop** and **rock**; also **R&B** and **gospel**. Produced *Bottle's Almost Gone* (album) and "Black Gold" (single), written and recorded by Mike Nelson (country), both released 1999 on ACR Records; and *Nashville Series* (album), written and recorded by various (country), released 1998 on ProJam Music.

Tips "Be professional. No living room tapes!"

✓ ◻ AIF MUSIC PRODUCTIONS

P.O. Box 691, Mamaroneck NY 10543. (914)381-3559. E-mail: aif@erols.com. Website: www.robertjackson. net/aif%20records.htm. **Contact:** Robert Jackson, president. Record producer. Estab. 1995. Produces 3 singles and 4 CDs/year. Fee derived from sales royalty when song or artist is recorded or outright fee from recording artist. "We work on a combination of fee basis, plus a percentage after the deal is made."

How to Contact Submit demo by mail. Unsolicited submissions are OK. Prefers CD or cassette. "Don't send photos, lyrics or press. We work on a fee plus percentage basis. Responds in 2-3 weeks.

Music Mostly **rock, hard rock** and **alternative**; also **metal, blues, folk, pop** and **country**. Does not want rap, dance, hip-hop, death/black metal, industrial or house. Produced "Much Better" (single by Nard) from *Highways, Biways* (album), recorded by Liquor Daddies (rock/alternative), released 2002 on PA/AIF; "Found A Way" (single by M. Lough) from *Spankin' America* (album), recorded by Young Spank (rock/alternative), released 2002 on Core; and "Eastern Sands" (single by R. Zucker) from *Time Waltz* (album), recorded by Rob Zucker (rock/instrumental), released 2002 on Grease/AIF. Other artists include First Spawn.

Tips "Contact us. If you like what we say, and we are compatible, we will work with you, period. For producing, you must travel to NY/NJ/CT tri-state area or pay for my transportation. My role in a project is to coach, coordinate and oversee music, lyrics, instrumentation, arrangements, restructuring of songs (if need be), and selection of studio musicians and facilities for recording, mixing and mastering. If you want a fantastic producer, contact me. I can hear everything, including your out-of-tune instrument."

☑ ⊘ STUART J. ALLYN

250 Taxter Rd., Irvington NY 10533. (212)486-0856. Fax: (914)591-5617. E-mail: adrstudios@adrinc.org. Website: www.advinc.org. **Associate:** Jack Walker. **Contact:** Jack Davis, general manager. **President:** Stuart J. Allyn. Record producer. Estab. 1972. Produces 6 singles and 3-6 CDs/year. Fee derived from sales royalty and outright fee from recording artist and record company.

How to Contact *Does not accept unsolicited submissions.*

Music Mostly **pop**, **rock**, **jazz** and **theatrical**; also **R&B** and **country**. Produced *Thad Jones Legacy* (album), recorded by Vanquard Jazz Orchestra (jazz), released 2000 on New World Records. Other artists include Billy Joel, Aerosmith, Carole Demas, Bob Stewart, The Dixie Peppers, Nora York, Buddy Barnes and various video and film scores.

☑ ⊘ AUDIO 911

(formerly Steve Wytas Productions), P.O. Box 212, Haddam CT 06438. (860)345-3300. E-mail: info@audio911.com. Website: www.audio911.com. **Contact:** Steven J. Wytas. Record producer. Estab. 1984. Produces 4-8 singles, 3 LPs, 3 EPs and 4 CDs/year. Fee derived from outright fee from recording artist or record company.

How to Contact Submit demo tape by mail. Unsolicited submissions are OK. Prefers CD or VHS videocassette with several songs and lyric or lead sheet. "Include live material if possible." Does not return material. Responds in 3 months.

Music Mostly **rock**, **pop**, **top 40** and **country/acoustic**. Produced *Already Home* (album), recorded by Hannah Cranna on Big Deal Records (rock); *Under the Rose* (album), recorded by Under the Rose on Utter Records (rock); and *Sickness & Health* (album), recorded by Legs Akimbo on Joyful Noise Records (rock). Other artists include King Hop!, The Shells, The Gravel Pit, G'nu Fuz, Tuesday Welders and Toxic Field Mice.

⊘ RON BAIRD ENTERPRISES

P.O. Box 42, 1 Main St., Ellsworth PA 15331. E-mail: ronssong@charterpa.net. **Contact:** Ron Baird, executive producer. Record producer, record company (La Ron Ltd. Records), music publisher (Baird Music Group). Estab. 1999. Produces 2-5 singles and 1-2 LPs/year.

● Also see the listing for Baird Music Group in the Music Publishers section of this book.

How to Contact Submit demo tape by mail. Unsolicited submissions are OK. "No certified mail." Prefers cassette only with 2-4 songs and lyric sheet. Does not return submissions. Responds only if interested.

Music Mostly **country** and **country rock**. Does not want hip-hop, gospel/religious or R&B. Produced "Big Time Dreams" (single by Ron Baird), recorded by Corey Christie (country), released 2004; "Back to Nashville" (single by Ron Baird) from *Here's Kim Early* (album), recorded by Kim Early (country), released 2004; and "My Texas Girl" (single by Ron Baird), recorded by Dale Such (country), released 2004, all on LaRon Ltd.

Tips "Our goal is to produce finished masters and shop these for major label deals. We want to produce legitimate hits."

🌐 BIG BEAR

Box 944, Birmingham, B16 8UT, United Kingdom. Phone: 44-21-454-7020. **Managing Director:** Jim Simpson. Record producer, music publisher (Bearsongs) and record company (Big Bear Records). Produces 10 LPs/year. Fee derived from sales royalty.

● Also see the listings for Bearsongs in the Music Publishers section of this book and Big Bear Records in the Record Companies section of this book.

How to Contact Write first about your interest, then submit demo tape and lyric sheet. Does not return material. Responds in 2 weeks.

Music **Blues**, **swing** and **jazz**.

◻ BLUES ALLEY RECORDS

Rt. 1, Box 288, Clarksburg WV 26301. (304)599-1055. Website: www.bluesalleymusic.com. **Contact:** Joshua Swiger, producer. Record producer, record company and music publisher (Blues Alley Publishing/BMI). New Christian record label (Joshua Tree Records/BMI). Produces 4-6 LPs and 2 EPs/year. Fee derived from sales royalty when song or artist is recorded.

How to Contact Submit demo by mail. Unsolicited submissions are OK. Prefers CD with 4 songs and lyric and lead sheets. Does not return material. Responds in 6 weeks.

Music Mostly **Christian**, **alternative** and **pop**. Produced *Hard Road* (album), recorded by The New Relics (acoustic rock), released 2003; *Sons of Sirens* (album), recorded by Amity (rock), released 2004; and *It's No Secret* (album), recorded by Samantha Caley (pop country), released 2004, all on Blues Alley Records.

☒ ☑ CACOPHONY PRODUCTIONS

2400 VaSanta Way, Los Angeles CA 90068. (917)856-8532. Producer: Steven Miller. Record producer and music publisher (In Your Face Music). Estab. 1981. Fee derived from sales royalty when song or artist is recorded, or outright fee from recording artist or record company.

How to Contact *Call first and obtain permission to submit.* Prefers CD with 3 songs and lyric sheet. "Send a cover letter of no more than three paragraphs giving some background on yourself and the music. Also explain specifically what you are looking for Cacophony Productions to do." Does not return material. Responds only if interested.

Music Mostly **progressive pop/rock**, **singer/songwriter** and **progressive country**. Produced Dar Williams, Suzanne Vega, John Gorka, Michael Hedges, Juliana Hatfield and Medeski-Martin & Wood.

☑ ☑ CANDYSPITEFUL PRODUCTIONS

2051 E. Cedar St., #8, Tempe AZ 85281. (480)468-7017. E-mail: mandrakerocks@yahoo.com. Website: www.ca ndyspiteful.com. **Contact:** William Ferraro, president. Record producer, record company (Candyspiteful Productions), music publisher (Candyspiteful Productions). Estab. 2000. Produces 12 singles, 2 albums per year. Fee derived from outright fee from recording artist.

- Also see the listings for Candyspiteful Productions in the Record Companies section of this book and Major Entertainment in the Music Publishers section of this book.

How to Contact Submit demo tape by mail. Unsolicited submissions are OK. Prefers CD/CDR with 3 songs and lyric sheet and cover letter. Does not return material. Responds only if interested.

Music Mostly **progressive rock**, **rock/pop/R&B**and **smooth jazz/rock**. Produced *Cloud Nine* (album written by David Farnsworth), recorded by Thunderhead (hard rock), released 2001 on Candyspiteful Productions.

☐ JAN CELT MUSICAL SERVICES

4015 NE 12th Ave., Portland OR 97212. E-mail: flyheart@teleport.com. Website: http://home.teleport.com/ ~flyheart. **Contact:** Jan Celt, owner. Record producer, music producer and publisher (Wiosna Nasza Music/ BMI) and record company (Flying Heart Records). Estab. 1982. Produces 3-5 CDs/year.

- Also see the listing for Flying Heart Records in the Record Companies section of this book.

How to Contact Submit demo tape by mail. Unsolicited submissions are OK. Prefers high-quality cassette with 1-10 songs and lyric sheet. "SASE required for any response." Does not return materials. Responds in 4 months.

Music Mostly **R&B**, **rock** and **blues**; also **jazz**. Produced "Vexatious Progressions" (single), written and recorded by Eddie Harris (jazz); "Bong Hit" (single by Chris Newman), recorded by Snow Bud & the Flower People (rock); and "She Moved Away" (single by Chris Newman), recorded by Napalm Beach, all on Flying Heart Records. Other artists include The Esquires and Janice Scroggins.

☐ COACHOUSE MUSIC

P.O. Box 1308, Barrington IL 60011. (847)382-7631. Fax: (847)382-7651. E-mail: coachouse1@aol.com. **Contact:** Michael Freeman, president. Record producer. Estab. 1984. Produces 6-8 CDs/year. Fee derived from sales royalty when song or artist is recorded.

How to Contact *Write or e-mail first and obtain permission to submit.* Prefers cassette, DAT or CD with 3-5 songs and lyric sheet. Include SASE. Responds in 6 weeks.

Music Mostly **rock**, **pop** and **blues**; also **alternative rock** and **country/Americana/roots**. Produced *Casque Nu* (album), written and recorded by Charlelie Couture on Chrysalis EMI France (contemporary pop); *Time Will Tell*, recorded by Studebaker John on Blind Pig Records (blues); *Where Blue Begins* (album by various/D. Coleman), recorded by Deborah Coleman on Blind Pig Records (contemporary blues); *A Man Amongst Men* (album), recorded by Bo Diddley (blues); and *Voodoo Menz* (album), recorded by Corey Harris and Henry Butler. Other artists include Echosend, Eleventh Dream Day, Magic Slim, The Tantrums, The Pranks, The Bad Examples, Mississippi Heat and Supermint.

Tips "Be honest, be committed, strive for excellence."

☒ ☑ ☑ COLLECTOR RECORDS

P.O. Box 1200, 3260 AE Oud Beyerland, Holland, The Netherlands. Phone: 186-604266. Fax: 186-604366. E-mail: sales@collectorrec.com. **Contact:** Cees Klop, president. Record producer and music publisher (All Rock Music). Produces 25 CDs/year. Fee derived from outright fee from record company.

- Also see the listings for All Rock Music in the Music Publishers section and Collector Records in the Record Companies section of this book.

How to Contact Submit demo tape by mail. Unsolicited submissions are OK. Prefers cassette. SAE and IRC. Responds in 2 months.

Music Mostly **'50s rock**, **rockabilly** and **country rock**; also **piano boogie woogie**. Produced *When You Rock And Roll* (album), recorded by Marvin Jackson (1950s rockers); *Bobby Crown & The Kapers* (album), recorded by Bobby Crown (1950s rockers); and *Rock, Rock, Rockin' Tonight* (album), recorded by various artists (1950s rockers), all released 2004 on Collector Records.

Tips "Only send the kind of music we produce."

JOHNNY COPPIN/RED SKY RECORDS

P.O. Box 27, Stroud, Glos. GL6 0YQ United Kingdom. Phone/fax: 01453-836877. E-mail: johnny@johnnycoppin. co.uk. **Contact:** Johnny Coppin, producer. Record producer, music publisher (PRS) and record company (Red Sky Records). Estab. 1985. Produces 1 album/year. Fee derived from sales royalty when song or artist is recorded.

   • Also see the listing for Red Sky Records in the Record Companies section of this book.

How to Contact *Write first and obtain permission to submit.* Does not return material. Responds in 6 months.

Music Mostly **rock**, **modern folk** and **roots music**. Produced "A Country Christmas" and "Keep the Flame" written and recorded by Johnny Coppin; and "Dead Lively!," written and recorded by Paul Burgess, all on Red Sky Records. Other artists include David Goodland.

DOUGLAS CRAIG

(formerly Bewildering Music, Inc.), P.O. Box 302, Locust Valley NY 11560. (516)759-5560. E-mail: bminc@aol.c om. Website: http://members.aol.com/bminc/homepage.htm. **Contact:** Douglas W. Craig, producer. Record producer. Estab. 1992. Produces 1 or 2 EPs and 3-5 CDs/year. Fee derived from flat fee or hourly rate.

How to Contact Prefers cassette, CD or VHS videocassette with photo. All submissions are kept on file.

Music Mostly **solo artists**, **rock**, **electronic world beat**; also **remix**, **soundtrack work** (melodic preferred). Artist must live in the New York area and travel to the producer's studio. Other artists include Breakthru and Cuentos Blancos.

CHARLIE CRAIG PRODUCTIONS

P.O. Box 1448, Mt. Juliet TN 37121-1448. Website: www.charliecraig.com. **Contact:** Charlie Craig, producer. Record producer and music publisher (Song Machine/BMI, Walker Publishing Co. L.L.C./ASCAP/BMI). Estab. 2001. Produces 5 singles and 5 CDs/year. Fee derived from sales royalty and/or outright fee from recording artist.

   • Charlie Craig Productions received a Grammy nomination in 1991 and Song of the Year nominations in 1986 and 1991. Was inducted into the South Carolina Entertainment Hall of Fame in 1998.

How to Contact *Write or call first to arrange personal interview.* For song publishing submissions, prefers CD with 3 songs, lyric sheet and lead sheet. "Include e-mail address for response." Does not return submissions. Responds in 3 weeks via e-mail only.

Music Mostly **traditional country**, **new country** and **country pop**. Co-produced *The Nashville Super Pickers* (album), recorded by The Nashville Super Pickers Band (country), released 1972 on Royal American Records. "First Nashville writer to work with Alan Jackson. Extensively involved in getting a record deal for the Wilkinsons with Giant Records"

Tips "Be prepared to record only the best songs, even if it takes an extended length of time. We won't go into the studio until we have great songs. Vocals should be memorized before going into the studio. You need to express as much emotion as possible. Suggestions are welcome from artists and musicians, but final decisions are made by the Producer. We will make sure the vocals are perfect no matter how many takes are necessary. Be prepared to work."

JERRY CUPIT PRODUCTIONS

Box 121904, Nashville TN 37212. (615)731-0100. Fax: (615)731-3005. E-mail: billy@cupitmusic.com. Website: www.cupitrecords.com. **Contact:** Denise Roberts, creative assistant. Record producer and music publisher (Cupit Music). Estab. 1984. Fee derived from sales royalty when song or artist is recorded or outright fee from artist.

   • Also see the listing for Cupit Music Group in the Music Publishers section of this book.

How to Contact *Visit website for policy.* Prefers CD with bio and photo. Include SASE. Responds in 2 months.

Music Mostly **traditional and contemporary uptempo**, **country**, **Southern rock** and **gospel**. Produced "What If He's Right" (single by Jerry Cupit) from *Memarie* (album), recorded by Memarie (Christian country), released 2000 on HotSong.com Records; and "I'm Not Homeless" (single by Jerry Cupit/Ken Mellons/Randy Roberts) from *Wings of a Dove* (album), recorded by Ken Mellons (Christian country), released 2000 on Curb Records. Other artists include Jack Robertson and Jon Nicholson.

Tips "Be prepared to work hard and be able to take constructive/professional criticism."

DAP ENTERTAINMENT

PMB 364, 7100 Lockwood Blvd., Boardman OH 44512. (330)782-5031. Fax: (330)782-6954. Website: www.dape ntertainment.com. **Contact:** Darryl Alexander, producer. Record Producer and music publisher (Alexander Sr.

Music, BMI). Estab. 1997. Produces 12 singles and 2-4 CDs/year. Fee derived from sales royalty (producer points) when song or artist is recorded or outright fee from recording artist or record company.

• Also see the listing for Alexander Sr. Music in the Music Publishers section of this book.

How to Contact *Write first and obtain permission to submit.* Prefers CD with 2-4 songs and lyric sheet. Include SASE. Responds in 1 month. "No phone calls or faxes will be accepted."

Music Mostly **contemporary jazz**, **urban contemporary gospel**; also **R&B**. Produced "Plumb Line" (single by Herb McMullen/Darryl Alexander) from *Diamond In the Sky* (album); "Cafe Rio" and "Garden of My Heart" (singles) from *Diamond In the Sky*, written and recorded by Darryl Alexander (contemporary jazz), all released 2004 on DAP Entertainment. Other artists include Kathryn Williams.

☒ DAVINCI'S NOTEBOOK RECORDS

20 Admiral Rd., St. Catharines ON L2P 1G6 Canada. (905)359-1616. E-mail: admin@davincismusic.com. Website: www.davincismusic.com. Owner: Kevin Richard. Record producer, record company, music publisher, distributor and MIDI recording facility. Estab. 1992. Produces 1 cassette and 1 CD/year. Fee derived from outright fee from artist or commission on sales.

How to Contact Submit demo CD by mail. Unsolicited submissions are OK. Prefers CD and bio. Does not return material. Responds in 6 weeks.

Music Mostly **rock**, **instrumental rock**, **New Age** and **progressive-alternative**; also **R&B**, **pop** and **jazz**. Produced *Windows* (by Kevin Hotte/Andy Smith), recorded by Musicom on DaVinci's Notebook Records (power New Age); *Inventing Fire*, written and recorded by Kevin Richard on DNR/Independent (instrumental rock); and *The Cunninghams*, written and recorded by The Cunninghams on Independent (gospel).

Tips "DNR is an artist-run label. Local bands and performers will receive priority. Be more interested in getting a-foot-in-the-door exposure as opposed to making a fortune. Be satisfied with conquering the world using 'baby steps.' Indie labels don't have large corporate budgets for artist development. We are more about online distribution than artist development. Being a local act means that you can perform live to promote your releases. For indie artist, selling from the stage is probably going to bring you the biggest volume of sales."

☑ ☒ ⊘ EDWARD DE MILES

28 E. Jackson Bldg., 10th Floor #S627, Chicago IL 60604-2263. (773)509-6381. Fax: (312)922-6964. Website: www.edmsahara.com. **Contact:** Edward De Miles, president. Record producer, music publisher (Edward De Miles Music Co./BMI) and record company (Sahara Records and Filmworks Entertainment). Estab. 1981. Produces 5-10 CDs/year. Fee derived from sales royalty when song or artist is recorded.

• Also see the listing for Edward De Miles in the Music Publishers and Managers & Booking Agents sections, as well as Sahara Records and Filmworks Entertainment in the Record Companies section of this book.

How to Contact *Does not accept unsolicited submissions.*

Music Mostly **R&B/dance**, **top 40 pop/rock** and **contemporary jazz**; also **country**, **TV and film themes—songs and jingles**. Produced "Moments" and "Dance Wit Me" (singles) (dance), both written and recorded by Steve Lynn; and "Games" (single), written and recorded by D'von Edwards (jazz), all on Sahara Records. Other artists include Multiple Choice.

Tips "Copyright all material before submitting. Equipment and showmanship a must."

☑ ⊘ AL DELORY AND MUSIC MAKERS

3000 Hillsboro Rd. #11, Nashville TN 37215. (615)292-2140. Fax: (615)297-6031. E-mail: aldelory@mn.rr.com. Website: www.aldelory.com. **Contact:** Al DeLory, president. Record producer and career consultant (DeLory Music/ASCAP). Estab. 1987. Fee derived from outright fee from recording artist.

• Al DeLory has won two Grammy Awards and has been nominated five times.

How to Contact *Write or call first and obtain permission to submit or to arrange personal interview.* Prefers CD or VHS videocassette. Include SASE. Responds in 1 month.

Music Mostly **pop** and **Latin**. Produced "Gentle On My Mind" (single), "By the Time I Get to Phoenix" (single) and "Wichita Lineman" (single), all recorded by Glen Campbell. Other artists include Letter Men and Gary Puckett.

Tips "Seek advice and council only with professionals with a track record."

☒ ⊞ ⊘ DEMI MONDE RECORDS & PUBLISHING LTD.

Foel Studio, Llanfair Caereinion, Powys, SY21 0DS Wales. Phone/fax: 01938-810758. E-mail: demi.monde@dial .pipex.com. Website: www.demi.monde.co.uk/demimonde. **Contact:** Dave Anderson, managing director. Record producer, music publisher (PRS & MCPS) and record company (Demi Monde Records). Estab. 1982. Produces 5 singles, 15 12" singles, 15 LPs and 10 CDs/year. Fee derived from sales royalty or outright fee from record company.

• Also see the listings for Demi Monde records & Publishing in the Music Publishing and Record Companies sections of this book.

How to Contact Submit demo tape by mail. Unsolicited submissions are OK. Prefers cassette with 3 or 4 songs and lyric sheet. Does not return material. Responds in 6 weeks.

Music Mostly **rock, pop** and **blues**. Produced *Average Man*, recorded by Mother Gong (rock); *Frozen Ones*, recorded by Tangle Edge (rock); and *Blue Boar Blues* (by T.S. McPhee), recorded by Groundhogs (rock), all on Demi Monde Records. Other artists include Gong and Hawkwind.

⊘ JOEL DIAMOND ENTERTAINMENT

Dept. SM, 3940 Laurel Canyon Blvd., Suite 441, Studio City CA 91604. (818)980-9588. Fax: (818)980-9422. E-mail: jdiamond20@aol.com. Website: www.joeldiamond.com. **Contact:** Joel Diamond. Record producer, music publisher and manager. Fee derived from sales royalty when song is recorded or outright fee from recording artist or record company.

• Also see the listing for Silver Blue Music/Oceans Blue Music in the Music Publishers section of this book.

How to Contact Does not return material. Responds only if interested.

Music Mostly **dance, R&B, soul** and **top 40/pop**. Produced "One Night In Bangkok" (single by Robey); "I Think I Love You," recorded by Katie Cassidy (daughter of David Cassidy) on Artemis Records; "After the Loving" (single), recorded by E. Humperdinck; "Forever Friends," recorded by Vaneza (featured on Nickelodeon's "The Brothers Garcia"); and "Paradise" (single), recorded by Kaci.

⊘ LEO J. EIFFERT, JR.

P.O. Box 5412, Buena Park CA 90620. (909)941-8216. **Contact:** Leo J. Eiffert, Jr., owner. Record producer, music publisher (Eb-Tide Music/BMI, Young Country Music/BMI), management firm (Crawfish Productions) and record company (Plain Country). Estab. 1967. Produces 15-20 singles and 5 LPs/year. Fee derived from sales royalty when song or artist is recorded.

• Also see the listing for Young Country Records/Plain Country Records in the Record Companies section of this book and Crawfish Productions in the Managers and Booking Agents section of this book.

How to Contact Submit demo tape by mail. Unsolicited submissions are OK. Prefers cassette with 2-3 songs, lyric and lead sheet. Include SASE. Responds in 1 month.

Music Mostly **country** and **gospel**. Produced "Who Used Who?" (single by Leo J. Eiffert, Jr.), recorded by Pigeons, released 2004 on Young Country Records; "Easy" (single), written and recorded by Cleat Wooley, released 2004 on Eiffert Records; and "Un-Sung Heroes" (single by Joe Eiffert), recorded by Southern Spirit, released 2004 on Young Country. Other artists include Homemade, Crawfish Band, Brandi Holland, Mary T. Eiffert, Stiff Racoons, Steel Promises, Southern Spirit and David Busson.

Tips "Just keep it real country."

⊘ ESQUIRE INTERNATIONAL

P.O. Box 6032, Station B, Miami FL 33101-6032. (305)547-1424. Fax: (305)547-1424. E-mail: stuacr@aol.com. **Contact:** Jeb Stuart, president. Record producer, music publisher (Jeb Stuart Music) and management firm. Produces 6 singles and 2 LPs/year. Fee derived from sales royalty or independent leasing of masters and placing songs.

• Also see the listing for Jeb Stuart Music Co. in the Music Publishers section of this book.

How to Contact Submit demo tape by mail. Unsolicited submissions are OK. Prefers cassette or CD with 2-4 songs and lead sheet. Include SASE. Responds in 1 month.

Music Mostly **blues, church/religious, country, dance, gospel, jazz, rock, soul** and **top 40/pop**. Produced "Go to Sleep, Little Baby" (single by Jeb Stuart), recorded by Cafidia and Jeb Stuart; "Guns Guns (No More Guns)" (single) and "No One Should Be Alone on Christmas" (single), both written and recorded by Jeb Stuart; "Mr. Love Jinx" (single by Cafidia Stuart/Jeb Stuart) from *Children Need More Happiness* (album), recorded by Cafidia Stuart (blues/rock), released 2002, all on Esquire Int'l Records. Other artists include Moments Notice and Night Live.

⊘ THE ETERNAL SONG AGENCY

P.O. Box 121, Worthington OH 43085. E-mail: submissions@eternal-song-agency.com. Website: www.eternal-song-agency.com. **Contact:** Attn: A&R. Executive Producer: Leopold Crawford. Record producer, record company and music publisher (Fragrance Records, Song of Solomon Records, Emerald Records, Lilly Records, Ancient of Days Music and Dynasty Publishing). Estab. 1986. Produces 7-15 singles and 5 CDs/year. Fee derived from sales royalty when song or artist is recorded or outright fee from recording artist or record company.

How to Contact *Write first and obtain permission to submit.* Prefers cassette or videocassette with 3 songs and lyric or lead sheet. "Type all printed material. Professionalism of presentation will get you an ear with us." Include SASE. Responds in 6 weeks.

Music Pop, AOR, country, contemporary Christian, Christian inspirational and southern gospel music. Produced "The Ultimate Answer" (by Michael Higgins), recorded by Anna Jackson on Fragrance Records. Other artists include Bloodbought, Seventh Dynasty, Streets of Gold and Laura Sanders.

☒ ☑ FINAL MIX MUSIC

2219 W. Olive Ave., Suite 102, Burbank CA 91506. (818)840-9000. E-mail: finalmix@aol.com. **Contact:** Theresa Frank, A&R. Record producer/remixer/mix engineer, record company (3.6 Music, Inc.) and music publisher (Roachi World Music). Estab. 1989. Releases 12 singles and 3-5 LPs and CDs/year. Fee derived from sales royalty when song or artist is recorded.

How to Contact *Does not accept unsolicited submissions.*

Music Mostly **pop, dance, R&B** and **rap**. Produced Michael Bolton, K-Ci and Jo Jo (of Jodeci), Will Smith, Janet Jackson, Ice Cube, Queen Latifah, Tatyana Ali, Jennifer Paige and The Corrs.

☑ FLOW LIKE THAT PRODUCTIONS

111 Bristol Dr., Decatur IL 62521. (217)454-7671. E-mail: theflow1@insightbb.com. Website: www.theflowofficialwebsite.com. **Contact:** The Flow, producer. Record producer and music publisher (Feel Me Flow Publishing). Estab. 1983. Produces 150 singles, 3 CDs/year. Fee derived from outright fee from record company or outright fee from artist if not signed to a record company.

How to Contact Call first to arrange personal interview. No unsolicited submissions. Prefers CD, videocassette (VHS) or DVD with 4 songs, lyric sheet, lead sheet and cover letter. Responds in 1 week.

Music Mostly **hip-hop, R&B** and **contemporary gospel**. Produced "Gettin' Away with Murder" (single by The Flow) from *The Usual Suspects* (album), recorded by The Usual Suspects (hip-hop); "Around the World in Shady Ways" (single by The Flow/Asian Mafia) from *AM to FM* (album), recorded by Asian Mafia (hip-hop); and "Sympathy for the Devil" (single by The Flow) from *Flowmotion* (album), recorded by The Flow (hip-hop), all released 2003 on World Records. Other artists include Kings English and White Thrash.

Tips "Be creative, versatile and self-motivated. Learn music and the business side."

☑ HAILING FREQUENCY MUSIC PRODUCTIONS

7438 Shoshone Ave., Van Nuys CA 91406. (818)881-9888. Fax: (818)881-0555. E-mail: blowinsmokeband@ktb. net. Website: www.blowinsmokeband.com. President: Lawrence Weisberg. Vice President: Larry Knight. Record producer, record company (Blowin' Smoke Records), management firm (Blowin' Smoke Productions) and music publisher (Hailing Frequency Publishing). Estab. 1992. Produces 3 LPs and 3 CDs/year. Fee derived from sales royalty when song or artist is recorded or outright fee from artist.

- Also see the listing for Blowin' Smoke Productions/Records in the Managers & Booking Agents section of this book.

How to Contact *Write or call first and obtain permission to submit.* Prefers cassette or VHS ½" videocassette. "Write or print legibly with complete contact instructions." Include SASE. Responds in 1 month.

Music Mostly **contemporary R&B, blues** and **blues-rock**; also **songs for film, jingles for commercials** and **gospel (contemporary)**. Produced "Beyond the Blues Horizon" (single), recorded by Blowin' Smoke Rhythm & Blues Band, released 2004. Other artists include the Fabulous Smokettes.

☐ HAWORTH PRODUCTIONS

Rt. 1, Box 164, Sunrise Beach MO 65079. (573)374-1111. Fax: (775)522-1533. E-mail: mashred@yahoo.com. Website: www.geocities.com/mashred. **Contact:** Dann E. Haworth, president/producer. Record producer and music publisher (Southern Most Publishing/BMI). Estab. 1985. Produces 5 singles, 3 12" singles, 10 LPs, 5 EPs and 10 CDs/year. Fee derived from sales royalty when song or artist is recorded or outright fee from recording artist.

- Also see the listing for Southern Most Publishing Company in the Music Publishers section of this book.

How to Contact Submit demo tape by mail. Unsolicited submissions are OK. Prefers cassette or 7½ ips or 15 ips reel-to-reel or CD with 3 songs and lyric or lead sheets. Include SASE. Responds in 2 weeks.

Music Mostly **rock, country** and **gospel**; also **jazz, R&B** and **New Age**. Produced *Christmas Joy* (album by Esther Kreak) on Serene Sounds Records. Other artists include The Hollowmen, Jordan Border, Jim Wilson, Tracy Creech and Tony Glise.

Tips "Keep it simple and from the heart."

☑ ☑ HESFREE PRODUCTIONS & PUBLISHING COMPANY

3711 E. 29th, P.O. Box 1214, Bryan TX 77806-1214. (979)775-5261. Fax: (979)846-2328. E-mail: hesfreeprodandpubco@yahoo.com. Website: www.hesfreeproductions.com. President/CEO/Owner: Brenda M. Freeman-Heslip. Producer of songwriting: Jamie Heslip. Vice President/Owner: Rochelle Heslip. Senior Director of R&B, Gospel and Rap: Cyril Roberon. Record producer, music publisher and management agency. Estab. 2001. Fee derived from sales royalty when song or artist is recorded, outright fee from recording artist and outright fee from record company.

How to Submit *Only accepts material referred to by a reputable industry source (manager, entertainment attorney, etc.).* Include CD/CDR. Does not return submissions. Responds in 6 weeks only if interested.

Music Mostly **r&b**, **gospel**, **rap** and **rock**. Does not want country. "We will ensure that each project is complete with professionalism, with the highest technology methods possible. Additionally, our goal is to publish and record over 200 songs annually." Produced "Texas Boys" (single by Chris Idlebird) from *Texas Boys* (album), recorded by Chris Idlebird and Vicki Diggs (rap), released 2002; "Controversial Crossover" (single by "Mike-Ray" Ray Brooks) from *Controversial Crossover* (album), recorded by "Mike-Ray" Ray Brooks (r&b), released 2002; "Walk through the Rays" (single by Donell Travis), from *Dontray the Ghetto Prophet* (album), recorded by Conett Travis and Ralatraneka Mercer (rap), released 2002; "Feel My Pain" (single by Emmett Wilson), recorded by Li'l Dee (hip-hip); "Body Rock Your Block" (single by Marcus Franklin), recorded by Marky D, both released 2003. Also Donnise Williams; Damion Turner; "Michael-Wayne" Wells.

☒ ☑ HF PRODUCTIONS

P.O. Box 3742, Washington DC 20027. (202)415-7748. E-mail: info@hfproductions.com. Website: www.hfproductions.com. **Contact:** Blake Althen or Paula Bellenoit, producers/owners. Estab. 2001. Record producer. "Human Factor Productions is a full service music production company featuring the hottest multi-talented producers, engineers, and state-of-the-art studios. We work with labels, seasoned artists, and develop/shop new talent. Services include production, arranging, composition, recording services, mixing, mastering, artist development and artist label shop."

How to Contact *Please call or e-mail to get permission to submit.* "Solicited material only."

Music Mostly **adult contemporary**, **pop**, **singer/songwriter**, **rock (all types)**, **world/ethnic**, **techno/electronica**, **rap** and **soundtrack/film score**. Produced "Powergame," "Linger" and "Breathe" (by M. Sosnowitz), recorded by Michelangelo (hot A/C). Other artists include Korea (rock), Human Factor (adult contemporary), Scandelle (adult contemporary/techno/electronica), Tommy Wosyluk (singer/songwriter), Gate 22 (rock), Jennifer Cutting, Rhonda Everitt, Rhythms from the Heart, Matt Cheplic, Claudia DiNatale, Ethereal Journey, Rachel Panay (jazz/R&B), and Mark Bodino.

Tip "Get your goals clear in your mind and on paper. What do want a producer to do for you? Know the answer to this question, and it will guide you to the industry professionals who are right for you."

☑ ☑ INTEGRATED ENTERTAINMENT

1815 JFK Blvd. #1612, Philadelphia PA 19103. (215)563-7147. E-mail: gelboni@aol.com. **Contact:** Lawrence Gelburd, president. Record producer. Estab. 1991. Produces 6 EPs and 6 CDs/year. Fee derived from sales royalty when song or artist is recorded or outright fee from recording artist or record company.

How to Contact Submit demo CD by mail. Solicited submissions only. CD only with 3 songs. "Draw a guitar on the outside of envelope so we'll know it's from a songwriter." Responds in 2 months.

Music Mostly **rock** and **pop**. Produced *Gold Record* (album), written and recorded by Dash Rip Rock on Ichiban Records (rock); *Virus* (album), written and recorded by Margin of Error on Treehouse Records (modern rock); and *I Divide* (album), written and recorded by Amy Carr on Evil Twin Records (AAA). Other artists include Land of the Blind, Grimace, Harpoon, Sprawl, Lockdown and Tripe.

☑ ALEXANDER JANOULIS PRODUCTIONS/BIG AL JANO PRODUCTIONS

1957 Kilburn Dr., Atlanta GA 30324. (770)662-6661. E-mail: ajproductions@hottrax.com. **Contact:** Oliver Cooper, vice president of A&R. CEO: Alex Janoulis. Record producer. Produces 6 singles and 2 CDs/year. Fee derived from sales royalty when song or artist is recorded or outright fee from recording artist or record company.

● Also see the listing for Hottrax Records in the Record Companies section of this book.

How to Contact *Write first and obtain permission to submit.* "Letters should be short, requesting submission permission." Prefers cassette with 1-3 songs. Does not return material. Responds in 6 months.

Music Mostly **top 40**, **rock** and **pop**; also **black** and **disco**. Produced *Lady That Digs the Blues* (album), recorded by Big Al Jano's Blues Mafia Show; *Everythang & Mo'* (album), written and recorded by Sammy Blue (blues); and *Blues You Can't Refuse* (album), written and recorded by Big Al (blues), both released 2000 on Hottrax Records. Other artists include Bullitthead, Roger Hurricane Wilson, The Bob Page Project, Mike Lorenz and Chesterfield Kings.

☑ JAY JAY PUBLISHING & RECORD CO.

P.O. Box 41-4156, Miami Beach FL 33141. Phone/fax: (305)758-0000. Owner: Walter Jagiello. Associate: J. Kozak. Record producer, music publisher (BMI) and record company (Jay Jay Record, Tape and Video Co.). Estab. 1951. Produces 12 singles, 12 LPs and 12 CDs/year. Fee derived from sales royalty when song or artist is recorded.

How to Contact Submit demo by mail. Unsolicited submissions are OK. Prefers CD of cassette or VHS videocassette with 6 songs and lyric and lead sheet. "Quality cassette or reel-to-reel, sheet music and lyrics." Does not return material. Responds in 2 months.

Music Mostly **ballads**, **love songs**, **country music** and **comedy**; also **polkas**, **hymns**, **gospel** and **waltzes**. Produced seven Christmas albums in English and Polish, recorded by the S.P. Stanislaus Choral Group of Michigan City, IN and the Lucky Harmony Boys Orchestra. Other artists include Eddie & The Slovenes, Johnny Vandal, Wisconsin Dutchmen and Eddie Zima.

◑ JERICHO SOUND LAB

4 River Rd., P.O. Box 407, Jericho VT 05465. (802)899-3787. Website: http://members.aol.com/jerichosound lab/. **Contact:** Bobby Hackney, owner. Record producer, music publisher (Elect Music/BMI) and record company (LBI Records). Estab. 1988. Produces 5 singles, 2 12″ singles and 3 LPs/year. Fee derived from sales royalty when song or artist is recorded.

- Also see the listings for Elect Music Publishing in the Music Publishers section and LBI Records in the Record Companies section of this book.

How to Contact *Write first and obtain permission to submit.* Prefers CD, cassette or VHS videocassette with 3-4 songs and lyric sheet. Include SASE. Responds in 6 weeks.

Music Mostly **reggae**, **R&B** and **pop**; also **rock** and **jazz-poetry**. Produced "Spotlight on You" (by B. Hackney), and "Sharing and Caring," recorded by Lambsbread (reggae), both on LBI Records.

Tips "Make it plain and simple. Send only your best. Most producers know within 10 to 15 seconds if a song catches their attention."

▦ ◔ JUMP PRODUCTIONS

39 Paul Gilsonstraat, 8200 St-Andries Belgium. Phone: (050)31-63-80. **Contact:** Eddy Van Mouffaert, general manager. Record producer and music publisher (Jump Music). Estab. 1976. Produces 25 singles and 2 CDs/year. Fee derived from sales royalty when song or artist is recorded.

- Also see the listing for Happy Melody in the Music Publishers section of this book.

How to Contact Submit demo CD or tape by mail. Unsolicited submissions are OK. Prefers CD. Does not return material. Responds in 2 weeks.

Music Mostly **ballads**, **up-tempo**, **easy listening**, **disco** and **light pop**; also **instrumentals**. Produced *Evelien* (album by Eddy Govert), recorded by Evelien on Quartz Records (Flemish); *Liefde Komt En Liefde Gaat* (album by Les Reed), recorded by Lina on Scorpion Records; and "Father Damiaan" (single by Jan De Vuyst), recorded by Eigentijdse Jeugd on Youth Sound Records.

▦ ☑ ◔ JUNE PRODUCTIONS LTD.

"Toftrees," Church Rd., Woldingham, Surrey CR3 7JH England. Fax: 44(0)1883 652457. E-mail: david@mackay 99.plus.com. **Contact:** David Mackay, producer. Record producer and music producer (Sabre Music). Estab. 1970. Produces 6 singles, 3 LPs and 3 CDs/year. Fee derived from sales royalty.

How to Contact Submit demo tape by mail. Unsolicited submissions are OK. Prefers CD or cassette with 1-2 songs and lyric sheet. SAE and IRC. Responds in 2 months.

Music Mostly **MOR**, **rock** and **top 40/pop**. Produced *Web of Love* (by various), recorded by Sarah Jory on Ritz Records (country rock). Other artists include Bonnie Tyler, Cliff Richard, Frankie Miller, Johnny Hallyday, Dusty Springfield, Charlotte Henry and Barry Humphries.

☑ ◔ KAREN KANE PRODUCER/ENGINEER

(910)681-0220. E-mail: mixmama@total.net. Website: www.mixmama.com. **Contact:** Karen Kane, producer/engineer. Record producer and recording engineer. Estab. 1978. Produces 3-5 CDs/year. Fee derived from sales royalty when song or artist is recorded or outright fee from recording artist or record company.

How to Contact *E-mail first and obtain permission to submit.* Unsolicited submissions are *not* OK. "Please note: I am not a song publisher. My expertise is in album production." Does not return material. Responds in 1 week.

Music Mostly **rock**, **blues**, **pop**, **alternative**, **R&B/reggae**, **acoustic**, **country**, and **bluegrass**. Produced *Independence Meal* (album), recorded by Alix Olson (blues), released on Subtle Sister Records; *Topless* (Juno-nominated album), recorded by Big Daddy G, released on Reggie's Records. Mixed *Wise and Otherwise* (Juno-nominated album), recorded by Harry Manx (blues). Other artists include Tracy Chapman (her first demo), Chad Mitchell, Ember Swift, Laura Bird, Wishing Chair, Blue Mule, Barenaked Ladies (live recording for a TV special), and Ron Wiseman.

Tips "Get proper funding to be able to make a competitive, marketable product."

HF Productions

Seeking the Human Factor

Blake Althen and Paula Bellenoit started out as recording and performing artists with their Human Factor band project. They received positive notice right out of the gate, including an award in the 2003 Mid-Atlantic Song Contest, but they soon realized their true home was in the studio crafting songs and challenging themselves to develop creative sounds and arrangements. The long hours and cramped conditions of the road also took their toll and proved disillusioning and confining compared to the possibilities of the studio. The duo's love of the studio was also plain to their fellow artists and music business fellow travelers. Says Althen, "The other side is that everybody we talked to was saying, 'You guys should be producers.' "

So, back into the studio they went, and the sound they had developed for their own album as Human Factor proved key in drawing the attention of clients. "It started with Jennifer Cutting's Ocean Orchestra," says Althen. "She heard our record and said, 'Hey, can you do some drums and soundscape-type work for me?' We did it, somebody else heard that, and it just snowballed. The next thing we knew, managers were calling us and wanting to send their groups."

Althen and Bellenoit's style as a production team is an extension of their writing partnership, which usually flows out of demoed instrumental ideas begun by Althen. Bellenoit then comes in and develops melodies and lyrics over the top that feed off the produced vibe of the tracks. When asked to what degree production defines the direction of a song, she says, "They're pretty much intertwined. We do a lot of our writing right in the studio, and as we're writing we think, 'Ah, this would be cool with this effect on it!' "

Similarly, Althen and Bellenoit take complementary roles when working with an artist: Althen guides the studio process and works directly with the recording artist to develop the initial direction in sound and arrangement, while Bellenoit offers an extra set of ears to the tracks in progress and handles the business side of their relationship with the artist. According to Althen, the process is as much about psychology as it is engineering or musicianship. He says, "With singer/songwriter-type artists, they come in and I say to the artist, 'Play me what you've got.' And they play the piano and sing it with a click track. Then I'll say, 'Hey, have you ever thought about it like this . . .' And I'll rip the piano out or turn it into a Rhodes, and then I'll put a funky groove and then I'll watch them and watch their expression. It may be a funk groove. It may be a Gregorian Chant I put behind it. And I'm waiting for them to go, 'Yeah!' We put this smorgasbord song, this mess, together. It's usually way over the top, because I try to find all the things they like, and I try to figure out the artist. Some people like to groove really hard. Other people might want it to focus more on complex chords. Others may want it to be very simple or may want it over-produced. And then, after we get the foundation arrangement in place, Paula will show up and give us her take on it."

Of her role at this point in the process, Bellenoit says, "I'll come in once there's a basic arrangement, and I'll give my opinion at that point, because I haven't been sitting there the whole time and I'm not attached to it. I'm the fresh ears. I'm the consumer coming in and hearing it for the first time. How I comment depends on what I hear. Sometimes I'll be really specific and be like, 'The pronunciation of that word is not good.' And other times I'll be more vague, and it's just the general idea of the song."

Both acknowledge the impact a producer can have on the overall sound of a recording project with the combination of equipment choices and sound preferences. When asked to describe the Human Factor sound, Bellenoit sums it up as: "A combination of electronic and organic - an organic thing combined with new technology. A very full and rich sound. And we like to joke that I'm the human and he's the factor."

Althen is quick to point out, however, that the final sound achieved with any particular artist is often a compromise made necessary by individual circumstances and his own sonic preferences. Also, he makes it clear he does not consider himself a jack-of-all-trades. "There are two ways we work with people," he says. "We do project-based stuff where we are creating things from scratch, or you have live band situations. Live band tends to have more of a sound of its own, versus the project stuff, which tends to have more of a Human Factor music experience because you're in my own studio, with my sounds, my guitars, my microphones, etc. On the other hand, if you track a group, a lot of times we're going to another studio. Every studio has its own sort of 'thing' happening. But with a project in my studio with an individual artist I naturally gravitate toward the sounds I like. I don't think I would be very good recording a group like the White Stripes, but I might be much better suited for a Linkin Park, because I like a big sound. I like incorporating electronics and all kinds of elements like rap when I can."

Having seen the music business from both sides, both as artists and as producers, Althen and Bellenoit note that beginning artists can be dangerously uninformed about how the music industry works. Bellenoit says she finds beginning artists are often "very naïve. They don't understand what 'points' are on an album the first time they talk to us. The baby artists, at least the ones we've worked with, don't know anything about the industry. They don't realize that getting signed means you're essentially getting a loan. They think that once you're signed you're a rock star."

Althen also feels strongly that artists can do a lot for themselves to move their careers forward, and that small details count. They can take advantage of networking opportunities offered by music business organizations. "Paula and I both have stayed up until 2:30 a.m. stuffing press kits and had to go to work the next day. I see bad websites. How many artists have business cards? It's such a simple thing, yet I think I've gotten two in the entire time I've been doing this. Or writing your phone number on your CD. People don't do even do that. And if everyone was as serious as the amount of talk I hear, every Washington Area Music Association seminar would be jam-packed, but there are rarely more than 40 people. Every NARAS event would be jam-packed, but there are rarely more than a couple hundred, and most of them are lawyers. The music business is very competitive, but look at Human Factor. We played three shows and we were nominated for stuff—because we put a lot of work into our press kit and making it sound good."

On the other hand, Bellenoit points out that artists should not be afraid to knock on doors and ask questions. They may find advice and help in unexpected places. "A lot of what I know is due to my lawyer. But, being around it and talking to different people, you learn different things, and one way to learn the industry is just doing it. You learn things from a book when you have to, but most of it is sitting in front of an A&R guy at LAVA Records and talking to him, or going online and meeting people. We met a guy who works at *Billboard* just by sending him an e-mail, and next time we were in New York we went and said hello and sat down in his office. Put yourself out there and talk to people.''

When asked about the possibility of using outside songwriters for projects, both Blake and Bellenoit are open to the idea, depending upon the project. "That's something we've never done before,'' Bellenoit says. "Typically, the artists we've worked with have their own songs, and we haven't had a need for that. But I have talked with one or two people, artists who don't write, who have asked me, 'Do you have a library that I could just pick a song from?' So, it's something we're willing to consider.''

When it comes to the question of genre, Althen has a strong desire to combine and push the edges of various genres. Says Althen, "I look for hip and cool, and I don't care what style it is. I like cutting edge. I like attitude. It can be totally experimental. I get excited about is a cutting edge voice. What it comes down to, in my book, is the voice and the song. And then the thing that will send me over the top is the ability to be experimental and try new things. I like stuff with a hard edge. I think we can definitely fit into rock, electonica, and pop. And I like New Age.''

Still, Althen acknowledges that production trickery is still secondary to the quality of the song itself. "No A&R guy ever said, 'I can't sign your group because the kick drum doesn't sound good enough.' So, I want a great voice. I want a great song. And if the artist can let me do my thing and try to come up with cool and creative stuff, which I hope I can for them, that's what I'm excited about.''

—*Ian Bessler*

◐ KINGSTON RECORDS AND TALENT
15 Exeter Rd., Kingston NH 03848. (603)642-8493. E-mail: kingstonrecords@ttlc.net. Website: www.kingstonrecords.com. **Contact:** Harry Mann, coordinator. Record producer, music publisher (Strawberry Soda Publishing/ASCAP) and record company (Kingston Records). Estab. 1988. Produces 3-4 singles, 2-3 12″ singles, 2-3 LPs and 1-2 CDs/year. Fee derived from sales royalty when song or artist is recorded. Deals primarily with NE and local artists.
• Also see the listing for Kingston Records in the Record Companies section of this book.
How to Contact *Write first and obtain permission to submit.* Prefers cassette with 1-2 songs and lyric sheet. Does not return material. Responds in 2 months.
Music Mostly **rock**, **country** and **pop**; "no heavy metal.'' Produced *Count the Stars* (album), written and recorded by Doug Mitchell; *Time Machine* (album), written and recorded by Gratefull Ted, both released 1999 on Kingston Records. Other artists include Bob Moore, Candy Striper Death Orgy, Pocket Band, Jeff Walker, J. Evans, NTM, Miss Bliss, Ted Solovicus, Armand LeMay, Four On The Floor and Sumx4.

◐ L.A. ENTERTAINMENT, INC.
7095 Hollywood Blvd., #826, Hollywood CA 90028. (323)467-1496. Fax: (323)467-0911. E-mail: info@warriorrecords.com. Website: www.WarriorRecords.com. **Contact:** Jim Ervin, A&R. Record producer, record company (Warrior Records) and music publisher (New Entity Music/ASCAP, New Copyright Music/BMI, New Melody Music/SESAC). Estab. 1988. Fee derived from sales royalty when song or artist is recorded.
How to Contact Submit demo by mail. Unsolicited submissions are OK. Prefers CD and/or videocassette with original songs, lyric and lead sheet if available. "We do not review internet sites. Do not send MP3s, unless requested. All written submitted materials (e.g., lyric sheets, letter, etc.) should be typed.'' Does not return material unless SASE is included. Responds in 2 months only via e-mail or SASE.
Music All styles. "All genres are utilized with our music supervision company for Film & TV, but our original focus is on **alternative rock** and **urban genres** (e.g., **R&B**, **rap**, **gospel**).

▣ ◐ LANDMARK COMMUNICATIONS GROUP
P.O. Box 1444, Hendersonville TN 37077. E-mail: lmarkcom@bellsouth.net. **Contact:** Bill Anderson Jr., producer. Record producer, record company, music publisher (Newcreature Music/BMI) and TV/radio syndication. Produces 12 singles and 12 LPs/year. Fee derived from sales royalty.

- Also see the listings for Newcreataive Music in the Music Publishers section and Landmark Communications Group in the Record Companies section of this book.

How to Contact *Write first and obtain permission to submit.* Prefers 7½ ips reel-to-reel, cassette or videocassette with 4-10 songs and lyric sheet. Include SASE. Responds in 1 month.

Music Mostly **country crossover**; also **blues, country, gospel, jazz, rock** and **top 40/pop**. Produced *Vernon Oxford* (album), written and recorded by Vernon Oxford (country), released 1999 on Norway; *Cowboy Church* (album), written and recorded by various (Christian country), released 1999 on Landmark; and "Nothin' Else Feels Quite Like It" (single by B. Nash/K. Nash/B. Anderson), recorded on TV Theme Records (country). Other artists include Skeeter Davis, Gail Score and Joanne Cash Yates.

◙ LARI-JON PRODUCTIONS

P.O. Box 216, Rising City NE 68658. (402)542-2336. **Contact:** Larry Good, owner. Record producer, music publisher (Lari-Jon Publishing/BMI), management firm (Lari-Jon Promotions) and record company (Lari-Jon Records). Estab. 1967. Produces 10 singles and 5 LPs/year. Fee derived from sales royalty when song or artist is recorded.

- Also see the listings for other Lari-Jon companies in the Music Publishers, Record Companies, and Managers & Booking Agents sections of this book.

How to Contact Submit demo CD by mail. Unsolicited submissions are OK. "Must be a professional demo." Include SASE. Responds in 2 months.

Music Mostly **country, gospel-Southern** and **'50s rock**. Produced *Jesus is my Hero* (album), written and recorded by Larry Good on Lari-Jon Records (gospel). Other artists include Brenda Allen, Tom Campbell and Tom Johnson.

◻ LARK TALENT & ADVERTISING

P.O. Box 35726, Tulsa OK 74153. (918)786-8896. Fax: (918)786-8897. E-mail: janajae@janajae.com. Website: www.janajae.com. **Contact:** Kathleen Pixley, vice president. Owner: Jana Jae. Record producer, music publisher (Jana Jae Music/BMI) and record company (Lark Record Productions, Inc.). Estab. 1980. Fee derived from sales royalty when song or artist is recorded.

- Also see the listings for Jana Jae Music in the Music Publishers section, Lark Record Productions in the Record Companies section, and Jana Jae Enterprises in the Managers & Booking Agents section of this book.

How to Contact Submit demo tape by mail. Unsolicited submissions are OK. Prefers CD or VHS videocassette with 3 songs and lead sheet. Does not return material. Responds in 1 month only if interested.

Music Mostly **country, bluegrass** and **classical**; also **instrumentals**. Produced "Bussin' Ditty" (single by Steve Upfold); "Mayonnaise" (single by Steve Upfold); and "Flyin' South" (single by Cindy Walker), all recorded by Jana Jae on Lark Records (country). Other artists include Sydni, Hotwire and Matt Greif.

◻ LAZY BONES PRODUCTIONS/RECORDINGS, INC.

9594 First Ave. NE, Suite 449, Seattle WA 98115-2012. (206)447-0712. Fax: (425)821-5720. E-mail: lbrinc@earthl ink.net. Website: www.lazybones.com. **Contact:** Scott Schorr, president. Record producer, record company and music publisher (Lazy Bones Music/BMI, Cat from Guatemala Music/ASCAP). Estab. 1992. Produces 4-6 CDs/year. Fee derived from sales royalty when song or artist is recorded or outright fee from recording artist (if unsigned) or outright fee from record company (if signed) or publishing royalties when co-songwriting with artist.

How to Contact Submit demo tape by mail. Unsolicited submissions are OK. Prefers cassette, DAT or CD with 3 songs (minimum) and lyric sheet. "If you honestly believe you can do better, improve your project to its greatest potential before submitting. With the number of projects received, if the material is not truly special and unique, it will not be taken seriously by a legitimate company." Does not return material. Responds in 1 month only if interested.

Music Mostly **alternative** and **rock**; also **hip-hop**. Produced *No Samples* (album by Da Blasta/Ratboy), recorded by Turntable Bay (hip-hop); and *Headland II* (album by Dave Hadland), recorded by Headland (pop), both on Lazy Bones. Other artists include Blackhead, MFTJ, B. Chestnut and Alan Charing.

Tips "Have outstanding and unique talent!"

◻ LINEAR CYCLE PRODUCTIONS

P.O. Box 2608, Sepulveda CA 91393-2608. Phone/fax: (818)347-9880. E-mail: LCP@wgn.net. Website: www.we stworld.com/lcp/. **Contact:** Manny Pandanceski, producer. Record producer. Estab. 1980. Produces 15-25 singles, 6-10 12″ singles, 15-20 LPs and 10 CDs/year. Fee derived from sales royalty when song or artist is recorded.

How to Contact Submit demo tape by mail. Unsolicited submissions are OK. Prefers cassette, 7⅜ ips reel-to-reel or ½″ VHS or ¾″ videocassette. Include SASE. Responds in 6 months.

Music Mostly **rock/pop, R&B/blues** and **country**; also **gospel** and **comedy**. Produced "Lost In a Fog 4U" (single by B. Hitte/N. Nigle/P. Grippe, etc.), recorded by L'il Shette (pop/dance), released 2003 on WIPie; "Noz No Fippos" (single by G. Juan) from his self titled album, recorded by Glax Aleart (alternative), released 2003 on Swip; and "I Wanna F" (single by Washington/"P"/Jaletyme/Supick) from *Bitty & Beans* (album), recorded by Y78H 22A (3W) (rap/hip-hop), released 2004 on Blyacke.

Tips "We only listen to songs and other material recorded on quality tapes and CDs. We will not accept anything that sounds distorted, muffled and just plain bad! If you cannot afford to record demos on quality stock, or in some high aspects, shop somewhere else!"

✅ ⬚ LOVE & LAUGHTER MUSIC

14628 Cortina Dr., La Mirada CA 90638. (562)946-2022. Fax: (562)946-6413. E-mail: contact@loveandlaughterm usic.com. Website: www.loveandlaughtermusic.com. **Contact:** Joey Arreguin or Josh Arreguin, owners/producers. Record producer and music publisher (Love & Laughter Music/ASCAP). Estab. 1987. Produces 4-8 singles and 3-4 CDs. Fee derived from sales royalty when album is released, outright fee from recording artist and/or outright fee from record company.

- Love and Laughter music was the winner of the ASCAP Plus Award from 1998-2002. Also see the Love & Laughter Music (ASCAP) listing in the Music Publishers section of this book.

How to Contact Submit demo by mail. Unsolicited submissions are OK. Prefers CD with 3-4 songs, lyric sheet, lead sheet and cover letter. Does not return submissions. Responds only if interested.

Music Mostly **Latin**, **jazz** and **R&B**; also **rock**, **hip-hop**, **country** and **contemporary Christian**. Produced "Change" (single by Deirdre Hughes/Lisa Manor/J. Arreguin), recorded by Deirdre Hughes (country); *Del Pasado Al Presente* (album), recorded by Frankie Cendejas (Latin); and *Looking Beyond* (album), written and recorded by Patricia Moon (instrumental jazz), all released 2002 on Love & Laughter. Other artists include Marja Harmon (pop/AC) and Melody Encheff (pop).

✅ ⬚ HAROLD LUICK & COUNTRY MUSIC SHOWCASE INTL. ASSOCIATES

Box #368, Carlisle IA 50047. (515)989-3748. E-mail: haroldl@cmshowcase.org. Website: www.cmshowcase.o rg. Producer: Harold L. Luick. Record producer, music industry consultant, music print publisher and music publisher. Produces 20 singles and 6 LPs/year. Fee derived from sales royalty, outright fee from artist/songwriter or record company, and from consulting fees for information or services.

- Also see the listing for Country Music Showcase International in the Organizations section of this book.

How to Contact *Write or call first and obtain permission to submit.* Prefers cassette with 3-5 songs and lyric sheet. Include SASE. Responds in 3 weeks.

Music Mostly **traditional country**, **gospel**, **contemporary country** and **MOR**. "Over a 12-year period, Harold Luick has produced and recorded 412 singles and 478 albums, 7 of which charted and some of which have enjoyed independent sales in excess of 30,000 units."

Tips "If you are looking to place a song with us and have it considered for a recording, make sure you have a decent demo, and all legals in order."

⬚ MAC-ATTACK PRODUCTIONS

868 NE 81st St., Miami FL 33138. (305)949-1422. E-mail: GoMacster@aol.com. **Contact:** Michael McNamee, engineer/producer. Record producer and music publisher (Mac-Attack Publishing/ASCAP). Estab. 1986. Fee derived from outright fee from recording artist or record company.

How to Contact Submit demo tape by mail. Unsolicited submissions are OK. Prefers CD or cassette or VHS videocassette with 3-5 songs, lyric sheet and bio. Does not return material. Responds in up to 3 months.

Music Mostly **pop**, **alternative rock** and **dance**. Produced "Stranger's Words" (single by Oren Maisner/Brian Hernandez), recorded by Jacobs Ladder (rock), released 2002 on Dippy Records; "Never Gonna Let You Go" (single by Bruce Jordan/John Link/Michael McNamee), recorded by Bruce Jordan (pop), released 2002 on H.M.S. Records; "They Don't Want This" (single by Rip the Mic), recorded by Rip the Mic (hip-hop), released 2002 on Mac-Attack. Other artists include Blowfly, Forget the Name, Nina Llopis, The Lead, Girl Talk and Tyranny of Shaw.

🆕 ⬚ COOKIE MARENCO

P.O. Box 874, Belmont CA 94002. E-mail: cojema@aol.com. (650)595-8475. Record producer/engineer. Estab. 1981. Produces 10 CDs/year. Fee derived from sales royalty and outright fee from recording artist or record company.

How to Contact *Write first and obtain permission to submit.* Does not return material. Responds only if interested.

Music Mostly **alternative modern rock**, **country**, **folk**, **rap**, **ethnic** and **avante-garde**; also **classical**, **pop** and **jazz**. Produced *Off the Beaten Path* (album), written and recorded by Melissa Crabtree (folk), released 2002; *Winter Solstice II* (album), written and recorded by various artists; *Heresay* (album by Paul McCandless); and

Deep At Night (album by Alex DeGrassi), all on Windham Hill Records (instrumental). Other artists include Tony Furtado Band, Praxis, Oregon, Mary Chapin Carpenter, Max Roach and Charle Haden & Quartet West.
Tips "If you'd like to sign up to be on our studio or artist mailing list, please visit Blue Coast Records www.blueco astrecords.com)."

PETE MARTIN/VAAM MUSIC PRODUCTIONS

P.O. Box 29550, Hollywood CA 90029-0550. (323)664-7765. E-mail: vaampubl@aol.com or pmarti3636@aol.c om. **Contact:** Pete Martin, president. Record producer, music publisher (Vaam Music/BMI and Pete Martin Music/ASCAP) and record company (Blue Gem Records). Estab. 1982.
 • Also see the listings for Vaam Music Group in the Music Publishers section of this book and Blue Gem Records in the Record Companies section of this book.
How to Contact Send CD or cassette with 2 songs and a lyric sheet. Send small packages only. Include SASE. Responds in 1 month.
Music Mostly **top 40/pop**, **country** and **R&B**.
Tips "Study the market in the style that you write. Songs must be capable of reaching top 5 on charts."

MASTERSCORE MUSIC

Lexington KY 40514. (859)492-6403. E-mail: info@masterscoremusic.com. Website: www.masterscoremusic.c om. **Contact:** Eric Copeland, producer/writer. Record producer. Produces 5-10 singles and 8-15 albums/year. Fee derived from outright fee from recording artist or company. Other fees include critique/review services.
How to Contact *Contact first by e-mail to obtain permission to submit demo.* Prefers CD with 2-3 songs and lyric sheet and cover sheet. Does not return submissions. Responds only if interested.
Music Mostly **contemporary Christian**, **jazz**, and **instrumental**; also **R&B** and **pop/rock**. Does not want country, metal, punk, or hardcore. Produced *Steps* (album), recorded by Sienna (contemporary Christian): *Faith More Real* (album), recorded by Tom Dolan (contemporary Christian); *Glimpse* (album), recorded by Kristyn Leigh (contemporary Christian), all released 2004 on Creative Soul Records. Other artists include Bret Rush, Eleanor Riley, Jesse Laine Powell, and Amanda Fessant.
Tips "Contact us first by e-mail, but please do not send mp3s without e-mailing first. We will delete any unsolicited mp3s without listening. E-mail us and let's start talking about your music and ministry!"

SCOTT MATHEWS, D/B/A HIT OR MYTH PRODUCTIONS INC.

246 Almonte Blvd., Mill Valley CA 94941. Fax: (415)389-9682. E-mail: hitormyth@aol.com. Website: www.scott mathews.com. **Contact:** Mary Ezzell, A&R Director. President: Scott Mathews. Assistant: Tom Luekens. Record producer, song doctor, studio owner and music publisher (Hang On to Your Publishing/BMI). Estab. 1990. Produces 6-9 CDs/year. Fee derived from recording artist or record company (with royalty points). *"Not affiliated with scottmathewsmusic.com or scottmathewsproductions.com. Beware of these and other imposters using the name 'Scott Mathews.' "*
 • Scott Mathews has several gold and platinum awards for sales of over 12 million records. He has worked on several Grammy and Oscar winning releases. In 2004, a Scott Mathews-produced single by country artist J.J. Johns, "United We Fall," went to #1 on European radio. See his article on page 69.
How to Contact *"No phone calls or publishing submissions, please."* Submit demo by mail. Unsolicited submissions are OK. Prefers CD (mp3 and cassette accepted). Include SASE and e-mail address. Responds in 2 months.
Music Mostly **rock/pop**, **alternative** and **singer/songwriters of all styles**. Produced 4 tracks on *Anthology (Best of)*, recorded by John Hiatt (rock/pop), released 2001 on Hip-O; "United We Fall" (single by Heather Myles/J.J. Johns) from *Songs That Make the Jukebox Play* (album), recorded by J.J. Johns, released 2003 on Artistock; and *Lucky Break* (album), recorded by Karen Lehner (w/guess appearances by Van Dyke Parks and Steve Nieve), released 2004 on Grey Mause. Has produced Elvis Costello, Roy Orbison, Rosanne Cash, John Hiatt and many more. Has recorded platinum records with everyone from Barbra Streisand to John Lee Hooker, including Keith Richards, George Harrison, Mick Jagger, Van Morrison, Elvis Costello, Bonnie Raitt and Eric Clapton to name but a few, plus several Grammy and Oscar-winning projects.
Tips "Waiting for a major label to come tap you on the shoulder and say, 'It's your turn,' is the last thing a new artist should even be thinking of. In my humble opinion, today's A&R stands for 'Afraid & Running.' Sorry to all my friends in that department, but the cold truth is, huge corporations are interested only in pleasing the shareholders. Most labels are all about the bottom line, not the music. Recently, I had a president of a major label admit to me that he hates his job because he's not allowed to sign and develop what he wants. So, it's our job to develop our careers by making incredible masters on our own. Fair deals are born from artists being in control. Set your goal (EP or LP) and budget, find the right producer, and make a stellar CD that can compete with anything on the radio. Early on, you can do more for yourself than a label can. When you prove yourself, they offer the moon and as an artist, you are able to keep creataive control of your music. Developing new

artists that will sustain long careers is my main focus. Developing new artists who will sustain long careers is my main focus. Let me know if I can help. (Please check www.scottmathews.com for more info, and also check my entry at www.allmusic.com.)''

⊘ MEGA TRUTH RECORDS

P.O. Box 4988, Culver City CA 90231. E-mail: jonbare@aol.com. Website: www.jonbare.com. **Contact:** Jon Bare, CEO. Record producer and record company. Estab. 1994. Produces 2 CDs/year. Fee negotiable.

How to Contact Submit demo tape by mail. Unsolicited submissions are OK. Prefers CD. ''We specialize in recording world-class virtuoso musicians and bands with top players.'' Does not return material. Responds in 2 weeks only if interested.

Music Mostly **rock**, **blues** and **country rock**; also **swing**, **dance** and **instrumental**. Produced *Party Platter* recorded by Hula Monsters (swing); and *Killer Whales, Shredzilla and Orcastra* (by Jon Bare and the Killer Whales) (rock), all on Mega Truth Records. Other artists include The Rich Harper Blues Band, Aeon Dream & the Dream Machine and Techno Dudes.

Tips ''Create a unique sound that blends great vocals and virtuoso musicianship with a beat that makes us want to get up and dance.''

⊠ ⊙ MONTICANA PRODUCTIONS

P.O. Box 702, Snowdon Station, Montreal QC H3X 3X8 Canada. **Contact:** David Leonard, executive producer. Record producer, music publisher (Montina Music) and record company (Monticana Records). Estab. 1963. Fee derived from sales royalty when song or artist is recorded.

> • Also see the listings for Monticana Records in the Record Companies section and Montina Music in the Music Publishers section of this book.

How to Contact Submit demo tape by mail. Unsolicited submissions are OK. Prefers CD with maximum 4 songs. ''Demos should be as tightly produced as a master.'' Include SASE.

Music Mostly **top 40**; also **bluegrass**, **blues**, **country**, **dance-oriented**, **easy listening**, **folk**, **gospel**, **jazz**, **MOR**, **progressive**, **R&B**, **rock** and **soul**.

Tips ''Work creatively and believe passionately in what you do and aspire to be. Success comes to those who persevere, have talent, develop their craft and network.''

MUSTROCK PRODUCTIONZ WORLDWIDE

167 W. 81st St., Suite 5C, New York NY 10024-7200. (212)799-9268. E-mail: recordmode@hotmail.com. President: Ivan ''DOC'' Rodriguez. Record producer and recording/mixing/mastering engineer. Estab. 1980. Produces 5 singles, engineers 2 LPs, 3 EPs and 2 CDs/year. Fee derived from sales royalty when song or artist is recorded. *We do not shop deals.*

How to Contact *Call first and obtain permission to submit.* Prefers cassette or VHS videocassette and lyric sheet. Does not return material. Responds in 2 months.

Music Mostly **hip-hop**, **R&B** and **pop**; also **soul**, **ballads** and **soundtracks**. Produced ''Poor Georgie'' (by MC Lyte/DJ DOC), recorded by MC Lyte on Atlantic Records (rap). Other artists include Caron Wheeler, The Hit Squad, The Awesome II, Black Steel Music, Underated Productions, EPMD, Redman, Dr. Dre & Ed-Lover, Das-EFX, Biz Markie, BDP, Eric B & Rakim, The Fugees, The Bushwackass, Shai and Pudgee, Alisha Keys, 50 cent, Tiro de Garcia, etc.

Tips ''Services provided include production (pre/post/co), tracking, mixing, remixing, live show tapes, jingles, etc. Additional info available upon request. Go to www.allmusic.com, type 'Ivan Doc Rodriguez' under 'artist' and enter.''

⊡ NEU ELECTRO PRODUCTIONS

P.O. Box 1582, Bridgeview IL 60455. (630)257-6289. E-mail: neuelectro@email.com. Website: www.neuelectro. com. **Contact:** Bob Neumann, owner. Record producer and record company. Estab. 1984. Produces 16 singles, 16 12″ singles, 20 LPs and 4 CDs/year. Fee derived from outright fee from record company or recording artist.

How to Contact Submit demo tape by mail. Unsolicited submissions are OK. Prefers cassette or CD with 3 songs and lyric sheet or lead sheet. ''Provide accurate contact phone numbers and addresses, promo packages and photos.'' Include SASE for reply. Responds in 2 weeks. ''A production fee estimate will be returned to artist.''

Music Mostly **dance**, **house**, **techno**, **rap** and **rock**; also **experimental**, **New Age** and **top 40**. Produced ''Juicy'' (single), written and recorded by Juicy Black on Dark Planet International Records (house); ''Make Me Smile'' (single), written and recorded by Roz Baker (house); *Reactovate-6* (album by Bob Neumann), recorded by Beatbox-D on N.E.P. Records (dance); and *Sands of Time* (album), recorded by Bob Neumann (New Age). Other artists include Skid Marx and The Deviants.

⬛ NEW EXPERIENCE RECORDS

P.O. Box 683, Lima OH 45802. E-mail: just_chilling_2002@yahoo.com. **Contact:** A&R Department. Music Publisher: James L. Milligan Jr. Record producer, music publisher (A New Rap Jam Publishing/ASCAP), management firm (Creative Star Management) and record company (New Experience Records, Grand-Slam Records and Pump It Up Records). Estab. 1989. Produces 15-20 12″ singles, 2 LPs, 3 EPs and 2-5 CDs/year. Fee derived from sales royalty when song or artist is recorded or outright fee from record company, "depending on services required."

- Also see the listings for A New Rap Jam Publishing in the Music Publishers section and Creative Star Management in the Managers & Booking Agents section of this book.

How to Contact *Write first to arrange personal interview.* Address material to A&R Dept. or Talent Coordinator. Prefers CD with a minimum of 3 songs and lyric or lead sheet (if available). "If tapes are to be returned, proper postage should be enclosed and all tapes and letters should have SASE for faster reply." Responds in 6 weeks.

Music Mostly **pop**, **R&B** and **rap**; also **gospel**, **contemporary gospel** and **rock**. Produced "Get Your Own" and "Can't Play a Playa" (singles by David Fawcett) from *Enter the Mind* (album), recorded by Devicus 01 (rap), released 2002 on Pump It Up Records; "The Son of God" (single by James Milligan/Anthony Milligan/Melvin Milligan) from *The Final Chapter* (album), recorded by T.M.C. Milligan Conection (r&b gospel), released 2002 on New Experience/Pump It Up Records. Other artists include Qutina Milligan, Melvin Milligan and Venesta Compton.

Tips "Do your homework on the music business. Be aware of all the new sampling laws. There are too many sound alikes. Be yourself. I look for what is different, vocal ability, voice range and sound stage presence, etc. Be on the look out for our new blues label Rough Edge Records/Rough Edge Entertainment. blues material is now being reviewed. Send your best studio recorded material. Also be aware of the new sampling laws and the New Digital downloading laws. People are being jailed and fined for recording music that has not been paid for. Do your homework."

⬛ 〇 NIGHTWORKS RECORDS

355 W. Potter Dr., Anchorage AK 99518. (907)562-3754. Fax: (907)561-4367. E-mail: kurt@nightworks.com. Website: www.surrealstudios.com. Owner: Kurt Riemann. Record producer. Produces 16 CDs/year. Fees derived from sales royalty when song or artist is recorded.

How to Contact Submit demo CD by mail. Unsolicited submissions are OK. Prefers CD with 2-3 songs "produced as fully as possible. Send jingles and songs on separate CDs." Does not return material. Responds in 1 month.

Music Produces a variety of music from **native Alaskan** to **Techno** to **Christmas**.

〇 PANIO BROTHERS LABEL

P.O. Box 99, Montmartre SK S0G 3M0 Canada. (306)424-2258. Fax: (306)424-2269. E-mail: panioja@sk.sympati co.ca. **Contact:** John Panio, Jr., executive director. Record producer. Estab. 1977. Produces 1 single and 1 LP/year. Fee derived from sales royalty or outright fee from artist/songwriter or record company.

How to Contact Submit demo tape by mail. Unsolicited submissions are OK. Prefers cassette with any number of songs and lyric sheet. SAE and IRC. Responds in 1 month.

Music Mostly **country**, **dance**, **easy listening** and **Ukrainian**. Produced *Vlad Panio Sings* (album), written and recorded by Vlad Panio on PB Records.

⬛ PATTY PARKER

Comstock Records, Ltd., P.O. Box 19720, Fountain Hills AZ 85269. (480)951-3115. Fax: (480)951-3074. **Contact:** Patty Parker, producer. Record producer, music publisher (White Cat Music) and record company (Comstock Records). Estab. 1978. Produces 6-8 CD singles and 3-4 albums/year. Fee derived from outright fee from recording artist or recording company.

- Also see the listings for White Cat Music in the Music Publishers section and Comstock Records Ltd. in the Record Companies section of this book.

How to Contact Submit demo by mail. Submit CD by postal mail only. We do not accept audio files onlines. Unsolicited submissions are OK. Submit CD only (no cassettes) with 2-4 songs and lyric sheet. Voice up front on demos. Include SASE. Responds in 2 weeks.

Music Mostly **country—traditional** to **crossover**. Produced "Great American Country" (single by Paula Mengarelli/Tom Mengarelli/Jeff Hansel), recorded by Paula Mengarelli (country); "Down to the Wire" (single by Maria Carmi), recorded by Maria Carmi (country); and "Your Daddy Would be Proud" (single by Paul Gibson) from *Reason to Believe* (album), recorded by Derek Carle (country), all released on Comstock Records. Other artists include Jentille, R.J. McClintock, Beth Hogan.

Tips "To catch the ears of radio programmers worldwide, I need good medium to uptempo songs for all the artists coming from Europe, Canada and the U.S. that I produce sessions on in Nashville."

◻ PHILLY BREAKDOWN RECORDING CO.

216 W. Hortter St., Philadelphia PA 19119. (215)848-6725. E-mail: mattcozar@juno.com. **Contact:** Matthew Childs, president. Music Director: Charles Nesbit. Record producer, music publisher (Philly Breakdown/BMI) and record company. Estab. 1974. Produces 3 singles and 2 LPs/year. Fee derived from sales royalty when song or artist is recorded.

How to Contact *Contact first and obtain permission to submit.* Prefers cassette with 4 songs and lead sheet. Does not return material. Responds in 2 months.

Music Mostly **R&B, hip-hop** and **pop**; also **jazz, gospel** and **ballads**. Produced "Lonely River" (single by Clarence Patterson/M. Childs) from *Lonely River* (album), recorded by Gloria Clark; and *Taps* (album), recorded by H Factor, both released 2001 on Philly Breakdown. Other artists include Leroy Christy, Gloria Clark, Jerry Walker, Nina Bundy, Mark Adam, Emmit King, Betty Carol, The H Factor and Four Buddies.

Tips "If you fail, just learn from your past experience and keep on trying, until you get it done right. Never give up."

◪ JIM PIERCE

Dept. SM, 101 Hurt Rd., Hendersonville TN 37075. (615)824-5900. Fax: (615)824-8800. E-mail: jimpierce@bells outh.net. Website: www.jimpierce.net. **Contact:** Jim Pierce, president. Record producer, music publisher (Strawboss Music/BMI) and record company (Round Robin Records). Estab. 1974. Fee derived from sales royalty or outright fee from recording artist. "Many artists pay me in advance for my services." Has had over 200 chart records to date.

How to Contact *E-mail first and obtain permission to submit or to arrange personal interview.* Prefers CD with 3 songs and lyric sheet. Will accept cassettes. Does not return material. Responds only if interested. "All submissions should include their contact phone number and/or e-mail address."

Music Mostly **country, contemporary, country/pop, gospel** and **traditional country**. Artists include Tommy Cash, George Jones, Jimmy C. Newman, Margo Smith, Bobby Helms, Sammi Smith, Roy Drusky, Charlie Louvin and Melba Montgomery.

Tips "Industry is seeking good singers who can write songs. Viewing our website is highly suggested."

☑ ◻ PREJIPPIE MUSIC GROUP

P.O. Box 216, Van Buren Twp. MI 48152. (734)697-0945. E-mail: prejippie@comcast.net. Website: www.prejipp ie.com. **Contact:** Bruce Henderson, president. Record producer, music publisher and record company (PMG Records). Estab. 1990. Produces 5 12″ singles, 2 LPs and 2 EPs/year. Fee derived from sales royalty when song or artist is recorded.

• Also see the listings for Prejippie Music Group in the Music Publishers section and PMG Records in the Record Companies section of this book.

How to Contact Submit demo tape by mail. Unsolicited submissions are OK. No phone calls please. Prefers cassette or CD with 3-4 songs and lyric sheet. Include SASE. Responds in 6 weeks.

Music Mostly **alternative R&B, experimental, alternative rock** and **techno/house**. Produced "Is That Life Good?" (single) and "Why Me?" (single), written and recorded by Bourgeoisie Paper Jam (funk/rock); and "Astral Traveler (Part 1)" (single), written and recorded by Synthetic Living Organism (techno), all released 1999 on PMG Records. Other artists include Tony Webb.

◻ THE PRESCRIPTION CO.

P.O. Box 222249, Great Neck NY 11021. (415)553-8540. Fax: (415)553-8541. E-mail: mcdmike525@aol.com. **Contact:** David F. Gasman, president. San Francisco office: 525 Ashbury St., San Francisco CA 94117. (415)553-8540. VP Sales (West Coast warehouse): Bruce Brennan. Record producer and music publisher. Fee derived from sales royalty when artist or song is recorded or outright fee from record company.

• Also see the listing for Prescription Company in the Music Publishers section of this book.

How to Contact *Write or call first about your interest then submit demo.* Prefers cassette with any number of songs and lyric sheet. Include SASE. "Does not return material without SASE and sufficient postage."

Music Mostly **bluegrass, blues, children's, country, dance, easy listening, jazz, MOR, progressive, R&B, rock, soul** and **top 40/pop**. Produced "The World's Most Dangerous Man," "Here Comes Trouble" and "Automated People" (singles by D.F. Gasman) from *Special EP No. 1* (album), all recorded by Medicine Mike (rock), all released 2003 on Prescription.

◻ REEL ADVENTURES

9 Peggy Lane, Salem NH 03079. (603)898-7097. Website: www.reeladventures1.homestead.com. **Contact:** Rick Asmega, chief engineer/producer. Record producer. Estab. 1972. Produces 100 12″ singles, 200 LPs, 5 EPs and 40 CDs/year. Fee derived from sales royalty when song or artist is recorded, or outright fee from recording artist or record company.

How to Contact Submit demo tape by mail. Unsolicited submissions are OK. Prefers cassette or CD. Include SASE. Responds in 6 weeks.

Music Mostly **pop**, **funk** and **country**; also **blues**, **Christian reggae** and **rock**. Produced *Funky Broadway* (album), recorded by Chris Hicks; *Testafye* (album), recorded by Jay Williams; and "Acoustical Climate" (single by John G.). Other artists include The Bolz, Second Sinni, Larry Sterling, Broken Men, Melvin Crockett, Fred Vigeant, Monster Mash, Carl Armand, Cool Blue Sky, Ransome, Backtrax, Push, Too Cool for Humans and Burn Alley.

☐ ROAD RECORDS

P.O. Box 2620, Victorville CA 92393. E-mail: staf@askland.net. Website: www.roadrecords.com. **Contact:** Conrad Askland, president. Record producer, record company (Road Records) and music publisher (Askland Publishing). Estab. 1989. Produces 6 singles and 10 albums/year. Fee derived from sales royalty when song or artist is recorded.

• Also see the listing for Road Records in the Record Companies section of this book.

How to Contact *Write or call first and obtain permission to submit.* Prefers at least 3 songs with lyric and lead sheet. "We are looking for people that have a different, original sound." Does not return submissions. Responds in 3 weeks.

Music Mostly **alternative**, **modern country** and **dance**; also **orchestral instrumental**. Does not want jazz. "We supply music to Grand Ole Opry, United Airlines, Knoxbury Farm and G.T.E."

Tips "Do not submit what you think we are looking for. A lot of our projects are 'on the edge.' "

☑ ☐ RUSTRON MUSIC PRODUCTIONS

1156 Park Lane, West Palm Beach FL 33417-5957. (561)686-1354. E-mail: rmp_wmp@bellsouth.net. **Contact:** Sheelah Adams, office administrator. Executive Director: Rusty Gordon. A&R Director: Ron Caruso. Assistant A&R Director: Kevin Reeves. Record producer, record company, manager and music publisher (Rustron Music Publishers/BMI and Whimsong Publishing/ASCAP). Estab. 1970. Produces 10 CDs/year. Fee derived from sales royalty when song or artist is recorded or outright fee from record company. "This branch office reviews all material submitted for the home office in Connecticut."

• Also see the listings for Rustron Music Publishers in the Music Publishers section and Rustron Music Productions in the Record Companies and Managers & Booking Agents sections of this book.

How to Contact *Write or call to discuss your submission* or submit demo tape or CD by mail. Prefers CD with up to 15 songs that was produced to sell at gigs or cassette with 1-3 songs and typed lyric sheets. Also send cover letter clearly explaining your reason for submitting. "Songs should be 3½ minutes long or less and must be commercially viable for today's market. Exception: New Age fusion compositions 3-10 minutes each, ½ hour maximum. Singer/songwriters and collaborators are preferred." SASE required for all correspondence. No exceptions. Responds in 4 months.

Music Mostly **progressive country**, **pop** (ballads, blues, theatrical, cabaret), **folk/rock**, and **adult contemporary electric acoustic**; also **R&B, New Age instrumental fusions children's music, reggae**, and **women's music**. Produced "Everglades Everlasting" (single) from *Everglades Everlasting* (album), written and recorded by Song On A Whim (children's music), released 2003 on Rustron Records; "Banyon Tree Blues" (single) from *Banyon Tree Blues* (album), written and recorded by The Dinner Key Boys (folk/rock/blues), released 2004 on Whimsong Records; and "Jah Jah Jamaica" (single) from *Jah Jah Jamaica* (album), written and recorded by Jeremy White & Kalliope (yankee reggae), released 2003 on Whimsong Records. Other artists include Haze Coates, Star Smiley, Jayne Margo-Reby, Stacie Jubal, Deb Criss, Robin Plitt, Boomslang Swampsinger.

Tips "Be open to developing your own unique style. Write well-crafted songs with unpredictable concepts, strong hooks and definitive melodies. New Age composers: evolve your themes and use multiculturally diverse instruments to embellish your compositions/arrangements. Don't be predictable. Experiment with instrumental fusion with jazz and/or classical themes, pop themes and international styles. Send cover letter clearly explaining your reason for submitting."

☐ STEVE SATKOWSKI RECORDINGS

P.O. Box 3403, Stuart FL 34995. (772)225-3128. Website: www.clearsoulproductions.com/stevesatkowski.html. Engineer/producer: Steven Satkowski. Record producer, recording engineer, management firm and record company. Estab. 1980. Produces 20 CDs/year. Fee derived from outright fee from recording artist or record company.

How to Contact Submit demo tape by mail. Unsolicited submissions are OK. Prefers CD or cassette. Does not return material. Responds in 2 weeks.

Music Mostly **classical**, **jazz** and **big band**. Produced recordings for National Public Radio and affiliates. Engineered recordings for Steve Howe, Patrick Moraz, Kenny G and Michael Bolton.

☑ SEGAL'S PRODUCTIONS

16 Grace Rd., Newton MA 02159. (617)969-6196. Fax: (617)969-6614. **Contact:** Charles Segal. Record producer, music publisher (Segal's Publications/BMI and Samro South Africa) and record company (Spin Records). Produces 6 singles and 6 LPs/year. Fee derived from sales royalty when song or artist is recorded.

• Also see the listing for Segal's Publications in the Music Publishers section of this book.

How to Contact *Write first and obtain permission to submit or to arrange personal interview.* Prefers cassette, CD or videocassette with 3 songs and lyric sheet or lead sheet of melody, words, chords. "Please record keyboard/voice or guitar/voice if you can't get a group." Does not return material. Responds in 3 months only if interested.

Music Mostly **rock**, **pop** and **country**; also **R&B** and **comedy**. Produced "What Is This Love" (single by Paul/Motou), recorded by Julia Manin (rock); "Lovely Is This Memory" (single by Segal/Paul), recorded by Nick Chosn on AU.S. (ballad); and *There'll Come A Time* (album by Charles Segal), recorded by Jill Kirkland on Spin Records (ballad). Other artists include Art Heatley, Dan Hill and Melanie.

Tips "Make a good and clear production of cassette even if it is only piano rhythm and voice. Also do a lead sheet of music, words and chords."

☑ ☑ SHU'BABY MONTEZ MUSIC

P.O. Box 28816, Philadelphia PA 19151. (215)473-5527. E-mail: schubabyschular@yahoo.com. Website: http://smm.indiegroup.com. **Contact:** Shubaby, owner. Record producer. Estab. 1986. Produces 6 singles, 6 12″ singles and 3 LPs/year. Fee derived from outright fee from record company.

• Also see the listing for Shu'Baby Montez Music in the Music Publishers section of this book.

How to Contact Submit demo CD by mail. Unsolicited submissions are OK. Prefers CD with 4 songs and lyric sheet. Include SASE. Responds in 5 weeks.

Music Mostly **R&B**, **hip-hop** and **funk**. Produced "Special Lady" (single by Shubaby Schuler/Saleem Jefferson), recorded by Saleem (R&B); "Who Knowz" (single), written and recorded by Gary Lloyd (R&B); and "Money" (single by Tony Bennett/Shubaby Schuler), recorded by Tony Bennett (R&B), all released 2004 on Urban Logic Records.

Tips "Be on time with all projects."

☑ SOUND ARTS RECORDING STUDIO

8377 Westview Dr., Houston TX 77055. (713)464-GOLD. E-mail: sarsjef@aol.com. Website: soundartsrecording .com. **Contact:** Jeff Wells, president. Record producer and music publisher (Earthscream Music). Estab. 1974. Produces 12 singles and 3 LPs/year. Fee derived from sales royalty when song or artist is recorded.

• Also see the listings for Earthscream Music Publishing in the Music Publishers section and Surface Records in the Record Companies section of this book.

How to Contact Submit demo tape by mail. Unsolicited submissions are OK. Prefers cassette with 2-5 songs and lyric sheet. Does not return material. Responds in 6 weeks.

Music Mostly **pop/rock**, **country** and **blues**. Produced *Texas Johnny Brown* (album), written and recorded by Texas Johnny Brown on Quality (blues). Other artists include Tim Nichols, Perfect Strangers, B.B. Watson, Jinkies, Joe "King" Carasco (on Surface Records), Mark May (on Icehouse Records), The Barbara Pennington Band (on Earth Records), Tempest Under the Sun and Attitcus Finch.

☑ ○ SOUND WORKS ENTERTAINMENT PRODUCTIONS INC.

P.O. Box 6093, Gardnerville NV 89460. Phone/fax: (775)265-4512. E-mail: mike@musicjones.com. Website: www.musicjones.com. **Contact:** Michael E. Jones, president. Record producer, record company (Sound Works Records) and music publisher (Sound Works Music). Estab. 1989. Produces 16 singles, 2 LPs and 20 CDs/year. Fee derived from sales royalty when song or artist is recorded or outright fee from recording artist or record company.

How to Contact Submit demo tape by mail. Unsolicited submissions are OK. Prefers cassette with 3-6 songs and lyric sheet. "Please include short bio and statement of goals and objectives." Does not return material. Responds in 6 weeks.

Music Mostly **country**, **folk** and **pop**; also **rock**. Produced "Lonelyville," and "Alabama Slammer" (singles), both written and recorded by Wake Eastman; and "Good Looking Loser" (single), written and recorded by Renee Rubach, all on Sound Works Records (country). Other artists include Matt Dorman, Steve Gilmore, The Tackroom Boys, The Los Vegas Philharmonic and J.C. Clark.

Tips "Put your ego on hold. Don't take criticism personally. Advice is meant to help you grow and improve your skills as an artist/songwriter. Be professional and business-like in all your dealings."

☑ ◩ SPHERE GROUP ONE

921 Dolphin Court, Marco Island FL 34145. (239)398-6800. Fax: (239)597-5611. E-mail: spheregroupone@att.n et. **Contact:** Tony Zarrella, president. Talent Manager: Janice Salvatore. Record producer, artist development and management firm. Produces 5-6 singles and 3 CDs/year. Estab. 1986.

How to Contact Submit CD/video by mail. Unsolicited submissions are OK. Prefers cassette or VHS videocassette with 3-5 songs and lyric sheets. "Must include: photos, press, résumé, goals and specifics of project submitted, etc." Does not return material.

Music Mostly **pop/rock (mainstream)**, **progressive/rock**, **New Age** and **crossover country/pop**; also **film soundtracks**. Produced song titles: *Rock to the Rescue*, *Sunset At Night*, *Double Trouble*, *Take This Heart*, *It's Our Love* and *You and I* (albums by T. Zarrella), recorded by 4 of Hearts (pop/rock) on Sphere Records. Other artists include Frontier 9, Myth, Survivor and Wicked Lester/Kiss.

Tips "Be able to take direction and have trust and faith in yourself, your producer and manager. Currently seeking artists/groups incorporating various styles into a focused mainstream product. Groups with a following are a plus."

☑ ◻ SRS PRODUCTIONS/HIT RECORDS NETWORK

6633 Yucca St., Suite #311, Hollywood CA 90028. (323)467-4082. E-mail: GLB@hotmail.com. **Contact:** Greg Lewolt, Ernie Orosco and J.C. Martin, producers. Record producer, record company (Night City Records, Warrior Records and Tell International Records), radio and TV promotion and music publisher. Estab. 1984. Produces 4 singles, 2 12" singles, 4 LPs, 2 EPs and 2-4 CDs/year. Fee derived from outright fee from record company.

How to Contact Submit demo tape by mail. Unsolicited submissions are OK. Prefers cassette, CD or VHS videocassette with 4-8 songs, photos, bio and lyric sheet. Does not return material. Include SASE. Responds in 2 months.

Music Mostly **pop-rock**, **country** and **top 40**; also **top 40 funk**, **top 40 rock** and **top 40 country**. Produced "Do You Remember When" (single by Liehengood/B. Faith) from Legends of Rock (album), recorded by Bobby Harris (Drifters) and Greg Munford (Strawberry Alarm Clock) (pop), released 2002 on Hit Records Network; "Blond Adventure" (single by JC Martin) from *Blond Adventure* (album), recorded by Black Angel (r&b rock), released 2002 on Outsider-Hit Records Network; "Michael" (single by B. Faith/F. Towles/K. Dyer) from Anthology (album), recorded by Brian Faith/Nic St. Nicholas (Steppenwolf) (pop rock), released 2002 on All American Records. Other artists include New Vision, Jade, Ernie and the Emperors, Hollywood Heros, Tim Bogert (Vanilla Fudge, Jeff Beck), Peter Lewis, Jim Calire (America), Mike Kowalski, Greg Munford (Strawberry Alarm Clock), Bobby Harris (Drifters), Ernie Knapp (Beach Boys) and Jewel.

Tips "Keep searching for the infectious chorus hook and don't give up."

◻ STUDIO SEVEN

417 N. Virginia, Oklahoma City OK 73106. (405)236-0643. Fax: (405)236-0686. E-mail: cope@okla.net. Website: www.lunacyrecords.com. **Contact:** Dave Copenhaver, producer. Record producer, record company (Lunacy Records) and music publisher (Lunasong Music). Estab. 1990. Produces 10 LPs and CDs/year. Fee is derived from sales royalty when song or artist is recorded or outright fee from recording artist or record company. "All projects are on a customized basis."

How to Contact *Contact first and obtain permission to submit.* Prefers cassette with lyric sheet. Include SASE. Responds in 6 weeks.

Music Mostly **rock**, **jazz-blues** and **world-Native American**; also **country** and **blues**. Produced "Like A Lifetime (single) from *Where the Wind Blows* (album), written and recorded by Stephanie Musser (easy listening), released 2004 on Passio Productions; "Wouldn't Be the First Time" (single) from *Picasso's Clouds* (album), written and recorded by Dustin Pittsley (rock), released 2004 on Lunacy Records; and "On My Way" (single) from *On My Way* (album), written and recorded by Joe Merrick (country), all released 2004 on Lunacy Records. Other artists include Harvey Shelton, Steve Pryor and Ken Taylor.

◻ SWIFT RIVER PRODUCTIONS

P.O. Box 231, Gladeville TN 37071. (615)316-9479. E-mail: office@andymay.com. Website: www.swiftrivermus ic.com. **Contact:** Andy May, producer/owner. Record producer and record company. Estab. 1979. Produces 40 singles and 4 CDs/year. Fee derived from outright fee from recording artist or record company.

How to Contact *Write or call first and obtain permission to submit.* "Let us know your present goals and reason for contacting us so we can tell if we are able to help you. Demo should be clear and well thought out. Vocal plus guitar or piano is fine." Does not return material. Responds in up to 2 months.

Music Mostly **country**, **singer/songwriters** and **"roots"** (folk, acoustic, bluegrass and rock); also **instrumental**. Produced *Vintage 76* (album), recorded by Curtis McPeake (bluegrass), released 2002 on Lake; *Jeff Tyler* (album), recorded by Jeff Tyler (contemporary country), released 2002 on Swift River; and *Flyin' Fast* (album), recorded by Brycen Fast (country), released 2003 on Swift River. Other artists include Marinda Flom, Curtis McPeake, Rick Lee, Bryce Fast and Bill Mulroney.

Tips "I'm interested in artists who are accomplished, self-motivated and able to accept direction. I'm looking for music that is intelligent, creative and in some way contributes something positive."

☑ ⬭ TAMJAM PRODUCTIONS

101 N. Citrus Ave., Suite 2, Covina CA 91723-2029. E-mail: tamjam1111@adelphia.net. **Contact:** John Maellaro, producer. Record producer. Estab. 1985. Produces 10 singles and 5 CDs/year. Fee derived from sales royalty when song or artist is recorded, outright fee from recording artist and record company, depending on project.

How to Contact Submit demo tape by mail. Unsolicited submissions are OK. Prefers CD with 3 songs and lyric sheet. Clearly label contact name and number on all items submitted. Does not return material. Responds in 3 months.

Music Mostly **adult contemporary**, **pop** and **R&B**; also **Latin**, **jazz** and **blues**. Produced "Play the Memories" and "Jericho" (by Charles Hardman), *Songs*, recorded by Kingman (A/C), 2004 on Tamjam; "Body Boogie" (by Tom McDonald), recorded by Convertible Cowboys (country), 2003 on Tamjam. Other artists include Magnetic Mary and Kingman.

Tips "Have a clear idea of your direction and handle things in a business-like manner."

⬭ ROGER VINCENT TARI

P.O. Box 576, Piscataway NJ 08855. Phone/fax: (908)222-8978. E-mail: rogervtari@earthlink.net. **Contact:** Roger Vincent Tari, president/producer. Vice President: Mike Roze. A&R: Joe Tasi. Marketing Manager: Eva Castari. Record producer, record company (VT Records), music publisher (Vintari Music/ASCAP) and magazine publisher (*Music of the World for Youth Culture*). Estab. 1979. Produces 6-8 singles/year. Fee derived from sales royalty when song or artist is recorded or outright fee from recording artist.

How to Contact Submit demo tape by mail. Unsolicited submissions are OK. Prefers cassette or VHS videocassette with 3 songs and lyric sheet (videocassette is optional). "The artist should send any relevant literature and a simple black and white picture along with the 3-song cassette and lyric sheet." Include SASE. Responds in 1 month.

Music Mostly **indie-pop**, **new wave**, **synth-pop** and **punk pop**; also **world pop**, **J-pop**, **art rock** and **avant jazz**. Produced "Bad Apple" (single by Reiko Lai/Chung Ho J Lee), recorded by Flush (indie-pop/rock), released 2002 on VT Music/VR Records; "Notice of Death" (single by Scott Cheng), recorded by Scott Cheng (hard rock), released 2002 on VT Music/VT Records; and "No-Way" (single by Roger Vincent Tari), recorded by Scott Cheng/Roger V. Tari (pop/punk), released 2002 on VT Music/VT Records. Other artists include Mind Dope 63, Yaag Yang, Leeji Young, Fractured Glass, N.F. Inc., Ling Ling and East Coast Project (midi inc).

Tips "We seek artists from around the world. The music should be new and creative regardless of style. VT Records and *Music of the World* are distributed by Seven Gods/Benten in Tokyo. We are also a distributor for Benten/Sister Records in the East Coast of the U.S.A. Benten Bentoh Series, Hang On The Box and Mummy The Peepshow are all signed to Benten/Sister Records Japan."

⬭ TMC PRODUCTIONS

P.O. Box 12353, San Antonio TX 78212. (210)829-1909. Website: www.axbarmusic.com. **Contact:** Joe Scates, producer. Record producer, music publisher (Axbar Productions/BMI, Scates & Blanton/BMI and Axe Handle Music/ASCAP), record company (Axbar, Trophy, Jato, Prince and Charro Records) and record distribution and promotion. Produces 2-3 CDs/year. Fee derived from sales royalty.

How to Contact *Write or call first and obtain permission to submit.* Prefers cassette with 1-5 songs and lyric sheet. Does not return material. Responds "as soon as possible, but don't rush us."

Music Mostly **traditional country**; also **blues**, **novelty** and **rock (soft)**. Produced "Chicken Dance" (single) (traditional), recorded by George Chambers and "Hobo Heart" (single), written and recorded by Juni Moon, both on Axbar Records. Other artists include Jim Marshall, Caroll Gilley, Rick Will, Wayne Carter, Kathi Timm, Leon Taylor, Mark Chestnutt, Kenny Dale and Britney Hendrickson.

◐ TRAC RECORD CO.

170 N. Maple, Fresno CA 93702. (209)255-1717. E-mail: tracsell@aol.com. **Contact:** Stan Anderson, Bev Anderson, owners. Record producer, music publisher (Sellwood Publishing/BMI) and record company (TRAC Records). Estab. 1972. Produces 5 12″ singles, 5 LPs and 5 CDs/year. Fee derived from outright fee from recording artist or outside investor.

• Also see the listings for Trac Record Co. in the Record Companies section of this book and Sellwood Publishing in the Music Publishers section of this book.

How to Contact Submit demo by mail. Unsolicited submissions are OK. Prefers cassette or CD with 3 songs and lyric sheet. "Send professional studio demo." Include SASE. Responds in 3 weeks.

Music Mostly **country, all styles** and **southern gospel**. Produced "City Days & Country Nights" (single by Jon Jensen) from *Back to Country* (album); "Sweet Deliverance" (single by H.C. "Chuck" House/Mary Miller) from *Back to Country* (album); and "Headed Right Out The Wrong Door" (single by Johnny Spears) from *Back to Country* (album), all recorded by H.C. "Chuck" House (country), released 2004 on TRAC Records.

◻ THE TRINITY STUDIO

P.O. Box 1417, Corpus Christi TX 78403. (361)854-SING. E-mail: info@trinitystydio.com. Website: www.trinitystudio.com. **Contact:** Jim Wilken, owner. Record producer and recording studio. Estab. 1988. Fee derived from outright fee from recording artist or record company.
How to Contact Submit demo tape by mail. Unsolicited submissions are OK. Prefers cassette, CD or VHS videocassette. Does not return material. Responds in 1 month.
Music Mostly **Christian-country**. Produced *Miracle Man* (album), written and recorded by Merrill Lane (country Christian) on TC Records; and *Higher Love* (album by Merrill Lane/Becky Redels), recorded by Becky Redels (country Christian). Other artists include Kerry Patton, Patty Walker, Leah Knight, Lofton Kline, Rockports Gospel Force and Jackie Cole.

◪ VALTEC PRODUCTIONS

P.O. Box 6018, Santa Maria CA 93456. (805)928-8559. Website: www.valtec.net. **Contact:** Joe Valenta, producer. Record producer. Estab. 1986. Produces 20 singles and 10 CDs/year. Fee derived from sales royalty when song or artist is recorded.
How to Contact Submit demo tape by mail. Unsolicited submissions are OK. Prefers CD or DVD with 3 songs and lyric or lead sheet. Send photo. Does not return material (kept on file for 2 years). Responds in 6 weeks.
Music Mostly **country, Christian, pop/AC** and **rock**.

◻ CHARLES VICKERS MUSIC ASSOCIATION

P.O. Box 725, Daytona Beach FL 32015-0725. (904)252-4849. Fax: (904 or 386)252-7402. E-mail: CharlesVickers @USALink.com. Website: www.ZYWorld.com/CharlesVickers. President: Harold Vickers. Manager: Loris Doby. President/Producer: Dr. Charles H. Vickers D.M. Record producer, music publisher (Pritchett Publication/ BMI and Alison Music/ASCAP) and record company (King of Kings Records, L.A. International Records, Quicksilvers/Increase Records Inc. and Bell Records International). Produces 3 singles and 6 LPs/year. Fee derived from sales royalty when song or artist is recorded.
  • Also see the listings for Pritchett Publishing in the Music Publishers section and Pickwick/Mecca/International Records in the Record Companies section of this book.
How to Contact *Call first and obtain permission to submit.* Prefers 7½ ips reel-to-reel or cassette with 1-6 songs. Does not return material. Responds in 6 months.
Music Mostly **church/religious, gospel** and **hymns**; also **bluegrass, blues, classical, country, easy listening, jazz, MOR, progressive, reggae (pop), R&B, rock, soul** and **top 40/pop**. Produced *Run to Jesus While You Can* (album), written and recorded by Charles Vickers on Quicksilvers/Increase Records Inc. Other artists include James Franklin, Gladys Nighton and Charles Gardy.

◻ THE WEISMAN PRODUCTION GROUP

449 N. Vista St., Los Angeles CA 90036. (323)653-0693. E-mail: unclelenny@aol.com. **Contact:** Ben Weisman, owner. Record producer and music publisher (Audio Music Publishers). Estab. 1965. Produces 10 singles/year. Fee derived from sales royalty when song or artist is recorded.
  • Also see the listings for Audio Music Publishers and Queen Esther Music Publishers in the Music Publishers section of this book.
How to Contact Submit demo CD or tape by mail. Unsolicited submissions are OK. Prefers CD or cassette with 3-10 songs and lyric sheet. Include SASE. "Mention *Songwriter's Market*. Please make return envelope the same size as the envelopes you send material in, otherwise we cannot send everything back. Just send tape." Responds in 6 weeks.
Music Mostly **R&B, soul, dance, rap** and **top 40/pop**; also **gospel** and **blues**.

◪ WESTWIRES RECORDING

(formerly Westwires Digital USA), 1042 Club Ave., Allentown PA 18109. (610) 435-1924. E-mail: wayne.becker @westwires.com. Website: www.westwires.com. **Contact:** Wayne Becker, owner/producer. Record producer and production company. Fee derived from outright fee from record company or artist retainer.
How to Contact Submit demo tape by mail. Unsolicited submissions are OK. Prefers cassette, CD or VHS videocassette with 3 songs and lyric sheet. Does not return material. Responds in 1 month.
Music Mostly **rock, R&B, dance, alternative, folk** and **eclectic**. Produced *Trap Door* (album), recorded by Trad Door (dance), released on Interstellar. Also engineered *Live & Acoustic* (album), recorded by Zakk Wylde

(hard rock), released on Spitfire Records. Other artists include Weston, Anne Le Baron and Gary Hassay.
Tips ''We are interested in singer/songwriters and alternative artists living in the mid-Atlantic area. Must be able to perform live and establish a following.''

☑ ◙ WILBUR PRODUCTIONS

% Pilot Recording Studios 59 W. 19th St., New York NY 10011. (212)255-5544. E-mail: info@pilotrecording.com. Website: www.pilotrecording.com. **Contact:** Will Schillinger, president. Record producer and recording engineer/studio owner. Estab. 1989. Produces 50 singles, 20 LPs and 20 CDs/year. Fee derived from sales royalty when song or artist is recorded or outright fee from record company or from artist.
How to Contact Submit demo CD by mail. Prefers CD with 3-5 songs. Does not return material. Responds in 2 weeks.
Music Mostly **rock**, **jazz** and **alternative**. Worked with Marshall Crenshaw, Vanessa Williams, Sean Lennon, Yoko, Bo Diddley, God's Child, Junior Brown, Warren Zevon, Amy Fairchild, In the Groove, Jack Walrath and many others.
Tips ''Don't worry about your demo quality. Send good songs. Very interested in new bands as well.''

☑ ◙ FRANK WILLSON

P.O. Box 2297, Universal City TX 78148. (210)653-3989. E-mail: bswr18@wmconnect.com. **Contact:** Frank Willson, producer. Record producer, management firm (Universal Music Marketing) and record company (BSW Records/Universal Music Records). Estab. 1987. Produces 20-25 albums/year. Fee derived from sales royalty when song or artist is recorded.

- Also see the listings for BSW Records in the Music Publishers and Record Companies sections and Universal Music Marketing in the Managers & Booking Agents section of this book.

How to Contact Submit demo CD by mail. Unsolicited submissions are OK. Prefers cassette with 3-4 songs and lyric sheets. Include SASE. Responds in 1 month.
Music Mostly **country**, **blues**, **jazz** and **soft rock**. Produced *Follow the Roses* (album), written and recorded by Larry Butler on BSW Records (country). Other artists include Candee Land, Dan Kimmel, Brad Lee, John Wayne, Sonny Marshall, Bobby Mountain and Crea Beal.

☑ ◙ WLM MUSIC/RECORDING

2808 Cammie St., Durham NC 27705-2020. (919)471-3086. Fax: (919)471-4326. E-mail: wlm-musicrecording@nc.rr.com. **Contact:** Watts Lee Mangum, owner. Record producer. Estab. 1980. Fee derived from outright fee from recording artist. ''In some cases, an advance payment requested for demo production.''
How to Contact Submit demo CD by mail. Unsolicited submissions are OK. Prefers CD with 2-4 songs and lyric or lead sheet (if possible). Include SASE. Responds in 6 months.
Music Mostly **country**, **country/rock** and **blues/rock**; also **pop**, **rock**, **blues**, **gospel** and **bluegrass**. Produced ''911,'' and ''Petals of an Orchid'' (singles), both written and recorded by Johnny Scoggins (country); and ''Renew the Love'' (single by Judy Evans), recorded by Bernie Evans (country), all on Independent. Other artists include Southern Breeze Band and Heart Breakers Band.

◙ WORLD RECORDS

5798 Deer Trail Dr., Traverse City MI 49684. E-mail: jack@worldrec.org. Website: www.worldrec.org. **Contact:** Jack Conners, producer. Record producer, engineer/technician and record company (World Records). Estab. 1984. Produces 1 CD/year. Fee derived from outright fee from recording artist.
How to Contact *Write first and obtain permission to submit.* Prefers CD with 1 or 2 songs. Include SASE. Responds in 6 weeks.
Music Mostly **classical**, **folk** and **jazz**. Produced *Have You Heard?* (album by Traverse Symphony Orchestra), (classical), released 2003, and *Music From the Monastery* (album by Nancy Larson), (classical), released 2002. Other artists include The Murphy Brothers and The Camerata Singers.

ADDITIONAL RECORD PRODUCERS

The following companies are also record producers, but their listings are found in other sections of the book. See the General Index for page numbers, then read the listings for submission information.

A

Alias John Henry Tunes
AlliSongs Inc.
AlphaBeat
Ariana Records
Arkadia Entertainment Corp.
Atlan-Dec/Grooveline Records
Avita Records

B

Bacchus Group Productions, Ltd.
Bagatelle Music Publishing Co.
Banana Records
Barrett Rock 'n' Roll Enterprises, Paul
Belmont Records
Big Fish Music Publishing Group
Blue Wave Productions
BME Publishing
Bradley Music, Allan
Burnsongs

C

Capstan Record Production
Cellar Records
Chiaroscuro Records
Christopher Publishing, Sonny
CKB Records/Helaphat Entertainment
Cornelius Companies, The
Cosmotone Records
Creative Improvised Music Projects (CIMP)
    Records

D

Del Camino Music Publishing
Discmedia
Duane Music, Inc.

E

Ellis International Talent Agency, The
EMF Productions

F

Fireant
First Time Records & Music (Publishing) U.K.

Frick Enterprises, Bob Scott
Furrow Music

G

Garrett Entertainment, Marty
Generic Records, Inc.
Glad Music Co.
Groove Makers' Recordings
Gueststar Records/Entertainment Agency

H

Hammel Associates, Inc., R.L.
Hardison International Entertainment Corpo-
    ration
Heads Up Int., Ltd.
Hi-Bias Records Inc.
Hickory Lane Publishing and Recording
His Power Productions and Publishing

I

Iron Skillet Music

J

Ja/Nein Musikverlag GmbH
Jupiter Records

K

Kaupp Records
Kaysarah Music

L

Lake Transfer Productions & Music
LCS Music Group
Lineage Publishing Co.
Living Eye Productions Ltd.
Lock
Loggins Promotion/Backstage Entertainment
Lucifer Records, Inc.

M

Manuiti L.A.
Martin Productions/Easyway Music, Rick
Marvel Records, Andy
Mayfair Music

Record Producers

McCoy Music, Jim
McJames Music Inc.
Mighty Records
Music Room Publishing Group, The

N

Naked Jain Records

O

OCP Publications
Ontrax Companies
OTA Productions

P

P. & N. Records
Plateau Music
Playbones Records
Prescription Company

Q

QUARK, Inc.

R

R.T.L. Music
Renaissance Entertainment Group
Rival Records
Ruf Records

S

Salt Works Music
Sinus Musik Produktion, Ulli Weigel
Sound Cellar Music
Southland Records, Inc.
Starbound Publishing Co.
Succes
Supreme Enterprises Int'l Corp.
Survivor Records/Ten of Diamonds Music

T

T.C. Productions/Etude Publishing Co.
Tiki Enterprises, Inc.
Ton Records
Tower Music Group

W

Wagner Agency, William F.
Warehouse Creek Recording Corp.
Warner Productions, Cheryl K.
Wilder Artists' Management, Shane
World Beatnik Records
World Famous Music Co.

X

X.R.L. Records/Music

Managers & Booking Agents

Before submitting to a manager or booking agent, be sure you know exactly what you need. If you're looking for someone to help you with performance opportunities, the booking agency is the one to contact. They can help you book shows either in your local area or throughout the country. If you're looking for someone to help guide your career, you need to contact a management firm. Some management firms may also handle booking; however, it may be in your best interest to look for a separate booking agency. A manager should be your manager—not your agent, publisher, lawyer or accountant.

MANAGERS

Of all the music industry players surrounding successful artists, managers are usually the people closest to the artists themselves. The artist manager can be a valuable contact, both for the songwriter trying to get songs to a particular artist and for the songwriter/performer. A manager and his connections can be invaluable in securing the right publishing deal or recording contract if the writer is also an artist. Getting songs to an artist's manager is yet another way to get your songs recorded, since the manager may play a large part in deciding what material his client uses. For the performer seeking management, a successful manager should be thought of as the foundation for a successful career.

The relationship between a manager and his client relies on mutual trust. A manager works as the liaison between you and the rest of the music industry, and he must know exactly what you want out of your career in order to help you achieve your goals. His handling of publicity, promotion and finances, as well as the contacts he has within the industry, can make or break your career. You should never be afraid to ask questions about any aspect of the relationship between you and a prospective manager. Always remember that a manager works *for the artist*. A good manager is able to communicate his opinions to you without reservation, and should be willing to explain any confusing terminology or discuss plans with you before taking action. A manager needs to be able to communicate successfully with all segments of the music industry in order to get his client the best deals possible. He needs to be able to work with booking agents, publishers, lawyers and record companies. Keep in mind that you are both working together toward a common goal: success for you and your songs. Talent, originality, professionalism and a drive to succeed are qualities that will attract a manager to an artist—and a songwriter.

BOOKING AGENTS

The function of the booking agent is to find performance venues for their clients. They usually represent many more acts than a manager does, and have less contact with their acts. A booking agent charges a commission for his services, as does a manager. Managers usually ask for a 15-20% commission on an act's earnings; booking agents usually charge around 10%. In the area of managers and booking agents, more successful acts can negotiate lower percentage deals than the ones set forth above.

SUBMITTING MATERIAL TO MANAGERS & BOOKING AGENTS

The firms listed in this section have provided information about the types of music they work with and the types of acts they represent. You'll want to refer to the Category Index at the end of this section to find out which companies deal with the type of music you write, and the Geographic Index at the back of the book to help you locate companies near where you live. Then determine whether they are open to your level of experience (see A Sample Listing Decoded on page 11). Each listing also contains submission requirements and information about what items to include in a press kit and will also specify whether the company is a management firm or a booking agency. Remember that your submission represents you as an artist, and should be as organized and professional as possible.

Icons

For More Info

For more instructional information on the listings in this book, including explanations of symbols (N ✓ ♈ ✿ ⊕ ◯ ⬰ ⬰ ⬰), read the article *Songwriter's Market: How Do I Use It?* on page 7.

ADDITIONAL MANAGERS & BOOKING AGENTS

There are **more managers & booking agents** located in other sections of the book! On page 259 use the list of Additional Managers & Booking Agents to find listings within other sections who are also managers/booking agents.

◪ AIR TIGHT MANAGEMENT

115 West Rd., P.O. Box 113, Winchester Center CT 06094. (860)738-9139. Fax: (860)738-9135. E-mail: mainoffice@airtightmanagement.com. Website: www.airtightmanagement.com. **Contact:** Jack Forchette, president. A&R: Scott Fairchild. Management firm. Estab. 1969. Represents individual artists, groups or songwriters from anywhere; currently handles 8 acts. Receives 15-20% commission. Reviews material for acts.

How to Contact *Write e-mail first and obtain permission to submit.* Prefers cassette or VHS videocassette. If seeking management, press kit should include photos, bio and recorded material. "Follow up with a fax or e-mail, not a phone call." Does not return material. Responds in 1 month.

Music Mostly **rock**, **country** and **jazz**. Current acts include Johnny Colla (songwriter/producer, and guitarist/songwriter for Huey Lewis and the News), Jason Scheff (lead singer/songwriter for the group "Chicago"), Gary Burr (Nashville songwriter/producer), Nathan East (singer/songwriter/bassist—Eric Clapton, Michael Jackson, Madonna, 4-Play and others), Rocco Prestia (legendary R&B musician, "Tower of Power" bassist), and Steve Oliver (contemporary jazz/pop songwriter/guitarist/vocalist, recording artist).

☑ ◪ ALL STAR MANAGEMENT

P.O. Box 2103, Westerville OH 43086. (614)332-8063. Fax: (614)794-2103. E-mail: allstarmanage@msn.com. **Contact:** John or Mary Simpson, owners. Management firm. Estab. 1980. Represents individual artists, groups and songwriters from anywhere; currently handles 3 acts. Receives 20% commission. Reviews material for acts.

● Also see the listing for All Star Record Promotions in the Record Companies section of this book.

How to Contact Submit demo tape by mail. Unsolicited submissions are OK. Prefers cassette or videocassette with 3 songs and lyric or lead sheet. If seeking management, press kit should include audio cassette with 3 songs, bio, 8×10 photo or any information or articles written about yourself or group, and video if you have one. Does not return material. Responds in 2 months.

Music Mostly **country**, **Christian**, **adult contemporary**, **smooth jazz** and **pop rock**. Works primarily with bands and singers/songwriters. Current acts include Debbie Robins (singer/songwriter, Christian contemporary), Allen Austin (singer/songwriter, country rock) and Leon Seiter (country singer/songwriter).

☑ ◪ ALL STAR TALENT AGENCY

P.O. Box 717, White House TN 37188. (615)643-4208. Fax: (615)643-2228. E-mail: kirbyjoy@aol.com. **Contact:** Joyce Kirby, owner/agent. Booking agency. Estab. 1966. Represents professional individuals, groups and songwriters; currently handles 6 acts. Receives 15% commission. Reviews material for acts.

How to Contact Submit demo tape by mail. Unsolicited submissions are OK. Prefers cassette or VHS videocassette with 4 songs (can be cover songs) and lead sheet. If seeking management, press kit should include bios, cover letter, press clippings, demo and photos. Does not return material. Does not return long distance phone calls. Responds in 1 month.

Music Mostly **country**; also **bluegrass**, **gospel**, **MOR**, **rock (country)** and **top 40/pop**. Works primarily with dance, show and bar bands, vocalists, club acts and concerts. Current acts include Chris Hartley (country), Alek Houston (MOR) and Joe Trice (blues).

◪ MICHAEL ALLEN ENTERTAINMENT DEVELOPMENT

P.O. Box 111510, Nashville TN 37222. Phone/fax: (615)754-0059. E-mail: michael@michaelallencreates.com. Website: www.michaelallencreates.com. **Contact:** Michael Allen. Management firm and public relations. Represents individual artists, groups and songwriters; currently handles 2 acts. Receives 15-25% commission. Reviews material for acts.

How to Contact Submit demo tape by mail. Unsolicited submissions are OK. Prefers CD or cassette or VHS videocassette with 3 songs and lyric or lead sheets. If seeking management, press kit should include photo, bio, press clippings, letter and tape. Include SASE. Responds in 3 months.

Music Mostly **country**, and **pop**; also **rock** and **gospel**. Works primarily with vocalists and bands. Currently doing public relations for Shotgun Red, Ricky Lynn Gregg, Easy Street and Kyle Raines.

◪ AMERICAN ARTISTS ENTERTAINMENT

1143 Fitzgerald St., Philadelphia PA 19148-3611. E-mail: online@aaeg.com. Website: www.aaeg.com. **Contact:** A&R Department. Management firm, music publisher (David Music, BMI), record company (East Coast Records) and record and motion picture distribution. Represents individual artists, groups, actors and models from anywhere; currently handles 3 acts. Receives 20% commission. Reviews material for acts.

How to Contact Submit demo tape by mail. Unsolicited submissions are OK. Prefers cassette, videocassette or CD with 3 songs. If seeking management, press kit should include bio, press releases, photos, performing, training and background. Include SASE. Responds in 1 month.

Music Mostly **R&B**, **top 40**, **rap** and **country**; also **modern rock** and motion picture scores. Current acts include The Blue Notes (R&B), The Trammps (disco), Clarice Rose (country) and Bliss (Top 40).

✦ ⦿ AMOK ARTISTS AGENCY

Box 12, Fergus ON N1M 2W7 Canada. (519)787-1100. Fax: (519)787-0084. E-mail: amok@sentex.net. Website: www.amokmusic.com. **Contact:** Hugo Ranpen, owner. Management firm and booking agency. Estab. 1985. Represents groups from anywhere; currently handles 13 acts. Receives 15-20% commission.

How to Contact Submit demo tape by mail. Unsolicited submissions are OK. Prefers VHS videocassette or CD with lyric sheet. If seeking management, press kit should include bio, past performances, photo, cassette, CD or video. ''Due to the large amount of submissions we receive we can only respond to successful applicants.'' Does not return material.

Music Mostly **world beat**, **new roots**, **aboriginal** and **folk**. Works primarily with bands in the world music and new roots field; no mainstream rock/pop. Current acts include Amampondo (world beat, Melt 2000), Lester Quitzau (blues, Festival), Bill Bourne (roots), Madagascar Slim (world), Veda Hille (art rock), Tri-continental (root) and Nash the Slash (art rock).

☑ ⦿ ANGEL GOMEZ MUSIC

21724 Nowlin Ave., Dearborn MI 48123. (313)274-7000. Fax: (313)274-9255. E-mail: angel@angelgomez.com. Website: www.angelgomez.com. **Contact:** Angel Gomez, president. Management firm. Estab. 1979. Represents local and international individual artists, groups and songwriters; currently handles 9 acts. Receives 15-20% commission. Reviews material for acts.

How to Contact *Write first and obtain permission to submit.* Prefers cassette or videocassette of performance with 3-5 songs. If seeking management, include photo, tape/CD, bio, cover letter, press clippings and itinerary of dates. Does not return material. Responds in 2 months.

Music Mostly **rock**, **pop** and **top 40**; also **funk**. Works primarily with individual artists, groups and songwriters. Current artists include Kat McAllister (pop T-40), The Rev. Right Time and the First Cuzins of Funk (new funk) and Bridge (rock).

⦿ ARTIST REPRESENTATION AND MANAGEMENT

1257 Arcade St., St. Paul MN 55106. (651)483-8754. Fax: (651)776-6338. E-mail: ra@armentertainment.com. Website: www.armentertainment.com. **Contact:** Roger Anderson, agent/manager. Management firm and booking agency. Estab. 1983. Represents artists from anywhere; currently handles 10 acts. Receives 15% commission. Reviews material for acts.

How to Contact Submit CD and video by mail. Unsolicited submissions are OK. Please include minimum 3 songs. If seeking management, references, current schedule, bio, photo, press clippings should also be included. ''Priority is placed on original artists with product who are currently touring.'' Does not return material. Responds only if interested within 30 days.

Music Mostly **melodic rock**. Current acts include Knight Crawler (melodic rock), Great White, Warrant, Firehouse and Jesse Lang.

☑ ◯ ATCH RECORDS AND PRODUCTIONS

9894 Bissonnet, Ste 906, Houston TX 77036. (713)981-6540. Fax: (713)981-0083. Website: www.atchrecords.com. Chairman/CEO: Charles Atchison. Management firm, recording studio and record company. Estab. 1989. Represents local, regional and international individual artists, groups and songwriters; currently handles 2 acts. Receives 20% commission. Reviews material for acts.

How to Contact Submit demo by mail. Unsolicited submissions are OK. Prefers CD with 2 songs and lyric sheet. If seeking management, include cover letter, bio, photo, demo and lyrics. Does not return material. Responds in 3 weeks.

Music Mostly **R&B** and **gospel**; also **pop**, **rap** and **hip-hop**. Works primarily with vocalists and groups. Current acts include Prime Flo and Joy (rap).

Tips ''Send a good detailed demo with good lyrics. Looking for wonderful love stories, dance music.''

Ⓝ ⦿ BACCHUS GROUP PRODUCTIONS, LTD.

5701 N. Sheridan Rd., Suite 8-U, Chicago IL 60660. (773)334-1532. Fax: (773)334-1531. E-mail: bacchusgrp@uron.cc. Website: www.BacchusGroup.com. **Contact:** D. Maximilian, Managing Director and Executive Producer. Director of Marketing: M. Margarida Rainho. Management firm and record producer (D. Maximilian). Estab. 1990. Represents individual artists or groups from anywhere; currently handles 9 acts. Receives 15-25% commission. Reviews material for acts.

How to Contact *Does not accept unsolicited submissions.*

Music Mostly **pop**, **R&B/soul** and **jazz**; also **Latin** and **world beat**. Works primarily with singer/songwriters, composers, arrangers, bands and orchestras. Current acts include Orchestra of the Americas (international dance orchestra), Sorcerers of Swing (big band jazz dance orchestra) and Samba Samba 2000 (Carnival/Mardi Gras worldbeat dance orchestra).

✅ ◎ BACKSTREET BOOKING

5658 Kirby Ave., Cincinnati OH 45239. (513)542-9544. Fax: (513)542-9545. E-mail: backstreetbking@aol.com. Website: www.backstreetbooking.com. **Contact:** James Sfarnas, president. Booking agency. Estab. 1992. Represents individual artists and groups from anywhere; currently handles 30 acts. Receives 10-15% commission. Reviews material for acts.

How to Contact *Call first and obtain permission to submit.* Accepts only signed acts with product available nationally.

Music Mostly **niche-oriented music** and **rock**. Current acts include Billy Preston Acumen (progressive rock group), Cab (jazz fusion) and Spock's Beard (progressive rock).

Tips "Build a base on your own."

◎ BARNARD MANAGEMENT SERVICES (BMS)

228 Main St., Suite 3, Venice CA 90291. (310)399-8886. Fax: (310)450-0470. E-mail: bms@barnardus.com. **Contact:** Russell Barnard, president. Management firm. Estab. 1979. Represents artists, groups and songwriters; currently handles 2 acts. Receives 10-20% commission. Reviews material for acts.

How to Contact *Write first and obtain permission to submit.* Prefers cassette or CD with 3-10 songs and lead sheet. Artists may submit VHS videocassette (15-30 minutes) by permission only. If seeking management, press kit should include cover letter, bio, photo, demo tape/CD, lyric sheets, press clippings, video and résumé. Does not return material. Responds in 2 months.

Music Mostly **country crossover**, **blues**, **country**, **R&B**, **rock** and **soul**. Current acts include Mark Shipper (songwriter/author) and Sally Rose (R&B band).

Tips "Semi-produced demos are of little value. Either save the time and money by submitting material 'in the raw,' or do a finished production version."

🌐 ✅ ◎ PAUL BARRETT ROCK 'N' ROLL ENTERPRISES

16 Grove Place, Penarth, Vale of Glamorgan CF64 2ND United Kingdom. Phone: 02920-704279. Fax: 02920. E-mail: barrettrocknroll@amserve.com. **Contact:** Paul Barrett, director. Management firm, booking agency, music publisher (October), record company (Rock 'n' Roll Records) and record producer (Paul Barrett and Ray Thompson). Estab. 1969. Represents individual artists and groups from anywhere; currently handles 37 acts. Receives 10% commission. Reviews material for acts.

• This company only represents acts who perform '50s rock 'n' roll.

How to Contact Submit demo tape by mail. Unsolicited submissions are OK. Prefers CD or DAT with picture and bio (for performers). SAE and IRC. Responds in 3 weeks.

Music Mostly **50s rock 'n' roll**. Works primarily with "performers plus some writers." Current acts include The Jets (trio), Matchbox (rockabilly) and Crazy Caravan & The Rhythm Rockers (rockabilly).

Tips "We want good original slanted roots music that does not sound British! Performed by cool people with nonmop top, mod squad, silly haircuts or clothes."

✅ ◐ BASSLINE ENTERTAINMENT, INC.

P.O. Box 2394, New York NY 10185. E-mail: info@basslineinc.com. Website: www.basslineinc.com. **Contact:** Clarence Williams, vice president. Management firm. Estab. 1993. Represents local and regional individual artists, groups and songwriters. Receives 20-25% commission. Reviews material for acts.

How to Contact Submit demo tape by mail. Unsolicited submissions are OK. Prefers cassette, CD, DVD, or VHS videocassette. If seeking management, press kit should include cover letter, press clippings, bio, demo (cassette, CD or VHS video), picture and accurate contact telephone number. Include SASE. Responds in 3 weeks.

Music Mostly **pop**, **R&B**, **club/dance** and **hip-hop/rap**; some **Latin**. Works primarily with singer/songwriters, producers, rappers and bands. Current acts include Iceman (hip hop), Thrilla (rap) and Ralph G. (R&B/pop).

◎ BIG J PRODUCTIONS

2516 S. Sugar Ridge, Laplace LA 70068. (504)652-2645. **Contact:** Frankie Jay, agent. Booking agency. Estab. 1968. Represents individual artists, groups and songwriters; currently handles over 50 acts. Receives 15-25% commission. Reviews material for acts.

How to Contact *Call first and obtain permission to submit* (office hours Monday-Friday: noon-5 pm). Prefers cassette or VHS videocassette with 3-6 songs and lyric or lead sheet. "It would be best for an artist to lip-sync to a prerecorded track. The object is for someone to see how an artist would perform more than simply assessing song content.'' Artists seeking management should include pictures, biography, tape or CD and video. Does not return material. Responds in 2 weeks.

Music Mostly **rock**, **pop** and **R&B**. Works primarily with groups with self-contained songwriters. Current acts include Zebra (original rock group), Crowbar (heavy metal) and Kyper (original dance).

✓ ◐ BISCUIT PRODUCTIONS INC.

3315 E. Russell Rd., H-117, Las Vegas NV 89120. (702)967-6016. Website: www.freestyleLLC.com. President: Steve Walker. Management firm. Estab. 1989. Represents individual artists and groups from anywhere; currently handles 3 acts. Receives 20% commission. Reviews material for acts.

How to Contact Submit demo tape by mail. Prefers cassette or VHS videocassette. Does not return material. Responds in 2 months.

Music Mostly **rap**, **R&B** and **dance**; also **pop** and **alternative**. Current acts include Jamariah, Biscuit and Brand X.

ⓝ ◑ BLACK STALLION COUNTRY, INC.

P.O. Box 368, Tujunga CA 91043. (818)487-9863. Fax: (818)487-9803. E-mail: bscmgmt@aol.com. **Contact:** Kenn E. Kingsbury, Jr., president. Management firm, production company and music publisher (Black Stallion Country Publishing/BMI). Estab. 1979. Represents individual artists from anywhere; currently handles 20 acts. Receives 15-20% commission. Reviews material for acts.

How to Contact Submit demo tape by mail. Unsolicited submissions are OK. Prefers cassette with 3 songs and lyric sheet. If seeking management, press kit should include picture/résumé and audio and/or video tape. ''I would also like a one-page statement of goals and why you would be an asset to my company or me.'' Include SASE. Responds in 2 months.

Music Mostly **country**, **jazz** and **A/C**. Works primarily with country acts, variety acts and film/TV pictures/actors. Current acts include Lane Brody (singer country), Thom Bresh (musician), Rebecca Holden (actress/singer).

◐ BLANK & BLANK

1 Belmont Ave., Suite 320, Bala Cynwyd PA 19004-1604. (610)664-8200. Fax: (610)664-8201. **Contact:** E. Robert Blank, manager. Management firm. Represents individual artists and groups. Reviews material for acts.

How to Contact *Contact first and obtain permission to submit.* Prefers videocassette. If seeking management, press kit should include cover letter, demo tape/CD and video. Does not return material.

◐ BLOWIN' SMOKE PRODUCTIONS/RECORDS

7438 Shoshone Ave., Van Nuys CA 91406-2340. (818)881-9888. Fax: (818)881-0555. E-mail: blowinsmokeband @ktb.net. Website: www.blowinsmokeband.com. **Contact:** Larry Knight, president. Management firm and record producer. Estab. 1990. Represents local and West Coast individual artists and groups; currently handles 6 acts. Receives 15-20% commission. Reviews material for acts.

  • Also see the listing for Hailing Frequency Music Productions in the Record Producers section of this book.

How to Contact *Write or call first and obtain permission to submit.* Prefers cassette or CD. If seeking management, press kit should include cover letter, demo tape/CD, lyric sheets, press clippings, video if available, photo, bios, contact telephone numbers and any info on legal commitments already in place. Include SASE. Responds in 1 month.

Music Mostly **R&B**, **blues** and **blues-rock**. Works primarily with single and group vocalists and a few R&B/blues bands. Current acts include Larry ''Fuzzy'' Knight (blues singer/songwriter), King Floyd (R&B artist), The Blowin' Smoke Rhythm & Blues Band, The Fabulous Smokettes, and Joyce Lawson.

◙ THE BLUE CAT AGENCY

P.O. Box 4036, San Rafael CA 94913-4036. Phone/fax: (415)713-2538. E-mail: bluecat_agency@yahoo.com. Website: www.geocities.com/bluecat_agency. **Contact:** Karen Kindig, owner/agent. Management firm and booking agency. Estab. 1989. Represents individual artists and/or groups from anywhere; currently handles 2 acts. Receives 10-15% commission. Reviews material for acts.

How to Contact **E-mail only for permission to submit.** Prefers cassette or CD. If seeking management, press kit should include demo, CD or tape, bio, press clippings and photo. SASE. Responds in 2 months.

Music Mostly **rock/pop** ''en español'' and **jazz/latin jazz**. Works primarily with bands. Current acts include Kai Eckhardt, Alejandro Santos, Ania Paz, Gabriel Rosati.

◑ BLUE WAVE PRODUCTIONS

3221 Perryville Rd., Baldwinsville NY 13027. (315)638-4286. Fax: (315)635-4757. E-mail: bluewave@localnet.com. Website: www.bluewaverecords.com. **Contact:** Greg Spencer, owner/president. Management firm, music publisher (G.W. Spencer Music/ASCAP), record company (Blue Wave Records) and record producer (Blue

Wave Productions). Estab. 1985. Represents individual artists and/or groups and songwriters from anywhere; currently handles 5 acts. Receives 10% commission. Reviews material for acts.

• Also see the listing for Blue Wave in the Record Companies section of this book.

How to Contact Submit demo tape by mail. Unsolicited submissions are OK. Prefers CD or VHS videocassette with 3-6 songs. "Just the music first, reviews and articles are OK. No photos or lyrics until later." If seeking management, press kit should include cover letter and demo tape/CD. Include SASE. Responds in 1 month. No phone calls.

Music Mostly **blues**, **blues/rock** and **roots rock**. Current acts include Kim Lembo (female blues vocalist), Kim Simmonds (blues guitarist and singer/songwriter) and Downchild Bluesband (blues).

Tips "I'm looking for great singers with soul. Not interested in pop/rock commercial material."

☑ ◎ BOUQUET-ORCHID ENTERPRISES

P.O. Box 1335, Norcross GA 30091. (770)339-9088. **Contact:** Bill Bohannon, president. Management firm, booking agency, music publisher (Orchid Publishing/BMI) and record company (Bouquet Records). Represents individuals and groups; currently handles 3 acts. Receives 10-15% commission. Reviews material for acts.

• Also see the listing for Orchid Publishing in the Music Publishers section of this book.

How to Contact Submit demo tape by mail. Unsolicited submissions are OK. Prefers cassette, CD or videocassette with 3-5 songs, song list and lyric sheet. Include brief résumé. If seeking management, press kit should include current photograph, 2-3 media clippings, description of act, and background information on act. Include SASE. Responds in 1 month.

Music Mostly **country**, **rock** and **top 40/pop**; also **gospel** and **R&B**. Works primarily with vocalists and groups. Current acts include Susan Spencer, Jamey Wells, Adam Day and the Bandoleers.

◎ BREAD & BUTTER PRODUCTIONS

P.O. Box 1539, Wimberley TX 78676. (512)301-7117. E-mail: steve@cyberhouse.com. **Contact:** Steve Gladson, managing partner. Management firm and booking agency. Estab. 1969. Represents individual artists, songwriters and groups from anywhere; currently handles 6 acts. Receives 10-20% commission. Reviews material for acts.

How to Contact Submit demo tape by mail. Unsolicited submissions OK. Prefers cassette, videocassette or CD and lyric sheet. If seeking management, press kit should include cover letter, demo tape/CD, lyric sheets, press clippings, video, résumé, picture and bio. Does not return material. Responds in 1 month.

Music Mostly **alternative rock**, **country** and **R&B**; also **classic rock**, **folk** and **Americana**. Works primarily with singer/songwriters and original bands. Current acts include Lou Cabaza (songwriter/producer/manager), Duck Soup (band) and Gaylan Ladd (songwriter/singer).

Tips "Remember why you are in this biz. The art comes first."

☑ ◎ BROTHERS MANAGEMENT ASSOCIATES

141 Dunbar Ave., Fords NJ 08863. (732)738-0880. Fax: (732)738-0970. E-mail: bmaent@yahoo.com. Website: www.bmaent.com. **Contact:** Allen A. Faucera, president. Management firm and booking agency. Estab. 1972. Represents artists, groups and songwriters; currently handles 25 acts. Receives 15-20% commission. Reviews material for acts.

How to Contact *Write first and obtain permission to submit.* Prefers cassette/CD or VHS videocassette with 3-6 songs and lyric sheets. Include photographs and résumé. If seeking management, include photo, bio, tape and return envelope in press kit. Include SASE. Responds in 2 months.

Music Mostly **pop**, **rock**, **MOR** and **R&B**. Works primarily with vocalists and established groups. Current acts include Nils Lofgren and Danny Federici.

Tips "Submit very commercial material—make demo of high quality."

◎ BILL BUTLER MUSIC

P.O. Box 20, Hondo TX 78861-0020. Phone/fax: (830)426-2112. E-mail: billbmusic@aol.com. Owner: Bill Butler. Management firm and music publisher. Estab. 1982. Represents individual artists and songwriters; currently handles 2 acts. Receives 15% commission. Reviews material for acts.

• They have received a special Citation of Achievement from BMI for One Million Air Plays of "Baby Blue" and Two Million Air Plays "Love Without End, Amen" by George Strait.

How to Contact Submit demo by mail. Unsolicited submissions are OK. Prefers cassette or CD with 3 songs and lyric sheet. If seeking management, press kit should include bio, photo, tape or CD with 5 unreleased songs. "No cover tunes please." Does not return material. Responds in 3 months only if interested.

Music Mostly **country**, **R&B** and **tejano**. Works primarily with singer/songwriters and songwriters. Current acts include Frank Solesbee (country) and Keith Lutz (country).

Tips "Send quality demos that allow the lyric to be clearly understood. Include lyric sheets. Make sure your name, address and phone number are on both tape or CD and J-card. Don't try to contact us—we will contact you if we're interested.''

⊕ Ⓜ BUXTON WALKER P/L

(formerly Mr. Walker's Company), P.O. Box 2197, St. Kilda West, Vic 3182 Australia. Phone: (+61)3 9537-7155. Fax: (+61)3 9537-7166. E-mail: andrew@buxtonwalker.com. Website: www.buxtonwalker.com. **Contact:** Andrew Walker. Management firm, music publisher (Head Records Publishing) and record company (Head Records). Estab. 1995. Represents individual artists and groups from anywhere; currently handles 5 acts. Management company receives 20% commission.

How to Contact Submit demo by mail. Unsolicited submissions are OK. CD only. If seeking management, press kit should include CD, bio and history. Please ensure submission is accompanied with clear notice detailing reason for submission. ''Processing takes time. Contact by fax or e-mail is best as it allows for time differences to be no obstacle.'' SAE and IRC. Responds in 2 months.

Music Mostly **rock/pop**, **jazz** and **acoustic**; also **reggae**, **blues** and **world**. No mainstream pop. Works primarily with singers/songwriters and bands. Current acts include The Jaynes (rock), Black Sorrows (blues and jazz), The Revelators (blues), Tess McKenna (alt rock) and Jen Anderson (scores).

Tips ''We have low need for songs to be supplied to our artists. We are mostly interested in recorded artists/writers looking for distribution/release in Australia/New Zealand.''

⊕ Ⓞ CIRCUIT RIDER TALENT & MANAGEMENT CO.

123 Walton Ferry Rd., Hendersonville TN 37075. (615)824-1947. Fax: (615)264-0462. E-mail: dotwool@bellsouth.net. **Contact:** Linda S. Dotson, president. Consultation firm, booking agency and music publisher (Channel Music, Cordial Music, Dotson & Dotson Music Publishers, Shalin Music Co.). Represents individual artists, songwriters and actors; currently handles 10 acts. Works with a large number of recording artists, songwriters, actors, producers. (Includes the late multi-Grammy-winning producer/writer Skip Scarborough.) Receives 10-15% commission (union rates). Reviews material for acts (free of charge).

How to Contact *Write or call first and obtain permission to submit.* Prefers cassette or videocassette with 3 songs and lyric sheet. If seeking consultation, press kit should include bio, cover letter, résumé, lyric sheets if original songs, photo and tape with 3 songs. Videocassettes required of artist's submissions. Include SASE. Responds in 2 months.

Music Mostly **Latin blues**, **pop**, **country** and **gospel**; also **R&B** and **comedy**. Works primarily with vocalists, special concerts, movies and TV. Current acts include Razzy Bailey (award winning blues artist/writer), Clint Walker (actor/recording artist) and Ben Calder (comedy/novelty).

Tips ''Artists, have your act together. Have a full press kit, videos and be professional. Attitudes are a big factor in my agreeing to work with you (no egotists). This is a business, and we will be building your career.''

☑ Ⓞ CLASS ACT PRODUCTIONS/MANAGEMENT

P.O. Box 55252, Sherman Oaks CA 91413. (818)980-1039. Fax: (603)710-5527. E-mail: pkimmel@gr8gizmo.com. **Contact:** Peter Kimmel, president. Management firm. Estab. 1985. Currently handles 2 acts. Receives 20% commission. Reviews material for acts.

How to Contact Submit demo CD by mail. Unsolicited submissions are OK. Include cover letter, bio, lyric sheets (essential), CD in press kit. Include SASE. Responds in 1 month.

Music All styles. Current acts include Terpsichore (cyber dance/pop), Karma (classic-style rock).

Ⓞ CLOCKWORK ENTERTAINMENT MANAGEMENT AGENCY

227 Concord St., Haverhill MA 01830. (978)373-5677. E-mail: wjm227@hotmail.com. **Contact:** William J. Macek, esq., entertainment attorney, president. Management firm. Represents groups and songwriters throughout New England with mastered product who are looking for label deals and licensing in US and internationally. Fee is negotiated individually; currently handles multiple acts. Commissions vary. Reviews material for acts.

How to Contact Submit demo by mail. Unsolicited submissions are OK. Prefers cassette or CD with 3-12 songs. ''Also submit promotion and cover letter with interesting facts about yourself.'' If seeking management, press kit should include cover letter, tape or CD, photo, bio and press clippings. Include SASE. Responds in 1 month.

Music Mostly **rock (all types)** and **top 40/pop**. Works primarily with bar bands and original acts.

Ⓞ CLOUSHER PRODUCTIONS

P.O. Box 1191, Mechanicsburg PA 17055. (717)766-7644. Fax: (717)766-1490. E-mail: clousher@webtv.net. Website: www.clousherentertainment.com. **Contact:** Fred Clousher, owner. Booking agency and production company. Estab. 1972. Represents groups from anywhere; currently handles over 100 acts.

How to Contact Submit demo tape by mail. Unsolicited submissions are OK. Prefers VHS videocassette. If seeking management, press kit should include press clippings, testimonials, credits, glossies, video demo tape, references, cover letter, résumé and bio. Does not return material. "Performer should check back with us!"

Music Mostly **country**, **old rock** and **ethnic** (German, Hawaiian, etc.); also **dance bands** (regional) and **classical musicals**. "We work mostly with country, old time R&R, regional variety dance bands, tribute acts, and all types of variety acts." Current acts include Jasmine Morgan (country/pop vocalist), Robin Right (country vocalist) and Island Breeze (ethnic Hawaiian group).

Tips "The songwriters we work with are entertainers themselves, which is the aspect we deal with. They usually have bands or do some sort of show, either with tracks or live music. We engage them for stage shows, dances, strolling, etc. We do not publish music or submit performers to recording companies for contracts. We strictly set up live performances for them."

☑ CONCEPT 2000 INC.

P.O. Box 2950, Columbus OH 43216-2950. (614)276-2000. Fax: (614)275-0163. Florida office: P.O. Box 2070, Largo FL 33779-2070. (727)585-2922. Fax: (727)585-3835. E-mail: info2k@concept2k.com. Website: www.concept2k.com. **Contact:** Brian Wallace, president. Management firm and booking agency. Estab. 1981. Represents international individual artists, groups and songwriters; currently handles 4 acts. Receives 20% commission. Reviews material for acts.

How to Contact Submit demo tape by mail. Unsolicited submissions are OK. Prefers cassette with 4 songs. If seeking management, include demo tape, press clips, photo and bio. Does not return material. Responds in 2 weeks.

Music Mostly **country**, **gospel** and **pop**; also **jazz**, **R&B** and **soul**. Current acts include Bryan Hitch (contemporary gospel), Shades of Grey (R&B/soul), Dwight Lenox (show group) and Gene Walker (jazz).

Tips "Send quality songs with lyric sheets. Production quality is not necessary."

☑ CONCERTED EFFORTS, INC./FOGGY DAY MUSIC

P.O. Box 600099, Newtonville MA 02460. (617)969-0810. Fax: (617)969-6761. Website: www.concertedefforts.com. Owner: Paul Kahn. Management firm, booking agency and music publisher (Foggy Day Music). Represents individual artists, groups and songwriters from anywhere. Commission varies. Reviews material for acts.

How to Contact Submit demo tape by mail. Unsolicited submissions are OK *"but call first!"* Prefers CD, will accept cassette, with lyric sheet. "No management submissions." Does not return material.

Music **Folk**, **country** and **rock**; also **world music**, **zydeco** and **blues**. Current acts include Luther Johnson (blues singer), Holmes Brothers, Roseanne Cash and Orchestra Baobab.

Tips "Simple recorded demo is OK, with lyrics."

☑ CONSCIENCE MUSIC

P.O. Box 617667, Chicago IL 60661. (312)226-4858. E-mail: towrecords@aol.com. **Contact:** Karen M. Smith, consultant/personal manager. Management firm, Studio S and record company (TOW Records). Estab. 1985. Represents individual artists, groups and songwriters from anywhere; currently handles 1 act. Receives 20% commission.

How to Contact *Write first and obtain permission to submit.* Prefers CD with 2-3 songs and lyric sheet. If seeking management, info should include demo CD, lyric sheets, list of performance locations, and letter with band or artist objectives. "Cannot overemphasize the importance of having objectives you are ready to discuss with us." Include SASE. Responds in 4 months.

Music Mostly **rock** and **pop**; also **visual artists**, **writers** and **models**. Works primarily with indie bands in the States and Great Britain. Currently represents Lance Porter (drummer with the Flash Express). "Many clients are on a consulting basis only."

☑ ☑ COUNTRYWIDE PRODUCERS

2466 Wildon Dr., York PA 17403. (717)741-2658. E-mail: cwpent@wmconnect.com. **Contact:** Bob Englar, president. Booking agency. Represents individuals and groups; currently handles 8 acts. Receives 15% commission. Reviews material for acts.

How to Contact Query or submit demo tape by mail. Unsolicited submissions are OK. If seeking management, press kit should include photo and demo tape. Include SASE. Responds in 1 week.

Music Bluegrass, blues, classical, country and disco; also folk, gospel, jazz, polka, rock (light), soul and top 40/pop. Works primarily with show bands. Current acts include The Walls of Time (bluegrass), The W. Va. Connections (bluegrass), Shilha Ridge (bluegrass) and Iron Ridge (bluegrass).

☐ STEPHEN COX PROMOTIONS & MANAGEMENT

6708 Mammoth Ave., Van Nuys CA 91405. (818)377-4530. Fax: (818)782-5305. E-mail: stephencox@earthlink.net. **Contact:** Stephen Cox, president. Management firm. Estab. 1993. Represents individual artists, groups or songwriters from anywhere; currently handles 5 acts. Receives 15% commission. Reviews material for acts.

How to Contact *Call first and obtain permission to submit.* Prefers cassette or CD. If seeking management, press kit should include biographies, performance history and radio play. "Include a clear definition of goals in a thoughtful presentation." Include SASE. Responds in 2 weeks.

Music Mostly **rock**, **New Age/world** and **alternative**; also **blues**, **folk** and **progressive**. Works primarily with bands. Current acts include Joe Sherbanee (jazz), Val Ewell & Pulse (blues rock), Paul Micich & Mitch Espe (New Age/jazz), Covet (metal) and Jill Cohn (folk rock).

Tips "Establish goals based on research, experience and keep learning about the music business. Start the business as though it will always be you as an independent. Establish a foundation before considering alternative commitments. We aim to educate and consult to a level that gives an artist the freedom of choice to choose whether to go to the majors etc., or retain independence. Remember, promote, promote and promote some more. Always be nice to people, treat them as you would wish to be treated."

🌐 🖉 CRANIUM MANAGEMENT

P.O. Box 240, Annandale NSW 2038 Australia. E-mail: cranium@smartchat.net.au. Manager: Peter "Skip" Beaumont-Edmonds. Management firm. Estab. 1992. Represents individual artists, groups and songwriters from anywhere; currently handles 5 acts. Receives 20% commission. Reviews material for acts.

How to Contact *E-mail first and obtain permission to submit.* Send "The minimum number of best songs—don't waste money on being elaborate. Talent will show through. Be sensible—if it doesn't suit us don't send it." If seeking management, press kit should include photo (optional), demo tape, press clippings (minimal), bio and cover letter. Does not return material. Responds in 1 month.

Music Mostly **alternative** and **pop**; also **country**. Works primarily with pop/rock, alternative bands and singer/songwriters. Current acts include Dog Trumpet (alternative roots duo), Adam Harvey (country singer), David Mason-Cox (singer/songwriter), Karl Broadie (singer/songwriter), Rebecca Lavelle (singer) and Jane Walker (singer/songwriter).

🖉 CRAWFISH PRODUCTIONS

P.O. Box 5412, Buena Park CA 90620. (909)941-8216. E-mail: swampbasque@msn.com. Producer: Leo J. Eiffert, Jr. Management firm, music publisher (Young Country/BMI), record producer (Leo J. Eiffert) and record company (Plain Country Records). Estab. 1968. Represents local and international individual artists and songwriters; currently handles 4 acts. Commission received is open. Reviews material for acts.

- Also see the listings for Young Country Records/Plain Country Records in the Record Companies section of this book and Leo J. Eiffert, Jr. in the Record Producers section of this book.

How to Contact Submit demo tape by mail. Unsolicited submissions are OK. Prefers cassette with 2-3 songs and lyric sheet. Include SASE. Responds in 3 weeks.

Music Mostly **country** and **gospel**. Works primarily with vocalists. Current acts include Pigeons, Southern Spirit and Nashville Snakes.

☑ ◻ CREATIVE STAR MANAGEMENT

P.O. Gox 683, Lima OH 45802. E-mail: Just_chilling_2002@yahoo.com. President/Owner: James Milligan. Vice President: Sonya Koger. Management firm, booking agency, music publisher (Party House Publishing/BMI, A New Rap Jam Publishing/ASCAP), record company (New Experience Records/Grand Slam Records). Estab. 1989. Represents individual artists, groups and songwriters from anywhere; currently handles 6 acts. Receives 15-20% commission. Reviews material for acts.

- Creative Star Management's publishing company, A New Rap Jam Publishing (ASCAP), is listed in the Music Publishers section, and their record label, New Experience Records/Grand Slam Records, is listed in the Record Companies section.

How to Contact *Contact first and obtain permission to submit.* Prefers cassette, VHS, or DVD with 3-5 songs and lyric sheet. If seeking management, press kit should include press clippings, bios, résumé, 8×10 glossy photo, any information that will support material and artist. Include SASE. Responds in 6 weeks.

Music Mostly **R&B**, **pop** and **country**; also **rap**, **contemporary gospel** and **soul/funk**. Current acts include T.M.C. (gospel), James Junior (r&b singer) and Dennis Esapa (rap).

Tips "We are seeking '70s and '80s groups looking to re-sign and for management. Please include any releases of recordings and videos in support of all materials. Rap artists—we want clean positive material! Thanks."

◻ D&R ENTERTAINMENT

308 N. Park, Broken Bow OK 74728. (580)584-9429. **Contact:** Don Walton, president. Management firm. Estab. 1985. Represents individual artists from anywhere; currently handles 2 acts. Receives 15% commission. Reviews material for acts. Also reviews for other country singers.

How to Contact Submit demo tape by mail. Unsolicited submissions are OK. Prefers cassette and videocassette with lyric and lead sheet. If seeking management, press kit should include brief background of artist, videotape of performance, cover letter, résumé, photo, press clippings and cassette or CD. "Indicate whether you have any financial or prospective financial backing." Does not return material. Responds in 3 months.

Music Mostly **contemporary Christian**; also **country** and **pop**. Works primarily with young beginning singers. Current acts include Kristi Reed (positive country) and Thomas Wells (contemporary Christian).

Tips "I need songs (country) that would fit a young singer under 20. In other words no drinking, cheating, marrying songs. A pretty tough choice. Also Christian contemporary songs."

🌑 DAS COMMUNICATIONS, LTD.
83 Riverside Dr., New York NY 10024. (212)877-0400. Fax: (212)595-0176. Management firm. Estab. 1975. Represents individual artists, groups and producers from anywhere; currently handles 25 acts. Receives 20% commission.

How to Contact Responds in 2 months. Prefers demo with 3 songs, lyric sheet and photo. Does not return material.

Music Mostly **rock, pop, R&B, alternative** and **hip-hop**. Current acts include Joan Osborne (rock), Wyclef Jean (hip-hop), Black Eyed Peas (hip-hop), Spin Doctors (rock), Diana King (pop), The Bacon Brothers (rock), Bone Thugs & Harmony (hip-hop).

☑ 🄯 DCA PRODUCTIONS
330 W. 38th St., Suite 904, New York NY 10018. (212)245-2063. Fax: (212)245-2367. Website: www.dcaproducti ons.com. **Contact:** Jennifer LaPlaca, office manager. President: Daniel Abrahamsen. Vice President: Geraldine Abrahamsen. Management firm. Estab. 1975. Represents individual artists, groups and songwriters from anywhere; currently handles 14 acts.

How to Contact If seeking management, press kit should include cover letter, bio, photo, demo tape/CD and video. Prefers cassette or VHS videocassette with 2 songs. "All materials are reviewed and kept on file for future consideration. Does not return material. We respond only if interested."

Music Mostly **acoustic, rock** and **mainstream**; also **cabaret** and **theme**. Works primarily with acoustic singer/ songwriters, top 40 or rock bands. Current acts include Gabrielle (singer/songwriter), Sean Altman (singer/ songwriter) and 1910 Fruitgum Company (oldies band).

Tips "Please do not call for a review of material."

☑ 🌑 THE EDWARD DE MILES COMPANY
28 E. Jackson Bldg., 10th Floor, #S627, Chicago IL 60604-2263. (773)509-6381. Fax: (312)922-6964. Website: www.edmsahara.com. **Contact:** Edward de Miles, president. Management firm, booking agency, entertainment/ sports promoter and TV/radio broadcast producer. Estab. 1984. Represents film, television, radio and musical artists; currently handles 15 acts. Receives 10-20% commission. Reviews material for acts. Regional operations in Chicago, Dallas, Houston and Nashville through marketing representatives. Licensed A.F. of M. booking agent.
   • Also see listings for Edward De Miles in the Music Publishers and Record Producers sections, and Sahara Records and Filmworks Entertainment in the Record Companies section of this book.

How to Contact *Does not accept unsolicited materials.* Prefers cassette with 3-5 songs, 8x10 b&w photo, bio and lyric sheet. "Copyright all material before submitting." If seeking management, include cover letter, bio, demo cassette with 3-5 songs, 8×10 b&w photo, lyric sheet, press clippings and video if available in press kit. Include SASE. Does not return material. Responds in 1 month.

Music Mostly **country, dance, R&B/soul, rock, top 40/pop** and **urban contemporary**; also looking for material for television, radio and film productions. Works primarily with dance bands and vocalists. Current acts include Steve Lynn (R&B/dance), Multiple Choice (rap) and D'von Edwards (jazz).

Tips "Performers need to be well prepared with their presentations (equipment, showmanship a must)."

○ DMR AGENCY
Galleries of Syracuse, Suite 250, Syracuse NY 13202-2416. (315)475-2500. E-mail: david@dmrbooking.com. Website: www.dmrbooking.com. **Contact:** David M. Rezak. Booking agency. Represents individuals and groups; currently handles 50 acts. Receives 15% commission.

How to Contact Submit demo tape by mail. Unsolicited submissions are OK. Submit cassette or videocassette with 1-4 songs and press kit. Does not return material.

Music Mostly **rock (all styles), pop** and **blues**. Works primarily with cover bands. Current acts include Prime Time (R&B), Tom Townsley and the Backsliders (blues) and Los Blancos (blues).

Tips "You might want to contact us if you have a cover act in our region. Many songwriters in our area have a cover group in order to make money."

◩ ⊘ EAO MUSIC CORPORATION OF CANADA

P.O. Box 1240, Station "M," Calgary AB T2P 2L2 Canada. (403)228-9388. Fax: (403) 229-3598. E-mail: eao@telu splanet.net. Website: www.oliverio.ca. **Contact:** Edmund A. Oliverio, president. Management firm and record company. Estab. 1985. Represents individual artists, groups and songwriters from western Canada (aboriginal artists); currently handles 52 acts. Receives 15-20% commission. Reviews material for acts.

How to Contact Submit demo tape by mail. Unsolicited submissions are OK. Prefers cassette with 3 songs and lyric and lead sheets. If seeking management, press kit should include cover letter, résumé, b&w glossy photo, cassette tape, bio, media clippings and list of venues and festivals performed. SAE and IRC. Responds in 2 weeks.

Music Mostly **folk** and **native (aboriginal)**; also **rock**. Works primarily with singer/songwriters. Current acts include Activate (funky reggae), Feeding Like Butterflies (folk rock/Celtic), Katrina (country/folk) and Gloria K. MacRae (adult contemporary).

Tips "Be upfront and honest. Establish your long term goals and short term goals. Have you joined your music associations (i.e., CMA, etc.)? Recent demand for cowboy artists rather than country."

◻ THE ELLIS INTERNATIONAL TALENT AGENCY

5617 W. Melvina, Milwaukee WI 53216. Phone/fax: (414)444-3385. **Contact:** Darnell Ellis, CEO/president. Management firm, booking agency, music publisher (Ellis Island Music/ASCAP) record company (Safire Records) and record producer (Darnell Ellis). Estab. 1997. Represents individual artists, groups and songwriters from anywhere; currently handles 1 act. Receives 15-20% commission. Reviews material for acts.

● Also see the listing for Safire Records in the Record Companies section of this book.

How to Contact Submit demo tape by mail. Unsolicited submissions are OK. Prefers cassette or videocassette with 4-6 songs and press kit. If seeking management, press kit should include cassette tape or CD with 4-6 songs (demo), 8×10 photo, video tape and reviews. Does not return material. Responds in 6 weeks. "We will respond only if we are interested."

Music Mostly **country**, **pop**, **mainstream pop**, **rock** (all styles) and anything else except rap and hip-hop. Works primarily with singers, singer/songwriters, songwriters and bands. Current acts include Tracy Beck (acoustic, roots, blues, alt. country, pop, swing).

Ⓝ ◻ ENDANGERED SPECIES ARTIST MANAGEMENT

4 Berachah Ave., South Nyack NY 10960-4202. (845)353-4001. Fax: (845)353-4332. E-mail: muzik@jerizon.net. Website: www.musicandamerica.com. President: Fred Porter. Vice President: Suzanne Buckley. Management firm. Estab. 1979. Represents individual artists, groups and songwriters from anywhere; currently handles 3 acts. Receives 20% commission. Reviews material for acts.

How to Contact *Call first and obtain permission to submit.* Prefers CD with 3 or more songs and lyric sheet. "Please include a demo of your music, a clear, recent photograph as well as any current press, if any. A cover letter indicating at what stage in your career you are and expectations for your future. Please label the cassette and/or CD with your name and address as well as the song titles." If seeking management, press kit should include cover letter, bio, photo, demo/CD, lyric sheet and press clippings. Include SASE. Responds in 6 weeks.

Music Mostly **pop**, **rock** and **world**; also **Latin/heavy metal**, **R&B**, **jazz** and **instrumental**. Current acts include Jason Wilson & Tabarruk (pop/reggae, nominated for Juno award 2001), and Anna (teen singer).

Tips "Listen to everything, classical to country, old to contemporary, to develop an understanding of many writing styles. Write with many other partners to keep the creativity fresh. Don't feel your style will be ruined by taking a class or a writing seminar. We all process moods and images differently. This leads to uniqueness in the music."

◻ SCOTT EVANS PRODUCTIONS

P.O. Box 814028, Hollywood FL 33081-4028. (954)963-4449. E-mail: evansprod@aol.com. Website: www.theen tertainmentmall.com. **Contact:** Ted Jones, new artists. Management firm and booking agency. Estab. 1979. Represents local, regional or international individual artists, groups, songwriters, comedians, novelty acts and dancers; currently handles over 150 acts. Receives 10-50% commission. Reviews material for acts.

How to Contact Submit demo tape by mail. Unsolicited submissions are OK. Prefers cassette and/or ½″ video-cassette with 3 songs. If seeking management, include picture, résumé, flyers, cassette or video tape. Does not return material.

Music Mostly **pop**, **R&B** and **Broadway**. Deals with "all types of entertainers; no limitations." Current acts include Scott Evans and Company (variety song and dance), Dorit Zinger (female vocalist), Jeff Geist, Actors Repertory Theatre, Entertainment Express, Perfect Parties, Joy Deco (dance act), Flashback 2000 Revue (musical song and dance), Everybody Salsa (Latin song and dance) and Around the World (international song and dance).

Tips "Submit a neat, well put together, organized press kit."

☑ ◐ EXCLESISA BOOKING AGENCY

716 Windward Rd., Jackson MS 39206. Phone/fax: (601)366-0220. E-mail: exclesis@bellsouth.net. Website: www.exclesisabooking.com. **Contact:** Roy and Esther Wooten, booking managers/owners. Booking agency. Estab. 1989. Represents groups from anywhere; currently handles 8 acts. Receives 15% commission. Reviews material for acts.

How to Contact *Call first and obtain permission to submit.* Submit demo tape by mail. Unsolicited submissions are OK. Prefers CD or videocassette. If seeking management, press kit should include CD or cassette, videocassette, pictures, address and telephone contact and bio. Does not return material. Responds in 2 months.

Music Gospel only. Current acts include Slim & The Supreme Angels, The Pilgrim Jubilees, Spencer Taylor & the Highway QC's, Evangelist Bertha Jackson, The Annointed Jackson Singers, The Southern Sons and David R. Curry, Jr.

Tips "Make sure your demo is clear with a good sound so the agent can make a good judgement."

☑ ◐ S.L. FELDMAN & ASSOCIATES

1505 W. Second Ave. #200, Vancouver BC V6H 3Y4 Canada. (604)734-5945. Fax: (604)732-0922. E-mail: feldman@slfa.com. Website: www.slfa.com. Management firm and booking agency. Estab. 1970. Represents mostly Canadian artists and groups; currently handles over 200 acts.

How to Contact *Write or call first to obtain permission to submit a demo.* Prefers CD, photo and bio. If seeking management, include video in press kit. SAE and IRC. Responds in 2 months.

Music Current acts include Bryan Adams, The Chieftains, Joni Mitchell, Anne Murray, Sarah McLachlan, Diana Krall, Martina McBride, Barenaked Ladies, Norah Jones, Swollen Members and Nelly Furtado.

◐ FRED T. FENCHEL ENTERTAINMENT AGENCY

2104 S. Jefferson Avenue, Mason City IA 50401. (641)423-4177. Fax: (641)423-8662. **Contact:** Fred T. Fenchel, president. Booking agency. Estab. 1964. Represents local and international individual artists and groups; currently handles up to 10 acts. Receives 20% commission.

How to Contact Submit demo tape by mail. Unsolicited submissions are OK. Prefers cassette or videocassette. Does not return material. Responds in 3 weeks.

Music Mostly **country**, **pop** and some **gospel**. Works primarily with dance bands and show groups; "artists we can use on club dates, fairs, etc." Current acts include New Odyssey (comedy & music), Nerness Family (family, variety music) and The Buck Hollow Band (duo, huge variety of music). "We deal primarily with established name acts with recording contracts, or those with a label and starting into popularity."

Tips "Be honest. Don't submit unless your act is exceptional rather than just starting out, amateurish and with lyrics that are written under the pretense of coming from qualified writers."

☑ ◐ B.C. FIEDLER MANAGEMENT

53 Seton Park Rd., Toronto ON M3C 3Z8 Canada. (416)421-4421. Fax: (416)421-0442. E-mail: info@bcfiedler.com. **Contact:** B.C. Fiedler/Alysha Main. Management firm, music publisher (B.C. Fiedler Publishing) and record company (Sleeping Giant Music Inc.). Estab. 1964. Represents individual artists, groups and songwriters from anywhere; currently handles 3 acts. Receives 20-25% or consultant fees. Reviews material for acts.

How to Contact *Call first and obtain permission to submit.* Prefers CD or VHS videocassette with 3 songs and lyric sheet. If seeking management, press kit should include bio, list of concerts performed in past 2 years including name of venue, repertoire, reviews and photos. Does not return material. Responds in 2 months.

Music Mostly **classical/crossover**, **voice** and **pop**. Works primarily with classical/crossover ensembles, instrumental soloists, operatic voice and pop singer/songwriters. Current acts include Liona Boyd (classical guitar) and Pavlo (instrumental).

Tips "Invest in demo production using best quality voice and instrumentalists. If you write songs, hire the vocal talent to best represent your work. Submit CD and lyrics. Artists should follow up 6-8 weeks after submission."

⊕ ◐ FIRST TIME MANAGEMENT

Sovereign House, 12 Trewartha Rd., Praa Sands-Penzance, Cornwall TR20 9ST England. Phone: (01736)762826. Fax: (01736)763328. E-mail: panamus@aol.com. Website: www.songwriters-guild.co.uk. **Contact:** Roderick G. Jones, managing director. Management firm, record company (First Time Records) and music publisher (First Time Music). Estab. 1986. Represents local, regional and international individual aritsts, groups and songwriters; currently handles 114 acts. Receives 15-25% commission. Reviews material for acts.

- Also see the listings for First Time Music (Publishing) in the Music Publishers section and First Time Records in the Record Companies section of this book.

How to Contact Submit demo tape by mail. Unsolicited submissions are OK. Prefers cassette, CD or VHS videocassette with 3 songs and lyric sheets. If seeking management, press kit should include cover letter, bio, photo, demo tape/CD, press clippings and anything relevant to make an impression. Does not return material. Responds in 1 month.

Music Mostly **dance**, **top 40**, **rap**, **country**, **gospel** and **pop**; also **all styles**. Works primarily with songwriters, composers, vocalists, groups and choirs. Current acts include Willow (pop), Animal Cruelty (indie/heavy thrash) and Peter Arnold (folk/roots).

Tips ''Become a member of the Guild of International Songwriters and Composers. Keep everything as professional as possible. Be patient and dedicated to your aims and objectives.''

ℕ ⊘ MITCHELL FOX MANAGEMENT INC.

212 3rd Ave. N., Nashville TN 37201. (615)259-0777. Fax: (615)259-0063. E-mail: mitchell@mitchellfox.com. **Contact:** Mitchell Fox, president. Management firm. Estab. 1980. Represents individual artists, groups and songwriters from anywhere; currently handles 2 acts. Receives 10-15% commission. Reviews material for acts.

How to Contact *Call or write first for permission to submit a demo.* Prefers cassette with 2 songs and lyric sheet. If seeking management, press kit should include music, pictures and press clippings. Does not return material. Responds in 1 month.

Music All styles.

✓ ⊘ ERIC GODTLAND MANAGEMENT, INC.

18352 160th Pl. SE, Renton WA 98058. (415)522-5292. Fax: (415)522-5293. **Contact:** Wayne Ledbetter, manager. Management firm. Estab. 1995. Represents individual artists, groups or songwriters from anywhere; currently handles 8 acts. Receives 20% commission. Reviews material for acts.

How to Contact Submit demo tape by mail. Unsolicited submissions are OK. Prefers CD. If seeking management, press kit should include brief information on how to reach you. Does not return material.

Music Mostly **pop**, **rock** and **hip-hop**. Works primarily with bands, producers and songwriters. Current acts include Third Eye Blind (pop, rock), Retrograde (pop, rock) and Dakona (pop, rock).

✓ ◯ GUESTSTAR ENTERTAINMENT AGENCY

17321 Ritchie Ave. NE, Sand Lake MI 49343-9475. (616)636-5068. Fax: (775)743-4169. E-mail: gueststarww@wingsisp.com. Website: www.mountainmanww.com. **Contact:** Raymond G. Dietz, Sr., president. Management firm, booking agency, music publisher (Sandlake Music/BMI), record company (Gueststar Records, Inc.), record producer and record distributor (Gueststar Music Distributors). Represents individual artists, groups, songwriters and bands from anywhere; currently handles 3 acts. Receives 20% commission. Reviews material for acts.

- Also see the listing for Gueststar Records in the Record Companies section of this book. Mr. Dietz is also the editor of several music books, including *Everything You Should Know Before You Get into the Music Business*.

How to Contact Submit demo tape by mail ''and include your contact information.'' Unsolicited submissions are OK. Prefers CD, cassette or VHS videocassette with unlimited songs, but send your best with lyric or lead sheet. If seeking management, press kit should include shoulder shot photo, demo tape, bio, music résumé and VHS videocassette (live on stage) if possible and press clippings. Returns material after 1 year if SASE and correct postage are included. Responds in 6 months.

Music Mostly **traditional country**. Current acts include DJ & The Dawgs (country band, traditional), Ikinoram (2 country singers, new country) and Dee Dee ''D'' (country singer, country rock).

✓ ⊘ GURLEY & CO.

P.O. Box 150657, Nashville TN 37215. (615)269-0474. Fax: (615)385-2052. E-mail: gurley@aol.com. Website: www.gurleybiz.com. President: Cathy Gurley. Vice President: Meagan Gurley. Management firm and public relations/marketing. Estab. 1985. Represents individual artists, groups and songwriters from anywhere; currently handles 8 acts. Receives 15% commission. Reviews material for acts.

How to Contact *No longer accepting unsolicited submissions.*

⊘ BILL HALL ENTERTAINMENT & EVENTS

138 Frog Hollow Rd., Churchville PA 18966-1031. (215)357-5189. Fax: (215)357-0320. **Contact:** William B. Hall III, owner/president. Booking agency and production company. Represents individuals and groups; currently handles 20-25 acts. Receives 15% commission. Reviews material for acts.

How to Contact Submit demo tape by mail. Unsolicited submissions are OK. Prefers cassette or videocassette of performance with 2-3 songs ''and photos, promo material and record or tape. We need quality material, preferably before a 'live' audience.'' Does not return material. Responds only if interested.

Music Marching band, circus and novelty. Works primarily with ''unusual or novelty attractions in musical line, preferably those that appeal to family groups.'' Current acts include Fralinger and Polish-American Philadelphia Championship Mummers String Bands (marching and concert group), ''Mr. Polynesian'' Show Band

and Hawaiian Revue (ethnic group), the "Phillies Whiz Kids Band" of Philadelphia Phillies Baseball team, Paul Richardson (Phillies' organist/entertainer), Mummermania Musical Quartet, Philadelphia German Brass Band (concert band), Vogelgesang Circus Calliope, Kromer's Carousel Band Organ, Reilly Raiders Drum & Bugle Corps, Hoebel Steam Calliope, Caesar Rodney Brass Band, Rohe Calliope, Philadelphia Police & Fire Pipes Band, Larry Rothbard's Circus Band and Tim Laushey Pep & Dance Band.

Tips "Please send whatever helps us to most effectively market the attraction and/or artist. Provide something that gives you a clear edge over others in your field!"

▨ ✇ HANSEN ENTERPRISES, LTD.

855 E. Twain #123411, Las Vegas NV 89109. (702)896-8115. Fax: (702)792-1363. **Contact:** J. Malcom Baird. Management firm. Estab. 1971. Represents individual artists, groups and songwriters from anywhere; currently handles 3 acts. Receives 15-25% commission "or contracted fee arrangement." Reviews material for acts. **How to Contact** Submit demo tape by mail. Unsolicited submissions are OK. Prefers cassette. Include SASE. Responds in 3 weeks. We are looking for potential *hit songs* only: top 40, pop and Spanish. From time to time we need music for TV shows, commercials and films. Send SASE for requirements, which change from time to time depending upon the project(s).

Music Mostly **'50s & '60s rock** and **Spanish adult contemporary**. Current acts include The Ronettes, Pilita Corrales (top selling female Spanish recording star), Mandrake and Carmen Soriano.

◻ HARDISON INTERNATIONAL ENTERTAINMENT CORPORATION

P.O. Box 1732, Knoxville TN 37901-1732. Phone: (865)688-8680 Fax: (865)219-8094 (after 7 pm). E-mail: alt1010@aol.com. **Contact:** Dennis K. Hardison, CEO/founder. Management firm, booking agency, music publisher (Denlatrin Music), record company (Denlatrin Records) and record producer. Estab. 1984. Represents individual artists from anywhere; currently handles 3 acts. Receives 20% commission. Reviews material for acts.

● This company has promoted acts including New Edition, Freddie Jackson, M.C. Lyte and Kool Moe Dee. **How to Contact** Submit demo tape by mail. Unsolicited submissions are OK. Prefers cassette or CD with 3 songs. If seeking management, press kit should include bio, promo picture and cassette. Does not return material. Responds in 6 weeks to the best material.

Music Mostly **R&B**, **hip-hop** and **rap**. Current acts include Dynamo (hip-hop), Shorti (r&b singer) and Triniti (record producer, Public Enemy).

Tips "We have an in-house production staff to critique your music."

✇ M. HARRELL & ASSOCIATES

5444 Carolina, Merrillville IN 46410. (219)887-8814. Fax: (480)345-2255. E-mail: mhmkbmgs95@hotmail.com. **Contact:** Mary Harrell, owner. Management firm and booking agency. Estab. 1984. Represents individual artists, groups, songwriters, all talents—fashion, dancers, etc.; currently handles 30-40 acts. Receives 10-20% commission. Reviews material for acts.

How to Contact *Call first and obtain permission to submit.* Submit demo tape by mail. Prefers cassette or videocassette with 2-3 songs. Send résumé, bio, photo, demo tape/CD and press clippings. "Keep it brief and current." Does not return material. Responds in 1 month.

Music All types, **country**, **R&B**, **jazz**, **gospel**, **Big Band**, **light rock** and **reggae**. Current acts include Bill Shelton & 11th Avenue ('50s rock & roll), Bang (R&B/jazz) and Retroactive.

Tips "The bands listed can and do tour in the U.S. and Europe (variety, mostly R&B, jazz and top 40) as well as the Chicagoland area. They get steady work and repeat business, because they are good and and beat their competition. We also manage showbands."

☑ ✇ HESFREE PRODUCTIONS & PUBLISHING COMPANY

3709 E. 29th, P.O. Box 1214, Bryan TX 77806-1214. (979)268-3263. Fax: (979)775-5261. E-mail: hesfreeprodandp ubco@yahoo.com. Website: http://home1.gte.net/jbhes/. CEO/Owner: Brenda M. Freeman-Heslip. Producer of songwriting: Jamie Heslip. VP/Director of A&R/Owner: Rochelle Heslip. Management agency, record producer and music publisher. Estab. 2001. Represents individual artists, groups, songwriters. Works with individual artists, regional artists in the Bryan, TX and Brazos Valley Area. Currently handles 8 acts. Receives 40% commission.

● Also see the listings for Hesfree Production & Publishing Company in the Music Publishers and Record Producers sections of this book.

How to Submit *We only accept material referred to us by a reputable industry source (manager, entertainment attorney, etc.)* Include CD/CDR with 10 songs and lyric sheet, lead sheet and cover letter. Send resume and updated application for a management firm. Does not return submissions. Responds in 6 weeks only if interested. "Make sure you are serious about your career choice. Only serious clients need to contact us."

Music Mostly **r&b**, gospel, **rap** and **rock**. Does not want country. "We strive to make our professional performing artists the most successful artists possible." Represents "Mike-Ray" Ray Brooks (R&B dancer and singer); Ralatraneka Mercer (R&B and rap singer); Vicki Diggs (R&B and rap singer).

Tips "Only contact our company if you are seriously considering the entertainment field as a job possibility. Only the seriously inclined clients need apply."

⬯ HORIZON MANAGEMENT INC.

P.O. Box 8770, Endwell NY 13762. (607)785-9120. Fax: (607)785-4516. E-mail: hmi67@aol.com. **Contact:** New Talent Department. Management firm, booking agency and concert promotion. Estab. 1967. Represents regional, national and international artists, groups and songwriters; currently handles over 1,500 acts. Receives 20% commission. Reviews material for acts.

How to Contact *Call first and obtain permission to submit.* Prefers CD, cassette or VHS videocassette with 1-4 songs and lead sheet. Send cover letter, résumé, lead sheets, photo, bio, lyric sheets, equipment list, demo tape/CD, video, press clippings, reviews, etc. Does not return material. Responds in 1 week.

Music All styles, originals or covers. Current acts include Pete Best Band (The Beatles original drummer), Queen Makedah (reggae from Africa) and Mafalda Nogueira (Bralian music/jazz).

⬯ HOT STEAMING COFFEE FILMS

(formerly Earth Tracks Artists Agency), 7522 Ave. T, #1, Brooklyn NY 11234. E-mail: enigpublus@aol.com. **Contact:** David Krinsky, managing director-artist relations. Management firm. Estab. 1990. Represents individual artists, groups and (rarely) songwriters; currently does not represent any act. Receives 12-20% commission.

How to Contact Submit demo CD by mail. Unsolicited submissions are OK. Prefers CD with original songs and must include lyrics sheet. If seeking management, press kit should include cover letter, bio, video (if available), 1 group photo, all lyrics with songs, a CD of original songs and the ages of the artists. "All submissions must include lyric sheets or material will not be heard." **Does not return material.** Responds in 1 month. "We will contact artist if interested." Include e-mail address for reply. **No MP3 files!** Songs must be copyrighted to submit!

Music Commercial rock (all kinds), **pop** and **alternative** acoustic only. Absolutely no rap, R&B, hip-hop, metal, or hard modern rock. "Limp Bizkit is NOT what I want. I am a small company. I do not handle anyone presently. I am looking for a GREAT artist to work with exclusively. I am patient. I can wait until I find who I am looking for; so expect to be turned down." Works with original, solo artists and groups.

Tips "I am dedicated to artists I believe in. I act strictly as a personal manager for an artist which means I help them choose songs, submit songs, find a publisher, and/or a record company. Prefer artists who write and perform their own songs. I am currently seeking material. CDs, CDRs and CDRWs accepted. Young artists mainly considered for development (ages 16-25). Be original! I charge no upfront fees. HINT: I like poetic melodic rock (Bob Dylan, Jewel, etc.)—'singer-songwriters' so to speak—with artistic top 40 potential, but writes from the heart (not the wallet in mind). No 'American Idol' types. Not looking for singers, but artists who can develop a long career as a singer/songwriter and plays an instrument!"

☑ ⬯ ⬯ A HUGE PRODUCTION, INC.

138 Marston St., Lawrence MA 01841. (978)376-6952. E-mail: rippo@comcast.net. Website: www.rippo.com. **Contact:** Richard M. Gordon, president. Management firm, music publisher (Cat Butt Musik/BMI) and record company (2 Funky International Records). Estab. 1996. Represents regional groups from the northeast; currently handles 2 acts. Receives negotiable commission.

 • This company manages Rippopotamus, winner of 1996 Boston Music Award.

How to Contact *Write, e-mail, or call first and obtain permission to submit.* Prefers cassette with 3 songs and lyric sheet. If seeking management, press kit should include press, radio tracking, photo and CD. Include SASE. Responds in 1 month.

Music Mostly **pop/rock** and **funk**. Works with bands exclusively. Current acts include Rippopotamus (8 piece funk band—management), Dr. Akward (funk/rock—consulting) and Josh Cole (folk—consulting).

Tips "At this time we have restricted our activities to consulting and project management. Always call first. Promo packages are expensive, and you should always make sure we're actively seeking material, especially since most modern bands do their own songwriting. Being artists ourselves, we strongly recommend that you be very sure of people you work with and that they have same level of faith and confidence in the project that you do. Never give away the store and always make sure that you are aware of what is transpiring with your career, even if you have someone you trust handling it for you. Ultimately, no one has your interests as much at heart as you do, and thus you should always have your finger on your career's pulse."

⬯ ⬯ ⬯ IMMIGRANT MUSIC INC.

5141 6th Ave., Montreal QC H1Y 2P5 Canada. Phone/fax: (514)722-5859. E-mail: immigrant@videotron.ca. **Contact:** Dan Behrman, president. Management firm, booking agency and music publisher. Estab. 1979. Represents individual artists, groups and songwriters from anywhere; currently handles 4 acts. Receives 20% commission. Reviews material for acts.

How to Contact *Call first and obtain permission to submit or to arrange personal interview.* Prefers cassette, VHS videocassette, CD or vinyl with 4 songs. If seeking management, press kit should include bio, press clippings, photo, references, recordings, technical and personal rider and requirements if known. Does not return material. ("I also may use material on my radio program.") Responds in 1 month.

Music Mostly **world music**, **original ethnic** and **new acoustic music**; also **singer/songwriters**, **folk** and **ethnic/ambient**. Current acts include Simbi (Xenophile Records, vodou-roots band), B'net Houariyat (Gnawa trance music, women ensemble from Morocco), Kristi Stassinopoulou (contemporary Greek world/folk/electronica) and Atlas-Soul (Gnawafro-beat/latino band from Boston).

INTERNATIONAL ENTERTAINMENT BUREAU
3612 N. Washington Blvd., Indianapolis IN 46205-3592. (317)926-7566. E-mail: ieb@prodigy.net. Booking agency. Estab. 1972. Represents individual artists and groups from anywhere; currently handles 153 acts. Receives 20% commission.

How to Contact *No unsolicited submissions.*

Music Mostly **rock**, **country** and **A/C**; also **jazz**, **nostalgia** and **ethnic**. Works primarily with bands, comedians and speakers. Current acts include Five Easy Pieces (A/C), Scott Greeson (country), and Cool City Swing Band (variety).

J & V MANAGEMENT
143 W. Elmwood, Caro MI 48723. (989)673-2889. Manager/Publisher: John Timko. Management firm, booking agency and music publisher. Represents local, regional or international individual artists, groups and songwriters; currently handles 3 acts. Receives 10% commission. Reviews material for acts.

How to Contact *Write first and obtain permission to submit.* Prefers CD or cassette with 3 songs maximum and lyric sheet. If seeking management, include short reference bio, cover letter and résumé in press kit. Include SASE. Responds in 2 months.

Music Mostly **country**. Works primarily with vocalists and dance bands. Current acts include John Patrick (country), Alexander Depue (fiddle) and Most Wanted (country).

JANA JAE ENTERPRISES
P.O. Box 35726, Tulsa OK 74153. (918)786-8896. Fax: (918)786-8897. E-mail: janajae@janajae.com. Website: www.janajae.com. **Contact:** Kathleen Pixley, agent. Booking agency, music publisher (Jana Jae Publishing/BMI) and record company (Lark Record Productions, Inc.). Estab. 1979. Represents individual artists and songwriters; currently handles 12 acts. Receives 15% commission. Reviews material for acts.

• Also see the listings for Jana Jae Music in the Music Publishers section, Lark Record Productions in the Record Companies section and Lark Talent & Advertising in the Record Producers section of this book.

How to Contact Submit demo tape by mail. Unsolicited submissions are OK. Prefers CD or videocassette of performance. If seeking management, press kit should include cover letter, bio, photo, demo tape/CD, lyric sheets and press clippings. Does not return material.

Music Mostly **country**, **classical** and **jazz instrumentals**; also **pop**. Works with vocalists, show and concert bands, solo instrumentalists. Represents Jana Jae (country singer/fiddle player), Matt Greif (classical guitarist), Sydni (solo singer) and Hotwire (country show band).

SHELDON KAGAN INTERNATIONAL
35 McConnell, Dorval QC H9S 5L9 Canada. (514)631-2160. Fax: (514)631-4430. E-mail: sheldon@sheldonkagan.com. Website: www.sheldonkagan.com. **Contact:** Sheldon Kagan, president. Booking agency. Estab. 1965. Represents local individual artists and groups; currently handles 17 acts. Receives 10-20% commission. Reviews materials for acts.

How to Contact Submit demo tape by mail. Unsolicited submissions are OK. Prefers CD or VHS videocassette with 6 songs. Include SASE. Responds in 5 weeks.

Music Mostly **top 40**. Works primarily with vocalists and bands. Current acts include Quazz (jazz trio), City Lights (top 40 band), Jeux de Cordes (violin and guitar duo), The Soulmates (top 40) and Travelin' Band (top 40).

KENDALL WEST AGENCY
P.O. Box 173776, Arlington TX 76003-3776. (817)468-7800. E-mail: vellucci@flash.net. Contact: Michelle Vellucci. Booking agency and television producer. Estab. 1994. Represents individual artists and groups from anywhere. Receives 10% commission. Reviews material for acts.

How to Contact *Write first and obtain permission to submit or write to arrange personal interview.* Prefers CD or cassette with 5 songs and lead sheet. If seeking management, press kit should include bio, photo, cover letter, demo tape/CD and résumé. Include SASE. Responds in 1 month.

Music Mostly **country**, **blues/jazz** and **rock**; also **trios**, **dance** and **individuals**. Works primarily with bands. Current acts include Way Out West (country band), Breckenridge (variety band) and Jaz-Vil (jazz/blues).

⚫◻ KICKSTART MUSIC LTD.

12 Port House, Square Rigger Row, Plantation Wharf, London SW11 3TY England. Phone: (020)7223 3300. Fax: (020)7223 8777. E-mail: info@kickstart.uk.net. **Contact:** Frank Clark, director. Management/publishing Company. Estab. 1994. Represents individual artists, groups or songwriters from anywhere; currently handles 7 acts. Receives 20-40% commission, "depends on contract." Reviews material for acts.

How to Contact Submit demo by mail. Unsolicited submissions are OK. Prefers CD, cassette or DAT with 3 songs and lyric and lead sheet. If seeking management, press kit should include photograph and bio. SAE and IRC. Responds in 2 weeks.

Music All genres including **pop**, **dance**, **rock**, **country** and **blues**. Works primarily with bands who perform a live set of original music and talented singer/songwriters who can cross over to all types of music. Current acts include Pal Joey (rock band), Simon Fox (songwriter) and The Electric Blues Anthology (blues band).

Tips "We prefer songwriters whose songs can cross over to all types of music, those who do not write in one style only."

Ⓝ ◗ BOB KNIGHT AGENCY

185 Clinton Ave., Staten Island NY 10301. (718)448-8420. **Contact:** Bob Knight, president. Management firm, booking agency, music publisher and royalty collection firm. Estab. 1971. Represents artists, groups and songwriters; currently handles 4 acts. Receives 10-20% commission. Reviews material for acts and for submission to record companies and producers.

How to Contact Submit demo tape by mail. Unsolicited submissions are OK. Prefers cassette, CDs or videocassette (if available) with 5 songs and lead sheet "with bio and references." If seeking management, press kit should include bio, videocassette and audio cassette. Include SASE. Responds in 2 months.

Music Mostly **top 40/pop**; also **easy listening**, **MOR**, **R&B**, **soul**, **rock** (**nostalgia '50s and '60s**), **alternative**, **country**, **country/pop**, **jazz**, **blues** and **folk**. Works primarily with recording and name groups and artists— '50s, '60s and '70s acts, high energy dance and show groups. Current acts include Delfonics (R&B nostalgia), B.T. Express, Brass Construction and Main Ingredient.

Tips "We're seeking artists and groups with completed albums/demos."

◻ KUPER PERSONAL MANAGEMENT/RECOVERY RECORDINGS

P.O. Box 66274, Houston TX 77266. (713)520-5791. Fax: (713)520-5791. E-mail: recovery@wt.net. Website: www.recoveryrecordings.com. **Contact:** Ivan "Koop" Kuper, owner. Management firm, music publisher (Kuper-Lam Music/BMI and Uvula Music/BMI) and record label (Recovery Recordings). Estab. 1979/2002. Represents individual artists, groups and songwriters from Texas; currently handles 4 acts. Receives 20% commission. Reviews material for acts.

How to Contact Submit demo tape by mail. Unsolicited submissions are OK. Prefers cassette. If seeking management, press kit should include cover letter, press clippings, photo, bio (1 page) tearsheets (reviews, etc.) and demo tape/CD. Does not return material. Responds in 2 months.

Music Mostly **singer/songwriters**, **triple AAA**, **roots rock** and **Americana**. Works primarily with self-contained and self-produced artists. Current acts include Philip Rodriguez (singer/songwriter), David Rodriguez (singer/songwriter), U.S. Representative for The Watchman (Dutch singer/songwriter) and The Very Girls (Dutch vocal duo).

Tips "Create a market value for yourself, produce your own master tapes, create a cost-effective situation."

◗ LARI-JON PROMOTIONS

P.O. Box 216, Rising City NE 68658. (402)542-2336. **Contact:** Larry Good, owner. Management firm, music publisher (Lari-Jon Publishing Co./BMI) and record company (Lari-Jon Records). Represents individual artists, groups and songwriters; currently handles 3 acts. Receives 15% commission. Reviews material for acts.

How to Contact Submit demo tape by mail. Unsolicited submissions are OK. Prefers CD with 5 songs and lyric sheet. If seeking management, press kit should include 8×10 photos, cassette, videocassette and bio sheet. Include SASE. Responds in 2 months.

Music Mostly **country**, **gospel** and **'50s rock**. Works primarily with dance and show bands. Represents Kent Thompson (singer), Nebraskaland 'Opry (family type country show) and Brenda Allen (singer and comedienne).

◗ LEVINSON ENTERTAINMENT VENTURES INTERNATIONAL, INC.

1440 Veteran Ave., Suite 650, Los Angeles CA 90024. (323)663-6940. E-mail: leviinc@aol.com. President: Bob Levinson. **Contact:** Jed Leland, Jr. Management firm. Estab. 1978. Represents national individual artists, groups and songwriters; currently handles 4 acts. Receives 15-25% commission. Reviews material for acts.

How to Contact *Write first and obtain permission to submit.* Prefers cassette or VHS videocassette with 6 songs and lead sheet. If seeking management, press kit should include bio, pictures and press clips. Include SASE. Responds in 1 month.

Music Mostly **rock**, **MOR**, **R&B** and **country**. Works primarily with rock bands and vocalists.

Tips "Should be a working band, self-contained and, preferably, performing original material."

☑ ◙ RICK LEVY MANAGEMENT

4250 A1AS, D-11, St. Augustine FL 32080. (904)460-1225. Fax: (904)460-1226. E-mail: rick@ricklevy.com. Website: www.ricklevy.com. **Contact:** Rick Levy, president. Management firm, music publisher (Flying Governor Music/BMI) and record company (Luxury Records). Estab. 1985. Represents local, regional or international individual artists and groups; currently handles 5 acts. Receives 15-20% commission. Reviews material for acts.

How to Contact *Write or call first and obtain permission to submit.* Prefers cassette or VHS videocassette with 3 songs and lyric sheet. If seeking management, press kit should include cover letter, bio, demo tape/CD, VHS video, photo and press clippings. Include SASE. Responds in 2 weeks.

Music Mostly **R&B** (no rap), **pop**, **country** and **oldies**; also **children's** and **educational videos** for schools. Current acts include Jay & the Techniques ('60s hit group), The Original Box Tops ('60s), The Limits (pop), Freddy Cannon (60s), Sev7n (modern rock).

Tips "Rick Levy currently produces and promotes oldies shows nationally."

▢ LIVING EYE PRODUCTIONS LTD.

P.O. Box 12956, Rochester NY 14612. (585)425-3640. E-mail: c.kings@att.net. Website: www.chesterfieldkings. com. Secretaries: Monica or Carol. **Contact:** Andy Babiuk, president. Vice President: Greg Prevost. Management firm, music publisher (Pussy Galore Publishing/BMI) and record producers (Andy Babiuk and Greg Prevost). Estab. 1982. Represents individual artists, groups and songwriters from anywhere; currently handles 3 acts. Receives 20% commission. Reviews material for acts.

How to Contact Submit demo tape by mail. Unsolicited submissions are OK. Prefers CD and "what the artist feels necessary." If seeking management, press kit should include cover letter, bio, photo, demo tape/CD, lyric sheet, press clippings, video and résumé. Does not return material. Responds in 2 weeks.

Music Mostly **'60s rock**, **'50s rock** and **blues**; also **folk rock** and **surf**. Works primarily with bands that can tour to promote record releases. Current acts include The Chesterfield Kings (rock), The Mean Red Spiders (rock) and the Moviees ('60s rock).

Tips "We don't like trendy new stuff. Don't follow fads, create your own music by having good rock-n-roll influences."

▢ LOGGINS PROMOTION/BACKSTAGE ENTERTAINMENT

26239 Senator Ave., Harbor City CA 90710. (310)325-2800. Fax: (310)325-2560. E-mail: promo@logginspromoti on.com. Website: www.logginspromotion.com. **Contact:** Paul Loggins, CEO. Management firm and radio promotion. Represents individual artists, groups and songwriters from anywhere; currently handles 6 acts. Receives 20% commission. Reviews material for acts.

How to Contact If seeking management, press kit should include picture, short bio, cover letter, press clippings and CD (preferred). "Mark on CD which cut you, as the artist, feel is the strongest." Does not return material. Responds in 2 weeks.

Music Mostly **adult**, **top 40** and **AAA**; also **urban**, **rap**, **alternative**, **college**, **smooth jazz** and **Americana**. Works primarily with bands and solo artists.

◙ MANAGEMENT BY JAFFE

1560 Broadway, Suite 1103, New York NY 10036-0000. (212)869-6912. Fax: (212)869-7102. E-mail: jerjaf@aol.c om. President: Jerry Jaffe. Management firm. Estab. 1987. Represents individual artists and groups from anywhere; currently handles 2 acts. Receives 20% commission. Reviews material for acts "rarely." Reviews for representation "sometimes."

How to Contact *Write or call first to arrange personal interview.* Prefers CD or cassette and videocassette with 3-4 songs and lyric sheet. Does not return material. Responds in 2 months.

Music Mostly **rock/alternative**, **pop** and **Hot AC**. Works primarily with groups and singers/songwriters. Current acts include Joe McIntrye (pop) and Lucy Diamonds (pop/rap).

Tips "Create some kind of 'buzz' first."

☑ ▢ MANAGEMENT PLUS

1617 E. Commerce #4104, San Antonio TX 78205. (210)226-8450, ext. 205. Fax: (210)223-3251. E-mail: bill@boo kyourevent.com or bangelini12@prodigy.net. Website: www.bookyourevent.com. **Contact:** Bill Angelini, owner. Management firm and booking agency. Estab. 1980. Represents individual artists and groups from anywhere; currently handles 6 acts. Receives 10-15% commission. Reviews material for acts.

How to Contact Submit demo tape by mail. Unsolicited submissions are OK. Prefers cassette, VHS videocassette and bio. If seeking management, press kit should include pictures, bio, résumé and discography. Does not return material. Responds in 1 month.

Music Mostly **Latin American**, **Tejano** and **international**; also **Norteño** and **country**. Current acts include Jay Perez (Tejano), Ram Herrera (Tejano), Rodeo (Tejano) and Grupo Vida (Tejano).

THE MANAGEMENT TRUST LTD.

411 Queen St. W, 3rd Floor, Toronto ON M5V 2A5 Canada. (416)979-7070. Fax: (416)979-0505. E-mail: mail@mgmtrust.ca. Website: www.mgmtrust.ca. President: Jake Gold. General Manager: Shelley Stertz. Management firm. Estab. 1986. Represents individual artists and/or groups; currently handles 7 acts.

How to Contact Submit demo tape by mail (Attn: A&R Dept.). Unsolicited submissions are OK. If seeking management, press kit should include CD or tape, bio, cover letter, photo and press clippings. Does not return material. Responds in 2 months.

Music All types. Current acts include Gord Downie (alternative rock), Doctor (rock band), Sass Jordan (rock), Joey Serlin (producer/composer), The Populars (rock) and Jenny Gear (jazz/r&b).

RICK MARTIN PRODUCTIONS/EASYWAY MUSIC

125 Fieldpoint Road, Greenwich CT 06830. Phone/fax: (203)661-1615. E-mail: rick@easywaysystems.com. **Contact:** Rick Martin, president. Personal manager, music publisher, and independent producer. Held the Office of Secretary of the National Conference of Personal Managers for 22 years. Represents vocalists, songwriters, and actresses; currently produces pop music artists in private project studio. Receives 15% commission as a personal manager and/or customary production and publishing distributions.

How to Contact E-mail for initial contract and/or submit 2-3 songs and picture.

Music Top 40 and dance.

Tips "Your demo does not have to be professionally produced to submit to producers, publishers, or managers. In other words, save your money. It's really not important what you've done. It's what you can do now that counts."

PHIL MAYO & COMPANY

P.O. Box 304, Bomoseen VT 05732. (802)468-2554. Fax: (802)468-8884. E-mail: pmcamgphil@aol.com. **Contact:** Phil Mayo, President. Management firm and record company (AMG Records). Estab. 1981. Represents individual artists, groups and songwriters from anywhere; currently handles 4 acts. Receives 15-20% commission. Reviews material for acts.

How to Contact *Contact first and obtain permission to submit.* Prefers CD with 3 songs and lyric or lead sheet. If seeking management, include bio, photo and lyric sheet in press kit. Does not return material. Responds in 2 months.

Music Mostly **rock**, **pop** and **country**; also **blues** and **Christian pop**. Works primarily with dance bands, vocalists and rock acts. Current acts include John Hall, Guy Burlage, Jonell Mosser, Pam Buckland, Orleans, Gary Nicholson and Jon Pousette-Dart.

MAZUR ENTERTAINMENT/MAZUR PUBLIC RELATIONS

P.O. Box 2425, Trenton NJ 08607. (609)890-4550. Fax: (609)890-4556. E-mail: michael@mazurpr.com. Website: www.mazurpr.com. **Contact:** Michael Mazur. Management and PR firm. Estab. 1987. Represents groups from anywhere; currently handles 30 acts. Commission varies. Reviews material for acts.

How to Contact Submit demo tape by mail. Unsolicited submissions are OK. Prefers cassette, CD or VHS videocassette with 2 songs. If seeking management, press kit should include CD/cassette, photo, bio and video. Include SASE. "We try to reply." Responds in 1 month.

Music Current acts include international and national artists. See website.

Music Mostly **country**. Works primarily with vocalists. Current acts include Sierra Highway.

THE McDONNELL GROUP

27 Pickwick Lane, Newtown Square PA 19073. (610)353-8554. E-mail: frankmcdonn@aol.com. **Contact:** Frank McDonnell. Management firm. Estab. 1985. Represents individual artists, groups and songwriters from anywhere; currently handles 6 acts. Receives 20% commission. Reviews material for acts.

How to Contact *Write first and obtain permission to submit.* Prefers cassette or VHS videocassette with 4 songs and lyric sheet. If seeking management, include cover letter, lyric sheets, press, tape or video, recent photos and bio. Include SASE. Responds in 1 month.

Music Mostly **rock**, **pop** and **R&B**; also **country** and **jazz**. Current acts include Johnny Bronco (rock group), Mike Forte (producer/songwriter) and Pat Martino (jazz guitarist).

◑ MEDIA MANAGEMENT

P.O. Box 3773, San Rafael CA 94912-3773. (415)457-0700. Fax: (415)457-0964. E-mail: mediamanagement9@aol.com. **Contact:** Eugene, proprietor. Management firm. Estab. 1990. Represents local, regional or international individual artists, groups and songwriters; currently handles 4 acts. Receives 15-20% commission. Reviews material for acts.

How to Contact Submit demo by mail. Unsolicited submissions are OK. Prefers CD or cassette with lyric sheet. If seeking management, include lyric sheets, demo tape, photo and bio. Does not return material.

Music Mostly **rock**, **blues** and **pop**; also **R&B**. Works primarily with songwriting performers/bands. Current acts include Zakiya Hooker (r&b/blues/singer/songwriter), Greg Anton/Greggs Eggs (rock songwriter/group), John Lee Hooker Estate (blues) and Ollan Christopher Bell (producer).

Tips ''Write great *radio-friendly* songs.''

◯ MERRI-WEBB PRODUCTIONS

P.O. Box 5474, Stockton CA 95205. (209)948-8186. Fax: (209)942-2163. E-mail: kauppmusic@filmmusic.net. Website: www.makingmusic4u.com. **Contact:** Kristy Ledford, A&R coordinator. Management firm, music publisher (Kaupp's & Robert Publishing Co./BMI) and record company (Kaupp Records). Represents regional (California) individual artists, groups and songwriters; currently handles 13 acts. Receives 10-15% commission. Reviews material for acts.

  • Also see the listing for Kaupp & Robert Publishing Company in the Music Publishers section and Kaupp Records in the Record Companies section of the book.

How to Contact *Write first and obtain permission to submit or to arrange personal interview.* Prefers cassette or VHS videocassette with 3 songs maximum and lyric sheet. Include SASE. Responds in 3 months.

Music Mostly **country**, **A/C rock** and **R&B**; also **pop**, **rock** and **gospel**. Works primarily with vocalists, bands and songwriters. Current acts include Bruce Bolin (rock/pop singer), Nanci Lynn (country/pop singer) and Rick Webb (country/pop singer).

☑ ◑ METRO TALENT GROUP, INC.

83 Walton St., 3rd Floor, Atlanta GA 30303. (404)954-6620. Fax: (404)954-6681. E-mail: mail@metrotalentgroup.com. Website: www.metrotalentgroup.com. **Contact:** Jennifer Hatch. Booking agency. Represents individual artists and groups; currently handles 12-15 acts. Receives 10-15% commission. Reviews material for acts.

How to Contact *Write or call first and obtain permission to submit.* ''We prefer to be contacted via e-mail.'' Prefers cassette or CD. Include clubs/venues played, guarantees for each show and who you've opened for. Does not return material. Responds in 2 weeks.

Music Mostly **rock/alternative**, **blues** and **jazz**; also **acoustic**. Visit website for full roster of current acts.

☑ ◯ MIDCOAST, INC.

1002 Jones Rd., Hendersonville TN 37075. (615)400-4664. E-mail: mid-co@ix.netcom.com. Managing Director: Bruce Andrew Bossert. Management firm and music publisher (MidCoast, Inc./BMI). Estab. 1984. Represents individual artists, groups and songwriters; currently handles 2 acts. Reviews material for acts.

How to Contact Submit demo tape by mail. Unsolicited submissions are OK. Prefers CD, cassette, VHS videocassette or DAT with 2-4 songs and lyric sheet. If seeking management, press kit should include cover letter, ''short'' bio, tape, video, photo, press clippings and announcements of any performances in Nashville area. Does not return material. Responds in 6 weeks if interested.

Music Mostly **rock**, **pop** and **country**. Works primarily with original rock and country bands and artists. Current acts include Room 101 (alternative rock).

☑ ◑ MIDNIGHT MUSIC MANAGEMENT

816 S. Robertson Blvd., Los Angeles CA 90035. (310)289-3006. Fax: (310)289-3007. E-mail: bob-diamond@hotmail.com. Agents: Bob Diamond and Stuart Wax. Management firm. Estab. 1989. Represents individual artists, groups, songwriters and indie labels for film and TV; currently handles 5 acts. Receives 15-20% commission. Reviews material for acts.

How to Contact *Write or call first and obtain permission to submit.* Prefers cassette with 3 songs, lyric sheet and bios and press. If seeking management, press kit should include bio, press, tape and video (if available). Does not return material. Responds in 1 month.

Music All kinds. Works primarily with R&B/pop songwriters and producers, punk/alternative bands and acoustic rock bands. Current acts include Irene Cara (r&b singer/actress), Nancy Bryan (alternative pop) and Lauran G. (alternative pop). Songwriters: Michele Vice-Maslin, Ken Hirsch, Dorothy Sea Gazekey.

☑ ⊞ ◐ MUSIC MARKETING & PROMOTIONS

Post Office Kendenup 6323, South Perth 6951 Australia. Phone: (618)9851 4311. Fax: (618)9851 4225. E-mail: mmp@global.net.au. Website: www.global.net.au/~mmp/. **Contact:** Eddie Robertson. Booking agency. Estab. 1991. Represents individual artists and/or groups; currently handles 50 acts. Receives 20% commission. Reviews material for acts.

How to Contact *Write first and obtain permission to submit.* Unsolicited submissions are OK. Prefers cassette or videocassette with photo, information on style and bio. If seeking management, press kit should include photos, bio, cover letter, résumé, press clippings, video, demo, lyric sheets and any other useful information. Does not return material. Responds in 1 month.

Music Mostly **top 40/pop**, **jazz** and **'60s-'90s**; also **reggae** and **blues**. Works primarily with show bands and solo performers. Current acts include Faces (dance band), N.R.G. (show band) and C.J. & the Thorns (soul).

Tips "Send as much information as possible. If you do not receive a call after four to five weeks, follow up with letter or phone call."

◐ NIK ENTERTAINMENT CO.

274 N. Goodman St., Rochester NY 14607. (585)244-0331. Fax: (585)244-0356. E-mail: nikniceguy@aol.com. Website: www.nikentertainment.com. **Contact:** Dave Lawrence, recording manager. General Manager/President: Gary Webb. Management firm and booking agency. Estab. 1988. Represents groups from anywhere; currently handles 10 acts. Reviews material for acts.

How to Contact Submit demo tape by mail. Unsolicited submissions are OK. Prefers cassette, VHS videocassette or CD with lyric or lead sheet. If seeking management, press kit should include photo, bio and demo tape. Does not return material. Responds in 3 weeks.

Music Mostly **mainstream rock** and **pop**. Works primarily with bands. Current acts include Nik and the Nice Guys (pop show band), The Shag-adelics ('60s meets '90s), Fever-The Wrath of Polyester ('70s retro), Alpha Delta Nik (the world's only tribute to *Animal House*), The Blues Family (r&b review), Jazz Nik (basic jazz trio and more), The Bugzappers (swing band), Shamalama (oldies with an edge) and the Rochester Rat Pack (the cocktail culture revival).

◒ NOTEWORTHY ENTERPRISES

3829 NE 167th St., N. Miami Beach FL 33160. (305)949-9192. Fax: (305)949-9492. E-mail: ss@noteworthy.net. Website: www.Noteworthy.net. **Contact:** Sheila Siegel, president. Booking agency, music publisher (On the Water Publications/BMI) and talent buyer. Estab. 1987. Represents individual artists, groups and songwriters from anywhere. Receives 20% commission. Reviews material for acts.

How to Contact *Does not accept unsolicited submissions.* "Request via Internet, please—no faxes or phone calls."

Music Mostly **big band**. Works primarily with jazz artists. Current acts include Noteworthy Orchestra (big band), Southlanders Traditional Jazz Band, David Siegel and Jack Siegel.

◓ NOTEWORTHY PRODUCTIONS

124½ Archwood Ave., Annapolis MD 21401. (410)268-8232. Fax: (410)268-2167. E-mail: mcshane@mcnote.com. Website: www.mcnote.com. **Contact:** McShane Glover, president. Management firm and booking agency. Estab. 1985. Represents individual artists, groups and songwriters from everywhere; currently handles 6 acts. Receives 15-20% commission. Reviews material for acts.

How to Contact *Write first and obtain permission to submit.* Prefers CD/CDR with lyric sheet. If seeking management, press kit should include cassette or CD, photo, bio, venues played and press clippings (preferably reviews). "Follow up with a phone call 3-5 weeks after submission." Does not return material. Responds in 2 months.

Music Mostly **Americana**, **folk**, and **celtic**. Works primarily with performing singer/songwriters. Current acts include Seamus Kennedy (Celtic/contemporary), Sonia (pop/rock/folk) and the McKrells (celtic/bluegrass).

☑ ◐ ON THE LEVEL MUSIC!

P.O. Box 508, Owego NY 13827. (607)689-0122. Fax: (607)689-0478. E-mail: fredny2020@yahoo.com. **Contact:** Fred Gage, CEO/president. Management firm, booking agency and music publisher (On The Level Music! Publishing). Estab. 1970. Represents individual artists, groups and songwriters from anywhere; currently handles 30 acts. Receives 15% commission. Reviews material for acts.

How to Contact Submit demo tape by mail. Unsolicited submissions are OK. Prefers CDs, DAT or VHS videocassette with 4 songs and lyric or lead sheet. If seeking management, press kit should include cover letter, bio, demo tape/CD, lyric sheets, press clippings, 8×10 photo and video. Does not return material. Responds in 1 month.

Music Mostly **rock**, **alternative** and **jazz**; also **blues**. Current acts include Ice River Blues and Summer Jam 2004.

Managers & Agents

☑ OTA PRODUCTIONS

484 Lake Park Ave. #32, Oakland CA 94610. (510)339-3389. Fax: (510)339-0389. E-mail: music@melodia.com. Website: www.melodia.com. **Contact:** Scott Price, director. Management firm, record company and record producer (Scott Price). Estab. 1995. Represents individual artists and groups from anywhere; currently handles 3 acts. Receives 20% commission. Reviews material for acts.

How to Contact Submit demo tape by mail. Unsolicited submissions are OK. Prefers CD with 5 songs and lyric sheet. If seeking management, press kit should include cover letter, bio, photo, demo/CD, press clippings, video and résumé. Does not return material. Responds in 2 months.

Music Mostly **jazz**, **Latin** and **pop**. Works primarily with individual artists/groups. Current acts include Omar Sosa (Cuban pianist) and Madhouse (jazz quartet).

☒ ☐ OUTLAW ENTERTAINMENT INTERNATIONAL

#101-1001 W. Broadway, Dept. 400, Vancouver BC V6H 4E4 Canada. (604)878-1494. Fax: (604)878-1495. E-mail: info@outlawentertainment.com. Website: www.outlawentertainment.com. CEO/President: Tommy Floyd. Assistant President: Suzanne Marie. Management firm. Estab. 1995. Represents individual artists, groups and songwriters from anywhere; currently handles 3 acts. Receives 20% commission. Reviews material for acts.

How to Contact Submit demo CD by mail. Unsolicited submissions are OK. Prefers CD with 2-3 songs and lyric sheet. If seeking management, press kit should include 8×10 photo, bio and written statement of goals. SAE and IRC. Responds in 1 month.

Music Mostly **rock**, **metal** and **alt. country**. Works primarily with bands, "but welcomes dynamic singer/songwriters." Current acts include American Dog (hard rock act), Luba Dvorak (alt. country act) and Subsonic (heavy metal act).

Tips "Clearly define your target market. Write simple, emotional, primal songs."

⊕ ☑ GORDON POOLE AGENCY LIMITED

The Limes, Brockley, Bristol BS48 3BB England. Phone: +44 (0)1275 463222. Fax: +44 (0)1275 462252. E-mail: agents@gordonpoole.com. Website: www.gordonpoole.com. **Contact:** Gordon Poole, managing director. Booking agency. Estab. 1963. Represents individual artists and groups from anywhere; currently handles 100 acts. Receives 20% commission. Reviews material for acts.

How to Contact Submit demo tape by mail. Unsolicited submissions are OK. Prefers cassette or videocassette and lyric sheet. If seeking management, press kit should include cv, tape/CD, cover letter, bio, photo, press clippings and video. SAE and IRC. Responds in 1 month.

Music Mostly **MOR**. Works primarily with bands.

☑ ☐ PRECISION MANAGEMENT

110 Coliseum Crossing, #158, Hampton VA 23666-5902. (800)275-5336, ext. 0381042. E-mail: precisionmanagement@netzero.com. Website: www.pmmusicgroup.com. **Contact:** Cappriccieo Scates, operations director. Management firm and music publisher (Mytrell/BMI). Estab. 1990. Represents individual artists and/or groups and songwriters from anywhere; currently handles 3 acts. Receives 20% commission. Reviews material for acts.

How to Contact Submit demo tape by mail. Unsolicited submissions are OK. Prefers cassette or VHS videocassette with 3-4 songs and lyric sheet. If seeking management, press kit should include photo, bio, demo tape/CD, lyric sheets, press clippings and all relevant press information. Include SASE. Responds in 6 weeks.

Music Mostly **R&B**, **rap** and **gospel**; also **all types**. Current acts include Nastacia "Nazz" Kendall (DreamWorks), Darius Brooks (Grammy, Stellar, and Dove Award Winner) and David Broom (MTV Real World).

☒ ☑ PRESTIGE MANAGEMENT

8600 Wilbur Ave., Northridge CA 91324. (818)993-3030. Fax: (818)993-4151. E-mail: prestige@gte.net. **Contact:** Waddell Solomon, vice president. Management firm. Estab. 1987. Represents individual artists, groups and songwriters from anywhere; currently handles 2 acts. Receives 15% commission. Reviews material for acts.

How to Contact Submit demo tape by mail. Unsolicited submissions are OK. Prefers cassette with 3 songs, photo/bio and lyric sheet. If seeking management, press kit should include photos, bio, recent show dates and recent show reviews. Does not return material. Responds in 1 month.

Music Mostly **pop rock**, **hard rock**, **alternative rock**; also **R&B** and **AAA**. Works primarily with pop/rock bands with strong songs and live shows; also songwriters for film/TV projects. Current acts include Bosteo, McFly, and V.

☑ PRIME TIME ENTERTAINMENT

28 N. First St., Suite 701, San Jose CA 95113. (408)289-9333. Fax: (408)289-8333. E-mail: ptes@pacbell.net. Owner: Jim Douglas. Management firm and booking agency. Estab. 1988. Represents individual artists, groups and songwriters from anywhere. Receives 10-20% commission. Reviews material for acts.

How to Contact Submit demo tape by mail. Unsolicited submissions are OK. Prefers cassette with 3-5 songs. If seeking management, press kit should include 8×10 photo, reviews and CDs/tapes. Include SASE. Responds in 1 month.

Music Mostly **jazz**, **country** and **alternative**; also **ethnic**. Artists include Greg Adams (jazz), Jeff Berlin (fusion, rock), Ronnie Montrose (rock) and Dick Dale (surf).

Tips "A quality package states a commitment to the project at the outset."

☐ PRO TALENT CONSULTANTS

P.O. Box 233, Nice CA 95464. (707)349-1809. E-mail: pro_talent_artists@yahoo.com. **Contact:** John Eckert, coordinator. Management firm and booking agency. Estab. 1979. Represents individual artists and groups; currently handles 12 acts. Receives 15% commission. Reviews material for acts.

How to Contact Submit demo tape by mail. Unsolicited submissions are OK. Prefers cassette or VHS videocassette with at least 4 songs and lyric sheet. "We prefer audio cassette (4 songs). Submit videocassette with live performance only." If seeking management, press kit should include an 8×10 photo, a cassette or CD of at least 4-6 songs, a bio on group/artist, references, cover letter, press clippings, video and business card or a phone number with address. Does not return material. Responds in 5 weeks.

Music Mostly **country**, **country/pop** and **rock**. Works primarily with vocalists, show bands, dance bands and bar bands. Current acts include Ronny and the Daytonas (pop/rock-top 40 band), Daryl Myers (country singer) and Stephen Bishop (pop/easy listening vocalist).

☑ RAINBOW TALENT AGENCY

146 Round Pond Lane, Rochester NY 14626. (585)723-3334. Fax: (585)720-6172. E-mail: rtalent@frontiernet.net. **Contact:** Carl Labate, President. Management firm and booking agency. Represents artists and groups; currently handles 6 acts. Receives 15-20% commission.

How to Contact Submit demo tape by mail. Unsolicited submissions are OK. Prefers CD/CDR with minimum 3 songs. May send video if available; "a still photo would be good enough to see the Act; if you are a performer, it would be advantageous to show yourself or the group performing live. Theme videos are not helpful." If seeking management, include photos, bio, markets established, CD/DVD. Does not return material. Responds in 1 month.

Music Blues, **rock** and **R&B**. Works primarily with touring bands and recording artists. Current acts include Nancy Kelley (jazz singer), Ghost Riders (Southern rock), Lazo & The Radikals (reggae) and Spanky Haschmann Swing Orchestra (high energy swing).

Tips "My main interest is with groups or performers that are currently touring and have some product. And are at least 50% percent original. Strictly songwriters should apply elsewhere."

Ⓝ ☐ RENAISSANCE ENTERTAINMENT GROUP

P.O. Box 1222, Mountainside NJ 07092-1222. E-mail: regroup@hotmail.com. **Contact:** Kevin A. Joy, president/CEO. Management firm, booking agency, record company (Suburan Records) and record producer (Onyx Music and Bo²Legg Productions). Estab. 1992. Represents individual artists, groups and songwriters from anywhere; currently handles 10 acts. Receives 20% commission. Reviews material for acts.

How to Contact *Write first and obtain permission to submit.* Prefers cassette with 3 songs and lyric or lead sheet. If seeking management, press kit should include cover letter, demo tape/CD, lyric sheets, press clippings, pictures and bio. Does not return material. Responds in 5 weeks.

Music Mostly **R&B** and **rap**. Works primarily with R&B groups, rap and vocalists. Current acts include Paper Boy (rap), ASU (rap) and A Mother's Child (r&b).

☑ Ⓩ RHYTHMIC TEMPLE ENTERTAINMENT INC.

3315 E. Russell Rd., Suite H-117, Las Vegas NV 89120. (702)967-6016. Fax: (702)451-4809. Website: www.freestyleLLC.com. Vice President: Steve Buckley. Management firm and record producer. Estab. 1993. Represents individual artists and groups from anywhere; currently handles 3 acts. Receives 10-20% commission. Reviews material for acts.

How to Contact Submit demo tape by mail. Unsolicited submissions are OK. Prefers cassette or VHS videocassette. If seeking management, press kit should include cassette or CD, bio and pictures. Does not return material. Responds in 2 months.

Music Mostly **R&B**, **pop** and **gospel**; also **rap** and **contemporary Christian**.

✒ RIOHCAT MUSIC

P.O. Box 764, Hendersonville TN 37077-0764. (615)824-9313. Fax: (615)824-0797. E-mail: tachoir@bellsouth.n et. Website: www.tachoir.com. **Contact:** Robert Kayne, manager. Management firm, booking agency, record company (Avita Records) and music publisher. Estab. 1975. Represents individual artists and groups; currently handles 4 acts. Receives 15-20% commission.

- Also see the listing for Avita Records in the Record Companies section of this book.

How to Contact *Contact first and obtain permission to submit.* Prefers cassette and lead sheet. If seeking management, press kit should include cover letter, bio, photo, demo tape/CD and press clippings. Does not return material. Responds in 6 weeks.

Music Mostly **contemporary jazz** and **fusion**. Works primarily with jazz ensembles. Current acts include Group Tachoir (jazz), Tachoir/Manakas Duo (jazz) and Jerry Tachoir (jazz vibraphone artist).

✒ A.F. RISAVY, INC.

1312 Vandalia, Collinsville IL 62234. (618)345-6700. Fax: (618)235-0004. E-mail: swingcitymusic@ameritech.n et. Website: www.swingcitymusic.com. **Contact:** Art Risavy, president. Management firm and booking agency. Divisions include Artco Enterprises, Golden Eagle Records, Swing City Music and Swing City Sound. Estab. 1960. Represents artists, groups and songwriters; currently handles 35 acts. Receives 10% commission. Reviews material for acts.

How to Contact Submit demo tape by mail. Unsolicited submissions are OK. Prefers CD/CDR, cassette or VHS videocassette with 2-6 songs and lyric sheet. If seeking management, press kit should include pictures, bio and VHS videocassette. Include SASE. Responds in 3 weeks.

Music Mostly **rock**, **country**, **MOR** and **top 40**.

☐ ROCK OF AGES PRODUCTIONS

1001 W. Jasmine Dr., Suite K, Lake Park FL 33403-2119. (561)848-1500. Fax: (561)848-2400. President/Agency Director: Joseph E. Larson. Booking agent, literary agency and publisher. Estab. 1980. Represents individual artists and groups from anywhere; currently handles 500 acts. Receives 15-25% commission. Reviews material for acts.

How to Contact Submit demo tape by mail. Unsolicited submissions are OK. Prefers CD, cassette or VHS videocassette with 3 or more songs and lead sheet. If seeking management, press kit should include videocassette and/or audio cassette, lyric sheets, relevant press, bio, cover letter, résumé and recent photo. Include SASE. Responds in 3 months.

Music Mostly **top 40**, **country/western** and **rock**; also **gospel** and **opera**. Works primarily with bands, singers, singer/songwriters. Current acts include Adonis (solo Caribbean act), Johnny Violin (renowned violinist) and Barracuda (6-piece energy variety band).

☐ ROCK WHIRLED MUSIC MANAGEMENT

1423 N. Front St., Harrisburg PA 17102. (717)236-2386. E-mail: phil.clark@rockwhirled.com. Website: www.ro ckwhirled.com. **Contact:** Philip Clark, director. Management firm, booking agency and publicists. Estab. 1987. Represents individual artists and/or groups from anywhere; currently handles 12 acts. Receives 10-25% commission. Reviews material for acts.

How to Contact *Contact first and obtain permission to submit.* Prefers cassette. If seeking management, press kit should include bio, cover letter, demo tape/CD, photo, song list, venue list, description of performance frequency, equipment needed, goals. Include SASE. Responds in 6 weeks.

Music Mostly **rock**, **alternative** and **folk**. Works primarily with soloist singer/instrumentalists, duo acoustic acts, bands. Current acts include My World (modern rock), Cameron Molloy (country fusion) and Adria (celtic).

Tips "Be brief, clear, focused in approach. Approach a variety of other agents and managers to get a feel for which companies make the best match. We look for clients who wish to work specifically with us, not just any firm."

☑ ☐ RUSTRON MUSIC PRODUCTIONS

Send all artist song submissions to: 1156 Park Lane, West Palm Beach FL 33417-5957. (561)686-1354. E-mail: RMP_WMP@bellsouth.net. **Contact:** Sheelah Adams, office administrator. Main Office in Connecticut. ("Main office does not review artist submissions—only South Florida Branch office does.") Executive Director: Rusty Gordon. Artist Consultants: Rusty Gordon and Davilyn Whims. Composition Management: Ron Caruso. Management firm, booking agency, music publisher (Rustron Music Publishers/BMI and Whimsong Publishing/ASCAP), record company and record producer. Estab. 1970. Represents individuals, groups and songwriters; currently handles 20 acts. Receives 10-30% commission. Reviews material for acts.

- Also see listings for Rustron Music in the Music Publishers, Record Companies and Record Producers sections of this book.

How to Contact *Call to discuss submission.* Send CD or cassette with 10-15 songs (CD produced to sell at gigs with up to 15 songs preferred). Provide typed lyric sheets for every song in the submission. If seeking management, send press kit including: cover letter, bio, CD demo, typed lyric sheets and press clippings. "SASE required for all correspondence." Responds in 4 months.

Music Mostly **adult contemporary**, **electric acoustic**, **blues** (**country folk/urban**, **Southern**), **country** (**rock, blues, progressive**), **easy listening**, **Cabaret**, **soft rock** (**ballads**), **women's music**, **R&B**, **folk/rock**; also **New Age instrumentals** and **New Age folk fusion**. Current acts include Jayne Margo-Reby (folk rock), Star Smiley (country), Robin Plitt (historical folk), Lisa Cohen (Cabaret/pop/acapella), Song on A Whim (folk/world music), Jeremy White (yankee reggae), Haze Coates (ACGA) and Boomslang Swampsinger (Florida folk).

Tips "Carefully mix demo, don't drown the vocals, 3-6 songs in a submission. Prefer a for-sale CD made to sell at gigs with up to 15 songs. Send photo if artist is seeking marketing and/or production assistance. Very strong hooks, definitive melody, evolved concepts, unique and unpredictable themes. Flesh out a performing sound unique to the artist. Stage presence a must!"

☑ ◑ SAFFYRE MANAGEMENT

23401 Park Sorrento, #38, Calabasas CA 91302. (818)842-4368. E-mail: ebsaffyre@yahoo.com. **Contact:** Esta G. Bernstein, president. Management firm. Estab. 1990. Represents individual artists, groups and songwriters from anywhere; currently handles 2 acts. Receives 15% commission.

How to Contact *Call first and obtain permission to submit.* If seeking management, press kit should include cover letter, bio, photo, cassette with 3-4 songs and lyric sheets. Does not return material. Responds in 2 weeks only if interested.

Music **Alternative/modern rock** and **top 40**. "We work only with bands and solo artists who write their own material; our main objective is to obtain recording deals and contracts, while advising our artists on their careers and business relationships."

◑ ST. JOHN ARTISTS

P.O. Box 619, Neenah WI 54957-0619. (920)722-2222. Fax: (920)725-2405. Website: www.st.john-artists.com/ . **Contact:** Jon St. John and Gary Coquoz, agents. Booking agency. Estab. 1968. Represents local and regional individual artists and groups; currently handles 20 acts. Receives 15-20% commission. Reviews material for acts.

How to Contact *Call first and obtain permission to submit.* Prefers CD or VHS videocassette. If seeking management, press kit should include cover letter, bio, photo, demo tape/CD, video and résumé. Include SASE.

Music Mostly **rock** and **MOR**. Current acts include Tribute (variety/pop/country), Boogie & the Yo-Yo's ('60s to 2000s) and Da Poopers (musical comedy/novelty).

☑ ◑ SA'MALL MANAGEMENT

P.O. Box 261488, Encino CA 91426. (310)317-0322. Fax: (818)506-8534. E-mail: samusa@aol.com. Website: www.pplentertainmentgroup.com. **Contact:** Ted Steele, vice president of talent. Management firm, music publisher (Pollybyrd Publications) and record company (PPL Entertainment Group). Estab. 1990. Represents individual artists, groups and songwriters worldwide; currently handles 10 acts. Receives 10-25% commission. Reviews material for acts.

● Also see the listings for Pollybyrd Publications Limited and Zettitalia Music International in the Music Publishers section and PPL Entertainment Group in the Record Companies section of this book.

How to Contact *E-mail first and obtain permission to submit.* Prefers CD or cassette. If seeking management, press kit should include picture, bio and tape. Include SASE. Responds in 2 months.

Music **All types**. Current acts include Riki Hendrix (rock), Buddy Wright (blues), Fhyne, Suzette Cuseo, The Band AKA, LeJenz, B.D. Fuoco and Gary J.

☑ ◑ CRAIG SCOTT ENTERTAINMENT

P.O. Box 1722, Paramus NJ 07652-1722. (201)587-1066. Fax: (201)587-0481. E-mail: scott@craigscott.com. Website: www.craigscott.com. Management firm. Estab. 1985. Represents individual artists and/or groups from anywhere. Commission varies. Reviews material for acts.

How to Contact Submit demo tape by mail. Unsolicited submissions are OK. Prefers cassette or CD. If seeking management, press kit should include tape/CD, bio, picture, relevant press. Does not return material. Responds in 1 month.

Music **All styles**.

Ⓝ ◑ SDM, INC.

740 N. La Brea Ave., 1st Floor, Los Angeles CA 90038. (323)933-9977. Fax: (323)933-0633. E-mail: laurent_besen con@sdmmusic.com. Website: www.sdmmusic.com. **Contact:** Laurent Besencon. Management firm, music

publisher and record company. Estab. 1979. Represents individual artists, groups, songwriters from anywhere. Reviews material for acts.

How to Contact Prefers cassette with lyric sheet. Does not return material. Responds in 3 months.

Music Current acts include Joe, Alicia Keyes and Luther Vandross.

N ⊘ SENDYK, LEONARD & CO. INC.

532 Colorado Ave., Santa Monica CA 90401. (310)458-8860. Fax: (310)458-8862. **Contact:** Gerri Leonard, partner. Business management. Represents individual artists, groups and songwriters from anywhere; currently handles 75 acts. Receives 5% commission.

How to Contact "We do not solicit any songwriters for works to be submitted to artists, but are certainly interested in representing songwriters with respect to their financial affairs. We can also monitor their royalties; we have an extensive royalty administration department."

Music Current acts include Marilyn Manson (hard rock), Jonathon Butler (jazz/urban) and The Cranberries (alternative).

✔ ☇ ◐ SERGE ENTERTAINMENT GROUP

P.O. Box 2760, Acworth GA 30102. (678)445-0006. Fax: (678)494-9289. E-mail: sergeent@aol.com. Website: www.serge.org. **Contact:** Sandy Serge, president. Management and PR firm and song publishers. Estab. 1987. Represents individual artists, groups, songwriters from anywhere; currently handles 20 acts. Receives 20% commission for management. Monthly fee required for PR acts.

How to Contact *E-mail first for permission to submit.* Submit demo tape or CD by mail. Unsolicited submissions are OK. Prefers cassette or CD with 4 songs and lyric sheet. If seeking management, press kit should include 8×10 photo, bio, cover letter, lyric sheets, max of 4 press clips, VHS videocassette, performance schedule and CD. "All information submitted must include name, address and phone number on each item." Does not return material. Responds in 6 weeks if interested.

Music Mostly **rock**, **pop** and **country**; also **New Age**. Works primarily with singer/songwriters and bands. Current acts include Kelly Keeling (rock), Sarah Fimm (pop/rock) and Jeffrey Michael (world/New Age).

N ⊕ ◐ PHILL SHUTE MANAGEMENT PTY. LTD.

Box 273, Dulwich Hill NSW 2203 Australia. Phone: +61 2 95692152. Fax: +61 2 95692152. E-mail: phillshute@ optusanet.com.au. Website: www.big-rock.com.au. **Contact:** Phill Shute, CEO. Management firm, booking agency and record company (Big Rock Records). Estab. 1979. Represents local individual artists and groups; currently handles 8 acts. Receives 10% commission. Reviews material for acts.

How to Contact Submit demo tape by mail. Unsolicited submissions are OK. Prefers cassette with 4 songs and lyric sheet. If seeking management, press kit should include cover letter, bio, photo, demo tape/CD, press clippings and résumé. Does not return material. Responds in 1 month.

Music Mostly **rock**, **pop** and **R&B**; also **country rock**. Works primarily with rock bands, pop vocalists and blues acts (band and vocalists). Current acts include Phill Simmons (country), Two R More (pop/rock) and Now Hear This (rock).

Tips "Make all submissions well organized (e.g., bio, photo and experience of the act). List areas in which the act would like to work, complete details for contact."

✔ ◐ SIDDONS & ASSOCIATES

14727 Ventura Blvd., Penthouse Floor, Sherman Oaks CA 91403. (323)462-6156. Fax: (323)462-2076. E-mail: bill@coreentertainment.biz. **Contact:** Stuart Squires. President: Bill Siddons. Management firm. Estab. 1972. Represents individual artists and groups from anywhere; currently handles 4 acts. Receives 15-20% commission. Reviews material for acts.

How to Contact *Write first and obtain permission to submit.* Prefers CD or VHS videocassette with 3 songs and lyric sheet. If seeking management, press kit should include cassette of 3 songs, lyric sheet, VHS videocassette if available, biography, past credits and discography. Does not return material. Responds in 3 months.

Music All styles. Current acts include Elayne Boosler (comedian), Kurt Bestor (singer/songwriter), Jerry Cantrell (rock), Slow Motion Reign (band—Columbia Records), D-SiSive (rapper/songwriter), and BSG (formerly Little River Band).

N SIMMONS MANAGEMENT GROUP

P.O. Box 747, Oak Island NC 28465. (919)278-1033. Fax: (919)278-7982. E-mail: HarrySimmons@HarrySimmons.com. President: Harry Simmons. Management firm and music publisher. Represents producers, artists, groups and songwriters; currently handles 4 acts. Receives 15-20% commission. Reviews material for acts.

How to Contact *Write or call first and obtain permission to submit.* Prefers cassette, CD or VHS videocassette of performance with 3-6 songs and lyric sheet; also submit promotional material, photos and clippings. "Videocassette does not have to be professional. Any information helps.'' If seeking management, include 3-song demo (tape or CD) and photos in press kit. Does not return material. Responds in 2 months.

Music Mostly **modern pop**; also **modern rock**, **rock**, **metal**, **R&B**, **industrial**, **country** and **top 40/pop**. Works primarily with ''original music recording acts or those that aspire to be.'' Current acts include Don Dixon (producer, songwriter and recording artist) and Marti Jones (recording artist).

☑ ◖ T. SKORMAN PRODUCTIONS, INC.

5156 S. Orange Ave., Orlando FL 32809. (407)895-3000. Fax: (407)895-1422. E-mail: ted@talentagency.com. Website: www.talentagency.com. **Contact:** Ted Skorman, president. Management firm and booking agency. Estab. 1983. Represents groups; currently handles 40 acts. Receives 10-25% commission. Reviews material for acts.

How to Contact *E-mail first for permission to submit.* Prefers CD with 2 songs, or videocassette of no more than 6 minutes. ''Live performance—no trick shots or editing tricks. We want to be able to view act as if we were there for a live show.'' If seeking management, press kit should include cover letter, bio, photo and demo CD or video. Does not return material. Responds only if interested.

Music Mostly **top 40**, **dance**, **pop** and **country**. Works primarily with high-energy dance acts, recording acts, and top 40 bands. Current acts include Steph Carse (pop).

Tips ''We have many pop recording acts and are looking for commercial material for their next albums.''

◖ GARY SMELTZER PRODUCTIONS

603 W. 13th #2A, Austin TX 78701. (512)478-6020. Fax: (512)478-8979. E-mail: gsptalent@aol.com. **Contact:** Gary Smeltzer, president. Management firm and booking agency. Estab. 1967. Represents individual artists and groups from anywhere. Currently handles 20 acts. ''We book about 100 different bands each year—none are exclusive.'' Receives 20% commission. Reviews material for acts.

How to Contact Submit demo tape by mail. Unsolicited submissions are OK. Prefers cassette, videocassette or CD. If seeking management, press kit should include cover letter, résumé, cassette or CD, bio, picture, lyric sheets, press clippings and video. Does not return material. Responds in 1 month.

Music Mostly **alternative**, **R&B** and **country**. Current acts include Ro Tel & the Hot Tomatoes (nostalgic '60s showband).

Tips ''We prefer performing songwriters who can gig their music as a solo or group.''

◖ SOUTHEASTERN ATTRACTIONS

181 W. Valley Ave., Suite 105, Birmingham AL 35209. (205)942-6600. Fax: (205)942-7700. E-mail: staff@seattractions.com. Website: www.seattractions.com. **Contact:** Agent. Booking agency. Estab. 1967. Represents groups from anywhere; currently handles 200 acts. Receives 20% commission.

How to Contact Submit demo tape by mail. Unsolicited submissions are OK. Prefers CD or VHS videocassette. Does not return material. Responds in 2 months.

Music Rock, **alternative**, **oldies**, **country** and **dance**. Works primarily with bands. Current acts include Leaderdog (rock), Undergrounders (variety to contemporary), Style Band (Motown/dance), The Connection (Motown/dance), Space Wrangler (Widespread Panic cover band), The Spoons (groove band), Skydog (groove band), Uncle Bud's 'Lectrowood Experience (bluegrass) and Horse (rock).

◖ SP TALENT ASSOCIATES

P.O. Box 475184, Garland TX 75047. **Contact:** Richard Park, talent coordinator. Management firm and booking agency. Represents individual artists and groups; currently handles 7 acts. Receives 15% commission. Reviews material for acts.

How to Contact Submit demo tape by mail. Unsolicited submissions are OK. Prefers VHS videocassette with several songs. Send photo and bio. Does not return material. Responds as soon as possible.

Music Mostly **rock**, **nostalgia rock** and **country**; also **specialty acts** and **folk/blues**. Works primarily with vocalists and self-contained groups. Current acts include Joe Hardin Brown (country), Renewal (rock group) and Juan Madera & the Supple Grain Seeds.

◖ STAIRCASE PROMOTION

P.O. Box 211, East Prairie MO 63845. (573)649-2211. **Contact:** Tommy Loomas, president. Vice President: Joe Silver. Management firm, music publisher (Lineage Publishing) and record company (Capstan Record Production). Estab. 1975. Represents individual artists and groups from anywhere; currently handles 6 acts. Receives 25% commission. Reviews material for acts.

- Also see the listings for Lineage Publishing Co. in the Music Publishers section and Capstan Record Production in the Record Companies section of this book.

How to Contact Submit demo tape by mail. Unsolicited submissions are OK. Prefers cassette with 3 songs and lyric sheet. If seeking management, press kit should include bio, photo, audio cassette and/or video and press reviews, if any. "Be as professional as you can." Include SASE. Responds in 2 months.

Music Mostly **country**, **pop** and **easy listening**; also **rock**, **gospel** and **alternative**. Current acts include Skidrow Joe (country comedian, on Capstan Records), Vicarie Arcoleo (pop singer, on Treasure Coast Records) and Scarlett Britoni (pop singer on Octagon Records).

◙ STANDER ENTERTAINMENT

11838 Hamlin St., #A, N. Hollywood CA 91606. Phone/fax: (818)769-6365. E-mail: stander@earthlink.net. **Contact:** Jacqueline Stander, manager. Management firm, music publisher (DocRon Publishing), record company (Soaring Records) and consulting firm. Estab. 1970. Represents local individual artists, groups, film composers and songwriters; currently handles 6 acts. Receives 15% commission. Charges $50/hour consulting fee. Reviews material for acts. Places songs in film/TV.

How to Contact *Call first and obtain permission to submit.* Prefers cassette or VHS videocassette with 3-5 songs and lyric sheet. If seeking management, press kit should include photo, bio, press publicity, CD or cassette. Include SASE. Responds in 3 weeks.

Music Mostly **jazz**, **pop** and **R&B** (no rap); also **world music** and **Broadway**. Works primarily with national recording artists, film composers and singer/songwriters. Current and past acts include Bill Cunliffe (jazz pianist/producer), Freddie Ravel (contemporary Latin jazz keyboardist) and Lauren Wood (vocalist/songwriter).

Tips "Always looking for long term professionals who have worked to establish themselves in their market, yet want to go to the next level. For those who have something to offer and are just starting out, I am available for consulting by phone or in person. Please call for submission request."

◙ STARKRAVIN' MANAGEMENT

20501 Ventura Blvd., 217, Woodland Hills CA 91364. (818)587-6801. Fax: (818)587-6802. E-mail: bcmclane@aol .com. **Contact:** B.C. McLane, Esq. Management and law firm. Estab. 1994. Represents individual artists, groups and songwriters. Receives 20% commission (management); $200/hour as attorney.

How to Contact Submit demo tape by mail. Unsolicited submissions are OK. Does not return material. Responds in 1 month.

Music Mostly **rock**, **pop** and **R&B**. Works primarily with bands.

☑ ◙ OBI STEINMAN MANAGEMENT

5627 Sepulveda Blvd., #230, Van Nuys CA 91411. (818)787-4065. Fax: (818)787-4194. E-mail: STCmanagement @aol.com. Website: www.stcent.com. **Contact:** Obi Steinman, manager. Management firm. Represents individual artists and groups from anywhere; currently handles 13 acts. Receives 15-20% commission.

How to Contact Submit demo tape by mail. Unsolicited submissions are OK. Prefers cassette with 4 songs and lyric sheet. If seeking management, press kit should include 8×10 picture, press clippings and bio. "Concentrate more on the material enclosed than the flashy package." Include SASE. Responds in 5 weeks.

Music Mostly **pop R&B**, **pop rock**, **alternative** and **hard rock**. Works primarily with bands and self-contained artists (write own material, have own backing band). Current acts include Warrant (hard rock), L.A. Guns (hard rock) and Keaton Simon.

Tips "We are street level. We are looking for new acts."

ℕ ◯ STEVENS & COMPANY MANAGEMENT

P.O. Box 6368, Corpus Christi TX 78411. (361)888-7311. Fax: (361)888-7360. E-mail: steveco@flash.net. Website: www.fidelHernandez.co. **Contact:** Matt Stevens, owner. Management firm. Estab. 1995. Represents individual artists from anywhere. Currently handles 3 acts. Receives 20% commission. Reviews material for acts.

How to Contact Submit demo CD by mail. Unsolicited submissions are OK. Prefers CD with lyric sheet. Include SASE. Responds in 3 weeks.

Music Mostly **country** and some **Latin**. Works primarily with singers and individual artists. Current acts include Fidel Hernandez (country/Broken Bow Records—Nashville).

Tips "Send material every time you have something new, always leave phone number on tapes."

☑ ◙ STORMIN' NORMAN PRODUCTIONS

2 W. Front, Red Bank NJ 07701. (732)741-8733. (732)741-5353. E-mail: info@storminnormanproductions.com. Website: www.storminnormanproductions.com. **Contact:** Norman Seldin, Owner. Management firm, booking agency, music publisher (Noisy Joy Music/BMI) and record company (Ivory Records). Estab. 1967. Represents individual artists, groups and songwriters from anywhere; currently handles 6 acts. Receives 15-20% commission. Reviews material for acts.

How to Contact Submit demo tape by mail. Unsolicited submissions are OK. Prefers CD (but will accept cassette) with 2-4 songs and lyric sheet for all songs. If seeking management, press kit should include demo cassette or CD with cover and original songs, photo, song list, appearance credits, home base area, phone and address. Include SASE. Responds in 5 weeks.

Music Mostly **country**, **rock** and **reggae**; also **soft rock, dynamic blues** and **folk**. Current acts include Stormin' Norman Band (R&B/nostalgia/adult contemporary), Steel Breeze (Caribbean/Latin/blues), Bobby Vac & Everyone (adult contemporary) and Predator Dub Assassins (original reggae).

STRICTLY FORBIDDEN ARTISTS

320 Avenue Rd., Suite 144, Toronto ON M4V 2H3 Canada. (416)926-0818. Fax: (416)926-0811. E-mail: creative_ agency@yahoo.com. **Contact:** Brad Black, vice president of A&R. Management firm, booking agency and record company. Estab. 1986. Represents individual artists and groups from anywhere; currently handles 8 acts. Receives 20-30% commission. Reviews material for acts.

How to Contact Submit demo CD by mail. Unsolicited submissions are OK. Prefers CD and lyric sheet. If seeking management, press kit should include biography, press clippings, 8×10, photo and demo tape/CD. "Once you've sent material, don't call us, we'll call you." Does not return material. Responds in 6 weeks.

Music Mostly **alternative rock, art rock** and **grindcore**; also **electronic, hip-hop** and **experimental**. Works primarily with performing bands, studio acts and performance artists. Current acts include Sickos (experimental/art-rock), Lazer (coldwave/electronica) and Andy Warhead (punk rock/noise).

Tips "As long as you have faith in your music, we'll have faith in promoting you and your career."

T.L.C. BOOKING AGENCY

37311 N. Valley Rd., Chattaroy WA 99003. (509)292-2201. Fax: (509)292-2205. E-mail: tlcagent@ix.netcom.c om. Website: www.tlcagency.com. **Contact:** Tom or Carrie Lapsansky, agent/owners. Booking agency. Estab. 1970. Represents individual artists and groups from anywhere; currently handles 17 acts. Receives 10-15% commission. Reviews material for acts.

How to Contact *Call first and obtain permission to submit.* Prefers cassette with 3-4 songs. Does not return material. Responds in 3 weeks.

Music Mostly **rock**, **country** and **variety**; also **comedians** and **magicians**. Works primarily with bands, singles and duos. Current acts include Nobody Famous (variety), Menagerie (variety-duo) and Soul Patrol (variety/top 40).

TAKE OUT MANAGEMENT

5605 Woodman Ave. #206, Van Nuys CA 91401. (818)901-1122. Fax: (818)901-6513. E-mail: howie@howiewoo d.com. Website: www.howiewood.com. **Contact:** Craig Parker, artist relations. Management firm. Estab. 1985. Represents individual artists, groups and songwriters from anywhere; currently handles 4 acts. Receives 15-20% commission. Reviews material for acts.

How to Contact Submit demo tape by mail. Unsolicited submissions are OK. Prefers cassette or CD with any number of songs and lyric sheet. If seeking management, press kit should include tape or CD, picture, bio and cover letter. Does not return material. Responds in 1 week.

Music Mostly **pop**, **A/C** and **rock**; also **R&B** and **dance**. Works primarily with singer/songwriters, arrangers and bands. Current acts include Dan Hill (A/C) and Rodney Sheldon (R&B).

TAS MUSIC CO./DAVE TASSE ENTERTAINMENT

N2467 Knollwood Dr., Lake Geneva WI 53147-9731. E-mail: baybreeze@idcnet.com. Website: www.baybreezer ecords.com. **Contact:** David Tasse. Booking agency, record company and music publisher. Represents artists, groups and songwriters; currently handles 21 acts. Receives 10-20% commission. Reviews material for acts.

How to Contact Submit demo tape by mail. Unsolicited submissions are OK. Prefers cassette with 2-4 songs and lyric sheet. Include performance videocassette if available. If seeking management, press kit should include tape, bio and photo. Does not return material. Responds in 3 weeks.

Music Mostly **pop** and **jazz**; also **dance, MOR, rock, soul** and **top 40**. Works primarily with show and dance bands. Current acts include Max Kelly (philosophic rock) and L.J. Young (rap).

TEXAS SOUNDS ENTERTAINMENT

P.O. Box 1644, Dickinson TX 77535. (281)337-2473. Fax: (281)534-1127. E-mail: mikesandberg@texas-sounds.c om. Website: www.texas-sounds.com. **Contact:** Mike Sandberg or George M. DeJesus, co-owners. Management firm, booking agency. Estab. 1980. Represents individual artists, groups and songwriters from anywhere. Currently handles 60 acts. Receives 10% commission.

How to Contact *Write first and obtain permission to submit.* Prefers cassette with 3-4 songs and lyric and/or lead sheet. If seeking management, press kit should include bio, photo, accomplishments, demo tape. Does not return material.

Music Mostly **country**, **R&B** and **Latin pop**. Works primarily with bands, orchestras, singer/songwriters. Current acts include Johnny Lee (country singer), Chris Chitsey (country singer/songwriter), Patrick Murphy (country singer/songwriter), Hamilton Loomis (R&B singer/musician) and Jerry Hart (country).

◪ TRIANGLE TALENT, INC.
10424 Watterson, Louisville KY 40299. (502)267-5466. Fax: (502)267-8244. Website: www.triangletalent.com. **Contact:** David H. Snowden, president. Booking agency. Represents artists and groups; currently handles 85 acts. Receives 10-20% commission. Reviews material for acts.
How to Contact Submit demo tape by mail. Unsolicited submissions are OK. Prefers CD, cassette or VHS videocassette with 2-4 songs and lyric sheet. If seeking management, press kit should include photo, cassette of at least 3 songs, and video if possible. Does not return material. Responds in 1 month.
Music Mostly **rock/top 40** and **country**. Current acts include Lee Bradley (contemporary country), Karen Kraft (country) and Four Kinsmen (Australian group).

◪ UMBRELLA ARTISTS MANAGEMENT, INC.
2612 Erie Ave., P.O. Box 8369, Cincinnati OH 45208. (513)871-1500. Fax: (513)871-1510. E-mail: shertzman@cinci.rr.com. Website: www.stanhertzman.com. **Contact:** Stan Hertzman, president. Management firm. Represents artists and groups for specific circumstances.
How to Contact *E-mail or phone specific need.*
Music Mostly **progressive**, **rock** and **top 40/pop**. Works with contemporary/progressive pop/rock artists and writers on a per project basis.

Ⓝ ◪ UMPIRE ENTERTAINMENT ENTERPRIZES
1507 Scenic Dr., Longview TX 75604. (903)759-0300. Fax: (903)234-2944. **Contact:** Jerry Haymes, owner/president. Management firm, music publisher (Golden Guitar, Umpire Music) and record company (Enterprize Records). Estab. 1974. Represents individual artists, groups, songwriters and rodeo specialty acts; currently handles 4 acts. Receives 15% commission. Reviews material for acts.
  • Also see the listing for Enterprize Records-Tapes in the Record Companies section of this book.
How to Contact *Contact first and obtain permission to submit.* Prefers cassette with lyric and lead sheets. If seeking management, press kit should include cover letter, bio, picture, lyric sheets, video and any recordings. Does not return material. "Submissions become part of files for two years, then disposed of." Responds in 1 month.
Music Mostly **country, pop** and **gospel**. Artists include Johnny Patterson (instrumentalist), Larry McGuire (instrumentalist) and three vocal acts.

☑ ◯ UNIVERSAL MUSIC MARKETING
P.O. Box 2297, Universal City TX 78148. (210)653-3989. E-mail: bswrl8@txdirect.net. **Contact:** Frank Willson, president. Management firm, record company (BSW Records), booking agency, music publisher and record producer (Frank Wilson). Estab. 1987. Represents individual artists and groups from anywhere; currently handles 12 acts. Receives 15% commission. Reviews material for acts.
  • Also see the listings for BSW Records in the Music Publishers and Record Companies sections and Frank Wilson in the Record Producers section of this book.
How to Contact Submit demo tape by mail. Unsolicited submissions are OK. Prefers cassette or ¾″ videocassette with 3 songs and lyric sheet. If seeking management, include tape/CD, bio, photo and current activities. Include SASE. Responds in 6 weeks.
Music Mostly **country** and **light rock**; also **blues** and **jazz**. Works primarily with vocalists, singer/songwriters and bands. Current acts include Candee Land, Darlene Austin, Larry Butler, John Wayne, Sonny Marshall, Bobby Mountain, Crea Beal and Butch Martin (country).

▦ ☑ ◪ HANS VAN POL MANAGEMENT
Utrechtseweg 39B, 1381 GS Weesp, Netherlands. Phone: (0)294-413-633. Fax: (0)294-480-844. E-mail: hansvanpol@yahoo.com. Managing Director: Hans Van Pol. A&R/Producer: Jochem Fluitsma. Management firm, consultant (Hans Van Pol Music Consultancy), record company (J.E.A.H.! Records) and music publisher (Blue & White Music). Estab. 1984. Represents regional (Holland/Belgium) individual artists and groups; currently handles 7 acts. Receives 20% commission. Reviews material for acts.
How to Contact Submit demo tape by mail. Unsolicited submissions are OK. Prefers CD/DVD with 3 songs and lyric sheets. If seeking management, press kit should include demo, possible DVD, bio, press clippings, photo and release information. SAE and IRC. Responds in 1 month.
Music Mostly **MOR, dance: rap/swing beat/hip house/R&B/soul/c.a.r.** Current acts include Fluitsma & Van Tÿn (production, commercials, MOR), Tony Scott (rap) and MC Miker "G" (rap/R&B).

Managers & Agents

ⓃⓏ RICHARD VARRASSO MANAGEMENT

P.O. Box 387, Fremont CA 94500. (510)792-8910. Fax: (510)792-0891. E-mail: richard@varrasso.com. Website: www.varrasso.com. President: Richard Varrasso. A&R: Saul Vigil. Management firm. Estab. 1976. Represents individual artists, groups and songwriters from anywhere; currently handles several acts. Receives 10-20% commission. Reviews material for acts.

How to Contact Submit demo tape by mail. Unsolicited submissions are OK. Prefers cassette or CD. If seeking management, press kit should include photos, bios, cover letter, cassette, lyric sheets, press clippings, video, résumé and contact numbers. Good kits stand out. Does not return material. Responds in 2 months.

Music Mostly **rock**, **blues** and **young country**. Works primarily with concert headliners and singers. Current acts include Gary Cambra of the Tubes, Dave Meniketti Group, Famous Hits Band featuring Rich Varasso, Alameda Allstars (Greg Allman's backup band), Richie Barron of HWY2000, Tongue N Groove, Greg Douglass (songwriter) and Blunt Force Trauma.

Ⓩ WILLIAM F. WAGNER AGENCY

14343 Addison St. #221, Sherman Oaks CA 91423. (818)905-1033. **Contact:** Bill Wagner, owner. Management firm and record producer (Bill Wagner). Estab. 1957. Represents individual artists and groups from anywhere; currently handles 2 acts. Receives 15% commission. Reviews materials for acts.

How to Contact Submit demo tape or CD by mail. Unsolicited submissions are OK. Prefers cassette or CD with 5 songs and lead sheet. If seeking management, press kit should include cover letter, bio, picture, tape or CD with 5 songs. "If SASE and/or return postage are included, I will reply in 30 days."

Music Mostly **jazz**, **contemporary pop** and **contemporary country**; also **classical**, **MOR** and **film and TV background**. Works primarily with singers, with or without band, big bands and smaller instrumental groups. Current acts include Page Cavanaugh (jazz/pop/contemporary/pianist) and Sandy Graham (jazz singer).

Tips "Indicate in first submission what artists you are writing for, by name if possible. Don't send material blindly. Be sure all material is properly copyrighted. Be sure package shows 'all material herein copyrighted' on outside."

Ⓩ CHERYL K. WARNER PRODUCTIONS

P.O. Box 127, Hermitage TN 37076-0127. Phone: (615)847-1286. E-mail: cherylkwarner@comcast.net. Website: www.cherylkwarner.com. **Contact:** Cheryl K. Warner and David M. Warner. Recording and stage production, music consulting, music publisher. Estab. 1988. Currently works with 3 acts. Reviews material for acts.

How to Contact Submit demo CD/DVD by mail. Unsolicited submissions are OK. Prefers CD or DVD, but will accept cassette with 3 best songs, lyric or lead sheet, bio and picture. Press kit should include CD, DVD, video/audio cassette with up-to-date bio, cover letter, lyric sheets, press clippings, and picture. Does not return material. Responds in 6 weeks if interested.

Music Mostly **country/traditional and contemporary**, **Christian/gospel** and **A/C/pop**. Works primarily with singer/songwriters and bands with original and versatile style. Current acts include Cheryl K. Warner (Nashville recording artist/entertainer), Cheryl K. Warner Band (support/studio alt) and Cherry (rock/pop artist).

ⓃⓄ WE RECORDS & MANAGEMENT

P.O. Box 684721, Austin TX 78768-4721. (512)328-5756. E-mail: werecords@aol.com. Website: www.werecords.com. **Contact:** Jason Whitmire, president. Management firm, booking agency and record company (WE Records). Estab. 1995. Represents individual artists and groups from anywhere; currently handles 2 acts. Receives 20% commission. Reviews material for acts.

How to Contact Submit demo tape by mail. Unsolicited submissions are OK. Prefers CD. If seeking management, press kit should include cover letter, demo tape/CD, press clippings, photo and bio. "Explain, besides the music, what makes your act more appealing than others?" Does not return material. Responds in 2 months.

Music Mostly **electronic** and **techno**. Current acts include DJ Alchemy (down tempo) and Vertigo Blue (electronica).

Tips "Keep everyone updated on your status and keep your name in the public eye."

☑Ⓩ WEMUS ENTERTAINMENT

2006 Seaboard, Suite 400, Midland TX 79705. (432)689-3687. Fax: (432)687-0930. E-mail: wemus@aol.com. Website: www.wemus.com. **Contact:** Dennis Grubb, president. Management firm, booking agency and music publisher (Wemus Music, Inc.). Estab. 1983. Represents local and regional individual artists and groups; currently handles 4 acts. Receives 15-25% commission. Reviews material for acts.

How to Contact Submit demo tape by mail. Unsolicited submissions are OK. Prefers cassette, CD, DVD or VHS videocassette with 3-5 songs and lyric sheet. If seeking management, press kit should include glossy head and full body shots and extensive biography. "Make sure address, phone number and possible fax number is included in the packet, or a business card." Does not return material. Responds in 1 month if interested.

Music Mostly **country**. Current acts include The Image (variety), The Big Time (variety), The Pictures (variety) and Pryce Conner.

Tips "We preview and try to place good songs with national artists who are in need of good materials. We have a very tough qualification process and are very selective in forwarding materials to artists and their management."

☐ SHANE WILDER ARTISTS' MANAGEMENT

P.O. Box 335687, North Las Vegas NV 89033-0012. (702)395-5624. **Contact:** Shane Wilder, president. General Manager: Aaron Wilder. Management firm, music publisher (Shane Wilder Music/BMI) and record producer (Shane Wilder Productions). Represents artists and groups; currently handles 4 acts. Receives 10% commission. Reviews material for acts.

How to Contact Submit demo tape by mail. Unsolicited submissions are OK. Prefers cassette or videocassette of performance with 4-10 songs and lyric sheet. If seeking management, send cover letter, bio, lyric sheets, cassette with 4-10 songs, photos of individuals or groups, video if possible and any press releases. "Submissions should be highly commercial." Include SASE. Responds in 2 weeks.

Music Country. Works primarily with single artists and groups. Current acts include Isabel Marie (country), Craig Dodson (country), Darren Collier (rock), Ann Lee (country) and Lonnie Raynes (country).

N ⛄ ☐ WINTERLAND ENTERTAINMENT MANAGEMENT & PUBLISHING

(formerly T.J. Booker Ltd.), P.O. Box 969, Rossland BC V0G 1Y0 Canada. (250)362-7795. E-mail: winterland@ne tidea.com. **Contact:** Tom Jones, owner. Management firm, booking agency and music publisher. Estab. 1976. Represents individual artists, groups and songwriters from anywhere; currently handles 6 acts. Receives 15% commission. Reviews material for acts.

How to Contact Submit demo tape by mail. Unsolicited submissions are OK. Prefers CD, cassette or videocassette with 3 songs. If seeking management, include demo tape or CD, picture, cover letter and bio in press kit. Does not return material. Responds in 1 month.

Music Mostly **MOR**, **crossover**, **rock**, **pop** and **country**. Works primarily with vocalists, show bands, dance bands and bar bands. Current acts include Kirk Orr (folk/country), Mike Hamilton (rock/blues) and Larry Hayton (rock/blues).

☐ RICHARD WOOD ARTIST MANAGEMENT

69 North Randall Ave., Staten Island NY 10301. (718)981-0641. Fax: (718)273-0797. **Contact:** Richard Wood. Management firm. Estab. 1974. Represents musical groups; currently handles 3 acts. Receives 20% commission. Reviews material for acts.

How to Contact Submit demo tape by mail. Unsolicited submissions are OK. Prefers cassette and lead sheet. If seeking management, press kit should include demo tape, photo, cover letter and résumé. Include SASE. Responds in 1 month.

Music Mostly **dance**, **R&B** and **top 40/pop**; also **MOR**. Works primarily with "high energy" show bands, bar bands and dance bands.

✓ ⊘ WORLD WIDE MANAGEMENT

P.O. Box 536, Bronxville NY 10708. Fax: (914)337-5309. **Contact:** David Zeich, Marcy Drexler, directors. Management firm and music publisher (Neighborhood Music/ASCAP). Estab. 1971. Represents artists, groups, songwriters and actors; currently handles 5 acts. Receives 15-20% commission. Reviews material for acts.

How to Contact *Write first and obtain permission to submit.* Prefers CD, cassette or videocassete of performance with 3-4 songs. If seeking management, press kit should include cover letter, bio, reviews, press clippings, CD or cassette with lyrics and photo. Does not return material. Responds in 1 month.

Music Mostly **contemporary pop**, **folk**, **folk/rock** and **New Age**; also **A/C**, **rock**, **jazz**, **bluegrass**, **blues**, **country** and **R&B**. Works primarily with self-contained bands and vocalists. Current acts include Wendy Starland, Gretchen Witt and Lina Koutrakos.

✓ ⊘ WORLDSOUND, LLC

19743 1st Ave. South, Seattle WA 98148. (206)444-0300. Fax: (206)244-0066. E-mail: wmw@wyattworld.com. Website: www.worldsound.com. **Contact:** Warren Wyatt, A&R manager. Management firm. Estab. 1976. Represents individual artists, groups and songwriters from anywhere; currently handles 8 acts. Receives 20% commission. Reviews material for acts.

How to Contact Submit demo tape by mail. Unsolicited submissions are OK. Prefers CD or VHS videocassette with 2-10 songs and lyric sheet. If seeking management, press kit should include band biography, photos, video, members' history, press and demo reviews. Include SASE. Responds in 1 month.

Music Mostly **rock**, **pop** and **world**; also **heavy metal**, **hard rock** and **top 40**. Works primarily with pop/rock groups. Current acts include Carmine Appice (rock), Makana (world music) and Carbon 9 (tribal rock/industrial pop metal).

Tips "Always submit new songs/material, even if you have sent material that was previously rejected; the music biz is always changing."

◢ ZANE MANAGEMENT, INC.

1650 Market St., One Liberty Place, 21st Floor, Philadelphia PA 19103. (215)575-3803. Fax: (215)575-3801. E-mail: lzr@braverlaw.com. Website: www.zanemanagement.com. **Contact:** Lloyd Z. Remick, Esq., president. Entertainment/sports consultants and managers. Represents artists, songwriters, producers and athletes; currently handles 7 acts. Receives 10-15% commission.

How to Contact Submit demo tape by mail. Unsolicited submissions are OK. Prefers CD and lyric sheet. If seeking management, press kit should include cover letter, bio, photo, demo tape and video. Does not return material. Responds in 3 weeks.

Music Mostly **dance**, **easy listening**, **folk**, **jazz** (fusion), **MOR**, **rock** (hard and country), **soul** and **top 40/pop**. Current acts include Bunny Sigler (disco/funk), Peter Nero and Philly Pops (conductor), Cast in Bronze (rock group), Pieces of a Dream (jazz/crossover), Don't Look Down (rock/pop) and Christian Josi (pop-swing).

D. ZIRILLI MANAGEMENT

P.O. Box 255, Cupertino CA 95015-0255. (408)257-2533. Fax: (408)252-8938. E-mail: donzirilli@aol.com. Website: www.zirilli.com. Owner: Don Zirilli. Management firm. Estab. 1965. Represents groups from anywhere; currently handles 1 act. Receives 20% commission. Reviews material for acts.

How to Contact Submit demo tape by mail. Unsolicited submissions are OK. Prefers cassette, DAT, videocassette or CD. If seeking management, press kit should include video. Does not return material. Responds in 2 weeks.

Music Mostly **rock**, **surf** and **MOR**. Current acts include Papa Doo Run Run (band).

Tips "Less is more."

ADDITIONAL MANAGERS & BOOKING AGENTS

The following companies are also managers/booking agents, but their listings are found in other sections of the book. See the General Index for page numbers, then read the listings for submission information.

C

Clearwind Publishing

D

Deep South Entertainment
Delev Music Company
Diamond Entertainment, Joel

E

Edition Rossori
Esquire International

H

His Power Productions and Publishing

L

Lucifer Records, Inc.

M

Modal Music, Inc.™

N

Nightmare Records

S

Satkowski Recordings, Steve
Sphere Group One
Standard Music Publishing
Stuart Music Co., Jeb

T

Twin Towers Publishing Co.

Music Firms

Advertising, Audiovisual & Commercial

t's happened a million times—you hear a jingle on the radio or television and can't get it out of your head. That's the work of a successful jingle writer, writing songs to catch your attention and make you aware of the product being advertised. But the field of commercial music consists of more than just memorable jingles. It also includes background music that many companies use in videos for corporate and educational presentations, as well as films and TV shows.

SUBMITTING MATERIAL

More than any other market listed in this book, the commercial music market expects composers to have made an investment in the recording of their material before submitting. A sparse, piano/vocal demo won't work here; when dealing with commercial music firms, especially audiovisual firms and music libraries, high quality production is important. Your demo may be kept on file at one of these companies until a need for it arises, and it may be used or sold as you sent it. Therefore, your demo tape or reel must be as fully produced as possible.

The presentation package that goes along with your demo must be just as professional. A list of your credits should be a part of your submission, to give the company an idea of your experience in this field. If you have no experience, look to local television and radio stations to get your start. Don't expect to be paid for many of your first jobs in the commercial music field; it's more important to get the credits and exposure that can lead to higher-paying jobs.

Commercial music and jingle writing can be a lucrative field for the composer/songwriter with a gift for writing catchy melodies and the ability to write in many different music styles. It's a very competitive field, so it pays to have a professional presentation package that makes your work stand out.

Three different segments of the commercial music world are listed here: advertising agencies, audiovisual firms and commercial music houses/music libraries. Each looks for a different type of music, so read these descriptions carefully to see where the music you write fits in.

ADVERTISING AGENCIES

Ad agencies work on assignment as their clients' needs arise. Through consultation and input from the creative staff, ad agencies seek jingles and music to stimulate the consumer to identify with a product or service.

When contacting ad agencies, keep in mind they are searching for music that can capture and then hold an audience's attention. Most jingles are short, with a strong, memorable hook. When an ad agency listens to a demo, it is not necessarily looking for a finished product so much as for an indication of creativity and diversity. Many composers put together a reel of excerpts of work from previous projects, or short pieces of music that show they can write in a variety of styles.

AUDIOVISUAL FIRMS

Audiovisual firms create a variety of products, from film and video shows for sales meetings, corporate gatherings and educational markets, to motion pictures and TV shows. With the increase of home video use, how-to videos are a big market for audiovisual firms, as are spoken word educational videos. All of these products need music to accompany them. For your quick reference, companies working to place music in movies and TV shows (excluding commercials) have a ▨ preceding their listing (also see the Film & TV Index on page 423 for a complete list of these companies).

Like ad agencies, audiovisual firms look for versatile, well-rounded songwriters. When submitting demos to these firms, you need to demonstrate your versatility in writing special-ized background music and themes. Listings for companies will tell what facet(s) of the audiovisual field they are involved in and what types of clients they serve. Your demo tape should also be as professional and fully produced as possible; audiovisual firms often seek demo tapes that can be put on file for future use when the need arises.

COMMERCIAL MUSIC HOUSES & MUSIC LIBRARIES

Commercial music houses are companies contracted (either by an ad agency or the advertiser) to compose custom jingles. Since they are neither an ad agency nor an audiovisual firm, their main concern is music. They use a lot of it, too—some composed by inhouse songwriters and some contributed by outside, freelance writers.

Music libraries are different in that their music is not custom composed for a specific client. Their job is to provide a collection of instrumental music in many different styles that, for an annual fee or on a per-use basis, the customer can use however he chooses.

In the following listings, commercial music houses and music libraries, which are usually the most open to works by new composers, are identified as such by **bold** typeface.

The commercial music market is similar to most other businesses in one aspect: experience is important. Until you develop a list of credits, pay for your work may not be high. Don't pass up opportunities if a job is non- or low-paying. These assignments will add to your list of credits, make you contacts in the field, and improve your marketability.

Money and rights

Many of the companies listed in this section pay by the job, but there may be some situations where the company asks you to sign a contract that will specify royalty payments. If this happens, research the contract thoroughly, and know exactly what is expected of you and how much you'll be paid.

Depending on the particular job and the company, you may be asked to sell one-time rights or all rights. One-time rights involve using your material for one presentation only. All rights means the buyer can use your work any way he chooses, as many times as he likes. Be sure you know exactly what you're giving up, and how the company may use your music in the future.

In the commercial world, many of the big advertising agencies have their own publishing companies where writers assign their compositions. In these situations, writers sign contracts whereby they do receive performance and mechanical royalties when applicable.

ADDITIONAL LISTINGS

For additional names and addresses of ad agencies that may use jingles and/or commercial music, refer to the *Standard Directory of Advertising Agencies* (National Register Publishing).

Commercial Music Firms

For a list of audiovisual firms, check out the latest edition of *AV Marketplace* (R.R. Bowker). Both these books may be found at your local library. To contact companies in your area, see the Geographic Index at the back of this book.

THE AD AGENCY

P.O. Box 470572, San Francisco CA 94147. **Contact:** Michael Carden, creative director. Advertising agency and **jingle/commercial music production house**. Clients include business, industry and retail. Estab. 1971. Uses the services of music houses, independent songwriter/composers and lyricists for scoring of commercials, background music for video production, and jingles for commercials. Commissions 20 composers and 15 lyricists/year. Pays by the job or by the hour. Buys all or one-time rights.

How to Contact Submit demo tape of previous work. Prefers cassette with 5-8 songs and lyric sheet. Include SASE. Responds in 3 weeks.

Music Uses variety of musical styles for commercials, promotion, TV, video presentations.

Tips "Our clients and our needs change frequently."

ADVERTEL, INC.

P.O. Box 18053, Pittsburgh PA 15236-0053. (412)344-4700. Fax: (412)344-4712. E-mail: pberan@advertel.com. Website: www.advertel.com. **Contact:** Paul Beran, president/CEO. Telephonic/Internet production company. Clients include small and multi-national companies. Estab. 1983. Uses the services of music houses and independent songwriters/composers for scoring of instrumentals (all varieties) and telephonic production. Commissions 3-4 composers/year. Pay varies. Buys all rights and phone exclusive rights.

How to Contact Submit demo of previous work. Prefers CD. "Most compositions are 2 minutes strung together in 6, 12, 18 minute length productions." Does not return material; prefers to keep on file. Responds "right away if submission fills an immediate need."

Music Uses all varieties, including unusual; mostly subdued music beds. Radio-type production used exclusively in telephone and Internet applications.

Tips "Go for volume. We have continuous need for all varieties of music in two minute lengths."

ⓃⒸ ALLEGRO MUSIC

3990 Sunsetridge, Suite 203, Moorpark CA 93021-3756. E-mail: dannymuse@adelphia.net. Website: www.danielobrien.com. Owner: Daniel O'Brien. Scoring service, **jingle/commercial music production house**. Clients include film-makers, advertisers, network promotions and aerobics. Estab. 1991. Uses the services of independent songwriters/composers and lyricists for scoring of films, TV and broadcast commercials, jingles for ad agencies and promotions, and commercials for radio and TV. Commissions 3 composers and 1 lyricist/year. Pays 50% royalty. Buys one-time rights.

How to Contact Query with résumé of credits or submit demo tape of previous work. Prefers CD, cassette and lyric sheet. Include SASE. Responds in 1 month (if interested).

Music Varied: Contemporary to orchestral.

Ⓩ ANDERSON COMMUNICATIONS

Suite 202, 2245 Godby Rd., Atlanta GA 30349. (404)766-8000. President: Al Anderson. Producer: Vanessa Vaughn. Advertising agency and syndication operation. Estab. 1971. Clients include major corporations, institutions and media. Uses the services of music houses, independent songwriters/composers and lyricists for background music for commercials and jingles for syndicated radio programs. Commissions 5-6 songwriters or composers and 6-7 lyricists/year. Pays by the job. Buys all rights.

How to Contact Write first to arrange personal interview or submit demo tape of previous work. Prefers cassette. Does not return material. Responds in 2 weeks or "when we have projects requiring your services."

Music Uses a variety of music for music beds for commercials and jingles for nationally syndicated radio programs and commercials targeted at the black consumer market.

Tips "Be sure the composition plays well in a 60-second format."

BLATTNER/BRUNNER INC.

11 Stanwix St., 5th Floor, Pittsburgh PA 15222-1312. (412)995-9500. Broadcast Production Coordinator: Karen Smith. Clients include retail/consumer, service, high-tech/industrial/medical. Estab. 1975. Uses the services of music houses and independent songwriters/composers for background music for TV and radio spots and jingles for TV and radio spots. Commissions 2-3 composers/year. Pays by the job. Buys all rights or one-time rights, depending on the job.

How to Contact *"Call first to see if there is an exisitng opportunity."*

Music "Project-dependent and driven by script."
Tips "Send relevant work in conjunction to the advertising business—i.e., jingles."

BRg MUSIC WORKS

P.O. Box 202, Bryn Mawr PA 19010. (610)971-9490. Fax: (610)971-9630. E-mail: lnapier@brgmusicworks.com. Website: www.brgmusicworks.com. Creative Director: Doug Reed. **Contact:** Lee Napier. **Jingle producers/ music library producers**. Uses independent composers and music houses for background music for radio, TV and commercials and jingles for radio and TV. Commissions 20 songwriters/year. Pays per job. Buys all rights.
How to Contact Submit demo tape of previous work. Prefers cassette. "We are looking for quality jingle tracks already produced, as well as instrumental pieces between 2 and 3 minutes in length for use in AV music library." Include SASE. Responds in 2 weeks.
Music All types.
Tips "Send your best and put your strongest work at the front of your demo tape."

CANTRAX RECORDERS

Dept. CM, 2119 Fidler Ave., Long Beach CA 90815. (562)498-4593. Fax: (562)498-4852. E-mail: cantrax@earthli nk.net. **Contact:** Richard Cannata, owner. Recording studio. Clients include anyone needing recording services (i.e., industrial, radio, commercial). Estab. 1980. Uses the services of independent songwriters/composers and lyricists for scoring of independent features and films and background music for radio, industrials and promotions, commercials for radio and TV and jingles for radio. Commissions 10 composers/year. Pays fees set by the artist. "We take 15%."
How to Contact *"No phone calls, please."* Query with résumé of credits or submit demo CD of previous work. Prefers CD—no cassettes. Does not return material. Responds in 2 weeks if SASE is provided.
Music Uses jazz, New Age, rock, easy listening and classical for slide shows, jingles and soundtracks.
Tips "You must have a serious, professional attitude."

CEDAR CREST STUDIO

P.O. Box 28, Mountain Home AR 72653. (870)488-5777. Fax: (253)681-8194. E-mail: cedarcrest@springfield.n et. Website: www.oznet.com/cedarcrest. **Contact:** Bob Ketchum, owner. Audiovisual firm and **jingle/commercial music production house**. Clients include corporate, industrial, sales, music publishing, training, educational, legal, medical, music and Internet. Estab. 1973. Sometimes uses the services of independent songwriters/ composers for background music for video productions, jingles for TV spots and commercials for radio and TV. Pays by the job or by royalties. Buys all rights or one-time rights.
How to Contact Query with résumé of credits or submit demo tape of previous work. Prefers CD, cassette, DAT, 7.5 or 15 IPS reel-to-reel or videocassette. Does not return material. "We keep it on file for future reference." Responds in 2 months.
Music Uses up-tempo pop (not too "rocky"), unobtrusive—no solos for commercials and background music for video presentations.
Tips "Hang, hang, hang. Be open to suggestions. Improvise, adapt, overcome."

CINEVUE/STEVE POSTAL PRODUCTIONS

108 Carraway St., Palatka FL 32177-1150. (386)328-6656. E-mail: birdshum@aol.com. Website: www.hometow n.aol.com/cinemapostal/myhomepage/movies.html. **Contact:** Steve Postal, director/producer. Motion picture production company. Estab. 1955. Serves all types of film distributors. Uses the services of music houses, independent songwriters, composers and lyricists for scoring and background music for films and nature documentaries. Commissions 10 composers and 5 lyricists/year. Pays by the job. Buys all rights.
How to Contact Query with résumé of credits or submit demo tape of previous work ("good tape only!"). Submit manuscript showing music scoring skills. Prefers cassette or CD with 10 pieces and lyric or lead sheet. Only returns material if accompanied by SASE with sufficient postage for return of all materials. "Send good audio-cassette, then call me in a week." Responds in 2 weeks.
Music Uses all styles of music for features (educational films and slide presentations). "Need horror film music on traditional instruments—no electronic music."
Tips "Be flexible, fast—do first job free to ingratiate yourself and demonstrate your style. Follow up with two phone calls."

COMMUNICATIONS FOR LEARNING

395 Massachusetts Ave., Arlington MA 02474. (781)641-2350. E-mail: comlearn@thecia.net. Website: www.co mmunicationsforlearning.com. **Contact:** Jonathan L. Barkan, executive producer/director. Video, multimedia, exhibit and graphic design firm. Clients include multi-nationals, industry, government, institutions, local, national and international nonprofits. Uses services of music houses and independent songwriters/composers as

theme and background music for videos and multimedia. Commissions 1-2 composers/year. Pays $2,000-5,000/ job and one-time fees. Rights purchased varies.
How to Contact Submit demo of previous work. Prefers CD. Does not return material; prefers to keep on file. "For each job we consider our entire collection." Responds in 3 months.
Music Uses all styles of music for all sorts of assignments.
Tips "Please don't call. Just send good material and when we're interested, we'll be in touch. Make certain your name and phone number are on all submitted work itself, not only on the cover letter."

CREATIVE ASSOCIATES

Dept. SM, 44 Park Ave., Madison NJ 07940. (973)377-4440. **Contact:** Susan Graham, production coordinator. Audiovisual/multimedia firm and web content provider. Clients include commercial, industrial firms. Estab. 1975. Uses the services of music houses and independent songwriters/composers for scoring of video programs, background music for press tours and jingles for new products. Pays $300-5,000/job. Buys all or one-time rights.
How to Contact Submit demo tape of previous work demonstrating composition skills or query with résumé of credits. Prefers cassette, CD-ROM or ½" VHS videocassette. Prefers to keep material on file.
Music Uses all styles for many different assignments.

☑ 🎬 D.S.M. PRODUCERS INC.

P.O. Box 1160, Marco Island FL 39146-1166. (212)245-0006. President, CEO: Suzan Bader. **Contact:** Elber Maldonado, Director A&R. Scoring service, **jingle/commercial music production house** and original stock library called "All American Composers Library (administered world wide except USA by Warner/Chappell Music, Inc.)" Clients include networks, corporate, advertising firms, film and video, book publishers (music only). Estab. 1979. Uses the services of independent songwriters/composers for scoring of TV and feature films, background music for feature films and TV, jingles for major products and commercials for radio and TV. Pays 50% royalty. Buys all rights.
How to Contact Write first and enclose SASE for return permission. Prefers cassette or VHS videocassette with 2 songs and lyric or lead sheet. "Use a large enough return envelope to put in a standard business reply letter." Responds in 3 months.
Music Uses all styles including alternative, dance, New Age, country and rock for adventure films and sports programs.
Tips "Carefully label your submissions. Include a short bio/résumé of your works. Lyric sheets are very helpful to A&R. Only send your best tapes and tunes. Invest in your profession and get a local professional to help you produce your works. A master quality tape is the standard today. This is your competition so if you really want to be a songwriter, act like the ones who are successful—get a good tape of your tune. This makes it easier to sell overall. Never use 'samples' or any other copyrighted material in your works without a license."

dbF A MEDIA COMPANY

P.O. Box 2458, Waldorf MD 20604. (301)843-7110. E-mail: production@dbfmedia.com. Website: www.dbfmedi a.com. **Contact:** Randy Runyon, general manager. Advertising agency, audiovisual and media firm and audio and video production company. Clients include business and industry. Estab. 1981. Uses the services of music houses, independent songwriters/composers and lyricists for background music for industrial, training, educational and promo videos, jingles and commercials for radio and TV. Commissions 5-12 composers and 5-12 lyricists/year. Pays by the job. Buys all rights.
How to Contact Submit demo tape of previous work. Prefers cassette or CD or VHS videocassette with 5-8 songs and lead sheet. Include SASE, but prefers to keep material on file. Responds in 6 months.
Music Uses up-tempo contemporary for industrial videos, slide presentations and commercials.
Tips "We're looking for commercial music, primarily A/C."

🎬 DISK PRODUCTIONS

1100 Perkins Rd., Baton Rouge LA 70802. Fax: (225)343-0210. E-mail: joey_decker@hotmail.com. **Contact:** Joey Decker, director. **Jingle/production house.** Clients include advertising agencies, slide production houses and film companies. Estab. 1982. Uses the services of music houses, independent songwriters/composers and lyricists for scoring and background music for TV spots, films and jingles for radio and TV. Commissions 7 songwriters/composers and 7 lyricists/year. Pays by the job. Buys all rights.
How to Contact Submit demo tape of previous work. Prefers CD, cassette or DAT (or ½" videocassette). Does not return material. Responds in 2 weeks.
Music Needs all types of music for jingles, music beds or background music for TV and radio, etc.
Tips "Advertising techniques change with time. Don't be locked in a certain style of writing. Give me music that I can't get from pay needle-drop."

ENSEMBLE PRODUCTIONS

P.O. Box 2332, Auburn AL 36831. (334)703-5963. E-mail: info@epient.com. **Contact:** Barry J. McConatha, owner/producer/director. Interactive multimedia and video production/post production. Clients include corporate, governmental and educational. Estab. 1984. Uses services of music houses and independent songwriters/composers for background music for corporate public relations, educational and training videos. Commissions 0-5 composers/year. Pays $25-250/job depending upon project. Buys one-time rights or all rights.

How to Contact Send e-mail or submit demo tape of previous work demonstrating composition skills. "Needs are sporadic, write first if submission to be returned." Prefers cassette, CD or VHS videocassette with 3-5 songs. "Most needs are up-beat industrial sound but occasional mood setting music also. Inquire for details." Does not return material; prefers to keep on file. Responds in 3 months if interested. "Usually does not reply unless interested."

Music Uses up-beat, industrial, New Age, and mood for training, PR, education and multi-media.

Tips "Make sure your printed material is as precise as your music."

☑ ⬛ ENTERTAINMENT PRODUCTIONS, INC.

2118 Wilshire Blvd. PMB 744, Santa Monica CA 90403. (310)456-3143. Fax: (310)456-8950. **Contact:** Anne Bell, Music Director. Producer: Edward Coe. Motion picture and television production company. Clients include motion picture and TV distributors. Estab. 1972. Uses the services of music houses and songwriters for scores, production numbers, background and theme music for films and TV and jingles for promotion of films. Commissions/year vary. Pays by the job or by royalty. Buys motion picture, video and allied rights.

How to Contact Query with résumé of credits. Demo should show flexibility of composition skills. "Demo records/tapes sent at own risk—returned if SASE included." Responds by letter within 1 month, "but only if SASE is included."

Tips "Have résumé on file. Develop self-contained capability."

☑ ⬛ FINE ART PRODUCTIONS/RICHIE SURACI PICTURES, MULTIMEDIA, INTERACTIVE

67 Maple St., Newburgh NY 12550-4034. (914)527-9740. Fax: (845)561-5866. E-mail: rs7fap@bestweb.net. Website: www.idsi.net/~rs7fap/tentsales.htm. **Contact:** Richard Suraci, owner. Advertising agency, audiovisual firm, scoring service, **jingle/commercial music production house**, motion picture production company (Richie Suraci Pictures) and **music sound effect library**. Clients include corporate, industrial, motion picture and broadcast firms. Estab. 1987. Uses services of independent songwriters/composers for scoring, background music and jingles for various projects and commercials for radio and TV. Commissions 1-2 songwriters or composers and 1-2 lyricists/year. Pays by the job, royalty or by the hours. Buys all rights.

How to Contact Submit demo tape of previous work or tape demonstrating composition skills, query with résumé of credits or write or call first to arrange personal interview. Prefers cassette (or ½″, ¾″, or 1″ videocassette) with as many songs as possible and lyric or lead sheets. Include SASE, but prefers to keep material on file. Responds in 1 year.

Music Uses all types of music for all types of assignments.

⬛ GOLD & ASSOCIATES, INC.

6000 Sawgrass Village Circle #C, Ponte Vedra Beach FL 32082. Fax: (904)285-1579. E-mail: gold@strikegold.com. Website: www.strikegold.com. **Contact:** Keith Gold, Creative Director. Marketing, design and advertising firm. Clients include DeBeers, Harcourt, GEICO, The State of Florida and Time Warner. Estab. 1988. Uses the services primarily of music houses, but also independent songwriters/composers. Agency develops its own lyrics for scoring background music for presentations, Websites, radio and TV commercials, special events and CDs. Commissions 5-10 music projects/year. "We pay 2-3 firms $1,500-2,500 for demos. For the final production, we pay between $5,000 and $35,000. We normally buy all rights. However, sometimes one time rights, for a year or specific markets."

- Gold & Associates, Inc. has won over 850, national and international awards, including honors from the Clio Awards, New York Advertising Awards, London International Advertising Awards, Global Awards and The Telly Awards.

How to Contact Submit CD of previous work. Will keep submitted material on file. "Agency contacts writers and music houses only when we are ready to have music developed."

Music Uses every style.

Tips "Send demos once a year."

⬛ HAMMOND & ASSOCIATES

11307 Tawinee, Houston TX 77065. (281)955-5029. E-mail: mhammond@houston.rr.com. **Contact:** Michael Hammond, creative director. Audiovisual firm, **jingle/commercial music production house**, motion picture production company and recording studio. Clients include food store chains, land development, auto dealers, television stations. Estab. 1985. Uses the services of independent songwriters/composers and lyricists for movie scores, background music for educational/training films, jingles for TV, auto dealers, grocery stores etc., background music for educational and training films, and commercials for radio and TV. Pays per job. Buys all or one-time rights.

How to Contact Query with résumé of credits. Submit cassette or VHS videocassette with 3 songs and lyric sheet. Does not return material. Prefers to keep submitted material on file. Responds in 3 weeks.

Music Uses up tempo, R&B, country and gospel for jingles, educational and commercial songs.

THE HITCHINS COMPANY

22756 Hartland St., Canoga Park CA 91307-2604. (818)715-0510. Fax: (775)806-2687. E-mail: w.hitchins@socal. rr.com. **Contact:** W.E. Hitchins, president. Advertising agency. Estab. 1984. Uses the services independent songwriters/composers for jingles and commercials for radio and TV. Commissions 1-2 composers and 1-2 lyricists/year. Will negotiate pay. Buys all rights.

How to Contact Query with résumé of credits. Prefers cassette, CD or VHS videocassette. "Check first to see if we have a job." Does not return material; prefers to keep on file.

Music Uses variety of musical styles for commercials.

☑ HODGES ASSOCIATES, INC.

912 Hay St., Fayetteville NC 28305. (910)483-8489. Fax: (910)483-7197. E-mail: anna@hodgesassoc.com. Website: www.hodgesassoc.com. **Contact:** Anna Smith, President, or Wanda Bullard, Production Manager. Advertising agency. Clients include industrial, retail and consumer. ("We handle a full array of clientele.") Estab. 1974. Uses the services of music houses and independent songwriters/composers for background music for industrial films and slide presentations, and commercials for radio and TV. Commissions 1-2 composers/year. Pays by the job. Buys all rights.

How to Contact Submit demo tape of previous work. Prefers cassette or CD. Does not return material; prefers to keep on file. Responds in 3 months.

Music Uses all styles for industrial videos, slide presentations and TV commercials.

HOME, INC.

731 Harrison Ave., Boston MA 02118. (617)266-1386. Fax: (617)266-8514. E-mail: alanmichel@homeinc.org. Director: Alan Michel. Audiovisual firm and video production company. Clients include cable television, nonprofit organizations, pilot programs, entertainment companies and industrial. Uses the services of music houses and independent songwriters/composers for scoring of music videos, background music and commercials for TV. Commissions 2-5 songwriters/year. Pays up to $200-600/job. Buys all rights and one-time rights.

How to Contact Submit demo tape of previous work. Prefers cassette with 6 pieces. Does not return material; prefers to keep on file. Responds as projects require.

Music Mostly synthesizer. Uses all styles of music for educational videos.

Tips "Have a variety of products available and be willing to match your skills to the project and the budget."

K&R'S RECORDING STUDIOS

28533 Greenfield, Southfield MI 48076. (248)557-8276. E-mail: recordav@knr.net. Website: www.knr.net. **Contact:** Ken Glaza. Scoring service and **jingle/commercial music production house**. Clients include commercial and industrial firms. Services include sound for pictures (music, dialogue). Uses the services of independent songwriters/composers and lyricists for scoring of film and video, commercials and industrials and jingles and commercials for radio and TV. Commissions 1 composer/month. Pays by the job. Buys all rights.

How to Contact Submit demo tape of previous work. Prefers CD or VHS videocassette with 5-7 short pieces. "We rack your tape for client to judge." Does not return material.

Tips "Keep samples short. Show me what you can do in five minutes. Go to knr.net 'free samples' and listen to the sensitivity expressed in emotional music." Current projects: Proof and D12 soundtracks.

KEN-DEL PRODUCTIONS INC.

First State Production Center, 1500 First State Blvd., Wilmington DE 19804-3596. (302)999-1111. Estab. 1950. **Contact:** Edwin Kennedy, A&R manager. Clients include publishers, industrial firms and advertising agencies, how-to's and radio/TV. Uses services of songwriters for radio/TV commercials, jingles and multimedia. Pays by the job. Buys all rights.

How to Contact "Submit all inquiries and demos in any format to general manager." Does not return material. Will keep on file for 3 years. Generally responds in 1 month or less.

☑ LAPRIORE VIDEOGRAPHY

67 Millbrook St. Ste. 114, Worcester MA 01606. (508)755-9010. Website: www.lapriorevideo.com. **Contact:** Peter Lapriore, owner. Video production company. Clients include corporations, retail stores, educational and

sports. Estab. 1985. Uses the services of music houses, independent songwriters/composers for background music for marketing, training, educational videos and TV commercials and for scoring video. "We also own several music libraries." Commissions 2 composers/year. Pays $150-1,000/job. Buys all or one-time rights.

How to Contact Submit demo tape of previous work. Prefers cassette, CD, or VHS videocassette with 5 songs and lyric sheet. Does not return material; prefers to keep on file. Responds in 3 weeks.

Music Uses slow, medium, up-tempo, jazz and classical for marketing, educational films and commercials.

Tips "Be very creative and willing to work on all size budgets."

MALLOF, ABRUZINO & NASH MARKETING

765 Kimberly Dr., Carol Stream IL 60188. (630)929-5200. Fax: (630)752-9288. E-mail: emallof@manmarketing.c om. Website: www.manmarketing.com. **Contact:** Edward G. Mallof, president. Advertising agency. Works primarily with auto dealer jingles. Estab. 1980. Uses music houses for jingles for retail clients and auto dealers, and commercials for radio and TV. Commissions 5-6 songwriters/year. Pays $600-2,000/job. Buys all rights.

How to Contact Submit demo tape of previous work. Prefers cassette with 4-12 songs. Include SASE. Does not return material. Responds if interested.

Tips "Send us produced jingles we could re-lyric for our customers' needs."

N MARC USA

(formerly Caldwell Vanriper/Marc), 1314 N. Meridian, Indianapolis IN 46202. (317)632-6501. Fax: (317)632-4438. Website: www.marc-usa.com. **Contact:** Bryan Hadlock, vice president/executive creative director. Advertising agency and public relations firm. Clients include industrial, financial and consumer/trade firms. Uses the services of music houses for scoring of radio, TV and A/V projects, jingles and commercials for radio and TV.

How to Contact Submit demo tape of previously aired work on audio cassette. Does not return material. "Sender can follow up on submission. Periodic inquiry or demo update is fine."

Tips "We do not work directly with composers, we work with music production companies. Composers should contact the production companies directly."

PATRICK MOORE COMPOSITIONS

84 Harris Ave., Oshawa ON L1J 5K7 Canada. (905)576-9039. Website: www.patrickmoore.ca. **Contact:** Patrick Moore, owner/president. Scoring service and **jingle/commercial music production house**. Clients include producers of documentaries/films (educational). Estab. 1988. Uses the services of orchestrators for scoring of orchestral scores.

How to Contact Write first to arrange personal interview. Prefers cassette. Does not return material. Prefers to keep submitted material on file. Responds in 1 month.

Music "I specialize in combining ethnic music with current music for educational films/documentaries."

Tips "My needs are very specific and must meet the requirements of the producer and music editor on each project. It is not unusual for me to work with film producers and music writers from all over the world. I do a great deal of work by mailing video tapes, cassette tapes and CDs of rough drafts to producers and other professionals involved in a film or video production."

MUSIC LIBRARY: EDITORS CHOICE MUSIC LIBRARY

208 W. 30th St., Suite 1006, New York NY 10001. (212)643-0404. E-mail: www.editorschoicemusic.com. **Contact:** Gary Fitzgerald, composer/producer. **Commercial music production house**. "We service the advertising, film and television community." Estab. 1987. Uses the music of independent composers in library to be placed on TV, radio and industrials, background music for film and television, and jingles and commercials for radio and TV.

How to Contact Call first to obtain permission to submit demo tape. Will not open unsolicited submissions. Prefers CD. Include SASE, but prefers to keep on file. "A follow-up call must follow submission."

Music Uses all styles of music.

Tips "Complete knowledge of how music is used on TV and in the film business is essential."

NORTON RUBBLE & MERTZ, INC. ADVERTISING

205 W. Walker Dr., Suite 400, Chicago IL 60606. (312)422-9500. Fax: (312)422-9501. Website: www.nrmadv.c om. **Contact:** Anthony Salgado, vice president. Advertising agency. Clients include consumer products, retail, business to business. Estab. 1987. Uses the services of music houses and independent songwriters/composers for jingles and background music for radio/TV commercials. Commissions 2 composers/year. Pays by the job.

How to Contact Submit tape of previous work; query with résumé of credits. Prefers cassette or CD. Does not return materials; prefers to keep on file. "Please do not call."

Music Uses up-tempo and pop for commercials.

☑ NOVUS

121 E. 24th St., 12 Floor, New York NY 10010. (212)487-1377. Fax: (212)505-3300. E-mail: novuscom@aol.com. **Contact:** Robert Antonik, president/creative director. Marketing and communication agency. Clients include corporations, interactive products. Estab. 1986. Uses the services of music houses, independent songwriters/composers and lyricists for scoring and background music for documentaries, commercials, multimedia applications, website, film shorts, and commercials for radio and TV. Commissions 2 composers and 4 lyricists/year. Pay varies per job. Buys one-time rights.

How to Contact *Write first to arrange personal interview.* Query with résumé. Submit demo of work. Prefers cassette or CD with 2-3 songs. "Submissions should be short and to the point." Prefers to keep submitted material on file, but will return material if SASE is enclosed. Responds in 6 weeks.

Music Uses all styles for a variety of different assignments.

Tips "Always present your best and don't add quantity to your demo. Novus/FSI is a full service marketing and communications company. We work with various public relations, artists managements and legal advisors. We create multimedia events to album packaging and promotion."

OMNI COMMUNICATIONS

Dept. SM, P.O. Box 302, Carmel IN 46032-0302. (317)574-6664. E-mail: winston@omniproductions.com. Website: www.omniproductions.com. President: W. H. Long. Creative Director: S.M. Long. Production Manager: Jim Mullet. Television production and audiovisual firm. Estab. 1978. Serves industrial, commercial and educational clients. Uses the services of music houses and songwriters for scoring of films and television productions, CD-ROMs and Internet streams; background music for voice overs; lyricists for original music and themes. Pays by the job. Buys all rights.

How to Contact Submit demo tape of previous work. Prefers reel-to-reel, cassette or videocassette. Does not return material. Responds in 2 weeks.

Music Varies with each and every project; from classical, contemporary to commercial industrial.

Tips "Submit good demo tape with examples of your range to command the attention of our producers."

ON-Q PRODUCTIONS, INC.

1100 E. Gutierrez St., Santa Barbara CA 93103. (805)963-1331. Fax: (805)963-1333. E-mail: info@onqpro.com. Website: www.onqpro.com. President: Vincent Quaranta. Audiovisual firm. Clients include corporate accounts/sales conventions. Uses the services of music houses, independent songwriters/composers and lyricists for scoring, background music and jingles for AV shows. Commissions 1-5 composers and 1-5 lyricists/year. Buys all or one-time rights.

How to Contact Query with résumé of credits. Prefers cassette or 15 ips reel-to-reel or VHS videocassette. Prefers to keep material on file.

Music Uses up-tempo music for slide, video and interactive presentations.

☑ RH POWER AND ASSOCIATES, INC.

320 Osuna NE, Bldg. B, Albuquerque NM 87107. (505)761-3150. Fax: (505)761-3153. E-mail: info@rhpower.com. Website: www.rhpower.com. **Contact:** Creative Director. Advertising agency. Clients include RV, boat and automotive dealers and manufacturers. Estab. 1988. Uses the services of music houses and independent songwriters/composers for background music, and jingles and commercials for radio and TV. Pay varies per job. Buys all rights.

How to Contact Query with résumé or circular of credits by mail, e-mail or fax only. Writer first to arrange personal interview. "No need to include a submission package unless contacted from initial résumé or letter contact."

Music Uses contemporary, jazz and up-tempo for jingles, TV and radio, commercials and music-on-hold.

☑ QUALLY & COMPANY INC.

2 E. Oak, Suite 2903, Chicago IL 60611. (847)975-8247. **Contact:** Robert Qually, creative director. Advertising agency. Uses the services of music houses, independent songwriters/composers and lyricists for scoring, background music and jingles for radio and TV commercials. Commissions 2-4 composers and 2-4 lyricists/year. Pays by the job. Buys various rights depending on deal.

How to Contact Submit demo tape of previous work or query with résumé of credits. Prefers CD. Include SASE, but prefers to keep material on file. Responds in 2 weeks.

Music Uses all kinds of music for commercials.

☑ RAMPION VISUAL PRODUCTIONS

125 Walnut St., Watertown MA 02472. (617)972-1777. Fax: (617)972-9157. E-mail: info@rampion.com. Website: www.rampion.com. **Contact:** Steven V. Tringali, director/camera. Motion picture multi media production

company. Clients include educational, independent producers, corporate clients and TV producers. Estab. 1982. Uses the services of independent songwriters/composers for jingles, background music and scoring to longer form programming. Commissions 4-6 composers/year. Pays by the job. Buys all rights.

How to Contact Submit demo tape of previous work or query with résumé of credits. Prefers CD with variety of pieces. Does not return material; prefers to keep on file.

Music Uses all styles for corporate, educational and original programming.

Tips "Submit a varied demo reel showing style and client base."

☑ RODEO VIDEO, INC.

412 S. Main St., Snowflake AZ 85937-0412. Fax: (928)536-7120. E-mail: info@rodeovideo.com. Website: www.r odeovideo.com. Video and TV production company. Clients include rodeo contestants and fans. Estab. 1982. Uses the services of music houses, independent songwriters/composers and lyricists for background music for rodeo blooper videos and rodeo documentaries. Commissions 2 composers and 2 lyricists/year. Pay varies. Buys all rights or one-time rights.

How to Contact Submit demo tape of previous work. Prefers cassette or DAT with any number of songs. Mainly interested in country/western with rodeo theme. Does not return material. Responds only if interested.

Music Uses country/western for video backgrounds.

Tips "Looking for uptempo songs with rodeo theme—country/western or rock."

SOTER ASSOCIATES INC.

209 N. 400 W., Provo UT 84601. (801)375-6200. Fax: (801)375-6280. Website: www.soter.net. President: N. Gregory Soter. Creative Director: Sherrie Hall Everett. Advertising agency. Clients include financial, health care, municipal, computer hardware and software. Estab. 1970. Uses services of music houses, independent songwriters/composers and lyricists for background music for audiovisual presentations and jingles for radio and TV commercials. Commissions 1 composer, 1 lyricist/year. Pays by the job. Buys all rights.

How to Contact Submit tape demonstrating previous work and composition skills. Prefers cassette or VHS videocassette. Does not return submissions; prefers to keep materials on file.

☒ TRF PRODUCTION MUSIC LIBRARIES

Dept. SM, 747 Chestnut Ridge Rd., Chestnut Ridge NY 10977. (845)356-0800. Fax: (845)356-0895. E-mail: info@trfmusic.com. Website: www.trfmusic.com. **Contact:** Anne Marie Russo. **Music/sound effect libraries.** Estab. 1931. Uses the services of independent composers for all categories of production music for television, film and other media. Pays 50% royalty.

- ● Also see the listing for Alpha Music Inc. in the Music Publishers section of this book.

How to Contact Submit demo CD of new compositions. Prefers CD with 3-7 pieces. Can send audio cassette, DAT or CD with up to 12 tracks. Submissions are not returnable. Responds in 2 to 3 months after receipt.

Music Primarily interested in **acoustic instrumental** music suitable for use as production music, which is theme and background music for TV, film and AV/multimedia.

☑ ☒ UTOPIAN EMPIRE CREATIVEWORKS

P.O. Box 9, Traverse City MI 49685-0009. (231)943-5050. Hawaii address: P.O. Box 499, Kapa 'a HI 96746-0499. E-mail: songwriter@utopianempire.com. Website: www.UtopianEmpire.com. **Contact:** Ms. M'Lynn Hartwell, president. Web design, multimedia firm and motion picture/video production company. Serves commercial, industrial and nonprofit clients. We provide the following services: advertising, marketing, design/packaging, distribution and booking. Uses services of music houses, independent songwriters/composers for jingles and scoring of and background music for multi-image/multimedia, film and video. Negotiates pay. Buys all or one-time rights.

How to Contact Submit CD of previous work, demonstrating composition skills or query with résumé of credits. Prefers CD or good quality cassette. Does not return material; prefers to keep on file. Responds only if interested.

Music Uses mostly industrial/commercial themes.

VIDEO I-D, INC.

Dept. SM, 105 Muller Rd., Washington IL 61571. (309)444-4323. Fax: (309)444-4333. E-mail: videoid@videoid.c om. Website: www.VideoID.com. **Contact:** Gwen Wagner, manager, operations. Post production/teleproductions. Clients include law enforcement, industrial and business. Estab. 1977. Uses the services of music houses and independent songwriters/composers for background music for video productions. Pays per job. Buys one-time rights.

How to Contact Submit demo tape of previous work. Prefers CD or VHS videocassette with 5 songs and lyric sheet. Does not return material. Responds in 1 month.

VIS/AID MARKETING/ASSOCIATES

P.O. Box 4502, Inglewood CA 90309-4502. (310)399-0696. **Contact:** Lee Clapp, manager. Advertising agency. Clients include "companies in 23 SIC codes (workable)." Estab. 1965. Uses the services of music houses, independent songwriters/composers and lyricists for background music for films, and commercials, TV jingles for radio/TV and scoring new material. Commissions 1-2 composers and 1-2 lyricists/year. Pay is negotiable. Buys all or one-time rights.

How to Contact Query with résumé of credits. Call first to arrange personal interview or submit demo tape of previous work. Prefers cassette with 1-2 songs and lyric and lead sheet. "Do not send original material that if misplaced/lost cannot be duplicated." Does not return material. Responds in 2 weeks.

Music Uses up-tempo, pop, jazz and classical for educational films, slide presentations and commercials.

Play Producers & Publishers

Finding a theater company willing to invest in a new production can be frustrating for an unknown playwright. But whether you write the plays, compose the music or pen the lyrics, it is important to remember not only where to start but how to start. Theater in the U.S. is a hierarchy, with Broadway, Off Broadway and Off Off Broadway being pretty much off limits to all but the Stephen Sondheims of the world.

Aspiring theater writers would do best to train their sights on nonprofit regional and community theaters to get started. The encouraging news is there is a great number of local theater companies throughout the U.S. with experimental artistic directors who are looking for new works to produce, and many are included in this section. This section covers two segments of the industry: theater companies and dinner theaters are listed under Play Producers (beginning on this page), and publishers of musical theater works are listed under the Play Publishers heading (beginning on page 287). All these markets are actively seeking new works of all types for their stages or publications.

BREAKING IN

Starting locally will allow you to research each company carefully and learn about their past performances, the type of musicals they present, and the kinds of material they're looking for. When you find theaters you think may be interested in your work, attend as many performances as possible, so you know exactly what type of material each theater presents. Or volunteer to work at a theater, whether it be moving sets or selling tickets. This will give you valuable insight into the day-to-day workings of a theater and the creation of a new show. On a national level, you will find prestigious organizations offering workshops and apprenticeships covering every subject from arts administration to directing to costuming. But it could be more helpful to look into professional internships at theaters and attend theater workshops in your area. The more knowledgeable you are about the workings of a particular company or theater, the easier it will be to tailor your work to fit its style and the more responsive they will be to you and your work. (See the Workshops & Conferences section on page 351 for more information.) As a composer for the stage, you need to know as much as possible about a theater and how it works, its history and the different roles played by the people involved in it. Flexibility is the key to successful productions, and knowing how a theater works will only help you in cooperating and collaborating with the director, producer, technical people and actors.

If you're a playwright looking to have his play published in book form or in theater publications, see the listings under the Play Publishers section (page 287). To find play producers and publishers in your area, consult the Geographic Index at the back of this book.

PLAY PRODUCERS

ALLIANCE THEATRE COMPANY

1280 Peachtree St., Atlanta GA 30309. (404)733-4650. Fax: (404)733-4625. Website: www.alliancetheatre.org. **Contact:** Freddie Ashley, literary associate. Artistic Director: Susan V. Booth. Play producer. Estab. 1969. Produces 9-10 plays and 1 new musical/year. Audience is diverse, regional and young. Two performing spaces: 800-seat proscenium and a 200-seat flexible black box. Pays negotiable amount per performance.

How to Contact Query with synopsis, character breakdown and set description. Include SASE. Responds in 6 months.

Musical Theater They are primarily interested in new musicals, but also will consider works for children's theatre. Musicals for young audiences must be no longer than 1 hour in length and have a cast of 8 or fewer.

Productions *The Color Purple*, by Marsha Norman Brenda Russell, Allee Willis, and Stephen Bay (adaptation of Alice Walker novel); *Elaborate Lives: The Legend of Aida*, by Elton John and Tim Rice (musical theatre update of legend); and *Soul Possessed*, by Debbie Allen/James Ingram/Arturo Sandoval (musical dance drama set in bayous of Louisiana).

☑ AMAS MUSICAL THEATRE, INC.

450 W. 42nd St., Suite 2J, New York NY 10036. (212)563-2565. Fax: (212)268-5501. E-mail: amas@amasmusical .org. Website: www.amasmusical.org. Producing Director: Donna Trinkoff. Play producer. Estab. 1968. Produces 2 musicals/year and musical development series (Amas Six O'clock Musical Theatre Lab) produces 5-6 concert versions of new musicals. "We seek to reach a wide and diverse audience by presenting musicals that speak to different cultures." Performance space is on Off-off Broadway theater with 76-99 seats. Payment is standard agreement.

How to Contact Submit complete manuscript, score and tape of songs. Include SASE. Responds in 6 months.

Musical Theater Seeks "innovative, well-written, good music. We seek musicals that lend themselves to multi-racial casting."

Productions *Little Ham: A Harlem Jazzical*, by Dan Owens/Richard Engquist/Judd Woldin (the Harlem community in the '30s); *Starmites*, by Stuart Ross/Barry Keating (a sci-fi, pop-rock adventure); and *4 Guys Named José*, by Dolores Prida, concieved by David Coffman (a Latino review).

Tips "Submit works that speak to and about racial and cultural themes using a fresh, new, fun style."

AMERICAN LIVING HISTORY THEATER

P.O. Box 752, Greybull WY 82426. (307)765-9449. Fax: (307)765-9448. E-mail: ludwigunlimited@hotmail.com. **Contact:** Dorene Ludwig, president/artistic director. Play producer. Estab. 1975. Produces 1-2 new plays/year. Performs all over U.S.—conventions, schools, museums, universities, libraries, etc. Pays by royalty.

How to Contact Query first. Include SASE. Responds in 1 year.

Musical Theater "We use only primary source, historically accurate material: in music—*Songs of the Civil War* or *Songs of the Labor Movement*, etc.—presented as a program/production. We would like to keep a file of music historians who might be consulted on selection of material and accuracy."

Tips "Do not send fictionalized historical material. We use primary source material only."

AMERICAN MUSICAL THEATRE OF SAN JOSE

1717 Technology Dr., San Jose CA 95110-1305. (408)453-1545. Fax: (408)453-7123. E-mail: mjacobs@amtsj.org. Website: www.amtsj.org. **Contact:** Marc Jacobs, director of new works. Play producer. Estab. 1935. Produces 4 mainstage musicals/year. "Our season subscribers are generally upper-middle class families. Our main season is in the 2,600-seat San Jose Center for the Performing Arts." Pays variable royalty.

How to Contact Submit synopsis and tape of songs. Include SASE. Responds in 3-4 months.

Musical Theater "We are not looking for children's musicals, Christmas shows or puppet shows. We are looking for high quality (professional caliber) musicals to develop for our 2,600-seat main stage theatre, an 800-seat 2nd stage a national tour or possible Broadway production. Submissions from composers and writers with some previous track record only, please. The first thing we look for is quality and originality in the music and lyrics. Next we look for librettos that offer exciting staging possibilities. If writing original music to a pre-existing play please be sure all rights have been cleared."

Tips "We are a company with a $12 million per season operating budget and one of the largest subscription audiences in the country. We are looking for shows we can develop for possible main stage, 2nd stage, or Broadway productions. Therefore it is advisable that any composers or writers have professional production history before submitting to us."

ARDEN THEATRE COMPANY

40 N. Second St., Philadelphia PA 19106. (215)922-8900. E-mail: info@ardentheatre.org. Website: www.ardenth eatre.org. **Contact:** Amy Dugas Brown, associate artistic director. Play producer. Estab. 1988. Produces 3-4

plays and 1-2 musicals/year. Adult audience—diverse. Mainstage: 350+ seats, flexible. Studio: 175+ seats, flexible. Pay is negotiable.

How to Contact Query with synopsis, character breakdown and set description. Include SASE. Responds in 1 year.

Musical Theater Full length plays and musicals. The Arden Theatre Company is dedicated to bringing to life the greatest stories by the greatest storytellers of all time. We draw from any source that is inherently dramatic and theatrical—fiction, nonfiction, poetry, music and drama. Especially interested in literary adaptations. Also interested in musicals for children. Will consider original music for use in developing or pre-existing play. Composers should send samples of music on cassette.

Productions *Baby Case*, by Michael Ogborn (Lindbergh baby kidnapping/trial of Bruno Richard Hauptman); *James Joyce's The Dead*, by Richard Nelson (adaptation of Joyce's short story); and *Pacific Overtures*, by Sondheim (musical about Westernization of Japan).

☑ ARKANSAS REPERTORY THEATRE

601 Main, P.O. Box 110, Little Rock AR 72203. (501)378-0405. Fax: (501)378-0012. Website: www.therep.org. **Contact:** Brad Mooy. Play producer. Estab. 1976. Produces 6-10 plays and musicals/year. "We perform in a 354-seat house and also have a 99-seat 2nd stage." Pays 5-10% royalty or $75-150 per performance.

How to Contact Query with synopsis, character breakdown and set description. Include SASE. Responds in 6 months.

Musical Theater "Small casts are preferred, comedy or drama and prefer shows to run 1:45 to 2 hours maximum. Simple is better; small is better, but we do produce complex shows. We aren't interested in children's pieces, puppet shows or mime. We always like to receive a tape of the music with the book."

Productions *Radio Gals*, by Mike Craver/Mark Hardwick; and *Always . . . Patsy Cline*, by Ted Swindley (biomusical).

Tips "Include a *good* cassette of your music, *sung well*, with the script."

☑ ASOLO THEATRE COMPANY

Dept. SM, 5555 N. Tamiami Trail, Sarasota FL 34243. (941)351-9010. E-mail: corinne_gabrielson@asolo.org. Website: www.asolo.org. Associate Artistic Director: Corinne Gabrielson. Play producer. Produces 7-8 plays (1 musical)/year. Plays are performed at the Asolo Mainstage (500-seat proscenium house). Pays negotiated royalty.

How to Contact Query with synopsis, character breakdown, set description and one page of dialogue. Include SASE. Responds in 6 months.

Musical Theater "We want small to mid-size non-chorus musicals only. They should be full-length, any subject. There are no restrictions on production demands; however, musicals with excessive scenic requirements or very large casts may be difficult to consider."

Productions *Oh What A Lovely War*, by Joan Littlewood (WWI); and *Jane Eyre*, by Ted Davis/David Clark.

☑ BAILIWICK REPERTORY

Bailiwick Arts Center, 1229 W. Belmont, Chicago IL 60657. (773)883-1090. Fax: (773)883-2017. E-mail: david@bailiwick.org. Website: www.bailiwick.org. Director: David Zak. Producer: Rusty Hernandez. Play producer. Estab. 1982. Produces 5 mainstage, 5 one-act plays and 1-2 new musicals/year. "We do Chicago productions of new works on adaptations that are politically or thematically intriguing and relevant. We also do an annual director's festival which produces 50-75 new short works each year." Pays 5-8% royalty.

How to Contact "Review our manuscript submission guidelines or the professional page of our website." Responds in 6 months.

Musical Theater "We want innovative, dangerous, exciting material."

Productions *The Christmas Schooner*, by John Reeger and Julie Shannon (holiday musical); *Bonnie and Clyde*, by Pomerantz/Eickmann/Herron/Ritchie (Roaring 20s).

Tips "Be creative. Be patient. Be persistent. Make me believe in your dream."

☑ BARTER THEATRE

133 West Main St., Abingdon VA 24210. (276)628-3991. Fax: (276)619-3335. E-mail: barter@naxs.com. Website: www.bartertheatre.com. **Contact:** Evalyn Baron, associate artistic director. Play producer. Estab. 1933. Produces 15 plays and 5-6 musicals (1 new musical)/year. Audience "varies; middle American, middle age, tourist and local mix." 500-seat proscenium stage, 140-seat thrust stage. Pays 5% royalty.

How to Contact Query with synopsis, character breakdown, set description, and CD/cassette of the songs. "Make sure cassettes and CDs will play back properly." Include SASE. Responds in 1 year.

Musical Theater "We investigate all types. We are not looking for any particular standard. Prefer sellable titles with unique use of music. Prefer small cast musicals, although have done large scale projects with marketable titles or subject matter. We use original music in almost all of our plays." Does not wish to see "political or very urban material, or material with very strong language."

Productions *Something's Afoot*, by James McDonald, David Vos and Robert Girlach; *Oklahoma*, by Rodgers & Hammerstein; *South Pacific*, Rodgers & Hammerstein; and *Sundown*, Peter Link and Joe Bravaco.

Tips "Be patient. Be talented. Don't be obnoxious. Be original and make sure subject matter fits our audience. And make sure your CD or cassette will play before you send it in."

BIRMINGHAM CHILDREN'S THEATRE

P.O. Box 1362, Birmingham AL 35201-1362. (205)458-8181. Fax: (205)458-8895. E-mail: bertb@bct123.org. Website: www.bct123.org. **Contact:** Bert Brosowsky, executive director. Play producer. Estab. 1947. Produces 9 plays and 1-4 new musicals/year; "typically, original adaptations of classic children's stories for pre-school through grade 1, K-6, and junior and senior high school." "Wee Folks" Series: preschool through grade 1; Children's Series: K-6; Young Adult Series: junior and senior high. Performs in 1,072-seat flexible thrust mainstage theater, 250 seat black box theater and a 200 seat studio theater (touring venues vary). Pay is negotiable.

How to Contact Query with synopsis, character breakdown and set description. Include SASE. Responds in 3 months.

Musical Theater " 'Wee Folks' productions should be 40-45 minutes; Children's Series 55-60 minutes; Young Adult Series 85-95 minutes. 'Wee Folks' shows should be interactive; all others presentational. Most productions tour, so sets must be lightweight, simple and portable. 'Wee Folks' shows prefer cast of four. Touring Children's Series shows prefer cast of six. All others prefer cast of 12 or less. BCT traditionally ultilizes a great deal of music for underscoring, transitions, etc. We welcome submissions from prospective sound designers."

Productions "The Elves and the Shoemaker" book and lyrics by Jean Pierce and Betty Pewitt, music by Jay Trumminello; "The Princess and the Pea" adapted by Paul Laurakas; "Ferdinand the Bull" adapted by Deborah Wicks, music by Deborah Wicks LaPuma; "The Best Christmas Pageant Ever" by Barbara Robinson.

THE BLOWING ROCK STAGE COMPANY

P.O. Box 2170, Blowing Rock NC 28605. (828)295-9168. Fax: (828)295-9104. E-mail: info@blowingrockstage.com. Website: www.blowingrockstage.com. **Contact:** Kenneth Kay, producing director. Play producer. Estab. 1986. Produces 4 shows/year. "Blowing Rock Stage Company provides a professional summer theatre experience for the residents and the high volume of summer tourists." Performances take place in a 240-seat proscenium summer theater in the Blue Ridge Mountains. Pays flat fee/performance or 5-7% royalty.

How to Contact Query with synopsis, character breakdown, set description and music CD. Include SASE. Responds in up to 6 months.

Musical Theater "Casts of ten or less are preferred, with ideal show running time of two hours, intermission included. Limit set changes to three or less; or unit concept. Some comic relief, please. Not producing stark adult themes."

Productions *The Christmas Bus*, by Robert Inman (world premiere Christmas show 2003); *A Dash of Rosemary*, by Douglas Kampsen (SE Premiere of New Revue of Rosemary Clooney); and *Italian 101*, by John D'Aquino (1 man play about growing up Italian).

Tips "We're looking for inspiration. We enjoy supporting projects which are soulful and uplifting. We want light-hearted musicals with some comic relief."

BRISTOL RIVERSIDE THEATRE

Dept. SM, P.O. Box 1250, Bristol PA 19007. (215)785-6664. Fax: (215)785-2762. Website: www.brtstage.org. Producing Director: Susan D. Atkinson. Business Manager: Lori Braunstein. Play producer. Estab. 1986. Produces 5 plays and 2 musicals/year (1 new musical every 2 years) and summer concert series. "302-seat proscenium Equity theater with audience of all ages from small towns and metropolitan area." Pays 6-8% royalty.

How to Contact Submit complete manuscript, score and tape of songs. Include SASE. Responds in 18 months.

Musical Theater "No strictly children's musicals. All other types with small to medium casts and within reasonable artistic tastes. Prefer one-set; limited funds restrict. Do not wish to see anything catering to prurient interests."

Productions *Sally Blane, World's Greatest Girl Detective*, by David Levy/Leslie Eberhard (spoof of teen detective genre); *Moby Dick*, by Mark St. Germain, music by Doug Katsarous; and *Texas Flyer*, by Larry Gatlin.

Tips "You should be willing to work with small staff, open to artistic suggestion, and aware of the limitations of newly developing theaters."

▨ WILLIAM CAREY COLLEGE DINNER THEATRE

William Carey College, Hattiesburg MS 39401-5499. (601)582-6218. E-mail: thecom@wmcarey.edu. **Contact:** O.L. Quave, managing director. Play producer. Produces 2 musicals/year. "Our dinner theater operates only in summer and plays to family audiences." Payment negotiable.

How to Contact Query with synopsis, character breakdown and set description. Does not return material. Responds in 1 month.
Musical Theater "Plays should be simply-staged, have small casts (8-10 maximum), and be suitable for family viewing; two hours maximum length. Score should require piano only, or piano, synthesizer."
Productions *Smoke on the Mountain*; *Schoolhouse Rock Live*; and *Pump Boys and Dinettes*.

CENTENARY COLLEGE
Theatre Dept., Shreveport LA 71134-1188. (318)869-5075. Fax: (318)869-5760. E-mail: rbuseick@centenary.e du. **Contact:** Robert R. Buseick, chairman. Play producer. Produces 6 plays (1-2 new musicals)/year. Plays are presented in a 350-seat playhouse to college and community audiences. Pay is negotiable.
How to Contact Query with synopsis, character breakdown and set description. Does not return material. Responds as soon as possible.
Productions *Blood Brothers*; *Grand Hotel*; and *Funny Girl*.
Tips "Keep trying. It's not easy."

CIRCA '21 DINNER PLAYHOUSE
Dept. SM, P.O. Box 3784, Rock Island IL 61204-3784. (309)786-2667, ext. 303. Fax: (309)786-4119. Website: www.circa21.com. **Contact:** Dennis Hitchcock, producer. Play producer. Estab. 1977. Produces 1-2 plays and 4-5 musicals (1 new musical)/year. Plays produced for a general audience. Three children's works/year, concurrent with major productions. Payment is negotiable.
How to Contact Query with synopsis, character breakdown and set description or submit complete manuscript, score and tape of songs. Include SASE. Responds in 3 months.
Musical Theater "We produce both full length and one act children's musicals. Folk or fairy tale themes. Works that do not condescend to a young audience yet are appropriate for entire family. We're also seeking full-length, small cast musicals suitable for a broad audience." Would also consider original music for use in a play being developed.
Productions *A Closer Walk with Patsy Cline*, *Swingtime Canteen*, *Forever Plaid* and *Lost Highway*.
Tips "Small, upbeat, tourable musicals (like *Pump Boys*) and bright musically-sharp children's productions (like those produced by Prince Street Players) work best. Keep an open mind. Stretch to encompass a musical variety—different keys, rhythms, musical ideas and textures."

⃠ CREEDE REPERTORY THEATRE
P.O. Box 269, Creede CO 81130. (719)658-2540. Fax: (719)658-2343. E-mail: crt@creederep.com. Website: www.creederep.org. **Contact:** Maurice Lamee, producing/artistic director. Play producer. Estab. 1966. Produces 6 plays and 1 musical/year. Performs in 243-seat proscenium theatre; audience is ½ local support and ½ tourist base from Texas, Oklahoma, New Mexico and Colorado. Pays 7% royalty.
How to Contact Query first. Include SASE. Responds in 1 year.
Musical Theater "We prefer historical Western material with cast no larger than 11. Staging must be flexible as space is limited."
Productions *Baby Doe Tabor*, by Kenton Kersting (Colorado history); *A Frog in His Throat*, by Feydeau, adapted by Eric Conger (French farce); and *Tommyknockers*, by Eric Engdahl, Mark Houston and Chris Thompson (mining).
Tips "Songwriter must have the ability to accept criticism and must be flexible."

GEOF ENGLISH, PRODUCER, SADDLEBACK CIVIC LIGHT OPERA
Saddleback College, 28000 Marguerite Pkwy., Mission Viejo CA 92692. (949)582-4763. E-mail: genglish@saddle back.edu. Producer: Geofrey English. Play producer for musical theater. Produces 4 musicals/year. Community audience of mostly senior citizens. Pays by royalty and performance.
How to Contact Submit complete manuscript, score and tape of songs. Does not return material. Responds in 3 months.
Musical Theater "Looking for mainly family musicals. No limitations, open to options. It is important that music must be sent along with scripts. Best not to call. Just send materials."
Productions *Singin' in the Rain*, by Betty Comden & Adolph Green; *Gypsey*, by Arthur Laurents; and *Route 66*, by Roger Bean.
Tips "Submit materials in a timely manner—usually at least one year in advance."

☑ ENSEMBLE THEATRE
1127 Vine St., Cincinnati OH 45202. (513)421-3555. Fax: (513)562-4104. E-mail: etcin@aol.com. Website: www. cincyetc.com. **Contact:** D. Lynn Meyers, producing artistic director. Play producer. Estab. 1986. Produces 10

plays and at least 1 musical (1 new musical)/year. Audience is multi-generational and multi-cultural. 191 seats, ¾ stage. Pays 5-8% royalty (negotiable).

How to Contact Query with synopsis, character breakdown and set description or full script. Include SASE. Responds in 6 months.

Musical Theater "All types of musicals are acceptable. Cast not over ten; minimum set, please."

Productions *Hedwig & the Angry Inch*, by John Cameron Mitchel (rock star/transgender/love story); *Alice in Wonderland*, by David Kisor and Joe McDonough (update of the classic tale; and *Frog Princess*, by Joe McDonough and David Kisor (family retelling of classic tale).

Tips Looking for "creative, inventive, contemporary subjects or classic tales. Send materials as complete as possible."

FOOLS COMPANY, INC.

423 W. 46th St., New York NY 10036. (212)307-6000. E-mail: foolsco@nyc.rr.com. **Contact:** Jill Russell, Executive Director. Collaborative new and experimental works producer. Estab. 1970. Produces 1 play and 1 musical (1 new musicals)/year. "Audience is comprised of hip, younger New Yorkers. Plays are performed at our own mid-Manhattan theater." Pay is negotiable.

How to Contact Query first by e-mail. Include SASE. Responds in 1 month.

Musical Theater "We seek new and unusual, contemporary and experimental material. We would like small, easy-to-tour productions. Nothing classical, folkloric or previously produced." Would also consider working with composers in collaboration or original music for use in plays being developed.

Productions *Rug Burn*; *Cathleen's Corsage*(alternative performance); and *Blunt Passage* (original drama).

Tips "Come work in NYC!"

☑ THE GASLIGHT THEATRE

7010 E. Broadway, Tucson AZ 85710. (520)886-9428. Fax: (520)722-6232. E-mail: gaslighttheatre@gci-net.com. Website: www.gaslighttheatre.info. **Contact:** Bonnie Rexroat, general manager. Play producer. Estab. 1977. Produces 5 musical melodramas (2-3 new musicals)/year. "We cater to family audiences. Our musical melodramas are always fun. Ages from toddlers to senior citizens come to our shows." Performance space is 20′w × 15′d (not including the apron). Pays for outright purchase.

How to Contact Query with synopsis, character breakdown, set description. Submit complete ms and score. Include SASE. Responds in 2 months.

Musical Theater Prefers musical melodramas of 1 hour and 30 minutes; with an olio of 18-20 minutes. "Our shows always have a hero and villain." Cast size is usually 3 women and 5-6 men. Does not wish to see anything violent or sad. "Family entertainment only." Looking for slapstick comedy. "We always use fun sets, i.e., rolling rocks, underwater adventure, camels that move, horses, etc. Our musical melodrama is followed by a themed olio (song and dance show with jokes). Include lots of music to accompany the show."

Productions *The Belle of Tombstone* (western with "Belle" (a woman) trying to battle the bad guys to save her mine); *Prince Valiant or Surely You Joust* (medieval—knight-prince valiant wooing the fair maiden and overcoming the black knight; and *Space Rangers 2025, The Battle for the Galaxy* (Rich Rocket travels in space to save the world from the evil queen Spiderella), all by Peter Van Slyke.

Tips "Think fun and comedy! Our productions always have a villian and a hero. In the conflict the hero always wins. Always fun and family entertainment. Lots of music."

☑ THE WILL GEER THEATRICUM BOTANICUM

P.O. Box 1222, Topanga CA 90290. (310)455-2322. Fax: (310)455-3724. E-mail: info@theatricum.com. Website: www.theatricum.com. **Contact:** Ellen Geer, artistic director. Literary Director: Isreal Baran. Produces 4 plays, 1 new musical/year. Plays are performed in "large outdoor amphitheater with 60′x 25′ wooden stage. Rustic setting." Pays negotiable royalty.

How to Contact Query with synopsis, tape of songs and character breakdown. Include SASE. Responds as soon as can be read.

Musical Theater Seeking social or biographical works, and full length musicals with cast of up to 10 equity actors (the rest non-equity). Requires "low budget set and costumes. Union contract." Would also consider original music for use in a play being developed. Does not wish to see "anything promoting avarice, greed, violence or apathy."

Productions *Three Penny Opera*, by Brecht; *Robber Bridegroom*, by VHRY/Waldman (country folktale); and *Pie in the Sky*, by Alsop (nuclear/3 Mile Island); *Dory, a Musical Portrait*, adapted by Dory Previn and Ellen Greer; *Animal Farm*, adapted by Peter Hall/Richard Peaslee/Adrian Mitchell, etc.

HORIZON THEATRE CO.

P.O. Box 5376, Atlanta GA 31107. (404)523-1477. Fax: (404)584-8815. E-mail: horizonco@mindspring.com. Website: www.horizontheatre.com. **Contact:** Lisa and Jeff Adler, artistic directors. Play producer. Estab. 1983.

Produces 4 plays and 1 musical/year. ''Our audience is comprised mostly of young professionals looking for contemporary comedy with some social commentary. Our theater features a 185-seat facility with flexible stage.'' Pays 6-8% royalty.

How to Contact Query with synopsis, character breakdown and set description. Include SASE. Responds in 3 months (to query).

Musical Theater ''We prefer musicals that have a significant book and a lot of wit (particularly satire). Our casts are restricted to 10 actors. We prefer plays with equal number of male and female roles, or more female than male roles. We have a limited number of musicians available. No musical revues and no dinner theater fluff. We generally contract with a musician or sound designer to provide sound for each play we produce. If interested send résumé, synopsis, references, tape with music or sound design samples.''

Productions *Angry Housewives*, by A.M. Collins/Chad Henry; *A. . . . My Name Is Still Alice*, conceived by Julianne Boyd/Joan Micklin Silver; and *The Good Times Are Killing Me*, by Lynda Barry.

Tips ''Have patience and use subtle persistence. Work with other theater artists to get a good grasp of the form.''

N LA JOLLA PLAYHOUSE

P.O. Box 12039, La Jolla CA 92039. (858)550-1070. Fax: (858)550-1075. E-mail: ljp@ucsd.edu. Website: www.la jollaplayhouse.com. **Contact:** Allison Horsley, literary manager. Play producer. Estab. 1947. Produces 5 plays and 1 musical (1-2 new musicals)/year. Audience is University of California students to senior citizens. Performance spaces include a large proscenium theatre with 480 seats and a black box with 450 seats.

How to Contact Query with synopsis, character breakdown. Include SASE. Responds in 9-12 months.

Musical Theater ''We prefer contemporary music but not necessarily a story set in contemporary times. Retellings of classic stories can enlighten us about the times we live in. For budgetary reasons, we'd prefer a smaller cast size.''

Productions *Dracula, The Musical*, book and lyrics by Don Black and Christopher Hampton, music by Frank Wildhorn (adaptation of Bram Stoker's novel); *Thoroughly Modern Millie*, book by Richard Morris and Dick Scanlan, new music by Jeanine Tesori, new lyrics by Dick Scanlan (based on the 1967 movie); and *Jane Eyre*, book and additional lyrics by John Cairo, music and lyrics by Paul Gordon (adaptation of Charlotte Brontë's novel).

LOS ANGELES DESIGNERS' THEATRE

P.O. Box 1883, Studio City CA 91614-0883. (323)650-9600. T.D.D.: (323)654-2700. Fax: (323)654-3210. E-mail: ladesigners@juno.com. **Contact:** Richard Niederberg, artistic director. Play producer. Estab. 1970. Produces 20-25 plays and 8-10 new musicals/year. Audience includes Hollywood production executives in film, TV, records and multimedia. Plays are produced at several locations, primarily Studio City, California. Pay is negotiable.

How to Contact Query first. Does not return material. Responds only if interested. *Send proposals only.*

Musical Theater ''We seek out controversial material. Street language OK, nudity is fine, religious themes, social themes, political themes are encouraged. Our audience is very 'jaded' as it consists of TV, motion picture and music publishing executives who have 'seen it all'.'' Does not wish to see bland, 'safe' material. We like first productions. In the cover letter state in great detail the proposed involvement of the songwriter, other than as a writer (i.e., director, actor, singer, publicist, designer, etc.). Also, state if there are any liens on the material or if anything has been promised.''

Productions *St. Tim*, by Fred Grab (historical '60s musical); *Slipper and the Rose* (gang musical); and *1593— The Devils Due* (historical musical).

Tips ''Make it very 'commercial' and inexpensive to produce. Allow for non-traditional casting. Be prepared with ideas as to how to transform your work to film or videotaped entertainment.''

DON AND PAT MACPHERSON PRODUCTIONS

461 Parkway, Gatlinburg TN 37738. (865)436-4039. Fax: (865)436-4038. E-mail: sfatheatre@aol.com. Website: www.sweetfannyadams.com. **Contact:** Don MacPherson and Pat MacPherson, co-owners/producers. Play producer. Estab. 1977. Produces 2 musicals/year. Plays are performed at Sweet Fanny Adams Theatre, Gatlinburg, Tennessee to tourist audience. Pays $25/per performance.

How to Contact Query with synopsis, character breakdown and set description. Include SASE. Responds in 1 month.

Musical Theater ''Produce musicals that are funny, fast—in fact, silly; musical farces. Theater is 1890 style so shows should fit that period. Have done many westerns. Cast size limited to 7 or 8 with 2 musicians on taped music. Stage very small. Use old-time backdrops forsets. Shows should be no longer than 90 minutes.'' Does not wish to see ''shows that would not fit 1890s style.''

Productions *Phantom of the Opry*, by Don & Pat MacPherson/J. Lovensheimer (spoof of *Phantom of the Opera*);

Life & Times of Billy Kincaid, by MacPherson/Lovensheimer (western); and *Not Quite Frankenstein*, by Don and Pat MacPherson.
Tips ''See a production at Sweet Fanny Adams.''

🔃 MAGIC THEATRE

Ft. Mason Center, Bldg. D, San Francisco CA 94123. (415)441-8001. Fax: (415)771-5505. E-mail: LauraO@magict heatre.org. Website: www.magictheatre.org. **Contact:** Laura Owen, literary manager. Play producer. Estab. 1968. Produces 5-6 plays/year. Audience is educated/intelligent, willing to take risks. Two performance spaces: 155-seat modified thrust and 155-seat proscenium. Pays negotiable royalty.
How to Contact Query with synopsis, character breakdown and set description. ''We prefer a smaller cast size, and nothing larger than 7 or 8.'' Include SASE. Responds in 2 months.
Musical Theater Plays are innovative in form and structure. Chamber musicals are best. Cast size of 6-8. ''We have only recently decided to start producing musicals. We are interested in stories with a strong book as well as music.'' Considers original music for use in a play being developed or for use in a pre-existing play.
Productions *Hillary and Soon Yi Shop for Ties*, by Michelle Carter; *Schrödinger's Girlfriend*, by Matthew Wells; and *First Love*, by Charles Mee, Jr.

MANHATTAN THEATRE CLUB

311 W. 43rd St., New York NY 10036. (212)399-3030. E-mail: questions@mtc-nyc.org. Website: www.mtc-nyc.org. **Contact:** Clifford Lee Johnson III, director of musical theater program. Associate Artistic Director: Michael Bush. Artistic Director: Lynne Meadow. Play producer. Estab. 1971. Produces 8 plays and sometimes 1 musical/year. Plays are performed at the Manhattan Theatre Club before varied audiences. Pays negotiated fee.
How to Contact Query first. Include SASE. Responds in 4 months.
Musical Theater ''Original work.''
Productions *A Class Act*, by Ed Kleban/Lonny Price/Linda Kline; *The Wild Party*, by Andrew Lippa; and *Newyorkers*, by Stephen Weiner/Glenn Slater.
Tips ''Make sure your script is tightly and securely bound.''

MIXED BLOOD THEATRE CO.

1501 S. Fourth St., Minneapolis MN 55454. (612)338-0937. E-mail: czar@mixedblood.com. Website: www.mixe dblood.com. **Contact:** David Kunz, script czar. Play producer. Estab. 1976. Produces 4-5 plays/year and perhaps 1 new musical every 2 years. ''We have a 200-seat theater in a converted firehouse. The audience spans the socio-economic spectrum.'' Pays royalty or per performance.
How to Contact Query first (1-page cover letter, 1-page synopsis). Include SASE. Responds on queries in 2 months.
Musical Theater ''We want full-length, non-children's works with a message. Always query first. Never send unsolicited script or tape.''
Productions *Black Belts II*, musical revue (black female vocalists and their music); *Birth of the Boom* (do-wop/hip hop extravaganza); and *Vices* (musical sketch revue).
Tips ''Always query first. The direct approach is best. Be concise. Make it interesting. Surprise us. Contemporary comedies, politically-edged material and sports-oriented shows are usually of interest.''

✅ NEW REPERTORY THEATRE

P.O. Box 610418, Newton Highlands MA 02461-0418. (617)332-1646. Fax: (617)527-5217. E-mail: info@newrep. org. Website: www.NewRep.org. **Contact:** Rick Lombardo, producing artistic director. Play producer. Estab. 1984. Produces 5 plays and 1 musical/year. Audience is Metro-Boston based. Performance space is an intimate, 170-seat thrust stage with minimal space for musicians. Pays negotiable royalty.
How to Contact Query with synopsis, character breakdown and set description. Include SASE. Responds in 9 months.
Musical Theater Seeks small cast (under 7), unusual stories, small orchestra. Full-length with adult themes. Does not wish to see standard musical comedies.
Productions *Valley Song*, by Athol Fugard (South Africa); *Gifts of the Magi*, by Mark St. Germain and Randy Courrrts (musical of O'Henry); and *Moby Dick*, music by Doug Katsaros, libretto by Mark St. Germain.
Tips ''Be very clever in theatricality and style. Be unconventional.''

NEW YORK STATE THEATRE INSTITUTE

37 First St., Troy NY 12180. (518)274-3200. E-mail: nysti@capital.net. Website: www.nysti.org. **Contact:** Patricia Di Benedetto Snyder, producing artistic director. Play producer. Produces 5 plays (1 new musical)/year.

Plays performed for student audiences grades K-12, family audiences and adult audiences. Theater seats 900 with full stage. Pay negotiable.

How to Contact Query with synopsis, character breakdown, set description and tape of songs. Include SASE. *Do not send ms unless invited.* Responds in 6 weeks for synopsis, 4 months for ms.

Musical Theater Looking for "intelligent and well-written book with substance, a score that enhances and supplements the book and is musically well-crafted and theatrical." Length: up to 2 hours. Could be play with music, musical comedy, musical drama. Excellence and substance in material is essential. Cast could be up to 20; orchestra size up to 8.

Productions *A Tale of Cinderella*, by W.A. Frankonis/Will Severin/George David Weiss (adaptation of fairy tale); *The Silver Skates*, by Lanie Robertson/Byron Janis/George David Weiss (adaptation of book); *The Snow Queen*, by Adrian Mitchell/Richard Peaslee (adaptation of fairy tale); and *Magna Carta*, by Ed Lange/Will Severin/George David Weiss (new musical drama).

Tips "There is a great need for musicals that are well-written with intelligence and substance which are suitable for family audiences."

NEW YORK THEATRE WORKSHOP

79 E. Fourth St., New York NY 10003. (212)780-9037. Fax: (212)460-8996. E-mail: info@nytw.org. Website: www.nytw.org. **Contact:** James C. Nicola, artistic director. Play producer. Produces 4-6 mainstage plays and approximately 50 readings/year. "Plays are performed in our theater on East Fourth St. Audiences include: subscription/single ticket buyers from New York area, theater professionals, and special interest groups." Pays by negotiable royalty.

How to Contact Query with synopsis, character breakdown and set description. Include SASE. Responds in 5 months.

Musical Theater "As with our nonmusicals, we seek musicals of intelligence and social consciousness that challenge our perceptions of the world and the events which shape our lives. We favor plays that possess a strong voice, distinctive and innovative use of language and visual imagery. Integration of text and music is particularly of interest. Musicals which require full orchestrations would generally be too big for us. We prefer 'musical theater pieces' rather than straightforward 'musicals' per-se. We often use original music for straight plays that we produce. This music may be employed as pre-show, post-show or interlude music. If the existing piece lends itself, music may also be incorporated within the play itself. Large casts (12 or more) are generally prohibitive and require soliciting of additional funds. Design elements for our productions are of the highest quality possible with our limited funds."

Productions *The Waves*, adapted from Virginia Woolf's novel, music and lyrics by David Bucknam and text and direction by Lisa Peterson; *My Children! My Africa*, by Athol Fugard; and *Rent*, by Jonathan Larson.

Tips "Submit ten pages of the script and a one page synopsis which captures the heart of your piece; inject your piece with a strong voice and intent and try to surprise and excite us."

☑ NORTH SHORE MUSIC THEATRE

62 Dunham Rd., Beverly MA 01915. (978)232-7203. Fax: (978)921-7874. Website: www.nsmt.org. **Contact:** John La Rock, associate producer. Play producer. Estab. 1955. Produces 1 Shakespearian play and 6 musicals (2 new musicals)/year. General audiences. Performance space is an 1800-seat arena theatre, 120-seat workshop. Pays royalty (all done via individual commission agreements).

How to Contact Submit synopsis and CD of songs. Include SASE. Responds within 6 months.

Musical Theater Prefers full-length adult pieces not necessarily arena-theatre oriented. Cast sizes from 1-30; orchestra's from 1-16.

Productions *Tom Jones*, by Paul Leigh, George Stiles; *I Sent A Letter to My Love* by Melissa Manchester and Jeffrey Sweet; Just So, by Anthony Drewe & George Stiles (musical based on Rudyard Kipling's fables); *Letters from 'Nam*, by Paris Barclay (Vietnam War experience as told through letters from GI's); and *Friendship of the Sea*, by Michael Wartofsky & Kathleen Cahill (New England maritime adventure musical).

Tips "Keep at it!"

☑ ODYSSEY THEATRE ENSEMBLE

P.O. Box 1315, Gilroy CA 95021. (310)477-2055. Fax: (310)444-0455. E-mail: info@odysseytheatre.org. Website: www.odysseytheatre.org. **Contact:** Sally Essex-Lopresti, director of literary programs. Play producer. Estab. 1969. Produces 9 plays and 1 musical (1-2 new musicals)/year. Pays negotiable royalty.

How to Contact Query with synopsis, character breakdown, 8-10 pages of libretto, cassette of music and set description. Query should include résumé(s) of artist(s) and tape of music. Include SASE. "Unsolicited material is not read or screened at all." Responds to query in 2 weeks; ms in 6 months.

Musical Theater "We want nontraditional forms and provocative, unusual, challenging subject matter. We are not looking for Broadway-style musicals. Comedies should be highly stylized or highly farcical. Works should be full-length only and not requiring a complete orchestra (small band preferred). Political material and satire are great for us. We're seeking interesting musical concepts and approaches. The more traditional Broadway-style musicals will generally not be done by the Odyssey. If we have a work in development that needs music, original music will often be used. In such a case, the writer and composer would work together during the development phase. In the case of a pre-existing play, the concept would originate with the director who would select the composer.''

☑ THE OPEN EYE THEATER

P.O. Box 959, 960 Main St., Margaretville NY 12455. Phone/fax: (845)586-1660. E-mail: openeye@catskill.net. Website: www.theopeneye.org. **Contact:** Amie Brockway, producing artistic director. Play producer. Estab. 1972. Produces approximately 3 full length or 3 new plays for multi-generational audiences. Pays on a fee basis.
How to Contact Query first. ''A manuscript will be accepted and read only if it is a play for all ages and is: 1) Submitted by a recognized literary agent; 2) Requested or recommended by a staff or company member; or 3) Recommended by a professional colleague with whose work we are familiar. Playwrights may submit a one-page letter of inquiry including a very brief plot synopsis. Please enclose a self-addressed (but not stamped) envelope. We will reply only if we want you to submit the script (within several months).''
Musical Theater ''The Open Eye Theater is a not-for-profit professional company working in a community context. Through the development, production and performance of plays for all ages, artists and audiences are challenged and given the opportunity to grow in the arts. In residence, on tour, and in the classroom, The Open Eye Theater strives to stimulate, educate, entertain, inspire and serve as a creative resource.''
Productions *Twelfth Night or What You Will*, by William Shakespeare, music by Michael Anthony Worden; *The Wide Awake Princess*, adapted by David Paterson from the novel by Katherine Paterson, with music and lyrics by Steve Liebman; and *Pixies, Kings and Magical Things*, by Hans Christian Anderson, adapted by Ric Aver (four children's tales).

PLAYHOUSE ON THE SQUARE

51 S. Cooper, Memphis TN 38104. (901)725-0776. Fax: (901)272-7530. **Contact:** Jackie Nichols, executive producer. Play producer. Produces 12 plays and 4 musicals/year. Plays are produced in a 260-seat proscenium resident theater. Pays $500 for outright purchase.
How to Contact Submit complete manuscript, score and tape of songs. Unsolicited submissions OK. Include SASE. Responds in 6 months.
Musical Theater Seeking ''any subject matter—adult and children's material. Small cast preferred. Stage is 26' deep by 43' wide with no fly system.''
Productions *Children of Eden*; and *Tommy*, by The Who.

Ⓝ PLAYWRIGHTS' ARENA

514 S. Spring St., Los Angeles CA 90013. (213)485-1631. E-mail: jrivera923@juno.com. Website: www.playwrightsarena.org. **Contact:** Jon Lawrence Rivera, artistic director. Play producer. Estab. 1992. Produces 4 plays and 1 musical (1 new musical)/year. Audience is in their early 20s to 50s. Performance space is 26' deep × 30' wide proscenium stage with fly system. Pays 6% royalty.
How to Contact Submit complete manuscript, score and tape of songs. Include SASE. Responds in 6 months.
Musical Theater Seeking new musicals like *Rent*. Does not want old fashioned musicals.
Productions *War Music*, by Bryan Davidson; *Red Hat and Tales*, by Nick Salamone; and *Palm Fever*, by Jean Colonomos.

☑ PLAYWRIGHTS HORIZONS

416 W. 42nd St., New York NY 10036. (212)564-1235. Fax: (212)594-0296. Website: www.playwrightshorizons.org. **Contact:** Christie Evangelista, assistant literary manager. Artistic Director: Tim Sanford. Musical Theatre. Play producer. Estab. 1971. Produces about 5 plays and 1 new musical/year. ''Adventurous New York City theater-going audience.'' Pays general Off-Broadway contract.
How to Contact Submit complete manuscript and tape or CD of songs. Attn: Musical Theater Program. Include SASE. Responds in 8 months.
Musical Theater American writers. ''No revivals, one-acts or children's shows; otherwise we're flexible. We have a particular interest in scores with a distinctively contemporary and American flavor. We generally develop work from scratch; we're open to proposals for shows and scripts in early stages of development.''
Productions *My Life with Albertine*, by Richard Nelson, Ricky Ian Gordon (adapted from Proust's ''In Search of Lost Time''); *Wilder*, by Erin Cressida Wilson, Mike Craver, Jack Herrick (growing up in the Depression); and *The Spitfire Grill*, by James Valcq/Fred Alley (adapted from the movie).

PRIMARY STAGES

131 W. 45th St., 2nd Floor, New York NY 10036. (212)840-9705. Fax: (212)840-9725. E-mail: info@primarystage
s.com. Website: www.primarystages.com. **Contact:** Tyler Marchant, associate artistic director. Play producer.
Estab. 1984. Produces 4-5 plays/year. "New York theater-going audience representing a broad cross-section,
in terms of age, ethnicity, and economic backgrounds. 99-seat, Off-Broadway theater."
How to Contact Query first with synopsis, character breakdown, set description and tape. "No unsolicited
scripts accepted. Submissions by agents only." Include SASE. Responds in up to 8 months.
Musical Theater "We are looking for work of heightened theatricality, that challenges realism—musical plays
that go beyond film and televisions standard fare. We are looking for small cast shows under 6 characters total,
with limited sets. We are interested in original works, that have not been produced in New York."
Productions *I Sent a Letter to My Love*, by Melissa Manchester/Jeffrey Sweet; and *Nightmare Alley*, by Jonathan
Brielle.

THE REPERTORY THEATRE OF ST. LOUIS

P.O. Box 191730, St. Louis MO 63119. (314)968-7340. E-mail: mail@repstl.org. Website: www.repstl.org/.
Contact: Susan Gregg, associate artistic director. Play producer. Estab. 1966. Produces 9 plays and 1 or 2
musicals/year. "Conservative regional theater audience. We produce all our work at the Loretto Hilton The-
atre." Pays by royalty.
How to Contact Query with synopsis, character breakdown and set description. Does not return material.
Responds in 2 years.
Musical Theater "We want plays with a small cast and simple setting. No children's shows or foul language.
After a letter of inquiry we would prefer script and demo tape."
Productions *Almost September* and *Esmeralda*, by David Schechter and Steve Lutvak; *Jack*, by Barbara Field
and Hiram Titus; and *Young Rube*, by John Pielmeier and Nattie Selman.

SECOND STAGE THEATRE

307 W. 43rd St., New York NY 10036. (212)787-8302. Fax: (212)397-7066. **Contact:** Christopher Burney, associate artistic director. Play producer. Estab. 1979. Produces 4 plays and 1 musical (1 new musical)/year. Plays
are performed in a small, 108-seat Off Broadway House. Pays per performance.
How to Contact Query with synopsis, character breakdown, set description, tape of 5 songs (no more). No
unsolicited manuscripts. Include SASE. Responds in 6 months.
Musical Theater "We are looking for innovative, unconventional musicals that deal with sociopolitical themes."
Productions *Saturday Night*, by Stephen Sondheim; *Little Fish*, by Michael John LaChiusa; and *Crowns*, by
Regina Taylor (music-gospel traditional).
Tips "Submit through agent; have strong references; always submit the best of your material in small quantities:
5 outstanding songs are better than 10 mediocre ones."

☑ SHAKESPEARE SANTA CRUZ

Theater Arts Center, U.C.S.C., 1156 High Street, Santa Cruz CA 95064. (831)459-2121. Fax: (831)459-3316. E-
mail: iago@cats.ucsc.edu. Website: www.shakespearesantacruz.org. **Contact:** Paul Whitworth, artistic director.
Play producer. Estab. 1982. Produces 4 plays/year. Performance spaces are an outdoor redwood grove; and an
indoor 540-seat thrust. Pay is negotiable.
How to Contact Query first. Include SASE. Responds in 2 months.
Musical Theater "Shakespeare Santa Cruz produces musicals in its Winter Holiday Season (Oct-Dec). We are
also interested in composers' original music for pre-existing plays—including songs, for example, for Shakespeare's plays."
Productions *Cinderella*, by Kate Hawley (book and lyrics) and Gregg Coffin (composer); and *Gretel and Hansel*,
by Kate Hawley (book and lyrics) and composer Craig Bohmler (both are British pantomime treatment of fairy
tale).
Tips "Always contact us before sending material."

☑ SHENANDOAH INTERNATIONAL PLAYWRIGHTS

717 Quick's Mill Rd., Staunton VA 24401. (540)248-1868. Fax: (540)248-4113. E-mail: rgsmall@ntelos.net.
Contact: Robert G. Small, artistic director. Play producer. Estab. 1976. Develops 10-12 plays/year for family
audience.
How to Contact Submit complete manuscript, score and tape of songs. Include SASE. Responds in 4 months.
Tips "Submit full materials by February 1."

STAGE ONE

501 W. Main St., Louisville KY 40202. (502)589-5946. Fax: (502)588-5910. E-mail: stageone@stageone.org.
Website: www.stageone.org. **Contact:** J. Daniel Herring, artistic director. Play producer. Estab. 1946. Produces

7-8 plays and 0-2 new musicals/year. "Audience is mainly young people ages 5-18, teachers and families." Pays 5-7% royalty, flat fee or $25-75 per performance.

How to Contact Submit complete manuscript and tape of songs (cassette preferred). Include SASE. Responds in 4 months.

Musical Theater "We seek stageworthy and respectful dramatizations of the classic tales of childhood, both ancient and modern. Ideally, the plays are relevant to young people and their families, as well as related to school curriculum. Cast is rarely more than 12."

Productions *The Great Gilly Hopkins*, by David Paterson/Steve Liebman (foster home); *Pinocchio*, by Moses Goldberg/Scott Kasbaum (classic tale); and *Jack & the Beanstalk*, by Goldberg/Corrett (fairytale).

Tips "Stage One accepts unsolicited manuscripts that meet our artistic objectives. Please do not send plot summaries or reviews. Include author's résumé, if desired. In the case of musicals, a cassette tape is preferred. Cast size is not a factor, although, in practice, Stage One rarely employs casts of over 12. Scripts will be returned in approximately 3-4 months, if SASE is included. No materials can be returned without the inclusion of a SASE. Due to the volume of plays received, it is not possible to provide written evaluations."

STAGES REPERTORY THEATRE

3201 Allen Parkway, Houston TX 77019. (713)527-0220. Fax: (713)527-8669. E-mail: rbundy@stagestheatre.com. Website: www.stagestheatre.com. **Contact:** Rob Bundy, artistic director. Play producer. Estab. 1979. Produces 6 plays and 1 musical/year. Performance space includes 170-seat thrust and 230-arena theatre. Pays negotiable royalty.

How to Contact Query with synopsis, character breakdown and set description. Include SASE. Responds in 7 months.

Musical Theater Prefers edgy, theatrical, non-realistic stories, with a maximum cast size of 10, and single unit set with multiple locations.

Productions *Nixon's Nixon*, by Russell Lees; *Funny Girl*, by Jules Styne; and *The Pitchfork Disney*, by Philip Ridley.

SWINE PALACE PRODUCTIONS

The Reilly Theatre, Tower Dr.—LSU, Baton Rouge LA 70803. (225)578-3533. Fax: (225)578-9279. E-mail: info@swinepalace.org. Website: www.swinepalace.com. **Contact:** Kristin Sosnowsky, managing director. Play producer. Estab. 1991. Produces 3 productions/year. "Swine's audience is made up of the community of Louisiana which ranges from the upper-lower classes. Many college and high school students. Not for the blue-haired group. The brand new Reilly theatre is a traverse stage with an earth floor converted from an old livestock judging/viewing pavillion (hence "Swine" Palace). Audience sits across from each other a la stadium seating. 488 seats and one of the largest performing stages in North America. Truly unique, bold and original." Pay negotiated with the artistic staff.

How to Contact Submit complete ms, score and tape of songs. Include SASE. Responds in 6 months if interested.

Musical Theater "Swine Palace's commitment is to new work reflects the Deep South experience. Work must contain substance. No light musical comedies based on trite gimmicks. The Reilly theatre is an epic space and lends itself to large cast productions (i.e., operas are perfectly acceptable). Large casts are acceptable." Does not want works that are in no way related to the Deep South experience. Interested in musicals "that are new and rock. 5-7 piece instrumentation is best. Innovative, original and possibly dangerous material."

Productions *A Midsummer Night's Dream*, by Shakespeare; *Gumbo Ya-Ya*, by Swine Palace Company (adaptation with music of book from 1940s Federal writer's project); *Four Joans and a Fire-Eater*, by Elizabeth Dewberry (reexamination of folk-lore, 3 women and 1 drag queen in New Orleans discover that they were all Joan of Arc in a former life—new play premiered at Swine); and *Jesus Christ Superstar*, by Andrew Lloyd Weber (fall 2000).

Tips "Love the art in yourself not yourself in the art. Don't be afraid of work. Take the work seriously but not yourself. Andre' du Broc, music director for Swine Palace has been composing scores for Swine since 1993. His work focuses on use of music as the supporting cast member in the productions. Live music is almost always an essential part in all of Swine Palace's work whether it be Shakespeare or Beckett. Songs and original scoring are always included in our season and audiences expect excellence in our musical support. Intelligent music based on support of the text that has been worked in through the production process is a must. Composers do not 'phone in' our scores but work alongside the design team during the production process."

☑ TADA!

150 W. 28th St., 3rd Floor, New York NY 10001. (212)252-1619. Fax: (212)252-8763. E-mail: info@tadatheater.com. Website: www.tadatheater.com. **Contact:** Janine Nina Trevens, artistic director. Play producer. Estab. 1984. Produces 4 staged readings and 2-4 new musicals/year. "TADA! is a company producing works performed by children ages 6-17 for family audiences in New York City. Performances run approximately 30-45 performances. Pays varying royalty.

• Also see the listing for Free Staged Reading Series Playwriting Competition in the Contests and Awards section.

How to Contact Submit complete manuscript with synopsis, character breakdown, score and tape of songs. Include SASE. Responds in 1 year.

Musical Theater "We do not produce plays as full productions. At this point, we do staged readings of plays. We produce original commissioned musicals written specifically for the company."

Productions *The History Mystery*, by Janine Nina Trevens (kids time traveling through history)' *New York New Year*, by Gary Bagley (a young midwestern girl discovers New York and herself); and *Golly Gee Whiz*, by Erick Rockwell (based on the "Mickey & Judy film classics).

Tips "Musical playwrights should concentrate on themes and plots meaningful to children and their families as well as consider our young actors' abilities and talents as well. Vocal ranges of children 7-17 should be strongly considered when writing the score."

THE TEN-MINUTE MUSICALS PROJECT

P.O. Box 461194, West Hollywood CA 90046. Website: www.tenminutemusicals.org. **Contact:** Michael Koppy, producer. Play producer. Estab. 1987. All pieces are new musicals. Pays $250 advance.

How to Contact Submit complete manuscript, score and tape of songs. Include SASE. Responds in 3 months.

Musical Theater Seeks complete short stage musicals of 8-15 minutes in length. Maximum cast: 9. "No parodies—original music only."

Productions *Away to Pago Pago*, by Jack Feldman/Barry Manilow/John PiRoman/Bruce Sussman; *The Bottle Imp*, by Kenneth Vega (from the story of the same title by Robert Louis Stevenson); and *The Furnished Room*, by Saragail Katzman (from the story of the same title by O. Henry).

Tips "Start with a *solid* story—either an adaptation or an original idea—but with a solid beginning, middle and end (probably with a plot twist at the climax). We caution that it will surely take much time and effort to create a quality work. (Occasionally a clearly talented and capable writer and composer seem to have almost 'dashed' something off, under the misperception that inspiration can carry the day in this format. Works selected in previous rounds all clearly evince that considerable deliberation and craft were invested.) We're seeking short contemporary musical theater material, in the style of what might be found on Broadway, Off-Broadway or the West End. Think of shows like *Candide* or *Little Shop of Horrors*, pop operas like *Sweeney Todd* or *Chess*, or chamber musicals like *Once on this Island* or *Falsettos*. (Even small accessible operas like *The Telephone* or *Trouble in Tahiti* are possible models.) All have solid plots, and all rely on sung material to advance them. Of primary importance is to start with a strong story, even if it means postponing work on music and lyrics until the dramatic foundation is complete."

☑ THEATRE THREE, INC.

2800 Routh St., Suite 168, Dallas TX 75201. (214)871-3300. Fax: (214)871-3139. E-mail: admin@theatre3dallas.com. Website: www.theatre3dallas.com. **Contact:** Terry Dobson, musical director. Artistic Director: Jac Alder. Play producer. Estab. 1961. Produces 10-12 plays and 3-4 musicals (1 or 2 new musicals)/year. "Subscription audience of 4,500 enjoys adventurous, sophisticated musicals." Performance space is an "arena stage (modified). Seats 250 per performance. Quite an intimate space." Pays varying royalty.

How to Contact *Submit through agent only.* Include SASE. Responds in 2 months.

Musical Theater "Off the wall topics. We have, in the past, produced *Little Shop of Horrors*, *Angry Housewives*, *Sweeney Todd*, *Groucho*, *A Life in Revue*, *The Middle of Nowhere* (a Randy Newman revue) and *A . . . My Name Is Alice*. We prefer small cast shows, but have done shows with a cast as large as 15. Orchestrations can be problematic. We usually do keyboards and percussion or some variation. Some shows can be a design problem; we cannot do 'spectacle.' Our audiences generally like good, intelligent musical properties. Very contemporary language is about the only thing that sometimes causes 'angst' among our subscribers. We appreciate honesty and forthrightness . . . and good material done in an original and creative manner."

Productions *A Class Act*, by Ed Kleban, Lonny Price & Linda Klein; *Beguiled Again*, the songs of Rodgers & Hart; *Bat Boy, The Musical*, by Farley, Flemming & O'Keefe.

☑ THEATRE WEST VIRGINIA

P.O. Box 1205, Beckley WV 25802. (800)666-9142. E-mail: contact@theaterwestvirginia.com. Website: www.theatrewestvirginia.com. **Contact:** Marina Honley, artistic director. Play producer. Estab. 1955. Produces 5 plays and 2 musicals/year. "Audience varies from mainstream summer stock to educational tours (ages K-high school)." Pays 3-6% royalty, negotiable.

How to Contact Query with synopsis, character breakdown and set description; should include cassette tape. Include SASE. Responds in 3 months.

Musical Theater "Theatre West Virginia is a year-round performing arts organization that presents a variety of productions including community performances and statewide educational programs on primary, elementary and secondary levels. This is in addition to our summer, outdoor dramas of *Hatfields & McCoys* and *Honey in the Rock*, now in their 43rd year.'' Anything suitable for school tours. No more than 6 in cast. Play should be able to be accompanied by piano/synthesizer.

Productions *The Apple Tree*, by Sheldon Harnick and Jerry Bock (used for educational tour grades 7th-12th); *The Tinderbox*, by Mark LaPierre (musical adaptation, used for educational tour grades K-6th); and *The Sound of Music*, by Rodgers & Hammerstein.

THEATREWORKS/USA

151 W. 26th St., 7th Floor, New York NY 10001. (212)647-1100. Fax: (212)924-5377. Website: www.theatrework susa.org. Literary Manager: Michael Alltop. Play producer. Produces 10-13 plays, most are musicals (3-4 are new musicals)/year. Audience consists of children and families. Pays 6% royalty and aggregate of $1,500 commission-advance against future royalties.

How to Contact Query with synopsis, character breakdown and sample scene and song. Include SASE. Responds in 6 months.

Musical Theater ''One hour long, 5-6 adult actors, highly portable, good musical theater structure; adaptations of children's literature, historical or biographical musicals, issues, fairy tales—all must have something to say. We demand a certain level of literary sophistication. No kiddy shows, no camp, no fractured fables, no shows written for school or camp groups to perform. Approach your material, not as a writer writing for kids, but as a writer addressing any universal audience. You have one hour to entertain, say something, make them care— don't preach, condescend. Don't forget an antagonist. Don't waste the audience's time. We always use original music—but most of the time a project team comes complete with a composer in tow.''

Productions *Island of the Blue Dolphins*, book/lyrics by Beth Blatt, music by Jennifer Giering (literary adaptation); *The Mystery of King Tut*, book/lyrics by Mindi Dickstein, music by Dan Messé (original historical); *Gold Rush!*, book by David Armstrong, music by Dick Gallagher, lyrics by Mark Waldrop (original historical); and *Sarah, Plain and Tall*, book by Julia Jordan, music by Larry O'Keefe, and lyrics by Nell Benjamin.

Tips ''Write a good show! Make sure the topic is something we can market! Come see our work to find out our style.''

☑ THUNDER BAY THEATRE

400 N. Second Ave., Alpena MI 49707. (989)354-2267. E-mail: tbt@deepnet.com. Website: www.deepnet.com/ tt/. Artistic Director: Hal Adams. Play producer. Estab. 1967. Produces 12 plays and 6 musicals (1 new musical)/ year. Performance space is thrust/proscenium stage. Pays variable royalty or per performance.

How to Contact Submit complete manuscript, score and tape of songs. Include SASE. Responds in 3 months.

Musical Theater Small cast. Not equipped for large sets. Considers original background music for use in a play being developed or for use in a pre-existing play.

Productions *Wonderful Life*, by Holmes/Kroner/Willison (Christmas); *Smoke On the Mountain* (gospel); and *Forever Plaid*, by Stuart Ross.

☑ VIRGINIA STAGE COMPANY

P.O. Box 3770, Norfolk VA 23514. (757)627-6988. Fax: (757)628-5958. E-mail: rchelimsky@vastage.com. Website: www.vastage.com. **Contact:** Robert Chelimsky, managing director. Play producer. Estab. 1978. Produces 7-10 plays and 1-2 musicals (0-1 new musical)/year. ''We have a diverse audience. As home to a large, well-traveled population from NATO and the U.S. Navy, we serve many sophisticated theatregoers as well as those for whom theatre is not yet a habit. Located in Southeastern Virginia, we also play to a number of people from Southern backgrounds.'' Performance space is a 670-seat, Beaux-Arts proscenium theatre built in 1913—a national historic landmark. This hemp house features a proscenium opening 36' wide and 28' high with a stage depth of 28'. Pay is negotiable.

How to Contact Query with synopsis, character breakdown and set description. Include SASE. Responds in 6 months.

Musical Theater ''We have produced the world premieres of *The Secret Garden* and *Snapshots* (with music by Stephen Schwartz). Our tastes are eclectic and have covered a number of styles. We have recently expanded our programming for young audiences.'' At this time, shows with less than 20 in the cast have a better chance of production. They have commissioned original music and adaptations for plays including *Hamlet*, *Twelfth Night*, *Terra Nova* and *A Christmas Carol*.

Productions *Appalachian Strings*, by Randal Myler/Dan Wheetman (social history of the Appalachian region); *Snapshots*, by David Stern/Michael Scheman, music by Stephen Schwartz (a middle-aged couple trying to save their marriage); *Twelfth Night*, by Shakespeare (set in 18th century Ireland with live musicians playing Celtic music); and *Blues in the Night*, by Sheldon Epps.

Tips ''Be patient. We review material as quickly as possible. It also takes time to establish the relationships and resources needed to lead us into full, top-quality productions.''

WALNUT STREET THEATRE

825 Walnut St., Philadelphia PA 19107. (215)574-3550, ext. 515. Fax: (215)574-3598. E-mail: wstpc@wstonline. org. Website: www.wstonline.org. **Contact:** Literary Office. Play producer. Estab. 1809. Produces 7 plays and 3 musicals/year. Plays produced on a mainstage with seating for 1,078; and in studio theaters with seating for 90. Pays by royalty or outright purchase.

How to Contact *Unsolicited scripts accepted with professional reference/recommendation only.*

Musical Theater "We seek musicals with lyrical non-operatic scores and a solid book. We are looking for a small musical for springtime and one for a family audience at Christmas time. We remain open on structure and subject matter and would expect a tape with the script. Cast size: around 20 equity members (10 for smaller musical); preferably one set with variations." Would consider original music for incidental music and/ or underscore. This would be at each director's discretion.

Productions *She Loves Me*, Jerry Bock, music/Sheldon Harnick (musical); *The Sound of Music*, Richard Rodgers, music/Oscar Hammerstein II, lyrics (musical); *Evita* (scheduled for Spring 2003), Andrew Lloyd Webber, music/ Tim Rice, lyrics (musical).

WATERLOO COMMUNITY PLAYHOUSE

P.O. Box 433, Waterloo IA 50704. (319)235-0367. Fax: (319)235-7489. E-mail: wcpbhct@cedarnet.org. Website: www.cedarnet.org. **Contact:** Charles Stilwill, managing artistic director. Play producer. Estab. 1917. Produces 12 plays (1-2 musicals)/year. "Our audience prefers solid, wholesome entertainment, nothing risqué or with strong language. We perform in Hope Martin Theatre, a 366-seat house." Pays $15-150/performance.

How to Contact Submit complete manuscript, score and cassette tape of songs. Include SASE. Responds in 10 months.

Musical Theater "Casts may vary from as few as 6 people to 54. We are producing children's theater as well. We're *especially* interested in new adaptations of classic children stories."

Productions *Jesus Christ Superstar*; *Fiddler on the Roof*; and *Grease*.

Tips "The only 'new' musicals we are likely to produce are adaptations of name shows that would fit in our holiday slot or for our children's theater."

WEST COAST ENSEMBLE

P.O. Box 38728, Los Angeles CA 90038. (323)876-9337. Website: www.wcensemble.org. **Contact:** Les Hanson, artistic director. Play producer. Estab. 1982. Produces 4-8 plays and 1 new musical/year. "Our audience is a wide variety of Southern Californians. Plays will be produced in our theater in Hollywood." Pays $35-50 per performance.

● See the listing for West Coast Ensemble—Musical Stairs in the Contests & Awards section of this book.

How to Contact Submit complete manuscript, score and tape of songs. Include SASE. Responds in 8 months.

Musical Theater "There are no limitations on subject matter or style. Cast size should be no more than 12 and sets should be simple. If music is required we would commission a composer; music would be used as a bridge between scenes or to underscore certain scenes in the play."

Productions *Cabaret*, *Merrily We Roll Along* and *A New Brain*.

Tips "Submit work in good form and be patient. We look for musicals with a strong book and an engaging score with a variety of styles."

ⓃWEST END ARTISTS

18034 Ventura Blvd. #291, Encino CA 91316. (818)623-0040. Fax: (818)623-0202. E-mail: egaynes@aol.com. **Contact:** Pamela Hall, associate artistic director. Artistic Director: Edmund Gaynes. Play producer. Estab. 1983. Produces 5 plays and 3 new musicals/year. Audience "covers a broad spectrum, from general public to heavy theater/film/TV industry crowds. Pays 6% royalty.

How to Contact Submit complete manuscript, score and tape of songs. Include SASE. Responds in 3 months.

Musical Theater "Prefer small-cast musicals and revues. Full length preferred. Interested in children's shows also." Cast size: "Maximum 12; exceptional material with larger casts will be considered."

Productions *The Taffetas*, by Rick Lewis ('50s nostalgia, received 3 Ovation Award nominations); *Songs the Girls Sang*, by Alan Palmer (songs written for women now sung by men, received 1 Ovation Award nomination); *Crazy Words, Crazy Tunes*(played 2 years to Los Angeles and nationwide).

Tips "If you feel every word or note you have written is sacred and chiseled in stone and are unwilling to work collaboratively with a professional director, don't bother to submit."

☑WESTBETH THEATRE CENTER

111 W. 17th St., 3rd Floor, New York NY 10011. (212)691-2272. Fax: (212)924-7185. E-mail: general@westbethe nt.com. Website: www.westbethent.com. **Contact:** Jill Beckman, executive assistant. Producing Director: Arnold Engleman. Play producer. Estab. 1977. Produces 1-2 musicals/year. Audience consists of artists, New York

professionals and downtown theater goers. "We have five performance spaces, including a music hall and cafe theater." Pay varies. Uses usual New York showcase contract.

How to Contact Query with résumé, one page project proposal—or one page synopsis with cast and production requirements for scripted plays and any relevant audio/visual material. Include SASE. Does not return material from outside the US. Responds in 3 months. "Artists must reside in NYC or surrounding areas and be desirous of extensive development and intense collaboration."

Musical Theater "The New Works Program has expanded its focus to include performance proposals from a range of various disciplines including dancers, playwrights, musicians, and other performance artists. Proposals should be sharp, urban, and contemporary—period pieces or plays set in rural/regional locales will not be considered.

Productions *20th Century Man*, by Ray Davies (bio of rock group The Kinks); *Almost Famous*, by Bruce Vilanch; and *Exactly Like You*, by Cy Coleman/E. Hutchner (musical comedy).

Tips "Be open to the collaborative effort. We are a professional theater company, competing in the competitive world of Broadway and off-Broadway, so the work we present must reach for the highest standard of excellence."

THE WILMA THEATER

265 S. Broad St., Philadelphia PA 19107. (215)893-9456. Fax: (215)893-0895. E-mail: info@wilmatheater.org. Website: www.wilmatheater.org. **Contact:** Nakissa Etemad, literary manager. Play producer. Produces 4 shows/ year. Performance space is a 300-seat, state of the art proscenium theater, with full fly system and large backstage area. Pays royalty negotiated between managing director and agent.

How to Contact Submit through agent only. Include SASE. Responds in 6 months.

Musical Theater "We seek to produce the most adventurous work possible. Because this is a director-driven theater, the full-length projects must pose creative challenges that engage the imaginations of our two artistic directors. The eclectic tastes of the artistic directors make it almost impossible to identify specific styles or topics. We look for work that is original, bold, challenging and stimulating."

Productions *Bed and Sofa*, by Polly Pen/Laurence Klavan; *Tin Pan Alley Rag*, by Mark Saltzman; and *Threepenny Opera*, by Brecht/Weill.

Tips "Please be familiar with the Wilma's production history before submitting your material."

WINGS THEATRE CO.

154 Christopher St., New York NY 10014. (212)627-2960. Fax: (212)462-0024. E-mail: jcorrick@wingstheatre.c om. Website: www.wingstheatre.com. **Contact:** Tricia Gilbert, literary manager. Artistic Director: Jeffrey Corrick. Play producer. Estab. 1987. Produces 3-5 plays and 3-5 musicals/year. Performance space is a 74-seat O.O.B. proscenium; repertoire includes a New Musicals Series, a gay-play series—we produce musicals in both series. Pays $100 for limited rights to produce against 6% of gross box office receipts.

How to Contact Submit complete manuscript, score and tape of songs (score is not essential). Include SASE. Responds in 1 year.

Musical Theater "Eclectic. Entertaining. Enlightening. This is an O.O.B. theater. Funds are limited." Does not wish to see "movies posing as plays. Television theater."

Productions *Scott & Zelda*, by Dave Bates (The Fitzgeralds); *Cowboys*, by Clint Jefferies (gay western spoof); and *The Three Musketeers*, by Clint Jefferies (musical adaptation).

Tips "Book needs to have a well-developed plot line and interesting, fully-realized characters. We place emphasis on well-written scripts, as opposed to shows which rely exclusively on the quality of the music to carry the show. Also be patient—we often hold onto plays for a full year before making a final decision."

WOMEN'S PROJECT AND PRODUCTIONS

55 West End Ave., New York NY 10023. (212)765-1706. Fax: (212)765-2024. Website: www.womensproject.org. **Contact:** Lisa McNulty, associate artistic director. Producing Artistic Director: Loretta Greco. Estab. 1978. Produces 3 plays/year. Pays by outright purchase.

How to Contact *Agent submissions only.* "Adult audience."

Musical Theater "We usually prefer a small to medium cast. We produce few musicals and produce *mainly* women playwrights."

Productions *Ladies*, by Eve Ensler (homelessness); *O Pioneers!*, by Darrah Cloud (adapted from Willa Cather's novel); and *Frida: The Story of Frida Kahlo*, by Hilary Blecher/Migdalia Cruz (biography of Frida Kahlo).

Tips "Resist sending early drafts of work."

WOOLLY MAMMOTH THEATRE

917 M. St. NW, Washington DC 20001. (202)312-5270. E-mail: mary@woollymammoth.net. Website: www.wo ollymammoth.net. **Contact:** Mary Resing, literary manager. Play producer. Estab. 1978. Produces 5 plays/year. Royalties vary.

How to Contact *Submit through agent only.* We do not accept unsolicited manuscripts. Include SASE. Responds in 6 months.

Musical Theater ''We do unusual works, including musicals and plays with music. We do not wish to see one-acts.''

Productions *The Dark Kalamazoo*, by Oni Faida Lampley (coming of age/trip to Sierra Leone with African-based music); *Wanted*, by All Carmines (musical comedy about the FBI's golden years under J. Edgar Hoover); *The Rocky Horror Picture Show*.

Tips ''Know what we do. Read or see our plays.''

PLAY PUBLISHERS

ARAN PRESS

1036 S. Fifth St., Louisville KY 40203. (502)568-6622. Fax: (502)561-1124. E-mail: aranpres@aye.net. Website: http://members.aye.net/ ~ aranpres. **Contact:** Tom Eagan, editor/publisher. Play publisher. Estab. 1983. Publishes 5-10 plays and 1-2 musicals/year. Professional, college/university, community, summer stock and dinner theater audience. Pays 50% production royalty or 10% book royalty.

How to Contact Submit manuscript, score and tape of songs. Include SASE. Responds in 2 weeks.

Musical Theater ''The musical should include a small cast, simple set for professional, community, college, university, summer stock and dinner theater production.''

Publications *Whiskey & Wheaties*, by Bruce Feld; *Who Says Life is Fair*, by Mike Willis; and *Burning Bridges*, by Stephen Avery.

BAKER'S PLAYS

P.O. Box 699222, Quincy MA 02269-9222. (617)745-0805. Fax: (617)745-9891. E-mail: info@bakersplays.com. Website: www.bakersplays.com. **Contact:** John Welch, managing director and chief editor. Play publisher. Estab. 1845. Publishes 15-22 plays and 0-3 new musicals/year. Plays are used by children's theaters, junior and senior high schools, colleges and community theaters. Pays negotiated book and production royalty.

• See the listing for Baker's Plays High School Playwriting Contest in the Contests & Awards section.

How to Contact Submit complete manuscript, score and cassette tape of songs. Include SASE. Responds in 4 months.

Musical Theater ''Seeking musicals for teen production and children's theater production. We prefer large cast, contemporary musicals which are easy to stage and produce. Plot your shows strongly, keep your scenery and staging simple, your musical numbers and choreography easily explained and blocked out. Music must be camera-ready.'' Would consider original music for use in a play being developed or in a pre-existing play.

Productions *Oedipus/A New Magical Comedy*, by Bob Johnson.

Tips ''As we publish musicals that can be produced by high school theater departments with high school talent, the writer should know if their play can be done on the high school stage. I recommend that the writer go to performances of original high school musicals whenever possible.''

CONTEMPORARY DRAMA SERVICE

885 Elkton Dr., Colorado Springs CO 80907. (719)594-4422. E-mail: merpcds@aol.com. Website: www.contemp orarydrama.com. **Contact:** Arthur Zapel, associate editor. Play publisher. Estab. 1979. Publishes 40-50 plays and 4-6 new musicals/year. ''We publish for young children and teens in mainstream Christian churches and for teens and college level in the secular market. Our musicals are performed in churches, schools and colleges.'' Pays 10-50% book and performance royalty.

How to Contact *Query first* then submit complete manuscript, score and tape of songs. Include SASE. Responds in 1 month.

Musical Theater ''For churches we publish musical programs for children and teens to perform at Easter, Christmas or some special occasion. Our school musicals are for teens to perform as class plays or special entertainments. Cast size may vary from 15-25 depending on use. We prefer more parts for girls than boys. Music must be written in the vocal range of teens. Staging should be relatively simple but may vary as needed. We are not interested in elementary school material. Elementary level is OK for church music but not public school elementary. Music must have full piano accompaniment and be professionally scored for camera-ready publication.''

Publications *Lucky, Lucky Hudson and the 12th Street Gang*, by Tim Kelly, book, and Bill Francoeur, music and lyrics (spoof of old time gangster movies); *Is There A Doctor in the House?*, by Tim Kelly, book, and Bill Francoeur, music and lyrics (adapted from Moliere comedy); and *Jitterbug Juliet*, by Mark Dissette, book, and Bill Francoeur, music and lyrics (spoof of *Romeo and Juliet*).

Tips "Familiarize yourself with our market. Send $1 postage for catalog. Try to determine what would fit in, yet still be unique."

THE DRAMATIC PUBLISHING COMPANY

311 Washington St., Woodstock IL 60098. (815)338-7170. E-mail: plays@dramaticpublishing.com. Website: dramaticpublishing.com. **Contact:** Linda Habjan, acquisitions editor. Play publisher. Publishes 35 plays and 3-5 musicals/year. Estab. 1885. Plays used by professional and community theaters, schools and colleges. Pays negotiable royalty.

How to Contact Submit complete manuscript, score and tape of songs. Include SASE. Responds in 3 months.

Musical Theater Seeking "children's musicals not over 1¼ hours, and adult musicals with 2 act format. No adaptations for which the rights to use the original work have not been cleared. If directed toward high school market, large casts with many female roles are preferred. For professional, stock and community theater small casts are better. Cost of producing a play is always a factor to consider in regard to costumes, scenery and special effects." Would also consider original music for use in a pre-existing play, "if we or the composer hold the rights to the non-musical work."

Publications *The Little Prince*, by Rick Cummins/John Scoullar; *Hans Brinker*, by Gayle Hudson/Bobbe Bramson; and *Bubbe Meises, Bubbe Stories*, by Ellen Gould/Holly Gewandter (all are full-length family musicals).

Tips "A complete score, ready to go is highly recommended. Tuneful songs which stand on their own are a must. Good subject matter which has wide appeal is always best but not required."

ELDRIDGE PUBLISHING CO., INC.

P.O. Box 14367, Tallahassee FL 32317. (800)HI-STAGE. E-mail: info@histage.com. Website: www.histage.com. **Contact:** Susan Shore, musical editor. Play publisher. Estab. 1906. Publishes 60 plays and 2-3 musicals/year. Seeking "large cast musicals which appeal to students. We like variety and originality in the music, easy staging and costuming. Also looking for children's theater musicals which have smaller casts and are easy to tour. We serve the school and church market, 6th grade through 12th; also Christmas and Easter musicals for churches." Pays 50% royalty and 10% copy sales in school market.

How to Contact Submit manuscript, score or lead sheets and CD of songs. Include SASE. Responds in 1 month.

Publications *The Bard is Back*, by Stephen Murray ("a high school's production of Romeo & Juliet is a disaster!"); and *Boogie-Woogie Bugle Girls*, book by Craig Sodaro, music and lyrics by Stephen Murray (WWII themed musical).

Tips "We're always looking for talented composers but not through individual songs. We're only interested in complete school or church musicals. Lead sheets, CDs tape and script are best way to submit. Let us see your work!"

N THE FREELANCE PRESS

P.O. Box 548, Dover MA 02030. (508)785-8250. E-mail: info@freelancepress.org. Website: www.freelancepress.org. Managing Editor: Narcissa Campion. Play publisher. Estab. 1979. Publishes up to 3 new musicals/year. "Pieces are primarily to be acted by elementary/middle school to high school students (9th and 10th grades); large casts (approximately 30); plays are produced by schools and children's theaters." Pays 10% of purchase price of script or score, 50% of collected royalty.

How to Contact Query first. Include SASE. Responds in 6 months.

Musical Theater "We publish previously produced musicals and plays to be acted by children in the primary grades through high school. Plays are for large casts (approximately 30 actors and speaking parts) and run between 45 minutes to 1 hour and 15 minutes. Subject matter should be contemporary issues (sibling rivalry, friendship, etc.) or adaptations of classic literature for children (*Syrano de Bergerac*, *Rip Van Winkle*, *Pied Piper*, *Treasure Island*, etc.). We do not accept any plays written for adults to perform for children."

Publications *Tortoise vs. Hare*, by Stephen Murray (modern version of classic); *Tumbleweed*, by Sebastian Stuart (sleepy time western town turned upside down); and *Mything Links*, by Sam Abel (interweaving of Greek myths with a great pop score).

Tips "We enjoy receiving material that does not condescend to children. They are capable of understanding many current issues, playing complex characters, handling unconventional material, and singing difficult music."

SAMUEL FRENCH, INC.

45 W. 25th St., New York NY 10010. (212)206-8990. Fax: (212)206-1429. Hollywood office: 7623 Sunset Blvd., Hollywood CA 90046. (323)876-0570. Fax: (323)876-6822. Website: www.samuelfrench.com. President: Charles R. Van Nostrand. Play publisher. Estab. 1830. Publishes 40-50 plays and 2-4 new musicals/year. Amateur and professional theaters.

How to Contact Query first. Include SASE. Responds in 10 weeks.

Musical Theater "We publish primarily successful musicals from the NYC, London and regional stage."
Publications *Prince And The Pauper*, by Neil Berg, Bernie Garzia, Ray Roderick and John Glaudini; *Elegies: A Son Cycle*, by William Finn; *Golf: The Musical*, by Michael Roberts; and *Jewish Girlz*, by Elizabeth Swados.

☑ HEUER PUBLISHING CO.

211 First Ave., SE Suite 200, Cedar Rapids IA 52401. (319)364-6311. E-mail: editor@hitplays.com. Website: www.hitplays.com. Publisher: C. Emmett McMullen. Play publisher. Estab. 1928. Publishes plays, musicals, operas/operettas and guides (choreography, costume, production/staging) for amateur and professional markets, including junior and senior high schools, college/university and community theatres. Focus includes comedy, drama, fantasy, mystery and holiday. Pays by percentage royalty or outright purchase. Pays by outright purchase or percentage royalty.
How to Contact Query with musical CD/tape or submit complete manuscript and score. Include SASE. Responds in 2 months.
Musical Theater "We prefer one, two or three act comedies or mystery-comedies with a large number of characters."
Publications *Happily Ever After*, by Allen Koepke (musical fairytale); *Brave Buckaroo*, by Renee J. Clark (musical melodrama); and *Pirate Island*, by Martin Follose (musical comedy).
Tips "We are willing to review single-song submissions as cornerstone piece for commissioned works. Special interest focus in multicultural, historic, classic literature, teen issues, and biographies."

PIONEER DRAMA SERVICE

P.O. Box 4267, Englewood CO 80155. (303)779-4035. Fax: (303)779-4315. E-mail: playwrights@pioneerdrama.com. Website: www.pioneerdrama.com. **Contact:** Lori Conary, assistant editor. Play publisher. Estab. 1963. "Plays are performed by junior high and high school drama departments, church youth groups, college and university theaters, semi-professional and professional children's theaters, parks and recreation departments." Playwrights paid 50% royalty (10% sales).
How to Contact Query with character breakdown, synopsis and set description. Include SASE. Responds in 6 months.
Musical Theater "We seek full length children's musicals, high school musicals and one act children's musicals to be performed by children, secondary school students, and/or adults. We want musicals easy to perform, simple sets, many female roles and very few solos. Must be appropriate for educational market. We are not interested in profanity, themes with exclusively adult interest, sex, drinking, smoking, etc. Several of our full-length plays are being converted to musicals. We edit them, then contract with someone to write the music and lyrics."
Publications *The Stories of Scheherazade*, book by Susan Pargmon, music and lyrics by Bill Francoeur (musical *Arabian Nights*); *Hubba Hubba: The 1940s Hollywood Movie Musical*, by Gene Casey and Jan Casey (tribute to the 1940s Hollywood movie musical); and *Cinderella's Glass Slipper*, book by Vera Morris, music and lyrics by Bill Francoeur (musical fairy tale).
Tips "Research and learn about our company. Our website and catalog provide an incredible amount of information."

PLAYERS PRESS, INC.

P.O. Box 1132, Studio City CA 91614. (818)789-4980. Associate Editor: Karen Flathers. Vice President: Robert W. Gordon. Play publisher, music book publisher, educational publisher. Estab. 1965. Publishes 20-70 plays and 1-3 new musicals/year. Plays are used primarily by general audience and children. Pays variable royalty and variable amount/performance.
How to Contact Query first. Include SASE. Responds in 3-6 months (3 weeks on queries).
Musical Theater "We will consider all submitted works. Presently musicals for adults and high schools are in demand. When cast size can be flexible (describe how it can be done in your work) it sells better."
Publications *Indian Tales*, by William-Alan Landes (American Indian tales and music based on Indian themes); *Chocolate Soldier*, a new adaptation by George Bernard Shaw (lighthearted comedy set to music); and *The Mad Holmes*, by Ian Wilkes (Sherlock Holmes musical).
Tips "For plays and musicals, have your work produced at least twice. Be present for rehearsals and work with competent people. Then submit material asked for in good clear copy with good audio tapes."

Classical Performing Arts

Finding an audience is critical to the composer of orchestral music. Fortunately, baby boomers are swelling the ranks of classical music audiences and bringing with them a taste for fresh, innovative music. So the climate is fair for composers seeking their first performance.

Finding a performance venue is particularly important because once a composer has his work performed for an audience and establishes himself as a talented newcomer, it can lead to more performances and commissions for new works.

BEFORE YOU SUBMIT

Be aware that most classical music organizations are nonprofit groups, and don't have a large budget for acquiring new works. It takes a lot of time and money to put together an orchestral performance of a new composition, therefore these groups are quite selective when choosing new works to perform. Don't be disappointed if the payment offered by these groups is small or even non-existent. What you gain is the chance to have your music performed for an appreciative audience. Also realize that many classical groups are understaffed, so it may take longer than expected to hear back on your submission. It pays to be patient, and employ diplomacy, tact and timing in your follow-up.

In this section you will find listings for classical performing arts organizations throughout the U.S. But if you have no prior performances to your credit, it's a good idea to begin with a small chamber orchestra, for example. Smaller symphony and chamber orchestras are usually more inclined to experiment with new works. A local university or conservatory of music, where you may already have contacts, is a great place to start.

All of the groups listed in this section are interested in hearing new works from contemporary classical composers. Pay close attention to the music needs of each group, and when you find one you feel might be interested in your music, follow submission guidelines carefully. To locate classical performing arts groups in your area, consult the Geographic Index at the back of this book.

⊠ ACADIANA SYMPHONY ORCHESTRA

P.O. Box 53632, Lafayette LA 70505. (337)232-4277. Fax: (337)237-4712. E-mail: information@acadianasympho ny.org. Website: www.acadianasymphony.org. **Contact:** Geraldine Hubbel, executive director. Symphony orchestra. Estab. 1984. Members are amateurs and professionals. Performs 20 concerts/year, including 1 new work. Commissions 1 new work/year. Performs in 2,230-seat hall with "wonderful acoustics." Pays "according to the type of composition."

How to Contact Call first. Does not return material. Responds in 2 months.

Music Full orchestra: 10 minutes at most. Reduced orchestra, educational pieces: short, up to 5 minutes.

Performances Quincy Hilliard's *Universal Covenant* (orchestral suite); James Hanna's *In Memoriam* (strings/ elegy); and Gregory Danner's *A New Beginning* (full orchestra fanfare).

ADRIAN SYMPHONY ORCHESTRA

110 S. Madison St., Adrian MI 49221. (517)264-3121. Fax: (517)264-3833. E-mail: aso@lni.net. Website: www.a so.org. **Contact:** John Dodson, music director. Symphony orchestra and chamber music ensemble. Estab. 1981. Members are professionals. Performs 25 concerts/year including new works. 1,200 seat hall—"Rural city with remarkably active cultural life." Pays $200-1,000 for performance.

How to Contact Query first. Does not return material. Responds in 6 months.

Music Chamber ensemble to full orchestra. "Limited rehearsal time dictates difficulty of pieces selected." Does not wish to see "rock music or country—not at this time."

Performances Michael Pratt's *Dancing on the Wall* (orchestral—some aleatoric); Sir Peter Maxwell Davies' *Orkney Wedding* (orchestral); and Gwyneth Walker's *Fanfare, Interlude, Finale* (orchestral).

THE AMERICAN BOYCHOIR

19 Lambert Dr., Princeton NJ 08540. (609)924-5858. Fax: (609)924-5812. E-mail: jkaltenbach@americanboychoi r.org. Website: www.americanboychoir.org. General Manager: Janet B. Kaltenbach. Music Director: Vincent Metallo. Professional boychoir. Estab. 1937. Members are musically talented boys in grades 5-8. Performs 200 concerts/year, including 10-25 new works. Commissions 1 new work approximately every 3 years. Actively seeks high quality arrangements. Performs national and international tours, orchestral engagements, church services, workshops, school programs, local concerts, and at corporate and social functions.

How to Contact Submit complete score. Include SASE. Responds in 1 year.

Music Choral works in unison, SA, SSA, SSAA or SATB division; unaccompanied and with piano or organ; occasional chamber orchestra or brass ensemble. Works are usually sung by 28 to 60 boys. Composers must know boychoir sonority.

Performances *Four Seasons*, by Michael Torke (orchestral-choral); *Garden of Light*, by Aaron Kernis (orchestral-choral); *Reasons for Loving the Harmonica*, by Libby Larsen (piano); and *Songs Eternity*, by Steven Paulus (piano).

⊠ ⊠ AMERICAN JAZZ PHILHARMONIC

10811 Washington Blvd., Suite 300, Culver City CA 90232. (310)845-1900. Fax: (310)845-1909. Website: www.a mjazzphil.org. **Contact:** Mitch Glickman, executive director. Symphonic jazz orchestra (72 piece). Estab. 1979. Members are professionals. Performs 8 concerts/year, including 10 new works. Commissions 2-5 composers or new works/year. Performs in major concert halls nationwide: Avery Fisher (New York), Karen & Richard Carpenter Performing Arts Center (Long Beach), Royce Hall (Los Angeles), Pick-Staiger (Chicago). Pays $2,500-5,000 for commission.

How to Contact Query first then submit complete score and tape of piece(s) with résumé. Include SASE. "Newly commissioned composers are chosen each July. Submissions should be sent by June 15th, returned by August 15th."

Music "The AJP commissions 1-2 new symphonic jazz works annually. Decisions to commission are based on composer's previous work in the symphonic jazz genre. The AJP is a 72-piece symphonic jazz ensemble that includes a rhythm section and woodwinds who double on saxophones, plus traditional symphonic orchestra."

Performances John Clayton's *Three Shades of Blue* (solo tenor sax and orchestra); Lennie Niehaus' *Tribute to Bird* (solo alto sax and orchestra); and Eddie Karam's *Stay 'N See* (symphonic jazz overture).

Tips "The AJP has been a recipient of a Reader's Digest/Meet the Composer grant and has received awards from ASCAP and the American Symphony Orchestra League for its programming. The ensemble has also received a Grammy Award nomination for its debut album on GRP Records featuring Ray Brown and Phil Woods. The AJP has recently established the Henry Mancini Institute—a four week summer educational music program for talented young musicians and composer/arrangers chosen from auditions held nationally. Participants study and perform with the principal players of the AJP and guest artists and composers/conductors.

Program includes private lessons, ensemble rehearsals, panel discussions/clinics, master classes, soloist opportunities and performances in orchestra, big band, chamber ensembles and combos.''

☑ AMERICAN OPERA MUSICAL THEATRE CO.

400 W. 43rd St. #19D, New York NY 10036. (212)594-1839. Fax: (212)695-4350. E-mail: aomtc@mindspring.c om. Website: www.americanoperaco.com. **Contact:** Diana Corto, artistic director. Opera and musical theatre producing/presenting organization. Estab. 1995. Members are professionals with varying degrees of experience. Performs 2 operas, many concerts/year and 1 musical theatre production each year. Audience is sophisticated and knowledgeable about music and theatre. ''We rent performance spaces in New York, or are either sponsored by a presenter, or are paid performance fees for opera and concerts.'' Pays negotiable royalty.

How to Contact Submit tape ''of excerpts, not more than 15 minutes.'' Does not return material. Responds in up to 1 month.

Music ''Must be vocal (for opera or for music theatre). Cast should not exceed 10. Orchestration should not exceed 30, smaller groups preferred. No rock 'n' roll, brassy pop.''

Performances Puccini's *La Boheme*; Verdi's *Rigoletto*; *The Jewel Box*; *Iolanta*; *La Molinara* and *The World Goes Round*.

AMHERST SAXOPHONE QUARTET

64 Roycroft Blvd., Amherst NY 14226. (716)839-9716. E-mail: steve@caramaxstudio.com. Website: www.amhe rstsaxophonequartet.buffalo.edu. **Contact:** Steve Rosenthal, director. Chamber music ensemble. Estab. 1978. Performs 80 concerts/year including 10-20 new works. Commissions 1-2 composers or new works/year. ''We are a touring ensemble.'' Payment varies.

How to Contact Query first. Include SASE. Responds in 1 month.

Music ''Music for soprano, alto, tenor and baritone (low A) saxophone. We are interested in great music of many styles. Level of difficulty is commensurate with full-time touring ensembles.''

Performances Lukas Foss's *Saxophone Quartet* (new music); David Stock's *Sax Appeal* (new music); and Chan Ka Nin's *Saxophone Quartet* (new music).

Tips ''Professionally copied parts help! Write what you truly want to write.''

☑ ANDERSON SYMPHONY ORCHESTRA

P.O. Box 741, Anderson IN 46015. (765)644-2111. Fax: (765)644-7703. E-mail: aso@andersonsymphony.org or sowers@anderson.edu. Website: www.andersonsymphony.org. **Contact:** Dr. Richard Sowers, conductor. Executive Director: George W. Vinson. Symphony orchestra. Estab. 1967. Members are professionals. Performs 7 concerts/year. Performs for typical mid-western audience in a 1,500-seat restored Paramount Theatre. Pay negotiable.

How to Contact Query first. Include SASE. Responds in several months.

Music ''Shorter lengths better; concerti OK; difficulty level: mod high; limited by typically 3 full service rehearsals.''

☒ ARCADY

P.O. Box 955, Simcoe ON N3Y 5B3 Canada. (519)428-3185. E-mail: info@arcady.ca. Website: www.arcady.ca. **Contact:** Ronald Beckett, director. Semi-professional chorus and orchestra. Members are professionals, university music majors and recent graduates from throughout Ontario. ''Arcady forms the bridge between the student and the professional performing career.'' Performs 12 concerts/year including 1-2 new works. Commissions 1 composer or new work/year. Pay negotiable.

How to Contact Submit complete score and tape of piece(s). Does not return material. Responds in 3 months.

Music ''Compositions appropriate for ensemble accustomed to performance of chamber works, accompanied or unaccompanied, with independence of parts. Specialize in repertoire of 17th, 18th and 20th centuries. Number of singers does not exceed 30. Orchestra is limited to strings, supported by a professional quartet. No popular, commercial or show music.''

Performances Ronald Beckett's *I Am . . .* (opera); Ronald Beckett's *John* (opera); and David Lenson's *Prologue to Dido and Aeneas* (masque).

Tips ''Arcady is a touring ensemble experienced with both concert and stage performance.''

☒ ATLANTA POPS ORCHESTRA

P.O. Box 15037, Atlanta GA 30333. (770)435-1222. E-mail: ladkmusic@aol.com. Website: www.atlantapops.-com. **Contact:** Albert Coleman, musical director/conductor. Pops orchestra. Estab. 1945. Members are professionals. Performs 5-10 concerts/year. Concerts are performed for audiences of 5,000-10,000, ''all ages, all types.'' Composers are not paid; concerts are free to the public.

How to Contact Call to request permission to submit. Then send cassette, and score or music, if requested. Include SASE. Responds "as soon as possible."

Performances Vincent Montana, Jr.'s *Magic Bird of Fire*; Louis Alter's *Manhattan Serenade*; and Nelson Riddle's *It's Alright With Me*.

Tips "My concerts are pops concerts—no deep classics."

THE ATLANTA YOUNG SINGERS OF CALLANWOLDE

980 Briarcliff Rd. N.E., Atlanta GA 30306. (404)873-3365. Fax: (404)873-0756. E-mail: aysc@bellsouth.net. Website: www.aysc.org. **Contact:** Paige F. Mathis, music director. Community children's chorus. Estab. 1975. Members are amateurs. Performs 45 concerts/year including new works. Audience consists of community churches, retirement homes, schools. Performs most often at churches. Pay is negotiable.

How to Contact Submit complete score and tape of piece(s). Include SASE. Responds in accordance with request.

Music "Subjects and styles appealing to 3rd-12th grade boys and girls. Contemporary concerns of the world of interest. Unusual sacred, folk, classic style. Internationally and ethnically bonding. Medium difficulty preferred, with or without keyboard accompaniment."

Tips "Our mission is to promote service and growth through singing."

AUREUS QUARTET

22 Lois Ave., Demarest NJ 07627-2220. (201)767-8704. E-mail: AureusQuartet@aol.com. **Contact:** James J. Seiler, artistic director. Vocal ensemble (a cappella). Estab. 1979. Members are professionals. Performs 75 concerts/year, including 12 new works. Commissions 5 composers or new works/year. Pay varies for outright purchase.

How to Contact Query first. Include SASE. Responds in 2 months.

Music "We perform anything from pop to classic—mixed repertoire so anything goes. Some pieces can be scored for orchestras as we do pops concerts. Up to now, we've only worked with a quartet. Could be expanded if the right piece came along. Level of difficulty—no piece has ever been too hard." Does not wish to see electronic or sacred pieces. "Electronic pieces would be hard to program. Sacred pieces not performed much. Classical/jazz arrangements of old standards are great! Unusual Christmas arrangements are most welcome!"

Tips "We perform for a very diverse audience. Luscious, four part writing that can showcase well-trained voices is a must. Also, clever arrangements of old hits from '50s through '60s are sure bets. (Some pieces could take optional accompaniment)."

BILLINGS SYMPHONY

201 N. Broadway., Suite 350, Billings MT 59101-1936. (406)252-3610. Fax: (406)252-3353. E-mail: symphony@billingssymphony.org. Website: www.billingssymphony.org. **Contact:** Dr. Uri Barnea, music director. Symphony orchestra, orchestra and chorale. Estab. 1950. Members are professionals and amateurs. Performs 12-15 concerts/year, including 6-7 new works. Traditional audience. Performs at Alberta Bair Theater (capacity 1,416). Pays by outright purchase (or rental).

How to Contact Query first. Include SASE. Responds in 2 weeks.

Music Any style. Traditional notation preferred.

Performances Jim Cockey's *Symphony No. 2 (Parmly's Dream)* (symphony orchestra with chorus and soloists); Ilse-Mari Lee's *Cello Concerto* (concerto for cello solo and orchestra); and Jim Beckel's *Christmas Fanfare* (brass and percussion).

Tips "Write what you feel (be honest) and sharpen your compositional and craftsmanship skills."

BIRMINGHAM-BLOOMFIELD SYMPHONY ORCHESTRA

1592 Buckingham, Birmingham MI 48009. (248)645-2276. Fax: (248)645-2276, *51. Website: www.bbso.org. **Contact:** Felix Resnick, music director and conductor. President and Executive Director: Carla Lamphere. Symphony orchestra. Estab. 1975. Members are professionals. Performs 6 concerts including 1 new work/year. Commissions 1 composer or new work/year "with grants." Performs for middle-to-upper class audience at Temple Beth El's Sanctuary. Pays per performance "depending upon grant received."

How to Contact Query first. Does not return material. Responds in 6 months.

Music "We are a symphony orchestra but also play pops. Usually 3 works on program (2 hrs.) Orchestra size 65-75. If pianist is involved, they must rent piano."

Performances Brian Belanger's *Tuskegee Airmen Suite* (symphonic full orchestra); and Larry Nazer & Friend's *Music from "Warm" CD* (jazz with full orchestra).

☑ THE BOSTON PHILHARMONIC

295 Huntington Ave., #210, Boston MA 02115. (617)236-0999. Fax: (617)236-8613. E-mail: office@bostonphil.org. Website: www.bostonphil.org. Music Director: Benjamin Zander. Symphony orchestra. Estab. 1979. Mem-

bers are professionals, amateurs and students. Performs 2 concerts/year. Audience is ages 30-70. Performs at New England Conservatory's Jordan Hall, Boston's Symphony Hall and Sanders Theatre in Cambridge. Both Jordan Hall and Sanders Theatre are small (approximately 1,100 seats) and very intimate.

How to Contact *Does not accept new music at this time.*

Music Full orchestra only.

Performances Dutilleuxs' *Tout un monde lointain* for cello and orchestra (symphonic); Bernstein's *Fancy Free* (symphonic/jazzy); Copland's *El Salon Mexico* (symphonic); Gershwin's *Rhapsody in Blue*; Shostakovitch's *Symphony No. 10*; Harbison's *Concerto for Oboe*; Holst's *The Planet Suite*; Schwantner's *New Morning for the World*; Berg's *Seven Early Songs*; and Ive's *The Unanswered Question*.

BRAVO! L.A.

16823 Liggett St., North Hills CA 91343. (818)892-8737. Fax: (818)892-1227. E-mail: info@bravo-la.com. Website: www.bravo-la.com. **Contact:** Dr. Janice Foy, director. An umbrella organization of recording/touring musicians, formed in 1994. Includes the following musical ensembles: Celllissimo! L.A. (cello ensemble); Interstellar Strings (expandable string group with optional piano); Mesto Chamber Players; the New American Quartet (string quartet); The Ascending Wave (harp, soprano, cello or harp/cello duo); Cellissimo! L.A. (cello ensemble); Musical Combustion (harp, flute, cello); I Musicanti (singer, piano and cello); and the Sierra Chamber Players (piano with strings or mixed ensemble). Performs 4 concerts/year, including 1 new work. "We take care of PR. There is also grant money the composer can apply for."

How to Contact Submit complete score and tape of piece(s). Include SASE. Responds in a few months.

Music "Classical, Romantic, Baroque, Popular (including new arrangements done by Shelly Cohen, from the 'Tonight Show Band'), ethnic (including gypsy) and contemporary works (commissioned as well). The New American Quartet has a recording project which features music of Mozart's *Eine Kleine Nachtmusik*, Borodin's *Nocturne*, a Puccini Opera Suite (S. Cohen), Strauss' *Blue Danube Waltz*, *Trepak* of Tschaikovsky, 'El Choclo' (Argentinian tango), *Csardas!* and arrangements of Cole Porter, Broadway show tunes and popular classics."

Performances Joe Giarrusso's *Rhapsody for Cello and Piano* (concert piece modern romantic); Joe Giarrusso's *Cello Sonata* (concert piece); and Dan Bogley's *Foybles* (contemporary solo cello).

Tips "Please be open to criticism/suggestions about your music and try to appeal to mixed audiences. We also look for innovative techniques, mixed styles or entertaining approaches, such as classical jazz or Bach and pop, or ethnic mixes. There are four CD's currently available for purchase online for $20 each. There are also sound clips on the website."

☑ ☷ CALGARY BOYS CHOIR

5336 Lakeview Dr. SW, Calgary AB T3E 5R9 Canada. (403)217-7790. Fax: (403)217-7796. E-mail: info@calgaryboyschoir.ab.ca. Website: www.calgaryboyschoir.ab.ca. **Contact:** Jenny Haldeman, office administrator. Artistic Director: Arlie Langager. Boys choir. Estab. 1973. Members are amateurs age 6 and up. Performs 50-70 concerts/year including 1-2 new works. Pay negotiable.

How to Contact Query first. Submit complete score and tape of piece(s). Include SASE. Responds in 6 weeks. Does not return material.

Music "Style fitting for boys choir. Lengths depending on project. Orchestration preferable a cappella/for piano/sometimes orchestra."

Performances Dr. William Jordan's *City of Peace* (world premiere Wednesday September 11, 2002); Lydia Adam's arrangement of *Mi'kmaq Honour Song* (May 26, 2002); and Bruce Sled's *Jing-ga-lye-ya* (May 12, 2002).

☷ ☑ CANADIAN OPERA COMPANY

227 Front St. E., Toronto ON M5A 1E8 Canada. (416)363-6671. Fax: (916)363-2660. E-mail: sandrag@coc.ca. Website: www.coc.ca. **Contact:** Sandra J. Gavinchuk, music administrator. Opera company. Estab. 1950. Members are professionals. 50-55 performances, including a minimum of 1 new work/year. Pays by contract.

How to Contact Submit complete score and tapes of vocal and/or operatic works. "Vocal works please." Include SASE. Responds in 5 weeks.

Music Vocal works, operatic in nature. "Do not submit works which are not for voice. Ask for requirements for the Composers-In-Residence program."

Performances Dean Burry's *Brothers Grimm* (children's opera, 50 minutes long); Paul Ruders' *Handmaid's Tale* (full length opera, 2 acts, epilogue); Benjamin Britten's *Albert Herring* (opera in 3 acts, full length).

Tips "We have a Composers-In-Residence program which is open to Canadian composers or landed immigrants."

CANTATA ACADEMY

2441 Pinecrest Dr., Ferndale MI 48220. (248)358-9868. **Contact:** Phillip O'Jibway, business manager. Music Director: Dr. Michael Mitchell. music director. Vocal ensemble. Estab. 1961. Members are professionals. Per-

forms 10-12 concerts/year including 1-3 new works. "We perform in churches and small auditoriums throughout the Metro Detroit area for audiences of about 500 people." Pays variable rate for outright purchase.
How to Contact Submit complete score. Include SASE. Responds in 3 months.
Music Four-part a cappella and keyboard accompanied works, two and three-part works for men's or women's voices. Some small instrumental ensemble accompaniments acceptable. Work must be suitable for forty voice choir. No works requiring orchestra or large ensemble accompaniment. No pop.
Performances Charles S. Brown's *Five Spirituals* (concert spiritual); Kirke Mechem's *John Brown Cantata*; and Randol Alan Bass's *Gloria* (accompanied SATB).
Tips "Be patient. Would prefer to look at several different samples of work at one time."

CARMEL SYMPHONY ORCHESTRA

P.O. Box 761, Carmel IN 46082-0761. (317)844-9717. Fax: (317)844-9916. E-mail: cso@carmelsymphony.org. Website: www.carmelsymphony.org. **Contact:** Allen Davis, executive director. Symphony orchestra. Estab. 1976. Members are professionals and amateurs. Performs 15 concerts/year, including 1-2 new works. Audience is "40% senior citizens, 85% white." Performs in a 1,500-seat high school performing arts center. Pay is negotiable.
How to Contact Query first. Include SASE. Responds in 3 months.
Music "Full orchestra works, 10-20 minutes in length. Can be geared toward 'children's' or 'Masterworks' programs. 65-70 piece orchestra, medium difficulty."
Performances Jim Beckel's *Glass Bead Game* (full orchestra); Percy Grainger's *Molly on the Shore* (full orchestra); and Frank Glover's *Impressions of New England* (full orchestra and jazz quartet).

☑ CARSON CITY SYMPHONY

P.O. Box 2001, Carson City NV 89702-2001 or 191 Heidi Circle, Carson City NV 89701-6532. (775)883-4154. Fax: (775)883-4371. E-mail: dcbugli@aol.com. Website: www.ccsymphony.com. **Contact:** David C. Bugli, music director/conductor. Amateur community orchestra. Estab. 1984. Members are amateurs. Performs 5 concerts, including 2 new works/year. Audience is largely Carson City/Reno area residents, many of them retirees. "Most concerts are performed in the Carson City Community Center Auditorium, which seats 800." Pay varies for outright purchase.
How to Contact Submit complete score and tape or CD of works. Does not return material. Responds in 2 months.
Music "We want classical, pop orchestrations, orchestrations of early music for modern orchestras, concertos for violin or piano, holiday music for chorus and orchestra (children's choirs and handbell ensemble available), music by women, music for brass choir. Most performers are amateurs, but there are a few professionals who perform with us. Available winds and percussion: 2 flutes and flute/piccolo, 2 oboes (E.H. double sometimes), 2 clarinets, 1 bass clarinet, 2 bassoons, 4 horns, 3 trumpets, 3 trombones, 1 tuba, timpani, and percussion. Harp and piano. Strings: 8-8-5-6-3 (or fewer). Avoid music that lacks melodic appeal. Composers should contact us first. Each concert has a different emphasis. Note: Associated choral group, Carson Chamber Singers, performs several times a year with the orchestra and independently."
Performances Thomas Svoboda's *Overture of the Season* (minimalist overture); Gwyneth Walker's *A Concerto of Hymns and Spirituals for Trumpet and Orchestra*; and Jim Cockey's *A Land of Sage and Sun*.
Tips "It is better to write several short movements well than to write long, unimaginative pieces, especially when starting out. Be willing to revise after submitting the work, even if it was premiered elsewhere."

ℕ CHAMBER ORCHESTRA OF SOUTH BAY/CARSON-DOMINIQUEZ HILLS SYMPHONY

21 La Vista Verde, Rancho Palos Verdes CA 90275. (310)243-3947. E-mail: FSteiner@csudh.edu. **Contact:** Dr. Frances Steiner, music director. Symphony orchestra. Estab. 1972. Members are professionals (chamber orchestra); professionals and amatuers (symphony). Performs 10-11 concerts/year including 3-4 new works. Commissions 0-1 new works/year. Chamber orchestra audience is conservative in musical taste; symphony has an ethnically diverse and new student audience. Performance spaces seat 450-480. Pays ASCAP/BMI royalty or rental fee to publisher.
How to Contact Query first. Include SASE. Responds in 3 months.
Music Prefers 10-15 minute works for chamber orchestra, string orchestra and symphony orchestra (winds in pairs). Works should have "audience appeal" and not be too difficult to learn; there is special interest in works by women composers of diverse ethnicity.
Performances Michael Abels's *Global Warming* (ethinic, melodic ideas); Augusta Reid Thomas's *Flute Concerto #1* (contemporary); and Kevin O'Neal's *Japanese Sketches* (jazz and orchestra).

☑ CHARLOTTE PHILHARMONIC ORCHESTRA

P.O. Box 470987, Charlotte NC 28247-0987. (704)846-2788. Fax: (704)847-6043. E-mail: info@charlottephilharmonic.org. Website: www.charlottephilharmonic.org. **Contact:** Albert Moehring, music director. Symphony

Classical Arts

orchestra. Estab. 1991. Members are professionals. Performs 12 concerts/year including 2-4 new works. Audience consists of music lovers, educated and uneducated. "We regularly perform Broadway/movie soundtracks, also standard classical repertoire." Performance spaces are up to 2,500 seats. Pay is negotiable.

• The Charlotte Philharmonic Orchestra was voted Charlotte's Best Entertainment in 1998.

How to Contact Submit complete score and tape of piece(s). Does not return material. Responds in 6 weeks.

Music Seeks full orchestrations, lush strings always popular. Maximum 8-10 minutes. Would review classical styles, but also interested in Boston Pops type selections. Require lyrical music with interesting melodies and good rhythms. "We are not interested in atonal, dissonant styled music. We will neither perform it, nor bother to review it. Our audiences do not like it." Players are professional. Limited rehearsals. String passages playable in limited time. Full orchestra sound—excellent brass players. 75 piece orchestra. Always interested in fine Broadway styled arrangements. Look for strong, smooth transpositions/modulations.

Performances Davis Brown's *Battle of the Fire Ants* (part of a suite); Robert Kerr's *Irish Legend* (medley of Celtic style melodies).

Tips "With a new composer, we recommend pieces under 10 minutes, lyrical basis with definite melodies. Full use of 75 piece orchestra. Lush strings without exceedingly difficult passages for limited rehearsals. Variety of materials welcomed. Enjoy standard classics, bib band, ballroom dance-type music, ballet style. Also enjoy operatic arrangements. Use our own Philharmonic Chorus as well as regular vocalists. Good choral arrangements with full orchestra always of interest. Appreciate a tape when possible. If a composer submits during a really busy period of performances, please be patient. If there is no response in 4-6 weeks, they may contact us again."

☑ CHATTANOOGA GIRLS CHOIR

P.O. Box 6036, Suite 612 Maclellan Building, Chattanooga TN 37401. (423)266-9422. E-mail: office@chattanoogagirlschoir.com. Website: http://chattanoogagirlschoir.com. **Contact:** John E. Wigal, artistic director. Vocal ensemble. Estab. 1986. Members are amateurs. Performs 2 concerts/year including at least 1 new work. Audience consists of cultural and civic organizations and national and international tours. Performance space includes concert halls and churches. Pays for outright purchase or per performance.

How to Contact Query first. Include SASE. Responds in 6 weeks.

Music Seeks renaissance, baroque, classical, romantic, twentieth century, folk and musical theatre for young voices of up to 8 minutes. Performers include 5 treble choices: 4th grade (2 pts.); 5th grade (2 pts.) (SA); grades 6-9 (3 pts.) (SSA); grades 10-12 (3-4 pts.) (SSAA); and a combined choir: grades 6-12 (3-4 pts.) (SSAA). Medium level of difficulty. "Avoid extremely high Tessitura Sop I and extremely low Tessitura Alto II."

Performances Jan Swafford's *Iphigenia Book: Meagher* (choral drama); Penny Tullock's *How Can I Keep from Singing* (Shaker hymn).

ℕ CHEYENNE SYMPHONY ORCHESTRA

P.O. Box 851, Cheyenne WY 82003. (307)778-8561. Fax: (307)634-7512. E-mail: director@cheyennesymphony.org. Website: www.cheyennesymphony.org. **Contact:** Chloe Illoway, executive director. Symphony orchestra. Estab. 1955. Members are professionals. Performs 6 concerts/year including 1-3 new works. "Orchestra performs for a conservative, mid-to-upper income audience of 1,200 season members." Pay varies.

How to Contact Query first. Does not return material. Responds in 2 months.

Performances Bill Hill's *Seven Abstract Miniatures* (orchestral).

ℕ CIMARRON CIRCUIT OPERA COMPANY

P.O. Box 1085, Norman OK 73070. Phone: (405)364-8962. E-mail: info@ccocopera.org. Website: www.ccocopera.org. **Contact:** Kevin Smith or Jennifer Baker, music directors. Opera company. Estab. 1975. Members are semi professional. Performs 75 concerts/year including 1-2 new works. Commissions 1 or less new work/year. "CCOC performs for children across the state of Oklahoma and for a dedicated audience in central Oklahoma. As a touring company, we adapt to the performance space provided, ranging from a classroom to a full raised stage." Pay is negotiable.

How to Contact Query first. Does not return material. Responds in 6 months.

Music "We are seeking operas or operettas in English only. We would like to begin including new, American works in our repertoire. Children's operas should be no longer than 45 minutes and require no more than a synthesizer for accompaniment. Adult operas should be appropriate for families, and may require either full orchestration or synthesizer. CCOC is a professional company whose members have varying degrees of experience, so any difficulty level is appropriate. There should be a small to moderate number of principals. Children's work should have no more than four principals. Our slogan is 'Opera is a family thing to do.' If we cannot market a work to families, we do not want to see it."

Performances Menotti's *Amahl & the Night Visitors*; and Barab's *La Pizza Con Funghi*.

Tips "45-minute fairy tale-type children's operas with possibly a 'moral' work well for our market. Looking for works appealing to K-8 grade students. No more than four principles."

COMMONWEALTH OPERA INC.

140 Pine St., Florence MA 01062. (413)586-5026. Fax: (413)587-0380. E-mail: info@commonwealthopera.org. Website: www.commonwealthopera.org. **Contact:** Richard R. Rescia, artistic director. Opera company. Estab. 1977. Members are professionals and amateurs. Performs 4 concerts/year. "We perform at the Calvin Theatre Northampton in an 1,200-seat opera house. Depending on opera, audience could be family oriented or adult." Pays royalty.

How to Contact Query first. Does not return material. Response will take months.

Music "We are open to all styles of opera. We have the limitations of a regional opera company with local chorus. Principals come from a wide area. We look only at opera scores."

Performances Arnold Black's *The Phantom Tollbooth* (children's opera); *Diefledermaus*, and *The Magic Flute*.

Tips "We're looking for opera that is accessible to the general public and performable by a standard opera orchestra."

☑ CONNECTICUT CHORAL ARTISTS/CONCORA

52 Main St., New Britain CT 06051. (860)224-7500. Website: www.concora.org. **Contact:** Jane Penfield, executive director. Richard Coffey, artistic director. Professional concert choir, also an 18-voice ensemble dedicated to contemporary a cappella works. Estab. 1974. Members are professionals. Performs 15 concerts/year, including 3-5 new works. "Mixed audience in terms of age and background; performs in various halls and churches in the region." Payment "depends upon underwriting we can obtain for the project."

How to Contact Query first. "No unsolicited submissions accepted." Include SASE. Responds in 1 year.

Music Seeking "works for mixed chorus of 36 singers; unaccompanied or with keyboard and/or small instrumental ensemble; text sacred or secular/any language; prefers suites or cyclical works, total time not exceeding 15 minutes. Performance spaces and budgets prohibit large instrumental ensembles. Works suited for 750-seat halls are preferable. Substantial organ or piano parts acceptable. Scores should be very legible in every way."

Performances Wm. Schuman's *Carols of Death* (choral SATB); Charles Ives' *Psalm 90* (choral SATB); and Frank Martin's *Mass for Double Chorus* (regional premiere).

Tips "Use conventional notation and be sure manuscript is legible in every way. Recognize and respect the vocal range of each vocal part. Work should have an identifiable *rhythmic* structure."

Ⓝ DESERT CHORALE

811 St. Michael's Dr. Suite 208, Santa Fe NM 87504. (505)988-2282. Fax: (505)988-7522. E-mail: info@desertchorale.org. Website: www.desertchorale.org. Music Director: Dennis Shrock. Executive Director: Jillian Sandrock. Business Manager: Jay Reep. Box Office Manager: Natalia Chavez. Vocal ensemble. Members are professionals. Performs 35 concerts/year including 2 new works. Commissions 1 new composer or new work/year. "Highly sophisticated audiences who are eager for interesting musical experiences. We pay $5,000 to $2,000 for premieres, often as part of consortium."

How to Contact Query first. Submit complete score and tape *after* query. Does not return material. Responds in 2 years.

Music "Challenging chamber choir works 6 to 20 minutes in length. Accompanied works are sometimes limited by space—normally no more than 5 or 6 players. "We sing both a cappella and with chamber orchestra; size of choir varies accordingly (20-32). No short church anthem-type pieces."

Performances Edwin London's *Jove's Nectar* (choral with 5 instruments); Lanham Deal's *Minituras de Sor Juana* (unaccompanied); and Steven Sametz's *Desert Voices* (choral with 4 instruments).

Tips "Call me or see me and I'll be happy to tell you what I need and I will also put you in touch with other conductors in the growing professional choir movement."

DÚO CLÁSICO

4 Essex St., Clifton NJ 07014. (973)655-4379. E-mail: wittend@mail.montclair.edu. Website: www.montclair.edu/music/pages/faculty/specialists/dwitten.html. **Contact:** David Witten. Chamber music ensemble. Estab. 1986. Members are professionals. Performs 16 concerts/year including 4 new works. Commissions 1 composer or new work/year. Performs in small recital halls. Pays 10% royalty.

How to Contact Query first. Include SASE. Responds in 6 weeks.

Music "We welcome scores for flute solo, piano solo or duo. Particular interest in Latin American composers."

Performances Diego Luzuriaga's *La Múchica* (modern, with extended techniques); Robert Starer's *Yizkor & Anima Aeterna* (rhythmic); and Piazzolla's *Etudes Tanguistiques* (solo flute).

Tips "Extended techniques, or with tape, are fine!"

✅ 🌐 EUROPEAN UNION CHAMBER ORCHESTRA

Hollick, Yarnscombe EX31 3LQ United Kingdom. Phone: (44)1271 858249. Fax: (44)1271 858375. E-mail: eucorc hl@aol.com. Website: www.etd.gb.com. **Contact:** Ambrose Miller, general manager. Chamber orchestra. Members are professionals. Performs 70 concerts/year, including 6 new works. Commissions 2 composers or new works/year. Performs regular tours of Europe, Americas and Asia, including major venues. Pays per performance or for outright purchase, depending on work.

How to Contact Query first. Does not return material. Responds in 6 weeks.

Music Seeking compositions for strings, 2 oboes and 2 horns with a duration of about 8 minutes.

Performances S. Gardner's *More Pricks Than Kicks* (strings); F. Festa's *Pegasus* (flute, strings); and T. Agerfeldt's *Ground* (strings).

Tips "Keep the work to less than 15 minutes in duration, it should be sufficiently 'modern' to be interesting but not too difficult as this could take up rehearsal time. It should be possible to perform without a conductor."

📰 FONTANA CONCERT SOCIETY

359 S. Kalamazoo Mall, Suite 200, Kalamazoo MI 49007. (616)382-7774. Fax: (616)382-0812. E-mail: info@fonta nachamberarts.org. Website: www.fontanachamberarts.org/history.html. **Contact:** Ms. Anne Berquist, executive and artistic director. Chamber music ensemble presenter. Estab. 1980. Members are professionals. Fontana Chamber Arts presents over 45 events, including the 6-week Summer Festival of Music and Art, which runs from mid-July to the end of August. Regional and guest artists perform classical, contemporary, jazz and nontraditional music. Commissions and performs new works each year. Fontana Chamber Arts presents 7 classical and 2 jazz concerts during the Fall/Winter season. Audience consists of well-educated individuals who accept challenging new works, but like the traditional as well. Summer—180 seat hall; Fall/winter—various venues, from 400 to 1,500 seats.

How to Contact Submit complete score, résumé and tapes of piece(s). Include SASE. Responds in approximately 1 month.

Music Chamber music—any combination of strings, winds, piano. No "pop" music, new age type. Special interest in composers attending premiere and speaking to the audience.

Performances George Perle's *Duos for String Quartet & Horn* (commission); Dan Welches's *Dante Dances* (U.S. premiere); and C. Curtis-Smith's *Les Adieux* for horn and string quartet (collaboration with International Horn Society).

Tips "Provide a résumé and clearly marked tape of a piece played by live performers."

✅ FORT WORTH CHILDREN'S OPERA

1300 Gendy St., Fort Worth TX 76107. (817)731-0833, ext. 19. Fax: (817)731-0835. E-mail: tkostecki@fwopera.o rg. Website: www.fwopera.org. **Contact:** Tony Kostecki, director of education. Opera company. Estab. 1946. Members are professionals. Performs over 180 in-school performances/year." Audience consists of elementary school children; performs in major venues for district-wide groups and individual school auditoriums, cafetoriums and gymnasiums. Pays $40/performance.

How to Contact Submit complete score and tape of piece(s). Include SASE. Responds in 6 months.

Music "Familiar fairy tales or stories adapted to music of opera composers, or newly-composed music of suitable quality. Ideal length: 40-45 minutes. Piano or keyboard accompaniment. Should include moral, safety or school issues. Can be ethnic in subject matter and must speak to pre-K and grade 1-6 children. Prefer pieces with good, memorable melodies. Performed by young, trained professionals on 9-month contract. Requires work for four performers, doubled roles OK, SATB plus accompanist/narrator. Special interest in bilugal (Spanish/English) works."

GREAT FALLS SYMPHONY ASSOCIATION

P.O. Box 1078, Great Falls MT 59403. (406)453-4102. Fax: (406)453-9779. E-mail: info@gfsymphony.org. Website: www.gfsymphony.org. **Contact:** Gordon J. Johnson, music director and conductor. Symphony orchestra. Estab. 1959. Members are nine-member professional core, plus 60 per-service local musicians. Performs 2 youth concerts/year including 1-2 new works. Commissions 1-2 new works/year. "Our audience is conservative. Newer music is welcome; however, it might be more successful if it were programmatic." Plays in Civic Center Auditorium seating 1,764. Pays per performance.

How to Contact Query first. Include SASE. Responds in 2 months.

Music "Compositions should be for full orchestra. Should be composed idiomatically for instruments avoiding extended techniques. Duration 10-20 minutes. Avoid diverse instruments such as alto flute, saxophones, etc. Our orchestra carries 65 members, most of whom are talented amateurs. We have a resident string quartet and woodwind quintet that serve as principals. Would enjoy seeing a piece for quartet or quintet solo and orchestra. Send letter with clean score and tape (optional). We will reply within a few weeks."

Performances David Bukvich's *Suite for Viola & Orchestra*; David Mastanka's *String Quartet* (string quartet).

Tips "Music for orchestra and chorus is welcome. Cross cues will be helpful in places. Work should not require an undue amount of rehearsal time (remember that a concerto and symphony are probably on the program as well)."

GREATER GRAND FORKS SYMPHONY ORCHESTRA

P.O. Box 7084, Grand Forks ND 58202-7084. (701)777-3359. Fax: (701)777-3320. E-mail: ggfso@und.nodak.e du. Website: www.und.nodak.edu/org/ggfso. **Contact:** Timm Rolek, music director. Symphony orchestra. Estab. 1908. Members are professionals and/or amateurs. Performs 6 concerts/year. "New works are presented in 2-4 of our programs." Audience is "a mix of ages and musical experience. In 1997-98 we moved into a renovated, 420-seat theater." Pay is negotiable, depending on licensing agreements.

How to Contact Submit complete score or complete score and tape of pieces. Include SASE. Responds in 6 months.

Music "Style is open, instrumentation the limiting factor. Music can be scored for an ensemble up to but not exceeding: 3,2,3,2/4,3,3,1/3 perc./strings. Rehearsal time limited to 3 hours for new works."

Performances Michael Harwood's *Amusement Park Suite* (orchestra); Randall Davidson's *Mexico Bolivar Tango* (chamber orchestra); and John Corigliano's *Voyage* (flute and orchestra); Linda Tutas Haugen's *Fable of Old Turtle* (saxophone concerto).

HEARTLAND MEN'S CHORUS

P.O. Box 32374, Kansas City MO 64171-5374. (816)931-3338. Fax: (816)531-1367. E-mail: hmc@hmckc.org. Website: www.hmckc.org. **Contact:** Joseph Nadeau, artistic director. Men's chorus. Estab. 1986. Members are professionals and amateurs. Performs 3 concerts/year; 9-10 are new works. Commissions 1 composer or new works/year. Performs for a diverse audience at the Folly Theater (1,100 seats). Pay is negotiable.

How to Contact Query first. Include SASE. Responds in 2 months.

Music "Interested in works for male chorus (ttbb). Must be suitable for performance by a gay male chorus. We will consider any orchestration, or a cappella."

Performances Mark Hayes' "Two Flutes Playing" (commissioned song cycle); Alan Shorter's "Country Angel Christmas" (commissioned chidren's musical); Kevin Robinson's "Life is a Cabaret: The Music of Kander and Ebb" (commissioned musical).

Tips "Find a text that relates to the contemporary gay experience, something that will touch peoples' lives."

ⓃHELENA SYMPHONY

P.O. Box 1073, Helena MT 59624. (406)442-1860. E-mail: info@helenasymphony.org. Website: www.helenasy mphony.org. **Contact:** Erik Funk, music director and conductor. Symphony orchestra. Estab. 1955. Members are professionals and amateurs. Performs 7-10 concerts/year including new works. Performance space is an 1,800 seat concert hall. Payment varies.

How to Contact Query first. Include SASE. Responds in 3 months.

Music "Imaginative, collaborative, not too atonal. We want to appeal to an audience of all ages. We don't have a huge string complement. Medium to difficult okay—at frontiers of professional ability we cannot do."

Performances Eric Funk's *A Christmas Overture* (orchestra); Donald O. Johnston's *A Christmas Processional* (orchestra/chorale); and Elizabeth Sellers' *Prairie* (orchestra/short ballet piece).

Tips "Try to balance tension and repose in your works. New instrument combinations are appealing."

ⓃHENDERSONVILLE SYMPHONY ORCHESTRA

P.O. Box 1811, Hendersonville NC 28793. (828)697-5884. Fax: (828)697-5765. E-mail: hso@brinet.com. Website: www.hendersonvillesymphony.org. **Contact:** Sandie Salvaggio-Walker, general manager. Symphony orchestra. Estab. 1971. Members are professionals and amateurs. Performs 6 concerts/year. "We would welcome a new work per year." Audience is a cross-section of retirees, professionals and some children. Performance space is a 857-seat high school audiorium.

How to Contact Query first. Include SASE. Responds in 1 month.

Music "We use a broad spectrum of music (classical concerts and pops)."

Performances Nelson's *Jubilee* (personal expression in a traditional method); Britten's "The Courtly Dances" from Glorina (time-tested); and Chip Davis' arrangement for Mannheim Steamroller's *Deck the Halls* (modern adaptation of traditional melody).

Tips "Submit your work even though we are a community orchestra. We like to be challenged. We have the most heavily patronized fine arts group in the county. Our emphasis is on education."

☑HERMANN SONS GERMAN BAND

P.O. Box 162, Medina TX 78055. (830)589-2268. E-mail: herbert@festmusik.com. Website: www.festmusik.c om. **Contact:** Herbert Bilhartz, music director. Community band with German instrumentation. Estab. 1990.

Members are both professionals and amateurs. Performs 12 concerts/year including 6 new works. Commissions no new composers or new works/year. Performs for "mostly older people who like German polkas, waltzes and marches. We normally play only published arrangements from Germany."

How to Contact Query first; then submit full set of parts and score, condensed or full. Include SASE. Responds in 6 weeks.

Music "We like European-style polkas or waltzes (Viennese or Missouri tempo), either original or arrangements of public domain tunes. Arrangements of traditional American folk tunes in this genre would be especially welcome. Also, polkas or waltzes featuring one or two solo instruments (from instrumentation below) would be great. OK for solo parts to be technically demanding. Although we have no funds to commission works, we will provide you with a cassette recording of our performance. Also, we would assist composers in submitting works to band music publishers in Germany for possible publication. Polkas and waltzes generally follow this format: Intro; 1st strain repeated; 2nd strain repeated; DS to 1 strain; Trio: Intro; 32 bar strain; 'break-up' strain; Trio DS. Much like military march form. Instrumentation: Fl/Picc, 3 clars in Bb, 2 Fluegelhorns in Bb; 3 Tpts in Bb, 2 or 4 Hns in F or Eb, 2 Baritones (melody/countermelody parts; 1 in Bb TC, 1 in BC), 2 Baritones in Bb TC (rhythm parts), 3 Trombones, 2 Tubas (in octaves, mostly), Drum set, Timpani optional. We don't use saxes, but a German publisher would want 4-5 sax parts. Parts should be medium to medium difficult. All brass parts should be considered one player to the part; woodwinds, two to the part. No concert type pieces; no modern popular or rock styles. However, a 'theme and variations' form with contrasting jazz, rock, country, modern variations would be clever, and our fans might go for such a piece (as might a German publisher)."

Performances Darryl Lyman's *American Folk Music Waltz* medley and *American Folk Music Polka* medley; and David Lorrien's *Cotton-Eyed Joe* arrangement.

Tips "German town bands love to play American tunes. There are many thousands of these bands over there and competition among band music publishers in Germany is keen. Few Americans are aware of this potential market, so few American arrangers get published over there. Simple harmony is best for this style, but good counterpoint helps a lot. Make use of the dark quality of the Fluegelhorns and the bright, fanfare quality of the trumpets. Give the two baritones (one in TC and one in BC) plenty of exposed melodic material. Keep them in harmony with each other (3rds and 6ths), unlike American band arrangements, which have only one Baritone line. If you want to write a piece in this style, give me a call, and I will send you some sample scores to give you a better idea."

HERSHEY SYMPHONY ORCHESTRA

P.O. Box 93, Hershey PA 17033. (800)533-3088. E-mail: drdackow@aol.com. **Contact:** Dr. Sandra Dackow, music director. Symphony orchestra. Estab. 1969. Members are professionals and amateurs. Performs 8 concerts/year, including 1-3 new works. Commissions "possibly 1-2" composers or new works/year. Audience is family and friends of community theater. Performance space is a 1,900 seat grand old movie theater. Pays commission fee.

How to Contact Submit complete score and tape of piece(s). Include SASE. Responds in 3 months.

Music "Symphonic works of various lengths and types which can be performed by a non-professional orchestra. We are flexible but like to involve all our players."

Performances Paul W. Whear's *Celtic Christmas Carol* (orchestra/bell choir) and Linda Robbins Coleman's *In Good King Charlie's Golden Days* (overture).

Tips "Please lay out rehearsal numbers/letter and rests according to phrases and other logical musical divisions rather than in groups of ten measures, etc., which is very unmusical and wastes time and causes a surprising number of problems. Also, please do not send a score written in concert pitch; use the usual transpositions so that the conductor sees what the players see; rehearsal is much more effective this way. Cross cue all important solos; this helps in rehearsal where instruments may be missing."

HUDSON VALLEY PHILHARMONIC

35 Market St., 1st Floor, Poughkeepise NY 12601. (845)473-5288. Fax: (845)473-4259. E-mail: slamarca@bardav on.org. Website: www.bardavon.org. **Contact:** Stephen LaMarca, production manager. Symphony orchestra. Estab. 1969. Members are professionals. Performs 20 concerts/year including 1 new work. "Classical subscription concerts for all ages; Pops concerts for all ages; New Wave concerts—crossover projects with a rock 'n' roll artist performing with an orchestra. HVP performs in three main theatres which are concert auditoriums with stages and professional lighting and sound." Pay is negotiable.

How to Contact Query first. Include SASE. Responds in 8 months.

Music "HVP is open to serious classical music, pop music and rock 'n' roll crossover projects. Desired length of work between 10-20 minutes. Orchestrations can be varied by should always include strings. There is no limit to difficulty since our musicians are professional. The ideal number of musicians to write for would include up to a Brahms-size orchestra 2222, 4231, T, 2P, piano, harp, strings."

Performances Joan Tower's *Island Rhythms (serious classical work); Bill Vanaver's P'nai El* (symphony work with dance); and Joseph Bertolozzi's *Serenade* (light classical, pop work).

Tips "Don't get locked into doing very traditional orchestrations or styles. Our music director is interested in fresh, creative formats. He is an orchestrator as well and can offer good advice on what works well. Songwriters who are into crossover projects should definitely submit works. Over the past four years, HVP has done concerts featuring the works of Natalie Merchant, John Cale, Sterling Morrison, Richie Havens and R. Carlos Nakaì (Native American flute player), all reorchestrated by our music director for small orchestra with the artist."

INDIANA UNIVERSITY NEW MUSIC ENSEMBLE
Indiana University Bloomington, School of Music, Bloomington IN 47405-2200. E-mail: ddzubay@indiana.edu. Website: www.indiana.edu/ ~ nme. **Contact:** David Dzubay, director. Performs solo, chamber and large ensemble works. Estab.1974. Members are students. Presents 4 concerts/year.

Music Peter Lieberson's *Free and Easy Wanderer* ; Sven-David Sandstrom's *Wind Pieces*; Atar Arad's *Sonata*; and David Dzubay's
Dancesing in a Green Bay.

Ⓝ KENTUCKY OPERA
101 S. Eighth St. at Main, Louisville KY 40202. (502)584-4500. Fax: (502)584-7484. E-mail: info@kyopera.org. Website: www.kyopera.org. **Contact:** Kim Cherie Lloyd, director of music. Opera. Estab. 1952. Members are professionals. Performs 3 main stage/year. Performs at Whitney Hall, The Kentucky Center for the Arts, seating is 2,400; Bomhard Theatre, The Kentucky Center for the Arts, 620; Macauley Theatre, 1,400. Pays by royalty, outright purchase or per performance.

How to Contact *Write or call first before submitting. No unsolicited submissions.* Submit complete score. Include SASE. Responds in 6 months.

Music Seeks opera—1 to 3 acts with orchestrations. No limitations.

Performances *Turandot; Susannah!;* and *Rigaletto.*

Ⓒ KITCHENER-WATERLOO CHAMBER ORCHESTRA
86 Weber St. E., Kitchener ON N2H 1C7 Canada. (519)744-3828. E-mail: kwchamberorchest@aol.com. Website: http://members.rogers.com/kwchamberorchestra. **Contact:** Graham Coles, music director. Chamber Orchestra. Estab. 1985. Members are professionals and amateurs. Performs 5-6 concerts/year including 1-2 new works. "We perform mainly baroque and classical repertoire, so any contemporary works must not be too dissonant, long or far fetched." Pays per performance.

How to Contact "It's best to query first so we can outline what not to send. Include: complete cv—list of works, performances, sample reviews." Include SAE and IRC. Responds in March of each year.

Music "Musical style must be accessible to our audience and players (3 rehearsals). Length should be under 20 minutes. Maximum orchestration 2/2/2/2 2/2/0/0 Timp/or 1 Percussion String 5/5/3/4/2. We have limited rehearsal time, so keep technique close to that of Bach-Beethoven. We also play chamber ensemble works—octets, etc. We do not want choral or solo works."

Performances James Grant's *Lament* (string orchestra) and Reynaldo Hahn's *La Fete Chez Therese* (ballet suite).

Tips "If you want a first-rate performance, keep the technical difficulties minimal."

Ⓝ KNOX-GALESBURG SYMPHONY
Box 31, Knox College, Galesburg IL 61401. (309)343-0112, ext. 208. E-mail: bpolay@knox.edu. Website: www.knox.edu/kgs. **Contact:** Bruce Polay, music director. Symphony orchestra. Estab. 1951. Members are professionals and amateurs. Performs 7 concerts/year including 2-5 new works. Commissions 1 composer or new work/year on occasion. High diverse audience; excellent, recently renovated historical theater. Pay is negotiable.

How to Contact Submit complete score and tapes of piece(s). "Pops material also welcome." Include SASE. Responds in 8 months.

Music Moderate difficulty 3222/4331/T piano, harpsichord, celesta and full strings. No country.

Performances Winstin's *5th Symphony* (orchestral); Pann's "Bullfight" from "Two Portraits of Barcelona" (orchestral); and Polay's Concerto-Fantasie (piano and orchestra).

Tips "Looking for moderately difficult, 8-10 minute pieces for standard orchestra."

☑ LAMARCA AMERICAN VARIETY SINGERS
2655 W. 230th Place, Torrance CA 90505. (310)325-8708. E-mail: lamarcamusic@lycos.com. Website: www.lamarcamusic.tripod.lycos.com. **Contact:** Robert L. Cronquist, director. Youth to high school vocal ensembles. Estab. 1979. Members are professionals and amateurs. Performs 10 concerts/year including 3 new works. Performs at major hotels, conventions, community theaters, fund raising events, cable TV, community fairs and Disneyland. Pays showcase only.

Classical Arts

How to Contact Query first. Include SASE. Responds in 2 weeks.

Music "Seeks 3-10 or 15 minute medleys; a variety of musical styles from Broadway—pop styles to humorous specialty songs. Top 40 dance music, light rock and patriotic themes. No rap or anything not suitable for family audiences."

Performances *Disney Movie Music* (uplifting); *Children's Music* (educational/positive); and *Beatles Medley* (love songs).

N LEHIGH VALLEY CHAMBER ORCHESTRA

P.O. Box 20641, Lehigh Valley PA 18002-0641. (610)266-8555. E-mail: luco@fast.net. Website: www.luco.org. Music Director: Donald Spieth. Chamber orchestra. Estab. 1979. Performs 25 concerts/year including 2-3 new works. Members are professionals. Commissions 1-2 composers or new works/year. Typical orchestral audience, also youth concerts. Pays commission for first 2 performances, first right for recording.

How to Contact Submit complete score and tape of piece(s). Include SASE. Responds in 4 months.

Music "Classical orchestral; works for youth and pops concerts. Duration 10-15 minutes. Chamber orchestra 2222-2210 percussion, strings (66442). No limit on difficulty."

Performances February 15-16, 2002, Kyle Smith commissioned for new work.

Tips "Send a sample tape and score of a work(s) written for the requested medium."

LEXINGTON PHILHARMONIC SOCIETY

161 N. Mill St., Arts Place, Lexington KY 40507. (859)233-4226. Fax: (859)233-7896. Website: www.lexingtonphi lharmonic.org. **Contact:** Dr. George Zack, music director. Symphony orchestra. Estab. 1961. Members are professionals. Series includes "8 serious, classical subscription concerts (hall seats 1,500); 3 concerts called Pops the Series; 3 Family Concerts; 10 outdoor pops concerts (from 1,500 to 5,000 tickets sold); 5-10 run-out concerts ($\frac{1}{2}$ serious/$\frac{1}{2}$ pops); and 10 children's concerts." Pays via ASCAP and BMI, rental purchase and private arrangements.

How to Contact Submit complete score and tape of piece(s). Include SASE.

Music Seeking "good current pops material and good serious classical works. No specific restrictions, but overly large orchestra requirements, unusual instruments and extra rentals help limit our interest."

Performances "Visit our website for complete concert season listing."

Tips "When working on large-format arrangement, use cross-cues so orchestra can be cut back if required. Submit good quality copy, scores and parts. Tape is helpful."

N LIMA SYMPHONY ORCHESTRA

67 Town Square, P.O. Box 1651, Lima OH 45802. (419)222-5701. Website: www.limasymphony.com. Fax: (419)222-6587. **Contact:** Crafton Beck, music conductor. Symphony orchestra. Estab. 1953. Members are professionals. Performs 17-18 concerts including at least 1 new work/year. Commissions at least 1 composer or new work/year. Middle to older audience; also Young People's Series. Mixture for stage and summer productions. Performs in Veterans' Memorial Civic & Convention Center, a beautiful hall seating 1,670; various temporary shells for summer outdoors events; churches; museums and libraries. Pays $2,500 for outright purchase (Anniversary commission) or grants $1,500-5,000.

How to Contact Submit complete score if not performed; otherwise submit complete score and tape of piece(s). Include SASE. Responds in 3 months.

Music "Good balance of incisive rhythm, lyricism, dynamic contrast and pacing. Chamber orchestra to full (85-member) symphony orchestra." Does not wish to see "excessive odd meter changes."

Performances Frank Proto's *American Overture* (some original music and fantasy); Werner Tharichen's *Concerto for Timpani and Orchestra*; and James Oliverio's *Pilgrimage—Concerto for Brass* (interesting, dynamic writing for brass and the orchestra).

Tips "Know your instruments, be willing to experiment with unconventional textures, be available for in depth analysis with conductor, be at more than one rehearsal. Be sure that individual parts are correctly matching the score and done in good, neat calligraphy."

LITHOPOLIS AREA FINE ARTS ASSOCIATION

3825 Cedar Hill Rd., Canal Winchester OH 43110-8929. (614)837-8925. Website: www.cwda.net/LAFAA/. **Contact:** Virginia E. Heffner, series director. Performing Arts Series. Estab. 1973. Members are professionals and amateurs. Performs 6-7 concerts/year including 2-3 new works. "Our audience consists of couples and families 30-80 in age. Their tastes run from classical, folk, ethnic, big band, pop and jazz. Our hall is acoustically excellent and seats 400. It was designed as a lecture-recital hall in 1925." Composers "may apply for Ohio Arts Council Grant under the New Works category." Pays straight fee to ASCAP.

How to Contact Query first. Include SASE. Responds in 3 weeks.

Music "We prefer that a composer is also the performer and works in conjunction with another artist, so they could be one of the performers on our series. Piece should be musically pleasant and not too dissonant. It should be scored for small vocal or instrumental ensemble. Dance ensembles have difficulty with 15' high 15' deep and 27' wide stage. We do not want avant-garde or obscene dance routines. No ballet (space problem). We're interested in something historical—national or Ohio emphasis would be nice. Small ensembles or solo format is fine."

Performances Patsy Ford Simms' *Holiday Gloria* (Christmas SSA vocal); Andrew Carter's *A Maiden Most Gentle* (Christmas SSA vocal); and Luigi Zaninelli's *Alleluia, Silent Night* (Christmas SSA vocal).

Tips "Call in December of 2004 or January 2005 for queries about our 2005-2006 season. We do a varied program. We don't commission artists. Contemporary music is used by some of our artist or groups. By contacting these artists, you could offer your work for inclusion in their program."

LYRIC OPERA OF CHICAGO

20 N. Wacker Dr., Chicago IL 60606. (312)322-2244. Fax: (312)419-8345. E-mail: jgriffin@lyricopera.org. Website: www.lyricopera.org. **Contact:** Julie Griffin-Meadors, music administrator. Opera company. Estab. 1953. Members are professionals. Performs 80 operas/year including 1 new work in some years. Commissions 1 new work every 4 or 5 years. "Performances are held in a 3,563 seat house for a sophisticated opera audience, predominantly 30+ years old." Payment varies.

How to Contact Query first. Does not return material. Responds in 6 months.

Music "Full-length opera suitable for a large house with full orchestra. No musical comedy or Broadway musical style. We rarely perform one-act operas. We are only interested in works by composers and librettists with extensive theatrical experience. We have few openings for new works, so candidates must be of the highest quality. Do not send score or other materials without a prior contact."

Performances William Bolcom's *View from the Bridge*; John Corigliano's *Ghosts of Versailles*; and Leonard Bernstein's *Candide*.

Tips "Have extensive credentials and an international reputation."

MASTER CHORALE OF WASHINGTON

1200 29th St. NW, Suite LL2, Washington DC 20007. (202)471-4050. Fax: (202)471-4051. E-mail: singing@masterchorale.org. Website: www.masterchorale.org. **Contact:** Donald McCullough, music director. Vocal ensemble. Estab. 1967. Members are professionals and amateurs. Performs 8 concerts/year including 1-3 new works. Commissions one new composer or work every 2 years. "Audience covers a wide range of ages and economic levels drawn from the greater Washington DC metropolitan area. Kennedy Center Concert Hall seats 2,400." Pays by outright purchase.

How to Contact Submit complete score and tape of piece(s). Include SASE. Responds in 9 months.

Music Seeks new works for: 1) large chorus with or without symphony orchestras; 2) chamber choir and small ensemble.

Performances Stephen Paulus' *Mass*; Joonas Kokkonen's *Requiem* (symphonic choral with orchestra); Morten Lauridsen's *Lux Aeterna*; Donald McCullough's *Let My People Go!: A Spiritual Journey*; and Daniel E. Gawthorp's *In Quiet Resting Places*.

MESQUITE SYMPHONIC BAND

(formerly Mesquite Community Band), 1527 North Galloway, Mesquite TX 75149-2327. (972)216-8125. Fax: (972)288-4760. E-mail: mesquitesymphonicband@att.net. Website: http://home.att.net/~mesquitesymphonicband/. **Contact:** Dale Y. Coates, conductor. Community band. Estab. 1986. Members are both professionals and amateurs. Performs 9 (4 formal, 5 outdoor) concerts/year. Commissions 1 composer or new work/year. Audience is young-to-mature adult. Performance space is concert hall (Mesquite Arts Center). Pays variable rate for outright purchase.

How to Contact Submit complete score and tape of piece(s). Include SASE. Responds in 1 month.

Music Seeks full orchestration for band, approximately 4-5 minutes. "At this time we have approximately thirty-five members with the top level being level four." Does not want modern style.

Performances James Curnow's *Olympic Fanfare & Theme*.

Tips "Know the capability of the performing group."

ⓃMILWAUKEE YOUTH SYMPHONY ORCHESTRA

929 N. Water St., Milwaukee WI 53202. (414)272-8540. Fax: (414)272-8549. E-mail: general@myso.org. Website: www.myso.org. **Contact:** Frances Richman, executive director. Multiple youth orchestras and other instrumental ensembles. Estab. 1956. Members are students. Performs 12-15 concerts/year including 1-2 new works. "Our groups perform in Uihlein Hall at the Marcus Center for the Performing Arts in Milwaukee plus area sites. The audiences usually consist of parents, music teachers and other interested community members, with periodic reviews in the *Milwaukee Journal Sentinel*." Payment varies.

How to Contact Query first. Include SASE. Does not return material. Responds in 1 month.

Performances James Woodward's *Tuba Concerto*.

Tips "Be sure you realize you are working with *students* (albeit many of the best in southeastern Wisconsin) and not professional musicians. The music needs to be on a technical level students can handle. Our students are 8-18 years of age, in 2 full symphony orchestras, a wind ensemble and 2 string orchestras, plus two flute choirs, advanced chamber orchestra and 15-20 small chamber ensembles."

THE MIRECOURT TRIO

50 Orchard St., Jamaica Plain MA 02130. (617)524-2495. E-mail: tkingcello@aol,com. **Contact:** Terry King. Chamber music ensemble; violin, cello, piano. Estab. 1973. Members are professionals. Performs 2-4 concerts/ year including 1 new work. Commissions 1 composer or new work/year. Concerts are performed for university, concert series, schools, societies and "general chamber music audiences of 100-1,500." Pays for outright purchase, percentage royalty or per performance.

How to Contact Query first. Include SASE. Responds in 6 months.

Music Seeks "music of short to moderate duration (5-20 minutes) that entertains, yet is not derivative or clichéd. Orchestration should be basically piano, violin, cello, occasionally adding voice or instrument. We do not wish to see academic or experimental works."

Performances Otto Leuning's *Solo Sonata* (solo cello); Lukas Foss's *Three American Pieces* (cello, piano premiere); and Coolidge's *Dialectic No. 1 for piano trio*.

Tips "Submit works that engage the audience or relate to them, that reward the players as well."

☑ MOORES OPERA CENTER

Moores School of Music, University of Houston, Houston TX 77204-4201. (713)743-2255. E-mail: bross@www.o rpheus.music.uh.edu. Website: www.uh.edu/music/Mooresopera/. Director of Opera: Buck Ross. Opera/music theater program. Members are professionals, amateurs and students. Performs 12-14 concerts/year including 1 new work. Performs in a proscenium theater which seats 800. Pit seats approximately up to 75 players. Audience covers wide spectrum, from first time opera-goers to very sophisticated. Pays per performance.

How to Contact Submit complete score and tapes of piece(s). Include SASE. Responds in 6 months.

Music "We seek music that is feasible for high graduate level student singers. Chamber orchestras are very useful. No more than two and a half hours. No children's operas."

Performances John Corigliano's *The Ghosts of Versailles*; Carlisle Floyd's *Bilby's Doll*; Robert Nelson's *A Room With a View*; Conrad Susa's *The Dangerous Liaisons*; and Dominick Argento's *Casanova's Homecoming*.

Ⓝ NATIONAL ASSOCIATION OF COMPOSERS/USA (NACUSA)

P.O. Box 49256, Los Angeles CA 90049. (310)541-8213. E-mail: bia@flash.net. Website: www.music.usa.org/ nacusa. **Contact:** Marshall Bialosky, president. Chamber music ensemble and composers' service organization. Estab. 1932. Members are professionals. Performs 10-15 concerts/year in L.A.; 10-11 nationally with other chapters—all new works. Usually perform at universities in Los Angeles and at a mid-town church in New York. Paid by ASCAP or BMI (NACUSA does not pay composers).

How to Contact To submit, you must be a member of NACUSA. Submit complete score and tape of pieces. Include SASE. Responds in 3 months.

Music Chamber music for five or fewer players; usually in the 5-20 minute range. "Level of difficulty is not a problem; number of performers is solely for financial reasons. We deal in serious, contemporary concert hall music. No 'popular' music."

Performances Robert Linn's *Piano Variations*; Aurelio dela Vega's *Transparent Songs* (voice, piano); and Michelle Green's *At Ends* (solo violin).

Tips "Send in modest-sized pieces—not symphonies and concertos."

☑ OPERA MEMPHIS

6745 Wolf River Parkway, Memphis TN 38120. (901)257-3100. Fax: (901)257-3109. E-mail: david@operamemp his.org. Website: www.operamemphis.org. **Contact:** Michael Ching, artistic director. Opera company. Estab. 1955. Members are professionals. Performs 8-12 concerts/year including new works. Occasionally commissions composers. Audience consists of older, wealthier patrons, along with many students and young professionals. Pay is negotiable.

How to Contact Query first. Include SASE. Responds in 1 year or less.

Music Accessible practical pieces for educational or second stage programs. Educational pieces should not exceed 90 minutes or 4-6 performers. We encourage songwriters to contact us with proposals or work samples for theatrical works. We are very interested in crossover work.

Performances Mike Reid's *Different Fields* (one act opera); David Olney's *Light in August* (folk opera); and Sid Selvidge's *Riversongs* (one act blues opera).

Tips "Spend many hours thinking about the synopsis (plot outline)."

ORCHESTRA SEATTLE/SEATTLE CHAMBER SINGERS

1305 Fourth Ave. #402, Seattle WA 98101. (206)682-5208. E-mail: osscs@osscs.org. Website: www.osscs.org. **Contact:** Andrew Danilchik, librarian. Symphony orchestra, chamber music ensemble and community chorus. Estab. 1969. Members are amateurs and professionals. Performs 8 concerts/year including 2-3 new works. Commissions 1-2 composers or new works/year. "Our audience is made up of both experienced and novice classical music patrons. The median age is 45 with an equal number of males and females in the upper income range. Most concerts now held in Benaroya Hall."

How to Contact Query first. Include SASE. Responds in 1 year.

Performances Robert Kechley's *Trumpet Concerto* (classical concerto); Carol Sams's *Earthmakers* (oratorio); and Murl Allen Sanders's *Accordion Concerto* (classical concerto.

ⓃOREGON SYMPHONY

921 SW Washington St., Suite 200, Portland OR 97205. (503)228-4294. E-mail: symphony@orsymphony.org. Website: www.orsymphony.org. **Contact:** Susan Nielson, concert director. Symphony orchestra. Estab. 1896. Members are professionals. Performs 110 concerts/year including 5-10 new works. Commissions 1 composer or new work/every other year. "Classical concerts are attended predominantly by 35-60 year olds. Hall seats 2,776—renovated vaudeville house." Pay varies for outright purchase.

How to Contact Query first. Does not return material. Responds in 1 month.

Music "Classical 10-20 min.: 3333-5331 3 perc, 1 tmp, 1 harp, 1 keyboard, strings: 16-14-12-10-8; pops, jazz: same, except strings 12-10-8-6-4. No country. Send a list of other orchestras with whom you have performed."

Performances John Adam's *Violin Concerto* (classical); Aaron Vernis' *New Era Dance* (classical); and George Rochberg's *Oboe Concerto* (classical).

ⓃPALMETTO MASTERSINGERS

P.O. Box 7441, Columbia SC 29202. (803)765-0777. Fax: (928)441-6083. E-mail: info@palmettomastersingers.org. Website: www.palmettomastersingers.org. **Contact:** Walter Cuttino, music director. 80 voice male chorus. Estab. 1981 by the late Dr. Arpad Darasz. Members are professionals and amateurs. Performs 8-10 concerts/year. Commissions 1 composer of new works every other year (on average). Audience is generally older adults, "but it's a wide mix." Performance space for the season series is the Koger Center (approximately 2,000 seats) in Columbia, SC. More intimate venues also available. Fee is negotiable for outright purchase.

How to Contact Query first. Include SASE. Or e-mail to info@palmettomastersingers.org.

Music Seeking music of 10-15 minutes in length, "not too far out tonally. Orchestration is negotiable, but chamber size (10-15 players) is normal. We rehearse once a week and probably will not have more than 8-10 rehearsals. These rehearsals (2 hours each) are spent learning a 1½-hour program. Only 1-2 rehearsals (max) are with the orchestra. Piano accompaniments need not be simplified, as our accompanist is exceptional."

Performances Randal Alan Bass' *Te Deum* (12-minute, brass and percussion); Dick Goodwin's *Mark Twain Remarks* (40 minute, full symphony); and Randol Alan Bass' *A Simple Prayer* (a capella 6 minute).

Tips "Contact us as early as possible, given that programs are planned by July. Although this is an amateur chorus, we have performed concert tours of Europe, performed at Carnegie Hall, The National Cathedral and the White House in Washington, DC. We are skilled amateurs."

PICCOLO OPERA COMPANY INC.

24 Del Rio Blvd., Boca Raton FL 33432-4734. (800)282-3161. Fax: (561)394-0520. E-mail: leejon51@msn.com. **Contact:** Lee Merrill, executive assistant. Traveling opera company. Estab. 1962. Members are professionals. Performs 1-50 concerts/year including 1-2 new works. Commissions 0-1 composer or new work/year. Operas are performed for a mixed audience of children and adults. Pays by performance or outright purchase. Operas in English.

How to Contact Query first. Include SASE.

Music "Musical theater pieces, lasting about one hour, for adults to perform for adults and/or youngsters. Performers are mature singers with experience. The cast should have few performers (up to 10), no chorus or ballet, accompanied by piano or local orchestra. Skeletal scenery. All in English."

Performances Menotti's *The Telephone*; Mozart's *Cosi Fan Tutte*; and Puccini's *La Boheme* (repertoire of more than 22 productions).

PRINCETON SYMPHONY ORCHESTRA

P.O. Box 250, Princeton NJ 08542. Phone/Fax: (609)497-0020. E-mail: info@princetonsymphony.org. Website: www.princetonsymphony.org. **Contact:** Mark Laycock, music director. Symphony orchestra. Estab. 1980. Members are professionals. Performs 6-10 concerts/year including some new works. Commissions 1 composer or new work/year. Performs in a "beautiful, intimate 800-seat hall with amazing sound." Pays by arrangement.

How to Contact Submit through agent only. Include SASE. Responds in 6 months.
Music "Orchestra usually numbers 40-60 individuals."

PRISM SAXOPHONE QUARTET

257 Harvey St., Philadelphia PA 19144. (215)438-5282. E-mail: info@prismquartet.com. Website: www.prismq uartet.com. President, New Sounds Music Inc. Prism Quartet: Matthew Levy. Chamber music ensemble. Estab. 1984. Members are professionals. Performs 80 concerts/year including 10-15 new works. Commissions 4 composers or new works/year. "Ours are primarily traditional chamber music audiences." Pays royalty per performance from BMI or ASCAP or commission range from $100 to $15,000.
How to Contact Submit complete score (with parts) and tape of piece(s). Does not return material. Responds in 3 months.
Music "Orchestration—sax quartet, SATB. Lengths—5-25 minutes. Styles—contemporary, classical, jazz, crossover, ethnic, gospel, avant-garde. No limitations on level of difficulty. No more than 4 performers (SATB sax quartet). No transcriptions. The Prism Quartet places special emphasis on crossover works which integrate a variety of musical styles."
Performances David Liebman's *The Gray Convoy* (jazz); Bradford Ellis's *Tooka-Ood Zasch* (ethnic-world music); and William Albright's *Fantasy Etudes* (contemporary classical).

RIDGEWOOD SYMPHONY ORCHESTRA

P.O. Box 176, Ridgewood NJ 07451. (201)612-0118. Fax: (201)529-4343. E-mail: info@ridgewoodsymphony.o rg. Website: www.ridgewoodsymphony.org. **Contact:** Gary S. Fagin, musicdirector and conductor. Symphony orchestra. Estab. 1939. Members (95 plus) are professionals and amateurs. Performs 4-6 concerts/year and 3-5 children's concerts including 1-2 new works. Commissions possibly 1 new work/year. Audience is "sophisticated." Performance space is 744-seat school auditorium. Pays commission fee.
How to Contact Submit complete score and tape of piece(s). Include SASE. Responds in 3 months ("it depends on how busy we are").
Music "Symphonic works of various lengths and types which can be performed by a nonprofessional orchestra. We are flexible but would like to involve all of our players; very restrictive instrumentations do not suit our needs."
Performances Shostakovich's *Festive Overture*; Gerschwin's *Piano Concerto in F*; Gerschwin's *American in Paris* (rhapsody); Dvorak's *Symphony No. 7 in d Minor*; Mussorgsky's *Pictures at an Exhibition*; Schumann's *Symphony No. 2 in C Major*; Berlioz's *Symphonie Fantastique*; and Elgar's *Enigma Variations*.
Tips "Please lay out rehearsal numbers/letters and rests according to phrases and other logical musical divisions rather than in groups of ten measures, etc., which is very unmusical, wastes time and causes a surprising number of problems. Also, please *do not* send a score written in concert pitch; use the usual transpositions so that the conductor sees what the players see. Rehearsal is much more effective this way. Cross cue all important solos; this helps in rehearsal where instruments may be missing."

SACRAMENTO MASTER SINGERS

P.O. Box 417997, Sacramento CA 95841. (916)338-0300. Fax: (916)788-7464. E-mail: smscbarb@aol.com. Website: www.mastersingers.org. **Contact:** Ralph Hughes, conductor/artistic director. Vocal ensemble. Estab. 1984. Members are professionals and amateurs. Performs 9 concerts/year including 5-6 new works. Commissions 2 new works/year. Audience is made up of mainly college age and older patrons. Performs mostly in churches with 500-900 seating capacity. Pays $200 for outright purchase.
How to Contact Submit complete score and tape of piece(s). Include SASE. Responds in 5 weeks.
Music "A cappella works; works with small orchestras or few instruments; works based on classical styles with a 'modern' twist; multi-cultural music; shorter works probably preferable, but this is not a requirement. We usually have 38-45 singers capable of a high level of difficulty, but find that often simple works are very pleasing."
Performances Joe Jennings' *An Old Black Woman, Homeless and Indistinct* (SATB, oboe, strings, dramatic).
Tips "Keep in mind we are a chamber ensemble, not a 100-voice choir."

ST. LOUIS CHAMBER CHORUS

P.O. Box 11558, Clayton MO 63105. (636)458-4343. E-mail: maltworm@inlink.com. Website: www.chamberch orus.org. **Contact:** Philip Barnes, artistic director. Vocal ensemble, chamber music ensemble. Estab. 1956. Members are professionals and amateurs. Performs 6 concerts/year including 5-10 new works. Commissions 1-2 new works/year. Audience is "diverse and interested in unaccompanied choral work and outstanding architectural/acoustic venues." Performances take place at various auditoria noted for their excellent acoustics—churches, synagogues, schools and university halls. Pays by arrangement.

How to Contact Query first. Does not return material. "Panel of 'readers' submit report to Artistic Director. Responds in 3 months. 'General Advice' leaflet available on request."
Music "*Only a cappella* writing; no contemporary 'popular' works; historical editions welcomed. No improvisatory works. Our programs are tailored for specific acoustics—composers should indicate their preference."
Performances Sir Richard Rodney Bennett's *A Contemplation Upon Flowers* (a cappella madrigal); Stuart McIntosh's *Can Thou Lov'st Me, Lady?* (a cappella glee for men's voices); and Sasha Johnson Manning's *Dies Irae* (a cappella motet).
Tips "We only consider a cappella works which can be produced in five rehearsals. Therefore pieces of great complexity or duration are discouraged."

SALT LAKE SYMPHONIC CHOIR
P.O. Box 45, Salt Lake City UT 84110. (801)466-8701. Fax: (801)466-8780. E-mail: slsymchoir@juno.com. President: Greg Bettinson. Director: George Welch. Professional touring choir. Estab. 1949. Members are professionals and amateurs. Performs 3-15 concerts/year, including 2-4 new works. Commissions 1 new work or composer/year. "We tour throughout U.S. and Canada for community concert series, colleges and universities." Pay is negotiable.
How to Contact Query first. Does not return material. Responds in 4 months.
Music Seeking "4-8 part choral pieces for a 100-voice choir—from Bach to rock."
Performances Howard Hanson's *Song of Democracy*.

SAN FRANCISCO GIRLS CHORUS
44 Page Street, Suite 200, San Francisco CA 94102. (415)863-1752. E-mail: info@sfgirlschorus.org. Website: www.sfgirlschorus.org. **Contact:** Susan McMane, artistic director. Vocal ensemble. Estab. 1978. Volunteer chorus with a core of paid professionals. Performs 8-10 concerts/year including 3-4 new works. Commissions 2-3 composers or new works/year. Concerts are performed for "choral/classical music lovers, plus family audiences and audiences interested in international repertoire. Season concerts are performed in a 900-seat church with excellent acoustics and in San Francisco's Davies Symphony Hall, a 2,800-seat state-of-the-art auditorium." Pay negotiable for outright purchase.
● The San Francisco Girls Chorus was a featured guest performer on the San Francisco Symphony's recording of Stravinsky's *Persephone*, which won a 2000 Grammy Award for Best Classical Album and Best Orchestral Performance.
How to Contact Submit complete score. Does not return material. Responds in 6 months.
Music "Music for treble voices (SSAA); a cappella, piano accompaniment, or small orchestration; 3-10 minutes in length. Wide variety of styles; 45 singers; challenging music is encouraged."
Performances Lisa Bielawa's *Letter to Anna (1998)* (a cappella); Jake Heggie's *Patterns* (piano, mezzo-soprano soloist, chorus); and Chen Yi's *Chinese Poems* (a cappella).
Tips "Choose excellent texts and write challenging and beautiful music. The San Francisco Girls Chorus has pioneered in establishing girls choral music as an art form in the United States. The Girls Chorus is praised for its 'stunning musical standard' (*San Francisco Chronicle*) in performances in the San Francisco Bay Area and on tour. SFGC's annual concert season showcases the organization's concert/touring ensembles, Chorissima and Virtuose, in performances of choral masterworks from around the world, commissioned works by contemporary composers, and 18th-century music from the Venetian Ospedali and Mexican Baroque which SFGC has brought out of the archives and onto the concert stage. Chorissima and Virtuose tour through California with partial support provided by the California Arts Council Touring Program and have represented the U.S. and the City of San Francisco nationally and abroad. The choruses provide ensemble and solo singers for performances and recordings with the San Francisco Symphony and San Francisco Opera, Women's Philharmonic, and many other music ensembles. SFGC's discography includes four CD recordings, *I Never Saw Another Butterfly* (20th Century music); *A San Francisco Christmas* (Benjamin Britten's *A Ceremony of Carols* and other holiday music); a 1998 release, *Music from the Venetian Ospedali* (18th-century works for girls chorus) (called "fresh" by *The New Yorker*); and a 2000 release, *Crossroads* (a collection of international music)."

SINGING BOYS OF PENNSYLVANIA
P.O. Box 206, Wind Gap PA 18091. (610)759-6002. Fax: (727)526-6197. **Contact:** K. Bernard Schade, Ed. D., director. Vocal ensemble. Estab. 1970. Members are professional children. Performs 100 concerts/year including 3-5 new works. "We attract general audiences: family, senior citizens, churches, concert associations, university concert series and schools." Pays $300-3,000 for outright purchase.
How to Contact Query first. Does not return material. Responds in 3 weeks.
Music "We want music for commercials, voices in the SSA or SSAA ranges, sacred works or arrangements of American folk music with accompaniment. Our range of voices are from G below middle C to A (13th above middle C). Reading ability of choir is good but works which require a lot of work with little possibility of more

than one performance are of little value. We sing very few popular songs except for special events. We perform music by composers who are well-known and works by living composers who are writing in traditional choral forms. Works which have a full orchestral score are of interest. The orchestration should be fairly light, so as not to cover the voices. Works for Christmas have more value than some other, since we perform with orchestras on an annual basis."

Performances Don Locklair's *The Columbus Madrigals* (opera).

Tips "It must be appropriate music and words for children. We do not deal in pop music. Folk music, classics and sacred are acceptable."

SOLI DEO GLORIA CANTORUM

3402 Woolworth Ave., Omaha NE 68105. (402)341-4111. E-mail: cantorum@berkey.com. Website: www.berke y.com. **Contact:** Almeda Berkey, music director. Professional choir. Estab. 1988. Members are professionals. Performs 5-7 concerts/year; several are new works. Commissions 1-2 new works/year. Performance space: "cathedral, symphony hall, smaller intimate recital halls as well." Payment is "dependent upon composition and composer."

How to Contact Submit complete score and tape of piece(s). Include SASE. Responds in 2 months.

Music "Chamber music mixed with topical programming (e.g., all Celtic or all Hispanic programs, etc.). Generally a cappella compositions from very short to extended range (6-18 minutes) or multi-movements. Concerts are of a formal length (approx. 75 minutes) with 5 rehearsals. Difficulty must be balanced within program in order to adequately prepare in a limited rehearsal time. 28 singers. Not seeking orchestral pieces, due to limited budget."

Performances Jackson Berkey's *Native Am Ambience* (eclectic/classical); John Rutter's *Hymn to the Creator of Light* (classical); and Arvo Part's *Te Deum* (multi-choir/chant-based classical).

N SOUTHERN ARIZONA SYMPHONY ORCHESTRA

P.O. Box 43131, Tucson AZ 85733-3131. (520)323-7166. Fax: (480)585-4485. E-mail: info@sasomusic.org. Website: www.sasomusic.org. **Contact:** Warren Cohen, musical director. Symphony orchestra. Estab. 1979. Members are amateurs. Performs 9 concerts/year at least 2 new works every year. Commissions 1 composer or new work/year. Audience is a cross-section of Tucson as well as retirees. Perfoms in the 400-seat Berger Performing Arts Center and the 700-seat Saddlebrooke Arts Center. Pay varies. "We arrange each case differently, usually pay per performance."

How to Contact Submit complete score and tape of piece(s). Include SASE. Responds in 4 months "or longer."

Music Seeking works for a full symphony or chamber orchestra. Open to all styles of music, and will consider works of any length under 30 minutes. "Concertos are harder to program, as are works with chorus, but we will consider them. We have an amateur orchestra, but we have played a good deal of fairly difficult music. We could not, however, do Bruckner or Mahler symphonies. Most contemporary music has been fairly conservative in style, but we are open to things that are different, as long as it's not extremely difficult. Please keep orchestration fairly standard; no bass oboes or theremins."

Performances 1999-2000 season included world premiere of James Barnes' *Autumn Soliloquy*. Other performances include Richard Arnell's *Symphony No. 6*, and Malcolm Arnold's *Clarinet Concerto No. 2*.

Tips "Send a nice clean score. Don't get discouraged as we only have limited performance options. We appreciate knowing if you have orchestral parts available. We are especially excited by the possibility of discovering talented, unknown composers who have not had the opportunities available to those who are well-connected."

N SPACE COAST POPS, INC.

P.O. Box 3344, Cocoa FL 32924 or 2150 Lake Dr., Cocoa FL 32926. (321)632-7445. Fax: (321)632-1611. E-mail: popsorch@aol.com. Website: www.spacecoastpops.com. **Contact:** Robert Coleman, music director and conductor. Pops orchestra and chamber music ensemble. Estab. 1986. Members are professionals. Performs 7 concerts/year, including 1-2 new works. Concerts are performed for "average audience—they like familiar works and pops. Concert halls up to 2,000 seats."

How to Contact Query first. Include SASE. Responds in 6 months.

Music Seeks "pops and serious music for full symphony orchestra, but not an overly large orchestra with unusual instrumentation. We use about 60 musicians because of hall limitations. Works should be medium difficulty—not too easy and not too difficult—and not more than ten minutes long." Does not wish to see avant-garde music.

Performances Dussich's *First March* (march).

Tips "If we would commission a work it would be to feature the space theme in our area."

N STAR-SCAPE SINGERS

P.O. Box 793, Station F, Toronto ON M4Y 2N7 Canada. (905)951-3155 or (800)437-1454. Fax: (905)951-9712. E-mail: info@sun-scape.com. Website: www.sun-scape.com or www.kennethgmills.com. **Contact:** Ellen Mann, assistant to the conductor. A cappella choir (10-12 voices). Estab. 1976. Members are professionals. Performs 15 concerts/year including over 170 original works. Audience is appreciative of extraordinary technical ability of the ensemble and recognize that "this music, this art opens up the soul." Performances take place in concert halls and churches.

• See the listing for Sun-Scape Enterprises Limited in the Record Companies section.

How to Contact Query first. Include SASE.

Performances Kenneth G. Mills/Christopher Dedrick's *The Fire Mass* and arrangement of *The Battle Hymn of the Republic*; *He's Got The Whole World In His Hands* (spiritual); and Rachmaninoff's *Vespers*.

SUSQUEHANNA SYMPHONY ORCHESTRA

P.O. Box 485, Forest Hill MD 21050. (410)838-6465. E-mail: sheldon.bair@ssorchestra.org Website: www.ssorchestra.org. **Contact:** Sheldon Bair, music director. Symphony orchestra. Estab. 1978. Members are amateurs. Performs 6 concerts/year including 1-2 new works. Composers paid depending on the circumstances. "We perform in 1 hall, 600 seats with fine acoustics. Our audience encompasses all ages."

How to Contact Query first. Include SASE. Responds in 3 or more months.

Music "We desire works for large orchestra, any length, in a 'conservative 20th and 21st century' style. Seek fine music for large orchestra. We are a community orchestra, so the music must be within our grasp. Violin I to 7th position by step only; Violin II—stay within 5th position; English horn and harp are OK. Full orchestra pieces preferred."

Performances Derek Bourgeois' *Trombone Concerto*; Gwyneth Walker's *The Magic Oboe*; and Johan de Meij's *Symphony No. 1 "Lord of the Rings"*.

TORONTO MENDELSSOHN CHOIR

60 Simcoe St., Toronto ON M5J 2H5 Canada. (416)598-0422. Fax: (416)598-2992. E-mail: manager@tmchoir.org. Website: www.tmchoir.org. **Contact:** Eileen Keown, executive director. Vocal ensemble. Members are professionals and amateurs. Performs 25 concerts/year including 1-3 new works. "Most performances take place in Roy Thomson Hall. The audience is reasonably sophisticated, musically knowledgeable but with moderately conservative tastes." Pays by commission and ASCAP/SOCAN.

How to Contact Query first or submit complete score and tapes of pieces. Include SASE. Responds in 6 months.

Music All works must suit a large choir (180 voices) and standard orchestral forces or with some other not-too-exotic accompaniment. Length should be restricted to no longer than ½ of a nocturnal concert. The choir sings at a very professional level and can sight-read almost anything. "Works should fit naturally with the repertoire of a large choir which performs the standard choral orchestral repertoire."

Performances Holman's *Jezebel*; Orff's *Catulli Carmina*; and Lambert's *Rio Grande*.

TOURING CONCERT OPERA CO. INC.

228 E. 80th, New York NY 10021. (212)988-2542. Fax: (518)851-6778. E-mail: tcoc@mhonline.net. **Contact:** Anne DeFigols, director. Opera company. Estab. 1971. Members are professionals. Performs 30 concerts/year including 1 new work. Payment varies.

How to Contact Submit complete score and tape of piece(s). Does not return material. Response time varies.

Music "Operas or similar with small casts."

Tips "We are a touring company which travels all over the world. Therefore, operas with casts that are not large and simple but effective sets are the most practical."

TULSA OPERA INC.

1610 S. Boulder, Tulsa OK 74119-4479. (918)582-4035. Fax: (918)592-0380. E-mail: tulsaopera@tulsaopera.com. Website: www.tulsaopera.com. **Contact:** Carol I. Crawford, general director. Opera company. Estab. 1948. Members are professionals. Performs 3 concerts/year including 1 new work. Commissions 1 composer or new work/year. "We have a contract with the Performing Arts Center. It holds approximately 2,300." Pays for outright purchase or by royalty (negotiable).

How to Contact Query first. Include SASE. Responds in 2 months.

Music "At the present time we are looking for new material for student operas. They need to be approximately 45-50 minutes in length, with piano accompaniment. For our main stage productions we use the Philharmonic Orchestra and our Artistic Director auditions our singers. Our student performances are sometimes done by young artists. The student materials need to be adapted for four-five singers. These young artists are usually just beginning their careers therefore they are limited in difficulty of the music. Our main stage artists are adept in doing more difficult roles and roles of the classic operas."

Performances Seymour Barab's *Little Red Riding Hood* (children's 1-act opera).

Tips "Our Artistic Director is very open to ideas and materials. She is interested in new works to present for our opera season."

⬛ VANCOUVER CHAMBER CHOIR

1254 W. Seventh Ave., Vancouver BC V6H 1B6 Canada. E-mail: info@vancouverchamberchoir.com. Website: www.vancouverchamberchoir.com. **Contact:** Jon Washburn, artistic director. Vocal ensemble. Members are professionals. Performs 40 concerts/year including 5-8 new works. Commissions 2-4 composers or new works/year. Pays SOCAN royalty or negotiated fee for commissions.

How to Contact Submit complete score and tape of piece(s). Does not return material. Responds in 6 months if possible.

Music Seeks "choral works of all types for small chorus, with or without accompaniment and/or soloists. Concert music only. Choir made up of 20 singers. Large or unusual instrumental accompaniments are less likely to be appropriate. No pop music."

Performances The VCC has commissioned and premiered over 180 new works by Canadian and international composers, including Alice Parker's *That Sturdy Vine* (cantata for chorus, soloists and orchestra); R. Murray Schafer's *Magic Songs* (SATB a cappella); and Jon Washburn's *A Stephen Foster Medley* (SSAATTBB/piano).

Tips "We are looking for choral music that is performable yet innovative, and which has the potential to become 'standard repertoire.' Although we perform much new music, only a small portion of the many scores which are submitted can be utilized."

⬛ ⬛ VANCOUVER YOUTH SYMPHONY ORCHESTRA SOCIETY

3214 W. 10th Ave., Vancouver BC V6K 2L2 Canada. (604)737-0714. Fax: (604)737-0739. E-mail: vyso@telus.net. Website: www.vyso.web.com. Music Directors: Roger Cole (senior orchestra conductor), Jim Zhang (intermediate orchestra conductor), and Margerita Kress (introductory string orchestra and junior string orchestra conductor). Youth orchestra. "There are four divisions with students ranging from 8-21 years old." Estab. 1930. Members are amateurs. Performs 6-8 concerts/year. Performs in various venues from churches to major concert halls.

How to Contact Query first. Does not return material.

Music "The Senior Orchestra performs the standard symphony repertoire. Programs usually consist of an overture, a major symphony and perhaps a concerto or shorter work. The Christmas concert and tour programs are sometimes lighter works. Extensive repertoire for all divisions. Please contact the VYSO for specific information."

Performances Glen Morley's *Salish Lullaby*; Victor Davies' *The Big Top*; and Michael Conway Baker's *Challenge for the Future*.

⬛ VIRGINIA OPERA

P.O. Box 2580, Norfolk VA 23501. (757)627-9545. Fax:(757)622-0058. E-mail: info@vaopera.com. Website: www.vaopera.org. Director of Education: Jeff Corrirean. Artistic Director: Peter Mark. Opera company. Estab. 1974. Members are professionals. Performs more than 560 concerts/year. Commissions vary on number of composers or new works/year. Concerts are performed for school children throughout Virginia, grades K-5, 6-8 and 9-12 at the Harrison Opera House in Norfolk, and at public/private schools in Virginia. Pays on commission.

How to Contact Query first. Include SASE. Response time varies.

Music "Audience accessible style approximately 45 minutes in length. Limit cast list to three vocal artists of any combination. Accompanied by piano and/or keyboard. Works are performed before school children of all ages. Pieces must be age appropriate both aurally and dramatically. Musical styles are encouraged to be diverse, contemporary as well as traditional. Works are produced and presented with sets, costumes, etc." Limitations: "Three vocal performers (any combination). One keyboardist. Medium to difficult acceptable, but prefer easy to medium. Seeking only pieces which are suitable for presentation as part of an opera education program for Virginia Opera's education and outreach department. Subject matter must meet strict guidelines relative to Learning Objectives, etc. Musical idiom must be representative of current trends in opera, musical theater. Extreme dissonance, row systems not applicable to this environment."

Performances Seymour Barab's *Cinderella*; John David Earnest's *The Legend of Sleepy Hollow*; and Seymour Barab's *The Pied Piper of Hamelin*.

Tips "Theatricality is very important. New works should stimulate interest in musical theater as a legitimate art form for school children with no prior exposure to live theatrical entertainment. Composer should be willing to create a product which will find success within the educational system."

⬛ WHEATON SYMPHONY ORCHESTRA

(formerly City Symphony of Chicago), 344 Spring Ave., Glen Ellyn IL 60137. (630)858-5552. Fax: (630)790-9703. E-mail: dmattob@aol.com. **Contact:** Don Mattison, manager. Symphony orchestra. Estab. 1959. Members are professionals and amateurs. Performs 6 concerts/year including a varying number of new works. "No pay for performance but can probably record your piece."

How to Contact Query first. Include SASE. Responds in 1 month.

Music "This is a *good* amateur orchestra that wants pieces in a traditional idiom. Large scale works for orchestra only. No avant garde, 12-tone or atonal material. Pieces should be 20 minutes or less and must be prepared in 3 rehearsals. Instrumentation needed for woodwinds in 3s, full brass 4-3-3-1, 4 percussion and strings—full-instrumentation only. Selections for full orchestra only. No pay for reading your piece, but we will record it at our expense."

Performances Richard Williams's *Symphony in G Minor* (4 movement symphony); Dennis Johnson's *Must Jesus Bear the Cross Alone, Azon* (traditional); and Michael Diemer's *Skating* (traditional style).

Contests & Awards

Participating in contests is a great way to gain exposure for your music. Prizes vary from contest to contest, from cash to musical merchandise to studio time, and even publishing and recording deals. For musical theater and classical composers, the prize may be a performance of your work. Even if you don't win, valuable contacts can be made through contests. Many times, contests are judged by music publishers and other industry professionals, so your music may find its way into the hands of key industry people who can help further your career.

HOW TO SELECT A CONTEST

It's important to remember when entering any contest to do proper research before signing anything or sending any money. We have confidence in the contests listed in *Songwriter's Market*, but it pays to read the fine print. First, be sure you understand the contest rules and stipulations once you receive the entry forms and guidelines. Then you need to weigh what you will gain against what they're asking you to give up. If a publishing or recording contract is the only prize a contest is offering, you may want to think twice before entering. Basically, the company sponsoring the contest is asking you to pay a fee for them to listen to your song under the guise of a contest, something a legitimate publisher or record company would not do. For those contests offering studio time, musical equipment or cash prizes, you need to decide if the entry fee you're paying is worth the chance to win such prizes.

Be wary of exorbitant entry fees, and if you have any doubts whatsoever as to the legitimacy of a contest, it's best to stay away. Songwriters need to approach a contest, award or grant in the same manner as they would a record or publishing company. Make your submission as professional as possible; follow directions and submit material exactly as stated on the entry form.

Contests in this section encompass all types of music and levels of competition. Read each listing carefully and contact them if the contest interests you. Many contests now have websites that offer additional information and even entry forms you can print. Be sure to read the rules carefully and be sure you understand exactly what a contest is offering before entering.

☑ AFRICAN AMERICAN COMPOSER'S PROGRAM

(formerly Unisys African American Composer's Residency and National Symposium), 3711 Woodward Ave., Detroit MI 48201. (313)576-5111. Fax: (313)576-5109. E-mail: cburke@dso.org. Website: www.detroitsymphony.com. **Contact:** Charles Burke, director of education. Estab. 1989. For composers. Annual award.

Purpose "Program was designed to identify and perform significant orchestral works by contemporary African American Composers."

Requirements Send for application. Samples of work upon request. Pieces should be scored for traditional orchestra.

Awards Applications are judged by Adjudication Committee (conductor and resident conductor).

☑ AGO/ECS PUBLISHING AWARD IN CHORAL COMPOSITION

American Guild of Organists, 475 Riverside Dr., Suite 1260, New York NY 10115. (212)870-2310. Fax: (212)870-2163. E-mail: info@agohq.org. Website: www.agohq.org. **Contact:** Harold Calhoun, competitions coordinator. Biannual award.

Requirements Composers are invited to submit a work for SATB choir and organ in which the organ plays a significant and independent role. Work submitted must be unpublished and approximately 3.5 to 5 minutes in length. There is no age restriction. Deadline: TBA. Send for application.

Awards $2,000 cash prize, publication by ECS Publishing and premier performance at the AGO National Convention.

ALEA III INTERNATIONAL COMPOSITION PRIZE

855 Commonwealth Ave., Boston MA 02215. (617)353-3340. E-mail: kalogeras@earthlink.com. Website: www.aleaiii.com. For composers. Annual award.

Purpose To promote and encourage young composers in the composition of new music.

Requirements Composers born after January 1, 1963 may participate; 1 composition per composer. Works may be for solo voice or instrument or for chamber ensemble up to 15 members lasting between 6 and 15 minutes. Available instruments are: one flute (doubling piccolo or alto), one oboe (doubling English horn), one clarinet (doubling bass clarinet), one bassoon, one horn, one trumpet, one trombone, one tuba, two percussion players, one harp, one keyboard player, one guitar, two violins, one viola, one cello, one bass, tape and one voice. All works must be unpublished and must not have been publicly performed or broadcast, in whole or in part or in any other version before the announcement of the prize in late September or early October of 2003. Works that have won other awards are not eligible. Deadline: March 15. Send for application. Submitted work required with application. "Real name should not appear on score; a nom de plume should be signed instead. Sealed envelope with entry form should be attached to each score."

Awards ALEA III International Composition Prize: $2,500. Awarded once annually. Between 8-10 finalists are chosen and their works are performed in a competition concert by the ALEA III contemporary music ensemble. At the end of the concert, one piece will beselected to receive the prize. One grand prize winner is selected by a panel of judges.

Tips "Emphasis placed on works written in 20th century compositional idioms."

☑ AMERICAN SONGWRITER LYRIC CONTEST

50 Music Sq. West Suite 604, Nashville TN 37203. (615)321-6096. Fax: (615)321-6097. E-mail: info@americansongwriter.com. Website: www.americansongwriter.com. **Contact:** Office Administrator. Estab. 1984. For songwriters and composers. Award for each bimonthly issue of *American Songwriter* magazine, plus grand prize at year-end.

Purpose To promote the art of songwriting.

Requirements Lyrics must be typed and a check for $10 (per entry) must be enclosed. Deadlines: January 21, March 21, May 23, July 19, September 17, November 13. Call for required official form or get it from our website. Lyrics only, no cassettes.

Awards A Martin guitar to each contest winner. Awards airfare to Nashville and a demo session for yearly winner; certificates to all winners; and top 5 winning lyrics reprinted in each magazine. Lyrics judged by 6-7 industry people—songwriters, publishers, journalists.

Tips "You do not have to be a subscriber to enter or win. You may submit as many entries as you like."

☑ ARTISTS' FELLOWSHIPS

New York Foundation for the Arts, 155 Avenue of Americas, 14th Floor, New York NY 10013. E-mail: nyfaafp@nyfa.org. To receive an application, or contact the fellowship's department, call: (212)366-6900, ext. 217. Fax: (212)366-1778. E-mail: nyfaafp@artswire.org. Website: www.nyfa.org. **Contact:** Shawn Miller, program officer.

For songwriters, composers and musical playwrights. Annual award, but each category funded biennially. Estab. 1984.

Purpose "Artists' Fellowships are $7,000 grants awarded by the New York Foundation for the Arts to individual originating artists living in New York State. The Foundation is committed to supporting artists from all over New York State at all stages of their professional careers. Fellows may use the grant according to their own needs; it should not be confused with project support."

Requirements Must be 18 years of age or older; resident of New York State for 2 years prior to application; and cannot be enrolled in any graduate or undergraduate degree program. Applications will be available in July. Deadline: October. Samples of work are required with application. 1 or 2 original compositions on separate audiotapes or audio CDs and at least 2 copies of corresponding scores or fully harmonized lead sheets.

Awards All Artists' Fellowships awards are for $7,000. Payment of $6,300 upon verification of NY State residency, and remainder upon completion of a mutually agreed upon public service activity. Nonrenewable. "Fellowships are awarded on the basis of the quality of work submitted. Applications are reviewed by a panel of 5 composers representing the aesthetic, ethnic, sexual and geographic diversity within New York State. The panelists change each year and review all allowable material submitted."

Tips "Please note that musical playwrights may submit only if they write the music for their plays—librettists must submit in our playwriting category."

BAKER'S PLAYS HIGH SCHOOL PLAYWRITING CONTEST

Baker's Plays, P.O. Box 699222, Quincy MA 02269-9222. (617)745-0805. Fax: (617)745-9891. E-mail: info@bakersplay.com. Website: www.bakersplays.com. **Contact:** John Welch, managing director & chief editor. Estab. 1990. For high school students. Annual award.

Requirements Plays should be about the "high school experience," but may also be about any subject and of any length, so long as the play can be reasonably produced on the high school stage. Plays must be accompanied by the signature of a sponsoring high school drama or English teacher, and it is recommended that the play receive a production or a public reading prior to the submission. Multiple submissions and co-authored scripts are welcome. Teachers may not submit a student's work. The manuscript must be firmly bound, typed and come with a SASE. Include enough postage to cover the return of the manuscript. Scripts that do not come with an SASE will not be returned. Do not send originals; copies only. Deadline: January 30. Send for guidelines.

Awards 1st Place: $500 and the play will be published by Baker's Plays; 2nd Place: $250 and an Honorable Mention; 3rd Place: $100 and an Honorable Mention.

THE BLANK THEATRE COMPANY YOUNG PLAYWRIGHTS FESTIVAL

1301 Lucile Ave., Los Angeles CA 90026. (323)662-7734. Fax: (323)661-3903. E-mail: info@theblank.com. Website: www.youngplaywrights.com. Estab. 1993. For both musical and non-musical playwrights. Annual award.

Purpose "To give young playwrights an opportunity to learn more about playwriting and to give them a chance to have their work mentored, developed, and presented by professional artists."

Requirements Playwrights must be 19 years old or younger on March 15, 2005. Send legible, original plays of any length and on any subject (co-written plays are acceptable provided all co-writers meet eligibility requirements). Submissions must be postmarked by March 15, 2005 and must include a cover sheet with the playwright's name, date of birth, school (if any), home address, home phone number, e-mail address and production history. Pages must be numbered and submitted unbound (unstapled). For musicals, a tape or CD of a selection from the score should be submitted with the script. Manuscripts will not be returned. Please do not send originals. Semi-finalists and winners will be contacted in May.

Awards Winning playwrights receive a workshop presentation of their work.

BUSH ARTIST FELLOWS PROGRAM

E-900 First National Bank Bldg., 332 Minnesota St., St. Paul MN 55101. (651)227-5222. E-mail: kpolley@bushfound.org. Website: www.bushfoundation.org. **Contact:** Kathi Polley, program assistant. Estab. 1976. For songwriters, composers and musical playwrights. Applications in music composition are accepted in even-numbered years.

Purpose "To provide artists with significant financial support that enables them to further their work and their contribution to their communities."

Requirements Applicant must be a Minnesota, North Dakota, South Dakota or western Wisconsin resident for 12 of preceeding 36 months, 25 years or older, not a student. Deadline: late October. Send for application. Audio work samples required with application. "Music composition applications will not be taken again until the fall of 2004. Applications will be taken in the fall of 2004 in the following areas: music composition, scriptworks (screenwriting and playwriting), literature (creative non-fiction, fiction, poetry) and film/video.

Awards Fellowships: $44,000 stipend for a period of 12-24 months. "Five years after completion of preceeding fellowship, one may apply again." Applications are judged by peer review panels.

THE CLW MUSIC AWARD/LIAISON

P.O. Box 15712, Beverly Hills CA 90209. (310)775-1238. E-mail: hnigelson@yahoo.co.uk or bjackson@india.com. Website: www.cleoaward.20fr.com or www.cmc.nu3.net. **Contact:** Holly Nigelson, Brenda Jackson or Jeremiah Lyles, owners/partners (for information and an application). Estab. 2002. For Songwriters and Composers.

Purpose "To aid or further the careers of independent musicians, eligible enrolled music students and certain Native/African/Asian/American Organizations musically.

Requirements "Each song entered must be an original work. The songs may have multiple writers, but only one name need be on the application. The performer or performers must be the writers of the material submitted and must be the same individuals who are attend the Awards. Division of the prizes to any co-writers shall be the responsibility of the person named on the entry form as the leader of the Band or Group. No song previously recorded and released through national or any other type of distribution in any country will be eligible to win. Each entry must consist of: 1) A CD or audiocassette containing 1 song, which shall be 5 minutes in length or less. The side with the entry shall be cued to the beginning of the song and it shall be named or marked so. Failure to maintain this regulation shall result in disqualification; 2) The entry form must be signed in ink, in any color, no roller balls, felt tips, Magic Markers, or anything similar shall be accepted. Any non-legible entry forms shall be disqualified. All signatures must be the originals, and shall be verified; 3) If there are any lyrics included with a song, a lyric sheet must be typed or laser printed, no hand written or ink jet printed lyric sheets shall be accepted. Lyrics must have an English translation lyric sheet also, if applicable. Instrumental music shall not require either; 4) The entry fee of $25, payable by money order, Personal or Business check or Credit Card. Entry fees are not refundable. No solo entries or a-cappella entries shall be accepted. *Employees Family, friends, Affiliates and Associates of this contest are not eligible to win the Contest. Do not send Cash and if you use a major Credit Card, an additional $1.50 will be charged to your account! A Money Order is what we suggest.* There are 5 preliminary rounds of Judging and the Contest Final rounds. 1 Finalist from each category will be selected as a Finalist and 5 Finalists with the highest point totals from the rest of the field will be chosen as Finalists also. After Judging, the 15 Finalists shall be notified by mail and will be sent the proper affidavits, which must be returned not more than 40 Business Days after the date on the Congratulatory letter each shall receive. Any fraudulent or inaccurate information shall result in disqualification and an alternate winner shall be selected. Any printed or recorded submissions shall not be returned. Each contestant must be age 15 or older. Any Winners under the age of 21 shall require a parent or guardian present for the administering of prizes. In the instances where any entrants are younger than age 21, the parent or guardian must also sign the entry form. Winners shall be determined 3 months after the close of submissions for the current contest. The odds for winning the overall CLW Music Award are, at maximum, 12,000 to 1 based upon a person making 1 entry, of the 12,000 required to start the Judging round. The format of this contest does not allow these odds to be greater. If a person enters more than 1 recording, the odds for winning increase accordingly, if the entries are in the same contest. A person can enter more than once in any category but a separate fee is required for each entry. If a contestant does not make the finals they may enter a future contest if they choose to. If a contestant finishes in Third Place or lower and finishes no higher by replacing any finalists that may be disqualified by some means, that contestant may enter a future contest if they choose to. The CLW Music Award and Aubusson Music Publishing are not responsible for any late, lost, damaged or mishandled entries. The contest is open to all Amateur persons in the world who have not earned more than $5,000 from music royalties in the last 2 years. This rule shall apply to an individual or all members of a group or band collectively. If it is found that an entrant violates these requirements, the entrant shall be prosecuted for fraud, and in addition, any amount of winnings shall be returned and the contestant will be disqualified, with another winner being selected in place of the fraudulent one. 15 finalists will perform their entry song, or songs at the finals and be Judged. Those entrants who finish 3rd Place or lower and no higher, are eligible to enter again in the next contest. There are a total of 15 rounds of judging and the results remain unknown to everyone until the presentations. The Awards ceremony will be taped for Broadcast at a later date.

Awards Prizes: 1 CLW Music Award Winner, who will receive $30,000 cash and a Publishing Award; 1 Grand Prize Winner, who will receive $15,000 in cash and a Publishing Award; 1 First Prize Winner, who will receive $7,500 cash and a Publishing Award; 1 Second Prize Winner, who will receive $5,000 cash and a Publishing Award; 1 Third Prize Winner, who will receive $2,500 in cash only; 1 Fourth Prize Winner, who will receive $1,500 cash; 1 Honorary Native American Music Award; 1 Honorary Asian American Music Award; and 1 Honorary African-American Music Award. There will also be 5 Runners Up with the Runners Up each receiving $1,000 cash. No substitutions for any prizes can, or will be, made.

Tips "DO NOT PHOTOCOPY YOUR ENTRY FORM FOR SOMEONE ELSE, they must have their own contestant serial number on their application. Photocopies are only for you in other categories. Make sure you read the rules and prepare your recording properly. Judging has been configured so that all types of music DO have the same chance of winning this contest. Make sure that you can perform your song live and be prepared to come to do so."

COLUMBIA ENTERTAINMENT COMPANY'S JACKIE WHITE MEMORIAL PLAYWRITING CONTEST

309 Parkade Blvd., Columbia MO 65202. (573)874-5628. **Contact:** Betsy Phillips, director, CEC contest. For musical playwrights. Annual award.

Purpose "We are looking for top-notch scripts suitable for family audiences with 7 or more fully-developed roles."

Requirements "May be adaptations or plays with original story lines and cannot have been previously published. Please write or call for complete rules." Send SASE for application; then send scripts to address above. Full-length play, neatly typed. No name on title page, but name, address and name of play on a 3×5 index card and lead sheets, as well as tape of musical numbers. $10 entry fee.

Awards $500 1st Prize. Play may or may not be produced at discretion of CEC. "The judging committee is taken from members of Columbia Entertainment Company's Executive and Advisory boards, and from theater school parents. Readings by up to eight members, with at least three readings of all entries, and winning entries being read by entire committee. All plays will receive a written evaluation."

Tips "We especially like plays that deal with current day problems and concerns. However, if the play is good enough, any suitable subject matter is fine."

COMPOSERS GUILD ANNUAL COMPOSITION CONTEST

P.O. Box 586, Farmington UT 84025-0586. (801)451-2275. **Contact:** Ruth B. Gatrell, president. Estab. 1963. For songwriters, musical playwrights and composers. Annual award.

• Also see the Composers Guild listing in the Organizations section of this book.

Purpose "To stimulate musical composition and help composers through judge's comments on each composition submitted. Composers can broaden their creative skills by entering different categories. Categories: Arrangements (original in public domain or with composer's permission); music for children; choral; instrumental; jazz/New Age; keyboard; orchestra/band; popular (all types); vocal solo; young composer (18 or under on August 31)."

Requirements Score and/or cassette or CD. Entry fee: $20 for work 7 minutes or more in length (may include multimovements on compositions), $15 for work less than 7 minutes. Dues are $25/year. Member entry fees: $10 for work 7 minutes or more, $5 less than 7 minutes. Deadline: August 31. Send or call for application.

Awards Award of Excellence $500; 1st Prize in each category except Award of Excellence category $100; 2nd Prize in each category $50; 3rd Prize in each category $25; Honorable Mention certificates. Judge has a doctorate in music, plus compositions published and performed (usually has vast teaching experience). Same judge never used in successive years.

Tips "Submit good clear copies of score. Have cassette cued up. Only one composition per cassette/CD (each entry requires separate cassette/CD). No composer names to appear on score or cassette/CD. Enter as many categories and compositions as you wish. Separate entry fee for each. One check can cover all entries and dues."

☑ CRS NATIONAL COMPOSERS COMPETITION

724 Winchester Rd., Broomall PA 19008. (610)544-5920. Fax: (215)544-5921. E-mail: crsnews@verizon.net. Website: http://mysite.verizon.net/crsnews. **Contact:** Caroline Hunt, administrative assistant. Senior Representative: Jack Shusterman. Estab. 1981. For songwriters, composers and performing artists. College faculty. Annual award.

Requirements For composers, songwriters, performing artists and ensembles. The work submitted must be non-published (prior to acceptance) and not commercially recorded on any label. The work submitted must not exceed nine performers. Each composer may submit one work for each application submitted. (Taped performances are additionally encouraged.) Composition must not exceed twenty-five minutes in length. CRS reserves the right not to accept a First Prize Winner. Write with SASE for application or visit website. Add $3.50 for postage and handling. Deadline: February 28. Send a detailed résumé with application form. Samples of work required with application. Send score and parts on cassette or DAT. Application fee: $50.

Awards 1st Prize: Commercial recording grant. Applications are judged by panel of judges determined each year.

CUNNINGHAM COMMISSION FOR YOUTH THEATRE

(formerly Cunningham Prize for Playwriting), The Theatre School, DePaul University, 2135 N. Kenmore Ave., Chicago IL 60614. (773)325-7938. Fax: (773)325-7920. E-mail: lgoetsch@depaul.edu. Website: theatreschool.de paul.edu. **Contact:** Lara Goetsch, director of marketing/public relations. Estab. 1990. For playwrights. Annual award.

Purpose "The purpose of the Commission is to encourage the writing of dramatic works for young audiences that affirm the centrality of religion, broadly defined, and the human quest for meaning, truth, and community. The Theatre School intends to produce the plays created through this commission in its award-winning Chicago Playworks for Families and Young Audiences series at the historic Merle Reskin Theatre. Each year Chicago Playworks productions are seen by 35,000 students and families from throughout the Chicago area."

Requirements "Candidates for the commission must be writers whose residence is in the Chicago area, defined as within 100 miles of the Loop. Playwrights who have won the award within the last five years are not eligible. Deadline: annually by October 1. Candidates should submit a résumé, a 20 page sample of their work, and a brief statement about their interest in the commission. The submission should not include a proposal for a project the playwright would complete if awarded the commission. The writing sample may be from a play of any genre for any audience."

Awards $5,000. "Winners will be notified by May 1. The Selection Committee is chaired by the Dean of The Theatre School and is composed of members of the Cunningham Commission advisory committee and faculty of The Theatre School."

KENNETH DAVENPORT NATIONAL COMPETITION FOR ORCHESTRAL WORKS

School of Fine & Performing Arts, SUNY New Paltz, 75 S. Manheim Blvd., Suite 9, New Paltz NY 12561-2443. (845)257-3860. Fax: (845)257-3859. E-mail: fpa@newpaltz.edu. Website: www.newpaltz.edu. Estab. 1988. For composers. Biannual award.

Requirements Deadline: July. Send for application. Works requiring chorus or solo voice are not eligible.

Awards Panel of judges reviews all scores submitted. $5,000 award and performance of winning composition by the Hudson Valley Philharmonic and a weeklong residency in the Department of Music, SUNY New Paltz.

Tips "Apply for prize by sending your score for orchestral works. $45 entry fee."

DELTA OMICRON INTERNATIONAL COMPOSITION COMPETITION

12297 W. Tennessee Place, Lakewood CO 80228. (303)989-2871. Composition Competition Chairman: Judith L. Eidson. For composers. Triennial award.

Purpose "To encourage composers worldwide to continually add to our wonderful heritage of musical creativity instrumentally and/or vocally."

Requirements People from college age on (or someone younger who is enrolled in college). Work must be unpublished and unperformed in public. The composition should be for Solo Flute or Flute Quartet with a time length from a minimum of seven minutes to a maximum of fifteen minutes. Manuscripts should be legibly written in ink or processed, signed with *nom de plume*, and free from any marks that would identify the composer to the judges. Entry fee: $25. Deadline: all entries postmarked no later than March 20, 2005. Send for application. Samples of work are required with application.

Awards 1st Place: $600 and world premiere at Delta Omicron Triennal Conference. Judged by 2-3 judges (performers and/or composers).

EUROPEAN INTERNATIONAL COMPETITION FOR COMPOSERS/IBLA FOUNDATION

226 E. 2nd St., Suite 5D, New York NY 10009. (212)387-0111. Fax: (212)214-0701. E-mail: iblanyc@aol.com. Website: www.ibla.org. **Contact:** Mr. Gregory Naber, assistant director. Chairman: Dr. S. Moltisanti. Estab. 1995. For songwriters and composers. Annual award.

Purpose "To promote the winners' career through exposure, publicity, recordings with Athena Records and nationwide distribution with the Empire Group."

Requirements Deadline: March 15. Send for application. Samples of work are required with application.

Awards Winners are presented in concerts in Europe-Japan, USA.

FULBRIGHT SCHOLAR PROGRAM, COUNCIL FOR INTERNATIONAL EXCHANGE OF SCHOLARS

3007 Tilden St. NW, Suite 5L, Washington DC 20008-3009. (202)686-7877. E-mail: scholars@cies.iie.org. Website: www.cies.org. Estab. 1946. For composers and academics. Annual award.

Purpose "Awards for university lecturing and advanced research abroad are offered annually in virtually all academic disciplines including musical composition."

Requirements "U.S. citizenship at time of application; M.F.A., Ph.D. or equivalent professional qualifications; for lecturing awards, university teaching experience (some awards are for professionals non-academic)." Applications become available in March each year, for grants to be taken up 1½ years later. Application deadlines: August 1, all world areas. Write or call for application. Samples of work are required with application.

Awards "Benefits vary by country, but generally include round-trip travel for the grantee and for most full academic-year awards, one dependent; stipend in U.S. dollars and/or local currency; in many countries, tuition allowance for school age children; and book and baggage allowance. Grant duration ranges from 2 months-1 academic year.''

HARVEY GAUL COMPOSITION CONTEST

The Pittsburgh New Music Ensemble, Inc., P.O. Box 99476, Pittsburgh PA 15233. (412)889-7231. E-mail: pnme@pnme.org. Website: www.pnme.org. **Contact:** Jeffrey Nyfah, DMA, managing director. For composers. Biennial.

Purpose Objective is to encourage composition of new music. Winning piece to be premiered by the PNME.

Requirements ''Must be citizen of the US. New works scored for 6 to 16 instruments drawn from the following: flute, oboe, 2 clarinets, bassoon, horn, trumpet, trombone, tuba, 2 violins, cello, bass, 2 percussion, piano, harp, electronic tape.'' Deadline: September 30, 2004. Send SASE for application or download from www.pnme.org. Samples of work are required with application.Entry fee: $20.

Awards Harvey Gaul Composition Contest: $6,000.

GREAT AMERICAN SONG CONTEST

PMB 135, 6327-C SW Capitol Hill Hwy., Portland OR 97239-1937. E-mail: info@GreatAmericanSong.com. Website: www.GreatAmericanSong.com. **Contact:** Carla Starrett, event coordinator. Estab. 1998. For songwriters, composers and lyricists. Annual award.

• Also see the listing for Songwriters Resource Network in the Organizations section of this book.

Purpose To help songwriters get their songs heard by music-industry professionals; to generate educational and networking opportunities for participating songwriters; to help songwriters open doors in the music business.

Requirements Entry fee: $20. ''Annual deadline. Check our website for details or send SASE along with your mailed request for information.''

Awards Winners receive a mix of cash awards and prizes. The focus of the contest is on networking and educational opportunities. (All participants receive detailed evaluations of their songs by industry professionals.) Songs are judged by knowledgeable music-industry professionals, including prominent hit songwriters, producers and publishers.

Tips ''Focus should be on the song. The quality of the demo isn't important. Judges will be looking for good songwriting talent. They will base their evaluations on the song—not the quality of the recording or the voice performance.''

HENRICO THEATRE COMPANY ONE-ACT PLAYWRITING COMPETITION

P.O. Box 27032, Richmond VA 23273. (804)501-5115. (804)501-5115 or (804)501-5138. Fax: (804)501-5284. E-mail: per22@co.henrico.va.us. **Contact:** Amy A. Perdue, cultural arts coordinator. Cultural Arts Assistant: Cindy Warren. For musical playwrights, songwriters, composers and performing artists. Annual award.

Purpose Original one-act musicals for a community theater organization.

Requirements ''Only one-act plays or musicals will be considered. The manuscript should be a one-act original (not an adaptation), unpublished, and unproduced, free of royalty and copyright restrictions. Scripts with smaller casts and simpler sets may be given preference. Controversial themes and excessive language should be avoided. Standard play script form should be used. All plays will be judged anonymously; therefore, there should be two title pages; the first must contain the play's title and the author's complete address and telephone number. The second title page must contain only the play's title. The playwright must submit two excellent quality copies. Receipt of all scripts will be acknowledged by mail. Scripts will be returned if SASE is included. No scripts will be returned until after the winner is announced. The HTC does not assume responsibility for loss, damage or return of scripts. All reasonable care will be taken.'' Deadline: July 1st. Send for application first.

Awards 1st Prize $300; 2nd Prize $200; 3rd Prize $200.

☑ HOLTKAMP-AGO AWARD IN ORGAN COMPOSITION

American Guild of Organists, 475 Riverside Dr., Suite 1260, New York NY 10115. (212)870-2310. Fax: (212)870-2163. E-mail: info@agohq.org. Website: www.agohq.org. **Contact:** Harold Calhoun, competitions coordinator. For composers and performing artists. Biennial award.

Requirements Organ solo, no longer than 8 minutes in duration. Specifics vary from year to year. Deadline: TBA. Send for application.

Award $2,000 provided by the Holtkamp Organ Company; publication by Hinshaw Music Inc.; performance at the biennial National Convention of the American Guild of Organists.

Ⓝ INDIANA OPERA THEATRE/MACALLISTER AWARDS FOR OPERA SINGERS

P.O. Box 1941, Indianapolis IN 46206. (317)202-0634. E-mail: opera@iquest.net. Website: www.indianaoperatheatre.com/macallister.html. Artister/General Director: E. Bookwalter. Estab. 1980. For college and professional opera singers.

Requirements For professional and amateurs. Entry fee: $25 professional, free for college students. Send for application or visit website. Auditions are held throughout the year; check the website.
Awards "The Final Awards Program dates are August 23-25."

☑ JEROME COMPOSERS COMMISSIONING PROGRAM

(formerly Composers Commissioning Program), ACF, 332 Minnesota St., #E-145, St. Paul MN 55101. (651)251-2824. Fax: (651)291-7978. E-mail: wcollins@composersforum.org. Website: www.composersforum.org. **Contact:** Wendy Collins, program director. Estab. 1979. For songwriters, musical playwrights, composers and performers. Annual award.
Purpose "CCP provides grants to support the commissioning of new works by emerging composers."
Requirements Not for students. Deadline: end of July. Application available on website. Samples of work are required with application. Send score/tape.
Awards 18-22 commissioning grants of $1,500-8,000; each grant good for 5 years. Applications are judged by peer review panel (anonymous).
Tips "Composers pair up with performers: one party must be based in Minnesota or New York City."

KATE NEAL KINLEY MEMORIAL FELLOWSHIP

University of Illinois, College of Fine and Applied Arts, 608 E. Lorado Taft Dr. #100, Champaign IL 61820. (217)333-1661. Website: www.faa.uiuc.edu. **Contact:** Dr. Kathleen F. Conlin, chair. Estab. 1931. For students of architecture, art or music. Annual award.
Purpose The advancement of study in the fine arts.
Requirements "The Fellowship will be awarded upon the basis of unusual promise in the fine arts. Open to college graduates whose principal or major studies have been in the fields of architecture, art or music." Write or call for fall deadline. Send for application or call. Samples of work are required with application.
Awards "Two or three major Fellowships which yield the sum of $7,500 each which is to be used by the recipients toward defraying the expenses of advanced study of the fine arts in America or abroad." Good for 1 year. Grant is nonrenewable.

☑ L.A. DESIGNERS' THEATRE MUSIC AWARDS

P.O. Box 1883, Studio City CA 91614-0883. (323)650-9600. (323)654-2700 (T.D.D.). Fax: (323)654-3210. E-mail: ladesigners@juno.com. Artistic Director: Richard Niederberg. For songwriters, composers, performing artists, musical playwrights and rights holders of music.
Purpose To produce new musicals, operettas, opera-boufes and plays with music, as well as new dance pieces with new music scores.
Requirements Submit nonreturnable cassette, tape, CD or any other medium by first or 4th class mail. "*We prefer proposals to scripts.*" Acceptance: continuous. Submit nonreturnable materials with cover letter. No application form or fee is necessary.
Awards Music is commissioned for a particular project. Amounts are negotiable. Applications judged by our artistic staff.
Tips "Make the material 'classic, yet commercial' and easy to record/re-record/edit. Make sure rights are totally free of all 'strings,' 'understandings,' 'promises,' etc. ASCAP/BMI/SESAC registration is OK, as long as 'grand' or 'performing rights' are available."

THE JOHN LENNON SONGWRITING CONTEST

459 Columbus Ave., Box 120, New York NY 10024. Fax: (212)579-4320. E-mail: info@jlsc.com. Website: www.jlsc.com. **Contact:** Marc Hassan, associate director. Estab. 1996. For songwriters. Annual award.
Purpose "The purpose of the John Lennon Songwriting Contest is to promote the art of songwriting by assisting in the discovery of new talent as well as providing more established songwriters with an opportunity to advance their careers."
Requirements Each entry must consist of the following: completed and signed application; audio cassette or CD containing one song only, 5 minutes or less in length; lyric sheet typed or printed legibly (English translation is required when applicable); $30 entry fee. Deadline: September 28, 2004. Applications can be found in various music-oriented magazines and on our website. Prospective entrants can send for an application or contact the contest via e-mail at info@jlsc.com.
Awards Entries are accepted in the following 13 categories: rock, country, jazz, pop, world, gospel/inspirational, R&B, hip-hop, Latin, electronic, folk and children's music and new to the 2004 contest a lyrics only category. 2002 prize packages: 12 Grand Prize winners (one in each category) receive $2,000 in cash, $5,000 in Yamaha project studio equipment, and a $5,000 advance from EMI Music Publishing. One Grand Prize winner receives an additional $20,000 for the "Song of the Year" courtesy of Maxell. Finalists receive $1,000. 72 additional winners receive $100 from Musician's Friend. Winners are chosen by an Executive Committee comprised of

noted songwriters, producers and recording artists. Songs will be judged based upon melody, composition and lyrics (when applicable). The quality of performance and production will not be considered during the adjudication process.

☑ **MAXIM MAZUMDAR NEW PLAY COMPETITION**
One Curtain Up Alley, Buffalo NY 14202-1911. (716)852-2600. Fax: (716)852-2266. E-mail: newplays@alleyway. com. Website: www.alleyway.com. **Contact:** Literary Manager. For musical playwrights. Annual award.
Purpose Alleyway Theatre is dedicated to the development and production of new works. Winners of the competition will receive production and royalties.
Requirements Unproduced full-length work not less than 90 minutes long with cast limit of 10 and unit or simple set, or unproduced one-act work less than 15 minutes long with cast limit of 6 and simple set; prefers work with unconventional setting that explores the boundaries of theatricality; limit of 1 submission in each category; guidelines available, no entry form. $5 playwright entry fee. Script, résumé, SASE optional. Cassette mandatory. Deadline: July 1.
Awards Production for full-length play or musical with royalty and travel and housing determined on a yearly basis; and production for one-act play or musical.
Tips "Entries may be of any style, but preference will be given to those scripts which take place in unconventional settings and explore the boundaries of theatricality. No more than ten performers is a definite, unchangeable requirement."

MID-ATLANTIC SONG CONTEST

Songwriters' Association of Washington, PMB 106-137, 4200 Wisconsin Ave., NW, Washington DC 20016. (301)654-8434. E-mail: masc@saw.org. Website: www.saw.org. For songwriters and composers. Estab. 1982. Annual award.
  ● Also see the listing for Songwriters Association of Washington in the Organizations section, as well as the Insider Report in this section on the Mid-Atlantic Contest 2002 Awards Ceremony.
Purpose This is one of the longest-running contests in the nation; SAW has organized twenty contests since 1982. The competition is designed to afford rising songwriters in a wide variety of genres the opportunity to receive awards and exposure in an environment of peer competition.
Requirements Amateur status is important. Applicants should request a brochure/application using the contact information above. Rules and procedures are clearly explained in that brochure. Cassette or CD and 3 copies of the lyrics are to be submitted with an application form and fee for each entry. Reduced entry fees are offered to members of Songwriters' Association of Washington; membership can be arranged simultaneously with entering. Applications are mailed out and posted on their website in late spring; the submission deadline is usually sometime in August; awards are typically announced late in the fall.
Awards The two best songs in each of ten categories win prize packages donated by the contest's corporate sponsors: Writer's Digest Books, BMI, Oasis CD and Cassette Duplication, Omega Recording Studios, TAXI, Mary Cliff, Stage Right Studios at Jammia' Java and the Hard Rock Cafe. Winning songwriters are invited to perform in Washington, DC at the Awards Ceremony Gala, and the twenty winning songs are included on a compilation CD. The best song in each category is eligible for three grand cash prizes. Certificates are awarded to other entries meriting honorable mention.
Tips "Enter the song in the most appropriate category. Make the sound recording the best it can be (even though judges are asked to focus on melody and lyric and not on production.) Avoid clichés, extended introductions, and long instrumental solos."

THELONIOUS MONK INTERNATIONAL JAZZ COMPOSERS COMPETITION

sponsored by BMI, 5225 Wisconsin Ave. NW, #605, Washington DC 20015. (202)364-7272. Fax: (202)364-0176. E-mail: lebrown@tmonkinst.org. Website: www.monkinstitute.org. **Contact:** Leonard Brown, program director. Estab. 1993. For songwriters and composers. Annual award.
Purpose The award is given to an aspiring jazz composer who best demonstrates originality, creativity and excellence in jazz composition.
Requirements Deadline: August 1. Send for application. Samples of work are required with application. Send cassette. The composition features a different instrument each year.
Awards $10,000. Applications are judged by panel of jazz musicians. "The Institute will provide piano, bass, guitar, drum set, tenor saxophone, and trumpet for the final performance. The winner will be responsible for the costs of any different instrumentation included in the composition."

☑ NACUSA YOUNG COMPOSERS' COMPETITION

Box 49256 Barrington Station, Los Angeles CA 90049. (310)838-4465. E-mail: nacusa@music-usa.org. Website: www.music-usa.org/nacusa. **Contact:** Deon Price, president, NACUSA. Estab. 1978. For composers. Annual award.

• Also see the National Association of Composers/USA (NACUSA) listing in the Organization section.
Purpose To encourage the composition of new American concert hall music.
Requirements Entry fee: $20 (membership fee). Deadline: October 30. Send for application. Samples are not required.
Awards 1st Prize: $200; 2nd Prize: $50; and possible Los Angeles performances. Applications are judged by a committee of experienced NACUSA composer members.

SAMMY NESTICO AWARD/USAF BAND AIRMEN OF NOTE
201 McChord St., Bolling AFB, Washington DC 20032-0202. (202)767-1756. Fax: (202)767-0686. E-mail: alan.ba ylock@bolling.af.mil. **Contact:** Alan Baylock, master sergeant. Estab. 1995. For composers. Annual award.
Purpose To carry on the tradition of excellence of Sammy Nestico's writing through jazz composition. The winner will have their composition performed by the USAF Airmen of Note, have it professionally recorded and receive a $1,000 follow up commission for a second work.
Requirements Unpublished work for jazz ensemble instrumentation (5,4,4,4) style, form and length are unrestricted. Deadline: October 1, 2002. Send for application. Samples of work are required with full score and set of parts (or cassette recording).
Awards Performance by the USAF Band Airmen of Note; expense paid travel to Washington, DC for the performance; professionally produced recording of the winning composition; and $1,000 follow up commission for second work. Applications are judged by panel of musicians.

☑ NEW FOLK CONCERTS FOR EMERGING SONGWRITERS
P.O. Box 291466, Kerrville TX 78029. (830)257-3600. Fax: (830)257-8680. E-mail: info@kerrville-music.com. Website: www.kerrvillefolkfestival.com. **Contact:** Dalis Allen, producer. For songwriters. Annual award.
• Also see the listing for Kerrville Folk Festival in the Workshops section of this book.
Purpose "To provide an opportunity for unknown songwriters to be heard and rewarded for excellence."
Requirements Songwriter enters 2 original previously unrecorded songs on same side of rewound cassette tape with entry fee; no more than one tape may be entered; 6-8 minutes total for 2 songs. No written application necessary; no lyric sheets or press material needed. Submissions accepted between January 1-April 1 or first 600 entries received prior to that date. Call or e-mail to request rules. Entry fee: $20.
Awards New Folk Award Winner. 32 semi-finalists invited to sing the 2 songs entered during The Kerrville Folk Festival on May 24-25, 2003. 6 writers are chosen as award winners. Each of the 6 receives a cash award of $450 or more and performs at a winner's concert during the Kerrville Folk Festival on June 1, 2003. Initial round of entries judged by the Festival Producer. 32 finalists judged by panel of 3 performer/songwriters.
Tips "Make certain cassette is rewound and ready to play. Do not allow instrumental accompaniment to drown out lyric content. Don't enter without complete copy of the rules. Former winners and finalists include Lyle Lovett, Nanci Griffith, Hal Ketchum, John Gorka, David Wilcox, Lucinda Williams and Robert Earl Keen, Tish Hinojosa, Carrie Newcomer, Jimmy Lafave, etc."

☑ NSAI/CMT ANNUAL SONG CONTEST
1701 West End Ave, 3rd Floor, Nashville TN 37203. (615)256-3354. Fax: (615)256-0034. E-mail: deanie@nashvil lesongwriters.com. Website: www.nashvillesongwriters.com. **Contact:** Deanie Williams, director. Annual award for songwriters.
Purpose "A chance for aspiring songwriters to be heard by music industry decision makers. Winners are flown to Nashville for a recording session and an appointment with Music Row executives."
Requirements Entry fee: $35 for one entry; $50 for 2. In order to be eligible contestants must not be receiving income from any work submitted—original material only. Submissions must include both lyrics and melody. Deadline is different each year; check website or send for application. Samples are required with application in the format of cassette or CD.
Awards Varies from year to year; check website.

PLAYHOUSE ON THE SQUARE NEW PLAY COMPETITION
51 S. Cooper, Memphis TN 38104. (901)725-0776. **Contact:** Jackie Nichols, executive director. For musical playwrights. Annual award. Estab. 1983.
Requirements Send script, tape and SASE. "Playwrights from the South will be given preference." Open to full-length, unproduced plays. Musicals must be fully arranged for piano when received. Deadline: April 1.
Awards Grants may be renewed. Applications judged by 3 readers.

☑ PORTLAND SONGWRITERS ASSOCIATION ANNUAL SONGWRITING COMPETITION
P.O. Box 42389, Portland OR 97242. (503)914-1000. E-mail: info@pdxsongwriters.org. Website: www.pdxsong writers.org. **Contact:** JC Tubbs, President. Vice President: Bill Wood. Estab. 1991. For songwriters and composers. Annual award.

Purpose To provide opportunities for songwriters to improve their skills in the art and craft of songwriting, to connect our performing songwriters with the public through PSA sponsored venues and to create a presence and an avenue of approach for members' songs to be heard by industry professionals.

Requirements For information, send SASE. All amateur songwriters may enter. Deadline: September 30 postmark. Entry fee: $15 members; $20 nonmembers.

Awards Multiple awards totaling $1,000 in prizes. All songs will be reviewed by at least three qualified judges, including industry pros. Finalists may have their songs reviewed by celebrity judges.

PULITZER PRIZE IN MUSIC

709 Journalism Building, Columbia University, New York NY 10027. (212)854-3841. Fax: (212)854-3342. E-mail: pulitzer@pulitzer.org. Website: www.pulitzer.org. **Contact:** Music Secretary. For composers and musical playwrights. Annual award.

Requirements "For distinguished musical composition of significant dimension by an American that has had its American premiere between January 16 and January 15 of the one-year period in which it is submitted for consideration." Deadline: March 1. Samples of work are required with application, biography and photograph of composer, date and place of performance, score or manuscript and recording of the work, entry form and $50 entry fee.

Awards "One award: $7,500. Applications are judged first by a nominating jury, then by the Pulitzer Prize Board."

☑ ROCKY MOUNTAIN FOLKS FESTIVAL SONGWRITER SHOWCASE

P.O. Box 769, Lyons CO 80540. (800)624-2422 or (303)823-0848. Fax: (303)823-0849. E-mail: emily@bluegrass.com. Website: www.bluegrass.com. **Contact:** Steve Szymanski, director. Estab. 1993. For songwriters, composers and performers. Annual award.

Purpose Award based on having the best song and performance.

Requirements Deadline: June 27. Finalists notified by July 15. Rules available on website. Samples of work are required with application. Send CD or cassette with $10 entry fee.

Awards 1st Place is a custom Hayes Guitar, Festival Main Stage and $100; 2nd: $500 and Taylor Big Baby guitar; 3rd: $400 and Taylor Big Baby guitar; 4th: $300 and Taylor Big Baby guitar; 5th: $200 and Taylor Big Baby guitar; 6th-10th: $100. Applications judged by panel of judges.

RICHARD RODGERS AWARDS

American Academy of Arts and Letters, 633 W. 155th St., New York NY 10032. (212)368-5900. **Contact:** Lydia Kaim, coordinator. Estab. 1978. Deadline: First Monday of November. "The Richard Rodgers Awards subsidize full productions, studio productions, and staged readings by nonprofit theaters in New York City of works by composers and writers who are not already established in the field of musical theater. The awards are only for musicals—songs by themselves are not eligible. The authors must be citizens or permanent residents of the United States." Guidelines for this award may be obtained by sending a SASE to above address.

ROME PRIZE COMPETITION FELLOWSHIP

American Academy in Rome, 7 E. 60th St., New York NY 10022-1001. (212)751-7200. Fax: (212)751-7220. E-mail: info@aarome.org. Website: www.aarome.org. **Contact:** Programs Department. For composers. Annual award.

Purpose "Rome Prize Competition winners pursue independent projects."

Requirements "Applicants for 11-month fellowships must hold a bachelor's degree in music, musical composition or its equivalent." Deadline: November 1. Entry fee: $25. Application guidelines are available to download through the Academy's website.

Awards "Up to two fellowships are awarded annually. Fellowship stipend is $21,000 for 11-months, and includes room and board, and a study or studio at Academy facilities in Rome. In all cases, excellence is the primary criterion for selection, based on the quality of the materials submitted. Winners are announced in mid-April."

☑ TELLURIDE TROUBADOUR CONTEST

P.O. Box 769, Lyons CO 80540. (303)823-0848 or (800)624-2422. Fax: (303)823-0849. E-mail: emily@bluegrass.com. Website: www.bluegrass.com. **Contact:** Steve Szymanski, director. Estab. 1991. For songwriters, composers and performers. Annual award.

Purpose Award based on having best song and performance.

Requirements Deadline: must be postmarked by April 25; notified May 9, if selected. Rules available on website. Send cassette or CD and $10 entry fee.

Awards 1st: custom Shanti Guitar, $100 and Festival Main Stage Set; 2nd: $400 and Taylor Big Baby guitar;

3rd: $300 and Taylor Big Baby guitar; 4th: $200 and Martin Backpacker guitar; 5th: $100 and Martin Backpacker guitar. Applications judged by panel of judges.

THE TEN-MINUTE MUSICALS PROJECT

P.O. Box 461194, West Hollywood CA 90046. Website: www.tenminutemusicals.org. **Contact:** Michael Koppy, producer. For songwriters, composers and musical playwrights. Annual award.

Purpose "We are building a full-length stage musical comprised of complete short musicals, each of which play for between 8-14 minutes. Award is $250 for each work chosen for development towards inclusion in the project, plus a share of royalties when produced."

Requirements Deadline: August 31. Write for guidelines. Final submission should include script, cassette and lead sheets.

Awards $250 for each work selected. "Works should have complete stories, with a definite beginning, middle and end."

U.S.A. SONGWRITING COMPETITION

4331 N. Federal Hwy., Suite 403A, Ft. Lauderdale FL 33308. (954)776-1577. Fax: (954)776-1132. E-mail: info@songwriting.net. Website: www.songwriting.net. **Contact:** Contest Manager. Estab. 1994. For songwriters, composers, performing artists and lyricists. Annual award.

Purpose "To honor good songwriters/composers all over the world, especially the unknown ones."

Requirements Open to professional and beginner songwriters. No limit on entries. Each entry must include an entry fee, a cassette tape of song(s) and lyric sheet(s). Judged by music industry representatives. Past judges have included record label representatives and publishers from Arista Records, EMI and Warner/Chappell. Deadline: To be announced. Entry fee: To be announced. Send SASE with request or e-mail for entry forms at any time. Samples of work are not required.

Awards Prizes include cash and merchandise in 15 different categories: pop, rock, country, Latin, R&B, gospel, folk, jazz, "lyrics only" category, instrumental and many others.

Tips "Judging is based on lyrics, originality, melody and overall composition. CD quality production is great but not a consideration in judging."

☑ U.S.-JAPAN CREATIVE ARTISTS EXCHANGE FELLOWSHIP PROGRAM

Japan-U.S. Friendship Commission, 1110 Vermont Ave., NW, Suite 800, Washington DC 20005. (202)418-9800. Fax: (202)418-9802. E-mail: artists@jusfc.gov. Website: www.jusfc.gov. **Contact:** Sylvia Dandridge, executive. Estab. 1980. For all creative artists. Annual award.

Purpose "For artists to go as seekers, as cultural visionaries, and as living liaisons to the traditional and contemporary life of Japan."

Requirements "Artists' works must exemplify the best in U.S. arts." Deadline: June. Send for application and guidelines. Applications available via Internet. Samples of work are required with application. Requires 2 pieces on cassette or CD, cued to the 3-5 minute section to be reviewed.

Awards Five artists are awarded a six-month residency anywhere in Japan. Awards monthly stipend for living expenses, housing and professional support services; up to $6,000 for pre-departure costs, including such items as language training and economy class roundtrip airfare. Residency is good for 1 year. Applications are judged by a panel of previous recipients of the awards, as well as other arts professionals with expertise in Japanese culture.

Tips "Applicants should anticipate a highly rigorous review of their artistry and should have compelling reasons for wanting to work in Japan."

☑ ⊞ U.S.-MEXICO FUND FOR CULTURE

Berline 18, 5th Floor, Colonia Juárez, C.P. 06600, México D.F., Mexico. (52-55)5535-6735 or (52-55)5592-5386. Fax: (52-55)5566-8071. E-mail: contacto@contacocultural.org. Website: www.fidemexusa.org.mx. **Contact:** Viviana Aguirre, grant coordinator. Estab. 1991. For composers, choreographers, musical playwrights and performers. Annual award.

Purpose "The U.S.-Mexico Fund for Culture, an independent body created through a joint initiative of the Bancomer Cultural Foundation, The Rockefeller Foundation and Mexico's National Fund for Culture and the Arts, provides financial support for the development of cultural binational projects in music, theater, dance, visual arts, cultural studies, literary and cultural publications, media arts and libraries."

Requirements Deadline: April 16, 2001 (postmarked). Send for application with SASE (8½×11 envelope) or contact us at our website. Samples of work are required with application in duplicate.

Awards Range from $2,000-25,000. Award is good for 1 year. Judged by binational panel of experts in each of the disciplines, one from Mexico and one from the USA.

Tips "Proposals must be binational in character and have a close and active collaboration with artists from Mexico. The creation of new works is highly recommendable."

UNISONG INTERNATIONAL SONG CONTEST

5198 Arlington Ave., PMB 513, Riverside CA 92504. (213)673-4067. E-mail: entry@unisong.com. Website: www.unisong.com. Founders: Alan Roy Scott and David Stark. London office: P.O. Box 13383, London, NW3 5ZR United Kingdom. (44)(0208)387-9293. Estab. 1997. For songwriters, composers and lyricists. Annual songwriting contest.

Purpose "Unisong was created by songwriters for songwriters."

Requirements Send for an entry form or request one by phone or e-mail. Download entry form from website or enter online. Send cassette or CD only. No DATs. Entries also accepted via MP3.

Awards Over $50,000 in cash and prizes. Grand Prize winner to write with professional writers and artists through Music Bridges Around The World. Songs judged on song quality only, not demo.

Tips "Please make sure your song is professionally presented. Make sure lyrics are typed or printed clearly. Print your personal information clearly. Enter your song in the most appropriate categories."

WEST COAST ENSEMBLE–MUSICAL STAIRS

P.O. Box 38728, Los Angeles CA 90038. (323)876-9337. Website: www.wcensemble.org. **Contact:** Les Hanson, artistic director. For composers and musical playwrights. Annual award.

  • Also see the listing for West Coast Ensemble in the Play Producers section of this book.

Purpose To provide an arena and encouragement for the development of new musicals for the theater.

Requirements No entry fee. Submit book and a cassette or CD of the score to the above address.

Awards The West Coast Ensemble Musical Stairs Competition Award includes a production of the selected musical and $500 prize. Panel of judges reads script and listen to cassette or CD. Final selection is made by Artistic Director.

Tips "Submit libretto in standard playscript format along with professional sounding cassette or CD of songs."

Y.E.S. FESTIVAL OF NEW PLAYS

Northern Kentucky University Dept. of Theatre, FA-205, Highland Heights KY 41099-1007. (859)572-6303. Fax: (859)572-6057. E-mail: forman@nku.edu. **Contact:** Sandra Forman, project director. Estab. 1983. For musical playwrights. Biennial award (odd numbered years).

Purpose "The festival seeks to encourage new playwrights and develop new plays and musicals. Three plays or musicals are given full productions."

Requirements "No entry fee. Submit a script with a completed entry form. Musicals should be submitted with a piano/conductor's score and a vocal parts score. Scripts may be submitted May 1 through Oct. 31, for the New Play Festival occuring April. Send for application."

Awards Three awards of $500. "The winners are brought to NKU at our expense to view late rehearsals and opening night." Submissions are judged by a panel of readers.

Tips "Plays/musicals which have heavy demands for mature actors are not as likely to be selected as an equally good script with roles for 18-25 year olds."

✓ YOUNG COMPOSERS AWARDS

% NGCSA and the Hartt School, University of Hartford, 200 Bloomfield Ave., West Hartford CT 06117. (860)768-7768, ext. 8558. E-mail: youngcomp@hartford.edu. Website: www.nationalguild.org. **Contact:** Carissa Reddick, director. For composers. Open to students age 13-18. Annual award.

Purpose "To encourage young students to write music, so that the art of composition—with no restrictions as to the category of music in which the works are written—will once again occupy the place in the center of music education where it belongs. It takes tons of ore to extract one ounce of gold: by focusing on the inventiveness of many students, the Awards may lead to the discovery of genuine creative talents—that is the eventual goal." Young Composers Awards was established by the late Dr. Herbert Zipperin in 1985 with the initial support of the Rockefeller Foundation. Since 1985, awards in the amount of $42,500 have been granted to 67 young composers.

Requirements "Applicants must be enrolled in a public or private secondary school, in a recognized musical institution, or be engaged in the private study of music with an established teacher. No compositions will be considered without certification by the applicant's teacher. Student composers must not be enrolled in an undergraduate program when they apply. This competition is open to residents of the United States and Canada. Each applicant may submit only one work. Deadline: all submissions must be postmarked on or before early April 2002. Check website for exact date. Send for application. Samples of work are required with application. Four photocopies of the work must be submitted. All manuscripts must be in legible form and may be submitted on usual score paper or reduced under a generally accepted process. The composer's name must not appear on the composition submitted. The composition must be marked with a pseudonym on the manuscript. Copies must be submitted with a check in the amount of $5 made payable to the Hartt School. One copy of score will be returned if entrant sends SASE with application. Entrants must be certain postage purchased has no expiration date. Composers retain full and all legal rights to their submitted composition. Students who have previously won this award are not eligible to reapply."

Awards Herbert Zipper Prizes: 2 separate categories—age group 13-15 (Junior) and 16-18 (Senior). 2 prizes are awarded in each of the Senior and Junior categories—Senior: 1st Place: $1,000; 2nd Place: $500. Junior: 1st Place: $500; 2nd Place: $250. "Announcement of the Awards are made no later than mid-June each year. In the event that no entry is found to be worthy of the $1,000 Prize, the jury may award one or both of the other prizes or none at all. NGCSA appoints an independent jury to review all entries submitted. The jury consists of not less than three qualified judges. Prizes shall be awarded at the discretion of the jury. The decision of the judges is final."

Tips "Paramount would be neatness and legibility of the manuscript submitted. The application must be complete in all respects."

Contests & Awards

Organizations

One of the first places a beginning songwriter should look for guidance and support is a songwriting organization. Offering encouragement, instruction, contacts and feedback, these groups of professional and amateur songwriters can help an aspiring songwriter hone the skills needed to compete in the ever-changing music industry.

The type of organization you choose to join depends on what you want to get out of it. Local groups can offer a friendly, supportive environment where you can work on your songs and have them critiqued in a constructive way by other songwriters. They're also great places to meet collaborators. Larger, national organizations can give you access to music business professionals and other songwriters across the country.

Most of the organizations listed in this book are non-profit groups with membership open to specific groups of people—songwriters, musicians, classical composers, etc. They can be local groups with a membership of less than 100 people, or large national organizations with thousands of members from all over the country. In addition to regular meetings, most organizations occasionally sponsor events such as seminars and workshops to which music industry personnel are invited to talk about the business, and perhaps listen to and critique demo tapes.

Check the following listings, bulletin boards at local music stores and your local newspapers for area organizations. If you are unable to locate an organization within an easy distance of your home, you may want to consider joining one of the national groups. These groups, based in New York, Los Angeles and Nashville, keep their members involved and informed through newsletters, regional workshops and large yearly conferences. They can help a writer who feels isolated in his hometown get his music heard by professionals in the major music centers.

In the following listings, organizations describe their purpose and activities, as well as how much it costs to join. Before joining any organization, consider what they have to offer and how becoming a member will benefit you. To locate organizations close to home, see the Geographic Index at the back of this book.

AARON ENTERPRISES SONGWRITERS GROUP

4411 Red Gate Dr., Disputanta VA 23842. (804)733-5908. **Contact:** Cham Laughlin, founder. Estab. 1997. "Songwriters of all ages, all styles and all skill levels are welcome to join. Applicants must have an interest in songwriting—music writing, lyric writing or co-writing. The main purpose of this organization is to educate songwriters about the business of songwriting, the art and craft of songwriting, lyric writing and structure, musical composition, song structure or arranging and professional presentation of your songs." Offers newsletter, evaluation services, seminars, discounts on demos and leads to publishers. Applications accepted year-round. Membership fee: $25/year with discounts for multiple years.

Tips "Networking is a very important part of this business. Members are offered a large amount of information and that information is explained to them through free seminars, the newsletter or one-on-one phone consultations to ensure the best possible support network for their songwriting careers."

☑ ACADEMY OF COUNTRY MUSIC

4100 W. Alameda Ave., Suite 208, Burbank CA 91505. (818)842-8400. Fax: (818)842-8535. E-mail: membership @acmcountry.com. Website: www.acmcountry.com. **Contact:** Fran Boyd, executive director. Estab. 1964. Serves producers, artists, songwriters, talent buyers and others involved with the country music industry. Eligibility for professional members is limited to those individuals who derive some portion of their income directly from country music. Each member is classified by one of the following categories: artist/entertainer, club operator/employee, musician/trend leader, DJ, manager/booking agent, composer, music publisher, promotion, publications, radio, TV/motion picture, record company or affiliated (general). The purpose of ACM is to promote and enhance the image of country music. The Academy is involved year-round in activities important to the country music community. Some of these activities include charity fund-raisers, participation in country music seminars, talent contests, artist showcases, assistance to producers in placing country music on television and in motion pictures and backing legislation that benefits the interests of the country music community. The ACM is governed by directors and run by officers elected annually. Applications are accepted throughout the year. Membership is $60/year.

ALABAMA SONGWRITER'S GUILD

P.O. Box 272, Garden City AL 35070. (256)352-4873. E-mail: lithics@hiwaay.net. **Contact:** Dennis N. Kahler. Estab. 1992. "The Alabama Songwriter's Guild is comprised of songwriters and their supporters, with no restrictions. We have members who are just beginning to write, and others who have number one hits under their belts on the *Billboard* charts. We welcome all genres of songwriting, and count several non-writers as members of our network efforts. The main purpose of the ASG is to help link Alabama and outside songwriters to information on seminars, showcases, publishing and song-plugging opportunities, local associations, workshops, and other events from one end of the state to the other. We help spread word of the induction ceremonies and other events at the Alabama Music Hall of Fame, report on the annual Frank Brown International Songwriter's Festival in Gulf Shores/Orange Beach every November, and help link writers together with like-minded individuals for co-writes. Any purpose that serves the songwriter is of interest to us." Queries welcomed anytime.

Tips "Networking is crucial! Wherever you live, develop your network. If you need songwriting contacts in Alabama, contact us."

ALL SONGWRITERS NETWORK (ASN)

(formerly American Songwriters Network), Dept A95, Box 23912, Ft. Lauderdale FL 33307. (954)537-3463. E-mail: asn@tiac.net. Website: http://home.tiac.net/~asn. **Contact:** Network Manager. Estab. 1995. Serves "professional level songwriters/composers with monthly music industry leads tipsheet. The tipsheet includes the most current listing of producers, A&R managers, record labels, entertainment attorneys, agents and publishing companies looking for specific material for their projects/albums. Any songwriter from any part of the country or world can be a member of this organization. The purpose of this organization is to foster a better professional community by helping members to place their songs." Membership fee: $140/year.

Tips "Please send SASE or e-mail for application form."

☑ AMERICAN COMPOSERS FORUM

332 Minnesota St., Suite East 145, St. Paul MN 55101. (651)228-1407. Fax: (651)291-7978. Website: www.compo sersforum.org. **Contact:** Wendy Collins, member services manager. Estab. 1973. "The American Composers Forum links communities with composers and performers, encouraging the making, playing and enjoyment of new music. Building two-way relationships between artists and the public, the Forum develops programs that educate today's and tomorrow's audiences, energize composers' and performers' careers, stimulate entrepreneurship and collaboration, promote musical creativity, and serve as models of effective support for the arts.

Programs include residencies, fellowships, commissions, producing and performance opportunities, a recording assistance program and a widely-distributed recording label. The Forum's members, more than 1,200 strong, live in 49 states and 16 countries; membership is open to all." Membership dues: Regular (U.S.): $50; Student/ Senior (U.S.): $35; Regular (Outside U.S.): $60; Student/Senior (Outside U.S.): $45.

AMERICAN MUSIC CENTER, INC.
30 W. 26th St., Suite 1001, New York NY 10010-2011. (212)366-5260. Fax: (212)366-5265. E-mail: center@amc.net. Website: www.amc.net. **Contact**: Membership Department. The American Music Center, founded by a consortium led by Aaron Copland in 1939, is the first-ever national service and information center for new classical and jazz music in the world. The Center has a variety of innovative new programs and services, including a montly Internet magazine (www.newmusicbox.org) for new American music, an online catalog of new music for educators specifically targeted to young audiences, a series of professional development workshops, and an online listening library (www.newmusicjukebox.org). Each month, AMC provides its over 2,500 members with a listing of opportunities including calls for scores, competitions, and other new music performance information. Last year, AMC's Information Services Program fielded over 35,000 requests concerning composers, performers, data, funding, and support programs. AMC Library presently includes over 60,000 scores and recordings, many unavailable elsewhere. "AMC also continues to administer several grant programs: the Aaron Copland Fund for Music; the Henry Cowell Performance Incentive Fund; and its own programs Live Music for Dance and the Composer Assistance Program." Members are also eligible to link their artists' pages to the center's website. The American Music Center is not-for-profit and has an annual membership fee.

AMERICAN SOCIETY OF COMPOSERS, AUTHORS AND PUBLISHERS (ASCAP)
One Lincoln Plaza, New York NY 10023. (212)621-6000 (administration); (212)621-6240 (membership). E-mail: info@ascap.com. Website: www.ascap.com. President and Chairman of the Board: Marilyn Bergman. CEO: John LoFrumento. Executive Vice President/Membership: Todd Brabec. **Contact**: Member Services at (800)95-ASCAP. **Regional offices: West Coast:** 7920 Sunset Blvd., 3rd Floor, Los Angeles CA 90046, (323)883-1000; **Nashville:** 2 Music Square W., Nashville TN 37203, (615)742-5000; **Chicago:** 1608 N. Milwaukee Ave., Suite 1007, Chicago IL 60647, (773)394-4286; **Atlanta:** PMB 400-541 10th St. NW, Atlanta GA 30318, (404)351-1252; **Florida:** 420 Lincoln Rd., Suite 385, Miami Beach FL 33139, (305)673-3446; **United Kingdom:** 8 Cork St., London WIX 1PB England, 011-44-202-439-0909; **Puerto Rico:** 654 Ave. Muñoz Rivera, IBM Plaza Suite 1101 Boz, Hato Rey, Puerto Rico 00918, (787)281-0782. ASCAP is a membership association of over 180,000 composers, lyricists, songwriters, and music publishers, whose function is to protect the rights of its members by licensing and collecting royalties for the nondramatic public performance of their copyrighted works. ASCAP licensees include radio, television, cable, live concert promoters, bars, restaurants, symphony orchestras, new media, and other users of music. ASCAP is the leading performing rights society in the world, with 2003 revenues of more than $668 million. All revenues, less operating expenses, are distributed to members (about 86 cents of each dollar). ASCAP was the first US performing rights organization to distribute royalties from the Internet. Founded in 1914, ASCAP is the only society created and owned by writers and publishers. The ASCAP Board of Directors consists of 12 writers and 12 publishers, elected by the membership. ASCAP's Member Card provides exclusive benefits geared towards working music professionals. Among the benefits are health, musical instrument and equipment, tour and studio liability, term life and long term care insurance, discounts on musical instruments, equipment and supplies, access to a credit union, and much more. ASCAP hosts a wide array of showcases and workshops throughout the year, and offers grants, special awards, and networking opportunities in a variety of genres. Visit their website listed above for more information.

ARIZONA SONGWRITERS ASSOCIATION
P.O. Box 678, Phoenix AZ 85001-0678. (602)973-1988. E-mail: punkfolker@aol.com. Website: www.punkfolker.com. **Contact**: Gavan Wieser, membership director. Estab. 1977. Members are all ages with wide variety of interests; beginners and those who make money from their songs. Most members are residents of Arizona. Purpose is to educate about the craft and business of songwriting and to facilitate networking with business professionals and other local songwriters. Offers instruction, newsletter, lectures, workshops and performance opportunities. Applications accepted year-round. Membership fee: $25/year.

☑ ◪ ASSOCIATION DES PROFESSIONEL.LE.S DE LA CHANSON ET DE LA MUSIQUE
292 Montréal Rd, Suite 200, ON K1L 6B7 Canada. (613)745-5642. Fax: (613)745-9715. E-mail: info-apcm@rogers.com. Website: www.apcm.ca. **Contact**: Jean-Emmanuel Simiano, agent de communication. Director: Laurent de Crombruggne. Estab. 1989. Members are French Canadian singers and musicians. Members must be French singing and may have a CD to be distributed. Purpose is to gather French speaking artists (outside of Quebec, mainly in Ontario) to distribute their material, other workshops, instructions, lectures, etc. Offers instruction,

newsletter, lectures, workshops, and distribution. Applications accepted year-round. Membership fee: $50 (Canadian).

ASSOCIATION OF INDEPENDENT MUSIC PUBLISHERS

Los Angeles Chapter: P.O. Box 69473, Los Angeles CA 90069. (818)771-7301. New York Chapter: % Burton Goldstein & Co., LLC., 156 W. 56th St., Suite 1803, New York NY 10019. (212)582-7622. Fax: (212)582-8273. E-mail: LAinfo@aimp.org or NYinfo@aimp.org. Website: www.aimp.org. Estab. 1977. Purpose is to educate members on new developments in the music publishing industry and to provide networking opportunities. Offers lectures, workshops and evaluation services. Applications accepted year-round. Membership fee: NY: $75/year; LA: $65/year.

N ⚏ ATLANTIC CANADIAN COMPOSERS ASSOCIATION

22 Portledge Ave., Moncton NB E1C 5C6 Canada. (506)388-4224. E-mail: gibsonr@umoncton.ca. **Contact:** Richard Gibson, member at large. Estab. 1980. ''Our membership consists of people who write 'serious' (as opposed to commercial, pop, jazz, industrial) music. An applicant must be resident in one of the four Atlantic Canadian provinces and must be able to demonstrate a fluency with a variety of genres of notated music. An applicant must be prepared to submit five completed scores.'' Offers performance opportunities. Applications accepted year-round. Membership fee is 35 Canadian dollars.

☑ AUSTIN SONGWRITERS GROUP

P.O. Box 2578, Austin TX 78768. (512)442-TUNE. E-mail: info@austinsongwriter.org. Website: www.austinson gwriter.org. **Contact:** Adam Donmoyer or Lee Duffy, co-presidents. Estab. 1986. Serves all ages and all levels, from just beginning to advanced. Perspective members should have an interest in the field of songwriting, whether it be for profit or hobby. The main purpose of this organization is ''to educate members in the craft and business of songwriting; to provide resources for growth and advancement in the area of songwriting; and to provide opportunities for performance and contact with the music industry.'' The primary benefit of membership to a songwriter is ''exposure to music industry professionals, which increases contacts and furthers the songwriter's education in both craft and business aspects.'' Offers competitions, instruction, lectures, library, newsletter, performance opportunities, evaluation services, workshops and ''contact with music industry professionals through special guest speakers at meetings, plus our yearly 'Austin Songwriters Conference,' which includes instruction, song evaluations, and song pitching direct to those pros currently seeking material for their artists, publishing companies, etc.'' Applications accepted year-round. Membership fee: $40/year.
Tips ''Our newsletter is top-quality—packed with helpful information on all aspects of songwriting—craft, business, recording and producing tips, and industry networking opportunities.''

☑ BALTIMORE SONGWRITERS ASSOCIATION

P.O. Box 22496, Baltimore MD 21203. (410)813-4039. E-mail: baltimoresongwriters@yahoo.com. Website: www.baltimoresongwriters.com. **Contact:** Paul Iwancio, president. Estab. 1997. ''The BSA is an inclusive organization with all ages, skill levels and genres of music welcome.'' Offers instruction, newsletter, lectures, workshops, performance opportunities, music publishing. Applications accepted year-round; membership not limited to location or musical status. Membership fee: $20.
Tips ''We are trying to build a musical community that is more supportive and less competitive We are dedicated to helping songwriters grow and become better in their craft.''

N THE BLACK ROCK COALITION

P.O. Box 1054, Cooper Station, New York NY 10276. (212)713-5097. Website: www.blackrockcoalition.org. **Contact:** LaRonda Davis, president. Estab. 1985. Serves musicians, songwriters—male and female ages 18-40 (average). Also engineers, entertainment attorneys and producers. Looking for members who are ''mature and serious about music as an artist or activist willing to help fellow musicians. The BRC independently produces, promotes and distributes Black alternative music acts as a collective and supportive voice for such musicians within the music and record business. The main purpose of this organization is to produce, promote and distribute the full spectrum of black music along with educating the public on what black music is. The BRC is now soliciting recorded music by bands and individuals for Black Rock Coalition Records. Please send copyrighted and original material only.'' Offers instruction, newsletter, lectures, free seminars and workshops, monthly membership meeting, quarterly magazine, performing opportunities, evaluation services, business advice, full roster of all members. Applications accepted year-round. Bands must submit a tape, bio with picture and a self-addressed, stamped envelope before sending their membership fee. Membership fee: $25 per individual/$100 per band.

THE BOSTON SONGWRITERS WORKSHOP

(617)499-6932. Website: www.bostonsongwriters.org. Estab. 1988. "The Boston Songwriters Workshop is made up of a very diverse group of people, ranging in age from late teens to people in their sixties, and even older. The interest areas are also diverse, running the gamut from folk, pop and rock to musical theater, jazz, R&B, dance, rap and classical. Skill levels within the group range from relative newcomers to established veterans that have had cuts and/or songs published. By virtue of group consensus, there are no eligibility requirements other than a serious desire to pursue one's songwriting ventures, and availability and interest in volunteering for the various activities required to run the organization. The purpose of the BSW is to establish a community of songwriters and composers within the greater Boston area, so that its members may better help each other to make further gains in their respective musical careers." Offers performance opportunities, instruction, newsletter, workshops and bi-weekly critique sessions. Applications accepted year-round. Membership: $35/year; newsletter subscription only: $10/year; guest (nonmember) fees: free, limited to two meetings.

☑ BROADCAST MUSIC, INC. (BMI)

New York: 320 W. 57th St., New York NY 10019. (212)586-2000. E-mail: newyork@bmi.com; **Los Angeles:** 8730 Sunset Blvd., Los Angeles CA 90069, (310)659-9109. E-mail: losangeles@bmi.com. Website: www.bmi. com; **Nashville:** 10 Music Square East, Nashville TN 37203, (615)401-2000. E-mail: nashville@bmi.com; **Miami:** 5201 Blue Lagoon Dr., Suite 310, Miami FL 33126, (305)266-3636. E-mail: miami@bmi.com; **Atlanta:** Tower Place 100, 3340 Peachtree Rd., NE, Suite 570, Atlanta GA 30326. (404)261-5151. E-mail: atlanta@bmi.com; **Puerto Rico:** BankTrust Plaza, Suite A-262/East Wing, 255 Ponce De Leon Ave., San Juan PR 00917. (787)754-5490; **United Kingdom:** 54 Harley House, Marylebone Rd., London NW1 5HN, United Kingdom. 011-44-207-486-2036. E-mail: london@bmi.com; President and CEO: Del R. Bryant. President Emeritus: Frances W. Preston. Senior Vice Presidents, New York: Phillip Graham, Writer/Publisher Relations; Alison Smith, Performing Rights. Vice President, New York: Charlie Feldman. Vice Presidents, Los Angeles: Barbara Cane and Doreen Ringer Ross; Vice President, Nashville: Paul Corbin. Assistant Vice President, Miami: Diane J. Almodovar: Assistant Vice President, Atlanta: Catherine Brewton. Senior Executive, London: Brandon Bakshi. BMI is a performing rights organization representing approximately 300,000 songwriters, composers and music publishers in all genres of music, including pop, rock, country, R&B, rap, jazz, Latin, gospel and contemporary classical. "Applicants must have written a musical composition, alone or in collaboration with other writers, which is commercially published, recorded or otherwise likely to be performed." Purpose: BMI acts on behalf of its songwriters, composers and music publishers by insuring payment for performance of their works through the collection of licensing fees from radio stations, Internet outlets, broadcast and cable TV stations, hotels, nightclubs, aerobics centers and other users of music. This income is distributed to the writers and publishers in the form of royalty payments, based on how the music is used. BMI also undertakes intensive lobbying efforts in Washington D.C. on behalf of its affiliates, seeking to protect their performing rights through the enactment of new legislation and enforcement of current copyright law. In addition, BMI helps aspiring songwriters develop their skills through various workshops, seminars and competitions it sponsors throughout the country. Applications accepted year-round. There is no membership fee for songwriters; a one-time fee of $150 is required to affiliate an individually-owned publishing company; $250 for partnerships, corporations and limited-liability companies. "Visit our website for specific contacts, e-mail addresses and additional membership information."

CALIFORNIA LAWYERS FOR THE ARTS

Fort Mason Center, C-255, San Francisco CA 94123. (415)775-7200. Fax: (415)775-1143. E-mail: cla@calawyersf orthearts.org. **Southern California:** 1641 18th St., Santa Monica CA 90404. (310)998-5590. Fax: (310)998-5594. E-mail: usercla@aol.com. **Sacramento Office:** 926 J St., Suite 811, Sacramento CA 95814. (916)442-6210. Fax: (916)442-6281. E-mail: clasacto@aol.com. **Oakland Office:** 1212 Broadway St., Oakland CA 94612. (510)444-6351. Fax: (510)444-6352. E-mail: oakcla@there.net. Website: www.calawyersforthearts.org. **Contact:** Alma Robinson, executive director. Systems Coordinator: Josie Porter. Estab. 1974. "For artists of all disciplines, skill levels, and ages, supporting individuals and organizations, and arts organizations. Artists of all disciplines are welcome, whether professionals or amateurs. We also welcome groups and individuals who support the arts. We work most closely with the California arts community. Our mission is to establish a bridge between the legal and arts communities so that artists and art groups may handle their creative activities with greater business and legal competence; the legal profession will be more aware of issues affecting the arts community; and the law will become more responsive to the arts community." Offers newsletter, lectures, library, workshops, mediation service, attorney referral service, housing referrals, publications and advocacy. Membership fee: $20 for senior citizens and full-time students; $25 for working artists; $40 for general individual; $55 for panel attorney; $100 to $1,000 for patrons. Organizations: $45 for small organizations (budget under $50,000); $80 for large organizations (budget of $50,000 or more); $100 to $1,000 for corporate sponsors.

☑ 🗘 CANADA COUNCIL FOR THE ARTS/CONSEIL DES ARTS DU CANADA

350 Albert St., P.O. Box 1047, Ottawa ON K1P 5V8 Canada. (613)566-4414, ext. 5060. E-mail: info@canadacounc il.ca. Website: www.canadacouncil.ca. **Contact:** Michelle Legaut, Danielle Sarault, or Lise Rochon, information officers. Estab. 1957. An independent agency that fosters and promotes the arts in Canada by providing grants and services to professional artists including songwriters and musicians. "Individual artists must be Canadian citizens or permanent residents of Canada, and must have completed basic training and/or have the recognition as professionals within their fields. The Canada Council offers grants to professional musicians to pursue their individual artistic development and creation. There are specific deadline dates for the various programs of assistance." Call or write for more details.

🗘 CANADIAN ACADEMY OF RECORDING ARTS & SCIENCES (CARAS)

355 King St. W, Suite 501, Toronto ON M5V 1J6 Canada. (416)485-3135 or (888)440-JUNO. Fax: (416)485-4978. E-mail: caras@juno-awards.ca. Website: www.juno-awards.ca. **Contact:** Brenna Knought, project coordinator. President: Melanie Berry. Manager, Awards and Events: Leisa Peacock. Manager, Marketing and Communica- tions: Tammy Watson. Membership is open to all employees (including support staff) in broadcasting and record companies, as well as producers, personal managers, recording artists, recording engineers, arrangers, composers, music publishers, album designers, promoters, talent and booking agents, record retailers, rack jobbers, distributors, recording studios and other music industry related professions (on approval). Applicants must be affiliated with the Canadian recording industry. Offers newsletter, nomination and voting privileges for Juno Awards and discount tickets to Juno awards show. "CARAS strives to foster the development of the Canadian music and recording industries and to contribute toward higher artistic standards." Applications accepted year-round. Membership fee is $50/year (Canadian) + GST = $53.50. Applications accepted from individuals only, not from companies or organizations.

🗘 CANADIAN COUNTRY MUSIC ASSOCIATION (CCMA)

5 Director Court, Unit 102, Woodbridge ON L4L 4S5 Canada. (905)850-1144. Fax: (905)850-1330. E-mail: countr y@ccma.org. Website: www.ccma.org. **Contact:** Amanda Power, communications manager. Estab. 1976. Mem- bers are artists, songwriters, musicians, producers, radio station personnel, managers, booking agents and others. Offers newsletter, workshops, performance opportunities and the CCMA awards every September. "Through our newsletters and conventions we offer a means of meeting and associating with artists and others in the industry. The CCMA is a federally chartered, nonprofit organization, dedicated to the promotion and development of Canadian country music throughout Canada and the world and to providing a unity of purpose for the Canadian country music industry." See website for membership information.

☑ 🗘 CANADIAN MUSICAL REPRODUCTION RIGHTS AGENCY LTD.

56 Wellesley St. W, #320, Toronto ON M5S 2S3 Canada. (416)926-1966. Fax: (416)926-7521. E-mail: inquiries@c mrra.ca. Website: www.cmrra.ca. **Contact:** Michael Mackie, membership services. Estab. 1975. Members are music copyright owners, music publishers, sub-publishers and administrators. Representation by CMRRA is open to any person, firm or corporation anywhere in the world, which owns and/or administers one or more copyrighted musical works. CMRRA is a music licensing agency—Canada's largest—which represents music copyright owners, publishers and administrators for the purpose of mechanical and synchronization licensing in Canada. Offers mechanical and synchronization licensing. Applications accepted year-round.

CENTER FOR THE PROMOTION OF CONTEMPORARY COMPOSERS

P.O. Box 631043, Nacogdoches TX 75963. E-mail: cpcc@under.org. Website: www.under.org/cpcc. Director: Dr. Stephen Lias. Estab. 1996. "Our members range from student composers to composers with international reputations." Purpose is to promote the works and activities of contemporary composers by creating custom composer web pages, posting composer opportunities (competitions, calls for scores, grants, faculty openings, etc.), maintaining a catalogue of members' works and a calendar of upcoming performances of new music. Offers competitions, newsletter, performance opportunities and custom web pages and listings in online catalog. Applications accepted year-round. Membership fee: $12 regular; $10/month resident ($120/year).

☑ CENTRAL CAROLINA SONGWRITERS ASSOCIATION (CCSA)

1144 Amber Acres Lane, Knightdale NC 27545. (919)266-5791. E-mail: ccsa_raleigh@yahoo.com. Website: www.centralcarolinasongwritersassociation.com. **Contact:** Shantel R. Davis, Founder. Vice President: Dawn Williams. Estab. 1996. "CCSA welcomes both beginner and published songwriters from North Carolina to join our group. Our members' musical background varies covering a wide array of musical genres. All songwriters and musicians can find benefit in joining CCSA. We meet monthly in Raleigh, NC. We are open to songwriters in the state of North Carolina (sorry, applications cannot be accepted from incarcerated persons or those who do not reside in the state of North Carolina). Our group's primary focus is on songwriters who are able to attend meetings, workshops, and other functions—to ensure members get the best value for their yearly dues. CCSA strives to provide each songwriter and musician a resourceful organization where members are able to grow musically by networking and sharing with one another. We want to reach every interested songwriter we can and attend to his/her musical needs. For those members who are unable to attend the monthly meetings in Raleigh, CCSA does offer a Critique-By-Mail service. Offers instruction, newsletter, library, workshops, evaluation services, open-mic nights and musicians/collaborators network. Applications are accepted year round. Dues are $12/year, with annual renewal each January. For new members, dues are pro-rated for the first year at $1/month by date of application.

☑ CENTRAL OREGON SONGWRITERS ASSOCIATION

15484 SW Hahlen Ave., Powell Butte OR 97753. (541)548-2387. E-mail: cosapresident@lycos.com. Website: www.centraloregonmusic.com. **Contact:** Ellen Jakab, president. Organizer: Earl Richards. President: Matt Engle. Estab. 1993. "Our members range in age from their 20s into their 80s. Membership includes aspiring beginners, accomplished singer/songwriter performing artists and all in between. Anyone with an interest in songwriting (any style) is invited to and welcome at COSA. COSA is a nonprofit organization to promote, educate and motivate members in the skills of writing, marketing and improving their craft." Offers competitions, instruction, newsletter, lectures, library, workshops, performance opportunities, songwriters round, awards, evaluation services and collaboration. Applications accepted year-round. Membership fee is $25.

CHICAGO ALLIANCE FOR PLAYWRIGHTS

1225 W. Belmont, Chicago IL 60657. (773)929-7367, ext. 60. Website: www.geocities.com/caplays. **Contact:** Joanne Koch, president. Estab. 1990. "Organizational members include Chicago Dramatists Workshop, Writer Bloc, New Tuners and Studio Z; there are over 150 individual members. Members must be Chicago-area residents (past or present); no pro status is required. CAP is a service organization that establishes a network for Chicago-area playwrights and others committed to the development of new work for the stage. The Alliance sponsors forums of interest to writers and publishes an annual directory of CAP members and their works." Offers instruction, newsletter, lectures, workshops and annual directory of CAP members. Applications accepted year-round. Membership fee: $25/year individual, $100/year organization.

CHICAGO DANCE AND MUSIC ALLIANCE

(formerly Chicago Music Alliance), 410 S. Michigan Ave., Suite 819, Chicago IL 60605. (312)987-9296. Fax: (312)987-1127. E-mail: info@chicagoperformances.org. Website: www.chicagoperformances.org. Executive Director: Matthew Brockmeier. Estab. 1984. "Chicago Dance and Music Alliance provides direct services to members engaged in all genres of dance and music in the Chicago area, acts as an advocate on their behalf, and disseminates information about their activities to the general public. The alliance includes administrators, composers, choreographers, performers, students, performers, educators and others, as well as groups from the smallest ensemble to full symphony orchestras and major dance companies. Members generally have a direct connection to Chicago, with most organizational members based in the Chicago metropolitan area. As a service organization the Alliance is committed to meeting the needs of members. Services for individual members include ticket and merchandise discounts, credit union membership and résumé/career counseling. The Alliance also publishes a monthly Newsletter, and offers occasional workshops or topical meetings. The Newsletter includes audition and employment notices. The website includes a searchable performance directory and a teaching directory. The teaching directory is available to members as well as to for-profit schools. Applications accepted year-round. All memberships expire December 31. Individual dues are $40 per year. Fees for ensembles vary by budget size.

CLEVELAND COMPOSERS GUILD

Website: www.en.com/users/jaquick/ccg.html. **Contact:** Daniel McCarthy, President; Ty Emerson, Vice President of Records; Katharine O'Connell, Vice President of Publicity. Estab. 1920. Offers performance opportunities and evaluation services for composers living in Northeast Ohio. Applications accepted year-round. Membership fee: $40/year.

THE COLLEGE MUSIC SOCIETY

312 E. Pine St., Missoula MT 59802. (406)721-9616. Fax: (406)721-9419. E-mail: cms@music.org. Website: www.music.org. Estab. 1959. Serves college, university and conservatory professors, as well as independent musicians. "The College Music Society is a consortium of college, conservatory, university and independent musicians and scholars interested in all disciplines of music. Its mission is to promote music teaching and learning, musical creativity and expression, research and dialogue, and diversity and interdisciplinary interaction." Offers journal, newsletter, lectures, workshops, performance opportunities, job listing service, databases

of organizations and institutions, music faculty and mailing lists. Applications accepted year-round. Membership fee: $60 (regular dues), $30 (student dues).

COLORADO MUSIC ASSOCIATION

8 E. First Ave., #107, Denver CO 80203. (720)570-2280. Website: http://coloradomusic.org. **Contact:** David Barber, president. Estab. 1999. Members are musicians of all ages and skill levels, songwriters, recording studios, music business merchants, teachers, performers, attorneys, agents, managers, publicists, promoters, venue owners and operators, and others connected to local music communities. Purpose is to support the local music community and encourage the development of skills, creativity and production. Offers instruction, lectures, workshops, performance and showcase opportunities, evaluation services, music directory, and free UPC (barcode) numbers for CD and other music products. Applications accepted year-round. Membership fee: $35/individual; $60/band; $115/business.

Tips "We meet monthly in Denver and present speakers on topics of interest to the group. Our Internet site is being expanded to provide extensive educational features relative to the music biz.

COMPOSERS GUILD

40 N. 100 West, P.O. Box 586, Farmington UT 84025-0586. (801)451-2275. **Contact:** Ruth Gatrell, president. Estab. 1963.

 • Also see the listing for the Composers Guild Annual Composition Contest in the Contests and Awards section of this book.

Serves all ages, including children. Musical skill varies from beginners to professionals. An interest in composing is the only requirement. The purpose of this organization is to "help composers in every way possible through classes, workshops and symposiums, concerts, composition contests and association with others of similar interests." Offers competitions, instruction, lectures, newsletter, performance opportunities, evaluation services and workshops. Applications accepted year-round. Membership fee is $25/year. Associate memberships for child, spouse, parent, grandchild or grandparent of member: $15. "Holds four concerts/year. See our listing in the Contests & Awards section for details."

☑ CONNECTICUT SONGWRITERS ASSOCIATION

P.O. Box 511, Mystic CT 06355. (860)945-1272. E-mail: info@ctsongs.com. Website: www.ctsongs.com. **Contact:** Bill Pere, executive director. Vice President: Robert Williams. "We are an educational, nonprofit organization dedicated to improving the art and craft of original music. Founded in 1979, CSA had almost 2,000 active members and has become one of the best known and respected songwriters' associations in the country. Membership in the CSA admits you to 12-18 seminars/workshops/song critique sessions per year at 3-5 locations in Connecticut. Out-of-state members may mail in songs for free critiques at our meetings. Noted professionals deal with all aspects of the craft and business of music including lyric writing, music theory, music technology, arrangement and production, legal and business aspects, performance techniques, song analysis and recording techniques. CSA offers song screening sessions for members (songs which are voted on by the panel). Songs that 'pass' are then eligible for inclusion on the CSA sampler anthology CD series. Thirteen compilation recordings have been released so far are for sale at local retail outlets and are given to speakers and prospective buyers. CSA also offers showcases and concerts which are open to the public and designed to give artists a venue for performing their original material for an attentive, listening audience. CSA benefits help local soup kitchens, group homes, hospice, world hunger, libraries, nature centers, community centers and more. CSA shows encompass ballads to bluegrass and Bach to rock. Our monthly newsletter, *Connecticut Songsmith*, offers free classified advertising for members, and has been edited and published by Bill Pere since 1980. In addition, CSA offers members free web pages on their website. Annual dues: $40; senior citizen and full time students $30; organizations $80. Memberships are tax-deductible as business expenses or as charitable contributions to the extent allowed by law."

☑ COUNTRY LEGENDS ASSOCIATION

Corporate Offices, P.O. Box 136592, Fort Worth TX 76136. (218)626-9044. Fax: (218)626-2796. E-mail: cla@clalonestar.com. Website: www.clalonestar.com. **Contact:** Frank Dell, president. Estab. 1997. Members are professional/nonprofessional industry people, fans of classic country music. Members must be active in the country music industry (country music)—artists, songwriters, promoters, record companies, merchandisers, musicians, country radio station disc jockeys and fans of country music. Purpose is to promote classic country music, educate, establish the country classic legends Hall of Fame in Fort Worth, Texas, help new talent, hold annual conventions and award shows. Offers competitions, instruction, newsletter, lectures, workshops, performance opportunities and evaluation services. Applications accepted year-round. Membership fee: $100/industry; $50/artist, musician, songwriters; $25/fans; $20 senior citizens.

COUNTRY MUSIC ASSOCIATION OF TEXAS

P.O. Box 549, Troy TX 76579. (254)938-2454. Fax: (254)938-2049. **Contact:** Bud Fisher, founder/director. Estab. 1989. Open to songwriters, singers, pickers, fans and other professionals of all ages from all over the world. Members are interested in country music, especially traditional, classics. Purpose is to promote traditional and independent country music. Offers performance opportunities and evaluation services. Applications accepted year-round. Membership fee: $29.95/year.

Tips "Membership has grown to over 4,000 fans, musicians and songwriters, making it one of the largest state organizations in America. We hold numerous functions throughout the year and we have helped many local recording artists chart their releases nationwide and in Europe. Texas country music is hot!"

COUNTRY MUSIC SHOWCASE INTERNATIONAL, INC.

P.O. Box 368, Carlisle IA 50047. (515)989-3748. E-mail: haroldl@cmshowcase.org. Website: www.cmshowcase. org or www.cmshowcase.org/doorway.htm. **Contact:** Harold L. Luick, CEO. "We are an online nonprofit website for public use, supported by donations, free will offerings, and operated, maintained entirely by volunteers."

☑ DALLAS SONGWRITERS ASSOCIATION

Sammons Center for the Arts, 3630 Harry Hines, Box 20, Dallas TX 75219. (214)750-0916. Fax: (214)692-1392. E-mail: info@dallassongwriters.org. Website: www.dallassongwriters.org. **Contact:** Alex Townes, membership director. President: Ron Grimes. Founding President Emeritis: Barbara McMillen. Estab. 1986. Serves songwriters and lyricists of Dallas/Ft. Worth metroplex. Members are adults ages 18-65, Dallas/Ft. Worth area songwriters/lyricists who are or aspire to be professionals. Purpose is to provide songwriters an opportunity to meet other songwriters, share information, find co-writers and support each other through group discussions at monthly meetings; to provide songwriters an opportunity to have their songs heard and critiqued by peers and professionals by playing cassettes and providing an open mike at monthly meetings and by offering contests judged by publishers; to provide songwriters opportunities to meet other music business professionals by inviting guest speakers to monthly meetings and the Dallas Songwriters Seminar; and to provide songwriters opportunities to learn more about the craft of songwriting and the business of music by presenting mini-workshops at each monthly meeting. "We offer a chance for the songwriter to learn from peers and industry professionals and an opportunity to belong to a supportive group environment to encourage the individual to continue his/her songwriting endeavors." Offers competitions (including the Annual Song Contest with over $5,000 in prizes, and the Quarterly Lyric Contest), field trips, instruction, lectures, newsletter, performance opportunities, social outings, workshops and seminars. "Our members are eligible for discounts at several local music stores and seminars." Applications accepted year-round. Membership fee: $45. "When inquiring by phone, please leave complete mailing address and phone number where you can be reached day and night."

THE DRAMATISTS GUILD OF AMERICA, INC.

(formerly The Dramatists Guild, Inc.), 1501 Broadway, Suite 701, New York NY 10036. (212)398-9366. Fax: (212)944-0420. E-mail: membership@dramaguild.com. Website: www.dramatistsguild.com. **Contact:** Tom Epstein, membership director. "For over three-quarters of a century, The Dramatists Guild has been the professional association of playwrights, composers and lyricists, with more than 6,000 members across the country. All theater writers, whether produced or not, are eligible for Associate membership ($75/year); those who are engaged in a drama-related field but are not a playwright are eligible for Subscribing membership ($25/year); students enrolled in writing degree programs at colleges or universities are eligible for Student membership ($35/year); writers who have been produced on Broadway, Off-Broadway or on the main stage of a LORT theater are eligible for Active membership ($125/year). The Guild offers its members the following activities and services: use of the Guild's contracts (including the Approved Production Contract for Broadway, the Off-Broadway contract, the LORT contract, the collaboration agreements for both musicals and drama, the 99 Seat Theatre Plan contract, the Small Theatre contract, commissioning agreements, and the Underlying Rights Agreements contract; advice on all theatrical contracts including Broadway, Off-Broadway, regional, showcase, Equity-waiver, dinner theater and collaboration contracts); a nationwide toll-free number for all members with business or contract questions or problems; advice and information on a wide spectrum of issues affecting writers; free and/or discounted ticket service; symposia led by experienced professionals in major cities nationwide; access to a health insurance programs and a group term life insurance plan; and a spacious meeting room which can accommodate up to 50 people for readings and auditions on a rental basis. The Guild's publications are: *The Dramatist*, a bimonthly journal containing articles on all aspects of the theater (which includes *The Dramatists Guild Newsletter*, with announcements of all Guild activities and current information of interest to dramatists); and an annual resource directory with up-to-date information on agents, grants, producers, playwriting contests, conferences and workshops.

THE FIELD

161 Sixth Ave., New York NY 10013. (212)691-6969. Fax: (212)255-2053. E-mail: info@thefield.org. Website: www.thefield.org. **Contact:** Jay House, manager, programs & outreach. Estab. 1986. "The Field gives independent performing artists the tools to develop and sustain their creative and professional lives, while allowing the public to have immediate, direct access to a remarkable range of contemporary artwork. The organization was started by eight emerging artists who shared common roots in contemporary dance and theater. Meeting regularly, these artists created a structure to help each other improve their artwork, and counter the isolation that often comes with the territory of an artistic career. The Field offers a comprehensive program structure similar to an urban artists' residency or graduate program. Participants select from a broad array of programs and services including art development workshops, performance opportunities, career management training and development, fundraising consultations, fiscal sponsorship, informational publications, and artist residencies. The Field's goal is to help artists develop their best artwork by deepening the artistic process and finding effective ways to bring that art into the marketplace. Most Field programs cost under $150, and tickets to our performance events are $19. In addition, since 1992, The Field has coordinated a network of satellite sites in Atlanta, Chicago, Houston, Miami, North Adams (MA), Philadelphia, Plainfield (MA), Phoenix, Rochester (NY), Salt Lake City, San Francisco, Seattle, Tucson, Richmond (VA), Washington, DC and Tokyo, Japan. The Field is the only organization in New York that provides comprehensive programming for independent performing artists on a completely non-exclusive basis. Programs are open to artists from all disciplines, aesthetic viewpoints, and levels of development." Offers workshops and performance opportunities on a seasonal basis. Applications accepted year-round. Membership fee: $85/year.

Tips "There are two new additions to the field: IPARC (Independent Artists Resource Center) and GoTour. Located at The Field's office, IPARC offers fund-raising resources and hands-on assistance, including databases such as the Foundation Directory Online, computer workstations, and a library of books, journals, and information directories. One-on-one assistance and consultations are also available to guide users through grant writing and other fund-raising endeavors. GoTour (www.gotour.org) is a free website offering independent artists the resources they need to take their show on the road. Visitors log on for free and access a national arts network where they can search for venues, network with artists nationwide, find media contacts, read advice from other artists and arts professionals, add information on their local arts community, post tour anecdotes, and list concert informaton and classified ads."

☑ FILM MUSIC NETWORK

10601 Wilshire Blvd., Los Angeles CA 90025. 1-888-456-5020 or (310)575-1820. E-mail: info@filmmusic.net. Website: www.filmmusicworld.com or www.filmmusic.net. L.A. Chapter Manager: Joy Taylor. NY Chapter Manager: Beth Krakower. SF Chapter Manager: Thomas Dowrie.

THE FOLK ALLIANCE (North American Folk Music and Dance Alliance)

962 Wayne Ave., Suite 902, Silver Springs MD 20910-4480. (301)588-8185. Fax: (301)588-8186. E-mail: fa@folk.org. Website: www.folk.org. **Contact:** Tony Ziselberger, member services director. Executive Director: Phyllis Barney. Estab. 1989.

  • Also see the listing for Folk Alliance Annual Conference in the Workshops section of this book.

Members are organizations and individuals involved in traditional and contemporary folk music and dance in the US and Canada (in any genre—blues, bluegrass, Celtic, Latino, old-time, singer/songwriter, etc.). The Folk Alliance hosts its annual conference (which includes performance showcases) in late February at different locations throughout US and Canada. The conferences include workshops, panel discussions, the largest all folk exhibit hall and showcases. The Folk Alliance also serves members with their newsletter and through education, advocacy and field development. Memberships accepted year-round. Membership fee: $70 ($90 Canadian)/year for individual (voting); $150-505 ($230-700 Canadian)/year for organizational. "We do not offer songwriting contests, but do host performance showcases."

☑ FORT WORTH SONGWRITERS ASSOCIATION

P.O. Box 162443, Fort Worth TX 76161. (817)654-5400. E-mail: info@fwsa.com. Website: www.fwsa.com. President: John Terry. Executive Vice President: Neely Reynolds. Vice President Publications: Scott Davis. Estab. 1992. Members are ages 18-83, beginners up to and including published writers. Interests cover gospel, country, western swing, rock, pop, bluegrass and blues. Purpose is to allow songwriters to become more proficient at songwriting; to provide an opportunity for their efforts to be performed before a live audience; to provide songwriters an opportunity to meet co-writers. "We provide our members free critiques of their efforts. We provide a monthly newsletter outlining current happenings in the business of songwriting. We offer competitions and mini workshops with guest speakers from the music industry. We promote a weekly open 'mic' for singers of original material, and hold invitational songwriter showcase events a various times throughout the year. Each year, we hold a Christmas Song Contest, judged by independent music industry professionals.

We also offer free web pages for members or links to member websites." Applications accepted year-round. Membership fee: $35.

☑ GEORGIA MUSIC INDUSTRY ASSOCIATION, INC.

P.O. Box 550314, Atlanta GA 30355. (404)633-7772. E-mail: gmia_att@bellsouth.net. Website: www.gmia.org. **Contact:** Janelaine Eller, president. Vice President: Sandra Ponder. Estab. 1978. "The Georgia Music Industry Association (GMIA), formerly the Atlanta Songwriter's Association, was formed in 1979 by a group of songwriters to provide an outlet to create and collaborate with fellow songwriters, and to provide an avenue for networking within the music community. The group's main purpose has always been to promote and encourage the craft of songwriting and to offer opportunities to those writers and performers who have set goals for themselves in the music business. GMIA does this by tying together talented performance artists and songwriters with music industry professionals, media representatives, and financial institutions. GMIA has formed alliances with an advisory board that is national in scope and that offers expertise to GMIA members at educational panels, seminars, and showcases." Events include songwriting showcase competitions, "Georgia's Best" Performance Showcase, Monthly Song Critiques, and a cyber-newsletter.

GOSPEL MUSIC ASSOCIATION

1205 Division St., Nashville TN 37203. (615)242-0303. E-mail: joy@gospelmusic.org. Website: www.gospelmusic.org. **Contact:** Joy T. Fletcher, vice president of events and programming. Estab. 1964. Serves songwriters, musicians and anyone directly involved in or who supports gospel music. Professional members include advertising agencies, musicians, agents/managers, composers, retailers, music publishers, print and broadcast media, and other members of the recording industry. Associate members include supporters of gospel music and those whose involvement in the industry does not provide them with income. The primary purpose of the GMA is to expose, promote, and celebrate the Gospel through music. A GMA membership offers a music library, newsletters, performance experiences and workshops, as well as networking opportunities. Applications accepted year-round. Membership fee: $85/year (professional); $60/year (associate); and $25/year (college student).

🌐 THE GUILD OF INTERNATIONAL SONGWRITERS & COMPOSERS

Sovereign House, 12 Trewartha Rd., Praa Sands, Penzance, Cornwall TR20 9ST England. Phone: (01736)762826. Fax: (01736)763328. E-mail: songmag@aol.com. Website: www.songwriters-guild.com. **Contact:** C.A. Jones, secretary. Serves songwriters, musicians, record companies, music publishers, etc. "Our members are amateur and professional songwriters and composers, musicians, publishers, studio owners and producers. Membership is open to all persons throughout the world of any age and ability, from amateur to professional. The Guild gives advice and services relating to the music industry. A free magazine is available upon request with an SAE or 3 IRCs. We provide contact information for artists, record companies, music publishers, industry organizations; free copyright service; *Songwriting & Composing Magazine*; and many additional free services." Applications accepted year-round. Annual dues: £45 in the U.K.; £50 in E.E.C. countries; £50 overseas (subscriptions in pounds sterling only).

HAWAI'I SONGWRITERS ASSOCIATION

P.O. Box 10248, Honolulu HI 96816. (808)988-6878. Fax: (808)988-6236. E-mail: stanrubens@aol.com Website: www.stanrubens.com. **Contact:** Stan Rubens, secretary. Estab. 1972. "We have two classes of membership: Professional (must have had at least one song commercially published and for sale to general public) and Regular (any one who wants to join and share in our activities). Both classes can vote equally, but only Professional members can hold office. Must be 18 years old to join. Our members include musicians, entertainers and record producers. Membership is world-wide and open to all varieties of music, not just ethnic Hawaiian. President, Stan Rubens, has published 4 albums." Offers competitions, instruction, monthly newsletter, lectures, workshops, performance opportunities and evaluation services. Applications accepted year-round. Membership fee: $24.

HOUSTON FORT BEND SONGWRITERS ASSOCIATION

(formerly Fort Bend Songwriters Association), P.O. Box 1273, Richmond TX 77406. (281)573-5318. E-mail: tony@katrose.com. Website: www.hfbsa.org. President: Gary Taylor. Vice President: Monty West. Estab. 1991. Serves "any person, amateur or professional, interested in songwriting or music. Our members write pop, rock, country, rockabilly, gospel, R&B, children's music and musical plays." Open to all, regardless of geographic location or professional status. The FBSA provides its membership with help to perfect their songwriting crafts. The FBSA provides instruction for beginning writers and publishing and artist tips for the more accomplished writer. The FBSA networks with producers, publishers, music industry professionals and other songwriting groups to help members place songs. Offers competitions, field trips, instruction, lectures, newsletter, performance opportunities, workshops, mail-in critiques and collaboration opportunities. Applications accepted year-round. Membership fees are: Regular: $35; Renewals; $25; Band: $45; Associate: $20; and Lifetime: $250. For more information send SASE.

⋈ THE INDIANAPOLIS SONGWRITERS ASSOCIATION, INC.

P.O. Box 26203, Indianapolis IN 46226. E-mail: president@indysongwriters.net. Website: www.indysongwriters .net. **Contact:** Jody FitzGibbon, president. Estab. 1983. Purpose is "to create an affiliation of serious-minded songwriters, promote the artistic value of the musical composition, the business of music and recognition for the songwriter and his craft." Sponsors quarterly newsletter, monthly meetings, periodic showcases and periodic seminars and workshops. "The monthly critiques are helpful for improving songwriting skills. The meetings offer opportunities to share information concerning publishing, demos, etc. Also offers monthly tip sheets. In addition, it provides the opportunity for members to meet co-writers." Membership fees: Regular $20/year; Family/Bank: $30/year.

✓ INTERNATIONAL BLUEGRASS MUSIC ASSOCIATION (IBMA)

2 Music Circle South, Suite 100, Nashville TN 37203. 1(888)GET-IBMA. Fax: (615)256-0450. E-mail: info@ibma. org. Website: www.ibma.org. Member Services: Jill Snider. Estab. 1985. Serves songwriters, musicians and professionals in bluegrass music. "IBMA is a trade association composed of people and organizations involved professionally and semi-professionally in the bluegrass music industry, including performers, agents, songwriters, music publishers, promoters, print and broadcast media, local associations, recording manufacturers and distributors. Voting members must be currently or formerly involved in the bluegrass industry as full or part-time professionals. A songwriter attempting to become professionally involved in our field would be eligible. Our mission statement reads: "IBMA: Working together for high standards of professionalism, a greater appreciation for our music, and the success of the world-wide bluegrass music community." IBMA publishes a bi-monthly *International Bluegrass*, holds an annual trade show/convention with a songwriters showcase in the fall, represents our field outside the bluegrass music community, and compiles and disseminates databases of bluegrass related resources and organizations. Market research on the bluegrass consumer is available and we offer Bluegrass in the Schools information and matching grants. The primary value in this organization for a songwriter is having current information about the bluegrass music field and contacts with other songwriters, publishers, musicians and record companies." Offers workshops, liability insurance, rental car discounts, consultation and databases of record companies, radio stations, press, organizations and gigs. Applications accepted year-round. Membership fee: for a non-voting patron $40/year; for an individual voting professional $65/year; for an organizational voting professional $150/year.

⊕ INTERNATIONAL SONGWRITERS ASSOCIATION LTD.

37b New Cavendish St., London WI England. (0171)486-5353. E-mail: jliddane@songwriter.iol.ie. Website: www.songwriter.co.uk. **Contact:** Anna M. Sinden, membership department. Serves songwriters and music publishers. "The ISA headquarters is in Limerick City, Ireland, and from there it provides its members with assessment services, copyright services, legal and other advisory services and an investigations service, plus a magazine for one yearly fee. Our members are songwriters in more than 50 countries worldwide, of all ages. There are no qualifications, but applicants under 18 are not accepted. We provide information and assistance to professional or semi-professional songwriters. Our publication, *Songwriter*, which was founded in 1967, features detailed exclusive interviews with songwriters and music publishers, as well as directory information of value to writers." Offers competitions, instruction, library, newsletter and a weekly e-mail newsletter *Songwriter Newswire*. Applications accepted year-round. Membership fee for European writers is £19.95; for non-European writers, US $30.

✓ INTERNATIONAL SONGWRITERS GUILD

5108 Louvre Ave., Orlando FL 31028. (407)851-5328. E-mail: isg2000@yahoo.com. **Contact:** Russ Robinson, president. Estab. 1977.
Members are lyricists, composers, performers, arrangers, publishers, songwriters of all ages, backgrounds and skill levels. Open to anyone interested in songwriting and in improving their songwriting skills. The main purpose of the organization is to guide and educate those people wanting to write commercial music successfully. We use monthly critiquing sessions of approximately 10 songs, where the top 5 winners are announced in the next monthly newsletter, "Guild Tidings." Offers competitions, lectures, performance opportunities, instruction, evaluation services, newsletters, workshops and industry contacts. Applications accepted year-round. Membership fee: $35 annually.
- Russ Robinson, President of the Guild, played piano for Judy Garland and Frank Sinatra, among others, and was a member of "The Modernairs" (five-part harmony vocals). He is a writer of national commercials, and is well-known in the music and film industry.

IRISH MUSIC RIGHTS ORGANISATION
Copyright House, Pembroke Row, Dublin 2 Ireland. Phone: +353 1 6614544. Fax: +353 1 6613789. E-mail: info@imro.ie. Website: www.imro.ie. Membership Department: Justin Dowling. Estab. 1988. "For songwriters, composers and publishers who must have one work which has been recorded and released for sale, or broadcast on radio or television in the past two years, or who have had their works performed at a live performance." The main purpose of this organization is "the collection and distribution of royalties for the public performance of copyright music." Offers newsletter and workshops. Applications accepted year-round.

JUST PLAIN FOLKS MUSIC ORGANIZATION
(www.jpfolks.com), 1315 N. Butler, Indianapolis IN 46219. (317)513-6557. E-mail: info@jpfolks.com. Website: www.jpfolks.com. **Contact:** Brian Austin Whitney (brian@jpfolks.com), founder or Linda Berger (linda@jpfolks.com), projects director. Estab. 1998. "Just Plain Folks is among the world's largest Music Organizations. Our members cover nearly every musical style and professional field, from songwriters, artists, publishers, producers, record labels, entertainment attorneys, publicists and PR experts, performing rights organization staffers, live and recording engineers, educators, music students, musical instrument manufacturers, TV, Radio and Print Media and almost every major Internet Music entity. Representing all 50 US States and over 90 countries worldwide, we have members of all ages, musical styles and levels of success, including winners and nominees of every major music industry award, as well as those just starting out. A complete demographics listing of our group is available on our website. Whether you are a #1 hit songwriter or artist, or the newest kid on the block, you are welcome to join. Membership does require an active e-mail account." The purpose of this organization is "to share wisdom, ideas and experiences with others who have been there, and to help educate those who have yet to make the journey. Just Plain Folks provides its members with a friendly networking and support community that uses the power of the Internet and combines it with good old-fashioned human interaction. We help promote our members ready for success and educate those still learning." Offers special programs to members, including:
- *Just Plain Notes Newsletter:* Members receive our frequent e-mail newsletters full of expert info on how to succeed in the music business, profiles of members successes and advice, opportunities to develop your career and tons of first-person networking contacts to help you along the way. (Note: we send this out 2-3 times/month via e-mail only.)
- *Just Plain Mentors:* We have some of the friendliest expert educators, writers, artists and industry folks in the business who volunteer their time as part of our Mentor Staff. Included are John and JoAnn Braheny, Jason Blume, Harriet Schock, Pat and Pete Luboff, Derek Sivers, Jodi Krangle, Steve Seskin, Alan O'Day, Walter Egan, Sara Light, Danny Arena, Barbara Cloyd, Michael Laskow, Anne Leighton, Mark Keefner, Valerie DeLaCruz, Karen Angela Moore, Ben McLane, Jack Perricone, Pat Pattison, Mark Baxter, Harold Payne, Joey Arreguin, John Beland, Susan Gibson, Art Twain, Diane Rapaport, Nancy Moran, Fett, Mike Dunbar, R. Chris Murphy, Bobby Borg, Paul Reisler, and many others.
- *JPFolks.com Website:* Our home page serves as your pathway to the resources and members of the group worldwide. With message boards, lyric feedback forums, featured members music, member profiles, member contact listings, member links pages, chapter homepages, demographics information, our Internet radio station and all the back issues of our newsletter, "Just Plain Notes."
- *Roadtrips:* We regularly tour the US and Canada, hosting showcases, workshops and friendly member gatherings in each city we visit. We provide opportunities for all our members, at all levels and welcome everyone to our events. Most events are free of charge.
- *Chapters:* Just Plain Folks has over 100 active local chapters around the world run by local member volunteer coordinators. Each chapter is unique but many host monthly networking gatherings, showcases, educational workshops and community service events. To join a chapter, or start one in your city, please visit the chapter section of the jpfolks.com website for a current list of chapters and guidelines.
- *Music Awards:* Just Plain Folks has one of the largest and most diverse Member Music Awards programs in the world. The most recent awards involved over 10,000 albums and 140,000 songs in over 50 genres. Music Award nominees and winners receive featured performance slots at showcases around the world throughout the year. Current submission instructions can be found on the website in the Awards section.

Membership requests are accepted year-round. "To become a member, simply send an e-mail to join@jpfolks.com with the words 'I Want To Join Just Plain Folks.' In the e-mail, include your name, address, website (if applicable) and phone number for our files." There are currently no membership fees.
Tips "Our motto is 'We're All In This Together!'"

KNOXVILLE SONGWRITERS ASSOCIATION
P.O. Box 603, Knoxville TN 37901. (865)673-4778. E-mail: greatsongs@yahoo.com. **Contact:** Dana Correll, Newsletter Editor. President: Richard McKee. Estab. 1982. Serves songwriters of all ages. "Some have been members since 1982, others are beginners. Members must be interested in learning the craft of songwriting.

Not only a learning organization but a support group of songwriters who wants to learn what to do with their song after it has been written. We open doors for aspiring writers. The primary benefit of membership is to supply information to the writer on how to write a song. Many members have received major cuts.'' Offers showcases, instruction, lectures, library, newsletter, performance opportunities, evaluation services and workshops. Applications accepted year-round. Membership fee: $30/year.

THE LAS VEGAS SONGWRITERS ASSOCIATION

P.O. Box 42683, Las Vegas NV 89116-0683. (702)223-7255. E-mail: azsongwriters@cox.net. Website: www.lasv egassongwriters.com. **Contact:** Betty Kay Miller, president. Secretary: Barbara Jean Smith. Estab. 1980. ''We are an educational, nonprofit organization dedicated to improving the art and craft of the songwriter. We want members who are serious about their craft. We want our members to respect their craft and to treat it as a business. Members must be at least 18 years of age. We offer quarterly newsletters, monthly information meetings, workshops three times a month and quarterly seminars with professionals in the music business. We provide support and encouragement to both new and more experienced songwriters. We critique each song or lyric that's presented during workshops, we make suggestions on changes—if needed. We help turn amateur writers into professionals. Several of our songwriters have had their songs recorded on both independent and major labels.'' Dues: $30/year.

☑ LOS ANGELES MUSIC NETWORK

P.O. Box 2446, Toluca Lake CA 91610-2446. (818)769-6095. E-mail: info@lamn.com. Website: www.lamn.com. **Contact:** Tess Taylor, president. Membership Director: Roslynn Cobarrubias. Estab. 1988. ''Connections. Facts. Career advancement. All that is available with your membership in the Los Angeles Music Network (LAMN). Our emphasis is on sharing knowledge and information, giving you access to top professionals and promoting career development. LAMN an association of music industry professionals, i.e., artists, singers, songwriters, and people who work in various aspects of the music industry with an emphasis on the creative. Members are ambitious and interested in advancing their careers. LAMN promotes career advancement, communication and continuing education among music industry professionals and top executives. LAMN sponsors industry events and educational panels held bi-monthly at venues in the Los Angeles area, and now in other major music hubs around the country (New York, Las Vegas, Chicago).'' Offers instruction, newsletter, lectures, seminars, music industry job listings, career counseling, résumé publishing, mentor network, résumé resource guide and many professional networking opportunities. See our website for current job listings and a calendar of upcoming events. Applications accepted year-round. Annual membership fee is $110 (subject to change without notice).

LOUISIANA SONGWRITERS ASSOCIATION

P.O. Box 80425, Baton Rouge LA 70898-0425. (504)443-5390. E-mail: zimshah@aol.com. Website: www.lasong writers.org. **Contact:** Connie Zimmerman, membership coordinator. Serves songwriters. ''LSA was organized to educate songwriters in all areas of their trade, and promote the art of songwriting in Louisiana. LSA is honored to have a growing number of songwriters from other states join LSA and fellowship with us. LSA membership is open to people interested in songwriting, regardless of age, musical ability, musical preference, ethnic background, etc. ''This year marks our 20th anniversary and also a new direction for our organization. Our group is now driven by special projects (short term), which are coordinated and implemented by our membership. This arms our members with the knowledge and experience necessary to succeed within the industry.'' LSA offers competitions, lectures, library, newsletter, directory, marketing, performance opportunities, workshops, discounts on various music-related books and magazines, discounts on studio time, and we are developing a service manual that will contain information on music related topics, such as copyrighting, licensing, etc.'' Also offers regular showcases in Baton Rouge and New Orleans. General membership dues: $25/year, 45/2 years.

☑ ✎ MANITOBA AUDIO RECORDING INDUSTRY ASSOCIATION (MARIA)

1-376 Donald St., Winnipeg MB R3B 2J2 Canada. (204)942-8650. Fax: (204)942-6083. E-mail: info@manitobamu sic.com. Website: www.manitobamusic.com. **Contact:** Hal Brolund, member services/office coordinator. Estab. 1987. Organization consists of ''songwriters, producers, agents, musicians, managers, retailers, publicists, radio, talent buyers, media, record labels, etc. (no age limit, no skill level minimum). Must have interest in the future of Manitoba's sound recording industry.'' The main purpose of MARIA is to foster growth in all areas of the Manitoba music industry primarily through education, promotion and lobbying. Offers newsletter, lectures, directory of Manitoba's music industry, workshops and performance opportunities; also presents demo critiquing sessions and comprehensive member discount program featuring a host of participating Manitoba businesses. MARIA is also involved with the Prairie Music Weekend festival, conference and awards show. Applications accepted year-round. Membership fee: $50 (Canadian funds).

MEET THE COMPOSER

75 Ninth Ave, 3R Suite C, New York NY 10011. (212)645-6949. Fax: (212)645-9669. E-mail: mtrevino@meetthec omposer.org. Website: www.meetthecomposer.org. Estab. 1974. "Meet The Composer serves composers working in all styles of music, at every career stage, through a variety of grant programs and information resources. A nonprofit organization, Meet The Composer raises money from foundations, corporations, individual patrons and government sources and designs programs that support all genres of music—from folk, ethnic, jazz, electronic, symphonic, and chamber to choral, music theater, opera and dance. Meet The Composer awards grants for composer fees to non-profit organizations that perform, present, or commission original works. This is not a membership organization; all composers are eligible for support. Meet The Composer was founded in 1974 to increase artistic and financial opportunities for composers by fostering the creation, performance, dissemination, and appreciation of their music." Offers grant programs and information services. Deadlines vary for each grant program.

☑ MEMPHIS SONGWRITERS' ASSOCIATION

4746 Spottswood, #191, Memphis TN 38117-4815. Website: www.memphissongwriters.org. **Contact:** Jon Dillard, president. Estab. 1973. "MSA is a nonprofit songwriters organization serving songwriters nationally. Our mission is to dedicate our services to promote, advance, and help songwriters in the composition of music, lyrics and songs; to work for better conditions in our profession; and to secure and protect the rights of MSA songwriters. We also supply copyright forms. We offer critique sessions for writers at our monthly meetings. We also have monthly open mic songwriters night to encourage creativity, networking and co-writing. We host an annual songwriter's seminar and an annual songwriter's showcase, as well as a bi-monthly guest speaker series, which provide education, competition and entertainment for the songwriter. In addition, our members receive a bimonthly newsletter to keep them informed of MSA activities, demo services and opportunities in the songwriting field." Annual fee: $50; Student/Senior: $35.

MINNESOTA ASSOCIATION OF SONGWRITERS

P.O. Box 333, Chicago City MN 55013. (651)254-9779. E-mail: info@mnsongwriters.org. Website: www.mnsong writers.org. "Includes a wide variety of members, ranging in age from 18 to 80; type of music is very diverse ranging from alternative rock to contemporary Christian; skill levels range from beginning songwriters to writers with recorded and published material. Main requirement is an interest in songwriting. Although most members come from the Minneapolis-St. Paul area, others come in from surrounding cities, nearby Wisconsin, and other parts of the country. Some members are fulltime musicians, but most represent a wide variety of occupations. MAS is a nonprofit community of songwriters which informs, educates, inspires and assists its members in the art and business of songwriting." Offers instruction, newsletter, lectures, workshops, performance opportunities and evaluation services. Applications accepted year-round. Membership fee: Individual: $25; Business: $65.

Tips "Members are kept current on resources and opportunities. Original works are played at meetings and are critiqued by involved members. Through this process, writers hone their skills and gain experience and confidence in submitting their works to others."

☑ MUSICIANS CONTACT

P.O. Box 788, Woodland Hills CA 91365. (818)888-7879. Fax: (818)340-1446. E-mail: info@musicianscontact.c om. Website: www.musicianscontact.com. **Contact:** Howard Stirling, president. Estab. 1969. "The primary source of paying jobs for musicians and vocalists nationwide. Job opportunities are posted daily on the Internet. Also offers exposure to the music industry for solo artists and complete acts seeking representation."

NASHVILLE SONGWRITERS ASSOCIATION INTERNATIONAL (NSAI)

1701 W. End Ave., 3rd Floor, Nashville TN 37203. (615)256-3354 or (800)321-6008. Fax: (615)256-0034. E-mail: nsai@nashvillesongwriters.com. Website: www.nashvillesongwriters.com. Executive Director: Barton Herbison. Purpose: a not-for-profit service organization for both aspiring and professional songwriters in all fields of music. Membership: Spans the United States and several foreign countries. Songwriters may apply in one of four annual categories: Active ($100—for songwriters who have at least one song contractually signed to a publisher affiliated with ASCAP, BMI or SESAC); Associate ($100—for songwriters who are not yet published or for anyone wishing to support songwriters); Student ($80—for full-time college students or for students of an accredited senior high school); Professional ($100—for songwriters who derive their primary source of income from songwriting or who are generally recognized as such by the professional songwriting community); Foreign ($75—for Active, Associate, and Student members residing outside the US). Membership benefits: music industry information and advice, song evaluations by mail, quarterly newsletter, access to industry professionals through weekly Nashville workshop and several annual events, regional workshops, use of office facilities, discounts on books and discounts on NSAI's three annual events. There are also "branch" workshops of NSAI. Workshops must meet certain standards and are accountable to NSAI. Interested coordinators may apply to NSAI.

- Also see the listing for NSAI Songwriters Symposium (formerly NSAI Spring Symposium) in the Workshops section of this book.

☑ NATIONAL ACADEMY OF POPULAR MUSIC (NAPM)

330 W. 58th St., Suite 411, New York NY 10019-1827. (212)957-9230. Fax: (212)957-9227. E-mail: 73751.1142@compuserve.com. Website: www.shof.org. **Contact:** Bob Leone, projects director. Managing Director: April Anderson. Estab. 1969. "The majority of our members are songwriters, but also on NAPM's rolls are music publishers, producers, record company executives, music attorneys, and lovers of popular music of all ages. Professional members are affiliated with ASCAP, BMI and/or SESAC; or are employed by music industry firms. Associate membership, however, merely requires a completed application and $25 dues. NAPM was formed to determine a variety of ways to celebrate the songwriter (e.g., induction into the Songwriters Hall of Fame). We also provide educational and networking opportunities to our members through our workshop and showcase programs." Offers newsletter, workshops, performance opportunities, networking meetings with industry pros and scholarships for excellence in songwriting. Applications accepted year-round. Membership fee: $25 and up.

THE NATIONAL ASSOCIATION OF COMPOSERS/USA (NACUSA)

P.O. Box 49256, Barrington Station, Los Angeles CA 90049. E-mail: nacusa@music-usa.org. Website: www.music-usa.org/nacusa. **Contact:** Deon Nielsen Price, president. Estab. 1932. Serves songwriters, musicians and classical composers. "We are of most value to the concert hall composer. Members are serious music composers of all ages and from all parts of the country, who have a real interest in composing, performing, and listening to modern concert hall music. The main purpose of our organization is to perform, publish, broadcast and write news about composers of serious concert hall music—mostly chamber and solo pieces. Composers may achieve national notice of their work through our newsletter and concerts, and the fairly rare feeling of supporting a non-commercial music enterprise dedicated to raising the musical and social position of the serious composer." Offers competitions, lectures, performance opportunities, library and newsletter. Applications accepted year-round. Membership fee: National (regular): $25; National (students/seniors): $15.

- Also see the listing for NACUSA Young Composers' Competition in the Contests section of this book.

Tips "99% of the money earned in music is earned, or so it seems, by popular songwriters who might feel they owe the art of music something, and this is one way they might help support that art. It's a chance to foster fraternal solidarity with their less prosperous, but wonderfully interesting classical colleagues at a time when the very existence of serious art seems to be questioned by the general populace."

☑ NATIONAL SOCIETY OF MEN AND WOMEN OF THE MUSIC BUSINESS (WOMB)

P.O. Box 5170, Beverly Hills CA 90209-5170. (323)210-1515. Fax: (323)467-8468. Website: www.YuleJam.org. **Contact:** Director. Estab. 1996. "WOMB is a non-profit organization of top music industry professionals keeping music education and dreams alive for kids who attend inner-city high schools and community organizations around the U.S. Music industry professionals are encouraged to participate and make a difference in a child's life!" Programs include "WOMB's School Music Network": top music industry professionals volunteer 2-3 hours to visit inner-city high schools; "WOMB's Music for Music": organizes music instrument and material donation drives for schools through corporate sponsorships and events; Yule Jam, a charity concert and music instrument drive with proceeds going to local school music departments. Offers corporate sponsorships, events, performance opportunities and an e-mail newsletter. Future programs include afterschool music programs, college scholarships and special events. Volunteers, music instrument, material donations and corporate sponsorships accepted year-round.

NORTH FLORIDA CHRISTIAN MUSIC WRITERS ASSOCIATION

P.O. Box 61113, Jacksonville FL 32236. (904)786-2372. E-mail: justsongs@aol.com Website: www.christiansongwriter.com. **Contact:** Jackie Hand, president. Estab. 1974. "Members are people from all walks of life who promote Christian music—not just composers or performers, but anyone who wants to share today's message in song with the world. No age limit. Anyone interested in promoting Christian music is invited to join. If you are talented in several areas you might be asked to conduct a training session or workshop. Your expertise is wanted and needed by our group. The group's purpose is to serve God by using our God-given talents and abilities and to assist our fellow songwriters, getting their music in the best possible form to be ready for whatever door God chooses to open for them concerning their music. Members' works are included in songbooks published by our organization—also biographies." Offers competitions, performance opportunities, field trips, instruction, newsletter, workshops and critiques. This year we offer a new website featuring song clips by members as well as a short bio. Also featured is a special "Memorial Members" list honoring deceased members by keeping their music alive. The one time fee of $100 to place loved ones on the list includes a song clip on our website and entry privileges in our songwriting contest. Applications accepted year-round. Membership fee: $25/year ($35 for outside US), $35 for husband/wife team ($45 for outside US). "The 25th Anniversary Edition songbook of our members music (plus our 25 years as a songwriting organization) is $10 plus $3.00 S&H. White Tee Shirt with black graphic and message, "North Florida Christian Music Writers Association" and a graphic of a beautiful piano and other instruments on front is also $10 plus $3.00 S&H." Make checks payable to Jackie Hand.

Tips "If you are serious about your craft, you need fellowship with others who feel the same. A Christian songwriting organization is where you belong if you write Christian songs. We are now in a position to offer Sound Trax of your original music. Contact Winston Miller at #14 Blanding Blvd., Orange Park FL 32073 for prices. Phone him at (904)276-5022 or fax (904)276-2840."

OKLAHOMA SONGWRITERS & COMPOSERS ASSOCIATION

105 S. Glenn English, Cordell OK 73632. Website: www.oksongwriters.com. **Contact:** Ann Wilson, membership. Estab. 1983. Serves songwriters, musicians, professional writers and amateur writers. "A nonprofit, all-volunteer organization sponsored by Rose State College providing educational and networking opportunities for songwriters, lyricists, composers and performing musicians. All styles of music. We sponsor major workshops, open-mic nights, demo critiques and the *OSCA News*. Throughout the year we sponsor contests and original music showcases." Applications accepted year-round. Membership fee: $25 for new members, $15 for renewal, $15 for out of state newsletter only.

✔ OPERA AMERICA

1156 15th St., NW, Suite 810, Washington DC 20005-1704. (202)293-4466. Fax: (202)393-0735. E-mail: frontdesk @operaamerica.org. Website: www.operaamerica.org. **Contact:** Harv Wileman, membership coordinator. Estab. 1970. Members are composers, librettists, musicians, singers, and opera/music theater producers. "OPERA America maintains an extensive library of reference books and domestic and foreign music periodicals, and the most comprehensive operatic archive in the United States. OPERA America draws on these unique resources to supply information to its members." Offers conferences. Publishes online database of opera/music theater companies in the US and Canada, online directory of opera and musical performances world-wide and US, and an online directory of new works created and being developed by current-day composers and librettists, to encourage the performance of new works. Applications accepted year-round. Publishes 40-page magazine 10 times/year. Membership fee is on a sliding scale by membership level.

OUTMUSIC

P.O. Box 376, Old Chelsea Station, New York NY 10113-0376. (212)330-9197. E-mail: info@outmusic.com. Website: www.outmusic.com. **Contact:** Ed Mannix, communications director. Estab. 1990. "OUTMUSIC is comprised of gay men, lesbians, bisexuals and transgenders. They represent all different musical styles from rock to classical. Many are writers of original material. We are open to all levels of accomplishment—professional, amateur, and interested industry people. The only requirement for membership is an interest in the growth and visibility of music and lyrics created by the LGBT community. We supply our members with support and networking opportunities. In addition, we help to encourage artists to bring their work 'OUT' into the world." Offers newsletter, lectures, workshops, performance opportunities, networking, industry leads and monthly open mics. Sponsors Outmusic Awards. Applications accepted year-round. For membership information go to www.outmusic.com.

Tips "OUTMUSIC has spawned *The Gay Music Guide*, The Gay and Lesbian American Music Awards (GLAMA), several compilation albums and many independent recording projects."

✔ ⚏ PACIFIC MUSIC INDUSTRY ASSOCIATION

.#501-425 Carrall St., Vancouver BC V6B 6E3 Canada. (604)873-1914. Fax: (604)873-9686. E-mail: info@musicb c.org. Website: www.pmia.org. Estab. 1990. Serves "mostly young adults and up from semi-pro to professional. Writers, composers, performers, publishers, engineers, producers, broadcasters, studios, retailers, manufacturers, managers, publicists, entertainment lawyers and accountants, etc. Must work in some area of music industry." The main purpose of this organization is "to promote B.C. music and music industry; stimulate activity in B.C. industry; promote communication and address key issues." Offers competitions, newsletters, ongoing professional development and directory for the BC music industry. Applications accepted year-round. Membership fee: $50 Canadian (plus 7% GST).

PACIFIC NORTHWEST SONGWRITERS ASSOCIATION

P.O. Box 98564, Seattle WA 98198. (206)824-1568. E-mail: pnsapals@hotmail.com. "PNSA is a nonprofit organization, serving the songwriters of the Puget Sound area since 1977. Members have had songs recorded by national artists on singles, albums, videos and network television specials. Several have released their own albums and the group has done an album together. For only $45 per year, PNSA offers monthly workshops, a quarterly newsletter and direct contact with national artists, publishers, producers and record companies. New members are welcome and good times are guaranteed. And remember, the world always needs another great song!"

☑ PITTSBURGH SONGWRITERS ASSOCIATION

523 Scenery Dr., Elizabeth PA 15037. (412)751-9584. E-mail: vstragand@aol.com. Website: www.pittsburghson gwritersassociation.com. **Contact:** Van Stragand, president. Estab. 1983. "We are a non-profit organization dedicated to helping its members develop and market their songs. Writers of any age and experience level welcome. Current members are from 20s to 50s. All musical styles and interests are welcome. Our organization wants to serve as a source of quality material for publishers and other industry professionals. We assist members in developing their songs and their professional approach. We provide meetings, showcases, collaboration opportunities, instruction, industry guests, library and social outings. Annual dues: $25. We have no initiation fee. Prospective members are invited to attend two free meetings. Interested parties please call Van Stragand at (412)751-9584."

POP RECORD RESEARCH

10 Glen Ave., Norwalk CT 06850. E-mail: horar@earthlink.net. **Director:** Gary Theroux. Estab. 1962. Serves songwriters, musicians, writers, researchers and media. "We maintain archives of materials relating to music, TV and film, with special emphasis on recorded music (the hits and hitmakers 1877-present): bios, photos, reviews, interviews, discographies, chart data, clippings, films, videos, etc." Offers library and clearinghouse for accurate promotion/publicity to biographers, writers, reviewers, the media. Offers programming, annotation and photo source for reissues or retrospective album collections on any artist (singers, songwriters, musicians, etc.), also music consultation services for film or television projects. "There is no charge to include publicity, promotional or biographical materials in our archives. Artists, writers, composers, performers, producers, labels and publicists are always invited to add or keep us on their publicity/promotion mailing list with career data, updates, new releases and reissues of recorded performances, etc. Fees are assessed only for reference use by researchers, writers, biographers, reviewers, etc. Songwriters and composers (or their publicists) should keep or put us on their publicity mailing lists to ensure that the information we supply others on their careers, accomplishments, etc. is accurate and up-to-date."

☑ PORTLAND SONGWRITERS ASSOCIATION

P.O. Box 42389, Portland OR 97242. (503)914-1000. E-mail: info@pdxsongwriters.org. Website: www.pdxsong writers.org. Estab. 1991. **Contact:** JC Tubbs, President. "The PSA is a nonprofit organization providing education and opportunities that will assist writers in creating and marketing their songs. The PSA offers an annual National Songwriting Contest, monthly workshops, songwriter showcases, special performance venues, quarterly newsletter, mail-in critique service, discounted seminars by music industry pros." Annual dues: $35 (no eligibility requirements).

Tips "Although most of our members are from the Pacific Northwest, we offer services that can assist songwriters anywhere. Our goal is to provide information and contacts to help songwriters grow artistically and gain access to publishing, recording and related music markets. For more information, please call, write or e-mail."

☑ RHODE ISLAND SONGWRITERS' ASSOCIATION (RISA)

P.O. Box 367, Harmony RI 02829. (401)949-0747. E-mail: risa@risongwriters.com or hearingri@ids.net. Website: www.risongwriters.com. **Co-Chairs:** John Fuzek and Bill Furney. Estab. 1993. "Membership consists of novice and professional songwriters. RISA provides opportunities to the aspiring writer or performer as well as the established regional artists who have recordings, are published and perform regularly. The only eligibility requirement is an interest in the group and the group's goals. Non-writers are welcome as well." The main purpose is to "encourage, foster and conduct the art and craft of original musical and/or lyrical composition through education, information, collaboration and performance." Offers instruction, newsletter, lectures, workshops, performance opportunities and evaluation services. Applications accepted year-round. Membership fee: $25/year. "The group holds twice monthly critique sessions; twice monthly performer showcases (one performer featured) at a local coffeehouse; songwriter showcases (usually 6-8 performers); weekly open mikes; and a yearly songwriter festival called 'Hear In Rhode Island,' featuring approximately 50 Rhode Island acts, over two days."

☑ SAN DIEGO SONGWRITERS GUILD

3368 Governor Dr., Suite F-326, San Diego CA 92122. (619)615-8874. E-mail: sdsongwriters@hotmail.com. Website: www.sdsongwriters.org. **Contact:** Joseph Carmel, membership/correspondence. Estab. 1982. "Members range from their early 20s to senior citizens with a variety of skill levels. Several members perform and work full time in music. Many are published and have songs recorded. Some are getting major artist record cuts. Most members are from San Diego county. New writers are encouraged to participate and meet others. All musical styles are represented." The purpose of this organization is to "serve the needs of songwriters and artists, especially helping them in the business and craft of songwriting through industry guest appearances." Offers competitions, newsletter, workshops, performance opportunities, discounts on services offered by fellow members, in-person song pitches and evaluations by publishers, producers and A&R executives. Applications accepted year-round. Membership dues: $50 full; $30 student; $135 corporate sponsorship. Meeting admission for non-members: $20 (may be applied toward membership if joining within 30 days).

Tips "Members benefit most from participation in meetings and concerts. Generally, one major meeting held monthly on a Monday evening, at the Doubletree Hotel, Hazard Center, San Diego. Call for meeting details. Can join at meetings."

☑ SAN FRANCISCO FOLK MUSIC CLUB

885 Clayton, San Francisco CA 94117. (415)661-2217. E-mail: sffolk@aol.com. Website: www.sffmc.org. **Contact:** Membership Coordinator. Serves songwriters, musicians and anyone who enjoys folk music. "Our members range from ages 2 to 80. The only requirement is that members enjoy, appreciate and be interested in sharing folk music. As a focal point for the San Francisco Bay Area folk music community, the SFFMC provides opportunities for people to get together to share folk music, and the newsletter *The Folknik* disseminates information. We publish two songs an issue (six times a year) in our newsletter, our meetings provide an opportunity to share new songs, and at our camp-outs there are almost always songwriter workshops." Offers library, newsletter, informal performance opportunities, annual free folk festival, social outings and workshops. Applications accepted year-round. Membership fee: $10/year.

SESAC INC.

New York: 152 W. 57th St., 57th Floor, New York NY 10019. (212)586-3450. Fax: (212)489-5699. **Nashville:** 55 Music Square East, Nashville TN 37203. (615)320-0055. Fax: (615)329-9627. **Los Angeles:** 501 Santa Monica Blvd., Suite 450, Santa Monica CA 90401. (310)393-9671. Fax: (310)393-6497. **London:** 6 Kenrich Place, London WIH 3FF United Kingdom. (020)74869994. Website: www.sesac.com. **Contact:** Tim Fink, associate vice president writer/publisher relations. Chief Operating Officer: Pat Collins. Coordinator-Writer/Publisher Relations: Mandy Reilly. SESAC is a selective organization taking pride in having a repertory based on quality rather than quantity. Serves writers and publishers in all types of music who have their works performed by radio, television, nightclubs, cable TV, etc. Purpose of organization is to collect and distribute performance royalties to all active affiliates. As a SESAC affiliate, the individual may obtain equipment insurance at competitive rates. Tapes are reviewed upon invitation by the Writer/Publisher Relations dept.

☑ THE SINGER SONGWRITER INFORMATION LINE

9 Music Square S. #145, Nashville TN 37203. Information Hotline: (800)345-2694. Office: (615)792-2222. E-mail: cjstarlit@aol.com. Website: www.StarliteRecords.net. **Contact:** C.J. Reilly, owner. Estab. 1988. Purpose is to give advice over a free 1-800 number to anyone who writes music. All callers will receive a free publisher's list. Offers instruction, performance opportunities and evaluation services. Demo services and promotional videos for singers are also available.

Tips "We are a Nashville-based company. When people call, we try to answer questions regarding music publishing and record production."

☑ SOCIETY OF COMPOSERS & LYRICISTS

400 S. Beverly Dr., Suite 214, Beverly Hills CA 90212. (310)281-2812. Fax: (310)284-4861. E-mail: execdir@thescl.com. Website: www.thescl.com. The professional nonprofit trade organization for members actively engaged in writing music/lyrics for films, TV, and/or video games, or are students of film composition or songwriting for film. Primary mission is to advance the interests of the film and TV music community. Offers an award-winning quarterly publication, educational seminars, screenings, special member-only events, and other member benefits. Applications accepted year-round. Membership fee: $135 Full Membership (composers, lyricists, songwriters—film/TV music credits must be submitted); $85 Associate/Student Membership for composers, lyricists, songwriters without credits only; $135 Sponsor/Special Friend Membership (music editors, music supervisors, music attorneys, agents, etc.).

☑ SOCIETY OF COMPOSERS, AUTHORS AND MUSIC PUBLISHERS OF CANADA/SOCIÉTÉ CANADIENNE DES AUTEURS, COMPOSITEURS ET ÉDITEURS DE MUSIQUE (SOCAN)

, Head Office: 41 Valleybrook Dr., Toronto ON M3B 2S6 Canada. (800)55-SOCAN. Fax: (416)445-7108. Website: www.socan.ca. CEO: André LeBel. Vice President, Quebec & Atlantic Division and National Licensing: France Lafleur. Vice President, West Coast Division and National Member Services: Kent Sturgeon. The Society licenses public performance of music and distributes performance royalties to composers, lyricists, authors and music publishers. ASCAP, BMI and SESAC license the public performance of SOCAN's repertoire in the US.

SOCIETY OF COMPOSERS, INC.

Old Chelsea Station Box 450, New York NY 10113-0450. E-mail: secretary@societyofcomposers.org. Website: www.societyofcomposers.org. **Contact:** Gerald Warfield, General Manager, SCI National Office. Offers promotion of composition, performance opportunities and instruction for composers and performers both inside and out of academia. Applications accepted year-round. Membership fee: $50/year.

◪ SODRAC INC.

759 Victoria Square, Suite 420, Montreal QC H2Y 2J7 Canada. (514)845-3268. Fax: (514)845-3401. E-mail: sodrac@sodrac.com. Website: www.sodrac.com. **Contact:** Chantál Beaúdoin, membership department (author, composer and publisher) or Anita Raymond, membership department (visual artist and rights owner). Estab. 1985. "Sodrac was founded in 1985 on the initiative of songwriters and composers in order to manage the reproduction rights of authors, composers and publishers of musical repertoire of about 83 countries and more than 5,000 Canadian members, as well as over 25,000 national and international visual artists. SODRAC is the only Reproduction Rights Society in Canada where both songwriters and music publishers are represented, equally and directly." Serves those with an interest in songwriting and music publishing no matter what their age or skill level is. "Members must have written or published at least one musical work that has been reproduced on an audio (CD, cassettte, LP) or audio-visual support (TV, DVD, video). The new member will benefit of a society working to secure his reproduction rights (mechanicals) and broadcast mechanicals." Applications accepted year-round.

☑ SONGWRITERS & LYRICISTS CLUB

% Robert Makinson, P.O. Box 605, Brooklyn NY 11217-0605. E-mail: makinsonrobert@hotmail.com. Website: www.angelfire.com/biz7/rbmakinson/index.htlm.**Contact:** Robert Makinson, founder/director. Estab. 1984. Serves songwriters and lyricists. Gives information regarding songwriting: creation of songs, reality of market and collaboration. Only requirement is the ability to write lyrics or melodies. Beginners are welcome. The club tends to concentrate on classical, inspirational, folk, country and humorous novelty. The primary benefits of membership for the songwriter are opportunities to collaborate and assistance with creative aspects and marketing of songs through publications and advice. Offers newsletter and assistance with demos. *Songwriters & Lyricists Club Newsletter* is an irregular publication. Latest issue and some back issues will be sent to new members. Other publications, such as *Climbing the Songwriting Ladder* and *Roster of Songs by Members* are mailed to new members upon joining. Applications accepted year-round. Dues: $35/year; remit to Robert Makinson. Write with SASE for more information.
Tips "Plan and achieve realistic goals. We specialize in classical, folk, country, inspirational, and humorous novelty songs and lyrics."

SONGWRITERS AND POETS CRITIQUE

P.O. Box 21065, Columbus OH 43221. (614)777-0326. E-mail: spcmusic@yahoo.com. Website: www.songwriterscritique.com. **Contact:** Brian Preston. Estab. 1985. Serves songwriters, musicians, poets, lyricists and performers. Meets second and fourth Friday of every month to discuss club events and critique one another's work. Offers seminars and workshops with professionals in the music industry. "We critique mail-in submissions from long-distance members. Our goal is to provide support and opportunity to anyone interested in creating songs or poetry." Applications are accepted year-round. Annual dues: $30.

SONGWRITERS ASSOCIATION OF WASHINGTON

PMB 106-137, 4200 Wisconsin Ave. NW, Washington DC 20016. (301)654-8434. E-mail: membership@SAW.org. Website: www.SAW.org. Estab. 1979. "SAW is a nonprofit organization operated by a volunteer board of directors. It is committed to providing its members opportunities to learn more about the art of songwriting, to learn more about the music business, to perform in public, and to connect with fellow songwriters. SAW sponsors various events to achieve these goals: workshops, open mics, songwriter exchanges, and showcases. In addition, SAW organizes the Mid-Atlantic Song Contest open to entrants nationwide each year; "the competition in 2003 was the twentieth contest SAW has adjudicated since 1982." (Contest information masc@saw.org). As well as maintaining a website, SAW publishes *SAW Notes*, a bimonthly newsletter for members containing information on upcoming local events, member news, contest information, and articles of interest. Joint introductory membership with the Washington Area Music Association is available at a savings. Use the contact information above for membership inquiries.

THE SONGWRITERS GUILD OF AMERICA(SGA)

New York Office: 1560 Broadway, Suite #1306, New York NY 10036. (212)768-7902. Fax: (212)768-9048. E-mail: ny@songwritersguild.com. Website: www.songwritersguild.com. **Los Angeles Office:** 6430 Sunset Blvd., Suite 705, Hollywood CA 90028, (323)462-1108. Fax: (323)462-5430. E-mail: la@songwritersguild.com. **Nashville Office:** 1222 16th Ave. S., Suite 25, Nashville TN 37203, (615)329-1782. Fax: (615)329-2623. E-mail: nash@songwritersguild.com. **SGA Administration:** 1500 Harbor Blvd., Wechawken NJ 07086. (201)867-7603. Fax: (201)867-7535.

● Also see the listings for The Songwriters Guild Foundation in the Workshops & Conferences section. President: Rick Carnes. Executive Director: Lewis M. Bachman. National Projects Director: George Wurzbach. West Coast Regional Director: Aaron Meza. Southern Regional Director: Rundi Ream. Estab. 1931. ''The Songwriters Guild of America (SGA) is a voluntary songwriter association run by and for songwriters. It is devoted exclusively to providing songwriters with the services and activities they need to succeed in the business of music. The preamble to the SGA constitution charges the board to take such lawful actions as will advance, promote and benefit the profession. Services of SGA cover every aspect of songwriting including the creative, administrative and financial.'' A full member must be a published songwriter. An associate member is any unpublished songwriter with a desire to learn more about the business and craft of songwriting. The third class of membership comprises estates of deceased writers. Membership dues: Gold Membership: $60/year; Platinum membership: $85/year; Diamond Membership: $108, plus sliding royalty percentage up to $1,750/year. The Guild contract is considered to be the best available in the industry, having the greatest number of built-in protections for the songwriter. The Guild's Royalty Collection Plan makes certain that prompt and accurate payments are made to writers. The ongoing Audit Program makes periodic checks of publishers' books. For the self-publisher, the Catalogue Administration Program (CAP) relieves a writer of the paperwork of publishing for a fee lower than the prevailing industry rates. The Copyright Renewal Service informs members a year in advance of a song's renewal date. Other services include workshops in New York and Los Angeles, free Ask-A-Pro sessions with industry pros, critique sessions, collaborator service and newsletters. In addition, the Guild reviews your songwriter contract on request (Guild or otherwise); fights to strengthen songwriters' rights and to increase writers' royalties by supporting legislation which directly affects copyright; offers a group medical and life insurance plan; issues news bulletins with essential information for songwriters; provides a songwriter collaboration service for younger writers; financially evaluates catalogues of copyrights in connection with possible sale and estate planning; operates an estates administration service; and maintains a nonprofit educational foundation (The Songwriters Guild Foundation).''

☑ SONGWRITERS OF OKLAHOMA

P.O. Box 4121, Edmond OK 73083-4121. E-mail: furrowmusic@sbcglobal.net. **Contact:** Harvey Derrick, president. Offers information on the music industry: reviews publishing/artist contracts, where and how to get demo tapes produced, presentation of material to publishers or record companies, royalties and copyrights. Also offers information on the craft of songwriting: co-writers, local songwriting organizations, a written critique of lyrics, songs and compositions on tapes/CDs as long as a SASE is provided for return of critique. All of these services are free to current members. Membership dues: $25/year. A SASE must be included with all submissions/inquiries.

☑ SONGWRITERS OF WISCONSIN INTERNATIONAL

P.O. Box 1027, Neenah WI 54957-1027. (920)725-5129. E-mail: sowi@new.rr.com. Website: www.sowi.cjb.net. **Contact:** Tony Ansems, president. Workshops Coordinator: Mike Heath. Estab. 1983. Serves songwriters. ''Membership is open to songwriters writing all styles of music. Residency in Wisconsin is recommended but not required. Members are encouraged to bring tapes and lyric sheets of their songs to the meetings, but it is not required. We are striving to improve the craft of songwriting in Wisconsin. Living in Wisconsin, a songwriter would be close to any of the workshops and showcases offered each month at different towns. The primary value of membership for a songwriter is in sharing ideas with other songwriters, being critiqued and helping other songwriters.'' Offers competitions (contest entry deadline: May 15), field trips, instruction, lectures, newsletter, performance opportunities, social outings, workshops and critique sessions. Applications accepted year-round. Membership dues: $30/year.

Tips ''Critique meetings every last Thursday of each month, January through October, 7 p.m.-10 p.m. at The Hampton Inn, 350 N. Fox River Dr., Appleton, WI.''

SONGWRITERS RESOURCE NETWORK

PMB 135, 6327-C SW Capitol Hill, Portland OR 97239-1937. E-mail: info@SongwritersResourceNetwork.com. Website: www.SongwritersResourceNetwork.com. **Contact:** Steve Cahill, president. Estab. 1998. ''For songwriters and lyricists of every kind, from beginners to advanced.'' No eligibility requirements. ''Purpose is to provide free information to help songwriters develop their craft, market their songs, and learn about songwriting opportunities.'' Sponsors the annual Great American Song Contest, offers marketing tips and website access to music industry contacts. "We provide leads to publishers, producers and other music industry professionals." Visit website or send SASE for more information.

- Also see the listing for Great American Song Contest in the Contests and Awards section of this book.

SOUTHEAST TEXAS BLUEGRASS MUSIC ASSOCIATION

130 Willow Run, Lumberton TX 77657-9210. (409)755-0622. E-mail: PickNBow@aol.com. **Contact:** Edy Mathews, editor. Estab. 1976. Members are musicians and listeners of all ages. Purpose is to promote bluegrass, gospel and old time music. Offers newsletter and monthly shows which are free. Applications accepted year-round. Membership fee: $12/year.

SOUTHEASTERN COMPOSERS LEAGUE

113 Joy Springs Rd., Columbus MS 39701. Website: www.runet.edu/~ scl-web. **Contact:** Richard Montalto, vice president. Estab. 1950. Offers performance opporunities, workshops, evaluation services and a newsletter. Applications accepted year-round. Membership fee: $30/year.

☑ SOUTHERN SONGWRITERS GUILD, INC.

P.O. Box 52656, Shreveport LA 71136-2656. E-mail: songguild@aol.com. Website: http://members.aol.com/ songguild. **Contact:** Cathy Williams, president. Estab. 1984. "The purpose of the Southern Songwriters Guild is to promote the art and craft of songwriting through all available educational and charitable means and to endeavor to uphold its objectives in harmony with society. SSG hosts an annual Awards Banquet that features winners of our 'Song of the Year' contest that provides cash prizes; and to induct new members into 'SSG Songwriters Hall of Fame', who may have local or regional roots in either heritage or career development. SSG has monthly Board and General Membership meetings aimed toward education. Fundraiser benefits are occasionally conducted for specific needs. A small educational scholarship program is infrequently available for those who meet certain criteria for need and purpose. SSG offers an opportunity to network or collaborate with other songwriters and songwriter organizations and encourages dual or multi-memberships with other organizations whose purposes are consistent with those of SSG. A newsletter is distributed to the membership and to non-member related entities. Performance opportunities, open mic sessions, songwriting workshops, clinics, annual family picnic, Christmas party and song critiques are additional functions. Please send SASE for membership application or other information." Applications accepted year-round. Membership fee: $30/year, $25 for each additional family member, $100 for organization or institution.

SOUTHWEST CELTIC MUSIC ASSOCIATION

4340 N. Central Expressway, Suite E104, Dallas TX 75206-6550. Website: www.scmatx.org. **Contact:** John Hebley, president. Estab. 1983. Persons interested in promotion and preservation of Celtic music. Musicians and Celtic music lovers are members (not necessary to be a musician to join). No eligibility requirements, although membership is primarily in Texas and surrounding states. Purpose is to promote, preserve and provide education about Celtic music, dance and culture in Texas and the Southwest region of the US. Offers instruction, newsletter, lectures, workshops, performance opportunities and sponsorships and scholarships. Applications accepted year-round. Membership fee: $15/family; $25/organization; $50/friendship; $100/sponsor; $300/lifetime member.
Tips "We are the producers of the second largest Irish Festival in the U.S."

☑ SOUTHWEST VIRGINIA SONGWRITERS ASSOCIATION

P.O. Box 698, Salem VA 24153. Phone/fax: (540)745-6771. E-mail: kirasongs@aol.com. **Contact:** Britt Mistele. Estab. 1981. 80 members of all ages and skill all levels, mainly country, folk, gospel, contemporary and rock but other musical interests too. "The purpose of SVSA is to increase, broaden and expand the knowledge of each member and to support, better and further the progress and success of each member in songwriting and related fields of endeavor." Offers performance opportunities, evaluation services, instruction, newsletter, workshops, monthly meetings and monthly newsletter. Application accepted year-round. Membership fee: $18/year.

☑ SPARS (Society of Professional Audio Recording Services)

9 Music Square South, Suite 222, Nashville TN 37203. 1-800-771-7727. Fax: (615)846-5123. E-mail: spars@spars .com. Website: www.spars.com. **Contact:** Larry Lipman, executive director. Estab. 1979. Members are recording studios, manufacturers of audio recording equipment, individual project studio owners, mastering engineers, regular audio engineers, providers of services to the audio recording industry. Call for application/brochure describing membership. Non-profit professional organization focused on the business issues of multimedia facility ownership; management and operations; and educational networking and communion. Offers newslet-

ter, publications, workshops, evaluation services and SPARS test. Applications accepted year-round. Call or write for information.

▣ SPNM—PROMOTING NEW MUSIC

(formerly Society for the Promotion of New Music (SPNM))St. Margarets House, 4th Floor, 18-20 Southwark St., London SE1 1TJ United Kingdom. Phone: 020 7407 1640. Fax: 020 7403 7652. E-mail: spnm@spnm.org.uk. Website: www.spnm.org.uk. Executive Director: Abigail Pogson. Administrator: Jo-Ann Naish. Estab. 1943. "All ages and backgrounds are welcome, with a common interest in the innovative and unexplored. We enable new composers to hear their works performed by top-class professionals in quality venues." Offers newsletter, lectures, workshops, special offers and concerts. Annual selection procedure, deadline September 30. "From contemporary jazz, classical and popular music to that written for film, dance and other creative media, spnm is one of the main advocates of new music in Britain today. Through its eclectic program of concerts, workshops, education projects and collaborations and through its two publications, *new notes* and *Beat Magazine*, spnm brings new music in all guises to many, many people." Other calls for specific events throughout year. Membership fee: Ordinary: £25; Concessions: £10; Friend: £35.

Tips "Most calls for pieces are restricted to those living and/or studying in UK/Ireland, or to British composers living overseas."

☑ THE TENNESSEE SONGWRITERS INTERNATIONAL

P.O. Box 2664, Hendersonville TN 370772664. TSA Hotline: (615)969-5967. (615)824-4555. E-mail: asktsai@aol. com Website: www.clubnashville.com/tsai.htm. **Contact:** Margie Reeves, membership director. Executive Director: Jim Sylvis. Serves songwriters. "Our membership is open to all ages and consists of both novice and experienced professional songwriters. The only requirement for membership is a serious interest in the craft and business of songwriting. Our main purpose and function is to educate and assist the songwriter, both in the art/craft of songwriting and in the business of songwriting. In addition to education, we also provide an opportunity for camaraderie, support and encouragement, as well a chance to meet co-writers. We also critique each others' material and offer suggestions for improvement, if needed. We offer the following to our members: Informative monthly newsletters; 'Pro-Rap'—once a month a key person from the music industry addresses our membership on their field of specialty. They may be writers, publishers, producers and sometimes even the recording artists themselves; 'Pitch-A-Pro'—we schedule a publisher, producer or artist who is currently looking for material to come to our meeting and listen to songs pitched by our members; 'Legends Night'— several times a year, a 'legend' in the music business will be our guest speaker. Annual Awards Dinner— honoring the most accomplished of our TSAI membership during the past year; Tips—letting our members know who is recording and how to get their songs to the right people. Workshops are held at Belmont University, Wedgewood Ave., Nashville TN in the Massey Business Center Building, Room 200-B on Wednesday evenings from 7-9 p.m. Other activities—a TSAI summer picnic, parties throughout the year, and opportunities to participate in music industry-related charitable events." Applications accepted year-round. Membership runs for one year from the date you join. Membership fee is $50/year in the U.S. and $65 in all foreign countries.

TEXAS ACCOUNTANTS & LAWYERS FOR THE ARTS

1540 Sul Ross, Houston TX 77006-4730. (713)526-4876 or (800)526-TALA. Fax: (713)526-1299. E-mail: info@tal arts.org. Website: www.talarts.org. **Contact:** Jane S. Lowery, executive director. Estab. 1979. TALA's members include accountants, attorneys, museums, theatre groups, dance groups, actors, artists, musicians and filmmakers. Our members are of all age groups and represent all facets of their respective fields. TALA is a nonprofit organization that provides pro bono legal and accounting services to income-eligible artists from all disciplines and to nonprofit arts organizations. TALA also provides mediation services for resolving disputes as a low cost-nonadversarial alternative to litigation. Offers newsletter, lectures, library and workshops. Applications accepted year-round. Membership fee for artists: $30.

Tips TALA's speakers program presents low-cost seminars on topics such as The Music Business, Copyright and Trademark, and The Business of Writing. These seminars are held annually at a location in Houston. TALA's speaker's program also provides speakers for seminars by other organizations.

TEXAS MUSIC OFFICE

P.O. Box 13246, Austin TX 78711. (512)463-6666. Fax: (512)463-4114. E-mail: music@governor.state.tx.us. Website: www.governor.state.tx.us/music. **Contact:** Casey Monahan, director. Estab. 1990. "The main purpose of the Texas Music Office is to promote the Texas music industry and Texas music, and to assist music professionals around the world with information about the Texas market. The Texas Music Office serves as a clearinghouse for Texas music industry information using their seven databases: Texas Music Industry (5,800 Texas music businesses in 94 music business categories); Texas Music Events (700 Texas music events); Texas Talent Register (900 Texas recording artists); Texas Radio Stations (733 Texas stations); U.S. Record Labels; Classical

Texas (detailed information for all classical music organizations in Texas); and International (450 foreign businesses interested in Texas music). Provides referrals to Texas music businesses, talent and events in order to attract new business to Texas and/or to encourage Texas businesses and individuals to keep music business in-state. Serves as a liaison between music businesses and other government offices and agencies. Publicizes significant developments within the Texas music industry.'' Publishes the *Texas Music Industry Directory* (see the Publications of Interest section for more information).

TEXAS SONGWRITERS ASSOCIATION

3503 Forrestwood Dr., Bryan TX 77807. (409)775-0729. President: Kay Mayfield. Estab. 1986. ''Writing songs and learning how to improve on writing skills is the main reason people join T.S.A. Some members have written songs for many years, whereas, some have only written a few. Age varies from teenage to senior citizens. Purpose is to educate the songwriter to become better writers; to know the business of songwriting; and to learn how to properly pitch their songs. Offers instruction, lectures, library, workshops, performance opportunities and evaluation services. Applications accepted year-round. Membership fee: $25/year.
Tips ''We encourage those who join TSA to take seriously their gift of songwriting. We also believe that TSA is a valuable asset to our community as well as to each writer. We recognize and respect all forms of music and promote each other as fellow members.''

⬛ TORONTO MUSICIANS' ASSOCIATION

15 Gervais Dr., Suite 500, Toronto ON M3C 1Y8 Canada. (416)421-1020 or 1-800-ROAD-GIG. Fax: (416)421-7011. E-mail: info@torontomusicians.org. Website: www.torontomusicians.org. Executive Director: Bill Skolnick. Estab. 1887. Serves musicians—*All* musical styles, background, areas of the industry. ''Must be a Canadian citizen, show proof of immigration status, or have a valid work permit for an extended period of time.'' The purpose of this organization is ''to unite musicians into one organization, in order that they may, individually and collectively, secure, maintain and profit from improved economic, working and artistic conditions.'' Offers newsletter. Applications accepted year-round. Joining fee is $235.

⬛ VICTORY MUSIC

P.O. Box 2254, Tacoma WA 98401. (253)428-0832. E-mail: info@victorymusic.org. Website: www.victorymusic .org. **Contact:** Deb Seymour, coordinator. Estab. 1969. All-volunteer organization serves songwriters, audiences and local acoustic musicians of all music styles. Victory Music provides places to play, showcases, opportunities to read about the business and other songwriters, referrals and seminars. Produced 6 albums of NW songwriters. Offers library, magazine (including previews of members' concerts), newsletter, performance opportunities, business workshops, music business books and a musician referral service. Applications accepted year-round. Membership fee: $30/year single; $80/year business; $40/family; $250 lifetime.

VOLUNTEER LAWYERS FOR THE ARTS

1 E. 53rd St., 6th Floor, New York NY 10022. (212)319-ARTS (2787), ext. 1 (Monday-Friday 9:30-12 and 1-4 EST). Fax: (212)752-6575. E-mail: vlany@vlany.org. Website: www.vlany.org. **Contact:** Elena M. Paul, esq., executive director. Estab. 1969. Serves songwriters, musicians and all performing, visual, literary and fine arts artists and groups. Offers legal assistance and representation to eligible individual artists and arts organizations who cannot afford private counsel and a mediation service. VLA sells publications on arts-related issues and offers educational conferences, lectures, seminars and workshops. In addition, there are affiliates nationwide who assist local arts organizations and artists. Call for information.
Tips ''VLA now offers a monthly copyright seminar, 'Copyright Basics,' for songwriters and musicians as well as artists in other creative fields.''

WASHINGTON AREA MUSIC ASSOCIATION

1101 17th St. NW, Suite 1100, Washington DC 20036. (202)338-1134. Fax: (703)393-1028. E-mail: dcmusic@wamadc.com. Website: www.wamadc.com. **Contact:** Mike Schreibman, president. Estab. 1985. Serves songwriters, musicians and performers, managers, club owners and entertainment lawyers; ''all those with an interest in the Washington music scene.'' The organization is designed to promote the Washington music scene and increase its visibility. Its primary value to members is its seminars and networking opportunities. Offers lectures, newsletter, performance opportunities and workshops. WAMA sponsors the annual Washington Music Awards (The Wammies) and The Crosstown Jam or annual showcase of more than 300 artists at 60 venues in the DC area. Applications accepted year-round. Annual dues: $30.

WEST COAST SONGWRITERS

(formerly Northern California Songwriters Association), 1724 Laurel St., Suite 120, San Carlos CA 94070. (650)654-3966. Fax: (650)654-2156, or (800)FORSONG (California and Nashville only). E-mail: ian@westcoasts ongwriters.org. Website: www.westcoastsongwriters.org. **Contact:** Ian Crombie, executive director. Serves songwriters and musicians. Estab. 1979. "Our 1,200 members are lyricists and composers from ages 16-80, from beginners to professional songwriters. No eligibility requirements. Our purpose is to provide the education and opportunities that will support our writers in creating and marketing outstanding songs. WCS provides support and direction through local networking and input from Los Angeles and Nashville music industry leaders, as well as valuable marketing opportunities. Most songwriters need some form of collaboration, and by being a member they are exposed to other writers, ideas, critiquing, etc." Offers annual West Coast Songwriters Conference, "the largest event of its kind in northern California. This 2-day event held the second hand in September features 16 seminars, 50 screening sessions (over 1,200 songs listened to by industry professionals) and a sunset concert with hit songwriters performing their songs." Also offers monthly visits from major publishers, songwriting classes, competitions, seminars conducted by hit songwriters ("we sell audio tapes of our seminars—list of tapes available on request"), mail-in song-screening service for members who cannot attend due to time or location, a monthly e-newsletter, monthly performance opportunities and workshops. Applications accepted year-round. Dues: $40/year, student; $75/year, regular membership; $150/year, pro-membership; $250/year, contributing membership.

Tips "WCS's functions draw local talent and nationally recognized names together. This is of a tremendous value to writers outside a major music center. We are developing a strong songwriting community in Northern and Southern California. We serve the San Jose, Monterey Bay, East Bay, San Francisco, Los Angeles, and Sacramento areas and we have the support of some outstanding writers and publishers from both Los Angeles and Nashville. They provide us with invaluable direction and inspiration."

WISCONSIN ALLIANCE FOR COMPOSERS

653 Charles Lane, Madison WI 53711. Website: www.wiscomposers.org. **Contact:** David Drexler. Estab. 1993. Offers performance opportunities for new music compositions. Applications accepted year-round. Membership fee: $20/year.

☑ WOMEN IN MUSIC

P.O. Box 441, Radio City Station, New York NY 10101. (212)459-4580. E-mail: wim@womeninmusic.org. Website: www.womeninmusic.org. Estab. 1985. Members are professionals in the business and creative areas: record company executives, managers, songwriters, musicians, vocalists, attorneys, recording engineers, agents, publicists, studio owners, music publishers and more. Purpose is to support, encourage and educate as well as provide networking opportunities. Offers newsletter, lectures, workshops, performance opportunities and business discounts. Presents annual "Touchstone Award" luncheon helping to raise money to support other organizations and individuals through WIM donations and scholarships. Applications accepted year-round. Membership fee: VIP: $100; Professional: $75; Affiliate: $45; Student: $25.

Workshops & Conferences

For a songwriter just starting out, conferences and workshops can provide valuable learning opportunities. At conferences, songwriters can have their songs evaluated, hear suggestions for further improvement and receive feedback from music business experts. They are also excellent places to make valuable industry contacts. Workshops can help a songwriter improve his craft and learn more about the business of songwriting. They may involve classes on songwriting and the business, as well as lectures and seminars by industry professionals.

Each year, hundreds of workshops and conferences take place all over the country. Songwriters can choose from small regional workshops held in someone's living room to large national conferences such as South by Southwest in Austin, Texas, which hosts more than 6,000 industry people, songwriters and performers. Many songwriting organizations—national and local—host workshops that offer instruction on just about every songwriting topic imaginable, from lyric writing and marketing strategy to contract negotiation. Conferences provide songwriters the chance to meet one on one with publishing and record company professionals and give performers the chance to showcase their work for a live audience (usually consisting of industry people) during the conference. There are conferences and workshops that address almost every type of music, offering programs for songwriters, performers, musical playwrights and much more.

This section includes national and local workshops and conferences with a brief description of what they offer, when they are held and how much they cost to attend. Write or call any that interest you for further information. To find out what workshops or conferences take place in specific parts of the country, see the Geographic Index at the end of this book.

Get the most from a conference

BEFORE YOU GO:

- **Save money.** Sign up early for a conference and take advantage of the early registration fee. Don't put off making hotel reservations either—the conference will usually have a block of rooms reserved at a discounted price.

- **Become familiar with all the pre-conference literature.** Study the maps of the area, especially the locations of the rooms in which your meetings/events are scheduled.

- **Make a list of three to five objectives you'd like to obtain,** e.g., what you want to learn more about, what you want to improve on, how many new contacts you want to make.

AT THE CONFERENCE:

- **Budget your time.** Label a map so you know where, when and how to get to each session. Note what you want to do most. Then, schedule time for demo critiques if they are offered.

- **Don't be afraid to explore new areas.** You are there to learn. Pick one or two sessions you wouldn't typically attend. Keep your mind open to new ideas and advice.

- **Allow time for mingling.** Some of the best information is given after the sessions. Find out "frank truths" and inside scoops. Asking people what they've learned at the conference will trigger a conversation that may branch into areas you want to know more about, but won't hear from the speakers.

- **Attend panels.** Panels consist of a group of industry professionals who have the capability to further your career. If you're new to the business you can learn so much straight from the horse's mouth. Even if you're a veteran, you can brush up on your knowledge or even learn something new. Whatever your experience, the panelist's presence is an open invitation to approach him with a question during the panel or with a handshake afterwards.

- **Collect everything:** especially informational materials and business cards. Make notes about the personalities of the people you meet to later remind you who to contact and who to avoid.

AFTER THE CONFERENCE:

- **Evaluate.** Write down the answers to these questions: Would I attend again? What were the pluses and minuses, e.g., speakers, location, food, topics, cost, lodging? What do I want to remember for next year? What should I try to do next time? Who would I like to meet?

- **Write a thank-you letter** to someone who has been particularly helpful. They'll remember you when you later solicit a submission.

Resources

APPEL FARM ARTS AND MUSIC FESTIVAL
P.O. Box 888, Elmer NJ 08318. (856)358-2472. Fax: (856)358-6513. E-mail: appelarts@aol.com. Website: www. appelfarm.org. **Contact:** Sean Timmons, artistic director. Estab. Festival: 1989; Series: 1970. "Our annual open air festival is the highlight of our year-round Performing Arts Series which was established to bring high quality arts programs to the people of South Jersey. Festival includes acoustic and folk music, blues, etc." Past performers have included Indigo Girls, John Prine, Ani DiFranco, Randy Newman, Jackson Browne, Mary Chapin Carpenter, David Gray, Nanci Griffith and Shawn Colvin. In addition, our Country Music concerts have featured Toby Keith, Joe Diffie, Ricky Van Shelton, Doug Stone and others. Programs for songwriters and musicians include performance opportunities as part of Festival and Performing Arts Series. Programs for musical playwrights also include performance opportunities as part of Performing Arts Series. Festival is a one-day event held in June, and Performing Arts Series is held year-round. Both are held at the Appel Farm Arts and Music Center, a 176-acre farm in Southern New Jersey. Up to 20 songwriters/musicians participate in each event. Participants are songwriters, individual vocalists, bands, ensembles, vocal groups, composers, individual instrumentalists and dance/mime/movement. Participants are selected by CD submissions. Applicants should send a press packet, CD and biographical information. Application materials accepted year round. Faculty opportunities are available as part of residential Summer Arts Program for children, July/August.

ARCADY MUSIC FESTIVAL
P.O. Box 780, Bar Harbor ME 04609. Phone/fax: (207)288-2141. E-mail: arcady@arcady.org. Website: www.arcady.org. **Contact:** Dean Stein, executive director. Artistic Director: Masanobu Ikemiya. Estab. 1980. Promotes classical chamber music, chamber orchestra concerts, master classes and a youth competition in Maine. Offers programs for performers. Workshops take place year-round in several towns in Eastern Maine. 30-50 professional, individual instrumentalists participate each year. Performers selected by invitation. "Sometimes we premiere new music by songwriters but usually at request of visiting musician."

ASCAP MUSICAL THEATRE WORKSHOP
1 Lincoln Plaza, New York NY 10023. (212)621-6234. Fax: (212)621-6558. E-mail: mkerker@ascap.com. Website: www.ascap.com. **Contact:** Michael A. Kerker, director of musical theatre. Estab. 1981. Workshop is for musical theatre composers and lyricists only. Its purpose is to nurture and develop new musicals for the theatre. Offers programs for songwriters. Offers programs annually, usually April through May. Event took place in New York City. Four musical works are selected. Others are invited to audit the workshop. Participants are amateur and professional songwriters, composers and musical playwrights. Participants are selected by demo tape submission. Send for application. Deadline: mid-March. Also available: the annual ASCAP/Disney Musical Theatre Workshop in Los Angeles. It takes place in January and February. Deadline is late November. Details similar to New York workshop as above.

ASCAP WEST COAST/LESTER SILL SONGWRITER'S WORKSHOP
7920 Sunset Blvd., 3rd Floor, Los Angeles CA 90046. (323)883-1000. Fax: (323)883-1049. E-mail: chard@ascap.com. Website: www.ascap.com. Estab. 1963. Offers programs for songwriters. Offers programs annually. Event takes place mid-January through mid-February. 14 songwriters/musicians participate in each event. Participants are amateur and professional songwriters. Participants are selected by demo tape submission or by invitation. "Send in two songs with lyrics, bio and brief explanation why you'd like to participate." Deadline: November 10.

BMI-LEHMAN ENGEL MUSICAL THEATRE WORKSHOP
320 W. 57th St., New York NY 10019. (212)830-2508. Fax: (212)262-2824. E-mail: jbanks@bmi.com. Website: www.bmi.com. **Contact:** Jean Banks, senior director of musical theatre. Estab. 1961. "BMI is a music licensing company which collects royalties for affiliated writers. We have departments to help writers in jazz, concert, Latin, pop and musical theater writing." Offers programs "to musical theater composers, lyricists and librettists. The BMI-Lehman Engel Musical Theatre Workshops were formed in an effort to refresh and stimulate professional writers, as well as to encourage and develop new creative talent for the musical theater." Each workshop meets 1 afternoon a week for 2 hours at BMI, New York. Participants are professional songwriters, composers and playwrights. "BMI-Lehman Engel Musical Theatre Workshop Showcase presents the best of the workshop to producers, agents, record and publishing company execs, press and directors for possible option and production." Call for application. Tape and lyrics of 3 compositions required with application. "BMI also sponsors a jazz composers workshop. For more information call David Sanjek at (212)586-2000."

☑ BONK FESTIVAL OF NEW MUSIC
% Bonk Inc., 407 W. Frances Ave., Tampa FL 33602. E-mail: bonk@music.org. Website: www.bonkfest.org. **Contact:** Festival Director. Estab. 1994. Offers programs for composers and performers. Offers programs annu-

ally. Event takes place in March. Participants are amateur and professional composers and instrumentalists. Participants are selected by demo tape audition. Demo tape criteria available on Web site. Include SASE. Deadline: September 30.

☑ BROADWAY TOMORROW PREVIEWS

% Science of Light, Inc., 191 Claremont Ave., Suite 53, New York NY 10027. E-mail: btomorrow.1@juno.com. Website: www.solministry.com/bway_tom.html. **Contact:** Elyse Curtis, artistic director. Estab. 1983. Purpose is the enrichment of American theater by nurturing new musicals. Offers series in which composers living in New York city area present scores of their new musicals in concert. 2-3 composers/librettists/lyricists of same musical and 1 musical director/pianist participate. Participants are professional singers, composers and opera/ musical theater writers. Submission is by audio cassette of music, synopsis, cast breakdown, résumé, reviews, if any, acknowledgement postcard and SASE. Participants selected by screening of submissions. Programs are presented in fall and spring with possibility of full production of works presented in concert. Membership fee: $50.

Ⓝ ☒ CANADIAN MUSIC WEEK

P.O. Box 42232, 128 St. S, Mississauga ON L5M 4Z0 Canada. Website: www.cmw.net. **Contact:** Phil Klygo, festival coordinator. Estab. 1985. Offers annual programs for songwriters, composers and performers. Event takes place mid-March in Toronto. 100,000 public, 300 bands and 1,200 delegates participate in each event. Participants are amateur and professional songwriters, vocalists, composers, bands and instrumentalists. Participants are selected by submitting demonstration tape. Send for application and more information. Concerts take place in 25 clubs and 5 concert halls, and 3 days of seminars and exhibits are provided. Fee: $375 (Canadian).

Ⓝ CMJ MUSIC MARATHON, MUSICFEST & FILMFEST

151 W. 25th St., 12th Floor, New York NY 10001. (917)606-1908. Fax: (917)606-1914. Website: www.cmj.com/ Marathon. **Contact:** Operations Manager. Estab. 1981. Premier annual alternative music gathering of more than 9,000 music business and film professionals. Fall, NYC. Features 4 days and nights of more than 50 panels and workshops focusing on every facet of the industry; exclusive film screenings; keynote speeches by the world's most intriguing and controversial voices; exhibition area featuring live performance stage; over 1,000 of music's brightest and most visionary talents (from the unsigned to the legendary) performing over 4 evenings at more than 50 of NYC's most important music venues. Participants are selected by submitting demonstration tape. Go to website for application.

CUTTING EDGE MUSIC BUSINESS CONFERENCE

1524 N. Claiborne Ave., New Orleans LA 70116. (504)945-1800. Fax: (504)945-1873. E-mail: cut_edge@bellsout h.net. Website: www.jass.com/cuttingedge. Executive Producer: Eric L. Cager. Showcase Producer: Nathaniel Franklin. Estab. 1993. "The conference is a five-day international conference which covers the business and educational aspects of the music industry. As part of the conference, the New Works showcase features over 200 bands and artists from around the country and Canada in showcases of original music. All music genres are represented." Offers programs for songwriters and performers. "Bands and artists should submit material for consideration of entry into the New Works showcase." Event takes place during August in New Orleans. 1,000 songwriters/musicians participate in each event. Participants are songwriters, vocalists and bands. Send for application. Deadline: June 1. Fee: $175 general registration; $25 showcase registration. "The Music Business Institute offers a month-long series of free educational workshops for those involved in the music industry. The workshops take place each October. Further information is available via our website."

PETER DAVIDSON'S WRITER'S SEMINAR

P.O. Box 497, Arnolds Park IA 51331. (712)332-9329. E-mail: peterdavidson@mchsi.com. **Contact:** Peter Davidson, seminar presenter. Estab. 1985. "Peter Davidson's Writer's Seminar is for persons interested in writing all sorts of materials, including songs. Emphasis is placed on developing salable ideas, locating potential markets for your work, copyrighting, etc. The seminar is not specifically for writers of songs, but is very valuable to them, nevertheless." Offers programs year-round. One-day seminar, 9:00 a.m.-4:00 p.m. Event takes place on various college campuses. In even-numbered years offers seminars in Minnesota, Iowa, Nebraska, South Dakota, Kansas, Colorado and Wyoming. In odd-numbered years offers seminars in Minnesota, Iowa, Nebraska, South Dakota, Missouri, Illinois, Arkansas and Tennessee. Anyone can participate. Send SASE for schedule. Deadline: day of the seminar. Fee: $45 to $59. "All seminars are held on college campuses in college facilities— various colleges sponsor and promote the seminars."

FILM & TV MUSIC CONFERENCE

%The Hollywood Reporter, 5055 Wilshire Blvd., Los Angeles CA 90036-4396. (323)525-2000. Website: www.bill boardevents.com/billboardevents/filmtv. **Contact:** Special Events Coordinator. Estab. 1995. Promotes all music

421,72,director.

for film and television. Offers programs for songwriters and composers. Offers programs annually in April. Held at the Directors Guild of America. More than 350 songwriters/musicians participate in each event. Participants are professional songwriters, composers, plus producers, directors, etc. Conference panelists are selected by invitation. For registration information, call the Special Events Dept. at Hollywood Reporter. Fee: $425/person.

FOLK ALLIANCE ANNUAL CONFERENCE

962 Wayne Ave., Suite 902, Silver Spring MD 20910. (301)588-8185. Fax: (301)588-8186. E-mail: fa@folk.org. Website: www.folk.org. **Contact:** Tony Ziselberger, membership services director. Estab. 1989. Conference/workshop topics change each year. Conference takes place mid-February and lasts 4 days at a different location each year. 2,000 attendees include artists, agents, arts administrators, print/broadcast media, folklorists, folk societies, merchandisers, presenters, festivals, recording companies, etc. Artists wishing to showcase should contact the office for a showcase application form. Closing date for application is May 31. Application fee is $20 for 2005 conference. Additional costs vary from year to year. Housing is separate for the event, scheduled for Feb. 16-19, 2006 in Austin, TX.

 • Also see the listing for The Folk Alliance in the Organizations section of this book.

☑ GENESIUS THEATRE GUILD

520 Eighth Ave., 3rd Floor, Suite 329, New York NY 10018. (212)244-5404. E-mail: info@genesiusguild.org. Website: www.genesiusguild.org. **Contact:** David Leidholdt, director of new musicals development. Estab. 1994. Purpose is to create and develop new musical theatre, opera, dance and other musical performance art. Offers programs for songwriters, composers and musical playwrights. Offers programs year round including stage reading series, workshops, productions, roundtable sessions and cabaret program. Event takes place at various venues in New York City. Participants are professional songwriters, vocalists, composers, bands, musical playwrights and instrumentalists. Participants are selected by demo tape submission. Send CD of music, script, synopsis, résumé/bio and letter. Series takes place at various venues and theatre spaces with 100-200 seats.

I WRITE THE SONGS

PMB 208, 2250 Justin Rd., Suite 108, Highland Village TX 75077-7164. (972)317-2760. Fax: (972)317-4737. E-mail: info@iwritethesongs.com. Website: www.iwritethesongs.com. **Contact:** Sarah Marshall, administrative director. Estab. 1996. "I Write the Songs is an on-the-air songwriting seminar. It is a syndicated radio talk show available both on the radio and on the Internet. A detailed description of the program and its hosts, Mary Dawson and Sharon Braxton, can be found on the website. The website address will also link you to the Internet broadcasts and list the radio stations that carry the program. You can also hear current and archived shows covering INSTRUCTION on the craft and business of songwriting; INTERVIEWS with famous and 'soon-to-be-famous' songwriters; and CRITIQUES of original songs submitted by our listeners. I Write the Songs has been created to inspire and instruct aspiring songwriters of all genres of music." Offers programs, including weekly programs on radio and the Internet, for songwriters, composers and performers. "We hold regular contests and competitions. All aspiring songwriters earning less than $5,000 annually from song royalties are eligible." I Write the Songs features "Critique Shows" every 4-6 weeks. Songwriters can submit demos on cassette or CD with typed lyric sheet. Does not return material. Featured songs are selected at random. Writers whose songs are selected for a show will receive a taped copy of the program on which their song is critiqued. Mary Dawson conducts songwriting seminars across the country and internationally. For a list of upcoming seminars, check the website.

☑ INDEPENDENT MUSIC CONFERENCE

(formerly Philadelphia Music Conference), 304 Main Ave., PMB 287, Norwalk CT 06851. (203)606-4649. Fax: (215)587-9552. E-mail: info@gopmc.com. Website: www.gopmc.com. Executive Director: Noel Ramos. Estab. 1992. "The purpose of the IMC is to bring together rock, hip hop and acoustic music for of panels and showcases. Offers programs for songwriters, composers and performers. 250 showcases at 20 clubs around the city. Also offer a DJ cutting contest." Held annually at the Sheraton Society Hill Hotel in Philadelphia in September. 3,000 amateur and professional songwriters, composers, individual vocalists, bands, individual instrumentalists, attorneys, managers, agents, publishers, A&R, promotions, club owners, etc. participate each year. Send for application. Fee(s): $30 showcase application fee; $150 conference registration.

KERRVILLE FOLK FESTIVAL

Kerrville Festivals, Inc., P.O. Box 291466, Kerrville TX 78029. (830)257-3600. E-mail: info@kerrville-music.com. Website: www.kerrvillefolkfestival.com. **Contact:** Dalis Allen, producer. Estab. 1972. Hosts 3-day songwriters' school, a 4-day music business school and New Folk concert competition sponsored by *Performing Songwriter* magazine. Festival produced in late spring and late summer. Spring festival lasts 18 days and is held outdoors at Quiet Valley Ranch. 110 or more songwriters participate. Performers are professional songwriters and bands. Participants selected by submitting demo, by invitation only. Send cassette, or CD, promotional material and list of upcoming appearances. ''Songwriter and music schools include lunch, experienced professional instructors, camping on ranch and concerts. Rustic facilities. Food available at reasonable cost. Audition materials accepted at above address. These three-day and four-day seminars include noon meals, handouts and camping on the ranch. Usually held during Kerrville Folk Festival, first and second week in June. Write or check the website for contest rules, schools and seminars information, and festival schedules. Also establishing a Phoenix Fund to provide assistance to ill or injured singer/songwriters who find themselves in distress.''

- Also see the listing for New Folk Concerts For Emerging Songwriters in the Contests & Awards section of this book.

LAMB'S RETREAT FOR SONGWRITERS
presented by SPRINGFED ARTS, a nonprofit organization, P.O. Box 304, Royal Oak MI 48068-0304. (248)589-1594. Fax: (248)589-3913. E-mail: johndlamb@ameritech.net. Website: www.springfed.org. **Contact:** John D. Lamb, director. Estab. 1995. Offers programs for songwriters on annual basis; November 4-7, 2004 at The Birchwood Inn, Harbor Springs, MI. 60 songwriters/musicians participate in each event. Participants are amateur and professional songwriters. Anyone can participate. Send for application or e-mail. Deadline: two weeks before event begins. Fee: $240-445, includes all meals. Facilities are single/double occupancy lodging with private baths; 2 conference rooms and hospitality lodge. Offers song assignments, songwriting workshops, song swaps, open mic and one-on-one mentoring. Faculty are noted songwriters, such as Michael Smith and Bob Franke. Partial scholarships may be available by writing: Blissfest Music Organization, % Jim Gillespie, P.O. Box 441, Harbor Springs, MI 49740. Deadline: day before event.

MANCHESTER MUSIC FESTIVAL
P.O. Box 33, Manchester VT 05254. (802)362-1956 or (800)639-5868. Fax: (802)362-0711. E-mail: info@mmfvt.o rg. Website: www.mmfvt.org. **Contact:** Robyn Madison, managing director. Estab. 1974. Offers classical music education and performances. Summer program for young professional musicians offered in tandem with a professional concert series in the mountains of Manchester, VT. Up to 23 young professionals, age 18 and up, are selected by audition for the Young Artists Program, which provides instruction, performance and teaching opportunities, with full scholarship for all participants. Printable application available on website. Application fee: $40. Commissioning opportunities for new music, and performance opportunities for professional chamber ensembles and soloists for both summer and fall/winter concert series. ''Celebrating 28 years of fine music.''

⃞N MUSIC BUSINESS SOLUTIONS/CAREER BUILDING WORKSHOPS
P.O. Box 230266, Boston MA 02123-0266. (888)655-8335. E-mail: peter@mbsolutions.com. Website: www.mbs olutions.com. **Contact:** Peter Spellman, director. Estab. 1991. Workshop titles include ''Discovering Your Music Career Niche,'' ''How to Release an Independent Record'' and ''Promoting and Marketing Music in the 21st Century.'' Offers programs for music entrepreneurs, songwriters, musical playwrights, composers and performers. Offers programs year-round, annually and bi-annually. Event takes place at various colleges, recording studios, hotels, conferences. 10-100 songwriters/musicians participate in each event. Participants are both amateur and professional songwriters, vocalists, music business professionals, composers, bands, musical playwrights and instrumentalists. Anyone can participate. Call or write (regular or e-mail) for application. Fee: varies. ''Music Business Solutions offers a number of other services and programs for both songwriters and musicians including: private music career counseling, business plan development and internet marketing; publication of *Music Biz Insight: Power Reading for Busy Music Professionals*, a bimonthly e-zine chock full of music management and marketing tips and resources. Free subscription with e-mail address.''

NASHVILLE MUSIC FESTIVAL
P.O. Box 291827, Nashville TN 37229-1827. (615)252-8202. Fax: (615)321-0384. E-mail: c4promo@aol.com. Website: www.radiocountry.org (festivals). **Contact:** Ambassador Charlie Ray, director. Estab. 2000. Offers 100 booth spaces for makers of instruments, craftspeople, independent record companies, and unsigned artists; seminars by successful music industry professionals; contests; and stages on which to perform. ''Nashville record companies big and small are looking for new talent. A lot of them will have talent scouts at the festival. If they see you on stage and like what they see, you could be signed to a recording contract. There will also be a songwriter's stage each year. This is an annual event. It takes place Memorial Day weekend each year. It has been expanded to 4 days. It always starts on Friday and ends about 10 p.m. the last Monday in May. Complete directions to festival location will be mailed with your tickets and posted on our webpage.'' Fee: $75, adult 3-day ticket; $100 adult 4-day ticket.

☑ NATIONAL ACADEMY OF POPULAR MUSIC SONGWRITING WORKSHOP PROGRAM

330 W. 58th St. Suite 411, New York NY 10019. (212)957-9230. Fax: (212)957-9227. E-mail: 73751.1142@compu serve.com. Website: www.shof.org. **Contact:** Bob Leone, projects director. Estab. 1969. "For all forms of pop music, from rock to R&B to dance." Offers programs for member lyricists and composers including songwriting workshops (beginning to master levels) and songwriter showcases. "The Abe Olman Scholarship for excellence in songwriting is awarded ($1,200) to a student who has been in our program for at least 4 quarters." Offers programs 3 times/year: fall, winter and spring. Event takes place mid-September to December, mid-January to April, mid-April to July (10 2-3 hour weekly sessions) at New York Spaces, 131 W. 72nd St., New York. Also offers networking meetings with industry pros and open mics. 50 students involved in 4 different classes. Participants are amateur and professional lyricists and composers. Some participants are selected by submitting demonstration tape, and by invitation. Send for application. Deadline: first week of classes. Annual dues: $25 and up. Sponsors songwriter showcases in March, June, September and December.

☑ NEMO MUSIC SHOWCASE & CONFERENCE

560 Harrison Ave., Suite 404, Boston MA 02118. (617)348-2899. E-mail: info@nemoboston.com. Website: www.nemoboston.com. **Contact:** Candace Avery, founder/director. Estab. 1996. Music showcase and conference, featuring the Boston Music Awards and 3 days/nights of a conference with trade show and more than 200 nightly showcases in Boston. Offers showcases for songwriters. Offers programs annually. Event takes place in October. 1,500 songwriters/musicians participate at conference; 3,000 at awards show; 20,000 at showcases. Participants are professional songwriters, vocalists, composers, bands and instrumentalists. Participants are selected by invitation. Send for application or visit website. Fees: Gold Badge: $150 (early registration), $250 (walk-up registration); Conference Only: $100 (early registration), $200 (walk-up registration); College Student: $75; High School Student: $50.

THE NEW HARMONY PROJECT

P.O. Box 441062, Indianapolis IN 46244-1062. (317)464-1103. E-mail: newharmony@newharmonyproject.org. Website: www.newharmonyproject.org. **Contact:** Joel Grynheim, conference director. Estab. 1986. Selected scripts receive various levels of development with rehearsals and readings, both public and private. "Our mission is to nurture writers and their life-affirming scripts. This includes plays, screenplays, musicals and TV scripts." Offers programs for musical playwrights. Event takes place in May/June in southwest Indiana. Participants are amateur and professional writers and media professionals. Send for application.

☑ ☒ NEW MUSIC WEST

1062 Homer St., #300, Vancouver BC V6B 2W9 Canada. (604)684-9338. Fax: (604)688-7155. E-mail: info@new musicwest.com. Website: www.newmusicwest.com. Producer: Frank Weipert. Estab. 1990. A four day music festival and conference held May each year in Vancouver, BC. The conference offers songwriter intensive workshops; demo critique sessions with A&R and publishers; information on the business of publishing; master producer workshops: "We invite established hit record producers to conduct three-hour intensive hands-on workshops with 30 young producers/musicians in studio environments." The festival offers songwriters in the round and 250 original music showcases. Largest music industry event in the North Pacific Rim. Entry fee: Full Pass: $150; Student: $50; Registered Artists (not selected for showcase): $70. Check website for most recent festival dates.

NORFOLK CHAMBER MUSIC FESTIVAL

September-May address: 165 Elm St., Suite 101, Box 208246, New Haven CT 06520. (203)432-1966. Fax: (203)432-2136. June-August address: Ellen Battell, Stoeckel Estate, Box 545, Norfolk CT 06058. (860)542-3000. Fax: (860)542-3004. E-mail: norfolk@yale.edu. Website: www.yale.edu/norfolk. **Contact:** Deanne E. Chin, operations manager. Estab. 1941. Festival season of chamber music. Offers programs for composers and performers. Offers programs summer only. Approximately 45 fellows participate. Participants are up-and-coming composers and instrumentalists. Participants are selected by following a screening round. Auditions are held in New Haven, CT. Send for application. Deadline: January 16. Fee: $50. HEld at the Ellen Battell Stoeckel Estate, the Festival offers a magnificent Music Shed with seating for 1,000, practice facilities, music library, dining hall, laundry and art gallery. Nearby are hiking, bicycling and swimming.

☑ ☒ NORTH BY NORTHEAST MUSIC FESTIVAL AND CONFERENCE (NXNE)

189 Church St., Lower Level, Toronto ON M5B 1Y7 Canada. (416)863-6963. Fax: (416)863-0828. E-mail: info@n xne.com. Website: www.nxne.com. **Contact:** Travis Bird, festival coordinator. Estab. 1995. "Our festival takes place mid-June at over 25 venues and 2 outdoor stages in downtown Toronto, drawing over 2,000 conference delegates, 400 bands and 50,000 music fans. Musical genres include everything from folk to funk, roots to rock, polka to punk and all points in between, bringing exceptional new talent, media front-runners, music business

heavies and music fans from all over the world to Toronto." Participants include emerging and established songwriters, vocalists, composers, bands and instrumentalists. Festival performers are selected by submitting a CD or tape and accompanying press kit. Application forms are available by website or by calling the office. Submission period each year is from November 1 to the third weekend in January. Submissions fee: $20. Conference registration fee: $115-195 (US), $145-250 (Canadian). "Our conference is held at the deluxe Holiday Inn King and the program includes mentor sessions—15-minute one-on-one opportunities for songwriters and composers to ask questions of industry experts. North By Northeast 2003 will be held June 5-7, 2003 and North By Northeast 2004 will be held June 10-12, 2004."

☑ NSAI SONG CAMPS

1701 West End Ave., Nashville TN 37023. 1-800-321-6008 or (615)256-3354. Fax: (615)256-0034. E-mail: songcamps@nashvillesongwriters.com. Website: www.nashvillesongwriters.com. **Contact:** Alicia Jones, director of song camps. Estab. 1992. Offers programs strictly for songwriters. Event held 4 times/year in Nashville. "We provide most meals and lodging is available. We also present an amazing evening of music presented by the faculty." Camps are 3 days long, with 36-112 participants, depending on the camp. "There are different levels of camps, some having preferred prerequisites. Each camp varies. Please call, e-mail or refer to website. It really isn't about the genre of music, but the quality of the song itself. Song Camp strives to strengthen the writer's vision and skills, therefore producing the better song. Song Camp is known as 'boot camp' for songwriters. It is guaranteed to catapult you forward in your writing! Participants are all aspiring songwriters led by a pro faculty. We do accept lyricists only and composers only with the hopes of expanding their scope." Participants are selected through submission of 2 songs with lyric sheet. Song Camp is open to NSAI members, although anyone can apply and upon acceptance join the organization. There is no formal application form. See website for membership and event information.

● Also see the listing for Nashville Songwriters Association International (NSAI) in the Organizations section of this book.

NSAI SONGWRITERS SYMPOSIUM

1701 West End Ave., Nashville TN 37203. (615)256-3354. Fax: (615)256-0034. E-mail: membership@NashvilleSongwriters.com. Website: www.nashvillesongwriters.com. Covers "all types of music. Participants take part in publisher evaluations, as well as large group sessions with different guest speakers." Offers annual programs for songwriters. Event takes place in April in downtown Nashville. 300 amateur songwriters/musicians participate in each event. Send for application.

☑ 🎵 ORFORD FESTIVAL

Orford Arts Centre, 3165 Chemim DuParc, Orford QC J1X 7A2 Canada. (819)843-9871 or 1-800-567-6155. Fax: (819)843-7274. E-mail: centre@arts-orford.org. Website: www.arts-orford.org. **Contact:** Judith Munger, registrar/information manager. Artistic Director: Agnes Grossmann. Estab. 1951. "Each year, the Orford Arts Centre produces up to 35 concerts in the context of its Music Festival. It receives artists from all over the world in classical and chamber music." Offers master classes for music students, young professional classical musicians and chamber music ensembles. New offerings include master classes for all instruments,voice, and opera. Master classes last 2 months and take place at Orford Arts Centre from the end of June to the middle of August. 350 students participate each year. Participants are selected by demo tape submissions. Send for application. Closing date for application is mid to late March. Check our website for specific dates and deadlines. Scholarships for qualified students. Registration fees $50 (Canadian). Tuition fees $260 (Canadian)/week. Accommodations $265 (Canadian)/week.

☑ THE SONGWRITERS GUILD FOUNDATION

6430 Sunset Blvd., Suite 705, Hollywood CA 90028. (323)462-1108. Fax: (323)462-5430. E-mail: lasga@aol.com. Website: www.songwritersguild.com. West Coast Regional Director: B. Aaron Meza. Assistant West Coast Regional Director: Eric Moromisato. Nashville office: 1222 16th Ave., S, Nashville TN 37212. (615)329-1782. Fax: (615)329-2623. Southern Regional Director: Rundi Ream. Assistant Southern Regional Director: Evan Shoemake. E-mail: sganash@aol.com. New York office: 200 W. 72nd Street, New York NY 10023. (212)768-7902. Fax: (212)768-9048. National Projects Director: George Wurzbach. Offers a series of workshops with discounts to members. "There is a charge for each songwriting class. Charges vary depending on the class. SGA members receive discounts! Also, the Re-write workshop and Ask-A-Pro/Song Critique are free!"

● Also see the Songwriters Guild of America listing in the Organizations section.

Ask-A-Pro/Song Critique (Hollywood and Nashville offices) SGA members are given the opportunity to present their songs and receive constructive feedback from industry professionals. A great chance to meet industry people, make contacts, ask questions and get your song heard! Free to SGA members. Reservations required. Call for schedule. Free.

Phil Swan Song Styles/Songwriting Workshops (Hollywood and Nashville offices) This 8-week workshop taught by Phil Swann, Dreamworks SKG staff writer is perfect for those writers who want to become better songwriters in the country, pop, and rock genres as well as more savvy the changing marketplaces. Fee.

Special Seminars and Workshops Other special seminars have been presented by such industry professionals as Dale Kawashima, John Braheny and Dr. George Gamez. Fee.

Building a Songwriting Career A 3-day workshop for songwriters, musicians and recording artists, etc. to help them discover how they can establish a career in the exciting world of songwriting. Features SGA professional songwriters and music business executives in panel discussions about intellectual property, creativity, the craft and business of songwriting and more. Fee.

Re-Write Workshop (Hollywood office) (Hollywood office)Conducted by Michael Allen. Songwriters will have the chance to have their songs critiqued by their peers with an occasional guest critique. Free.

Harriet Schock Songwriting Workshop (Hollywood office) A 10-week course consisting of nine lessons which help create a solid foundation for writing songs effortlessly. Fee.

Jai Josefs Writing Music For Hit Songs (Hollywood office) This 10-week course will show songwriters how to integrate the latest chord progressions, melodies, and grooves from all styles of music into their writing.

Song Critique New York's oldest ongoing song critique. Guild songwriters are invited to either perform their song live or present a cassette demo for feedback. A Guild moderator is on hand to direct comments. Nonmembers may attend and offer comments. Free.

Street Smarts (New York office) Street Smarts is a 3-hour orientation session for new SGA members. It introduces the basics in areas such as: contracts, copyrights, royalties, song marketing and more. The session is free to members and is scheduled whenever there is a minimum of 8 participants.

Pro-Shop For each of 6 sessions an active publisher, producer or A&R person is invited to personally screen material from professional Guild writers. Participation is limited to 10 writers, and audit of 1 session. Audition of material is required. Coordinator is producer/musician/award winning singer, Ann Johns Ruckert. Fee; $75 (SGA members only).

SGA Week Held in spring/summer of each year, this is a week of scheduled events and seminars of interest to songwriters at each of SGA's regional offices. Events include workshops, seminars and showcases. For schedule and details contact the SGA office beginning several weeks prior to SGA Week.

SONGWRITERS PLAYGROUND®

75-A Lake Rd., #366, Congers NY 10920. (845)267-0001. E-mail: heavyhitters@earthlink.net. **Contact:** Barbara Jordan, director. Estab. 1990. "To help songwriters, performers and composers develop creative and business skills through the critically acclaimed programs *Songwriters Playground®*, *The 'Reel' Deal on Getting Songs Placed in Film and Television*, and the *Mind Your Own Business* Seminars. We offer programs year-round. Workshops last anywhere from 2-15 hours. Workshops are held at various venues throughout the United States. Prices vary according to the length of the workshop." Participants are amateur and professionals. Anyone can participate. Send or call for application.

SOUTH BY SOUTHWEST MUSIC CONFERENCE (SXSW)

SXSW Headquarters, P.O. Box 4999, Austin TX 78765. (512)467-7979. Fax: (512)451-0754. E-mail: sxsw@sxsw. com. Website: www.sxsw.com. **Contact:** Conference Organizer. **Europe:** Mementomori Ltd., Cill Ruan, 7 Ard na Croise, Thurles, Co. Tipperary, Ireland. Phone: 353-504-26488. Fax: 353-504-26787. E-Mail: una@sxsw.com **Contact:** Una Johnston. **Asia:** Meijidori Bldg. 403, 2-3-21 Kabuki-cho Shinjuku-ku, Tokyo 160-0021, Japan. Phone: +82 3-5292-5551. Fax: +82 3-5292-5552. E-Mail: benten@jk9.so-net.ne.jp. **Contact:** Hiroshi Asada. **Australia / New Zealand / Hawaii:** 20 Hordern St., Newtown NSW 2042, Australia. Phone: 61-2-9557-7766. Fax: 61-2-9557-7788. E-mail: musicpro@tpg.com.au. **Contact:** Phil Tripp. Estab. 1987. "South by Southwest (SXSW, Inc.) is a private company based in Austin, Texas, with a year-round staff of professionals dedicated to building and delivering conference and festival events for entertainment and related media industry professionals. Since 1987, SXSW has produced the internationally-recognized music and media conference and festival. As the entertainment business adjusted to issues of future growth and development, in 1993, SXSW added conferences and festivals for the film industry (SXSW Film) as well as for the blossoming interactive media (SXSW Interactive Festival). Now three industry events converge in Austin during a Texas-sized week, mirroring the ever increasing convergence of entertainment/media outlets." The next conference will be held March 16-20, 2005 in Austin, TX. Offers panel discussions, "Crash Course" educational seminars and showcases. The 2004 Keynote speaker was Little Richard. "The South By Southwest Music Conference seeks out speakers who have developed unique ways to create and sell music. With our Wednesday Crash Courses and introductory panels, the basics will be covered in plain English. From Thursday through Saturday, the conference includes over fifty sessions including a panel of label heads discussing strategy, interviews with notable artists, topical discussions, demo listening sessions and the mentor program. And when the sun goes down, a multitude of performances by musicians and songwriters from across the country and around the world populate the SXSW

Music Festival, held in venues in central Austin.'' Write, e-mail or visit website for dates and registration instructions.

Tips ''SXSW is also involved in North by Northeast (NXNE), held in Toronto, Canada in late Spring.''

THE SWANNANOA GATHERING—CONTEMPORARY FOLK WEEK

Warren Wilson College, P.O. Box 9000, Asheville NC 28815-9000. Phone/fax: (828)298-3434. E-mail: gathering @warren-wilson.edu. Website: www.swangathering.com. Director: Jim Magill. ''For anyone who ever wanted to make music for an audience, we offer a comprehensive week in artist development, divided into four major subject areas: Songwriting, Performance, Sound & Recording and Vocal Coaching, along with daily panel discussions of other business matters such as promotion, agents and managers, logistics of touring, etc. 2002 staff includes Steve Seskin, Kim and Reggie Harris, Ray Chesna, John Smith, Tena Moyer, Penny Nichols, Mae Robertson, Sloan Wainwright, Eric Garrison, Christine Kane, Tom Paxton, Crow Johnson, Billy Jonas and Doc & Jean Russell. For a brochure or other info contact Jim Magill, Director, The Swannanoa Gathering, at the phone number/address above. Tuition: $340. Takes place last week in July. Housing (including all meals): $260. Annual program of The Swannanoa Gathering Folk Arts Workshops.''

THE TEN-MINUTE MUSICALS PROJECT

P.O. Box 461194, West Hollywood CA 90046. Website: www.tenminutemusicals.org. **Contact:** Michael Koppy, producer. Estab. 1986. Promotes short complete stage musicals. Offers programs for songwriters, composers and musical playwrights. ''Works selected are generally included in full-length 'anthology musical'—11 of the first 16 selected works are now in the show *Stories 1.0*, for instance.'' Awards a $250 royalty advance for each work selected. Participants are amateur and professional songwriters, composers and musical playwrights. Participants are selected by demonstration tape, script, lead sheets. Send for application. Deadline: August 31st annually.

TUNESMITH SUMMER & WINTER SEMINARS

E-mail: info@tunesmith.net. Website: www.tunesmith.net. **Contact:** Nancy Cassidy, Tunesmith owner and seminar organizer. Estab. 2001. Offers programs twice a year. ''The event is open to all songwriters, from hobbyist to more advanced. Learn how to impress publishers with your songs and yourself. Learn about the craft of commercial songwriting from professional hit songwriters. Learn the art of networking as it pertains to the music business and how to make connections down on Music Row.'' At our seminars you will write a song during the seminar and the winning song will be pitched to Nashville publishers. E-mail or visit website for dates and fees.

☑ UNDERCURRENTS

P.O. Box 94040, Cleveland OH 44101-6040. (216)392-4136. E-mail: music@undercurrents.com. Website: www. undercurrents.com. **Contact:** John Latimer, president. Estab. 1989. A yearly music industry expo with online exposure featuring seminars, trade show, media center and showcases of rock, alternative, metal, folk, jazz and blues music. Offers programs for songwriters, composers, music industry professionals and performers. Contact for dates and deadlines. Participants are selected by demo tape, biography and 8×10 photo audition. Send for application. Fee: $25 for 3-day event.

☑ WEST COAST SONGWRITERS CONFERENCE

(formerly Northern California Songwriters Association Conference), 1724 Laurel St., Suite 120, San Carlos CA 94070. (650)654-3966 or (800)FOR-SONG. Fax: (650)654-2156. E-mail: info@westcoastsongwriters.org. Website: www.westcoastsongwriters.org. **Contact:** Ian Crombie, executive director. Estab. 1980. ''Conference offers opportunity and education. 16 seminars, 50 song screening sessions (1,500 songs reviewed), performance showcases, one on one sessions and concerts.'' Offers programs for lyricists, songwriters, composers and performers. ''During the year we have competitive open mics. Winners go into the playoffs. Winners of the playoffs perform at the sunset concert at the conference.'' Event takes place second weekend in September at Foothill College, Los Altos Hills, CA. Over 500 songwriters/musicians participate in this event. Participants are songwriters, composers, musical playwrights, vocalists, bands, instrumentalists and those interested in a career in the music business. Send for application. Deadline: September 1. Fee: $110-315. ''See our listing in the Organizations section.''

☑ WINTER MUSIC CONFERENCE INC.

3450 NE 12 Terrace, Ft. Lauderdale FL 33334. (954)563-4444. Fax: (954)563-1599. E-mail: info@wintermusiccon ference.com. Website: www.wintermusicconference.com. President: Margo Possenti. Estab. 1985. Features educational seminars and showcases for dance, hip hop, alternative and rap. Offers programs for songwriters and performers. Offers programs annually. Event takes place March of each year in Miami, Florida. 3,000 songwriters/musicians participate in each event. Participants are amateur and professional songwriters, composers, musical playwrights, vocalists, bands and instrumentalists. Participants are selected by submitting demo tape. Send SASE, visit website or call for application. Deadline: February. Event held at either nightclubs or hotel with complete staging, lights and sound. Fee: $200-350.

Retreats & Colonies

This section provides information on retreats and artists' colonies. These are places for creatives, including songwriters, to find solitude and spend concentrated time focusing on their work. While a residency at a colony may offer participation in seminars, critiques or performances, the atmosphere of a colony or retreat is much more relaxed than that of a conference or workshop. Also, a songwriter's stay at a colony is typically anywhere from one to twelve weeks (sometimes longer), while time spent at a conference may only run from one to fourteen days.

Like conferences and workshops, however, artists' colonies and retreats span a wide range. Yaddo, perhaps the most well-known colony, limits its residencies to artists "working at a professional level in their field, as determined by a judging panel of professionals in the field." The Brevard Music Center offers residencies only to those involved in classical music. Despite different focuses, all artists' colonies and retreats have one thing in common: They are places where you may work undisturbed, usually in nature-oriented, secluded settings.

SELECTING A COLONY OR RETREAT

When selecting a colony or retreat, the primary consideration for many songwriters is cost, and you'll discover that arrangements vary greatly. Some colonies provide residencies as well as stipends for personal expenses. Some suggest donations of a certain amount. Still others offer residencies for substantial sums but have financial assistance available.

When investigating the various options, consider meal and housing arrangements and your family obligations. Some colonies provide meals for residents, while others require residents to pay for meals. Some colonies house artists in one main building; others provide separate cottages. A few have provisions for spouses and families. Others prohibit families altogether.

Overall, residencies at colonies and retreats are competitive. Since only a handful of spots are available at each place, you often must apply months in advance for the time period you desire. A number of locations are open year-round, and you may find planning to go during the "off-season" lessens your competition. Other colonies, however, are only available during certain months. In any case, be prepared to include a sample of your best work with your application. Also, know what project you'll work on while in residence and have alternative projects in mind in case the first one doesn't work out once you're there.

Each listing in this section details fee requirements, meal and housing arrangements, and space and time availability, as well as the retreat's surroundings, facilities and special activities. Of course, before making a final decision, send a SASE to the colonies or retreats that interest you to receive their most up-to-date details. Costs, application requirements and deadlines are particularly subject to change.

MUSICIAN'S RESOURCE

For other listings of songwriter-friendly colonies, see *Musician's Resource* (available from Watson-Guptill Publications, 1695 Oak St., Lakewood NJ 08701, 1-800-451-1741), which not only provides information about conferences, workshops and academic programs but also residencies and retreats. Also check the Publications of Interest section in this book for newsletters and other periodicals providing this information.

☑ BREVARD MUSIC CENTER

P.O. Box 312, Brevard NC 28712. (828)862-2140. Fax: (828)884-2036. E-mail: bmc@brevardmusic.org. Website: www.brevardmusic.org. **Contact:** Dorothy Knowles, admissions coordinator. Estab. 1936. Offers 6-week residencies from June through the first week of August. Open to professional and student composers, pianists, vocalists, collaborative pianists and instrumentalists of classical music. A 2-week jazz workshop is offered June 8-22, 2003. 2003 composers-in-residence will be Bright Sheng, Claude Baker and Gunther Schuller. Accommodates 400 at one time. Personal living quarters include cabins. Offers rehearsal, teaching and practice cabins.
Costs $3,750 for tuition, room and board. Scholarships are available.
Requirements Call for application forms and guidelines. $50 application fee. Participants are selected by audition or demonstration tape and then by invitation. There are 80 different audition sites throughout the US.

BYRDCLIFFE ARTS COLONY

34 Tinker St., Woodstock NY 12498. (845)679-2079. Fax: (845)679-4529. E-mail: wguild@ulster.net. Website: www.woodstockguild.org. **Contact:** Carla T. Smith, executive director. Estab. 1991. Offers 1-month residencies June-September. Open to composers, writers and visual artists. Accommodates 10 at one time. Personal living quarters include single rooms, shared baths and kitchen facilities. Offers separate private studio space. Composers must provide their own keyboard with headphone. Activities include open studio, readings, followed by pot luck dinner once a month. The Woodstock Guild, parent organization, offers music and dance performances, gallery exhibits and book signings.
Costs $600/month. Residents are responsible for own meals and transportation.
Requirements Send SASE for application forms and guidelines. Accepts inquiries via fax or e-mail. $5 application fee. Submit a score of at least 10 minutes with 2 references, résumé and application.

DORSET COLONY HOUSE

P.O. Box 510, Dorset VT 05251-0510. (802)867-2223. Fax: (802)867-0144. E-mail: theatre@sover.net. Website: www.dorsetcolony.org. **Contact:** John Nassivera, executive director. Estab. 1980. Offers up to 1-month residencies October-November and April-mid-May. Open to writers, composers, directors, designers and collaborators of the theatre. Accommodates 9 at one time. Personal living quarters include single rooms with desks with shared bath and shared kitchen facilities.
Costs $150/week. Meals not included. Transportation is residents' responsibility.
Requirements Send SASE for application forms and guidelines. Accepts inquiries via fax or e-mail. Submit letter with requested dates, description of project and résumé of productions.

☑ ⊕ THE TYRONE GUTHRIE CENTRE

Annaghmakerrig, Newbliss, County Monaghan, Ireland. Phone: (353)(047)54003. Fax: (353)(047)54380. E-mail: thetgc@indigo.ie. Website: www.tyroneguthrie.ie. **Contact:** Program Director. Estab. 1981. Offers year-round residencies. Artists may stay for anything from 1 week to 3 months in the Big House, or for up to 6 months at a time in one of the 5 self-catering houses in the old farmyard. Open to artists of all disciplines. Accommodates 15 at one time. Personal living quarters include bedroom with bathroom en suite. Offers a variety of workspaces. There is a music room for composers and musicians, a photographic darkroom and a number of studios for visual artists. At certain times of the year it is possible, by special arrangement, to accommodate groups of artists, symposiums, master classes, workshops and other collaborations.
Costs Artists who are not Irish residents must pay £600 per week, all found, for a residency in the Big House and £300 per week for one of the self-catering farmyard houses. To qualify for a residency, it is necessary to show evidence of a significant level of achievement in the relevant field.
Requirements Send SAE and IRC for application forms and guidelines. Accepts inquiries via fax or e-mail. Fill in application form with cv to be reviewed by the board members at regular meetings.

☑ THE HAMBIDGE CENTER

P.O. Box 339, Rabun Gap GA 30568. (706)746-5718. Fax: (706)746-9933. E-mail: center@hambidge.org. Website: www.hambidge.org. **Contact:** Fran Lanier, residency director. Estab. 1934 (Center); 1988 (residency). Offers 2-week to 2-month residencies year round. Open to all artists. Accommodates 8 at one time. Personal living quarters include a private cottage with kitchen, bath, and living/studio space. Offers composer/musical studio equipped with piano. Activities include communal dinners February through December and nightly or periodic sharing of works-in-progress.

Costs $125/week.

Requirements Send SASE for application forms and guidelines, or available on website. Accepts inquiries via fax and e-mail. Application fee: $20. Deadlines: October 1 for February to August; May 1 for September to December.

ISLE ROYALE NATIONAL PARK ARTIST-IN-RESIDENCE PROGRAM

800 E. Lakeshore Dr., Houghton MI 49931. (906)487-0984. Fax: (906)482-8753. E-mail: Greg_Blust@nps.gov. Website: www.nps.gov/ISRO/. **Contact:** Greg Blust, coordinator. Estab. 1991. Offers 2-3 week residencies from mid-June to mid-September. Open to all art forms. Accommodates 1 artist with 1 companion at one time. Personal living quarters include cabin with solar powered generators for enough electricity for computer use; shared outhouse. A canoe is provided for transportation. Offers a guest house at the site that can be used as a workroom. The artist is asked to contribute a piece of work representative of their stay at Isle Royale, to be used by the park in an appropriate manner. During their residency, artists will be asked to share their experience (1 presentation per week of residency, about 1 hour/week) with the public by demonstration, talk, or other means.

Requirements Send for application forms and guidelines. Accepts inquiries via fax or e-mail. A panel of professionals from various disciplines, and park representatives will choose the finalists. The selection is based on artistic integrity, ability to reside in a wilderness environment, a willingness to donate a finished piece of work inspired on the island, and the artist's ability to relate and interpret the park through their work.

KALANI OCEANSIDE RETREAT

RR 2 Box 4500, Pahoa-Beach Road HI 96778-9724. (808)965-7828. Fax: (808)965-0527. E-mail: kalani@kalani.com. Website: www.kalani.com. **Contact:** Richard Koob, director. Estab. 1980. Offers 2-week to 2-month residencies. Open to all artists who can verify professional accomplishments. Accommodates 120 at one time. Personal living quarters include private cottage or lodge room with private or shared bath. Full (3 meals/day) dining service. Offers shared studio/library spaces. Activities include opportunity to share works in progress, ongoing yoga, hula and other classes; beach, thermal springs, Volcanos National Park nearby; olympic pool/spa on 113-acre facility.

Cost $55-120/night lodging with 50% stipend. Meals separate at $43/day. Transportation by rental car from $25/day, Kalani service $50/trip, or taxi $70/trip. 50% discount ("stipend") on lodging only.

Requirements Send SASE for application forms and guidelines. Accepts inquiries via fax or e-mail. $10 application fee.

THE MACDOWELL COLONY

100 High St., Peterborough NH 03458. (603)924-3886. Fax: (603)924-9142. E-mail: info@macdowellcolony.org. Website: www.macdowellcolony.org. **Contact:** Admissions Coordinator. Estab. 1907. Offers year-round residencies of up to 2 months (average length is 6 weeks). Open to writers, composers, film/video makers, visual artists, architects and interdisciplinary artists. Personal living quarters include single rooms. Offers private studios on 450-acre grounds.

Cost None (contributions accepted).

Requirements Send SASE or visit website for application forms and guidelines. Composers should send 2 clearly reproduced scores, one of which was completed in the last 5 years, along with audiocassette (1 piece per cassette) or both works on 1 CD. Application deadline: January 15, April 15 and September 15.

NORTHWOOD UNIVERSITY ALDEN B. DOW CREATIVITY CENTER

4000 Whiting Dr., Midland MI 48640-2398. (989)837-4478. Fax: (989)837-4468. E-mail: creativity@northwood.edu. Website: www.northwood.edu/abd. **Contact:** Director. Estab. 1979. Offers 10-week summer residencies (mid-June through mid-August). Fellowship Residency is open to individuals in all fields (the arts, humanities or sciences) who have innovative, creative projects to pursue. Accommodates 4 at one time. Each Fellow is given a furnished apartment on campus, complete with 2 bedrooms, kitchen, bath and large living room. Fellows' apartments serve as their work space as well as their living quarters unless special needs are requested.

Cost $10 application fee. Room and board is provided plus a $750 stipend to be used toward project costs or personal needs. "We look for projects which are innovative, creative, unique. We ask the applicant to set accomplishable goals for the 10-week residency."

Requirements Send for application information and guidelines. Accepts inquiries via fax or e-mail. Applicants submit 2-page typed description of their project; cover page with name, address, phone numbers plus summary

(30 words or less) of project; support materials such as tapes, CDs; personal résumé; facilities or equipment needed; and $10 application fee. Application deadline: December 31 (postmarked).

SITKA CENTER FOR ART & ECOLOGY

P.O. Box 65, Otis OR 97368-0065. (541)994-5485. Fax: (541)994-8024. E-mail: info@sitkacenter.org. Website: www.sitkacenter.org. **Contact:** Randall Koch, executive director. Estab. 1971. Offers 4-month residencies in October through January or February through May; shorter residencies are available upon arrangement. Open to artists or naturalists who have earned a BA, BS, BFA and/or MA, MS, MFA, PhD degree, or equivalent professional experience. Personal living quarters include 3 living quarters, each self-contained with a sleeping area, kitchen and bathroom. Offers 4 studios. Workshops or presentations are encouraged; an exhibition/ presentation to share residents' works is held in January and May.

Cost The resident is encouraged to hold an open studio or community outreach program at Sitka one day per month during the residency, exceptions by arrangements with the director. The resident is asked to provide some form of community service on behalf of Sitka.

Requirements Send SASE for application forms and guidelines. Accepts inquiries via fax. Send completed application with résumé, 2 letters of recommendation, work samples and SASE.

✅ VIRGINIA CENTER FOR THE CREATIVE ARTS

154 San Angelo Dr., Amherst VA 24521. (434)946-7236. Fax: (434)946-7239. E-mail: vcca@vcca.com. Website: www.vcca.com. **Contact:** Sheila Gulley Pleasants, director of artists' services. Estab. 1971. Offers residencies year-round, typical residency lasts 2 weeks to 1 month. Open to originating artists: composers, writers and visual artists. Accommodates 22 at one time. Personal living quarters include 20 single rooms, 2 double rooms, bathrooms shared with one other person. All meals are served. Kitchens for fellows' use available at studios and residence. Activities include trips in the VCCA van twice a week into town. Fellows share their work regularly. Three studios have pianos.

Cost No transportation costs are covered. The suggested daily fee is $30 which includes meals.

Requirements Send SASE for application forms and guidelines or call the above number. Applications are reviewed by a panel of judges. Application fee: $25. Deadline: May 15 for October-January residency; September 15 for February-May residency; January 15 for June-September residency.

State & Provincial Grants

A rts councils in the United States and Canada provide assistance to artists (including poets) in the form of fellowships or grants. These grants can be substantial and confer prestige upon recipients; however, **only state or province residents are eligible**. Because deadlines and available support vary annually, query first (with a SASE).

UNITED STATES ARTS AGENCIES

Alabama State Council on the Arts, 201 Monroe St., Montgomery AL 36130-1800. (334)242-4076. E-mail: staff@arts.state.al.us. Website: www.arts.state.al.us.

Alaska State Council on the Arts, 411 W. Fourth Ave., Suite 1-E, Anchorage AK 99501-2343. (907)269-6610 or (888)278-7424. E-mail: aksca_info@eed.state.ak.us. Website: www.educ.state.ak.us/aksca.

Arizona Commission on the Arts, 417 W. Roosevelt, Phoenix AZ 85003-1326. (602)255-5882. E-mail: general@arizonaarts.org. Website: www.arizonaarts.org.

Arkansas Arts Council, 1500 Tower Bldg., 323 Center St., Little Rock AR 72201. (501)324-9766. E-mail: info@arkansasarts.com. Website: www.arkansasarts.com.

California Arts Council, 1300 I St., Suite 930, Sacramento CA 95814. (916)322-6555 or (800)201-6201. E-mail: cac@cwo.com. Website: www.cac.ca.gov.

Colorado Council on the Arts, 1380 Lawrence St., Suite 1200, Denver CO 80204. (303)866-2723. E-mail: coloarts@state.co.us. Website: www.coloarts.state.co.us.

Connecticut Commission on the Arts, 755 Main St., 1 Financial Plaza, Hartford CT 06103. (860)566-4770. E-mail: artsinfo@ctarts.org. Website: www.ctarts.org.

Delaware Division of the Arts, Carvel State Office Building, 820 N. French St., Wilmington DE 19801. (302)577-8278. E-mail: delarts@state.de.us. Website: www.artsdel.org.

District of Columbia Commission on the Arts & Humanities, 410 Eighth St. NW, 5th Floor, Washington DC 20004. (202)724-5613. E-mail: dcarts@dc.gov. Website: http://dcarts.dc.gov.

Florida Arts Council, Division of Cultural Affairs, Florida Dept. of State, 1001 DeSoto Park Dr., Tallahassee FL 32301. (850)245-6470. Website: www.florida-arts.org.

Georgia Council for the Arts, 260 14th St. NW, Suite 401, Atlanta GA 30318-5793. (404)685-2787. E-mail: goarts@gaarts.org. Website: www.gaarts.org.

Hawaii State Foundation on Culture & Arts, 250 S. Hotel St., 2nd Floor, Honolulu HI 96813. (808)586-0300. E-mail: ken.hamilton@hawaii.gov/sfca. Website: www.state.hi.us/sfca.

Idaho Commission on the Arts, 2410 North Old Penitentiary Rd., Boise ID 83712. (208)334-2119 or (800)278-3863. E-mail: mestrada@ica.state.id.us. Website: www2.state.id.us/arts.

Illinois Arts Council, 100 W. Randolph, Suite 10-500, Chicago IL 60601. (312)814-6750. E-mail: info@arts.state.il.us. Website: www.state.il.us/agency/iac.

Indiana Arts Commission, 402 W. Washington St., Indianapolis IN 46204-2243. (317)232-1268. E-mail: arts@state.in.us. Website: www.state.in.us/iac.

Iowa Arts Council, 600 E. Locust, Capitol Complex, Des Moines IA 50319-0290. (515)281-6412. E-mail: linda.lee@iowa.gov. Website: www.iowaartscouncil.org.

Kansas Arts Commission, 700 SW Jackson, Suite 1004, Topeka KS 66603. (785)296-3335. E-mail: KAC@arts.state.ks.us. Website: http://arts.state.ks.us.

Kentucky Arts Council, Old Capital Annex, 300 W. Broadway, Frankfort KY 40601-1980. (502)564-3757. E-mail: kyarts@ky.gov. Website: www.kyarts.org.

Louisiana State Arts Council, P.O. Box 44247, Baton Rouge LA 70804-4247. (225)342-8180. E-mail: arts@crt.state.la.us. Website: www.crt.state.la.us/arts.

Maine Arts Commission, 193 State St., 25 State House Station, Augusta ME 04333-0025. (207)287-2724. E-mail: mainearts.info@maine.gov. Website: www.mainearts.com.

Maryland State Arts Council, 175 West Ostend Street, Suite E, Baltimore MD 21230. (410)767-6555. E-mail: msac@msac.org. Website: www.msac.org.

Massachusetts Cultural Council, 10 St. James Ave., 3rd Floor, Boston MA 02116-3803. (617)727-3668. E-mail: web@art.state.ma.us. Website: www.massculturalcouncil.org.

Michigan Council for Arts & Cultural Affairs, 722 West Kalamazoo Street, P.O. Box 30159, Lansing, MI 48909. (517)373-1820. E-mail: artsinfo@cis.state.mi.us. Website: www.michigan.gov/hal/.

Minnesota State Arts Board, Park Square Court, 400 Sibley St., Suite 200, St. Paul MN 55101-1928. (651)215-1600. E-mail: msab@state.mn.us. Website: www.arts.state.mn.us.

Mississippi Arts Commission, 239 N. Lamar St., Suite 207, Jackson MS 39201. (601)359-6030. E-mail: hedgepet@arts.state.ms.us. Website: www.arts.state.ms.us.

Missouri Arts Council, 111 N. Seventh St., Suite 105, St. Louis MO 63101-2188. (314)340-6845. E-mail: moarts@ded.mo.gov. Website: www.missouriartscouncil.org.

Montana Arts Council, P.O. Box 202201, Helena MT 59620-2201. (406)444-6430. E-mail: mac@state.mt.us. Website: www.art.state.mt.us.

National Endowment for the Arts, 1100 Pennsylvania Ave. NW, Washington DC 20506. (202)682-5400. E-mail: webmgr@arts.endow.gov. Website: www.arts.endow.gov.

Nebraska Arts Council, 3838 Davenport St., Omaha NE 68131-2329. (402)595-2122. E-mail: khardin@nebraskaartscouncil.org. Website: www.nebraskaartscouncil.org.

Nevada State Council on the Arts, 716 N. Curry St., Carson City NV 89701. (775)687-6680. E-mail: kjodonne@clan.lib.nv.us. Website: www.dmla.clan.lib.nv.us/docs/arts/

New Hampshire State Council on the Arts, 2½ Beacon St., 2nd Floor, Concord NH 03301-

4974. (603)271-2789. E-mail: mdurkee@nharts.state.nh.us. Website: www.state.nh.us/nharts.

New Jersey State Council on the Arts, P.O. Box 306, 225 W. State St., Trenton NJ 08625. (609)292-6130. E-mail: njsca@arts.sos.state.nj.us. Website: www.njartscouncil.org.

New Mexico Arts Division, P.O. Box 1450, Santa Fe NM 87504. (505)827-6490. E-mail: vcastell@oca.state.nm.us. Website: www.nmarts.org.

New York State Council on the Arts, 175 Varick St., 3rd Floor, New York NY 10014. (212)627-4455. E-mail: msc@nysca.org. Website: www.nysca.org.

North Carolina Arts Council, Department of Cultural Resources and Service Center, Raleigh NC 27699-4632. (919)733-2111. E-mail: ncarts@ncmail.net. Website: www.ncarts.org.

North Dakota Council on the Arts, 1600 East Century Avenue, Suite 6, Bismarck ND 58503. (701)328-7579. E-mail: comserv@state.nd.us. Website: www.state.nd.us/arts.

Ohio Arts Council, 727 E. Main St., Columbus OH 43205-1796. (614)466-2613. E-mail: shannon.ford@oac.state.oh.us. Website: www.oac.state.oh.us.

Oklahoma Arts Council, P.O. Box 52001-2001, Oklahoma City OK 73152-2001. (405)521-2931. E-mail: okarts@arts.state.ok.us. Website: www.state.ok.us/~arts.

Oregon Arts Commission, 775 Summer St. NE, Suite 200, Salem OR 97301-1284. (503)986-0082. E-mail: oregon.artscomm@state.or.us. Website: www.oregonartscommission.org.

Pennsylvania Council on the Arts, Room 216, Finance Bldg., Harrisburg PA 17120. (717)787-6883. E-mail: ngriffiths@state.pa.us. Website: www.artsnet.org/pca.

Institute of Puerto Rican Culture, P.O. Box 9024184, San Juan PR 00902-4184. (787)725-5137. E-mail: IPRAC@aspira.org. Website: http://iprac.aspira.org.

Rhode Island State Council on the Arts, One Capitol Hill, 3rd Floor, Providence RI 02908. (401)222-3880. E-mail: info@risca.state.ri.us. Website: www.risca.state.ri.us.

South Carolina Arts Commission, 1800 Gervais St., Columbia SC 29201. (803)734-8696. E-mail: burnette@arts.state.sc.us. Website: www.state.sc.us/arts.

South Dakota Arts Council, 800 Governors Dr., Pierre SD 57501-2294. (605)773-3131. E-mail: sdac@stlib.state.sd.us. Website: www.state.sd.us/deca/sdarts.

Tennessee Arts Commission, 401 Charlotte Ave., Nashville TN 37243-0780. (615)741-1701. Website: www.arts.state.tn.us.

Texas Commission on the Arts, P.O. Box 13406, Austin TX 78711-3406. (512)463-5535. E-mail: front.desk@arts.state.tx.us. Website: www.arts.state.tx.us.

Utah Arts Council, 617 E. South Temple, Salt Lake City UT 84102-1177. (801)236-7555. E-mail: swaddingham@utah.gov. Website: http://arts.utah.gov/.

Vermont Arts Council, 136 State St., Drawer 33, Montpelier VT 05633-6001. (802)828-3291. E-mail: info@vermontartscouncil.org. Website: www.vermontartscouncil.org.

Virgin Islands Council on the Arts, 41-42 Norre Gada, P.O. Box 103, St. Thomas VI 00802. (340)774-5984. E-mail: adagio@islands.vi. Website: www.vicouncilonarts.org/.html.

Virginia Commission for the Arts, Lewis House, 2nd Floor, 223 Governor St., Richmond VA 23219-2010. (804)225-3132. E-mail: arts@state.va.us. Website: www.arts.state.va.us/.

Washington State Arts Commission, P.O. Box 42675, Olympia WA 98504-2675. (360)753-3860. E-mail: markg@arts.wa.gov. Website: www.arts.wa.gov.

West Virginia Arts Commission, Cultural Center, 1900 Kanawha Blvd. E., Charleston WV 25305-0300. (304)558-0220. E-mail: barbie.anderson@wvculture.org. Website: www.wvculture.org.

Wisconsin Arts Board, 101 E. Wilson St., 1st Floor, Madison WI 53702. (608)266-0190. E-mail: artsboard@arts.state.wi.us. Website: www.arts.state.wi.us.

Wyoming Arts Council, 2320 Capitol Ave., Cheyenne WY 82002. (307)777-7742. E-mail: ebratt@state.wy.us. Website: http://wyoarts.state.wy.us.

CANADIAN PROVINCES ARTS AGENCIES

Alberta Foundation for the Arts, 901 Standard Life Centre, 10405 Jasper Ave., Edmonton, Alberta T5J 4R7. (780)427-6315. E-mail: afa@mcd.gov.ab.ca. Website: www.cd.gov.ab.ca/affta.

British Columbia Arts Council, P.O. Box 9819, Stn Prov Govt, Victoria, British Columbia V8W 9W3. (250)356-1718. E-mail: bcartscouncil@gems2.gov.bc.ca. Website: www.bcartscouncil.ca.

Manitoba Arts Council, 525 - 93 Lombard Ave., Winnipeg, Manitoba R3B 3B1. (204)945-2237. E-mail: info@artscouncil.mb.ca. Website: www.artscouncil.mb.ca.

New Brunswick Department of Economic Development, Tourism & Culture, Arts Branch, P.O. Box 6000, Fredericton, New Brunswick E3B 5H1. (506)453-3984. E-mail: www@gnb.ca. Website: www.gnb.ca.

Newfoundland & Labrador Arts Council, P.O. Box 98, St. John's, Newfoundland A1C 5H5. (709)726-2212. E-mail: nlacmail@newcomm.net. Website: www.nlac.nf.ca.

Nova Scotia Arts Council, (902)424-1593. Website: www.novascotiaartscouncil.ns.ca.

The Canada Council, 350 Albert St., P.O. Box 1047, Ottawa, Ontario K1P 5V8. (613)566-4414. Website: www.canadacouncil.ca.

Ontario Arts Council, 151 Bloor St. W., 5th Floor, Toronto, Ontario M5S 1T6. (416)961-1660. E-mail: info@arts.on.ca. Website: www.arts.on.ca/.

Prince Edward Island Council of the Arts, 115 Richmond, Charlottetown, Prince Edward Island C1E 1H7. (902)368-4410. E-mail: peiarts@peiartscouncil.com. Website: www.peiartscouncil.com.

Saskatchewan Arts Board, 2135 Broad St., Regina, Saskatchewan S4P 3V7. (306)787-4056. E-mail: sab@artsboard.sk.ca. Website: ww.artsboard.sk.ca.

Yukon Arts Branch, Box 2703, Whitehorse, Yukon Y1A 2C6. (867)667-5036. E-mail: arts@gov.yk.ca. Website: www.btc.gov.yk.ca/cultural/arts.

Publications of Interest

K nowledge about the music industry is essential for both creative and business success. Staying informed requires keeping up with constantly changing information. Updates on the evolving trends in the music business are available to you in the form of music magazines, music trade papers and books. There is a publication aimed at almost every type of musician, songwriter and music fan, from the most technical knowledge of amplification systems to gossip about your favorite singer. These publications can enlighten and inspire you and provide information vital in helping you become a more well-rounded, educated, and, ultimately, successful musical artist.

This section lists all types of magazines and books you may find interesting. From songwriters' newsletters and glossy music magazines to tip sheets and how-to books, there should be something listed here that you'll enjoy and benefit from.

PERIODICALS

The Album Network, 110 West Spazier, Burbank CA 91502. (818)842-2600. Website: www. musicbiz.com. *Weekly music industry trade magazine.*

American Songwriter Magazine, 50 Music Square W., Suite 604, Nashville TN 37203-3227. (615)321-6096. E-mail: info@americansongwriter.com. Website: www.americansongwrit er.com. *Bimonthly publication for and about songwriters.*

Back Stage East, 770 Broadway, 4th Floor, New York NY 10003. (646)654-5700.

Back Stage West, 5055 Wilshire Blvd., Los Angeles CA 90036. (323)525-2358 or (800)745-8922. Website: www.backstage.com. *Weekly East and West Coast performing artist trade papers.*

Bass Player, P.O. Box 57324, Boulder CO 80323-7324. (800)234-1831. E-mail: bassplayer@n eodata.com. Website: www.bassplayer.com. *Monthly magazine for bass players with lessons, interviews, articles, and transcriptions.*

Billboard, 1515 Broadway, New York NY 10036. (800)745-8922. E-mail: bbstore@billboard.c om. Website: www.billboard.com. *Weekly industry trade magazine.*

Canadian Musician, 23 Hannover Dr., Suite 7, St. Catharines, Ontario L2W 1A3 Canada. (877)746-4692. Website: www.canadianmusician.com. *Bimonthly publication for amateur and professional Canadian musicians.*

Chart, 200-41 Britain St., Toronto, Ontario M5A 1R7 Canada. (416)363-3101. E-mail: chart@c hartnet.com. Website: www.chartnet.com. *Monthly magazine covering the Canadian and international music scenes.*

CMJ New Music Report, 151 W. 25th St., 12 Floor, New York NY 10001. (917)606-1908. E-mail: subscriptions@cmj.com. Website: www.cmjmusic.com. *Weekly college radio and alternative music tip sheet.*

Country Line Magazine, 16150 S. IH-35, Buda TX 78610. (512)295-8400. E-mail: editor@cou ntrylinemagazine.com. Website: http://countrylinemagazine.com. *Monthly Texas-only country music cowboy and lifestyle magazine.*

Daily Variety, 5700 Wilshire Blvd., Suite 120, Los Angeles CA 90036. (323)857-6600. Website: www.variety.com. *Daily entertainment trade newspaper.*

Dramalogue, 1456 N. Gordon, Hollywood CA 90028. *L.A.-based entertainment newspaper with an emphasis on theatre and cabaret.*

The Dramatist, 1501 Broadway, Suite 701, New York NY 10036. (212)398-9366. Fax: (212)944-0420. Website: www.dramaguild.com. *The quarterly journal of the Dramatists Guild, the professional association of playwrights, composers and lyricists.*

Entertainment Law & Finance, New York Law Publishing Co., 345 Park Ave. S., 8th Floor, New York NY 10010. (212)545-6174. E-mail: leader@ljextra.com. *Monthly newsletter covering music industry contracts, lawsuit filings, court rulings and legislation.*

Exclaim!, 7-B Pleasant Blvd., Suite 966, Toronto, Ontario M4T 1K2 Canada. (416)535-9735. E-mail: exclaim@exclaim.ca. Website: http://exclaim.ca. *Canadian music monthly covering all genres of non-mainstream music.*

Fast Forward, Disc Makers, 7905 N. Rt. 130, Pennsauken NJ 08110-1402. (800)468-9353. Website: www.discmakers.com/music/ffwd. *Quarterly newsletter featuring companies and products for performing and recording artists in the independent music industry.*

The Gavin Report, 140 Second St., 5th Floor, San Francisco CA 94105. (415)495-1990. Website: www.gavin.com. *Weekly listing of radio charts.*

Guitar Player, 1601 W. 23rd St., Suite 200, Lawrence KS 60046-0127. (800)289-9839. E-mail: guitarplayer@neodata.com. Monthly guitar magazine with transcriptions, columns, and interviews, including occasional articles on songwriting.

Hits Magazine, 14958 Ventura Blvd., Sherman Oaks CA 91403. (818)501-7900. Website: www.hitsmagazine.com. *Weekly music industry trade publication.*

Jazztimes, 8737 Colesville Rd., 9th Floor, Silver Spring MD 20910-3921. (301)588-4114. Website: http://jazztimes.com. 10 issues/year magazine covering the American jazz scene.

The Leads Sheet, Allegheny Music Works, 1611 Menoher Blvd., Johnstown PA 15905. (814)255-4007. Website: www.alleghenymusicworks.com. Monthly tip sheet.

Lyricist Review, 4535 W. Sahara Ave., Suite 100A-638, Las Vegas NV 89102. 1-888-732-1176. E-mail: info@virtualstudiosystems.com. Website: www.virtualstudiosystems.com. Quarterly commentaries on song lyrics and previously unpublished lyrics available to performing musicians.

Music Books Plus, P.O. Box 670, 240 Portage Rd., Lewiston NY 14092. (800)265-8481. E-mail: mail@nor.com. Website: www.musicbooksplus.com.

Music Business International Magazine, 1 Penn Plaza, 11th Floor, New York NY 10119. (212)615-2925. E-mail: mbi@dotmusic.com. *Bimonthly magazine for senior executives in the music industry.*

Music Connection Magazine, 16130 Ventura Blvd., Suite 540, Encino CA 91436. (818)795-0101. E-mail: contactMC@musicconnection.com. Website: www.musicconnection.com. *Biweekly music industry trade publication.*

Music Morsels, P.O. Box 672216, Marietta GA 30006-0037. (770)850-9560. Fax: (770)850-9646. E-mail: musmorsels@aol.com. Website: www.serge.org/musicmorsels.htm. *Monthly songwriting publication.*

Music Row Magazine, P.O. Box 158542, Nashville TN 37215. (615)321-3617. E-mail: news @musicrow.com. Website: www.musicrow.com. *Biweekly Nashville industry publication.*

Offbeat Magazine, OffBeat Publications, 421 Frenchman St., Suite 200, New Orleans LA 70116-2506. (504)944-4300. E-mail: editor@offbeat.com. Website: www.offbeat.com. *Monthly magazine covering Louisiana music and artists.*

Performance Magazine, 1203 Lake St., Suite 200, Fort Worth TX 76102-4504. (817)338-9444. E-mail: sales@performancemagazine.com. Website: www.performancemagazine.c om. *Weekly publication on touring itineraries, artist availability, upcoming tours, and production and venue news.*

The Performing Songwriter, P.O. Box 40931, Nashville TN 37204. (800)883-7664. E-mail: order@performingsongwriter.com. Website: www.performingsongwriter.com. *Bimonthly songwriters' magazine.*

Producer Report, 415 S. Topanga Canyon Blvd., Suite 114, Topanga CA 90290. (310)455-0894. Fax: (310)455-0894. E-mail: web@mojavemusic.com. Website: www.mojavemusic. com. *Semimonthly newsletter covering which producers are working on which acts, and upcoming, current and recently completed projects.*

Professional Sound, 23 Hannover Dr., Suite 7, St. Catharine's, Ontario L2W 1A3 Canada. (800)265-8481. Fax: (905)641-1648. E-mail: mail@nor.com. Website: www.professional-sound.com. *Bimonthly publication for professionals in the sound and light industry.*

Public Domain Report, P.O. Box 3102, Margate NJ 08402. (609)822-9401. Website: www.pu bdomain.com. *Monthly guide to significant titles entering the public domain.*

Radio and Records, 10100 Santa Monica Blvd., 3rd Floor, Los Angeles CA 90067-4004. (310)553-4330. Fax: (310)203-9763. E-mail: mailroom@rronline.com. Website: www.rron line.com. *Weekly newspaper covering the radio and record industries.*

Radir, Radio Mall, 2412 Unity Ave. N., Dept. WEB, Minneapolis MN 55422. (800)759-4561. E-mail: info@bbhsoftware.com. Website: www.bbhsoftware.com. *Quarterly radio station database on disk.*

Sing Out!, P.O. Box 5460, Bethlehem PA 18015. (888)SING-OUT. Fax: (610)865-5129. E-mail: info@singout.org. Website: www.singout.org. *Quarterly folk music magazine.*

Songcasting, 15445 Ventura Blvd. #260, Sherman Oaks CA 91403. (818)377-4084. *Monthly tip sheet.*

Songlink International, 23 Belsize Crescent, London NW3 5QY England. E-mail: david@son glink.com. Website: www.songlink.com. *10 issues/year newsletter including details of re-*

cording artists looking for songs; contact details for industry sources; also news and features on the music business.

Songwriter Magazine, P.O. Box 25879, Colorado Springs CO 80936. *Monthly magazine especially for songwriters.*

Songwriter Products, Ideas and Necessities, 2520 CR 427 North, Suite 100, Longwood FL 32750. (407)834-8555. Fax: (407)834-9997. E-mail: info@songwriterproducts.com. Website: www.songwriterproducts.com. *Free semi-annual catalog of songwriting tips, tools and accessories, including tapes, CDs, duplication products and music business career packages.*

Songwriter's Monthly, The Stories Behind Today's Songs, 332 Eastwood Ave., Feasterville PA 19053. (215)953-0952. E-mail: a1foster@aol.com. *Monthly songwriters' magazine.*

The Texas Polka News, P.O. Box 800183, Houston TX 77280. (281)480-8624. Fax: (713)462-7213. Website: www.angelfire.com/folk/polka/news.html. *Monthly publication on Texas dancehalls, record releases, festival and dance listings, and radio station information.*

Variety, 5700 Wilshire Blvd., Suite 120, Los Angeles CA 90036. (323)857-6600. Fax: (323)857-0494. Website: www.variety.com. *Weekly entertainment trade newspaper.*

Words and Music, 41 Valleybrook Dr., Don Mills, Ontario M3B 2S6 Canada. (416)445-8700. Website: www.socan.ca. *Monthly songwriters' magazine.*

BOOKS & DIRECTORIES

88 Songwriting Wrongs & How to Right Them, by Pat & Pete Luboff, Writer's Digest Books, 4700 E. Galbraith Rd., Cincinnati OH 45236. (800)448-0915. Website: www.writers digest.com.

The A&R Registry, by Ritch Esra, SRS Publishing, 7510 Sunset Blvd. #1041, Los Angeles CA 90046-3418. (800)377-7411 or (800)552-7411. E-mail: musicregistry@compuserve.com.

Attention: A&R, by Teri Muench and Susan Pomerantz, Alfred Publishing Co. Inc., P.O. Box 10003, Van Nuys CA 91410-0003. (818)892-2452. Website: www.alfredpub.com.

The Billboard Guide to Music Publicity, revised edition, by Jim Pettigrew, Jr., Billboard Books, 1695 Oak St., Lakewood NJ 08701. (800)344-7119.

Breakin' Into Nashville, by Jennifer Ember Pierce, Madison Books, University Press of America, 4501 Forbes Rd., Suite 200, Lanham MD 20706. (800)462-6420.

CMJ Directory, 151 W. 25th St., 12th Floor, New York NY 10001. (917)606-1908. Website: www.cmj.com.

Contracts for the Music industry, P.O. Box 952063, Lake Mary FL 32795-2063. (407)834-8555. E-mail: info@songwriterproducts.com. Website: www.songwriterproducts.com. *Book and computer software of a variety of music contracts.*

The Craft and Business of Songwriting, by John Braheny, Writer's Digest Books, 4700 E. Galbraith Rd., Cincinnati OH 45236. (800)448-0915. Website: www.writersdigest.com.

The Craft of Lyric Writing, by Sheila Davis, Writer's Digest Books, 4700 E. Galbraith Rd., Cincinnati OH 45236. (800)448-0915. Website: www.writersdigest.com.

Creating Melodies, by Dick Weissman, Writer's Digest Books, 4700 E. Galbraith Rd., Cincinnati OH 45236. (800)448-0915. Website: www.writersdigest.com.

Directory of Independent Music Distributors, by Jason Ojalvo, Disc Makers, 7905 N. Rt. 130, Pennsauken NJ 08110. (800)468-9353. E-mail: discman@discmakers.com. Website: www.discmakers.com.

Easy Tools for Composing, by Charles Segal, Segal's Publications, 16 Grace Rd., Newton MA 02159. (617)969-6196.

FILM/TV MUSIC GUIDE, by Ritch Esra, SRS Publishing, 7510 Sunset Blvd. #1041, Los Angeles CA 90046-3418. (800)552-7411. E-mail: musicregistry@compuserve.com or srspubl@aol.com. Website: www.musicregistry.com.

Finding Fans & Selling CDs, by Veronique Berry and Jason Ojalvo, Disk Makers, 7905 N. Rt. 130, Pennsauken NJ 08110-1402. (800)468-9353. E-mail: discman@diskmakers.com. Website: www.discmakers.com.

Guide to Independent Music Publicity, by Veronique Berry, Disc Makers, 7905 N. Rt. 130, Pennsauken NJ 08110-1402. (800)468-9353. E-mail: discman@discmakers.com.

Guide to Master Tape Preparation, by Dave Moyssiadis, Disk Makers, 7905 N. Rt. 130, Pennsauken NJ 08110-1402. (800)468-9353. E-mail: discman@discmakers.com.

Hollywood Creative Directory, 3000 W. Olympic Blvd. #2525, Santa Monica CA 90404. (800)815-0503. Website: www.hcdonline.com. *Lists producers in film and TV.*

The Hollywood Reporter Blu-Book Production Directory, 5055 Wilshire Blvd., Los Angeles CA 90036. (323)525-2150. Website: www.hollywoodreporter.com.

Hot Tips for the Home Recording Studio, by Hank Linderman, Writer's Digest Books, 4700 E. Galbraith Rd., Cincinnati OH 45236. (800)448-0915. Website: www.writersdigest.com.

How to Promote Your Music Successfully on the Internet, by David Nevue, Midnight Rain Productions, P.O. Box 21831, Eugene OR 97402. Website: www.rainmusic.com.

How You Can Break Into the Music Business, by Marty Garrett, Lonesome Wind Corporation, P.O. Box 2143, Broken Arrow OK 74013-2143. (800)210-4416.

Louisiana Music Directory, OffBeat, Inc., 421 Frenchmen St., Suite 200, New Orleans LA 70116. (504)944-4300. Website: www.offbeat.com.

Music Attorney Legal & Business Affairs Registry, by Ritch Esra and Steve Trumbull, SRS Publishing, 7510 Sunset Blvd. #1041, Los Angeles CA 90046-3418. (800)552-7411. E-mail: musicregistry@compuserve.com or srspubl@aol.com.

Music Directory Canada, seventh edition, Norris-Whitney Communications Inc., 23 Hannover Dr., Suite 7, St. Catherines, Ontario L2W 1A3 Canada. (877)RING-NWC. E-mail: mail@nor.com. Website: http://nor.com.

Music Law: How to Run Your Band's Business, by Richard Stin, Nolo Press, 950 Parker St., Berkeley CA 94710-9867. (510)549-1976. Website: www.nolo.com.

Music, Money and Success: The Insider's Guide to the Music Industry, by Jeffrey Brabec and Todd Brabec, Schirmer Books, 1633 Broadway, New York NY 10019.

The Music Publisher Registry, by Ritch Esra, SRS Publishing, 7510 Sunset Blvd. #1041, Los Angeles CA 90046-3418. (800)552-7411. E-mail: musicregistry@compuserve.com or srspubl@aol.com.

Music Publishing: A Songwriter's Guide, revised edition, by Randy Poe, Writer's Digest

Books, 4700 E. Galbraith Rd., Cincinnati OH 45236. (800)448-0915. Website: www.writersdigest.com.

The Musician's Guide to Making & Selling Your Own CDs & Cassettes, by Jana Stanfield, Writer's Digest Books, 4700 E. Galbraith Rd., Cincinnati OH 45236. (800)448-0915. Website: www.writersdigest.com.

Musicians' Phone Book, The Los Angeles Music Industry Directory, Get Yourself Some Publishing, 28336 Simsalido Ave., Canyon Country CA 91351. (805)299-2405. E-mail: mpb@earthlink.net. Website: www.musiciansphonebook.com.

Nashville Music Business Directory, by Mark Dreyer, NMBD Publishing, 9 Music Square S., Suite 210, Nashville TN 37203. (615)826-4141. E-mail: nmbd@nashvilleconnection.com. Website: www.nashvilleconnection.com.

Nashville's Unwritten Rules: Inside the Business of the Country Music Machine, by Dan Daley, Overlook Press, One Overlook Dr., Woodstock NY 12498. (845)679-6838. E-mail: overlook@netstep.net.

National Directory of Independent Record Distributors, P.O. Box 452063, Lake Mary FL 32795-2063. (407)834-8555. E-mail: info@songwriterproducts.com. Website: www.songwriterproducts.com.

The Official Country Music Directory, ICMA Music Directory, P.O. Box 271238, Nashville TN 37227.

Radio Stations of America: A National Directory, P.O. Box 452063, Lake Mary FL 32795-2063. (407)834-8555. E-mail: info@songwriterproducts.com. Website: www.songwriterproducts.com.

The Real Deal—How to Get Signed to a Record Label from A to Z, by Daylle Deanna Schwartz, Billboard Books, 1695 Oak St., Lakewood NJ 08701. (800)344-7119.

Recording Industry Sourcebook, Music Books Plus, P.O. Box 670, 240 Portage Rd., Lewiston NY 14092. (800)265-8481. Website: www.musicbooksplus.com.

The Songwriters Idea Book, by Sheila Davis, Writer's Digest Books, 4700 E. Galbraith Rd., Cincinnati OH 45236. (800)448-0915. Website: www.writersdigest.com.

Songwriter's Market Guide to Song & Demo Submission Formats, Writer's Digest Books, 4700 E. Galbraith Rd., Cincinnati OH 45236. (800)448-0915. Website: www.writersdigest.com.

Songwriter's Playground—Innovative Exercises in Creative Songwriting, by Barbara L. Jordan, Creative Music Marketing, 1085 Commonwealth Ave., Suite 323, Boston MA 02215. (617)926-8766.

Songwriting and the Creative Process, by Steve Gillette, Sing Out! Publications, P.O. Box 5640, Bethlehem PA 18015-0253. (888)SING-OUT. E-mail: singout@libertynet.org. Website: www.singout.org/sopubs.html.

Songwriting: Essential Guide to Lyric Form and Structure, by Pat Pattison, Berklee Press, 1140 Boylston St., Boston MA 02215. (617)747-2146. E-mail: info@berkleepress.com. Website: www.www.berkleepress.com.

The Soul of the Writer, by Susan Tucker with Linda Lee Strother, Journey Publishing, P.O. Box 92411, Nashville TN 37209. (615)952-4894. Website: www.journeypublishing.com.

Successful Lyric Writing, by Sheila Davis, Writer's Digest Books, 4700 E. Galbraith Rd., Cincinnati OH 45236. (800)448-0915. Website: www.writersdigest.com.

This Business of Music Marketing and Promotion, by Tad Lathrop and Jim Pettigrew, Jr., Billboard Books, Watson-Guptill Publications, 770 Broadway, New York NY 10003. E-mail: info@watsonguptill.com.

Tim Sweeney's Guide to Releasing Independent Records, by Tim Sweeney, TSA Books, 31805 Highway 79 S., Temecula CA 92592. (909)303-9506. E-mail: info@tsamusic.com. Website: www.tsamusic.com.

Tim Sweeney's Guide to Succeeding at Music Conventions, by Tim Sweeney, TSA Books, 31805 Highway 79 S., Temecula CA 92592. (909)303-9506. Website: www.tsamusic.com.

Texas Music Industry Directory, Texas Music Office, Office of the Governor, P.O. Box 13246, Austin TX 78711. (512)463-6666. E-mail: music@governor.state.tx.us. Website: www.governor.state.tx.us/music.

Tunesmith: Inside the Art of Songwriting, by Jimmy Webb, Hyperion, 77 W. 66th St., 11th Floor, New York NY 10023. (800)759-0190.

Volunteer Lawyers for the Arts Guide to Copyright for Musicians and Composers, One E. 53rd St., 6th Floor, New York NY 10022. (212)319-2787.

Writing Better Lyrics, by Pat Pattison, Writer's Digest Books, 4700 E. Galbraith Rd., Cincinnati OH 45236. (800)448-0915. Website: www.writersdigest.com.

The Yellow Pages of Rock, The Album Network, 120 N. Victory Blvd., Burbank CA 91502. (800)222-4382. Fax: (818)955-9048. E-mail: ypinfo@yprock.com.

Websites of Interest

The Internet can provide a wealth of information for songwriters and performers, and the number of sites devoted to music grows each day. Below is a list of some websites that can offer you information, links to other music sites, contact with other songwriters and places to showcase your songs. Since the online world is changing and expanding at such a rapid pace, this is hardly a comprehensive list, and some of these addresses may be obsolete by the time this book goes to print. But it gives you a place to start on your journey through the Internet to search for opportunities to get your music heard.

About.com Musicians' Exchange: http://musicians.miningco.com
Site featuring headlines and articles of interest to independent musicians, as well as numerous links.

American Music Center: www.amc.net
Classical/jazz archives, includes a list of composer organizations and contacts.

American Society of Composers, Authors and Publishers (ASCAP) www.ascap.com
Database of performed works in ASCAP's repertoire. Also includes songwriter, performer and publisher information, ASCAP membership information and industry news.

Ampcast.com: www.ampcast.com
Online musicians community and music hosting site.

ARCANA, Artist Research, Composer's Aid & Network Access: www.musicnotes.com
Reference site for classical composers and musicians, including collaboration opportunities, contests and music archives, in addition to industry news.

The Bandit A&R Newsletter: www.banditnewsletter.com
Offers newsletter to help musicians target demos and press kits to labels, publishers, managers and production companies actively looking for new talent.

Bandstand: www.bandstand.com
Music news and links.

The Bard's Crier: http://thebards.net/crier/
A free guerilla music marketing e-zine.

The Blues Foundation: www.blues.org
Information on the foundation, its membership and events.

Broadcast Music, Inc. (BMI): www.bmi.com
Offers lists of song titles, songwriters and publishers of the BMI repertoire. Also includes BMI membership information, and general information on songwriting and licensing.

The Buzz Factor: www.thebuzzfactor.com
Offers press kit evaluation, press release writing, guerrilla music marketing, tips and weekly newsletter.

CDBABY: www.cdbaby.com
An online CD store dedicated solely to independent music.

CDstreet.com: www.cdstreet.com
Offers secure online ordering support to artist websites for a 15% commission.

Chorus America: www.chorusamerica.org
The website of Chorus America, a national service organization for professional and volunteer choruses, including job listings and professional development information.

Composers Concordance: www.musicnotes.com
The website of the ARCANA-sponsored group which promotes performance of new American music through concert series and public awareness.

CPCC: www.under.org/cpcc
Website for the Center for the Promotion of Contemporary Composers.

Creative Musicians Coalition (CMC): www.aimcmc.com
Website of the CMC, an international organization dedicated to the advancement of independent musicians, links to artists, and tips and techniques for musicians.

DIY Tour Guide: http://industrial.org
Directory of venues and promoters.

Ensemble 21: www.ensemble21.com/e21.html
Website of the New York contemporary music performance group dedicated to promotion and performance of new orchestral compositions.

Film Music: www.filmmusic.com
Website relating to film and TV music composition.

Fourfront Media and Music: www.knab.com
This site by music industry consultant Christopher Knab offers in-depth information on product development, promotion, publicity and performance.

Gajoob Magazine: www.gajoob.com
Online magazine offering information on labels looking for artists, radio stations looking for independent artists, festivals, publications, collaborations, etc.

Getsigned.com: www.getsigned.com
Interviews with industry executives, how-to business information and more.

Government Liaison Services: www.trademarkinfo.com
An intellectual property research firm. Offers a free online trademark search.

Guitar Nine Records: www.guitar9.com
Offers articles by music professionals and insiders.

Harry Fox Agency: www.nmpa.org/hfa/licensing.html
Offers a comprehensive FAQ about licensing songs for use in recording, performance and film.

Independent Artists' Services: www.idiom.com/ ~ upend/
Full of information including searchable databases of bands and booking/touring information and other resources.

Independent Distribution Network: www.idnmusic.com/
Website of independent bands distributing their music, with advice on everything from starting a band to finding labels.

Independent Songwriter Web Magazine: www.independentsongwriter.com
Independent music reviews, classifieds, message board and chat sessions.

Indie Centre: www.indiecentre.com
An independent label information site created to share ideas on releasing albums, including creating a label, distribution and touring.

Indie-Music.com: http://indie-music.com
Full of how-to articles, record label directory, radio links and venue listing.

Internet Underground Music Archive (IUMA): www.iuma.com
Online musicians community and music hosting site.

Jazz Composers Collective: www.jazzcollective.com
Industry information on composers, projects, recordings, concerts and events.

Jazz Corner: www.jazzcorner.com
Website for musicians and organizations featuring links to 70 websites for jazz musicians and organizations and the Speakeasy, an interactive conference area.

Just Plain Folks: www.jpfolks.com
Online songwriting organization featuring messageboards, lyric feedback forums, member profiles, featured members' music, contact listings, chapter homepages, and an Internet radio station. (See the Just Plain Folks listing in the Organizations section).

Kathode Ray Music: www.kathoderaymusic.com
Specializes in marketing and promotion consultation and offers a business forum, e-newsletter and a free classified ads board.

Law Cybercenter: www.hollywoodnetwork.com/research/legal
Tips on negotiating and dealing with songwriting contracts.

Li'l Hank's Guide for Songwriters in L.A.: www.halsguide.com
Website for songwriters with information on clubs, publishers, books, etc. as well as links to other songwriting sites.

Los Angeles Goes Underground: http://lagu.somaweb.org
Website dedicated to underground rock bands from Los Angeles and Hollywood.

Los Angeles Music Access (LAMA): http://lama.com
Database of Los Angeles bands, clubs and resources sponsored by a group that promotes independent artists.

Lyrical Line: www.lyricalline.com
Offers places to market your songs, critique service, industry news and more.

Lyricist.com: www.lyricist.com
Jeff Mallet's songwriter site offering contests, tips and job opportunities in the music industry.

Media Bureau: www.mediabureau.com
Live Internet radio programs where guests perform and talk about songwriting.

MI2N (THE MUSIC INDUSTRY NEWS NETWORK): www.mi2n.com
Offers news on happenings in the music industry and career postings.

MP3.com: www.mp3.com
Currently the most well-known online musicians community and music hosting site with thousands of songs available for free download.

The Muse's Muse: www.musesmuse.com
Classifieds, catalog of lyric samples, songwriting articles, organizations and chat room.

Music & Audio Connection: www.musicandaudio.com
Guide to Canadian artists, associations and other resources from Norris-Whitney Communications, Inc.

Music Publishers Association: http://host.mpa.org
Provides a copyright resource center, directory of member publishers and information on the organization.

Music Yellow Pages: www.musicyellowpages.com
Phone book listings of music-related businesses.

Musicians Assistance Site (MAS): www.musicianassist.com
Features site reviews and databases of venues, contacts, promoters, manufacturers and record labels. Also includes an archive of music business articles, columns, and pre-made contracts and agreements.

The Musicians Guide Through the Legal Jungle: www.legaljungleguide.com/resource.htm
Offers articles on copyright law, music publishing and talent agents.

National Association of Composers USA (NACUSA): www.music-usa.org/nacusa
Website of the organization dedicated to promotion and performance of new music by Americans, featuring a young composers' competition, concert schedule, job opportunities and more.

National Music Publishers Association: www.nmpa.org
The organization's online site with information about copyright, legislation and other concerns of the music publishing world.

Online Rock: www.onlinerock.com
Offers e-mail, marketing and free webpage services. Also features articles, chat rooms, links, etc.

Opera America: www.operaam.org
Website of Opera America, featuring information on advocacy and awareness programs, publications, conference schedules and more.

Outersound: www.outersound.com
Information on finding a recording studio, educating yourself in the music industry, and a list of music magazines to advertise in or get reviewed by.

Public Domain Music: www.pdinfo.com
Articles on public domain works and copyright, including public domain song lists, research resources, tips and a FAQ.

PUMP AUDIO: www.pumpaudio.com
License music for film and TV on a non-exclusive basis. (See the Insider Report with singer/songwriter Bibi Farber on page 160.)

Rhythm Net: www.rhythmnet.com
Information on artists, labels, entertainment establishments and more.

SESAC Inc.: www.sesac.com
Includes SESAC performing rights organization information, songwriter profiles, organization news, licensing information and links to other sites.

Song Shark: www.geocities.com/songshark
Website of information on known song sharks.

Songcatalog.com: www.songcatalog.com
Online song catalog database for pitching and licensing.

Songfile.com: www.songfile.com
Online song catalog database for pitching and licensing.

Songlink: www.songlink.com
Offers opportunities to pitch songs to music publishers for specific recording projects, also industry news.

Songnet.com: www.songnet.com
Information, bulletin boards and links related to songwriting.

Songscape: www.songscape.com
Music database and music industry news service.

Songscope.com: www.songscope.com
Online song catalog database for pitching and licensing.

Songwriter Products Ideas & Necessities (SPIN): www.songwriterproducts.com
Offer songwriting tips, tools and accessories, including tapes, CDs, duplication products and music business career packages.

Songwriter's Guild of America (SGA): www.songwriters.org
Offers industry news, members services information, newsletters, contract reviews and more.

Songwriter's Resource Network: www.songwritersresourcenetwork.com
Online information and services designed especially for songwriters.

The Songwriting Education Resource: www.craftofsongwriting.com
An educational site for Nashville songwriters offering discussion boards, articles and links.

Sonic Net: www.sonicnet.com
Music news, chat and reviews.

Stompingground: www.stompinground.com
Provides bands with Real Audio concerts, free listings, promotion and a list of record labels.

Studio Finder: www.studiofinder.com
Locate more than 5,000 recording studios anywhere in the U.S.

TAXI: www.taxi.com
Independent A&R vehicle that shops tapes to A&R professionals.

Ultimate Band List: www.ubl.com
Lists record labels and their artists, posts calendar of events, festivals and club dates for artists nationwide; also includes chart information and artist news.

United States Copyright Office: http://lcweb.loc.gov/copyright
The homepage for the U.S. copyright office, offering information on registering songs.

Yahoo!: www.yahoo.com/Entertainment/Music/
Use this search engine to retrieve over 20,000 music listings.

ONLINE SHOWCASES

These sites offer places for you to post your music for a fee as a way of marketing your songs to music executives.

Internet Underground Music Archive (IUMA): www.iuma.com.

Kaleidospace: http://kspace.com

Glossary

A cappella. Choral singing without accompaniment.

AAA form. A song form in which every verse has the same melody; often used for songs that tell a story.

AABA, ABAB. A commonly used song pattern consisting of two verses, a bridge and a verse, or a repeated pattern of verse and bridge, where the verses are musically the same.

A&R Director. Record company executive in charge of the Artists and Repertoire Department who is responsible for finding and developing new artists and matching songs with artists.

A/C. Adult contemporary music.

Advance. Money paid to the songwriter or recording artist, which is then recouped before regular royalty payment begins. Sometimes called "up front" money, advances are deducted from royalties.

AFIM. Association for Independent Music (formerly NAIRD). Organization for independent record companies, distributors, retailers, manufacturers, etc.

AFM. American Federation of Musicians. A union for musicians and arrangers.

AFTRA. American Federation of Television and Radio Artists. A union for performers.

AIMP. Association of Independent Music Publishers.

Airplay. The radio broadcast of a recording.

AOR. Album-Oriented Rock. A radio format that primarily plays selections from rock albums as opposed to hit singles.

Arrangement. An adaptation of a composition for a recording or performance, with consideration for the melody, harmony, instrumentation, tempo, style, etc.

ASCAP. American Society of Composers, Authors and Publishers. A performing rights society. (See the Organizations section.)

Assignment. Transfer of rights of a song from writer to publisher.

Audio Visual Index (AVI). A database containing title and production information for cue sheets which are available from a performing rights organization. Currently, BMI, ASCAP, SOCAN, PRS, APRA and SACEM contribute their cue sheet listings to the AVI.

Audiovisual. Refers to presentations that use audio backup for visual material.

Background music. Music used that creates mood and supports the spoken dialogue of a radio program or visual action of an audiovisual work. Not feature or theme music.

b&w. Black and white.

Bed. Prerecorded music used as background material in commercials. In rap music, often refers to the sampled and looped drums and music over which the rapper performs.

Black box. Theater without fixed stage or seating arrangements, capable of a variety of formations. Usually a small space, often attached to a major theater complex, used for workshops or experimental works calling for small casts and limited sets.

BMI. Broadcast Music, Inc. A performing rights society. (See the Organizations section.)

Booking agent. Person who schedules performances for entertainers.

Bootlegging. Unauthorized recording and selling of a song.

Business manager. Person who handles the financial aspects of artistic careers.

Buzz. Attention an act generates through the media and word of mouth.

b/w. Backed with. Usually refers to the B-side of a single.

C&W. Country and western.

Catalog. The collected songs of one writer, or all songs handled by one publisher.

CD. Compact Disc (see below).

CD-R. A recordable CD.

CD-ROM. Compact Disc-Read Only Memory. A computer information storage medium capable of holding enormous amounts of data. Information on a CD-ROM cannot be deleted. A computer user must have a CD-ROM drive to access a CD-ROM.

Chamber music. Any music suitable for performance in a small audience area or chamber.

Chamber orchestra. A miniature orchestra usually containing one instrument per part.

Chart. The written arrangement of a song.

Charts. The trade magazines' lists of the best-selling records.

CHR. Comtemporary Hit Radio. Top 40 pop music.

Collaboration. Two or more artists, writers, etc., working together on a single project; for instance, a playwright and a songwriter creating a musical together.

Compact disc. A small disc (about 4.7 inches in diameter) holding digitally encoded music that is read by a laser beam in a CD player.

Composers. The men and women who create musical compositions for motion pictures and other audio visual works, or the creators of classical music composition.

Co-publish. Two or more parties own publishing rights to the same song.

Copyright. The exclusive legal right giving the creator of a work the power to control the publishing, reproduction and selling of the work. Although a song is technically copyrighted at the time it is written, the best legal protection of that copyright comes through registering the copyright with the Library of Congress.

Copyright infringement. Unauthorized use of a copyrighted song or portions thereof.

Cover recording. A new version of a previously recorded song.

Crossover. A song that becomes popular in two or more musical categories (e.g., country and pop).

Cut. Any finished recording; a selection from a LP. Also to record.

DAT. Digital Audio Tape. A professional and consumer audio cassette format for recording and playing back digitally-encoded material. DAT cassettes are approximately one-third smaller than conventional audio cassettes.

DCC. Digital Compact Cassette. A consumer audio cassette format for recording and playing back digitally-encoded tape. DCC tapes are the same size as analog cassettes.

Demo. A recording of a song submitted as a demonstration of a writer's or artist's skills.

Derivative work. A work derived from another work, such as a translation, musical arrangement, sound recording, or motion picture version.

Distributor. Wholesale marketing agent responsible for getting records from manufacturers to retailers.

Donut. A jingle with singing at the beginning and end and instrumental background in the middle. Ad copy is recorded over the middle section.

E-mail. Electronic mail. Computer address where a company or individual can be reached via modem.

Engineer. A specially-trained individual who operates recording studio equipment.

Enhanced CD. General term for an audio CD that also contains multimedia computer information. It is playable in both standard CD players and CD-ROM drives.

EP. Extended play record or cassette containing more selections than a standard single, but fewer than a standard album.

Exploit. To seek legitimate uses of a song for income.

Final mix. The art of combining all the various sounds that take place during the recording session into a two-track stereo or mono tape. Reflects the total product and all of the energies and talents the artist, producer and engineer have put into the project.

Fly space. The area above a stage from which set pieces are lowered and raised during a performance.

Folio. A softcover collection of printed music prepared for sale.

Following. A fan base committed to going to gigs and buying albums.

Foreign rights societies. Performing rights societies other than domestic which have reciprocal agreements with ASCAP and BMI for the collection of royalties accrued by foreign radio and television airplay and other public performance of the writer members of the above groups.

Harry Fox Agency. Organization that collects mechanical royalties.

Grammy. Music industry awards presented by the National Academy of Recording Arts and Sciences.

Hip-hop. A dance oriented musical style derived from a combination of disco, rap and R&B.

Hit. A song or record that achieves top 40 status.

Hook. A memorable "catch" phrase or melody line that is repeated in a song.

House. Dance music created by remixing samples from other songs.

Hypertext. Words or groups of words in an electronic document that are linked to other text, such as a definition or a related document. Hypertext can also be linked to illustrations.

Indie. An independent record label, music publisher or producer.

Infringement. A violation of the exclusive rights granted by the copyright law to a copyright owner.

Internet. A worldwide network of computers that offers access to a wide variety of electronic resources.

ips. Inches per second; a speed designation for tape recording.

IRC. International reply coupon, necessary for the return of materials sent out of the country. Available at most post offices.

Jingle. Usually a short verse set to music designed as a commercial message.

Lead sheet. Written version (melody, chord symbols and lyric) of a song.

Leader. Plastic (non-recordable) tape at the beginning and between songs for ease in selection.

Libretto. The text of an opera or any long choral work. The booklet containing such text.

Listing. Block of information in this book about a specific company.

LP. Designation for long-playing record played at $33\frac{1}{3}$ rpm.

Lyric sheet. A typed or written copy of a song's lyrics.

Market. A potential song or music buyer; also a demographic division of the record-buying public.

Master. Edited and mixed tape used in the production of records; the best or original copy of a recording from which copies are made.

MD. MiniDisc. A 2.5 inch disk for recording and playing back digitally-encoded music.

Mechanical right. The right to profit from the physical reproduction of a song.

Mechanical royalty. Money earned from record, tape and CD sales.

MIDI. Musical instrument digital interface. Universal standard interface that allows musical instruments to communicate with each other and computers.

Mini Disc. (See **MD** above.)

Mix. To blend a multi-track recording into the desired balance of sound, usually to a 2-track stereo master.

Modem. MOdulator/DEModulator. A computer device used to send data from one computer to another via telephone line.

MOR. Middle of the road. Easy-listening popular music.

MP3. File format of a relatively small size that stores audio files on a computer. Music saved in a MP3 format can be played only with a MP3 player (which can be downloaded onto a computer).

Ms. Manuscript.

Multimedia. Computers and software capable of integrating text, sound, photographic-quality images, animation and video.

Music bed. (See **Bed** above.)

Music jobber. A wholesale distributor of printed music.

Music library. A business that purchases canned music, which can then be bought by producers of radio and TV commercials, films, videos and audiovisual productions to use however they wish.

Music publisher. A company that evaluates songs for commercial potential, finds artists to record them, finds other uses (such as TV or film) for the songs, collects income generated by the songs and protects copyrights from infringement.

Music Row. An area of Nashville, TN, encompassing Sixteenth, Seventeeth and Eighteenth avenues where most of the major publishing houses, recording studios, mastering labs, songwriters, singers, promoters, etc. practice their trade.

NARAS. National Academy of Recording Arts and Sciences.

The National Academy of Songwriters (NAS). The largest U.S. songwriters' association. (See the Organizations section.)

Needle-drop. Refers to a type of music library. A needledrop music library is a licensed library that allows producers to borrow music on a rate schedule. The price depends on how the music will be used.

Network. A group of computers electronically linked to share information and resources.

NMPA. National Music Publishers Association.

One-off. A deal between songwriter and publisher which includes only one song or project at a time. No future involvement is implicated. Many times a single song contract accompanies a one-off deal.

One-stop. A wholesale distributor of who sells small quantities of records to "mom and pop" record stores, retailers and jukebox operators.

Operetta. Light, humorous, satiric plot or poem, set to cheerful light music with occasional spoken dialogue.

Overdub. To record an additional part (vocal or instrumental) onto a basic multi-track recording.

Parody. A satirical imitation of a literary or musical work. Permission from the owner of the copyright is generally required before commercial exploitation of a parody.

Payola. Dishonest payment to broadcasters in exchange for airplay.

Performing rights. A specific right granted by U.S. copyright law protecting a composition from being publicly performed without the owner's permission.

Performing rights organization. An organization that collects income from the public performance of songs written by its members and then proportionally distributes this income to the individual copyright holder based on the number of performances of each song.

Personal manager. A person who represents artists to develop and enhance their careers. Personal managers may negotiate contracts, hire and dismiss other agencies and personnel relating to the artist's career, review material, help with artist promotions and perform many services.

Piracy. The unauthorized reproduction and selling of printed or recorded music.

Pitch. To attempt to solicit interest for a song by audition.

Playlist. List of songs a radio station will play.

Points. A negotiable percentage paid to producers and artists for records sold.

Producer. Person who supervises every aspect of a recording project.

Production company. Company specializing in producing jingle packages for advertising agencies. May also refer to companies specializing in audiovisual programs.

Professional manager. Member of a music publisher's staff who screens submitted material and tries to get the company's catalog of songs recorded.

Proscenium. Permanent architectural arch in a theater that separates the stage from the audience.

Public domain. Any composition with an expired, lapsed or invalid copyright, and therefore belonging to everyone.

Purchase license. Fee paid for music used from a stock music library.

Query. A letter of inquiry to an industry professional soliciting his interest.

R&B. Rhythm and blues.

Rack Jobber. Distributors who lease floor space from department stores and put in racks of albums.

Rate. The percentage of royalty as specified by contract.

Release. Any record issued by a record company.

Residuals. In advertising or television, payments to singers and musicians for use of a performance.

RIAA. Recording Industry Association of America.

Royalty. Percentage of money earned from the sale of records or use of a song.

RPM. Revolutions per minute. Refers to phonograph turntable speed.

SAE. Self-addressed envelope (with no postage attached).

SASE. Self-addressed stamped envelope.

SATB. The abbreviation for parts in choral music, meaning Soprano, Alto, Tenor and Bass.

Score. A complete arrangement of all the notes and parts of a composition (vocal or instrumental) written out on staves. A full score, or orchestral score, depicts every orchestral part on a separate staff and is used by a conductor.

Self-contained. A band or recording act that writes all their own material.

SESAC. A performing rights organization, originally the Society of European Stage Authors and Composers. (See the Organizations section.)

SFX. Sound effects.

Shop. To pitch songs to a number of companies or publishers.

Single. 45 rpm record with only one song per side. A 12″ single refers to a long version of one song on a 12″ disc, usually used for dance music.

Ska. Fast tempo dance music influenced primarily by reggae and punk, usually featuring horns, saxophone and bass.

SOCAN. Society of Composers, Authors and Music Publishers of Canada. A Canadian performing rights organization. (See the Organizations section.)

Solicited. Songs or materials that have been requested.

Song plugger. A songwriter representative whose main responsibility is promoting uncut songs to music publishers, record companies, artists and producers.

Song shark. Person who deals with songwriters deceptively for his own profit.

SoundScan. A company that collates the register tapes of reporting stores to track the actual number of albums sold at the retail level.

Soundtrack. The audio, including music and narration, of a film, videotape or audiovisual program.

Space stage. Open stage that features lighting and, perhaps, projected scenery.

Split publishing. To divide publishing rights between two or more publishers.

Staff songwriter. A songwriter who has an exclusive agreement with a publisher.

Statutory royalty rate. The maximum payment for mechanical rights guaranteed by law that a record company may pay the songwriter and his publisher for each record or tape sold.

Subpublishing. Certain rights granted by a U.S. publisher to a foreign publisher in exchange for promoting the U.S. catalog in his territory.

Synchronization. Technique of timing a musical soundtrack to action on film or video.

Take. Either an attempt to record a vocal or instrument part, or an acceptable recording of a performance.

Tejano. A musical form begun in the late 1970s by regional bands in south Texas, its style reflects a blended Mexican-American culture. Incorporates elements of rock, country, R&B and jazz, and often features accordion and 12-string guitar.

Thrust stage. Stage with audience on three sides and a stagehouse or wall on the fourth side.

Top 40. The first 40 songs on the pop music charts at any given time. Also refers to a style of music which emulates that heard on the current top 40.

Track. Divisions of a recording tape (e.g., 24-track tape) that can be individually recorded in the studio, then mixed into a finished master.

Trades. Publications covering the music industry.

12″ Single. A 12-inch record containing one or more remixes of a song, originally intended for dance club play.

Unsolicited. Songs or materials that were not requested and are not expected.

VHS. ½″ videocassette format.

Vocal score. An arrangement of vocal music detailing all vocal parts, and condensing all accompanying instrumental music into one piano part.

Website. An address on the World Wide Web that can be accessed by computer modem. It may contain text, graphics and sound.

Wing space. The offstage area surrounding the playing stage in a theater, unseen by the audience, where sets and props are hidden, actors wait for cues, and stagehands prepare to chance sets.

World music. A general music category which includes most musical forms originating outside the U.S. and Europe, including reggae and calypso. World music finds its roots primarily in the Caribbean, Latin America, Africa and the south Pacific.

World Wide Web (WWW). An Internet resource that utilizes hypertext to access information. It also supports formatted text, illustrations and sounds, depending on the user's computer capabilities.

Category Indexes

The Category Indexes are a good place to begin searching for a markets. They break down the listings by section (music publishers, record companies, etc.) and by the type of music they are interested in. For example, if you write country songs, and are looking for a publisher to pitch them, go to the Music Publishers heading and then check the companies listed under the Country subheading. The music categories cover a wide range of variations within each genre, so be sure to read each listing thoroughly to make sure your own unique take on that genre is a good match. Some listings do not appear in these indexes because they did not cite a specific preference. Listings that were very specific, or whose music descriptions don't quite fit into these categories also do not appear. (Category listings for **Music Publishers** begin on this page, **Record Companies** on page 396, **Record Producers** on page 403 and **Managers & Booking Agents** begin on page 408.)

MUSIC PUBLISHERS

Adult Contemporary (also easy listening, middle of the road, AAA, ballads, etc.)

Dance (also house, hi-NRG, disco, club, rave, techno, trip-hop, trance, etc.)

Folk (also acoustic, Celtic, etc.)

Instrumental (also background music, musical scores, etc.)

Jazz (also fusion, bebop, swing, etc.)

R&B (also soul, black, urban, etc.)

Rap (also hip-hop, bass, etc.)

World Music (also reggae, ethnic, calypso, international, world beat, etc.)

RECORD COMPANIES

Adult Contemporary (also easy listening, middle of the road, AAA, ballads, etc.)

Dance (also house, hi-NRG, disco, club, rave, techno, trip-hop, trance, etc.)

World Music (also reggae, ethnic, calypso, international, world beat, etc.)

RECORD PRODUCERS

Adult Contemporary (also easy listening, middle of the road, AAA, ballads, etc.)

Alternative (also modern rock, punk, college rock, new wave, hardcore, new music, industrial, ska, indie rock, garage, etc.)

R&B (also soul, black, urban, etc.)

Rap (also hip-hop, bass, etc.)

Rock (also rockabilly, AOR, rock 'n' roll, etc.)

World Music (also reggae, ethnic, calypso, international, world beat, etc.)

Openness to Submissions Index

Use this index to find companies open to your level of experience. It is recommended to use this index in conjunction with the Category Indexes found on page 388. Once you have compiled a list of companies open to your experience and music, read the information in these listings, paying close attention to the **How to Contact** subhead. (Also see A Sample Listing Decoded on page 11.)

○ OPEN TO BEGINNERS

Music Publishers

Record Companies

Record Producers

Openness Index

Managers & Booking Agents

◑ PREFERS EXPERIENCED, BUT OPEN TO BEGINNERS

Music Publishers

Record Companies

Record Producers

Managers & Booking Agents

◉ OPEN TO PREVIOUSLY PUBLISHED/WELL-ESTABLISHED

Music Publishers

Record Companies

Openness Index

Film & TV Index

This index lists companies who place music in motion pictures and TV shows (excluding commercials). To learn more about their film/TV experience, read the information under **Film & TV** in their listings. It is recommended to use this index in conjunction with the Openness to Submissions Index beginning on page 415.

Geographic Index

This Geographic Index will help you locate companies by state, as well as those in countries outside of the U.S. It is recommended to use this index in conjunction with the Openness to Submissions Index on page 415. Once you find the names of companies in this index you are interested in, check the listings within each section for addresses, phone numbers, contact names and submission details.

Record Producers

Managers & Booking Agents

Advertising, Audiovisual & Commercial Music Firms

Play Producers & Publishers

Advertising, Audiovisual & Commercial Music Firms
Mallof, Abruzino & Nash Marketing 267
Norton Rubble & Mertz, Inc. Advertising 267
Qually & Company Inc. 268
Video I-D, Inc. 269

Play Producers & Publishers
Bailiwick Repertory 273
Circa '21 Dinner Playhouse 275
Dramatic Publishing Company, The 288

Classical Performing Arts
Knox-Galesburg Symphony 301
Lyric Opera of Chicago 303
Wheaton Symphony Orchestra 310

Contests & Awards
Cunningham Commission for Youth Theatre 316
Kinley Memorial Fellowship, Kate Neal 319

Organizations
American Society of Composers, Authors and Publishers (ASCAP) 328
Chicago Alliance for Playwrights 332
Chicago Dance and Music Alliance 332

INDIANA
Music Publishers
Hammel Associates, Inc., R.L. 105
Ontrax Companies 119

Record Companies
Dale Productions, Alan 156

Managers & Booking Agents
Harrell & Associates, M. 239
International Entertainment Bureau 241

Advertising, Audiovisual & Commercial Music Firms
Marc USA 267
Omni Communications 268

Classical Performing Arts
Anderson Symphony Orchestra 292
Carmel Symphony Orchestra 295
Indiana University New Music Ensemble 301

Contests & Awards
Indiana Opera Theatre/MacAllister Awards for Opera Singers 318

Organizations
Indianapolis Songwriters Association, Inc., The 337
Just Plain Folks 338

Workshops & Conferences
New Harmony Project, The 357

IOWA
Music Publishers
JoDa Music 109

Record Producers
Luick & Country Music Showcase Intl. Associates, Harold 212

Managers & Booking Agents
Fenchel Entertainment Agency, Fred T. 237

Play Producers & Publishers
Heuer Publishing Co. 289
Waterloo Community Playhouse 285

Organizations
Country Music Showcase International, Inc. 334

Workshops & Conferences
Davidson's Writer's Seminar, Peter 354

KANSAS
Music Publishers
Dave Music, Jof 98

KENTUCKY
Music Publishers
Holy Spirit Music 107
Just a Note 110

Record Producers
Masterscore Music 213

Managers & Booking Agents
Triangle Talent, Inc. 255

Play Producers & Publishers
Aran Press 287
Stage One 281

Idol Records Publishing 167
Inner Soul Records, Inc. 167
Southland Records, Inc. 188
Surface Records 189
Texas Music Café 190
World Beatnik Records 193

Record Producers
ACR Productions 199
Hesfree Productions & Publishing 205
Sound Arts Recording Studio 218
TMC Productions 220
Trinity Studio, The 221
Willson, Frank 222

Managers & Booking Agents
Atch Records and Productions 228
Bread & Butter Productions 231
Butler Music, Bill 231
Hesfree Productions & Publishing Company 239
Kendall West Agency 241
Kuper Personal Management/Recovery Recordings 242
Management Plus 243
Smeltzer Productions, Gary 252
SP Talent Associates 252
Stevens & Company Management 253
Texas Sounds Entertainment 254
Umpire Entertainment Enterprizes 255
Universal Music Marketing 255
WE Records & Management 256
Wemus Entertainment 256

Advertising, Audiovisual & Commercial Music Firms
Hammond & Associates 265

Play Producers & Publishers
Stages Repertory Theatre 282
Theatre Three, Inc. 283

Classical Performing Arts
Fort Worth Children's Opera 298
Hermann Sons German Band 299
Mesquite Symphonic Band 303
Moores Opera Center 304

Contests & Awards
New Folk Concerts for Emerging Songwriters 321

Organizations
Austin Songwriters Group 329
Center for the Promotion of Contemporary Composers 331
Country Legends Association 333
Country Music Association of Texas 334
Dallas Songwriters Association 334
Fort Worth Songwriters Association 335
Houston Fort Bend Songwriters Association 336
Southeast Texas Bluegrass Music Association 347
Southwest Celtic Music Association 347
Texas Accountants & Lawyers for the Arts 348
Texas Music Office 348
Texas Songwriters Association 349

Workshops & Conferences
I Write the Songs 355
Kerrville Folk Festival 355

Retreats & Colonies
South by Southwest Music Conference 359

UTAH
Music Publishers
A Ta Z Music 84

Advertising, Audiovisual & Commercial Music Firms
Soter Associates, Inc. 269
Salt Lake Symphonic Choir 307

Contests & Awards
Composers Guild Annual Composition Contest 316

Organizations
Composers Guild 333

Record Producers
Big Bear 200
Coppin, Johnny/Red Sky Records 202
June Productions Ltd. 207

Managers & Booking Agents
Barrett Rock 'n' Roll Enterprises, Paul 229
First Time Management 237
Kickstart Music Ltd. 242
Poole Agency Limited, Gordon 247

Classical Performing Arts
European Union Chamber Orchestra 298

Organizations
American Society of Composers, Authors and
    Publishers (ASCAP) 328
Broadcast Music, Inc. (BMI) 330

Guild of International Songwriters & Compos-
    ers, The 336
International Songwriters Association Ltd.
    337
SESAC Inc. 344
Spnm—Promoting New Music 348

U.S. VIRGIN ISLANDS
Music Publishers
Island Culture Music Publishers 108

WALES
Record Companies
Boulevard Music & Publishing 150

Record Producers
Demi Monde Records & Publishing Ltd. 203

General Index

Use this index to locate specific markets and resources. Also, we list companies that appeared in the 2004 edition of *Songwriter's Market*, but do not appear this year. Instead of page numbers beside these markets you will find two-letter codes in parentheses that explain why these markets no longer appear. The codes are (**ED**)—Editorial Decision, (**NS**)—Not Accepting Submissions, (**NR**)No (or late) Response to Listing Request, (**OB**)—Out of Business, (**RR**)—Removed by Listing's Request, (**UC**)—Unable to Contact.

General Index

Songwriter's Market
Feedback

If you have a suggestion for improving *Songwriter's Market*, or would like to take part in a reader survey we conduct from time to time, please make a photocopy of this form (or cut it out of the book), fill it out, and return it to:

Songwriter's Market Feedback
4700 East Galbraith Road
Cincinnati, OH 45236
Fax: (513) 531-2686

○ **Yes!** I'm willing to fill out a short survey by mail or online to provide feedback on *Songwriter's Market* or other books on songwriting.

○ **Yes!** I have a suggestion to improve *Songwriter's Market* (attach a second sheet if more room is necessary):

_____
_____
_____
_____
_____
_____
_____
_____

Name: _____
Address: _____
City: _____ State: _____ Zip: _____
Phone: _____ Fax: _____
E-mail: _____ Website: _____

I am a

○ songwriter
○ performing songwriter
○ musician
○ other: _____

NOTES

NOTES

NOTES

NOTES